R. F. HARROD

# The Life of
# John Maynard Keynes

PENGUIN BOOKS

Penguin Books Ltd, Harmondsworth, Middlesex, England
Penguin Books Australia Ltd, Ringwood, Victoria, Australia

—

First published by Macmillan 1951
Published in Pelican Books 1972

—

This book is copyright in all countries which are signatories to the
Berne Convention

—

Made and printed in Great Britain
by Hazell Watson & Viney Ltd
Aylesbury, Bucks
Set in Linotype Georgian

TO
F.A.K.

# Contents

# Preface

WHEN I decided, at the suggestion of Mr Geoffrey Keynes, to undertake the task of writing a Life of his brother, John Maynard, I was fully conscious of the serious difficulties with which I should be confronted. Maynard Keynes made contributions to the theory of economics which have had great influence, and was playing an important part in public affairs during the period immediately before his death. In regard to both these activities it may be said that the time has not yet come when we can form a final estimate; we need a longer perspective. This objection to an early Life is certainly a weighty one. There appeared to me to be considerations which outweighed it.

Keynes's contributions to the theory of economics tended to be closely related to his practical proposals, and these in turn were also influenced by his general philosophy. An understanding of the background of his thought is indispensable for a correct interpretation of his conclusions. Furthermore, I venture to think that those who come after will be interested in Keynes, not only on account of his teachings and influence, but also for what he was in himself. If I am right in supposing that he was one of the greatest Englishmen of his age, then it is expedient that an attempt should be made to bring together all the varied aspects of his character and interests into a single biography.

Once that is granted, it follows that there is some need for haste. There are relevant matters of which there is no published record. Many of those who knew Keynes well in his early days may have passed from the scene in ten or twenty years from now. If I have made mistakes of emphasis in regard to economic theory or historical events, through lack of sufficient perspective, these can be corrected by future students. My task has been to save them from mistakes, which there would later be no one to correct. I cannot conceive how a future student, however conscientious and able, who had had first-hand knowledge neither of Keynes nor of the intellectual circles which formed his environment, could fail to fall into grievous errors of interpretation. It is my hope that at least some of these may be rendered impossible by this book.

An objection of a more trivial kind which occurred to me was the fact that I am an Oxford man. There are in Cambridge economists of high standing who were naturally in closer contact with Keynes than I. There is something to be said for the relative detachment of an Oxford observer; his attention is inevitably struck by certain features in the Cambridge scene, good or bad, which a Cambridge man would overlook because he took them for granted. In further extenuation I would add that I spent a term in Cambridge studying under Keynes, that I have maintained fairly regular contact since, and that I am conscious of owing much to Cambridge. Oxford has its own glories and precious qualities which are unique; on the purely intellectual plane I tended in my early years to feel a closer affinity with Cambridge.

One of my senior colleagues recently remarked to me that he supposed that my book would be in the nature of an encomium. Throughout my labours, I have set it steadily before me as my objective to present all materials which would enable the reader to form a balanced judgement. In one respect I rest comfortably in the confidence that my book contains too little, not too much, praise. In a man of genius, of intense individuality, alive in every pore, there is a vital spirit which no biography can portray. If any reader is impressed by my representation, I can assure him that he would have been much more impressed by the man himself. No words can recapture the living essence.

In regard to his faults, I am not conscious of any suppression. Criticisms have been made by the malicious or ill-informed which have no foundation in fact. At various points in the pages that follow I have drawn attention to failings, and I believe that in one passage or another I have made reference to all that are well authenticated.

One cause of embarrassment has been the necessity to refer to, and even to give character sketches of, living persons. In so far as their qualities affected Keynes, they are part of his story. My observations on living people have been made without their permission; any other course would have made my task impossible. I would ask the reader to remember that when some character walks across these pages, I have only referred to qualities or actions which in some way influenced Keynes; these may have been governed by the peculiar conditions of the incidents which brought them into contact with one another, and may have been quite uncharacteristic or unimportant in relation to the life of the individual in question considered as a whole.

I hope that I have not done damage to any reputation! Only in regard to one case have I any uneasiness. By a chapter of accidents a distinguished American came into sharp conflict with Keynes in the final phase and played a part which is bound to appear unsympathetic to the reader. It would be impertinent and beyond my competence to attempt an assessment of his career as a whole; I will only say that to the best of my knowledge he is a man of most distinguished gifts, who has served his country notably and may yet render still greater service. Despite their difference, Keynes continued to think well of him and to wish him well.

Reference to the living has also involved me in a stylistic embarrassment: I have chosen to use the past tense, on the ground that I am only concerned with the attributes of people as they were during Keynes's life and as they affected him. Their survival, however welcome, is irrelevant to my story. Thus if the reader finds the words 'X was a clever man', he must not infer either that X is dead or that he has, in my judgement, ceased to be clever!

Another colleague expressed astonishment when I told him that I had written more than a third of the book and was in fact dealing with the year 1919. 'I should have thought that that would have been your first chapter,' he replied; 'no one had heard of Keynes before 1919.' In fact Keynes did work of no little importance before that year. I confess, however, that I have been at pains to dwell at some length on the formative period, for it is precisely here that materials can be provided which will be inaccessible to the future historian. Early influences remained of great importance throughout Keynes's life.

Many of those who worked with him – not his intimate personal friends – have informed me that they detected what they deemed an improvement in his character, a progress from a sharply critical and intolerant attitude to greater mellowness. No doubt there was such a development. It is perhaps natural for a man of great powers to enter upon life with ardent enthusiasm and intolerance of the follies of his contemporaries and a certain measure of arrogance, and to become in due course less self-opinionated and more comprehending. The first set of attributes enables him to make a place for himself in the world, and the second to use it wisely. Yet the early phase may be as essential a part of the nature of the whole man as the later, and may be quite as creditable. Virtues are relative to the environment; in one's youth it may be right to be intransigent in the advocacy of one's own beliefs. I confess to retaining a certain affection for the early Keynes; I suppose that when I first knew him, he may be reckoned to have been in the later part of his early phase. His passionate espousal of good causes, his fierce and obliterating contempts, his supreme confidence in the powers of his own reasoning – I see all these as splendid attributes in the young knight-errant; I would not have wished him otherwise. If we are to understand him as a whole – and this applies to his character as well as to his economic doctrines – we must not view him at one point of time, but as evolving throughout his life, not replacing imperfection by perfection, but adapting himself to the successive functions he had to fulfil. I hope that the reader will feel that I have been justified in dwelling at some length on the earlier phases.

In expressing my debts of gratitude, which are many and weighty, it is more than usually necessary to give a warning that none of those whom I shall mention as having helped me are responsible for the interpretation or emphasis that I have given. In covering a vast field, partly undocumented, I have had to rely much upon my own judgement, not only in regard to Keynes himself, but also in regard to those whose careers affected his. I have sought out the best authorities and endeavoured to follow them; I have not at every point been able to do so. Intensive and continued study of his published work and of his vast collection of papers – he was something of a hoarder – has given me the sense that I do for the moment know more about his mind than anyone else. In the interpretation of his motives on a particular occasion, I have sought to bring to bear all my collateral knowledge, and it has sometimes happened that I have felt compelled to prefer my judgement to that of one who had more direct knowledge of the occasion in question.

First and foremost, thanks must be rendered to his mother, Mrs Keynes, not only for her tireless efforts to assist me in my labours, but also for her lifelong zeal in preserving letters and other papers relating to her son's career. The newspaper cuttings, which she pasted in, occupy thirty-four large volumes. She has allowed me to see the great mass of letters written by her son to herself and to her husband, the late Dr J. N. Keynes. She has been through this book, first in typescript, then in galley proof, and made many corrections on small points of fact and helpful suggestions. Now in her ninetieth year, she has retained a memory of youthful freshness and a wise judgement. In those few cases where she has wished for a change of emphasis, she has always willingly left the matter to my final decision. It may be surmised that these fine qualities, which have proved so invaluable to the biographer, also played their part in encouraging and helping her son in his career, which she always followed with an intelligent interest.

Lady Keynes, Maynard's widow, has been kindness itself. She has allowed me to use her drawing-room as my workshop, she has given me access to all papers, she has helped me in a number of other material ways, and often given me good cheer on my progress by words of encouragement. It should be recorded, however, that I have not had her assistance in the actual composition of the narrative which follows; statements relating to the Russian Ballet, or to the many other matters of which she had cognizance, do not have the benefit of her confirmation.

Mr Geoffrey Keynes (brother) has given me access to all materials and helped in every possible way, and he and Mrs A. V. Hill (sister) have read through the galley proofs.

These have also been read by Mr R. F. Kahn. He is a high authority on the development of Keynes's thought on economics during the crucial period from 1929 to 1939. It was a great source of comfort to me to have my account subjected to his careful scrutiny, and I am grateful for a number of valuable suggestions. It must not be inferred that he would endorse my distribution of emphasis in the work as a whole.

For the sake of economy in what has been a very laborious task, I have, on occasions when I had documentary evidence or first-hand knowledge, omitted to consult certain prime authorities. In the field of pure economic doctrine another principle has also been at work. Keynes's views have for many years constituted an important part of my mental life, and I have discussed them over and over again with many experts. I accordingly judged that the best result would be achieved in a biography, which has to be very selective in its treatment of pure theory, if I put on paper my mature views without a fresh round of discussion. It is proper therefore that I should supplement my record of direct indebtedness by mentioning certain high authorities, whom I have not used as sources in chief in writing this Life (although some of them have helped me on ancillary matters), but with whom I have had discussions in earlier years – for the development of Keynes's economic thought in the twenties, Professor D. H. Robertson, for the thirties Mrs (Joan) Robinson, Mr P. Sraffa, Professor E. A. G. Robinson and Professor J. E. Meade.

Next I must express my thanks to Mr Duncan Grant and Mr and Mrs Clive Bell. I have spent more than one weekend in their house, gossiping about times past and reviving old memories. This was a part of my work which I enjoyed most. They have supplied valuable information and corrected my thoughts when they went astray. In this connection, however, I should mention that I have not relied primarily on these visits, or indeed upon any recent talks with Keynes's 'Bloomsbury' friends, for the impressions which I have put on paper. By good luck, through certain Oxford friends, and quite independently of Keynes, I was brought into touch with a number of members of the 'Bloomsbury' circle when I was a young man in the twenties. They made a sharp and indelible impression on my mind. This section of my book has something of the character of an autobiography, being an attempt to give form to the impressions which I received twenty-five years ago. My account is certainly a fragmentary and imperfect one, but it is first-hand. I have, however, been helped by having been allowed to read the large two-way correspondence between Keynes and Mr Duncan Grant and Mrs Bell.

To Mr James Strachey I am grateful for permitting me to see and use letters which passed between his brother, Lytton Strachey, and Keynes, and for helping me in a number of ways. Keynes, Mr James Strachey and I agreed at least on one point – our profound admiration for Lytton Strachey. Posterity will be able to judge one side of his genius from his written works. There was also another side – a certain quality, highly individual, exciting, strangely compelling, yet elusive, which was manifested in conversation with his friends. This quality, which created a great impression at the time, will probably never be conveyed to future generations – unless we have some yet unknown writer of genius among us. My own task has been limited to putting down to the best of my ability what seemed relevant to Keynes's great friendship with him. Mr James Strachey has helped me in many ways, but is by no means responsible for what I have said about his brother.

Next I must thank Professor Lionel Robbins, who has read through the last four chapters and been good enough to write out many pages of detailed comments upon them and to spend many hours with me discussing these matters. I owe a great deal to him. I must also thank Lord Brand and Mr Frank Lee, who have read through these four chapters and helped me with their observations. I had the privilege of an interview with Field-Marshal the Rt Hon. J. C. Smuts, who has subsequently read through Chapters 7 and 8 and given me the benefit of his views upon them. Mr Richard Braithwaite saw the first version of my two sections on Probability and saved me from a number of mistakes – he may still think that my final version contains some! Mr John Ryan has read through Chapter 10, section 2 (on the Cotton Industry).

I must express thanks to Mr J. R. Sargent (Christ Church), who has made laborious statistical calculations for me in connection with the French estimates on damage in World War I, and with Post-War Credits.

I am grateful to the Provost and Fellows of King's College for bearing with me on frequent visits and for many other kindnesses. Perhaps I should here mention the greatest kindness of all: when I came as a stranger from Oxford in 1922, Sir John Sheppard, not yet Provost, and the other Fellows welcomed me and made me feel completely at home in my new surroundings. But for the quite unusual warmth of their hospitality, I might have failed to maintain my continuing connection with King's, and this book might never have been written.

I am grateful to the Treasury for having allowed me to inspect the official records of Lord Keynes's work in the department, and to publish certain extracts from them, and for the promptness with which it has tended to my needs. It has, however, no responsibility for, and would not necessarily endorse, the conclusions which I have drawn from the study of these papers.

I am grateful also to the Rockefeller Foundation for having provided me with a timely supply of dollars, thus enabling me to make a longer stay in the United States than would otherwise have been possible. Had it not been for this generosity I should inevitably have been much less well equipped to write the four concluding chapters of this book.

Many others have helped me. It would make an excellent 'parlour game' to place the names of those I wish to thank in their true order of merit. Some have borne with me through several interviews, some have written notes for my guidance. The quality of the testimony given would have to be balanced against its quantity. I have included the name of one with whom I only had talk for a few minutes; her evidence was so crisp and lucid that it enabled me to make up my mind about a point on which I had long been in doubt, and on which many witnesses had given conflicting testimony. It seems better to arrange the names in alphabetical order and express my heartfelt thanks to the following:

Professor F. E. Adcock, Sir John Anderson, Mrs Bagenal, Mr T. Balston, Mr Cyril Beaumont, Professor Sir J. D. Beazley, Lady Violet Bonham-Carter, Mrs Harold Bowen, Madame Bussy, Mr Arthur Cole, Messrs Angus and Douglas Davidson, Mr R. H. Dundas, Mr O. T. Falk, Mr C. R. Fay, Mr David Garnett, Miss Mary Glasgow, Mr C. W. Guillebaud, Lord Halifax, Mr W. H. Haslam, Professor R. G. Hawtrey, Professor Agnes Headlam-Morley, Sir Hubert and Lady Henderson, Mr Norman Higgins, Sir Arthur Hobhouse, Mr W. H. Hope-Jones, Sir Richard Hopkins, Lord Layton, Mr S. G. Lubbock, Mr and Mrs Desmond

MacCarthy, Sir Andrew MacFadyean, Mr A. Mackworth-Young, the Revd Basil Maine, the late Sir Henry Marten, Mr Kingsley Martin, Mr J. C. Masterman, Professor H. O. Meredith, Mr M. Montagu-Nathan, Mr A. N. L. Munby, Sir Otto Niemeyer, Mr W. M. Page, Mr Alwyn Parker, Lord Perth, Professor A. C. Pigou, Dr J. Plesch, Professor D. H. Robertson, Professor E. A. G. Robinson, Mr A. Rose, Mr G. Rylands, Mr F. C. Scott, Sir J. T. Sheppard, Mr S. Sidney-Turner, Field-Marshal J. C. Smuts, Professor W. J. H. Sprott, Mr R. Stone, the Misses Marjorie, Pernel and Philippa Strachey, Mr B. W. Swithinbank, Mr G. M. Trevelyan, Mr R. Trouton, Sir David Waley, Mr Dudley Ward, Professor Geoffrey Webb, Sir Charles Webster, Mr G. Winthrop Young, Mr Leonard Woolf. And on the American side: Professor J. W. Angell, Mr A. Berle, jun., Mr E. M. Bernstein, Mr W. Chatfield-Taylor, Mr W. L. Clayton, Mr Frank Coe, Mr Ben Cohen, Mr E. G. Collado, Mr Oscar Cox, Mr Lauchlin Currie, Mr Marriner Eccles, Mr Herbert Feis, Justice F. Frankfurter, Mr W. Gardner, Mr E. A. Goldenweiser, M. Camille Gutt, Professor Alvin Hansen, Professor S. E. Harris, Mr H. Hawkins, Mr Quentin Keynes (nephew), Mr R. C. Leffingwell, Mr A. F. Luxford, Mr A. Maffry, Professor D. McCord Wright, Mr Henry Morgenthau, Mr Norman Ness, Mr R. Opie (who has to be reckoned on this side now), Mr L. Pasvolsky, Mrs F. D. Roosevelt, Mr A. Sachs, Mr W. S. Salant, Mr Walter Stewart, Professor J. Viner, Chief Justice F. M. Vinson, Professor J. H. Williams, and Mr J. H. Willits.

These are my living authorities. My documentation has mainly consisted of Keynes's own papers. I will forbear to mention the large mass of literature which I have consulted, with one exception, namely, the admirable books on the Russian Ballet by Mr Cyril Beaumont.

I am grateful to Mr Geoffrey Winthrop Young for having written out for me and allowed me to use a description of Keynes when he was a boy at Eton (Ch. 1, 3), to Mr E. A. G. Robinson for two extracts from his obituary notice of Keynes in the *Economic Journal* (Ch. 4, 1 and Ch. 11, 1), to Colonel Terence Maxwell for having allowed me to publish letters by the late Mr Austen Chamberlain (Ch. 4, 3 and Ch. 6, 3), to Mrs Brooksbank for having allowed me to inspect the diary of her brother, Sir Basil Blackett, and to publish certain extracts from it (Ch. 6, 1), to Sir Frederick Kenyon (for the British Academy), Sir Richard Hopkins and Sir Otto Niemeyer for having allowed me to publish extracts from the obituary notice in the *Proceedings of the British Academy* (Ch. 6, 1), to Mr Alwyn Parker for his account of a character sketch of Keynes by the late Sir Eyre Crowe (Ch. 6, 3), to Mrs Allyn Young for having dug out an important letter from Keynes to her late husband (Ch. 8, 1), to the Provost of King's and Mr Hugh Durnford for the extract from the King's College brochure on Keynes (Ch. 10, 3), to Mr Walter Lippmann for allowing me to publish a letter by him (Ch. 11, 1) and to Professor Lionel Robbins for having allowed me to publish extracts from his Journal (Ch. 13, 4).

I am grateful to Mr E. M. Bernstein for having given me access to the files of the International Monetary Fund, and allowed me to spend some days working there; to Mr Kingsley Martin for having allowed me to work for several days at a desk in the offices of the *New Statesman*; to Sir Philip Hendy for having supplied me with a list of the works purchased at the Degas sale (1917); to Mr Geoffrey Crowther for letting me inspect the Minute Book of the Tuesday Club.

Mr Dundas, Keynes's old friend of Eton days, came into service and applied his meticulous scrutiny to my galley proofs. I am grateful also to Mr H. Dobell, who volunteered to place his exceptional gifts at my disposal at the page-proof stage. Mrs Stephens, who was Keynes's secretary for twelve years, spent more than a year on the heroic task of getting his papers into order before I appeared on the scene. She also typed the book, kept track of the numerous successive corrections in the various copies and performed the same service at the galley-proof stage. I am grateful to my wife for her continuing encouragement and for taking the hardest share in constructing the index.

*Christ Church, Oxford*
*June 1950*

R. F. HARROD

# [1]

## Home and Eton

I

JOHN MAYNARD KEYNES[1] was born on 5 June 1883, at 6
Harvey Road, a solid, roomy Victorian house in a quiet
Cambridge street. His parents, who survived him,[2] continued to live there throughout his sixty-three years. During all
his active and, at times, tempestuous career in the realms of
thought and practical affairs, he was able to return to this
house, full of fond memories, and to his parents, whom he
loved. They were loving parents; they also had qualities of
intellectual eminence and personal distinction, so that, great
man as he was, he did not outgrow them. His roots were
deep in 6 Harvey Road, which embodied the stable values
of the civilization in which he was bred.

In 1883 his father, John Neville Keynes, was a young
Cambridge don of rising reputation as a lecturer in logic
and political economy and as an administrator. Life was full
of pleasant activity and of the promise of good things to
come. His gifted wife, Florence Ada, was destined to make
her own mark in local affairs and with her pen, and had tact
and sagacity which enabled her to be an unfailing support
to her son. On 4 February 1885 Margaret was born, and on
25 March 1887, Geoffrey. Here was a happy, late-Victorian
family, living in moderate circumstances but solid comfort,
the house well staffed with domestic servants, the passing
days full of activity and the future secure.

In Cambridge, the pulse of life beat strongly. The home of
ancient traditions, which still flourished, it was a progressive
place; its pre-eminence in the natural sciences ensured that.

1. Pronounced Canes.
2. Dr Keynes, his father, died on 15 November 1949, at the age of
97.

The social sciences also were gaining recognition. University reforms were under way. There was the problem of the relation of the University to the Colleges. The provision of lectures had been reorganized, the curricula revised. Cambridge was throwing out tentacles over the country through her system of extension lectures and external examinations: John Neville Keynes was at this time assistant secretary to the 'Syndicate for local examinations and lectures'. There was the unfolding drama of the advent of women to Cambridge and their admission to lectures, examinations and other privileges. Henry Sidgwick had been the hero in that story; he was also the hero of the Keynes family. He seemed to embody many of the virtues of the great Victorian age. His resignation of his Fellowship at Trinity on grounds of religious doubt had been an important landmark in the struggle for the abolition of religious tests at the University. His combination of eminence as a philosopher, personal integrity, free thinking, and tireless attention to the small details of University reform, made him a typical Victorian of the time; and how should he not be dear to the heart of the Keyneses, since Mrs Keynes had been one of the early pupils at Newnham, whose inception owed so much to him? Their attitude towards him was almost one of veneration. We shall see that Maynard, in his adult years, came to hold a somewhat different view – a change typical of the transition from the late Victorian outlook to that of the twentieth century.

If Cambridge combined a deep-rooted traditionalism with a lively progressiveness, so too did England. She was in the strongly upward trend of her material development; her overseas trade and investment were still expanding; the great pioneers of social reform were already making headway in educating public opinion. On the basis of her hardly won, but now solidly established, prosperity, the position of the British Empire seemed unshakable. Reforms would be within a framework of stable and unquestioned social values. There was ample elbow-room for experiment with-

out danger that the main fabric of our economic well-being
would be destroyed. It is true that only a minority enjoyed
the full fruits of this well-being; but the consciences of the
leaders of thought were not unmindful of the hardships of
the poor. There was great confidence that, in due course, by
careful management, their condition would be improved
out of recognition. The stream of progress would not cease
to flow. While the reformers were most earnestly bent on
their purposes, they held that there were certain strict rules
and conventions which must not be violated; secure and
stable though the position seemed, there was a strong sense
that danger beset any changes. In the period that followed,
some of the rules came to seem absurd and the fears and
hesitations groundless. The life of Keynes lies athwart these
two periods; in his own thoughts he passed through the
transition, and, indeed, he contributed much to it. Those
who live half a century later, in a period when the tempo of
progress has increased but the world is full of perils, may
wonder whether all the old conventions were in fact completely foolish and the hesitations groundless. Have we yet
devised good new rules to replace the old rules? This is a
problem on which study of the development of Keynes's
thought should throw light.

Cambridge was an important constituent of England. She
trained a large proportion of those destined to guide public
opinion and to execute policy. There were personal links
between the University and those high in public affairs;
Mrs Henry Sidgwick was herself the sister of Mr Balfour,
who became Prime Minister. Thus Cambridge, where Keynes
spent his childhood, was an active, purposeful place. With
her strong traditionalism, her security, her earnestness, she
was an epitome of England. Reform, in the larger, as in the
smaller, sphere, was to be achieved primarily and principally
by the discussion of intelligent people. In all vital matters
their view would prevail. Public opinion would be wisely
guided. The existing stability, the need none the less for
caution in advance, and the certainty that advances on a

cumulative scale would be achieved, were taken for granted. They were the presuppositions of life, and the justification alike of one's work and one's leisure. Pleasures could be sipped with a clear conscience. Were not all good men day by day ensuring through their efforts that in due course those pleasures would be widely diffused and multiplied?

If I achieve my purpose, the life-work of Keynes will be seen, in part, as an expression of this Cambridge civilization, both in its stability and self-confidence and in its progressiveness. Will that life-work in due course have to be regarded as a splendid afterglow of a civilization fast disappearing, or may it perhaps be a link between one phase of British civilization and the next, stretching across a period of confusion and uncertainty?

Keynes's make-up would qualify him to be such a link. His mind was keenly receptive, and the events through which he lived made sharp and immediate impressions upon it. He became aware of changes in contemporary thought and contemporary practice as soon as they occurred. That was why, to those who had met him two or three times only, or had dipped into his writing without deep study, he presented a chameleon-like appearance. It was the chop and change of our age which they saw reflected in him, before they had had the wit to appreciate its significance themselves. But beneath this appearance of variability was a continuity of thought and purpose, which may be traced back to early influences. He continued to value those elements in our civilization which he had been brought up to value as a boy. Just because he was so quickly aware of new forces which might serve to disrupt this civilization, he felt how urgently needful it was for us to adapt ourselves without delay to the changes proceeding. If time were wasted, much might be lost beyond recovery. His mind was constantly seeking new methods of accommodation, new recipes.

World War I did much to undermine the stable and secure conditions of the British Empire and the presuppositions of 6 Harvey Road. As time went on, Keynes had to rely more and more on his own resources in devising policies he could support. On the one side were those of conservative temperament who did not understand the extent to which adaptation was necessary if old values were to be preserved in the new environment. On the other side were those who had little regard for the old values. To many of the former, Keynes may have seemed a mischievous radical; many of the latter, while welcoming him for his modernity, failed, to a large extent, to understand the purport of his message, lacking his presuppositions. Not all Englishmen fell into these two categories; he had many followers, who understood fairly well what he was about; his legacy remains with us. In what follows, some attempt will be made to interpret it.

Meanwhile, across the waters, there was a civilization in which the old self-confidence remained and was nourished by its own successes and growth of power. The American civilization is widely different from that of Harvey Road. On the material side one may perhaps put down the combination of modest, unostentatious living with ample domestic service and domestic comforts as the basis of cultured life of the old British type. Intellectual Cambridge may have had its counterpart in the United States; but it cannot be deemed to have resembled the more usual American pattern. Keynes was not predisposed to admire the American way of life. Later influences, strongly and typically British, coming from his circle of Bloomsbury friends, made him still less predisposed to take a kindly view of American civilization. And yet it was destined to happen that, when he crossed the Atlantic repeatedly, amid the grim and terrible circumstances of World War II, to discuss affairs of the utmost gravity, he found something that he had long missed in Britain. He found there men who had retained their intellectual poise, men of strong conviction, men who had their settled presuppositions, which, albeit not the same as those of Harvey Road, were first cousins to them, men who believed that by rational discussion one could plan and achieve reform and carry foward the progress of mankind.

Britain had, in the interval, become somewhat scatter-brained; events had moved too quickly for her, and most of her leading men had lost their grip. The continued security and prosperity of America had sustained that purposeful-ness, that self-confidence and that faith that the reasonable solution can be made to prevail which were the characteris-tics of late Victorian England, and which, because of Maynard Keynes's terrific innate mental vigour, had, despite all the storms, remained characteristic of him. And so it happened that he came at long last to appreciate that the United States was also a great civilization. Close cooperation was possible, almost easy.

Will these two nations continue in a joint endeavour for progress and reform on a world-wide scale? Did Keynes reach a point of view in this matter, as in so many others, in which his fellow-countrymen will follow him? Will the positive achievements of Bretton Woods endure and proli-ferate? Or will the heroic efforts of his last days prove vain?

When at Eton, Keynes, perhaps spurred by emulation of his distinguished compeers, devoted some time to tracing his family ancestry. There is a tree drawn out in his hand, which is headed 'William de Keynes, 1066'. A good begin-ning! One may conjure up the image of a long line of Keyneses who, behind the scenes on which puppet Planta-genets and Tudors played their parts, were in effect ruling the country all the while. At 1066 the correct spelling was Cahagnes, a place in Vire, Normandy. The modern spelling first occurs in 1300, and Kaynes in the reign of King John. They did not rule the country. But they were for several centuries persons of considerable substance, and may be traced in local names, such as Horsted-Keynes and Milton-Keynes. One line had estates in Sussex which included Tilton, of which Maynard obtained a life tenancy in order to make it his country home, without previously knowing of its connection with the family.[3] The Keyneses showed their proclivity to intellectual independence by remaining Catholics in the sixteenth and seventeenth centuries, and thereby they lost much of their position.[4] Maynard's grandfather lived at Salisbury, first as a manufacturer and then as a nurseryman. He prospered considerably, and bred and exhibited many new varieties of flowers. He married, as his second wife, Anna Neville of the Essex family of that name, and of that marriage John Neville, born in 1853, was the only child.

John Neville was educated at Amersham Hall School and University College, London, and having obtained a scholarship in mathematics at Pembroke College, Cambridge, was 'Senior Moralist' in 1875 and was awarded a Fellowship at Pembroke in 1876.[5] Six years later he married Florence Brown, one of the early Newnham students. She was a daughter of a well-known Congregationalist divine, John Brown, who was the minister for thirty years of Bunyan's chapel at Bedford, the author of an authoritative life of Bunyan and of other works on the history of puritanism, and received a doctorate from the University of Yale. One of his sons, Sir Walter Langdon-Brown, became Regius Professor of Physics in Cambridge. Maynard claimed to be the first son of the marriage of a Cambridge Fellow with a member of Newnham.

Seven months after the happy event of Maynard's birth, Neville Keynes published the first edition of his book on *Formal Logic*. This underwent successive revisions until the edition of 1906. It is a notable work: thorough, lucid and

3. The same ancestor who owned property at Tilton also acquired property in the parish of Barton, of which King's was tithe-owner. Maynard, as bursar, took an active interest in this church, while probably unconscious of its connection with his family.

4. For a full account of the Keynes pedigree and also of Maynard's ancestors on his mother's side, see *Gathering up the Threads*, by F. A. Keynes. Publ. Heffer & Sons, 1950.

5. He was also awarded a Fellowship at University College, London, which he held for life without stipend.

7

authoritative, and may well attain a permanent place in the history of thought. It is an exposition of the system of deductive logic, of which Aristotle was the inventor and which for some twenty-two centuries has constituted the main part of what teachers and scholars have understood by logic. It carried a stage further the work of the nineteenth-century masters – Mill, De Morgan, Jevons and Venn. It appeared on the eve of that great displacement which has been caused by the rapid and spectacular development of 'mathematical logic'. The practitioners of this new branch claim that old deductive logic is now dead and buried.

A final verdict cannot yet be given. Maynard, who promoted or was associated with so many great changes of thought and practice in his time, was also a close and interested spectator of this more recondite but very fundamental change in our theory of the principles of human thought. The condition of logical studies has not yet reached a new equilibrium. Few now doubt that the mathematical logicians have achieved a mighty synthesis, which will not be challenged in essentials and has far-reaching implications. But the new system, imprisoned, as in a manner it is, in its own symbolism, fails to answer satisfactorily many philosophical problems about deductive thought. Neville Keynes's book has a sure place as the most complete and polished exposition of the old system. It is still commonly used as a text-book in Cambridge, and still often recommended, when teachers in the sister university overcome their insularity, for reading in Oxford. It is likely that, when the study of thought as such recovers its wind after the formidable impact of the symbolists, many of the lines of inquiry which we find in Neville Keynes's treatise will be taken up again for further development.

One of the closest friends of the family was the logician W. E. Johnson. By comparison with the graciousness and warmth of John Neville, Johnson appeared to many to be rather a dry stick. But he had his charm for those who knew him well; G. K. Chesterton was a great friend, and, when he came on one of his periodic visits, there was no lack of fun in the Johnson home. To the notice by Professor Broad in the *Proceedings of the British Academy,* Maynard contributed a description:

He used, when I was a child, regularly to lunch at Harvey Road with my father, I should think almost once a week. My father was then writing a book on logic [strictly, this should be, revising his book], which would frequently be a matter of discussion. They seemed to me in those days to sit endlessly over the meal, and I would be in a fidget to be allowed to get up and go. His voice and manner were quite unchanged in my memory from those days, more than forty years ago, up to the end of his life.

Maynard remembered his fidgets as a little boy; but it is recalled that when he was no longer quite such a little boy he used to join in the argument between his father and Johnson. Unhappily, we do not know what precisely the arguments were about or which side Maynard took. A profound student of thought might be able, by the diligent study of the logical writings of Keynes father, Keynes son and Johnson, to elucidate this matter, and thereby perhaps to explain characteristic tendencies (even perversities!) in the economic writings of Maynard, for this precocious initiation into debate on the higher mysteries of logic would surely implant a lasting intellectual bias.

Maynard retained a great regard for Johnson. When I asked him in 1922 how much mathematics it was needful for an economist to know, he replied that Johnson, in his article in the *Economic Journal*,[6] had carried the application of mathematical analysis to economic theory about as far as it was likely to be useful to carry it.[7]

6. December 1913: 'The Pure Theory of Utility Curves'.

7. He had evidently written the matter off in his mind thus. Mathematical economists of the younger school may have felt in more recent years that he did not sufficiently appreciate the value of their original work. His dictum about Johnson's contribution was clearly not meant to have finality. It may have been a shrewd assessment of what was likely to be useful to himself in his own economic explorations within his own span of life.

Meanwhile, in the years immediately following 1883 even Maynard could not be expected to know anything of logic or mathematical economics. His father kept a diary which preserves for us contemporary notes about the progress of the infant. Readers of *The General Theory of Employment, Interest and Money* may like to know that in 1888, at the age of four and a half, Maynard, on being asked what is meant by interest, said, 'If I let you have a halfpenny and you kept it for a very long time, you would have to give me back that halfpenny and another too. That's interest.' In April 1890 (age six) there is an entry about the future logician: 'Maynard much interested in his brain. "Just now," he says, "it is wondering how it thinks. It ought to know."' In March 1891 (age seven) we find the entry, 'His father having remarked that he was not behaving so well at lunch as he had done the day before when Dr James Ward came to lunch, "That," he said, "was by a great effort. I had been preparing for it for days. I cannot always make so great an effort!"' There is a delightfully happy feeling in the diary. His father remarks that he is a 'thoroughly interesting companion'.

Meanwhile, John Neville was going from strength to strength. He was an economist as well as a logician. In the year of Maynard's birth, Alfred Marshall writes, 'I am delighted indeed to see that you are examiner at London' (a permanent appointment). 'If I had to select the man out of all England whom I should have liked to have there, I should have chosen you.'

Marshall's regard for Keynes as an economist is further testified by a voluminous correspondence, in which Marshall consulted him, as one whose verdict would have great weight, on various points in economics, which had to be settled for his forthcoming *magnum opus, The Principles of Economics*. Keynes was in correspondence also with most of the leading economists of the day. There was some idea that he might become Professor of Political Economy in Oxford, and a letter from Professor Foxwell (15 January 1888) is worth quoting:

I should regret it for many reasons, though I expect it would be the best thing for Oxford . . .

Pray don't go. It is much better that a study be concentrated in a particular place. There arise many of the same advantages as in the localization of an industry. Your departure would leave a nasty ragged wound in our Moral Sciences Organization.

What is the use of being a settled family man if you are to drift from your moorings in this fashion? Think of the effect your move may have on your son. He may grow up flippantly epigrammatical and end by becoming the proprietor of a Gutter Gazette, or the hero of a popular party; instead of emulating his father's noble example, becoming an accurate, clear-headed Cambridge man, spending a life in the valuable and unpretentious service of his kind, dying beloved of his friends, venerated by the wise and unknown to the masses, as true merit and worth mostly are.

John Neville stayed at Cambridge. Maynard's career did not exactly correspond to Foxwell's prescription, but, for all the epigrams and even flippancies that he subsequently perpetrated, he was, at the centre of his being, 'an accurate and clear-headed Cambridge man'. It was the combination of the solid worth with the epigrammatic brilliance that enabled him to render his unique service to mankind. Would Oxford indeed have caused him to cultivate his taste for epigrams over-much?

In 1890 the British Economic Association was founded, with John Neville as an original member of the Council, and in March 1891 the first issue of the *Economic Journal* appeared, under the editorship of F. Y. Edgeworth. Maynard was destined to become its editor for a period of no less than thirty-three years. It is interesting to know that his father was strongly pressed by Alfred Marshall and others to become the first editor. 'I promise not to worry you any more about editorship of the *Economic Journal*. . . . Foxwell asked whether there was any use in putting pressure on you for the last time. *Everyone* would *very much* prefer you.'[8]

8. Letter to J. N. Keynes from Alfred Marshall, 7 February 1889.

In 1890 appeared the first edition of *The Scope and Method of Political Economy*. This, like *Formal Logic*, became and remained for many years the standard English treatise on the subject. It has not been replaced by a work of comparable scope. It has the same qualities as *Formal Logic*, accuracy of thought, lucidity of style, thorough scholarship, balanced judgement and fairness to all parties in matters of controversy. It does not claim to blaze a new trail. It is modest, and therewith has authority. The reader has the comfortable feeling that he is on solid ground, that a widely read scholar and master of precise thinking is carrying him to the limit, but not beyond the limit, of what can safely be accepted, and that no touch of egoism is biasing the author. In June 1891 he was awarded a Doctorate of Science by Cambridge University, and Maynard (aged eight) was present at the ceremony. Maynard, with his varied gifts, has captured the imagination of mankind and succeeded in influencing the course of history to a notable extent; but John Neville has also his own special claims to be remembered by future generations.

In 1890 Maynard was sent to the Perse School Kindergarten; one does not learn much at institutions of this kind, and Maynard was given his elementary instruction at home. In 1892 he began his more public life by going as a day boy to St Faith's preparatory school, of which Mr Goodchild was headmaster. In the same year, his father made a step forward in his career of varied interests, by being promoted to be Secretary of the Local Examinations and Lectures Syndicate. For eighteen years he was the organizer of the important and rapidly developing work for which this Syndicate was responsible. In due course he became the leading administrator in the University and held the supreme position of Registrary from 1910 to 1925.[9] Many tributes

9. In 1892 he was elected to the Council of the Senate. In 1893 he became its honorary secretary, a position which seems at that time to have been more influential than that of the Registrary. When Keynes became Registrary in 1910 the two offices were combined.

have been paid to his excellent work in this capacity. It may be most appropriate to quote his son, whose words, even if biased on this subject, are of interest to us. In August 1942 Dr and Mrs Neville Keynes celebrated the diamond anniversary of their wedding. There are some very rough notes in pencil of what Maynard proposed to say at the family gathering. After touching tributes to his mother and his father, he proceeds to say of the latter:

Let me look at him more from the outside for a moment. I saw him for a long period as he was in the University. For thirty-three years he was one of the best administrators there ever was and during those years this University was a better place in my judgement than it has ever been before or since. Perfect order and accuracy without a shadow of pedantry and red tape, the machine existing for the sake of the University and not the other way round as it sometimes seems to be now. He really helped to create a framework within which learning and science and education could live and flourish without feeling restraint or a hampering hand, and he combined this with himself possessing learning and science and education at the highest level – which no one now seems to be able to do.

While Dr Keynes was thus busy, his wife had many practical activities of her own. She was one of the first to plan a Juvenile Labour Exchange, which was afterwards taken over by the local authority and finally absorbed in the national scheme. She was also concerned with the establishment of Papworth Village Settlement which revolutionized the lives of those suffering from chronic tuberculosis. Small pensions were given by the Charity Organization Society, of which she was the local secretary for many years, to old people living in great penury. She had much to do with helping families back on to their feet when they had been thrown into the workhouse on account of the bread-winner's unemployment, the help being especially needed because he was not allowed out of the workhouse unless he took his family with him, and some arrangements for this had to be made in advance. All these reforms proceeded slowly and with great difficulty owing to the parsimony of the government in providing funds for the social services.

Mrs Keynes was in fact a great pioneer. It may well be that her practical humanity made a deeper impression on Maynard's young mind than the abstract doctrines of the social philosophers, who were sometimes a little remote from the sordid realities. In her activities Maynard could see the reforming spirit of Cambridge taking effect and bringing solace to afflicted persons.

Whilst the Keyneses were thus much occupied on active work in their several spheres, their main interest remained centred upon their home. They had no great love of social entanglements, reserving their leisure hours for their best friends, and, above all, for their children. Reading aloud was a favourite entertainment, the father reading Dickens to the family, or Maynard poetry to his sister; there were trips to London to see plays, carefully chosen to suit the awakening powers of the boy; Dr Keynes had a special love for the theatre, a trait inherited by Maynard.

There were no signs of the infant prodigy in Maynard's early years at Mr Goodchild's. There were fairly good reports, and reports not so good, which contained complaints of carelessness. There were indeed references at the age of eight to his being quick at arithmetic and algebra and to his large vocabulary. But on the whole, progress appears to have been slow. There was more than the usual allowance of colds, coughs, temperatures and headaches. The diary has a reference to the school driving him too hard, to his being away from school for a large part of one term in 1893, and to his taking a whole term away from school in the autumn of that year. There seems to have been some frailty of constitution, which continued to give rise to anxiety until the age of fifteen, and less frequently thereafter. He was not robust. Up to a point he was careful in this matter; throughout his life he did much of his work while lying in bed in the morning. But his tireless mind and fiery spirit took charge, dominated his body, made it sustain labours that would soon have broken a much stronger man – and in the end he overtaxed it.

He does not appear to have made many friends at Mr Goodchild's. None the less he seems to have had the power to exert influence in a characteristic way. We hear of a 'slave' who walked behind him, at a respectful distance, carrying his books home from school. This service was given in return for protection during scrapes or assistance at work. With another boy he made what he called a 'commercial treaty'. This boy was uncongenial. So he made an arrangement to place a book from the circulating library on the top of a pillar-box regularly each week, on the understanding that the boy would never approach within fifteen yards of him at any time.

Harvey Road was itself full of recently married dons' children who careered about on their bicycles. At the age of nine Maynard had a serious accident, owing to collision with a hansom-cab. Fenner's cricket ground was at the end of the road, and he spent many hours watching the players and keeping records of their scores. For a considerable time he retained an intense interest in cricket, although he never became adept at the game in practice.

Only when he was eleven is there a record that he was first in the class (June 1894). In December of that year, things began to look up; he was first again, and a mathematical master, who was of somewhat higher attainment than is usual at a preparatory school, reports that 'he does really brilliant work'; but adds that he 'soon tires and has not perseverance in the face of difficulty'. How unlike what Maynard was so soon to become! After this, progress was more marked, and physically he became more robust. As he approached the age of thirteen, he began to grow very rapidly. Mr Goodchild reports of his work at the end of 1896 that Maynard is 'head and shoulders above all the other boys in the school', and feels confident that he will get a scholarship for Eton. This became an important aim. Special tutors were engaged for a brief period. Mr Robert

Walter Shackle, father of the well-known economist Mr G. L. S. Shackle, coached him in mathematics, and reported that he was 'so delightful a pupil'. For a time Maynard rose at 7 a.m. to work before breakfast, because the Eton examination was due to begin at that hour. Poor Maynard!

On 28 June is an entry in Dr Keynes's diary:

It is a grief to me to think that the dear boy will not in any case do his work very much longer with me in the study.

Working together in the same study! One cannot but be reminded of those other two economists, James Mill and John Stuart Mill.

He had to face his ordeal on 5 July 1897, then already fourteen and rather older than the average. On 4 July is the entry, 'Maynard not well'. The next day his parents took him to Eton, and the examination lasted three days. The Vice-Chancellor[10] was one of the examiners. The entry for the 12th summarizes the anguish of how many millions of parents!

July 12th. Expect telegram from Vice-Chancellor 2 to 3 p.m. Nothing came. Gave up hope. At 5.30, telegram arrived. Maynard tenth out of twenty elected.

Maynard had been bracketed first in mathematics. Dillwyn Knox, aged twelve, had been head of the list.

After that there had to be much preparation and measuring for Eton clothes. At Eton, boys were each assigned a tutor, in addition to their house-master and form-master. Apparently it was possible to negotiate under this head. Mr Samuel Gurney (Jimbo) Lubbock had just been appointed a master at Eton. He recalls how Dr Keynes came to pay a call on him one morning in King's College, and stated that he would like him to be Maynard's tutor. Lubbock protested – after all, he was a new hand at this himself and surely Dr Keynes would prefer to have an experienced master. But Dr Keynes overbore him with a courteous firmness. He had

10. Mr Charles Smith, Master of Sidney Sussex College.

made inquiries of the authorities at King's College.[11] They, with their traditional faith in the virtues of the young, assured Dr Keynes that he could not do better than choose Mr Lubbock. The choice proved a fortunate one, for in the struggle over Maynard's soul, which was later to develop at Eton, Lubbock took the broad view that he should not specialize too much in mathematics, his best subject, at the expense of a more general education.

Mr Lubbock was indeed an ideal tutor, a man of culture, wide interests, fine tact and sensitiveness, the very type of English gentleman, tall and handsome, and a most success-ful schoolmaster. Something of the Lubbock quality is known to a wider world through the published works of his brother, Mr Percy Lubbock, a writer with an exquisite deli-cacy, power of observation, and sense of beauty. One may believe that these same qualities were present in Jimbo Lubbock and channelled by him into the loving surveillance of many generations of Eton schoolboys.

Maynard was due to go to Eton on 22 September, but on 19 September he had a feverish attack and had to go to school three days late.

*Mrs Keynes to Dr J. N. Keynes*, 26 September 1897

I very much wish you were here so that I could tell you our experiences yesterday ... I am sure you will be glad to hear first of all that the dear boy seemed very much better and when I left him said that he felt hardly more tired than he would have done under ordinary circumstances ... By the way, Miss Hackett says she believes Maynard is bigger than his fag-master (Macnagh-ten)! This is a relief to mother [his grandmother] who seems to be under the impression that fags are beaten and generally ill-treated by their masters ...

Maynard played up by writing one letter to his father and another to his mother on that same first day, giving an

11. King's has a close connection with Eton, as twin foundation of Henry VI, and has a number of closed scholarships for Eton boys.

hourly narrative of events. Admission to college is described
as 'something like having your degree'.

The letters to his father continued as a matter of weekly
routine. At first they were a little thin, suggesting an attempt,
not always successful, to cover four pages of writing-paper.
But in his second year at school the letters thickened and
became much more interesting and lively, bristling with
news and views. A paradox. The trend with schoolboys is
usually the other way. With adolescence and the crowding
in of new interests, thoughts, friendships and intellectual
adventures, there is apt to be a falling-off in the zeal for
writing home. For this week's letter there is no time; the
next week's is a little perfunctory; one must write to one's
parents, but the duty is found a trifle burdensome. If Maynard moved in the opposite direction, that is certainly a
tribute to his father's sympathy and fond interest in every
detail of school life. It is also symptomatic of certain qualities
in Maynard. For one thing, there was that extraordinary
intellectual capaciousness. If a thousand other interests were
pressing in, there was still ample room for a full and growing
communication of thoughts with his father. So it was all
through his life; the new interests did not drive out the old;
both could be accommodated together. It was also, perhaps,
a symptom of the strength and magisterial quality of Maynard's mind. His ideas were so well founded and strong in
good sense, that he was not bashful, as schoolboys so often
are, of showing them to his parents. He had enough self-
confidence to believe they would be interesting. And so the
full flow of correspondence continued and grew.

Every detail of school affairs was discussed: what work
was being done – sometimes mathematical problems were
transcribed in full – what games were played, what school
events were taking place, how the other boys were pro-
gressing, the pros and cons of changes in curricula. The
father got to know about Maynard's contemporaries so well
that he could give a comprehensive forecast of their order
in the Newcastle Prize examination.

The letters show extremely clearly how absorbingly interested Maynard was in the work, the games and the whole
life of the school. It became his passion. It may certainly be
claimed that Eton greatly helped his development. He found
there associates who were congenial to him, youths of intellectual distinction with whom he could quickly get on to
terms of intimacy on the basis of common interests. They
had self-confidence, inquiring minds and a gay and carefree
outlook. His own great fund of gaiety, of fun and satire,
found scope. It is not clear that there are many schools in the
world where one can find a wide choice of companions of
this quality; it is clear that he needed this society and that
in his school-days his imagination was already stimulated
and taking wing.

2

His mother had taken him there and left him, rather anxious
about his health and strength, knowing his charming, kindly
character and his excellent, clever companionship in the
home, pleased at the rapid progress which he had finally
made in the preparatory school, but with some doubts,
surely, as to how he would stand up to the exacting tests of a
larger world. We have seen how rapidly he had been growing physically in the previous year – 'taller' on arrival 'than
his fag-master'. It turned out that this gave him a good start.
Mr Hope-Jones, who was in his election as a scholar and
afterwards became a master at Eton for many years, recalls
the impression made by his tall stature on his contemporaries. He was a little their senior, not in years, but in months,
which are important at that time of life. His voice had
already broken. He seemed quite a young man in their
midst. They at once looked to him for leadership. If a group
was summoned for a misdemeanour by the authorities, it
was assumed, without pause or question, that he would be
their spokesman. This young boy, so carefully cherished in
the home, careful of his own comforts also, fastidious, ailing,

the product of a day-school only, suddenly became, by accidents of premature growth and a broken voice, the spokesman of his group at Eton. And what a spokesman! His friends could not at first have known what manner of man was among them. For of all the divine gifts none was lavished upon him so unstintingly, in no sphere has his talent been so peerless and undisputed, as spokesmanship. He became a natural leader at once. From St Faith's to Eton, the transition was easily made. His career now began in earnest.

### *J. M. Keynes to Dr J. N. Keynes*, 3 October 1897

. . . I like Mr Lubbock very much . . . He is going to read some Homer with me as private work . . . My fag-master is very nice to me, and if he has anything extra for me to do always asks me if I am sure I have nothing else I want to do. He does not want me to call him in the morning as most do.

### *J. M. Keynes to Mrs Keynes*, 11 October 1897

To my great surprise I have come out top of the division in the fortnightly order . . . My cold is very much better.

There are a good many reassurances about health in these early letters.

### *J. M. Keynes to Dr J. N. Keynes*, 17 October 1897

. . . On my last prose I had (I think) 'Style good but too many mistakes'. And on the verse 'Better but too many blunders'. Do not laugh and say 'careless as usual'.

Still the child in this letter.

### *ibid.*

Last night we had chamber singing which was a glorious rag lasting an hour and a half. All fags are required to sing, but not many of the older ones are present, and after the fags have finished, several are called upon and the night is made hideous with the row.

I will leave you to guess what I sang, but it was the success of the evening (as far as the fags go) and was the only one to be encored later in the evening.

This notable song, which became a standard item, was entitled 'Three Blue Bottles'.

### *J. M. Keynes to Dr J. N. Keynes*, 6 December 1897

Last night College Pop Supper took place and I and three other fags were deputed to wait. They had a glorious feed, turkey, champagne, etc. When they got to the dessert stage, we fags retired to Lower Tea Room and made a supper off the remains and a bottle of champagne. As one of the fags did not take any, the other three had to do their duty and finish it.

When we had finished, we went in again and songs etc. proceeded for about an hour. I was called on to sing 'T.B.B.'. Afterwards we handed coffee round. In fact we had a very fine time.

### *J. M. Keynes to Dr J. N. Keynes*, 12 December 1897

I was not the fag who abstained from champagne ...

Maynard was not corrupted by this early initiation; throughout his life he was always abstemious in such matters. But in his last two or three years he was in the habit of saying on festive occasions that the only thing he seriously regretted about the way in which he had managed his life was that he had not drunk more champagne! Was he recalling these early celebrations of his schooldays? Probably not, as he lived essentially in the moment. Perhaps there was some semi-conscious reminiscence. The past lives on and colours the present. Who is that interesting looking man, with a glass of champagne in his hand, talking so animatedly at the wedding party? Is it a great statesman, upon whose wisdom the financial solvency of Britain herself depends, as by a thread, a man gravely ill, although so talkative and gay, a man barely kept alive by medical skill and the tireless devotion of his wife? Or is it a young man, tall beyond his years, his voice only recently broken, partaking in the festivities of College Pop?

At the end of his first 'half'[12] he came out first for classics. He had been pushed up three divisions at the end of the first fortnight in mathematics, but none the less came out second. He had evidently got into his stride. His curve of development, which had risen so sharply in his last year or two at St Faith's, was proceeding upwards and carrying him well beyond the level of the previous July, when he had only been elected tenth to Eton. In this first term, a copy of his verses was 'sent up for good'. By this Eton custom, good compositions and mathematical solutions were transcribed, bound up and deposited in the College Library. Numerous classical compositions and mathematical sums in Maynard's hand may be inspected there. Some may regret that the practice of preserving these fair copies has been discontinued.

At the end of this term he was selected at the head of the list to Chamber Pop, a debating society for those in Chamber, i.e. who have not yet acquired rooms of their own. Excellent reports came in. Lubbock noted that he had 'a real healthy interest in all the doings of College, athletic and otherwise'.

Next term was interrupted by measles and absence. Despite this, progress appears to have been made. In the following term he was captain of Chamber and won the Junior Mathematical Prize. 'Maynard will be returning to you with his honours thick upon him . . . I have been delighted to see that he takes no half-hearted interest in his own games and those of the school.'[13] Characteristic touches began to appear in Maynard's letters.

*J. M. Keynes to Dr J. N. Keynes*, 11 October 1898

Tuck preached in Lower Chapel about bicycling, comparing it to life. He compared the telegraph posts to guardian angels. I

12. A 'half' is a term. Three halves make one year at Eton.
13. Mr S. G. Lubbock to Dr J. N. Keynes, 28 July 1898.

wish I could have been there. He promised one on football next
Sunday.

### J. M. Keynes to Dr J. N. Keynes, 5 February 1899

The Reverend the Provost preached today. He really ought not
to be allowed to ...

### J. M. Keynes to Dr J. N. Keynes, 30 April 1899

I had a short conversation with Professor Darwin[14] at the end of
the journey. His hands certainly looked as if he might be descended from an ape.

This is the first recorded reference to hands. Observation
of hands remained a lifelong interest; he thought that they
were the best guide to character. At one time he had casts
made of his own and his wife's hands, and even talked of
making a collection of his friends'.

### Extract from 'The Economic Consequences of the Peace'. Description of President Wilson

... and his hands, though capable and fairly strong, were wanting
in sensitiveness and finesse.[15]

### Extract from a description of President Roosevelt on his first meeting him in 1934

... But at first, of course, I did not look closely at these things.
For naturally my concentrated attention was on his hands. Rather
disappointing. Firm and fairly strong, but not clever or with
finesse, shortish round nails like those at the end of a businessman's fingers. I cannot draw them right, yet while not distinguished (to my eye) they are not of a common type. All the same,
they were oddly familiar. Where had I seen them before? I spent

14. Sir George Darwin.
15. Monsieur Etienne Mantoux in *The Carthaginian Peace*, a severe
criticism of Keynes's *Economic Consequences of the Peace*, took him
to task for regarding the shape of the President's hands as relevant.
'Why not also reveal to the world that Wilson wore pince-nez and that
Lloyd George had a grey moustache?'

ten minutes at least searching my memory as for a forgotten name, hardly knowing what I was saying about silver and balanced budgets and public works. At last it came to me. Sir Edward Grey. A more solid and Americanized Sir Edward Grey. The idea will probably mislead you, but there is a grain of significant truth in it. Much cleverer, much more fertile, sensitive, and permeable, but something all the same, which corresponded to those finger nails and carried me back to Sir Edward Grey.

Let it not be thought that the boyish joke about Professor Darwin implied any predisposition to be hostile to the theory of natural selection.

*J. M. Keynes to B. W. Swithinbank*, 13 May 1908

. . . Really the most substantial joys I get are from the perception of logical arguments, and, oh, from reading Darwin's life. How superb it is. Surely he was the greatest and best and happiest of men.

In the next half we learn that Maynard was awarded full marks for an essay on the 'Responsibilities of Empire'. Some responsibilities were to fall on him later! It is satisfactory to know that his opinions were considered quite perfect by Eton in 1899. His marks in the examination this half were considered remarkable – 1156 out of 1400 – and Mr Lubbock adds, 'in his work there is absolutely nothing of the mercenary, mark-getting feeling . . . He takes a real interest in anything which it is worth while to be interested in.'

His interest in the athletic side of things remained keen. 'I have been out on the river every day this week. I enjoyed rowing immensely and wonder now why anyone ever remains a drybob.'[16] 'I have never watched such an exciting match' (cricket match against Winchester) 'and at the end of it was a mental and physical wreck.'[17]

This term he was at the head of the select list in the Senior Mathematical Prize. On 5 August, Mr Lubbock wrote:

16. Letter from J. M. Keynes to Dr J. N. Keynes, 7 May 1899.
17. ibid., 25 June 1899.

. . . He is never unduly elated by the mere getting of a prize and seems to realize fully that handsomely bound volumes are not the most important result of learning. Moreover the manner in which his work is done and the attitude he takes towards his various masters are as nice and good as they can be and it says much for him that some very illiterate members of my pupil-room with whom he comes into contact, like and respect him a good deal.

This summer the family holiday was at Tintagel.

*Extract from Dr J. N. Keynes's Diary*, 6 August 1899

Our pleasure in our children has, I think, never been greater than it is now, and during the summer holiday, we have them so entirely with us. We are certainly a very happy quintet.

In the next half, the first of his third year – he was now already sixteen – he was up to Broadbent, a famous and rather formidable Eton master, distinguished scholar, occasional correspondent with Wilamowitz-Moellendorff himself. Maynard had a word of praise for him. He also began at this time to go for history to C. H. K. Marten, beloved of many generations, who eventually became Provost of Eton. This half we find him playing in the famous Eton College Wall game.

And now, while things proceeded thus placidly at Eton, Britain was involved in the Boer War. It is not clear to what extent deeper questions of right and wrong, such as harassed the mind in 1914, were pondered by the schoolboy. He took a common-sense view about his own position; he showed signs of that healthy optimism which was to serve him in good stead at more momentous crises; we see signs of the statistician peeping out.

*J. M. Keynes to Dr J. N. Keynes*, 22 October 1899

. . . I am no more jingo than I was previously, but now that war has begun one must perforce be reconciled to it. Besides, when

25

writing for such journals as the *Acorn*,[18] it is necessary to be a little rampant to keep up its circulation.

### J. M. Keynes to Dr J. N. Keynes, 17 December 1899

I agree with you that the news from South Africa is bad, especially this last reverse of Buller. But we console ourselves with history which makes our losses and reverses seem puny. In the battle of Albuera, nearly one hundred years ago in the Peninsular war, our losses were seven times as heavy per cent as at the Modder River, yet we won. People are so terribly eager to get up a scare that they make the failure of ours to make the Boers to evacuate a position as bad as if we ourselves had evacuated a position. It is rather deceptive too, including in the term losses, wounded and missing as well as killed.

It is hard luck on generals that news should be transmitted so quickly. The people do not see the result of the campaign but seem to gloat over every little loss. Seventy men killed in a battle is terrible for their families, but it is a tiny loss for a nation of 30 million.

### J. M. Keynes to Dr J. N. Keynes, 29 January 1900

This morning the Head gave us a stirring oration on the volunteer movement. He declared it to be in the present circumstances the duty of all to get what military training they could, and he said that he expected all boys of the right age to join our corps.

For once in a way his words have had effect and people are joining and being coerced into joining in throngs, including all sixth form and the greater part of College.

Am I to join?

I am not keen and the drills will be a nuisance, but I am perfectly willing to do so if I ought. It would be unpleasant to be almost the only non-shooter ...

### Extract from Dr Keynes's Diary, 31 January 1900

We pronounce no veto. He may do as he likes.

18. A domestic production, compiled by the Keynes children.

*J. M. Keynes to Dr J. N. Keynes*, 4 February 1900

... About the volunteers – I have not joined.

Taking into regard my feelings and the terms of your letter, I consulted people and they agreed that I should be justified in not joining.

I wavered a little and hey presto, it was done – or rather it was not done.

I think that without your letter which amounted to a refusal I think I should have been compelled to be engulfed in this marvellous martial ardour that has seized the school.

Some say that patriotism requires one to join the useless Eton shooters, but it seems to me to be the sort of patriotism that requires one to wave the Union Jack.

Ten more beaks have joined than were members before, including my beloved tutor.

There are well over 100 recruits.

*J. M. Keynes to Dr J. N. Keynes*, 11 February 1900

... As a matter of fact less than half our election have joined the shooters, but most of the people that I see much of have.

You can resign whenever you like, but the preliminary drills are a dreadful nuisance. You have to go directly after early school and get no proper breakfast and O so cold! We all agree that it is easier to die for your country than to go without your breakfast for it. There are about 130 recruits.

It may be conjectured that his anxious parents were unwilling for him to put this extra strain upon his physique.

At this age he was already showing independent literary judgement.

*J. M. Keynes to Dr J. N. Keynes*, 25 February 1900

... I have finished *Red Pottage*.[19]

It is quite readable and improves after about half-way, but it is not more than readable, and, to my mind, quite unworthy of the extravagant praise which has been lavished upon it.

19. By Mary Cholmondeley. Mr Percy Lubbock thought her worthy of a Memoir.

It has, as you said of Isabel Carnaby, the stamp of the 'lady writer' upon it. Many of the incidents are grossly impossible and the characters are inclined to be overdrawn. The whole book has an aroma of unreality about it, and it is rather the work of an amateur. Of course the heroine writes novels; that was inevitable from the beginning.

### J. M. Keynes to Dr J. N. Keynes, 18 March 1900

Broader has developed into a most consummate wag. He is quite the funniest man I have ever been up to, but at the same time the most supremely rude. I think that this arises from his candour. He does not mind telling a chap before the division if he considers him to have ability and at the same time he does not mind pointing out another chap as a muddle-headed imbecile.

Did he learn something from Broader?

### J. M. Keynes to Dr J. N. Keynes, 25 February 1900

. . . I was reading the other day the first volume of the proceedings of College Pop. The Revd C. K. Parr was master in College at the time of its foundation and he seems to have done a good deal to help it. He very frequently took part in the divisions. 1854 or 1855 was the date I think. Oscar Browning and the two Austen Leighs, one of whom would I suppose be the present Provost of King's, were among the original members.

A very large percentage of the questions they discussed were historical. 'Was the execution of Marshal Ney justifiable?' 'Is the character of Cromwell to be admired?' etc. etc. I am afraid that they are not so deadly serious now-a-days. I think that this was an epoch when the Eton boy was in danger of taking himself too seriously. There were no athletics to speak of and he would perambulate the country and enlarge on the beauties of nature. They upheld the slave system in America and condemned the ballot by a large majority.

As far as I remember O.B. was anti-slavery, but the Provost (at least either he or his brother) thought that the lot of the slave was better as it was.

They condemned the system of corporal punishment at Eton which seems to me extraordinary for this time.

*Extract from Dr. J. N. Keynes's Diary*, 26 April 1900

Maynard played golf with Sidgwick at Royston. He enjoyed Sidgwick's talk as much as his golf.

This was a few months before the tragic death of the philosopher.

The reports of Lubbock and others proceeded in a crescendo of praise, but there was one exception. In the summer half, Maynard was up to Mr X, a respected master and very famous cricketer, nearing the end of his time.

*J. M. Keynes to Dr J. N. Keynes*, 6 May 1900

As I said before, we are all up to X. I could hardly have imagined that a man could be so dull; anyhow I shall not suffer from want of sleep this half ...

*Report by Mr X*, July 1900

... Rather a provoking boy in school. Reads notes when he should be attending to the lesson. Apt to talk to his neighbour unless severly repressed. He gives one the idea of regarding himself as a privileged boy with perhaps a little intellectual conceit.

Neither the other masters nor his Eton contemporaries endorsed this view. On the contrary he seems to have taken his successes with perfect grace. But Mr X's report expresses a view that has often been held subsequently.[20]

*J. M. Keynes to Dr J. N. Keynes*, 20 May 1900

There was only one sane person in Eton yesterday morning and he was a pro-Boer. We did not get the news the evening before and Bob announced it to everyone as they were called. Instead of the customary 'Are you properly awake, sir?' it was 'Mafeking relieved, sir'. And I think this latter proved to be the more efficacious in waking people up. After early school it soon became apparent that Mafeking was going to be responsible for a good

20. Mr X broke down completely during the next half and had to give up his work at Eton.

many things. Feelings were first of all let off at Mr Broadbent's House, and it was found that windows and exuberence of heart were quite incompatible. When there were no more left to break, the Eton Society (there is nothing like Pop for keeping order on these occasions) drove off the mob.

Then successive waves of ideas passed over the school, affecting the lower boys most seriously. At 8.30 everyone was returning with Union Jack pocket handkerchiefs, at 8.45 with large flags of all descriptions, at 8.50 they were nailing scarlet bed coverlets on to goal posts and hoisting them out of the window, at 9.0 everyone was possessed of a trumpet or a horn or some diabolical wind instrument, by 9.15 people were becoming original and Japanese umbrellas and laurel wreaths were the order of the day.

Everything was just about six times its value and finally it cost a shilling even to hire a sixpenny flag. A fortune must have been spent.

In chapel we sang the National Anthem and as we were going into school a whole holiday was announced. This was fortunate for hardly a boy in the school had learnt his lesson.

Young and I, though we did not spend vast sums, got the best flag in College. We ambulated to Windsor and purchased three yards of art muslin at a draper's, a yard of each of the colours, red, white and blue, at 4¾d. a yard. We gave the man 1/3 and as there seemed no immediate prospect of his discovering what 3 times 4¾d. meant, we hurried from the shop for 11.30 absence.

Instead of absence, the Head gave us an oration from the top of chapel steps. I never heard such a voice. Without seemingly exerting himself he made the whole of the school yard resound.

It was the usual stuff. Ought to show our thankfulness; remember dignity of school; if anything done must be of best; as always before. And the outcome of it all was that we had been asked to take part in a huge torchlight procession that had been organized in Windsor: that torches had just been sent for, but that these would probably not be more than enough for the volunteers. Young and I got Moss to sew our muslin together. We nailed it on to a goal post and launched it from the top tower window. It was a symphony nine feet long.

At 8.30 we paraded in school yard for three quarters of an hour. We formed fours and manoeuvred and waited until the rest of the procession was ready for us.

Then out we filed, making with the rest a procession that must
have been a good mile long, some people say more.

Our course was through Eton and Windsor to the Long Walk
and up that glorious approach to the castle opposite the Long
Walk.

At one point the crowd was tremendous and was quite as much
as the police could manage. (London could not spare many special
ones to come down.)

You have heard me before on the Windsor crowd, but last
night it surpassed itself. The men were reeling drunk and the
women offensive and gross beyond words.

It was a good thing that it was Mafeking and not the Royal
Borough of Windsor that was besieged.

Dundas went on leave to London and told us of the state of
things there. It is evident that the whole nation has gone in for
what we call at Eton an organized rag. The papers call it a 'fervent thanksgiving from the heart'.

I do not think that we are quite such hypocrites here. Most of
us know that Mafeking is a glorious pretext for a whole holiday
and for throwing off all discipline. We do not break windows because we are mad with joy, but because we think that under the
circumstances we can do so with impunity.

But to return to the procession. We marched up into St
George's quad and it was there a really fine sight. The whole procession came up into it and the huge square was packed and
seemed to be sown with torches.

We manoeuvred a little and then swung past underneath the
Queen, who was seated in the same window as on the occasion of
the birthday celebrations. In darkness one could not see more
than her outline. Our shooters really marched past extremely well
and then we sang the first verse of God Save the Queen. We returned the same way as we had come and found the crowd much
as ever; perhaps a little hoarser and rather more drunk.

The town of Windsor is the fungus on the Royal Oak.

We got back to school yard at 11.0 and not to be done out of
'knavish tricks' and 'confound their politics' we tried with the
remains of voice still left to us to sing all three verses. As for the
procession itself, I necessarily saw very little of it, but amongst a
judicious blend of fire brigades and Church Lads' ditto, I saw an

31

impossible vehicle which called itself an ambulance, and the inevitable 'decorated' motors and cycles.

Decorating a cycle consists in hanging two chinese lanterns over the handlebars and swathing the wheels in paper until they will only just go round.

. . . On Friday I saw the Queen better than I have ever seen her before. She drove past just as we were going into school and though it was quite cold, she was very little wrapped up. She is very like her photographs, but, doubtless owing to the coldness of the day, her nose was unfortunately red.

. . . The squash racquet courts . . . have been open this week . . .

I find it an extremely good game and, though I am still putridly bad I played on Wednesday, Thursday, Friday and Saturday last week. [In the previous term he had been in the finals of College Fives.]

I have enjoyed *Richard Feverel* immensely. It is my first Meredith and I find it quite different from anything I have ever read. When I am reading it I get absorbed in a way that is not very usual with me. Is Meredith one of those dreadful people who think that a happy ending is inartistic?

X is as usual. We have not yet succeeded in probing the depths of his ignorance. It must, I think, be bottomless.

. . . For Sunday private my tutor read us Macaulay's description of the siege of Londonderry. The political consequences of its fall would have been much the same as those that would have followed the fall of Ladysmith. The siege only lasted about half as long as the siege of Mafeking, but the extremities to which they were reduced were terrible.

I expect that we shall find that Mafeking has been very much worse than we have heard . . .


## J. M. Keynes to Dr J. N. Keynes, 27 May 1900

I went to Queen's Eyot Club for the first time on Thursday and again yesterday. It is most excellent and I have come to think now, not a bit too far. We got our tea there, eggs, bread and butter and marmalade for a very small price, and there are innumerable other varieties of refreshment. They will eventually make it quite a palatial and large permanent building, bathing and every kind of convenience. It is a great thing to have an objective in one's rowing, and the appetite you, of course, acquire on the way ... I forgot to mention one incident of Mafeking Day in my last letter. The College subscribed to send a telegram of congratulations to B-P, and it was couched in the following terms:—Togati Etonienses Obsessis Gratulantur. Later in the day an official document was received saying that no cypher was allowed ... This week I have read de Quincey's *Confessions*. I have enjoyed them so much that I think I shall read another volume of his works.

*J. M. Keynes to Dr J. N. Keynes*, 24 June 1900

   ... I began the *Ring and the Book* today and have read about half the first volume. It goes without saying that I like it immensely ...

*J. M. Keynes to Dr J. N. Keynes*, 1 July 1900

   ... I have finished the second volume of *The Ring and the Book*. It is a grand poem.

Maynard's love of good literature was sustained through life. During the last hectic years of his great American negotiations, he read himself to sleep on Elizabethan authors. He was fond of poetry and of reading it aloud, which he did with feeling. I remember coming into his rooms in the autumn of 1922, to find that he was reading aloud *The Waste Land* by T. S. Eliot, a poet of whom I had so far not heard. His reading was intelligent and moving, and served to win one's admiration for this strange new form of expression.

   Maynard's mind jumped very quickly from thing to thing; the emotion of a moment before could be banished completely. There was some special quality in his constitution which allowed him to terminate one phase of feeling abruptly and redirect his mind to something else. This quality may be a key to his success in life. He had a heart, without which it is impossible to be a great man. But by reverting to an intellectual interest he could always terminate his heartache quickly.

And so we need not think that the schoolboy's pleasure in poetry was any less genuine because, all at once, the future statistician comes to the fore. The letter proceeds to give us some interesting information.

*ibid.*

. . . I made some investigations the other day about the comparative lengths of some long poems. This was among the longest, but I was surprised at the results on the whole.

The longest is W. Morris's *Earthly Paradise*, which comes approximately to 40,000 lines.

Then Spenser's *Faery Queen* (35,632), then in order, *The Ring and the Book* (21,116), *Canterbury Tales* (17,386), *The Iliad* (15,692), Dante's *Divine Comedy* (including Paradise, Purgatory, and the Inferno) (14,408), *Hudibras* (11,445), *Paradise Lost* (10,665) and the *Aeneid* (9,896). I did not look at the *Odyssey*. I should put it down at eleven or twelve thousand.

This term he won the Senior Mathematical Prize.

We have seen that from the beginning he established good relations with his contemporaries. He gained universal respect, and also affection. Men of genius or of great brains or in other ways out of the ordinary are often ragged at their public school – even at Eton. There was not the slightest hint of anything of this sort in Maynard's case.

Although his eminence was recognized, his exceptional maturity must have made him seem a little unusual to the schoolboys; and so at the end of his third year, he did not come out first in the esteem of those immediately above him.

*J. M. Keynes to Dr J. N. Keynes,* 29 July 1900

. . . the elections to College Pop took place last night and the only person in our election to get in was Dundas. I regarded him as almost certain all the time.

There are two vacancies to be filled up next half.

Robert Hamilton (Robin) Dundas was one of his greatest school friends. His Eton friendships were fervent and wholehearted. Within his own election there was a group of boys who were usually in the same form and had many interests in common. Their names occur over and over again in the letters.

Robin Dundas was a curious blend of Scottish puritanism and modern emancipation. He was often daring in talk, but one was conscious of a background of strict principle. His style of speaking and writing was lapidary and terse in the highest degree. He could single out one epithet, telling and often funny, which admirably summarized the complex character of a friend. He corresponded largely by postcard, partly out of an ingrained habit of Scottish carefulness, but also because he could say things on a postcard for which others would require four pages. Since he has published very little, it may be permitted to place on record one instance of the literary power of this remarkable friend of Maynard's school-days. He had to announce in an after-dinner speech the death of two Christ Church men by an accident, and then two suicides.

*Extract from Speech at Censors' Dinner; Christ Church,* December 1922

Those two were cut off by an accident of the body; and then there were another two who perished by an accident of the mind. The young of this generation are apt to expect much of life, and to be impatient if what she has to offer falls short of their hopes; these carried their impatience into action.

Dundas believed in blunt speaking; indeed it is rather amusing to think of these two great past-masters in the art of rudeness as cronies together at school. Were they armed against each other's shafts? They had very different styles of rudeness. There was something freezing and terrible about Maynard's; it was employed selectively against victims deserving punishment; and it punished. It was not usually meant to be unforgivable, but was often not forgiven.

Dundas's rudenesses were more frequent, and sometimes served, curiously enough, as a bridge to friendship. A new acquaintance, finding himself suddenly buffeted by apparent insults, would encounter the regard of kindly grey-blue eyes in a finely chiselled Roman face. They seemed to be well-intentioned and to plead: 'I am only telling you the truth; after all, that is the best mode of intercourse; why beat about the bush?' His manifest friendliness would lead to quick forgiveness; but to have forgiven a man is already to be in an emotional relationship with him, much more intimate than can usually be achieved by the normal small talk of first meetings.

These two did not maintain close contacts in later life. Dundas went to Oxford, as a scholar of New College, and has spent his life as a tutor in Greek History at Christ Church. He has been for many years a pillar of that college, succeeding by his industry and shrewd insight in getting to know far more of the characters and problems of under-graduates, whether his pupils or not, than most dons can achieve.

Best friend of all was Bernard Swithinbank. Tall and handsome, he had finely moulded features, well covered in youth, later revealed in their full dignity as he grew leaner. He was an elegant, even exquisite, schoolboy; not voluble in talk and of quiet habit of mind, he chose his words with precision and enunciated them caressingly, so that what he said about books or life seemed to have a quality of mellow and easy judgement. He had independence of mind and character, taking nothing on trust. His unassuming and gentle self-confidence diffused an atmosphere in which the schoolboys felt themselves already arbiters of taste. To Maynard's boyish enthusiasm he seemed a veritable king of men.

Throughout his life the claims of friendship came first with Maynard. When Swithinbank went to Balliol College, Oxford, Maynard made tremendous attempts, by letter and interchange of visits, to keep alive their communion of soul.

He introduced Swithinbank to his new friends at Cambridge. When finally in 1908 Swithinbank decided to take service in Burma (where he had a distinguished career, rising to be Commissioner of the Pegu Division, 1933–42, and afterwards adviser to the Secretary of State in London), Maynard regarded the prospective separation as a calamity. Lytton Strachey thought fit to send a telegram to him in the Orkneys to convey the doleful news. Maynard took prompt action:

*Telegram from J. M. Keynes to B. Swithinbank,* 9.15 a.m. 22 September 1908

My dear Swithinbank. Great Congratulations.[21] I do hope this quite alters your decision. Please stay in England. You will I am sure regret it otherwise. Perhaps this telegram unnecessary but please stay in England. There is no doubt you ought to and decision is irrevocable. Please telegraph to me. Keynes.

*Telegram from B. Swithinbank to J. M. Keynes,* 11.7 a.m. 22 September 1908

Sorry but I do really want to go to India if medical allows. Really want to fixedly but if I fail will wire. Swithinbank.

*Telegram from J. M. Keynes to B. Swithinbank,* 5 p.m. 22 September 1908

You see evident horrors of England too clearly but greater horrors of India are for you in a mist. Although doctors pass you I doubt your health and strength standing it. Forgive importunity. Do stay. I am sure you can be happy in England.

*Telegram from B. Swithinbank to J. M. Keynes,* 9.8 p.m. 22 September 1908

Please don't trouble about me any more. I am decided.

It is nice to have friends who really want you. That these

21. He was elected fourth in the Civil Service Examination, which gave him the opportunity to opt for the Home Civil Service.

telegrams still exist, kept by the two friends independently
of one another, is a tribute to an Eton friendship.

Then there was Dillwyn Knox, the most brilliant of a
family of brilliant brothers.[22] A superb classical scholar, he
was head of his election to Eton at the age of twelve, and
afterwards scholar and then Fellow of King's College, Cambridge. In this case Maynard was able to maintain his
friendship at King's. Dillwyn was a loyal and true friend.
Lean and light of build, he achieved his scholastic success
so easily, that his mind had plenty of leisure for pleasant
nothings. Often rotting and ragging about, with a touch of
inconsequence, always with a new limerick, witty and sharp,
he could be relied on to amuse and charm, and to prick any
bubble of pomposity in friend or foe. His first-rate brains
were enlisted in his country's intelligence service in World
War I and afterwards, to the benefit of the nation, but to the
detriment of literature and scholarship.

Granville Hamilton (afterwards Proby), good-looking and
charming, was of aristocratic connections. Maynard had an
especially warm spot for him. In later life he was Clerk to
the House of Lords for thirty years, Lord Lieutenant of
Huntingdonshire and an antiquary of repute. Gerard Mack-
worth Young was a boy of parts and presence, a scholar and
of the world. He also went on to King's, and subsequently
achieved two distinguished careers, one in the Indian Civil
Service (Secretary, Army Department, 1926–32) and one as a
writer on antiquities and Director of the British School at
Athens (1936–46). By a coincidence he was concerned at
Athens with the publication of the remains of Humfry
Payne, one of the best archaeologists of his generation and

22. Monsignor Ronald (Ronnie) Knox, author of *Studies in the
Literature of Sherlock Holmes* (republished in *Essays in Satire*, Sheed
Ward, 1923), and of more serious work, wittiest President of the
Oxford Union within living memory, translator of the *Vulgate*; E. V.
Knox (Evoe), editor of *Punch*; the Revd Wilfred Knox, Fellow of the
British Academy, Fellow of Pembroke College, Cambridge, author of
important contributions on Hellenistic Judaism and early Christ-
ianity.

pupil of Robin Dundas. Thomas Balston, elected second to Knox at Eton, was of the group, afterwards a distinguished writer and a publisher. Among these the tone was secular; but religion was represented by R. H. Lightfoot, who became a very learned divine and Professor of the Exegesis of Holy Scripture at Oxford. He did not hesitate to remind his boy friends of their common human frailties. He was supported by J. M. Duncan, less learned in theology, but severer in his churchmanship, and deeply interested in ritual. Then there was W. Hope-Jones, who returned to Eton, where he was a beloved house-master and tutor in mathematics, and at the same time made learned contributions in one of Maynard's fields of interest – statistical methods in biology. Among the next election Maynard was especially fond of Daniel Macmillan, publisher of this volume, who followed Swithinbank to Balliol.

These urbane and scholarly young men were impressed from the beginning by Maynard's great ability and his touch of genius; as his reading progressed he began to acquire a reputation of omniscience. Were they a little frightened of him? It does not seem so. After all, they were redoubtable people themselves. And he was essentially companionable, as Dr Keynes had recorded; he was ready to appreciate all forms of fun and was himself an unfailing fount of amusement. Were his opinions ill-regarded? He was, of course, a Liberal, but so were some of the others; it does not appear that his political views were extreme. Religion was more dangerous ground. Indifference was no doubt then prevalent; but the serious-minded Christians soon grasped that his free-thinking went deeper.

Sayings of his are remembered. Duncan having affirmed that Dissenters could by no means gain access to Heaven, Maynard was bound, if only having regard to his Congregationalist upbringing, to take up the challenge. Duncan had finally to succumb to his reasonings.

DUNCAN: 'Anyhow they won't be admitted to our *kind* of Heaven.'

39

KEYNES: 'Yes, but what we want to know is whether they will be admitted to our kind of Hell.'

Or again: 'I wish I could be the Angel of Death. I know a good many people I should gladly put out of the way.'

Despite the glories of her seventeenth-century pulpit, the Church of England has for a long time sadly neglected the art of preaching. If Maynard had doubts, what he heard at Eton was not likely to lead him back to the fold.

*J. M. Keynes to Dr J. N. Keynes*, 12 November 1899

... This morning I have heard a sermon which, putting my hand on my heart and without hesitation, I can call the worst I have ever had inflicted upon me. Sermons may be dull, but you can sleep; sermons may be old, but you can sleep; but this – there is no parliamentary language in which I can express my opinion of it.

I sat and writhed for twenty-five minutes ...

*J. M. Keynes to Dr J. N. Keynes*, 4 March 1900

... We had inflicted on us this morning another old reprobate in the person of the Revd ——. It was a revolting performance and an insult to the congregation. It is enough to make one think that the Church is the refuge for those who cannot preach.

They ought at least to make him an archdeacon at once. He has got all the qualifications ...

*J. M. Keynes to Dr J. N. Keynes*, 17 February 1901

... This morning an atrocity was perpetrated in the pulpit, a revolting and merciless atrocity in a loud voice. The criminal was the Revd —. [This preacher was subsequently elevated to a bishopric which he held for a great many years.]

But Maynard was not blind to true merit. Those who remember the beautiful sermons of Robert Hugh Benson, later converted to the Church of Rome, will recognize Maynard's discrimination.

*J. M. Keynes to Dr J. N. Keynes*, 27 February 1901

... Last Sunday we had an extremely good sermon from Benson's youngest brother. He is a real orator. He has joined some brotherhood in which one gives up one's earthly possessions and goes about preaching. I thought that he would preach well as soon as I saw that he had not brushed his hair ...

*J. M. Keynes to Dr J. N. Keynes*, 10 March 1901

I suppose that you have seen that Ford[23] has got the Headmastership of Repton; he will, I think, be a great loss to us. He is quite the best preacher we have and has been of late one of the most conspicuous figures among the masters ...

Pretty as a child, Maynard could not have been called handsome at Eton. He always had an interesting face. The lips were thick. If one added the inevitable epithet 'sensual', that would not convey quite the right impression, for sensual lips are lazy lips. His were highly sensitive and expressive. They came into play to an unusual extent when he spoke, rounding and modulating the words and seeming to give them a thoughtful emphasis. He grew a small moustache, which he retained through life. His large dark-blue eyes were very beautiful – steady, direct and full of kindness and wisdom.

These features were but the vehicle for the constant play of expression, animated and intelligent, and above all there was his sense of fun, seldom absent for long. Then at once his face became irradiated. He had a broad smile, the eyes sparkled and the eyebrows arched upwards. Little wrinkles at the corners of his eyes appeared. Seldom can a face have expressed a sense of the ridiculous so completely; and as he went about the world, he was, luckily for his friends, always finding matters worthy of ridicule. But there was nothing censorious or caustic about his facial comment; it was all pure gaiety and impishness. Certainly he had a very charming and interesting face. Strangers noticed it in a crowd. He

23. Later Head Master of Harrow.

was quite unlike anyone else. It was sympathetic, communi-
cative, winning.

He was tall; at school he was thin, but filled out later. He
sometimes walked with a slight stoop. His motions of body
were animated. He moved quickly about the room, tidying
or adjusting or dispatching business in hand with speed. But
then he liked to settle down on the sofa with his long legs
outstretched, and his attitude became one of complete
repose. There must be no discomfort that might impede the
interchange of ideas, which was, after all, the main pleasure,
perhaps the main object, in life. How would he have
described his own hands? They were smooth and the fingers
long and delicate. He had a habit of tucking each hand into
the sleeve of the arm opposite, so that they became invisible.
Thus he completed the sense of repose, like a cat with her
paws tucked up under her.

### 3

The summer of 1900 found the family at Tintagel again.
Maynard was reading Lecky's *History of the Eighteenth
Century*, which had a 'great attraction for him'. He suffered
from an attack of high fever and later from a bad knee,
which was deemed to be due to it.

In the Michaelmas Half he was up to Luxmoore; the
friends regarded him as 'quite the nicest master' they had
been up to. At the same time he was doing European History from 1509 to 1603 with Marten. Arguments were
beginning about the extent to which he ought to specialize
in mathematics. Mr Hurst, his mathematical master, wanted
as much of his time as possible, while Mr Lubbock pleaded
for his other interests. On the whole, Mr Lubbock, aided no
doubt by Maynard himself, seems to have got the better of
it. But Hurst was jealous, and Maynard, when doing some
other bits of work, trembled at the probable displeasure of
Hurst when he should get to know.

### *J. M. Keynes to Dr J. N. Keynes*, 21 October 1900

I am enjoying all my work now, and Lubbock says that my verses have greatly improved, but to really get on in Classics I ought now to do a lot of private reading.

It would be very pleasant getting through one's favourite Classical authors in that way, but it is absolutely impossible as well as Mathematical extras.

Like you, I should not mind thirty-six hours a day and fourteen days a week, etc. etc. . . .

Games meanwhile were continuing.

### *J. M. Keynes to Dr J. N. Keynes*, 14 October 1900

I played Wall Game on Monday under such conditions as I hope never to have to repeat.

The sun was blazing and the day more than reminiscent of summer, and yet we went and played a fairly hard Wall Game. I have never felt so bad in my life. I was of course dripping with sweat, but it was the absolute exhaustion and inability to breathe that was so awful . . .

On the next day I played in Mixed Wall in similar weather conditions, but we knew what we were in for and played slackly so that I got nothing worse than horribly hot.

He got some boils on his knee, perhaps connected with his holiday ailment, recovered, played another Wall Game, and then got boils on his other knee. The doctor said that his blood was not in good condition, but did not think him unfit to carry on with the Wall Game, and by the end of term he had won his College colours. His mother has since been somewhat doubtful of that doctor's verdict, and felt that the terrific strains of this formidable game may have done permanent injury and been a remote cause of his later heart troubles, which were to prove fatal.

He went home for Long Leave.

### *Extract from Dr Keynes's Diary*, 18 November 1900

Much enjoy having Maynard with us – in capital spirits bright and intelligent as he always is. Mr Lubbock came up for the

Greek play – says he considers Maynard safe for a first class in Classics if he reads Classics. He evidently thinks very highly of the child.

If Maynard's classics were good, so also was his history. He was first in his division. In the later part of this half, he competed for the Richards English Essay Prize. The subject was given out a couple of weeks in advance. On this occasion it was the character of the Stuarts. 'I cannot say that it is a very congenial subject.' On 25 November an essay on it had to be written in the School Library between the hours of 9.0 and 12.0. Maynard covered twenty-two pages; his hand-writing was small. He won the prize.

At the beginning of the Lent Half, Maynard was elected to College Pop.

*J. M. Keynes to Mrs J. N. Keynes*, 27 January 1901

Last night I was elected to College Pop and next Saturday I make my maiden speech that 'Women are more fitted to rule than men'.

I have just this morning received the rules to put up in my room framed in purple riband ... We are, I believe, to have a general post in the way of food in Hall under the auspices of the new Bursar.

Irish stew and veal that is tottering on to the verge of beef are to be among our weekly items.

There is also talk of a permanent early breakfast such as we have during trials, a hot roll and butter and tea for early school. This will be a real boon. My first attempt at making mustard has been too solid; I shall probably go to the other extreme next time ...

I am going to take the *Daily Mail* this half. This is a great sacrifice of Principle to Pocket.

He was playing fives 'almost every day'.

*J. M. Keynes to Dr J. N. Keynes*, 26 February 1901

I was given my Lower Boats yesterday and have got an oar in the St George ... This is a great surprise; I thought I might have had some slight chance of getting them next 4th June, but not the smallest hope of getting them this half.

The colour is white with narrow magenta stripes.

The economizer and the economist both appear in the following letter:

*J. M. Keynes to Dr J. N. Keynes,* 3 March 1901

Last night I put up a motion in Private Business in College Pop but was defeated by one vote. The facts were these: a fine of 6d. is exacted for every article left in Reading Room after 9.30. I left a pair of fives gloves and a double fine of 1s. was demanded of me. I held that a pair of fives gloves only constituted one article within the meaning of the Law. I was surprised at so nearly winning as it is almost impossible to make the House pass anything which will diminish its revenue from fines. Personally I don't think it good policy to make fines a source of revenue; it is an extremely vexatious form of indirect taxation and one which involves considerable trouble in collection. Quite a large amount of money is obtained in this way, but I should prefer a fixed subscription in lieu of fines.

Towards the end of this half it appeared that rowing, despite his enthusiasm, was getting too much of a good thing. The matter was happily solved in the following half.

*J. M. Keynes to Dr J. N. Keynes,* 12 May 1901

This afternoon I was given an oar in *Monarch* by the Captain of the Boats. This was at my own request as I had had it conveyed to him that I wanted it. It is nominally the first boat on the river, but it is generally recognized as the home of bad oars. Apart, however, from slight opprobrium it is all bliss. One has all the advantages of wet bobbing without any of its disadvantages.

One has all the privileges of a member of Upper Boats, sliding seats, bathing off Boveney, etc., and no races. One behaves exactly as one would in Lower Boats except that one has no bumping races. These are never things to look forward to, and it is particularly fortunate to escape them as they immediately precede the Tomline [the principal Mathematical Prize at Eton].

One, in fact, – to begin one more sentence with 'one' – buys cultured ease by giving up ambition.

There are three other Collegers in the *Ark*, as it is familiarly called: Gaselee, who got it at his own request two years ago; Mavrogordato; and Olphert, who has got it at his own request this year.

... By the way, I have got the Holiday Task Prize. So has Dundas in the division below; *he* spent the holidays reading it through carefully three times.

He won the Tomline, getting 437 out of 620 marks, the next man with 336. Dilly Knox, although primarily a classic, and a very outstanding classic, was in for it.

### *J. M. Keynes to Dr J. N. Keynes*, 9 June 1901

Knox shows his work up in a most loathsomely untidy, unintelligible, illegible condition ...

### *J. M. Keynes to Dr J. N. Keynes*, 15 June 1901

I am most surprised that Knox is only fourth; I am sure that he really has more mathematical ability than Bailey or Jones. These three were very close together and Knox seems to have been undone by his mechanics and his want of lucidity; especially, I think, the latter. He has got one of the most confused brains I have ever come across. Even in conversation he is wholly incapable of expressing the meaning he intends to convey. In addition to this he is quite abnormally untidy in his work and always forgets to write down the most necessary steps.

This is an interesting commentary on one of England's most illustrious 'intelligence experts'. There is corroboration for it. Knox's ideas came crowding into his mind in an untidy and confused jumble – all was seemingly chaos; in a Cambridge court he might be seen to pause midway on his course, and it was well known that his train of thinking had then become so confused that he did not know where he was or what he was doing. He remained stuck for a long time until he had sorted matters out with himself. Perhaps it was precisely this shower of irrelevant ideas impinging on a brain of the very highest quality that produced such successful results.

### J. M. Keynes to Dr J. N. Keynes, 16 June 1901

Hawtrey,[24] as perhaps you saw, was eighteenth in the Mathematical Tripos. Dyer – whose pupil he was – is very disappointed and thinks he ought to have taken a very high place, and Hurst holds him up before me as a dreadful example of a person who has tried to do too many things.

Maynard added that he thought that Hurst was wrong in holding that Hawtrey had 'lost his soul in knowing something besides Mathematics'.

There was an institution at Eton called 'Private Business', at which tutors gave some special instruction, rather in the university manner, to two or three pupils. There were also 'Sunday Privates'. This half, Mr Lubbock chose for study some translations which had been made by Dr J. M. Neale of the poetry of St Bernard of Cluny. They interested Maynard greatly. By his discriminating choice, Mr Lubbock kindled an interest in Maynard's mind, which was to occupy much of his spare time during the remainder of his spell at Eton and afterwards at Cambridge.

### Extract from Diary of Dr J. N. Keynes, 22 June 1901

Maynard for long leave. Mediaeval Latin poetry is now one of his hobbies.[25]

A year later he read a paper on St Bernard to the Literary Society.

24. This is Mr R. G. Hawtrey, the famous economist.
25. That autumn he was set to write a Latin hymn based on the Eighty-seventh Psalm – as a punishment for being late for prayers! So he wrote *two* versions.

*J. M. Keynes to Mrs J. N. Keynes,* 2 May 1902

I read my Bernard tomorrow at 8 p.m. Ramsay is ill – pneumonia I believe – and Luxmoore is taking the Society under his wing until the recovery of the Ram.

When I announced my subject he exclaimed 'Oh! That is my subject. I once read a paper on him.' Whereat I was greatly abashed for he is a rare one to contradict. Fortunately he had misheard me. It was Bernard of Clairvaux that his paper treated.

In an obituary notice of Stephen Gaselee in the *Proceedings of the British Academy*, Mr Andrew Gow wrote: 'He is remembered ... to have read a paper to a school society on the *De Contemptu Mundi* of Bernard of Morlaix'. Keynes at once took the matter up with him. It was he, not Gaselee, who had read the paper.[26]

At the end of this half Maynard won the Chamberlayne Prize, consisting of £60 a year for four years, for being first in the Higher Certificate Examination. He was first in mathematics, first in history, and first in the English essay.

*Mr Lubbock to Dr J. N. Keynes,* 2 August 1901

I must congratulate you once again on your boy's very excellent performances; and nothing about them is so admirable as the way in which he takes them. He rates prizes at their proper worth, is glad to get them, but fully recognizes that they are only of

26. *Proceedings of the British Academy* (1943), p. 442. Mr Gow obtained his information from a notice by Mr Ramsay in the *Cambridge Review*. He himself drew my attention to his mistake, and added, 'In justice to myself I may say, as I said to Keynes, that when I questioned Ramsay, he professed doubt as to whether Gaselee read the paper when at school or as an old boy. I then made inquiry from the Minute Book of the Essay Society (which proved to be lost) and had the files of the Eton College *Chronicle* searched without result; and therefore wrote not "he read", but "he is remembered to have read" – which was strictly true.' Mr Ramsay's inaccurate recollection was no doubt due to his illness. Mr Gow may be credited with a scholar's care in this matter, although whether what he wrote was 'strictly true' must depend on the philosophical theory of the meaning of the word 'remember'.

secondary consideration and importance. I am sure he will go far. He seems to have the power of being interested in everything and at the same time he seems incapable of doing anything in a dilettante manner ...

I confess I was fairly dazzled by the actual result. It is an extraordinary performance. He certainly does command success to an amazing extent, but then no one ever deserved it better. His way of accepting it is characteristic; just as quiet, frank and modest as ever, enhancing all the pleasure his successes give one. I hope he has not overdone himself and am glad to think of him beginning a complete rest ...

This time the family went off to Switzerland.

His last year had the usual pattern of those of successful schoolboys, first a blaze of triumphs, and then a period of more leisure – aristocratic dignity, living in the school rather as in one's own fine country house, and cooperating with one's friends in running it.

In a letter to his father he gave full details of changes in the teaching arrangements at school and proceeded:

*J. M. Keynes to Dr J. N. Keynes, 22 September 1901*

The Old Boy[27] thinks that within the next few years there will be considerable state re-organization in secondary education and that very critical examination will be made into the Public School system. So he is endeavouring to bring Eton up to scratch. He has been dilating on this subject both in his address to sixth form and in his sermon today.

In College also there have been changes. We are going to have hot suppers three days a week and the old hags who gather up the remnants in Hall have been abolished. They have, I believe, been given almshouses to comfort them.

The Bursar is going to meet sixth form this week for them to suggest any further changes they desire.

This half he still had before him the task of winning a scholarship at the university.

27. The Head Master.

### J. M. Keynes to Dr J. N. Keynes, 4 October 1901

Mr Marten and Hurst have within the last two days been urging me to go up for Trinity instead of King's. The latter wanted to know if you would be coming to Eton any time soon as he would like to see you about my work. I promised I would write and forward his remarks.

Hurst's case is briefly this:

He says that my having won the Chamberlayne puts a different complexion on matters; now that I have that, it would not so much matter if I only got a minor or exhibition at Trinity. His reason for wishing me to go to Trinity is that he thinks that Mathematics are at rather a low ebb at King's. They do chiefly Classics and Science there. There are not many doing Mathematics; Berry is entirely pure and I should have to go elsewhere for my applied. I should not get a mathematical atmosphere.

It is my very strong impression that he thinks that if I go to King's I shall be drawn from Mathematics altogether. Marten's reason was but a small one; he thinks that my History might count for something in the Trinity general paper.

For myself I still think that I would rather go to King's. I have been imagining myself going there for some time and it is difficult to dispel a 'fixed idea'. Besides, Trinity is altogether too risky. Lubbock has written to, I think, the Provost of King's, to find out whether the Chamberlayne is tenable with an Eton-King's scholarship.

If it is not, that is, I admit, a great argument in favour of Trinity ...

### J. M. Keynes to Dr J. N. Keynes, 13 October 1901

Lubbock has definitely heard from King's that the Certificate Scholarship is tenable as well as an Eton scholarship.

In the debate on the new system I spoke and voted against it. It is not of course by any means entirely bad, but I think there is a good deal to be said against it. Next Saturday I am opening a debate in which I am to abuse the Stuarts. I put up this debate chiefly because Hamilton is opposing. It is a subject upon which we hold very different views and it ought to make an amusing debate. I took History Extras chiefly because it does not really

take much time and is a pleasant change from the flood of
Mathematics. I rather wish now that I had taken Pindar.

Hurst has said no more about Trinity; Lubbock would very
much prefer me to go to King's and I would rather go there myself; so don't you think we had better definitely decide on the
latter? Hurst still does not want me even to take the Classical
papers. He says he thinks they may tire me for the Mathematics.
His jealousy of Classics is most curious and interesting. What do
you think of Kipling's grotesque effort in yesterday's *Times*?
What is 'the imperishable plinth of things'?

## J. M. Keynes to Dr J. N. Keynes, 20 October 1901

On Tuesday as you have seen in the *Chronicle*, we played the
masters; I have never been so dissatisfied at the result of a match
and I was very much annoyed at our being beaten ...

The letter in the *Chronicle* was by Turner.[28] It was most
thoroughly justified; in both the Wall Matches one or two of the
masters had disputed every decision of the Umpire in a most
unsportsmanlike manner, and it was high time that the matter
was publicly called attention to ... Yesterday was the first College Wall Match against Browning's scratch. After a tremendous
game, College succeeded in drawing; I have never enjoyed a
match so much. I did one hold which I am rather proud of and
I am sufficiently conceited to give you an extract from the
account of the match written in the College Wall Book by the
Keeper:

> 'At this point Keynes got well set and backed up by Olphert
> and the seconds did one of the best holds I have ever seen,
> remaining on the ball about eight minutes ... I knew he was
> a good holding wall, but I did not know that he could perform
> such prodigies of valour against such gigantic opponents.'

The walls who were trying to get me off weighed 13, 14 and 15
stone respectively, while the three College walls are in the aggregate about 32 stone.

At the Shakespeare Society in addition to the *Tempest*, we
have read the *Merchant* and tomorrow we begin *Twelfth Night*.
I am to be Malvolio.

28. Mr J. R. Turner, later Bursar of Westminster School.

*J. M. Keynes to Dr J. N. Keynes*, 24 November 1901

I have entered myself for £40 at King's as I want to go there anyhow. There is nowhere else worth going to at Cambridge which comes on later. And I do not want to go to Oxford at any price.

The half ended in triumphs, which came crowding in on two momentous days. He was elected to an Eton scholarship at King's, 'in Mathematics and Classics'. This was most unusual. Hurst's fears had been unnecessary.

The Eton Society, commonly known as Pop, is a self-elected body of boys, who have responsibilities in the school corresponding roughly to those of school monitors or school prefects in other places. The qualities which are required for election are those which make appeal to the boys themselves – athletics, no doubt, and general character; social standing may also play some part. These young men govern the school for the time – as they expect, many of them, or used to expect, to govern the country later. They are in fact our born leaders, people of substance and character, men of the world. One or two of the 'bookworms' in College may be among the chosen, but the bias is somewhat against them.

*J. M. Keynes to Dr J. N. Keynes*, 15 December 1901

You will scarcely believe me, I have been elected to Pop. I had absolutely no idea that I had the smallest chance, and did not even know that I was put up. The elections were held today, and I was told at Hall. Of Collegers, Olphert has also got in. Yesterday also was rather a red letter day in my calendar: I got the first news [of his scholarship] from a telegram from Dr James which I found awaiting me after 11.0 school. It was sent off fourteen minutes after yours, but arrived five minutes sooner. It was very good of him to telegraph. They have been very wily in King's in choosing those who cannot come up again. Bailey, Olphert and Young will all come up again next year; Hamilton is quite satisfied with £60 and is still faithful to King's after a week at Oxford.[29] In the afternoon I played for College at the

29. But in the end he went to Oxford.

Field[30] and after the match got my colours. I have got it 10th, higher than I have been before this half.

In the evening College supper came off. We had a most excellent dinner and I flatter myself that I managed the arrangements very satisfactorily.

Your claret was very especially appreciated as being extraordinarily good.

We had soup, fish, pilaugh, turkeys, partridges, plum puddings, mince pies, paté de foie gras, dessert, coffee, with claret, moselle and champagne.

I asked the Head for leave off early school for the rest of the half yesterday; he gave it like a lamb.

Among his successes, that in the Wall Game was clearly not regarded as a merely trivial matter. The following letter, written during the Christmas holidays, is characteristic for the fervent interest taken in the subject, the critical analysis of the essentials of the proposal and the suggestion of an alternative remedy.

### *J. M. Keynes to R. H. Dundas*, 19 January 1902

You seem to have been having a very giddy time at your godmother's; we have had a comparatively quiet time and I with consummate skill have got off all (*all* mind you) dances. Oh, what fair round lies have I told! . . . A little more than a week ago I heard from Turner to say that after all he was coming up to King's this term. For God's sake come thou and do likewise; I add as an appendix to this letter many sound and weighty arguments all of which you have heard before.

If you want to drown yourself in the Bosphorus, do so and be damned to you.

If not, I shall think very poorly of you if you cannot over-persuade your people to let you come into residence at the Royal Foundation.

I have seen a good deal of the King's people this week. I played bridge with Gaselee and friends a few nights ago (and won a shilling) and I play again this week. S. G. had his usual equipment of port, cigars and brandy and sodas.

George Lyttelton is going to revise the Wall rules.

30. The other Eton football game.

I have seen the correspondence on the subject, and it seems to me that all the changes are of no effect save that concerning hands (for the sake of which the whole thing is doubtless being done).

I cannot enter into details now, but the effect of the new rule is practically to abolish the use of hands.

To this I am strongly opposed; it means that it will become possible for a good wall to sit almost indefinitely (unless some new form of ruffianism such as slicking[31] is introduced). I told Muggins major the suggested rule and he thought that he personally could sit for the greater part of the day under these arrangements. It is impossible to make the Wall Game humane and one suitable for the newly shaved and tender usher; the present form of legalized ruffianism is, I think, the best condition under which one can play the glorious game.

I have suggested as a compromise that knuckling and not pushing be abolished; this would, I think, greatly reduce the ruffianism and at the same time leave the game fundamentally the same. It is a very important question, but more of this anon ...

Prizes at Eton took the form of books, newly bound in calf. Maynard's succession of awards led to much correspondence with his father concerning what books to buy. He became restive about the calf bindings. It did not escape his lucid mind that, if one is gathering books together with limited resources, the expenditure of a substantial fraction on new calf is not the best way of building up a fine library. Mr Lubbock, at his suggestion, persuaded the head master to change the rules.

In the market-place at Cambridge a certain Mr David, who ultimately became famous, had a stall in which were to be found old and rare books. From the age of twelve Maynard frequented it.

*J. M. Keynes to B. Swithinbank*, 31 December 1901

I bought an early edition (1820) of Wordsworth's *Excursion* yesterday from my secondhand bookseller for 1/-. It is a fine

31. viz. kicking or hacking.

large paper edition. I had a long talk with him about books, a subject he knows a good deal about.

It appears that I gave fully what it was worth for that Byron. It is only some of the shorter poems, whose first edition is of any real value.

I am spending a certain amount of time reading Church History for the Newcastle, and am getting a great deal of interest out of it. I have, I think, a certain bent towards theology. My interest in the subject delights my grandfather who is, as I think I once told you, a Non-Conformist clergyman.

I have also been studying some more family history and have written a short article on the derivation and spelling for the last thousand years of the name Keynes.

Maynard continued book collecting actively, but economically. He sought out products of the Aldine and Elzevir presses and other early printed editions of the classics, not usually going above 10s., but more often paying much less. He maintained frequent contacts with David. In these early days he inserted a number in his books, indicating the order of purchase. These numbers were only placed in books of substantial value or interest. From them we learn that by the time he first went up to Cambridge as an undergraduate in October 1902 he had already bought 329 such books.

Amid this multiplicity of intellectual interests, political economy was not entirely neglected. After the death of Henry Sidgwick, Dr Keynes was asked to edit a new edition of his *Principles of Political Economy*. Later in life, Maynard recalled[32] how his father had at this time given him the proof-sheets of that volume to correct.

His last two terms were filled with activities of a kind proper to one whose main struggle was over.

*J. M. Keynes to Dr J. N. Keynes*, 26 January 1902

I am going to do three extras this half, Lucretius with Ramsay, History with Marten and Mathematics with Hurst. For private

32. At the dinner given him by the Council of the Royal Economic Society on 21 June 1945, on his retirement from the editorship of the *Economic Journal*.

with Lubbock I am to read the *Choephoroe* of Aeschylus ...
We had College Pop P.B. on Saturday night and I spoke an
unconscionable number of times.

I was elected to the Athletic Committee (for making arrangements about the sports). Butler[33] and I have succeeded in reviving the Essay Society ...

### *J. M. Keynes to Dr J. N. Keynes*, 2 February 1902

On Friday the Head demanded of me to choose a speech at a
moment's notice; I gained an hour by not going to him, but I had
the greatest difficulty in finding anything that I cared for and
was at the same time suitable. Finally I produced three alternatives: Firstly a passage out of the Pope's speech in *The Ring and
the Book* (suggested in the Public School Speaker), but the Head
has always consistently refused to allow Browning, and he told
me he thought it would prove gibberish to the audience;
Secondly, 'The Case of Rumdrum the Barber' out of *The Shaving
of Shagpat*. This he seemed to think not sufficiently conventional. My third alternative, however, Burke's Panegyric on Fox
was thoroughly to his taste, and that I am to do. I think it is
right to at any rate ply the Head at first with what is a little less
dull and conventional than the old, old speeches.

A cousin of Young's – of the same name, has come to be an
usher here, and yesterday I went to tea with him ...

This was Geoffrey Winthrop Young, renowned as a mountain climber, renowned also later for scaling Alpine peaks
after he had lost a leg, as well as for great gallantry in
World War I, a poet and author of books on climbing, etc.
He has kindly written out for me his impressions of Maynard at Eton.

### *Description of Keynes by Mr Geoffrey Young*

When I went to Eton as a young Master, I heard of Maynard
as an outstanding mathematical scholar, in College; and I soon
met him among other sixth-form leaders. But it was at a literary
society that I first realized him. He was reading a paper on the
later Latin poets – of all subjects! – and he traversed the vast

33. Sir Harold Butler.

field of second-rate production with masterly scholarship. His reading had been immense, his selection was admirable, and wit and some well-calculated indiscretions illuminated an astonishingly mature performance. We were listening to something much beyond the range of the normal clever sixth-form boy; and the fineness of the delivery in a sympathetic voice that never lost through all his life its intimate gaiety, contributed further to the effect . . .

As a boy he was slim, agile, pale and dark-haired. He had no special athletic gift, but he suggested both in movement and talk, a keen dark-metal rapier, with light and shadow playing quickly over it. 'A dark ray', I once described him. His manner was polished, after an older fashion, and very lively: too urbane ever to be thought of as a boy's. The small head was finely modelled; the features distinctly ugly at first sight, with lips projecting and seeming to push up the well-formed nose and strong brows in slightly simian fashion. But the moment the eyes glanced up through long lashes, marvellously alive, with depths of almost superhuman intelligence – nothing else counted. When the quick gay smile followed, the whole face was alight, and it held one by an unusual charm, of sympathy and expression.

Soon after this, his Tutor sent him to me, to practise essays for scholarship purposes . . . His style was already lucid and trenchant, and his intellectual grasp in many fields far outdistanced mine. We treated essays as bases for discussions. He soon fell into the habit of dropping in, one or two evenings in each week, at my house in High Street; and there in my library we turned up references and talked over all things on earth and elsewhere.

His reading, as I have said, was astonishingly wide already. It covered the whole literature in some subjects; and while he read quickly he remembered accurately and with excellent selective taste. Not only the classics and notable authors, he had explored the arcana, and knew more of the private presses and editions and of the privately circulated books of authors known and unknown, than I had ever heard of.

In an attempt to balance his formidable combination of intellectualism and aestheticism, I introduced him [this was at a later date] to the world of open air adventure and of natural beauty, using the beauty of movement as a means. In mountain climbing he became particularly interested, even for a time enthusiastic. Delicacy of constitution prevented him maintaining the practice; which I regretted, since it might have kept the balance better. He would have mountaineered well. He joined me once in the Alps, and I sent him ahead up the Aiguille d'Agentière, alone with Joseph Knubel, while I followed with another rope. I watched him climbing upon the very steep snow and ice slope of the summit with smooth security and fine nerve. Obviously he was revelling in every minute of it. [In due course we shall give Maynard's own version of this experience.] Later, on my suggestion, he went on a walking tour to the Pyrenees, and wrote to me very critically as one climber to another of the poor technique of one of his companions, and of the unexpected speed and endurance he discovered in his brother.

## *J. M. Keynes to Dr J. N. Keynes*, 9 February 1902

Last night the Literary Society (as the Essay Society is technically called) had its first meeting and Butler read an exceedingly good paper on the British occupation of Egypt.

We are to have four papers altogether, the next three from Buxton, Swithinbank and Paul (the son of Herbert Paul the essay writer). At the close of the proceedings I was elected President ...

I have also been elected to the Committee of Management (composed of boys and masters) of the School Stores.

As far as I can make out I am elected chiefly as a person competent to check the financial affairs. I am finding that, like you, when I am appointed to a committee, I am inevitably made to do all the work.

Last week we carried through a good deal of work concerning the reform and expurgation of College Library ...

My speech came off yesterday after 12.0 in Upper School; clad as to my uppers in dress clothes, and as to my lowers in knee breeches and black silk stockings I declaimed some of one of Mr Burke's orations which I knew by no means perfectly, to an audience representative of Eton College ...

On Friday night I attended my first Pop debate on our old friend 'Capital Punishment'. I spoke twice and find that by now I have no modesty when on my legs, even before a strange audience.

I cannot say that the average of speaking was high. I might even go so far as to say that it was low ...

His claim that he 'had to do all the work' is confirmed by Mr Hope-Jones, who well remembers the heroic reform he carried out in the College Library, a landmark in the history of that institution. Mr C. R. Fay confirms the point with reference to Maynard's undergraduate days. 'What was so extraordinary was that while he seemed to us all to be leading such a lovely life, yet he never refused a dirty job.'

*J. M. Keynes to Dr J. N. Keynes*, 16 March 1902

Swithinbank read a paper last night on 'Ben Jonson'. His behaviour was typical; though he had several weeks in which to prepare it, he did not begin writing anything down until 5.15. He then wrote as hard as he could until 7.0, the hour at which he had to read. He had not, however, time to write a peroration; he was saved by a great stroke of genius. He read us out the peroration of an article on the same subject that he had got hold of ...

Last night the motion in College Pop was that 'There is a deplorable spirit of extravagance at Eton'. It was carried by the casting vote of the President; I voted in the minority.

In the Shakespeare we have been reading *Othello*. I have taken the title part ...

Meanwhile the Newcastle was about to come off, the greatest of the Eton prizes, mainly classical. Maynard could hardly hope to win. Kynaston was the Cambridge examiner, and Godley, a very well-known Oxford figure, came from that University.

*J. M. Keynes to Dr J. N. Keynes*, 23 March 1902

Kynaston looks an extremely nice old man, but Godley is rather terrible and apparently very nervous. He has the reputation of being the dullest man in Oxford to talk to, and of being the greatest wit in print ... Last night we had an essay from Paul on 'Charles Lamb'. It was very good and distinctly the best we have had ...

A few days ago some foolish individual went about an hour before early school and blocked up the key holes of all the doors of the school rooms with plaster of Paris. Fortunately it was discovered in time to prevent its interfering very much with trials. The culprit has not been discovered and the Head has declared that unless he gives himself up, no leave will be given to any of the school either this half or next. I am very sorry that the Head has acted thus. The principle of such a punishment is in my opinion atrociously bad and not at all consonant with his usual methods. It is not even certain that the offender was a present member of the school. Threats of this kind in a case where the rest of the school neither knows the culprit, nor has taken any part in the crime, seem to me most unwise and useless. Besides I don't suppose for a moment that he will be able to enforce it strictly.

Pallis won the Newcastle, and the order in the 'select' was Ainger, Dundas, Hamilton, Keynes...

### J. M. Keynes to Mrs J. N. Keynes, 2 May 1902

I have bought a perfect dove of a waistcoat, lavender with pale pink spots (Wycombe papers please copy) [34] ...

### J. M. Keynes to Dr J. N. Keynes, 11 May 1902

'The Mirror' as it is to be called, will come out on Tuesday; I have not had time to contribute anything for this first number, but I have got two or three things out of Swithinbank for it ...

Rehearsals for speeches are now in full swing, Butler and I are doing Act III scene iv ... of *The Rivals*; it is not at all easy ... I am *Acres* and Butler *Sir Lucius*.

We are doing *Hamlet* at the Shakespeare, and I am enacting the part of the melancholy Dane...

It is difficult to realize that the cataclysm at St Pierre is probably the greatest disaster of the kind that has taken place in the history of civilization. The destruction of Pompeii and Herculaneum was on a much smaller scale, they were much smaller cities; ... It is difficult to analyse the apathy with which one accepts such a stupendous event.

34. Maynard's sister, Margaret, was then at Wycombe Abbey School.

*J. M. Keynes to Dr J. N. Keynes*, 15 May 1902

The scenes that we are doing from *Much Ado About Nothing* are . . . Very much against my inclination I am being made to do 'Dogberry' . . .

On Tuesday I played in 'Aquatics'. This is a weekly game of cricket played by members of Upper Boats under Aquatic Rules . . .

*J. M. Keynes to Dr J. N. Keynes*, 15 June 1902

Last night Young read an extraordinarily good essay on Praed. I don't believe any other school could keep up so good a series of papers . . .

These are but a few items from a vast catalogue of interesting events which crowded the letters of this last term, despite the fact that some days were taken out of it by one of his feverish attacks. And at the end of term he was once again first in the school in the Higher Certificate Examination. During the course of it he found time to cover four pages of foolscap examination paper with a letter to his father.

| Eton College | Page 1 |
| --- | --- |
| Subject | J. M. Keynes, K.S. |
| Sunday Letter | Certificate Index No. 170 |

The end of this half will be made additionally miserable by the fact that Camp has been made compulsory and that therefore nearly everyone is going off on Tuesday morning. I have just reached a very melancholy stage. Last night I received a vote of thanks in College Pop, which I think I desired perhaps more than anything else that remains to be got here. Eton has been much kinder to me than I deserve . . .

He was not the only one to be miserable.

*R. H. Dundas to J. M. Keynes*, 3 August 1902

I think I have never spent a sadder day than on Tuesday. Your words on Monday night 'before we part' had brought home

to me rather forcibly that we were going to part in earnest, and
that the old Eton life was over as far as I was concerned, for
Eton will never be the same. You have always taken the chief
part in that time as far as I was concerned, but what applies to
you also applies more or less to all the others . . .

I hope I shall see you often . . .

Your affectionate friend,<br>
ROBERT HAMILTON DUNDAS

# [2]

## Undergraduate at Cambridge

### I

In October 1902 Maynard entered the Royal Foundation. Its outward aspect is indeed regal. On the right of the front court is the famous Chapel, with its matchless array of lights and buttresses unbroken by any transept. Facing the lodge is Gibbs's classic masterpiece, well known for the view of its other frontage which is obtained from the Backs. There is a great lawn in the front court, and the proportions are just, giving both a sense of splendid spaciousness and the right perspective to the buildings. Beyond Gibbs's Building is a still greater lawn, reaching to the river.

At first, however, he was somewhat removed from these glories. Passing through the Wilkins Building on the left, one goes into a mean court, surrounded by a confused jumble of ugly structures. Passing still beyond, down steps, through a wretched subway under King's Lane, one reaches a number of poky sets of rooms known as 'the Lane'.[1] Having arrived here, Maynard had to climb to the first floor. There he found his small rooms, by no means conducive to the comfortable life. It is understood that part of the money which he has bequeathed to King's College will be used to build better sets on this site.

None the less it was a privilege to be there. At Oxford freshmen are brought together into their colleges in their first year, in order to be easily initiated into the corporate life. In their third or fourth year, when the need for the concentrated study of books is at its height, they are sent out into their separate 'digs' in the town, in which the number of visits by friendly intruders is likely to be less.

1. The alternative name, 'the Drain', is a modern vulgarism unknown in 1902.

Cambridge has the custom, which to an Oxford man appears inferior, of leaving the men in lodgings outside college during their first and, possibly, second years, and only bringing them within the college walls subsequently. King's, however, made special arrangements for its scholars in their first year; they were given accommodation in the Lane; there, crowded together, they certainly had a good opportunity of getting to know one another.

On the landing above, Maynard found a fresh young man from the north, with rough-hewn features and tousled hair, a warm handshake and a hearty and earnest manner of speech. This was C. R. Fay.[2] At this moment Fay's life was a welter of excitement and triumph; educated at Merchant Taylors', Crosby, he had played rugger for Lancashire, and was now about to play for Cambridge University, thereby in his freshman term bringing honour to his college. He may have doubted whether the extremely urbane, grown-up, sophisticated and, evidently, most intellectual scholar from Eton would be interested in these delights; but the old Eton wall knew the thrill of them quite well. And he was delighted by Fay's brimming enthusiasm. They very soon became fast friends. Fay was working for the History Tripos, and was interested, then as always, in social and economic problems. Here was a new type, quite different from those who frequented Eton College or Harvey Road. Here was a point of view to be examined, and Maynard kept finding his way upstairs to take up the argument. They argued and argued.

In the next Summer vacation Fay took Maynard on a visit to his parents in Liverpool. They were people of strong Conservative and Low Church views. He recalls what pains Maynard was at to make himself an engaging guest and show a sympathetic understanding of all his parents' interests. Fay was thus able to be proud and pleased at the impression which his clever college friend was making. In fact it probably caused Maynard no trouble, for he would be

2. The well-known economic historian.

fascinated to get this glimpse of a different point of view, and
had a natural spontaneous sympathy with all manner of
men. It is appropriate to apply to him in this connection a
word that is falling into disuse, but has played no little part
in British history. Despite his devastating rudeness, which,
however, he had under control when he chose, he was every
inch a gentleman.

In the room opposite his was W. M. Page, also a mathematical scholar, destined to be above Maynard in the list of
Wranglers in 1905 and to be elected to a Fellowship at King's
in the year before Maynard was elected. They were sent together by the King's authorities to receive instruction from
Mr Hobson[3] ('Hobbema' always to Maynard), Fellow of
Christ's College, and afterwards Sadleirian Professor of Pure
Mathematics. Mr Hurst's fears that Maynard would be
frozen out by Berry's purities were needless; King's knew
its job; it dispatched its mathematical scholars in their first
year to one of the best coaches in Cambridge.

Maynard's logical faculty, his accuracy and his lightning
speed of thought made him a thoroughly competent mathematician. He had no specific genius for mathematics; he had
to take pains with his work; while showing efficiency and
good style within his range, he did not seek out those abstruse regions which are a joy to the heart of the professional
mathematician. From the beginning of his time at Cambridge he had many other interests, and only by diligent
industry did he achieve the required standard in mathematics. When Dr Keynes was a guest at the Founder's Feast at
King's in December 1904 it was not very comforting to be
told by Berry that he thought he 'could honestly say that
Maynard was devoting all his *spare* time to mathematics'!
Despite his earlier frailties, he showed remarkable powers of
work. Although he spent most evenings at some society and
afterwards in endless arguments with his friends, going to
bed at about 3 a.m., Mr Page recalls that he was always as

3. Father of Mr O. Hobson and M. C. K. Hobson, well-known
writers on economic questions.

fresh as a daisy when receiving instruction from Mr Hobson at 9 a.m. the next morning. This happened three times a week. As they walked back from Christ's, Maynard insisted on pausing for a while at David's bookstall and often made a purchase. Mr Page has carried in his mind an incident on their return journey. A young crippled girl was coming along King's Parade on crutches, and a high gust of wind carried off her hat and deposited it in front of a tram-car. 'Stay where you are!' and like a streak the old college wall retrieved the hat. A simple act of kindness, perhaps; but Page had the idea that undergraduate freshmen are not often so considerate, usually having their heads in the clouds.

Robin Furness, who dwelt opposite Fay above, must be written down as Maynard's best friend at King's during his undergraduate days. He was a young man of literary interests, and good taste and judgement, abounding in fancies, and of intellectual calibre to make an excellent companion for Maynard. He was also a boon companion, a pleasure-loving companion, and revelled in scandalous gossip and anecdote; their tongues wagged in that good old way that provides a natural and healthy outlet for the young; their ingenious minds often added such embroidery to the details, that the simple-hearted Fay sometimes thought they went a little too far.

On the ground floor was an old Eton friend, Capron. At this time he was deeply involved with his planchette-board and levitation. Pictures took themselves off his walls and mantelpiece and deposited themselves on the floor. Maynard certainly had an epitome of undergraduate life on his stair. Capron afterwards took Orders, and did faithful duty as Vicar of Scarborough, and elsewhere.

Intellectual fliers usually find it expedient to give up rowing when they reach the university. Not so Maynard. He was always most reluctant to abandon an old love, in order to make way for new interests. Harold Butler expressed his surprise from Balliol College, Oxford, to hear that Keynes was still 'toiling at the oar', but so it was. In the Michaelmas

term he rowed in Trial ('Crock') Eights, and, great glory, his
boat won, and he achieved a cup for his pains.

*J. M. Keynes to B. W. Swithinbank,* 27 November 1902

I have won a pot at rowing; tell it not among the heathen. I
sang a song before an audience of nearly fifty last night; tell it
not in Gath.

In the next term he was included in the 'Lent Boat'. But he
had to give it up in the end and relapse into milder forms of
exercise. He and Gaselee and two others used to play an extremely rudimentary game of lawn-tennis to their own great
amusement, and to that of others who happened to pass by.
He was a much better performer at golf; at one time he and
Mr Leonard Woolf played at Royston regularly every Saturday afternoon. He was also fond of riding. At a later
period he went out with Lowes Dickinson, who, we may believe, was not a very proficient horseman.

If we record that Maynard pursued mathematics as his
subject of study and kept fit by rowing on the river, we have
only scratched the surface of his undergraduate activities
at Cambridge.

It is to be emphasized that at Oxford and Cambridge the
main part of an undergraduate's education is imbibed from
other undergraduates. One may indeed acquire from lectures or laboratories the rudiments of a subject in which
one wishes to specialize. But the processes of higher education are subtler; it is a question of what gives the stimulus
to the creative or logical powers and of the mode by which
the mind makes a transition from the commonplace to the
mature outlook. This higher education has to provide our
society with men capable of initiating new thought, whether
in letters or in science, and with men who, by the breadth
and mellowness of their understanding, will be capable
eventually of valuable leadership in statesmanship, commerce and industry.

It is the general testimony of those who have achieved

distinction in these various fields that they learnt more of permanent value from their fellow-undergraduates than in any other way. There are the societies for debates and discussion, and there are certain traditions which the older generation of undergraduates hands on to its successors. Part of the tradition is a certain mode of frankness in discussion. The half-formed thought in a young mind may easily wither, smothered by the conventional platitudes of the market-place. At the university it is not allowed to die; it is drawn out, developed and tested in argument, so that each young man acquires self-confidence, and therewith the power to develop his gifts. The technique by which this is achieved – more ancient than the psychoanalyst's sofa – is peculiar to undergraduate life; it consists in a certain subtle blend of flippancy and intimacy. Then there is the clash of opinion. It is *de rigueur* in the university atmosphere to pretend to understand the merits of the opposite point of view; one ends by really doing so, and thereby becomes an educated man.

The dons form a background for these vital processes. They form a good background, because, although they may often be old-fashioned and crabbed in their general views, they are revolutionaries in their own subjects, no matter whether it is a question of splitting an atom or displacing a comma in an ancient text. Thus the pupil who receives instruction is made conscious of a dynamic world of new discovery, and of the fundamental insecurity of established orthodoxies. He gets a glimpse of the processes by which new truths are arrived at. It does not matter that dons are often poor teachers, for the aptitude to research, which is their fundamental business, may not be conjoined with the teacher's flair.

Imprinted upon the old fabrics of Oxford and Cambridge is the clear intention to provide convenient means for combining communal life with private life. Communal life is important – easy means for the continuous process of discussion by day and by night. But private life is equally important, the seclusion of one's own set of rooms, where one may turn over one's thoughts undisturbed. The oak may be sported, if necessary. The separate stairs without inter-communicating corridors are important in this connection. A central Authority granting funds for a hostel may plead that separate stairs are more expensive. But that is just the point at issue. Would that central Authority even conceive the possibility that it might be more truly in the interest of higher education to forgo six professorships and to spend the money thus saved on separate stairs – or on additional domestic service, to ensure that the characteristic mixture of communal and private life was successfully achieved?

One cannot look closely at Maynard's education at Cambridge without perceiving that, in so far as it contributed to his being the man he was, professors were of minor importance, while the particular kind of communal and private life he was able to lead in King's at that time was everything.

Its best known undergraduate society was the Walpole Debating Society, in which Maynard took an active part. There was a more select and august body known as Decemviri, consisting of only ten members, as its name implies. This was a mixed Society of Trinity men and King's men, and Maynard was soon elected. He was also, almost at the outset, elected to the Apennine Society, the oldest Literary Society in King's. Then there was the Union. He became a member on the nomination of Dr Keynes on 10 October. We find him speaking for the motion 'that the British system of government by party is becoming a hindrance to useful legislation'. *The Granta* noted that 'Mr Keynes, a maiden speaker and freshman, was quite excellent. He has that taking quiet manner, which is so rare in the Union, and interesting opinions even on a dull subject at a late hour; but he speaks a little too fast.' He supported the motion on the ground that individuals tended to be submerged in parties.

Edwin Montagu, a Liberal, and subsequently Secretary of

State for India, was President, and gave Maynard encouragement. Later in the term he had the honour of being tabled to speak 'on the paper'. He opposed the motion 'that this House welcomes the proposal that Mr Joseph Chamberlain should visit South Africa'. He objected to placing absolute power in the hands of a Cabinet Minister. 'It was a dangerous precedent to let Mr Chamberlain loose and uncontrolled over South Africa.' But Fay spoke on the other side. Maynard joined the Liberal Club and was in due course to be involved in much Liberal speaking, both at the University and elsewhere.

Scarcely had he arrived in Cambridge, when he decided to make a canvas of the scholarly colony in the Lane, to persuade them, whatever their subject of study, to come and hear McTaggart's lectures on general philosophy. The lectures were intended for such an audience; Maynard would have known of McTaggart's eminence from his father. Early in the following term he received an invitation from McTaggart to go to his 'Wednesday Evenings'. These were social evenings, but McTaggart lacked the gift of putting the young men at ease. Mr Leonard Woolf has rather grim memories of it; McTaggart might become lost in silent thought, unconscious of the passage of time, but the undergraduates were on tenterhooks, very much conscious of waiting for the great man. Woolf once actually timed one of these terrible silences, and found that it lasted no less than ten minutes. But if a somewhat senior man was present, the scene was quite transformed and the evening lively; Sanger in particular had a way with the redoubtable philosopher. Sanger was an interesting person, already down, but a frequent visitor; he had shown brilliant promise as an undergraduate and was much respected by Maynard and his friends. They always maintained contact with him.[4]

4. Keynes wrote a notice of him on his death, *Economic Journal*, March 1930. There is a fleeting vision of him under the name of Sandys in Virginia Woolf's *Night and Day*.

Maynard probably did not often go to these rather forbidding sessions; his philosophical allegiance soon began to shift. But he went to the lectures, and these stimulated him to write a paper on 'Time', which was read in Stephen Gaselee's rooms to the Parrhesiasts, one of the countless undergraduate societies. It was an astonishingly mature work for a freshman, not even a specialist in philosophy. Time was essentially relative. Its measurements depended on the unsupported assumption that the time intervals between recurring events of a certain character, e.g. the complete rotation of the earth, were equal. The scientists might allege that the tides were retarding the earth's spin to the extent of one second in a hundred thousand years; this proposition could only have meaning if there were other recurring events arbitrarily assumed by definition to be equidistant in time. If one wanted to criticize the regularity of these other events, then one must have some other standard which in its turn would be equally arbitrary. There was no absolute. It was just as true to say that the Sun moved round the Earth, as that the Earth moved round the Sun. (This was, of course, before the era of 'Relativity'.) More generally the concept of time was dependent on change. 'If you admit the existence of a background of empty time, beyond and apart from change, you have no right to deny the possibility of the elapse of a million million years between the utterance of my last two words.' He proceeded to a more general philosophical discussion. If there was purpose in the Universe, and Time stretched infinitely backwards, that purpose must be already achieved. If the Universe was the scene of a combat between two powers, Good and Evil, they must be of precisely identical strength – a peculiar condition. Were we in due course to enter into a timeless state? 'It is difficult to see in what sense an entry into such an existence would, from our present point of view, differ from complete extinction.' While he could not accept Kant's view of time, he concluded that the common-sense view of it was probably illusory. The paper was wonderfully undogmatic for a very young man. It posed the problems without claiming to solve them.[5]

One of the most influential of the younger dons at King's was Goldsworthy Lowes Dickinson ('Goldie'). He had to teach history and political subjects; he was not a great specialist, and it was a mark of enlightenment in King's to have this very stimulating teacher on its staff. He was a very sweet person, simple and friendly. Struggling with great problems in discussions with the young, he used sometimes to end with a little shrug of despair and a smile, which gave, and yet simultaneously seemed to appeal for, sympathy. How could we poor mortals ever find our way among these baffling problems? His style was straightforward and unadorned. His outstanding quality was one of which we shall have to take recurrent note among these distinguished Cambridge personalities, that of absolute integrity. He followed the thought where it led, and if it led to no solution – well, do not let us pretend! He was full of passionate yearnings, yet cool and balanced in judgement, and distrustful of the conclusions of enthusiasts. Mr E. M. Forster has given a fine sensitive portrait of him.[6]

He exerted a very strong influence on all the clever youth both in King's and beyond,[7] and thereby on Maynard, although the direct influence may not have been great. His mind lacked the keen cutting edge which Maynard loved. Though his interests were philosophical, yet in deep philosophy he was an amateur. Would he even have understood Maynard's freshman paper on 'Time'? His style of writing was lucid, and at times had considerable beauty. He seemed to state the case, or opposing cases, in plain language, entirely free from obscurity; yet perhaps it is not true that

5. Mr Page believes that this paper was read in Maynard's first term. The meeting of the Parrhesiasts which heard it was in May 1903, at the beginning of his third. But it may well have been read to more than one Society. Internal evidence shows that it was written before the close of McTaggart's course of lectures.

6. *Goldsworthy Lowes Dickinson*, by E. M. Forster. Publ. Arnold.

7. cf. p. 129 below.

style always reflects the mind, for in the last analysis there was a certain woolliness in his thought.

But his 'Discussion Society'[8] – which Maynard was naturally asked to join – was a forum for a select number of King's intellectuals, at which eminent philosophers from without, McTaggart, Bertrand Russell and G. E. Moore, occasionally appeared. There the problems of the hour were discussed, and eternal problems – religion, the significance of music and poetry, philosophy, the ideal social order. He was not dogmatic in politics, but he seemed to waft with him, in his gentle way, the atmosphere of the Fabians and others of the progressive vanguard, with whom he was associating in London. He was concerned in the foundation of the London School of Economics, and lectured there occasionally, and at a later date regularly. He was a founder also of the *Independent Review*, which was a vehicle for the thoughts of the younger progressives for a number of years. At Cambridge at this time, he was concerned with the inauguration of the new Economic Tripos, which included Political Science. Alfred Marshall was the real architect of this new degree, which was to give economics a place in the University curriculum alongside classics, history and the other great subjects of study. But Marshall was rather difficult in business, and it is thought that the necessary University legislation would not have been passed without further delay, save through the sweet reasonableness of Lowes Dickinson in persuading the Cambridge historians and others concerned to support it.

World War I was probably a more devastating blow to Dickinson than to any, save those who suffered the loss of their loved ones. Thereafter he was a changed man. Out of the wreckage of his shattered hopes and aspirations, he pieced together a new self, which stood forth as a flaming

8. Mr E. M. Forster (op. cit., p. 102) wrongly dates the foundation of this Society at 1904. Many remember it in earlier years, and it was a going concern when Lowes Dickinson went on his trip to America in 1901 and asked Berry to look after it in his absence.

crusader for peace. His whole being was concentrated on this one purpose. There was no more woolliness, no more aimless wandering in a world of unplumbed ideas. His thoughts were focused. When this quaint little figure, rather untidy, rather fragile, stood up to address a large audience, in simple, unadorned, at first rather stumbling sentences, speaking the language of everyday with his gift of pellucid expression, gradually building up an argument that all could understand, his absolute integrity shining forth, he succeeded in inspiring his audience with that passion for peace which had his own life in thrall. One felt that now indeed one was in the presence of a prophet of righteousness. That was the consummation of his powers. But the elements were always there; and one could see clearly what it was that, despite his shortcomings, stirred the hearts and minds of the young so strongly in his earlier days.

At the opposite extreme to Goldie in the King's scene was Maynard's old Etonian friend, Stephen Gaselee, with 'his bridge and port and brandy and soda'. When Gaselee arrived there the year before, he made a great impression as being already so mature and accomplished a man of the world. The general verdict, however, is that the similar impression made by Maynard a year later was even greater. Gaselee, it is true, was more interested than Maynard in matters of deportment. He liked to be well dressed, and clung to older fashions. Later, when an M.A. on a visit from London, he astonished spectators by coming to service at the college chapel in the old traditional style, namely, a tall hat and an M.A. gown. (Antiquaries have not unearthed this custom at Oxford.) During World War II he was to be seen proceeding from the Foreign Office, where he was the Librarian for many years, in spats, sponge-bag trousers, a bow tie and a starched upright collar, not white but bright bespeckled pink, its points boring into his lower jaw.

Maynard and Gaselee were widely opposed in opinions and temperament. Gaselee was a Tory and an unbending churchman. But they had much, as well as their maturity, in common. Gaselee had read widely and was a witty talker and shared Maynard's interests in later Latin. They were also both keen book collectors. Maynard soon made the acquaintance of Mr Arthur Cole, also one year senior, who shared the taste, and was his lifelong correspondent on these matters. Mr Charles Sayle, Deputy Librarian of Cambridge University Library, was eager to spot undergraduates with a book-loving taste. One day in 1903 he and Cole decided to form a society of book-lovers, which was named the Baskerville Club. Maynard and Gaselee were roped in on the following day, and two or three more were added. Their meetings were usually at breakfast time, Cole acting as secretary. Maynard was an active member and bought many Baskervilles during his undergraduate days. Maynard also spent much time with Dr Montague James,[9] a scholar of immense learning, who was a guide in questions relating to old books and manuscripts, and an expert in late Latin literature, to which Maynard was continuing to devote a considerable amount of his attention.

Gaselee was also a companion in amusement, particularly at the bridge table. Maynard was fond of bridge, both as an undergraduate and later as a don. Gaselee, while he was still up, Dilly Knox, Page and Adcock were among those who often played. After the annual Founder's Feast at King's Maynard always insisted upon what he called a 'Rubber *in Piam Memoriam*'. He was a respectable but not a great player, always ready to take a risk for the sake of trying out some new idea. Knox was first-rate in his knowledge of the game and the lie of the cards, and was equally ready to take risks, but he had a touch of genius in him, and his risks more often led to triumph than to crashes. Maynard thought out the situation with his usual lightning celerity, and he used to say, when the players took a little time to ponder upon the situation: 'What do you think about when you play bridge?' Professor Adcock recalls an occasion when Knox played an unusually surprising card which caused even

9. Provost of King's, 1905–18; Provost of Eton, 1918–36.

Maynard to pause. The same thought leapt simultaneously to the minds of the other three, and they turned upon him in chorus, 'What do you think about when you play bridge, Maynard?'

When he could not get a four, in later days, he sat in the Combination Room playing demon patience. I once challenged him on the ground that it lacked skill and therefore interest. He replied that it was all the better recreation for that, but that it had its excitement. It is a form of patience which comes out seldom, and he knew how often on average. He played to succeed twice running. His interest in the theory of probability made him intrigued to see if this double event occurred with the proper frequency. He went so far as to organize others in the Combination Room to play and to count their failures and successes. He even mentioned 'thrice running'; but I do not recollect if he claimed to have achieved it.

There was at this time an undergraduate at King's, two years senior to Maynard, who carried one forward on the road of higher education further than one could be led at Eton. He was a young man of cherubic countenance, who had been to school at Dulwich. In his early years, when he came to read the plays of Shakespeare, and when he proceeded to read the Greek dramatists, and to read Homer, the beauty of the poetry, the humanity of the characters, and the pattern and unity of the compositions, gripped and possessed him, and became for him then, as they continued to be, the most important facts of existence. This was Mr J. T. Sheppard. Not only was his soul fired by these ancient beauties, but he felt a strong inner impulse to convey his impression, to explain and expound, and to make others share his secret understanding. Mr A. H. Smith (now Warden of New College) remembers his early enthusiasms at Dulwich.[10]

Mr Sheppard has retained his cherubic lineaments during

10. Dulwich at this time seems to have been remarkably fertile in the production of men of strongly individual genius. In one year

the long years of his academic career; but his hair grew prematurely white, and, by a slight affectation, he made it a habit to stump about leaning on a stick, as though oppressed with his years. As one watched him in his vivid conversation, he seemed at one moment still the charming young schoolboy, at another the venerable sage. At times – was it possible? – one had the impression of the two qualities magically fused. That surely was as it should be in one who sought to convey the essence of Greek art, which itself so perfectly fused the passionate susceptibilities of youth with the wisdom of the ages.

He was an admirable performer on the stage. His undergraduate rendering of Peisthetairos in Aristophanes' *Birds* in 1903 is still remembered. The *Granta* wrote: 'Mr Sheppard was splendid throughout. His energy never flagged; we heard every word he said; he made all his points with most telling force; above all he was inimitably funny. In the scene with the Priest he was at his best. The way in which Peisthetairos attempted to join seriously in the ceremony of sacrifice, but was overcome first by his sense of humour, and then by boredom, brought the house down.' He became a classical tutor at King's. Over many years he has also devoted his gifts to productions of Greek plays, of which the most famous was that of Aeschylus' trilogy on Orestes in 1919. This ushered in a very notable era of theatrical productions in Cambridge.

---

there were three, of each of whom severally it could be said that, in type of mind and in mode of self-expression, they were utterly unlike any other human being, namely Mr P. G. Wodehouse, Mr J. T. Sheppard (Provost of King's College Cambridge), and Mr A. H. Smith (Warden of New College Oxford). Mr P. G. Wodehouse has conveyed his exquisite fancies to the million. But the smaller number who have sat at the feet of Mr Sheppard, and the still smaller number who have listened to the narrative style, or studied deeply in the philosophical work, of Mr A. H. Smith, will agree that these two have an originality not less intense than that of Wodehouse. And a few years before, Dulwich produced Mr G. E. Moore, the originality of whose genius was as strongly marked as that of the others.

There was a touch of the dramatic in his manner of lecturing. Besides the lectures intended for classical specialists, he gave some of a more general character which drew large audiences. As time went on, he became less restrained in his mannerisms and was led on to use violent gestures in his intense anxiety to convey his vision. He waved his arms and tore his white locks. I once saw him in a lecture on the *Frogs* of Aristophanes to a society of staid grammarians at Oxford, leap across the room with astonishing agility. Critics objected that it was not the spirit of the Greek authors, but his own, that he was interpreting. But is there any other way of conveying an aesthetic impression save by distilling it through one's own personality? Sheppard felt that he must adopt every device that lay to hand, in order to kindle his listeners' imagination. His lifelong assiduity in his missionary task, using in these later days the medium of the wireless with success, has been of notable value in keeping classical beauties alive in the minds of this generation.

As an undergraduate, he was also an accomplished speaker at the Union and became President in the term before Maynard. He was a dashing figure. In his postgraduate year he had a hansom cab on charter to convey him from place to place in Cambridge at his pleasure. He and Maynard soon became intimates. Their friendship was destined to ripen through a long period of cooperation as Fellows of King's College.

Maynard had been barely a month at King's when he wrote this letter to Swithinbank:

*J. M. Keynes to B. W. Swithinbank*, 13 November 1902

O Swithin, Swithin,

The reasons that I have not writ to thee is because I am too full for words.

I wanted to see you when I came down to wall, and then you and Macmillan (to whom give my love) go for leave like a pair of so-called owls.

I have never enjoyed myself so much before, Sir; and if I write I must needs gush, and gush in a letter is damned offensive.

I have very much increased my knowledge of the affairs of this world and even more of the next.

I know nice people. I have bought over fifty books this term.[11] I row hard every afternoon without exception, and I never go to bed.

What more can heaven offer me?

Take my programme last Sunday evening.

Immediately after hall I went to a Trinity Essay Society and heard a most brilliant satire on Christianity.[12] From there I went to an informal philosophical debating society of interesting people where I stayed till nearly twelve; I then went to see Monty James where I stayed till one; from there I went on to another man with whom I talked till half past four. At half past seven I got up and read the Lesson in Chapel.[13] I had four hours' work that morning, and rowed half a course in the afternoon. In the evening I went as a visitor to the Political Society to hear a paper on the Jesuits . . . and so on.

I am going down for St Andrew's Day.

The President of the Union has put me on the paper to speak next Tuesday,

Ever yours,

J. M. KEYNES

11. Later in the term he bought a magnificent edition of Vergil in three volumes which belonged originally to Adam Smith, and a set of about twenty Elzevirs.

12. This was a paper by Lytton Strachey, entitled 'Colloquies of Senrab', which created a sensation. 'Senrab' was the backward spelling of Barnes, a brother of the Bishop of Birmingham, who had previously read a paper on 'Intellectual Snobs', directed against Strachey and his friends.

13. Maynard read again on the following Sunday, by invitation. 'Cranage, the Sorleys, and others have spoken of M.'s reading in Chapel yesterday. He seems to have pitched his voice successfully and to have been heard well. Sorley tells F. [Mrs Keynes] that he hears M. is the most popular man in King's.' (Extract from Dr Keynes's diary.)

2

Towards the end of his first term, Maynard, responding to a knock on his door, found in the passage two men who were regarding him for the first time. One was lean and tall, the other leaner and taller and with moustache. They introduced themselves: Mr Leonard Woolf, Mr Lytton Strachey. They had come to pay a call. He bade them enter. They drew him out in conversation, and, we may be sure, he responded readily. After a time they rose to go, and, muttering something about the hope that he would come and have tea with them and meet the philosopher, Mr G. E. Moore, they took their leave. Very nice, rather flattering, but surely a little mysterious.

There used to exist at that time in Cambridge a club of considerable age, which was known as 'The Society'. It was founded in the eighteen-twenties by F. D. Maurice and his friends. Tennyson and Hallam were members together.

> Another name was on the door:
> > I linger'd; all within was noise
> > Of songs, and clapping hands, and boys
> That crash'd the glass and beat the floor;
>
> Where once we held debate, a band
> > Of youthful friends, on mind and art
> > And labour, and the changing mart,
> And all the framework of the land.[14]

The Society was very skilful in its choice of members; William Harcourt and Clerk-Maxwell had both belonged, and, at a period shortly before that in which we are interested, Maitland, Walter Raleigh, McTaggart, Alfred Whitehead, and Lowes Dickinson. At the beginning of the twentieth century the number of undergraduate members was very small, barely exceeding six. But the young dons who had been members continued to take part, and other young men

14. *In Memoriam*, canto 87.

made a point of going up from London rather frequently to attend its meetings. The Society was a secret one. But there have been a number of references to it in English literature, and, since it was remarkably successful in preserving its characteristics throughout the generations, it may be well to cite two descriptions of it.

Dean Merivale was a member at the same time as Tennyson. He was elected in 1830 immediately after taking his B.A. degree. He writes[15] of the autumn of 1830, as follows:

Most happily for myself, I fell just at that time into a society of able and studious youths of my own standing with most of whom I had little if any acquaintance before but with whom I soon became familiar, and lived in constant intercourse of the utmost intimacy; men, many of whom I felt to be much my superiors in ability, from most or all of whom I derived knowledge and insight into men and things, yet with all of whom I could more or less hold my own place and feel myself appreciated to my satisfaction. Many of this set have continued to be my close friends through life; several of them survive; from some, the inevitable changes and chances of life have separated me, far and long. But I am sure we all have ever felt and still feel a certain freemasonry of sympathy which binds us implicitly to one another as brethren of one family. Our common bond has been a common intellectual taste, common studies, common literary aspirations, and we have all felt, I suppose, the support of mutual regard and perhaps some mutual flattery. We soon grew, as such youthful coteries generally do, into immense self-conceit. We began to think that we had a mission to enlighten the world upon things intellectual and spiritual. We had established principles, especially in poetry and metaphysics, and set up certain idols for our worship. Coleridge and Wordsworth were our regular divinities, and Hare and Thirlwall were regarded as their prophets; or rather in this celestial hierarchy I should have put Shakespeare at the top of all, and I should have found a lofty pedestal for Kant and Goethe. It was with a vague idea that it should be our function to interpret the oracles of transcendental

15. *Autobiography of Charles Merivale*, ed. Judith Anne Merivale, privately printed Oxford 1898, pp. 98–9. Publ. Arnold, London, 1899, pp. 80–81.

wisdom to the world of Philistines, or Stumpfs, as we designated them, and from time to time to call forth from this world the great souls who might be found capable of sympathizing with them, that we piqued ourselves on the name of the 'Apostles' – a name given us, as we were sometimes told, by the envious and jeering vulgar, but to which we presumed that we had a legitimate claim, and gladly accepted it. We lived, as I said, in constant intercourse with one another, day by day, meeting over our wine or our tobacco; but every Saturday evening we held a more solemn sitting, when each member of the society, about twelve in number, delivered an essay on any subject, chosen by himself, to be discussed and submitted to the vote of the whole number. Alas! alas! what reckless joyous evenings those were. What solemn things were said, pipe in hand; how much serious emotion was mingled with alternate bursts of laughter; how everyone hit his neighbour, intellectually, right and left, and was hit again, and no mark left on either side; how much sentiment was mingled with how much humour! Who is the poet who says, and how aptly he might have said it of us? –

> Witty as youthful poets in their wine;
> Bold as a centaur at a feast; and kind
> As virgins that were ne'er beguiled with love.

The style of our lucubrations may be illustrated perhaps by a saying of one of our profound philosophers, Jack Kemble: 'The world is one great thought, and I am thinking it.'

Much of this description coincides exactly with the testimony of those who were members seventy years later.

Henry Sidgwick was elected in 1856–7. His own account is published in *A Memoir*.

I became a member of a discussion society – old and possessing historical traditions – which went by the name of 'The Apostles'. When I joined it the number of members was not large, and there is an exuberant vitality in Merivale's description to which I recall nothing corresponding. [Mid-Victorian solemnity evidently descended upon the Society for a time.] But the spirit, I think, remained the same, and gradually this spirit – at least as I apprehended it – absorbed and dominated me. I can only describe it as the spirit of the pursuit of truth with absolute devotion and unreserve by a group of intimate friends, who were perfectly frank with each other, and indulged in any amount of humorous sarcasm and playful banter, and yet each respects the other, and when he discourses tries to learn from him and see what he sees. Absolute candour was the only duty that the tradition of the society enforced. No consistency was demanded with opinions previously held – truth as we saw it then and there was what we had to embrace and maintain, and there were no propositions so well established that an Apostle had not the right to deny or question, if he did so sincerely and not from mere love of paradox. The gravest subjects were continually debated, but gravity of treatment, as I have said, was not imposed, though sincerity was. In fact it was rather a point of the apostolic mind to understand how much suggestion and instruction may be derived from what is in form a jest – even in dealing with the gravest matters.

I had at first been reluctant to enter this society when I was asked to join it. I thought that a standing weekly engagement for a whole evening would interfere with my work for my two Triposes. But after I had gradually apprehended the spirit as I have described it, it came to seem to me that no part of my life at Cambridge was so real to me as the Saturday evenings on which the apostolic debates were held; and the tie of attachment to the society is much the strongest corporate bond which I have known in life. I think, then, that my admission into this society and the enthusiastic way in which I came to idealize it really determined or revealed that the deepest bent of my nature was towards the life of thought – thought exercised on the central problems of human life.

A more elaborate description of the procedure and constitution is also to be found in the *Memoir*[16] on pages 29–32.

Strachey and Woolf had come to vet Maynard. He was elected in February 1903, and his membership of the Society during his undergraduate days had a profound influence on his whole life.

What were the characteristics of the Society, which made so deep an impression on distinguished men at widely different dates? Most notable was the sense of brotherhood and

16. By Mrs Sidgwick and Mr Arthur Sidgwick.

the 'utmost intimacy' into which its members fell quite naturally and at once. By what elixir did it succeed in preserving this happy feeling of comradeship through so many decades? We must accept this characteristic as a fact, for the testimony is unanimous. In the light of it, it is easy to see why the Society had such influence. To be able easily and openly to discuss profound questions, such as harass and perplex the spirit of young men, with others of the same age or somewhat more experienced, hand-picked for their intelligence and suitability of character, must needs be a godsend. One could unburden one's soul; one could bring one's most secret thoughts out into the open; one could subject them to wise and friendly comment. Quicker progress was possible in that way towards the achievement of inner harmony. One was brought into contact too with the problems of others, which might be new and strange and open out great vistas of thought.

In most undergraduate societies of purely intellectual purpose, there is a tendency for members when on the carpet in front of the fireplace to think that they must shine. (Cambridge, surely, cannot be totally different from Oxford in this respect.) Erudition may be brought out for display, designed to impress the audience with the speaker's extensive knowledge. This would not be well regarded by the Society. Any learned reference not arising spontaneously and necessitated by the train of thought, was considered to be in bad taste. Or again, in other societies, argumentation may be the strong point. It is up to X, having enunciated a certain proposition, to display his forensic ability in defending it against the onslaughts of Y; all ingenuities of dialectic are encouraged, even although X is beginning to suspect that he has the worse case. This was not in the tradition of the Society. It was understood that as soon as a member began to feel doubtful of his own opinion, he would express his doubts frankly, and perhaps retreat from it.

The primary aim of the discussion, which every member had steadily before his mind, was to achieve the truth. To this end all egoisms had to be suppressed. The subjects discussed were always of a fundamental kind, touching those central opinions which make the man. Tennyson's list is comprehensive; Merivale tends to stress transcendental philosophy. At the beginning of the twentieth century there was emphasis on philosophy, although no doubt the discussion would not normally have become involved in purely technical questions. It seems evident that Sidgwick's experience in the Society was not unconnected with his religious doubts. But by Maynard's time problems connected with orthodox creeds had receded into the background.

There is one point on which the testimony is not quite undivided. Some hold that a prime article of faith was unworldliness, so that a member would become disinclined to take pains and encompass manoeuvres directed towards a successful worldly career for himself. Others are inclined to be doubtful on this point. The coterie, known as 'Bloomsbury', of which we shall hear more, was undoubtedly unworldly in its outlook and was strongly influenced by some who had been members of the Society. It would be wrong, however, to argue from characteristics of Bloomsbury to the nature of the Society itself.

The truth is probably akin to, but subtly different from, that expressed by the creed of unworldliness. For the Society, truth was the paramount objective, and absolute intellectual integrity the means of achieving it. There was certainly a feeling that Apostles were different from ordinary mortals. For purposes of practical life an Apostle had also, of course, to be an ordinary mortal; and it might be that he would set himself to plan and contrive in order to win position and influence in the world. That was a matter of indifference to the Society, not of reproach. On the other hand, if an Apostle did none of these things, but devoted himself unostentatiously and with small worldly means to some line of thought or to achieving an inner spiritual harmony, that was excellent. As regards the ambitious, the saving clause would be that at heart they should be seeking to promote what they honestly believed to be a good cause.

Maynard fell in part into both categories. He certainly did not map out his life in its early stages in a way that would exploit to the full the power, which his brilliant gifts gave him, to achieve a great worldly position. On the other hand he can by no means be described as altogether unworldly. He desired to influence the course of events. He was not unmindful of valuable contacts and worldly ways and means for achieving desired results. He went beyond what the Bloomsbury coterie thought fitting for someone who sought the good life. There may have been a certain ambivalence in Maynard in this respect, some inner force which prevented him at times from adopting all the expedients which would come naturally to a worldly man, in the full sense of that word, in his endeavour to attain his ends. This ambivalence may have had important consequences at certain crucial points in his career. If we hold that the austere canons of the Society were in this respect some hindrance – and it may be deemed that humankind was the loser from any inhibitions he may have had in advancing himself – we must always remember that by his contact with the Society his faith and vision were sustained. And it is these, rather than any worldly success in Britain, that have contributed to his world-wide influence.

Of his sense of the importance of the Society to him there can be no doubt.[17] He always observed the rule of secrecy with extreme strictness, although he was by no means a person who rejoiced in exaggerating rules of 'official secrecy' beyond their usefulness. Many close friends were totally unaware of the existence of the Society. It would not be an exaggeration of language to say that it served him, in some respects, in place of a religion. The sense of brotherhood, the communion of souls, 'the mission to enlighten the world on things intellectual and spiritual', 'the established principles' making Truth the supreme objective of man, the canons of integrity and sincerity, the relative antiquity, cer-

17. cf. refs. on pp. 131–2 below.

tain rites carefully observed at meetings, the use of words with meanings not understood by the uninitiated, all responded to certain spiritual cravings which orthodox churches seek to satisfy.

### 3

Henry Sidgwick died of cancer in 1900 at the age of sixty-two. Other philosophers of eminence were already established in Cambridge. We have seen Maynard bidding his friends to go to the lectures of McTaggart. Alfred Whitehead and Bertrand Russell coming together at this time, but separating later, were engaged on those great philosophical speculations which will, no doubt, outlive other Cambridge philosophical productions of our period. In 1902 a new star had recently risen above the horizon, in the person of Mr G. E. Moore. For the time he had much the greatest influence on the intellectual youth. Undergraduate members of the Society chose their own new members – with most meticulous care. It was usually thought well to introduce them to the discriminating inspection of G. E. Moore, before deciding to put them forward. Moore was a paramount influence in the Society. But it is time to desist from prying into the affairs of that august body, for its members wished them to be secret, and those wishes should be respected, so far as our purpose allows. Moore's influence in Cambridge was of much wider ambit, and as such we may consider it. His views on moral questions were well known there some time before the publication of *Principia Ethica*.

This appeared in the autumn of 1903.[18]

*J. M. Keynes to B. Swithinbank*, 7 October 1903

I have just been reading Moore's *Principia Ethica*, which has been out a few days – a stupendous and entrancing work, *the greatest* on the subject.

Whence came his influence? There was his style. Readers

18. Students of Mr Forster's *Life of Lowes Dickinson* should note that the appearance of *Principia Ethica* is there misdated (p. 111).

of his works are familiar with the fascinating, indeed spell-binding, way in which, with twists and turns and elaborate convolutions of phrase, with plentiful use of italics, he suc-ceeds in conveying thought, clear, distilled, purified, its very quintessence finally expressed so that it is impossible to mistake his meaning. Maynard once told me that he thought that Moore had carried the use of ordinary speech as far as it would ever be possible to carry it, in conveying clear meaning. For still greater precision one would have to pro-ceed by mathematical symbols.[19]

And then there was the man himself. His devotion to truth was indeed palpable. In argument his whole frame was gripped by a passion to confute error and expose con-fusion. To watch him at work was an enthralling experience. Yet, when the heat of argument died down, he was the mildest and simplest of men, almost naïve in unphilosophi-cal matters. He was friendly to the young, approaching them on natural and equal terms. Despite his *naïveté*, he seemed to have understanding. In human questions he had none of that intolerance or crabbedness which so often marks the academic man of thought. He was happy and at ease in discussions beyond his proper range. There was no question of his being shocked, and the young had no inhi-bitions in his presence. When Strachey made one of his subtle, perhaps cynical, perhaps shocking, utterances, the flavour of which even his clever undergraduate friends did not at first appreciate at its full value, Moore was seen to be shaking with laughter. If the veneration which his young admirers accorded him almost matched that due to a saint, we need not think that they were mistaken. It does not follow that the doctrines set forth in *Principia Ethica* are infallible.

If questioned on Moore's most important contribution to ethics, his admirers – outside the ranks of professional philo-sophers – are apt to recall his doctrine that 'good' is an attribute, the meaning of which is indefinable. It may be

19. cf. *A Treatise on Probability*, by J. M. Keynes, p. 19.

held that Moore should not be regarded as the originator of this doctrine. He himself makes generous acknowledgement in the *Principia* to Henry Sidgwick. Sidgwick's arguments, however, are not so pointed as Moore's, nor collected into so formidable a battle array; they are to be found scattered about in his large volume on *The Methods of Ethics*; and his style is altogether less readable. I remember Alfred Whitehead telling me that he had read *The Methods of Ethics* as a young man and found it so stodgy that he had been deterred from ever reading any book on ethics since.[20]

This same doctrine was very familiar in the lecture rooms of Oxford when I was an undergraduate there (1919–22). It was sometimes enunciated in the proposition that 'the good can only be defined in terms which pre-suppose an understanding of what it is'. We need not consider whether this rigmarole is more or less precise than Moore's 'indefinable'. The arguments used in Oxford to sustain this position resembled fairly closely those which appear in *Principia Ethica*. They were propounded by an important group of philosophers, who had broken away from the older Oxford tradition of idealism, and had been strongly influenced by J. Cook-Wilson. It is not clear, however, what progress had already been made in Oxford in the development of this line of thought when *Principia Ethica* appeared.

The doctrine of indefinability has the consequence that decisions about what is good depend on direct intuition in each particular case. The interpretation given in Oxford to this consequence was widely different from that in Cambridge. In Oxford – no doubt owing partly to the special attention paid to Aristotle's *Ethics* – great reliance was placed on what may be called traditional morality, embodying the intuitions of wise men through the ages. In Cambridge the doctrine of intuition was interpreted – anyhow by those disciples who were to be for many years the inti-

20. Not having at that time a specialist interest in the development of Cambridge thought on these topics, I did not reply then, as I certainly should now: 'But surely you have read Mr Moore's book'.

mate intellectual companions of Keynes – as giving fairly complete licence to judge all things anew.

There was another important difference between the Oxford doctrine, as it developed in these years, and that of the *Principia*. Oxford philosophers produced for the edification of their pupils a second 'indefinable', namely duty. The arguments which they used in defence of the indefinability of duty were similar to those used in the case of 'the good'. The trouble about these indefinables is that, once you accept one of them, they tend to proliferate. In my own person I have never been convinced by the arguments used by Moore or by those used at Oxford.

The independent status given to the concept of duty by Oxford philosophers also fostered an outlook very different from that of the Cambridge intellectuals. In one's general view of things, when going out into the world to face the practical problems of life, it makes an enormous difference to one's point of view whether one holds that one must judge one's own actions according to whether or not they tend to promote some ultimate good which one may have in mind, or supposes oneself limited on every hand by a number of hard and fast duties, intuitively recognized as such.[21] This was relevant, as we shall see, to the great issues of conscience presented by World War I; Keynes himself thought it his duty to assist the war effort, but many of his greatest friends did not, and this had further consequences.

Moore had indeed a chapter (ch. 5) containing a discussion on moral obligation. During World War I some friends, many of whom belonged to this Cambridge period, founded a Club entitled 'The Memoir Club'. Two papers read to this Club by Keynes have been published.[22] In one of these

21. In a later work, *Ethics* (Home University Library, 1912), Moore appears to embrace the view that duty is also an indefinable. (See p. 173.) I am grateful to Sir David Ross for calling my attention to this development. It had, I believe, no influence on, if indeed it was noticed by, the intellectuals with whom we are concerned.

22. *Two Memoirs*, by J. M. Keynes. Publ. Rupert Hart-Davis, 1949.

memoirs ('Early Beliefs') he gave a full account of Moore's influence. Referring to the chapter on moral obligation, he wrote:

There was one chapter in the *Principia* of which we took not the slightest notice. We accepted Moore's religion, so to speak, and discarded his morals. Indeed, in our opinion, one of the greatest advantages of his religion was that it made morals unnecessary – meaning by 'religion' one's attitude towards oneself and the ultimate, and by 'morals' one's attitude towards the outside world and the intermediate.

Moore's disciples were not altogether to blame for this attitude. He wrote this chapter rather in the style of one making a concession to what was necessary, and as though he was not deeply interested. It is in marked contrast to the flaming advocacy of the other chapters. Furthermore the argument is somewhat halting, and it is evident that he had not thought deeply about the difficulty of relating the 'good', at which we should aim, to conduct in the practical affairs of life. There is in fact a very great gap in his treatise; one half, or more, of what is important for practical ethics is omitted.

While the doctrine of an indefinable good seemed to give emancipation from earlier preconceptions, positive direction to one's thoughts on ethical matters was to be found in Moore's chapter on 'The Ideal'. Keynes's memoir should be read in conjunction with this chapter. Here Moore set out what things are good in themselves. His list is a short one, containing two items – 'the enjoyment of beautiful objects', and 'the pleasures of human intercourse'. There is no need to quarrel with these items; they are both of them, undoubtedly, supreme goods. But what a world is left out! As Keynes observed in his memoir: 'it is remarkable how oblivious he managed to be of the qualities of the life of action, and also of the pattern of life as a whole'.[23]

23. The pleasure of personal human intercourse may be regarded as comprised by the general expression, Love, in the broadest sense of

Looked at from a broad point of view, Moore's list of 'goods' is cloistered and anaemic. This is not to deny that it may have been of great value in its own place and time. It challenged his readers to a revaluation; it made a clean sweep of the past; it stimulated the young to new thoughts and enthusiasms; it caused an intellectual ferment; it held out the promise of a new world of ideas to be conquered. The artist who created beautiful objects was put on a pillar of pre-eminence. Most philosophers, while having their chapters on aesthetics, seem merely to be paying lip service to it. And how much worse is the case of important men of affairs in regard to artistic matters, with their patronizing philistinism.

It may have been well, also, at that time to focus attention upon the problems of human relations and love. The severities of Victorian morality in placing all the stress on what was expedient, on what was necessary to sustain an ordered society, seemed in danger of losing sight of the purpose of society. If a home was unhappy – as many Victorian homes were – it was necessary to use the stiff upper lip, and endure sorrows for the good of the social order. But what was this good? It was certainly well to remind this great materialistic society, which was so harsh in its conventional morality, that after all the object of all these rules and conventions was precisely to achieve happy personal relations. A great revaluation was indeed due; but it was important that in this revolution of ideas we should not degenerate into a mere attitude of 'do as you like', but should have our standards

---

that word. Even his treatment of love is, however, unsatisfactory – and rather curious. He emphasizes the importance of corporeal qualities; it is a prime evil for anyone to be in a state of admiring contemplation of what is ugly; on the other hand, he is apt to speak of 'lust' as something to be condemned. By putting his doctrines together, one would reach the conclusion that one of the most evil things that can happen in the world, is to be carnally attracted by an ugly person. This is rather hard lines on a large minority of the human race! The matter would be made even worse if that person had faulty artistic taste.

maintained by the unworldliness of Moore's chapter on 'The Ideal', of which Keynes said: 'I know no equal to it in literature since Plato, and it is better than Plato because it is quite free from fancy. It conveys the beauty of the literalness of Moore's mind, the pure and passionate intensity of his vision, unfanciful and undressed up.'[24]

It must be noticed, however, that the practical value of Moore's concentration on these particular forms of 'good' depended upon what I have called the presuppositions of Harvey Road, namely the security and good order of the British Empire. That institution was maintained by many people acting in accordance with moral laws, the philosophical justification of which they may not have understood and would not have found explained in Moore. Within the framework of a secure society thus kept in being, it was possible and desirable to make new experiments, and to set one's eyes fixedly upon certain ideals, too long neglected. It might not matter if certain other principles necessary for the maintenance of an ordered society were temporarily overlooked.

But let there be a threat to this security. Where find in the *Principia* a guide to duty? Moore's book only comprises a fragment of the moral story. If his ideals are to retain their place, they must be integrated into a wider philosophy, which, while doing honour to them, would have something more adequate to say about the nature and rationale of the social obligations on which a civilized society rests.

In his memoir Maynard gives a critical analysis of the state of mind of himself and his friends in their youth.

We were amongst the last of the Utopians, or meliorists as they are sometimes called, who believe in a continuing moral progress by virtue of which the human race already consists of reliable, rational, decent people, influenced by truth and objective standards, who can be safely released from the outward restraints of convention and traditional standards and inflexible rules of con-

24. op. cit., p. 94.

duct, and left, from now onwards, to their own sensible devices, pure motives and reliable intuitions of the good.[25]

*

In short, we repudiated all versions of the doctrine of original sin, of there being insane and irrational springs of wickedness in most men. We were not aware that civilization was a thin and precarious crust erected by the personality and the will of a very few and only maintained by rules and conventions skilfully put across and guilefully preserved. We had no respect for traditional wisdom or the restraints of custom. We lacked reverence, as Lawrence[26] observed and as Ludwig[27] with justice also used to say – for everything and everyone. It did not occur to us to respect the extraordinary accomplishment of our predecessors in the ordering of life (as it now seems to me to have been) or the elaborate framework which they had devised to protect this order. Plato said in his *Laws* that one of the best of a set of good laws would be a law forbidding any young man to inquire which of them are right or wrong, though an old man remarking any defect in the laws might communicate this observation to a ruler or to an equal in years when no young man was present. That was a *dictum* in which we should have been unable to discover any point or significance whatever. As cause and consequence of our general state of mind we completely misunderstood human nature, including our own. The rationality which we attributed to it led to a superficiality, not only of judgement, but also of feeling.

The comment is just. But it may be that the imperfection of their view was due not only to this neglect of certain characteristics of human nature, but also to defects in their philosophical bible.

25. It has been pointed out to me, I judge correctly, that these friends did not actually attribute these high qualities to the majority of mankind; there was in fact a good deal of disdain for that majority. Nevertheless Maynard is right in holding that their ethical code – or lack of code – was only defensible on the assumption that these qualities were in fact present.

26. D. H. Lawrence.

27. Ludwig Wittgenstein.

4

Among the undergraduates who arrived at Trinity in the year 1899, five soon became intimate friends. When Maynard went up three years later, he found them there, a close circle, and was adopted by them. These men were Thoby Stephen, Clive Bell, Saxon Sydney-Turner, Leonard Woolf and Lytton Strachey. Very soon after their arrival they founded the 'Midnight Society' which gathered at twelve on Saturday evenings and proceeded to read some serious play. An arduous beginning to a lifelong intimacy!

Thoby Stephen, son of Leslie Stephen, was the most mundane of the party. He came of a cultivated home, was well read, and liked to talk to these friends about books; he was good-looking, had sporting interests, and formed a link with the wider world of Trinity. He had qualities which made him greatly beloved; but he was entirely unselfconscious about his charms; he was spontaneous in his friendship, and, by his poise and self-confidence, a pillar of strength in this intensely intellectual and somewhat introspective group. He was known to them as 'the Goth'. Of the other four, the closest to Thoby was perhaps Clive Bell, 'a gay and amiable dog', as Maynard calls him,[28] less oppressed by the cares of humanity than the others, full of life and sparkle, an unending source of cheerful gossip. He was deeply interested in the visual arts and this provided a link between him and Lytton Strachey. Saxon Sydney-Turner, 'the quietist', was the most scholarly. He was a classic, and later perpetrated more than one of those incredible *tours de force*, the Latin Epilogues performed after the production of a play by Plautus or Terence at his old school, Westminster. He shared with Leonard Woolf the view that human prospects were very black. He was of amiable disposition, and a staunch friend, and continued to be an intimate and highly valued member of this group, indispensable in any reunion. His life

28. op. cit., p. 81.

has been spent in the British Treasury. Leonard Woolf was an ardent spirit, then, as always, the fearless champion of the oppressed. In political opinions he was probably the most leftward of the party. Of sensitive and discriminating intelligence, and interested in art and literature as well as in politics, he was a delightful intellectual companion.

Lytton Strachey was one of a family of thirteen (ten surviving infancy). He was delicate in his childhood, and remained so. His school education was fragmentary; yet at nineteen he seemed in many respects more mature than most Cambridge freshmen. Two features of his youth stand out. One was his incessant reading from early years. His mother was devoted to Elizabethan literature, and she began to read Shakespeare and other Elizabethan playwrights aloud to him when he was barely three, and at an early age she introduced him to French literature. She was a woman of remarkable gifts, a friend of Huxley, George Eliot, Henry Maine and other illustrious men and women of the time. She was also interested in painting and music. Modern ideas began to infiltrate, for we learn that, before the end, Roger Fry was an occasional visitor. And there, in the bosom of the family, in addition to all the others, was the young cousin Duncan Grant, in the charge of Lady Strachey, his paternal aunt, while the Grants were in India. Duncan's painting activity began early.

The second characteristic was the incessant fun and laughter. To use a word not dignified but appropriate, Lytton seemed to his sisters to be giggling fairly continuously from the age of three to nineteen. There were the habitual jokes of childhood, fanciful nicknames, endless conversations in dog French, acting, ragging, playing jokes on visitors, not practical but subtle and disconcerting. The round of fun was hectic and delirious, and Lytton's inventiveness seemed endless.

Being delicate he was sent with two or three other boys to coach with Mr Forde at Poole Harbour. He had his youthful adventure; routine was broken by a trip, first to Gibraltar, and then through Egypt to the Cape, when he was twelve years old; there was some connection between this trip and the journeyings of his father, Sir Richard Strachey, who was a great Indian Administrator. Lytton had to travel alone with his older sister Dorothy (Madame Bussy) to Gibraltar. She recalls that his father gave instructions that, if anything went amiss in the Bay of Biscay, they were not to spare the champagne. Sitting together in the cabin they obeyed this instruction to the letter. Thus Lytton received his initiation even earlier than Maynard!

Having returned for a time to Mr Forde, he was sent by his mother to Abbotsholme, a school in Derbyshire, conducted on modern lines, somewhat under the influence of Edward Carpenter. It appears that this did not suit him. He was withdrawn after a term and proceeded to Leamington College, where he spent between three and four years. This was a small school, chosen for that, but run on more conventional lines than Abbotsholme. It may be well that his energies were not overtaxed there, and that his reading continued apace.

His next port of call was Liverpool University, to which he went at the age of seventeen. This was due to the presence of Sir Walter Raleigh, whose influence was important. It is pleasant to think of the mutual regard felt for one another by these two fine geniuses of literature.[29] We may be sure that Raleigh's beautiful dry humour was not lost upon Strachey. Raleigh was in the van of a shift of critical values. Cultivated persons of the late-Victorian period were no doubt well read in our earlier masterpieces, but they were inclined to be over-zealous in their admiration of the Victorian pontiffs; they gave the classics their meed of praise, but with an inflection which implied that the older masters were a little archaic, of the past, hardly really significant for current problems, having been superseded by the Victorian giants,

29. cf. *Letters of Sir Walter Raleigh*, edited by Lady Raleigh, ii, 479–82. In the letter of 13 May 1918 Raleigh suggested that Strachey should write the Life of Queen Victoria.

with their greater depth and more spiritual vision. Raleigh served to restore a sense of proportion, and Strachey in this sense may be regarded as his disciple.

But he was not officially studying literature at Liverpool; his subject was history; and he often expressed indebtedness to Professor Mackay. He was introduced also to social problems, being taken round the worst parts of Liverpool by Dr Stookes with whom he lodged. He made a lifelong friend in Lumsden Barkway, since Bishop of St Andrews. Although they were bound by ties of mutual amity, their intellectual points of view were not coincident. The Bishop has written a valuable treatise on *The Creed and its Credentials*. Strachey at one time thought of writing a Life of Christ, and is recalled as having given as his reason for abandoning the project 'that it was impossible to find evidence for his actual existence'.

His mother wished him to go to Balliol College, Oxford. The Balliol authorities were somewhat perplexed by the oral examination. Mr Strachan-Davidson told Lady Strachey that he would probably be happier at a smaller college. So she sent him instead to Trinity College, Cambridge.

His début there was not an unqualified success. Weird in appearance and in his manner of speaking, paradoxical in the substance of what he seemed to be saying, in so far as it was possible to make head or tail of it, he was an object of some doubt in the minds of many Trinity undergraduates. To balance this, he quickly gathered round him the circle of interesting friends whom I have already named. And senior men, such as Mr Desmond MacCarthy and Mr E. M. Forster, were not slow to be impressed by his fine intellect. A word should be said about his voice, which was a subject of general and unfavourable comment, being, on first acquaintance, his most noticeable characteristic. It broke late, and, to the end of his life, it went into a high pitch on the emphatic termination of a sentence. The complaint was that it was extremely affected, even being used by him to make an utterance sound impressive which had nothing else to commend it. On the whole, the charge of affectation is probably false. The intonation was certainly very peculiar, but this was a family characteristic. The brothers and sisters shared it with him, and were often recognized as Stracheys by total strangers in remote parts of the globe. It need not be denied, however, that he occasionally exaggerated his native inflections for effect. There are recollections of his uttering whole sentences in a monotonous falsetto which was certainly not natural to him. It may well have been done to tease. We must not forget that he had spent nineteen years in making the other members of the family laugh, and there was no reason why the atmosphere of Trinity should staunch his capacity for fun. But there was more to it than this. In his own thoughts he wished to bring about a revolution in many existing values. Thought and feeling are conveyed not only by grammatical forms but also by the inflections used in utterance. By choosing to stress those elements in a sentence which are not usually stressed, and conversely, one may produce in the mind of a hearer a revaluation of old truisms. When one wishes to persuade men to think or act differently – a hard task veritably – no artifice is to be despised. There was much more meaning in his curious inversions of stress than the undergraduates of Trinity, even his friends, at first understood. As evidence of this we may adduce the fact that in due course these peculiar intonations were adopted by a number of clever people, and used by them as an instrument to achieve their own quite different effects. The Strachey voice became the 'Bloomsbury voice', and was used by many who had never even heard Strachey speak.

The influence of Strachey at Trinity was not at once outstanding; his comment on life was subtle, and the flavour of it an acquired taste. His mode of asserting his own point of view was a peculiar one. He often sat silent in a corner, letting the ripples of general conversation flow over him. Then suddenly he piped up, perhaps in a high squeak. He might say something of devastating pointedness, which quite clearly confuted and confounded them all. Or he might say something which they hardly understood. Or what he said might on the face of it be so profoundly shocking, that they could scarcely believe that his words were to be taken seriously. Perhaps they were a joke; and yet, perhaps, he might mean them seriously. There could be something terrifying about his silences. There was no longer the ceaseless flow of gaiety of his boyhood days. He brooded, and polished his thoughts. He still had a great sense of the ludicrous. But it was distilled now and expressed in sudden sallies.

His friends did not at first apprehend that he was a man of outstanding genius. He stayed in Cambridge for six years, and before he went down his influence had become paramount among the intellectual youth. When Maynard arrived in 1902 Strachey was not yet at his zenith. If Maynard fell for him at once, that was by virtue of his own clever judgement; he always recognized the best when he saw it, with a lightning discernment. They also had certain affinities, which it is necessary to the story of Maynard to analyse. Lytton was unusually mature, for an undergraduate, in his literary and artistic judgements; Maynard had such interests. Hitherto he had not had for stimulus more than might come from a cultivated home and from Eton. This was not enough to satisfy his intense spirit. He had a passionate nature, and a craving for something high, for something perfect. But he could not be satisfied easily. He was, first and foremost, a very clever man, a deep thinker, a logician. A literary man, however accomplished, who could not see the force of a good argument, might win his affection, but would not do as a regular companion for him at this stage. He needed someone who could sufficiently understand his mental processes.

Lytton was such a person. This is not always appreciated by his readers. Some are beguiled by his poetic vision, by his fun and by the impressionistic touches in his historical writing, into supposing that he was an intellectual dilettante, fundamentally frivolous. This was by no means the case. He was a man of considerable intellectual and logical ability. His father had scientific interests, including meteorology. He was a Fellow of the Royal Society and Royal Medallist. He was President of the Meteorological Society; this was not merely an ornamental position; he took an active part in discussing with its experts the details of their activities. He and Lytton used to write letters to each other about mathematical problems. At Cambridge Lytton became deeply interested in the philosophies of McTaggart and Moore. There was a time when, in planning *Eminent Victorians*, he thought of including a series of studies of Victorian scientists, with the intention of raising these scientists in the popular esteem by as much as he depressed Manning and Arnold. If Maynard wanted to grapple with some exacting philosophical problem, Lytton could come at least part of the way with him.

But this is not the whole story; we must go deeper. Lytton was, in the world of ideas, a revolutionary. He wished to overthrow, to make a clean sweep, to value all things anew, and this appealed to something very deep in Maynard. Just at this juncture Lytton, both because he was three years senior and had had an unconventional education, had progressed further than Maynard in the quest for fresh values. At the moment he was in a position to help Maynard towards satisfying his cravings for a new vision of heaven and earth.

On the whole, nineteenth-century England remained under the sway of the Romantic movement, of Goethe and of that extraordinary galaxy of men of genius who wrote in English in the first quarter of the century. The great Victorians, for all their vitality and originality, their remarkable twists and turns of form and feeling, remained under the spell. The old vein was worked hard and exploited in new ways. This could not go on. By the end of the century the time was ripe for a great revolt.

Strachey's early immersion in the Elizabethans and the

French work of the seventeenth and eighteenth centuries was important; important also was the fact that these were his private enthusiasms. For Keynes at Eton, the older masters were part of what was venerable and established; Burke's oratory was the 'old, old' stuff. For one's private adventure, one went ahead of one's schoolmasters and admired Browning and Meredith. In cultivated London drawing-rooms the position was reversed. There the latest Victorian masters were the revered idols; to suggest that one's soul might be better nourished by reading Gibbon was indeed astonishing.

Strachey's revolt was not only literary. The religious question was central. Many of the great Victorians no longer accepted dogmatic theology. But had they faced the implications of rejection? They were worried and ambivalent. Were they also a little hypocritical? On these deep questions one must be absolutely honest, truthful, straightforward. If a clean sweep had to be made, let it be made. There was the consequential question of values and moral sentiments. Here again one found ambivalence, obscurity, fear to face the issues. Yes; it was time to make a clean sweep and to build again in the light of one's deepest convictions. At this point Moore stretched out a helping hand, with his idealism unequalled 'since Plato', and 'better than Plato because it is quite free from fancy'.

All this responded to something fundamental in Keynes. His mind was highly intolerant of anything ambiguous or makeshift. Confronted with an intellectual patchwork, with an old idea and a new idea incongruously held together, he could not fail to detect the incongruity with his quick penetration, and was left with a feeling of irritation and disgust. He, like Strachey, craved for the clean sweep, the bold new idea, the crisp and lucid. And then he deeply loved excitement and adventure. This revaluation – where would it lead? What new vistas would be opened to view? And he had a streak of iconoclasm. To tease, to flout, finally perhaps to overthrow, venerable authorities – that was a sport which had great appeal for him. And so it happened that he found in this clever Trinity undergraduate someone who shared many of his deeper tendencies; here indeed was an ideal friend.

The Collected Edition of Strachey's works consists of six volumes.[30] Of these, posterity may well attach the least value to *Eminent Victorians*, in which he gave full rein to his satire and sense of fun. Since it was through this book that he made his impact on a wider public, there are still too many who judge him by it. Turning to the other five, an admirer might claim, not with dogmatism but with confidence that he could not easily be refuted, that one would have to look back to Hazlitt to find work of comparable distinction in the field of biographical and literary *belles lettres*. But one who witnessed all the ferment of those days might have expected a greater achievement by the whole group, something as important for the coming time as the Romantic Movement had been a hundred years earlier. It has not so turned out.

Keynes also had within him the seeds of rebellion. Although his intellect reached its full development when he was very young, his creative impulse came to maturity slowly. In those days he did not know that he was to be an economist. In the end his influence extended further than Strachey's, for the products of his brain have become the everyday thoughts of many people all over the globe. He at least has carried the banner far afield. The ultimate outcome of Keynes's work is not yet decided. All we can now say is that he is decidedly in the running for the prize of having had a permanent influence 'on all the framework of the land'. This is a paradox, for social questions were not prominent in the discussions of that group. His wish to challenge authority was indigenous to him; but there is no doubt that the impulse to build all things anew was sustained and strengthened by the society of these Cambridge friends.

There is one final characteristic of Strachey which must be mentioned. This lanky, angular creature, a comic almost,

30. Publ. Chatto & Windus, 1948.

with his weird voice, and clever, critical, mocking mind, had in the highest measure the power of personal sympathy. He had a delicate understanding of the inmost recesses of the heart. Even with a close friend it is not always easy to confide; there is often some barrier, some fear – perhaps of shocking, perhaps of saying something that will disturb the friendship in an unforeseeable way. With Strachey there could be no fear of this sort. One could be sure that whatever one said would be received with perfect understanding. There could be no embarrassment, no awkwardness. As it were to compensate for his sharpness and satire in general company, and on intellectual topics, he was gentleness itself as a confidant. Whence came this quality? Was it all that fun and jest, which kept his relations with his family so easy and gay? Confucius held that one's power to maintain harmonious relations in one's own family precisely measured one's power to do so in a wider world. All the Strachey family had some gift of sympathy. But no doubt we must ascribe Lytton's high measure of it to his own peculiar genius, and associate it with those powers of interpretation and penetration which we find in his literary criticism and in his study of historical personages.

The reader may wonder how this could have been important for Maynard, who was so successful, so competent in all his own affairs, so much a master of life, so little in need of external support. This is only to look at the surface. From the outside he seemed all urbanity, suavity, self-possession. He appeared to some to be almost inhuman, so mechanical was the precision with which he achieved every objective. Yet underneath that urbanity he had an ardent, passionate nature. He had a great fund of affection which he wished to lavish and have reciprocated. But his other gifts, which raised him to a superior plane, became in the course of time in some sense a barrier. The ordinary run of mortals had so much respect for his powers, that it was not easy to be on simple terms of human fellowship with him. This problem hardly arose at Eton. At school a boy, however clever, provided that he is not gauche or egoistic, remains one of the family among his contemporaries in his house. Maynard was very companionable, and the schoolboy spirit of easy friendship permeated his daily intercourse. At the University distinctions begin to appear. The clever set becomes slightly apart. One may begin by rowing in the College boat, but that has to be given up for the sake of work and other pressures on one's time. A young man like Thoby Stephen, with his abundant charm and easy fellowship, would discharge and receive, in the course of his daily college doings, any amount of spontaneous affection. In such good comradeship, the cravings of nature received satisfaction, the person in question being scarcely aware of what was going on. A very clever young man slightly different, inevitably slightly aloof, lacks something that others have in their easy companionship. But if he be of an affectionate nature, as Maynard was, the lack sets up internal reactions; one's feelings become just a little intense and perhaps overwrought. One concentrates a stronger stream of affection upon one's particular friends. Then if anything goes wrong with the friendship, there may be acute distress. Under the polished surface of urbanity, his emotions ran strong.

Thus from time to time the woes of the world descended upon him, and his spirit would languish. It was therefore of very great value to have such a confidant as Strachey, who was not in the least frightened of him and who had a unique power of sympathetic understanding. To intellectual companionship was added a deeper communion of spirit.

Maynard did not forget his older friends; he strove to maintain his close relationship with Swithinbank; he wrote to him frequently, paid occasional visits to Balliol and was eager that he should be appreciated by his new friends. Strachey was greatly impressed by him. At Balliol, Swithinbank's most interesting contemporary was J. D. Beazley, and he reciprocated by introducing Beazley to Maynard. Although no great intimacy arose, Maynard showed a touching desire to bring this friend of Swithinbank into his circle also. There are often references to Beazley in his letters to Swithinbank – has he won such-and-such a prize? – what are his interests now? Swithinbank (accompanied by Dundas, who stayed at Harvey Road) brought Beazley on a visit to King's in the autumn of 1904. Incidentally, in the course of the visit, Beazley caught a cold. Such matters he usually took in his stride, and was amazed therefore to find Keynes putting him to bed, producing all sorts of cures and lavishing the greatest attention upon him. Beazley had the sense that he was nursing him 'like a mother'. 'Like a mother', he repeated to me with emphasis. Poor Maynard had much experience of colds, and of worse ailments following on colds, and of his own mother's loving care.

But before this disaster of the cold, Beazley found himself sitting by the fireside in a Cambridge study. Opposite him was a lanky, loose-limbed figure, outstretched in an easy-chair, in a position of the greatest repose; that was Keynes. On the carpet in front of the fire was a collection of still longer limbs, still more loosely joined together, stretching out indefinitely in different directions; that was Strachey. It is difficult to remember over the years the contents of brilliant conversations, but the following piece of nonsense happens to have remained in Beazley's mind:

STRACHEY (*from the hearthrug*): 'I have never in the whole course of my life read any book merely for pleasure. Have you, Keynes?'

KEYNES: 'No, never. Have you, Beazley?'

BEAZLEY: 'Oh yes. I read poems out of the Greek Anthology like eating chocolate creams out of a large box.'

This was a palpable hit. But later the conversation took a more serious turn, the subject being rococo. Beazley expressed a preference for the classical revival of Canova and Ingres. Keynes was on to him like a knife. 'Oh, do you really, Beazley? Now why is that? You must give us your reasons.' He seemed almost nettled, as though Beazley had invaded a strongly held conviction, trodden on sacred ground. Beazley does not recall that he made an adequate defence of his preference.

American and German scholars have given me their opinion that J. D. Beazley is the world's foremost classical scholar in this generation. His attribution of hundreds of Greek vases to various individual painters hitherto unknown, and its acceptance by all who are competent to judge upon the matter, may perhaps be regarded as the most notable achievement in the whole history of art criticism. Beazley has travelled far and wide wherever Greek antiquities are to be found, and met most of the eminent classical scholars and art connoisseurs of the various countries. His tribute therefore has some weight.

'When I went over to Cambridge at that time,' he has told me, 'I thought Keynes and Strachey were the two cleverest men I had ever met; and, looking back over the years, I still think that they are the two cleverest men I ever have met.' I asked him specifically whether he had the impression that one was leading or dominating the other. 'No,' he replied, 'they seemed to me to be equals, peers, different and complementary.'

### 5

Such was the setting and such the interests; and the terms at Cambridge passed rapidly by.

*J. M. Keynes to B. W. Swithinbank*, 10 December 1902

I am engaged upon the works of Peter Abelard, my intention being, at present, to write a paper upon the aforementioned gent.

\*

How go things with you? – I find so many nice people, who have periods when they come to the conclusion that the world is a damned bad concern: – a very bad habit, even if their conclusion is the right one, and a very difficult one to get out of – how go things with you?

The paper on Abelard was read to the Apennine Society

at the beginning of the following February. Those who heard it were astounded by the erudition of this mathematical philosopher. We learn from his father's diary that, while he was working on Abelard, he was devoting three hours each morning to mathematics.

### J. M. Keynes to B. W. Swithinbank, 31 December 1902

On Friday I am going metropoliswards to see two plays; later on I shall be in Manchester for a short time visiting relatives. An uncle is a Director of the Rylands Library (one of the best collections of rare books in the country) and I am to be given full access . . .

One of the plays was Forbes-Robertson's *Othello*, which he 'enjoyed immensely'. In the last years of his life many great honours came to Maynard, and many invitations to serve as President, or Vice-President, or what not, of various bodies which he had to refuse. But the invitation to be a Director of the Rylands Library he accepted, and it gave him great pleasure.

Next term he began going to Moore's lectures on Ethics; in addition to Hobson he had Richmond, a Fellow of King's, for mathematical instruction.

### J. M. Keynes to B. W. Swithinbank, 24 January 1903

Next Tuesday at the Union Sheppard proposes that the Disestablishment of the Church would be in accordance with the best interest both of herself and the nation; and Gaselee opposes.

Won't it be grand!

### J. M. Keynes to B. W. Swithinbank, 5 February 1903

The result of the Disestablishment debate was, I think, on the whole satisfactory; Sheppard made a very good speech indeed, but Gaselee, I thought, was a trifle disappointing; his was a good speech too, but he was clearly not at his ease and did not orate enough. Last night Sheppard, Strachey, and I dined with Verrall; he holds forth continuously and somewhat brilliantly withal, his wife and daughter forming an intelligent and well drilled chorus.

During the last week the whole of King's has been turned upside down by a religious controversy – as to what lines a mission, which it is proposed that the College should start, is to be run upon. It was, at one time, to be high church, but Sheppard and I and several others helped to organize a regular opposition and we finally carried in the College meeting by a majority of some 75 to 25 that the scheme should be on a purely *secular* basis. It was a tremendous triumph. But I will say no more about it; we have had enough of it here already. I had to make a speech before the Provost, almost the whole College, and a no. of dons including Professor Bury.

I read Abelard last Sunday.

I would ooze more ink, if I hadn't to speed off to tea with Strachey ...

The controversy mentioned in this letter shook the College to its foundation. After much negotiation, much intrigue, the formation of committees and of sub-committees, the hopes of a settlement were finally dashed and there was a great *ad hoc* meeting in the Hall of King's, which is still remembered. Mr H. O. Meredith and George Barger were brought up from London to speak. A word should be said of Meredith, who had just been elected to a Fellowship. He was resident in London at this time, but had recently been a person of considerable influence in King's. A man of noble mien, later with a beard, and of bright, flashing eye, he looked and was every inch a philosopher. With such an imposing appearance, he might be expected to roll forth resonant Victorian periods. Not so; his voice was very gentle, reflecting his subtle, finely tempered mind. He did not orate, but in a quiet insinuating way, with delicate touch, pushed your thought forward a little. Might not the matter be just a little different – like this? He was an early admirer of the works of Mr E. M. Forster, and enthusiastic in his appreciation of Lowes Dickinson.[31] Barger was the well-known

31. H. O. Meredith (known as 'Hom' in Maynard's circle) in 1911 became Professor of Political Economy at Queen's University, Belfast, where he was an important cultural influence both in the University and the city.

chemist. Grant and Gaselee were leaders on the other side.

Meredith has a clear recollection of the speeches made by Maynard and Sheppard on this occasion. Maynard's was a magnificent forensic display, cool and collected, the arguments well marshalled, the rights of the individual conscience clearly set out. It carried the votes of those who could be persuaded by logic, and his support gave his side the necessary respectability among Etonian Kingsmen. But Meredith judges that Sheppard's performance was the more effective with the majority. An experienced Union speaker, he delivered what he had to say with sober, reflective judgement. He had been much perplexed in mind by this affair. Drawing on his experiences in connection with the Dulwich Mission, he adjured his audience to choose the path of caution and safety. This motion was carried and Maynard was inevitably elected one of the twelve members of the Settlement Committee.

He spoke 'on the paper' at the Union at the first meeting of the term on the Venezuelan dispute, urging that it was 'not safe to trust Germany too implicitly'. Later, rather surprisingly, he spoke for a motion 'in favour of the support given by the present Government to the Principles of Imperialism'.

Next term he visited Oxford (Swithinbank was still at Eton; he went to Balliol the following autumn).

### *J. M. Keynes, Balliol College, Oxford, to B. W. Swithinbank,* 30 May 1903

As you will see from the preliminary emblazonment I am staying at the rival seat of the humanities, having made a dinner to Sir E. Grey, to which I was invited as a representative of the Cambridge Liberal League, an excuse for a first visit to Oxford.

I went to breakfast at All Souls this morning to meet him, and he strikes me as a very commanding and reliable statesman.

Butler is putting me up at Balliol.

I have been waxing quite political lately – a most amusing game, and a very adequate substitute for bridge.

\*

I am leaving Oxford this evening: it's all very mysterious, but rather pleasant.

Back in Cambridge he was first speaker for the motion at the Union that the House 'sincerely hopes that Home Rule for Ireland is beyond the sphere of practical politics'. According to the *Cambridge Review* he held that there were practical objections, both fiscal and strategical, that would render the granting of Home Rule an utter impossibility. 'Mr Keynes's forte is clearness, fluency and elegance of expression. He makes no attempt at oratory, and except in a well-educated audience he would be difficult to follow.' He made other speeches and was elected at the top of the list to the Standing Committee. Immediately after the end of term the family went for a holiday to Switzerland.

In his second year he was able to move into a fine set of rooms, formerly Gaselee's, on Staircase A, looking across the front court towards the Chapel. His mother had to think hard about furnishing them. The dining-room carpet and the drawing-room sofa were transferred from 6 Harvey Road. Cambridge has a pleasant habit of assembling undergraduates voluntarily for a period of residence during the long vacation. There are no lectures or official instruction; it is a reading party on a grand scale.[32] Maynard went with Page for some coaching to Mr Leathem of St John's.

During the course of the vacation he remembered that there was a subject, in which his father had no little interest, called Political Economy. He set himself to do the Civil Service Examination Paper, in which his father happened to be examining, and in the following weeks did some desultory reading in it. Towards the end of the vacation we find him going to a gathering organized by the Liberal Party at the Hotel Cecil, in London.

The fiscal question was becoming a burning issue at this

32. It is to be feared that the Cambridge scientists are, by making certain attendances at the laboratories compulsory (1950), insidiously tending to convert this into an extra term – to the detriment, some hold, of the proper studies of dons and undergraduates alike.

time. At the opening meeting of the Union Keynes was speaking on the Free Trade side. Towards the end of the term Swithinbank and Dundas came over to witness Sheppard's performance of Peithetairos. Dr Keynes notes that Maynard 'cannot be doing much work. For fourteen consecutive days he has only one free evening.' The impulse first given by Mr Lubbock died hard, and at this time he was again working at St Bernard.

Meanwhile Maynard's sister Margaret had completed her time at Wycombe Abbey and had gone for further education to Germany, where she stayed with the Baronin von Bissing at Wittenberg. In the following Easter Vacation Maynard went with his mother to fetch her home and they visited Dresden and Berlin.

*J. M. Keynes to B. W. Swithinbank*, 24 March 1904

Out of some three-thousand pictures I find I have marked 140 in my catalogue as supreme, and 24 as – well whatever the word is for the next stage up towards the ideal good. Every painter is here, but I find the Germans of the early sixteenth century most to my taste, – the Dürers, Holbeins, and Cranachs. I should like to analyse my reasons – if I have any. In Berlin we saw more pictures – especially one Holbein, and both here and there much statuary, Greek and Roman and later; at Berlin two most beautiful boys' busts of the Augustan period, and a most magnificent bust of Scipio Africanus – but the list is endless ... At Berlin we saw Ibsen's *Wild Duck* supremely acted. The more I contemplate it the greater does the play appear ... The book-sellers' shops in this country are rather an interesting contrast to ours – innumerable translations from French and English (particularly Bernard Shaw, and Maeterlinck), very little native modern literature, but the Classical writers of all languages translated and fabulously cheap. (I bought a copy of Ibsen's *Wild Duck* for 2d. and that is the normal price.)

In the next following Summer Term (1904) he showed in a very striking way his predilection for the best. He attended a course of lectures by Alfred Whitehead, given three times a week, *alone*. Not an easy task! *Experto crede*. There is some tendency to stay away, even if only to spare the lecturer his pains. In a letter written to me some thirty years later, Whitehead cited Bertrand Russell and Keynes as instances of his best pupils. At the time it puzzled me to know how Keynes had been his pupil. This solitary attendance for three hours a week surely justified the description.

Maynard continued to speak frequently at the Union. At the last meeting, with Sheppard, just elected President, already in the Chair, he spoke for a motion proposed by MacGregor[33] against Chamberlain's fiscal policy. On earlier occasions the House had tended to be favourable to Chamberlain. But this time the Free Traders carried the day.

At the end of this term he was elected Secretary of the Union, defeating Mr J. K. Mozley. By the custom which was then followed in Cambridge, the Secretaryship led automatically to the Vice-Presidency and the Presidency. Thus in effect he had been elected President. At the same time he also became President of the University Liberal Club. And in the May examination, a kind of College dress-rehearsal for the ordeal of the Tripos, which was to come a year later, he obtained a first-class in mathematics.

Quite a little bunch of successes! Did they recall that red-letter day at Eton when he was elected to Pop, obtained a King's scholarship, and his college colours? I hardly think so. Less than three years had elapsed, but in that time he had grown up. He had long since achieved maturity of speech and manners, but now he had achieved maturity of soul. He was to be President of the Union, yes; but his mind kept reverting to Moore's argument at the last meeting of the Society, and to Strachey's revelation at their talk over the fire a few nights ago. He had become the apostle of truth. To think aright, perhaps to influence the course of events, these were to be his goals in future. No worldly successes were to mean much to him, nor rebuffs either for that

33. D. H. MacGregor, Drummond Professor of Political Economy, Oxford, 1922–45.

matter. It is true that when, shortly before his death, he heard that he was to receive the Order of Merit, that gave pleasure. He may have felt that it was what he 'desired perhaps more than anything else that remains to be got here'. But with the mellowness of advancing years external honours regain something of the charm that they have for the imagination of boyhood. One recaptures a vision of the enchantments of fairyland.

In the Long Vacation he went with Woolf for a walking tour in North Wales, and they stayed with the Sangers. Towards the end of it he began working on his essay on Burke, which in the following term won him the 'Members' Prize'. The greatest merit of the essay was his mature restraint in not forcing the doctrines of Burke to yield clear-cut answers to the questions raised. He showed much sympathy for his author's point of view, including his defence of things established, criticizing him mainly for letting intrinsically good arguments carry him to extremes. It is interesting to compare this essay with his Memoir. In the latter he wrote of his youthful period that 'we were not aware that civilization was a thin and precarious crust', and 'it did not occur to us to respect the extraordinary accomplishment of our predecessors in the ordering of life (as it now seems to me to have been) or the elaborate framework which they had devised to protect this order'. But his essay shows clearly that he had known all about that at the time. He had never in his own person been a callow young idealist; he had had no illusions. If he went along with his friends in dreaming dreams, it is clear that he must have had his own mental reservations. It was part of his genius and his greatness that, while he could become the most polemical of partisans, he saw all sides of the case. This bewildered many, since they inferred fickleness. But it reassured the finest minds who met his, because they knew that, when it came to practical decisions, he would recognize the full strength of the opposition case – and indeed already knew it better than his opponents themselves! Thus, for all his exaggerations in controversy, he would be a safe guide in action.

He now approached the final year of his work for the mathematical Tripos. His comparative neglect of his proper subject of study had been a matter of recurrent anxiety to his father, who feared that the wrong subject had been chosen. Maynard continued to maintain outside interests. This Michaelmas term was the occasion of the Swithinbank-Beazley visit, and we find him still playing the Wall Game at Eton. His position at the Union inevitably absorbed much time, and he spoke frequently. He was due to hold office in each term in this last year, but by a stroke of luck he missed the Vice-Presidency. The President elected at the end of the Michaelmas term for the following term was not able to remain in Cambridge, and in consequence Maynard proceeded straight from the Secretaryship to the Presidency, and his Tripos term was thus clear of official duties at the Union.[34] One characteristic touch must be mentioned in connection with his term of Presidency. He was not so immersed in high Union politics as to take no thought of the staff. He set up a Committee to investigate the matter, and detailed instructions concerning hours of employment were embodied in the minutes of the Standing Committee during his term. And, determined that the matter should be properly buttoned up, he had a standing order passed that in future every Vice-President must make a report on staff conditions.

The Tripos was looming up, and what was to happen after that? Maynard had a wonderful capacity for living in the present, and we may believe that he was not obsessed, as some undergraduates are, with the problems of the future. He had, it is true, to make his own way. His father paid the preliminary fee for him to be entered at the Inner Temple, and in the next year he ate some dinners. This was a pre-

34. This accident has deprived the Union of records of his which they would otherwise have had: for it is the Vice-President who writes the terminal report, and who deals with complaints in the suggestion book.

caution, but it does not seem that he thought of the Bar very seriously as a career. The following letter is undated, but was evidently written while Maynard was an undergraduate.[35]

## G. M. Trevelyan to J. M. Keynes

I keep hearing from different people that you have made up your mind to go into the Civil Service. I don't know why at the stage you have now reached you should have made up your mind about your future career, and perhaps it is not true. But if you are already beginning to think seriously about it, do let me beg you to keep an open mind. Personally I think it is most distressing the way the civil service swallows nearly all the best Cambridge men, to the ruin of our political life. Only one or two people like Theodore Davies can make a *great* career out of the civil service. That needs both great luck, and very peculiar qualities.

You are born to be a politician I should guess. The only reason for rushing into the tomb of the civil service is that it offers safety from the beginning in the way of income. The Bar is not a *certainty* – that is its only disadvantage as against the civil service for a man like you. But surely you can feel confidence enough in yourself to be able to get on at the Bar, if by a fellowship you can secure enough to keep you for a few years. You live in a very unadventurous atmosphere at Cambridge, but ought you not to be a little more adventurous yourself? Why should not a fellowship lead to the bar, and the bar after many years to politics? It is on such choices, made in early youth, that the fate of the country in the future ultimately turns. Our supply of liberal aristocrats is running dry. Of course it is a risk and a venture, – but there are proverbs on the need of taking them. This is a venture many men take with less prospect of doing great things than you would have. I don't say that I am sure that you ought to do thus, I only say don't yet be sure you oughtn't. And let your soul revolve the matter in all its aspects. Don't answer this letter. It doesn't need an answer and is not written to draw one. Only do not forget it.

35. In a letter written to Strachey on 30 October 1907, Keynes refers to this letter as 'two years ago'. 'Two years', may be approximate: the reference to 'the stage you have now reached' suggests a slightly earlier date.

Weighty words. What shall we say? There is certainly a prophetic note in this letter. British politics have languished sadly since it was written, perhaps even beyond the expectations of the author. What if Maynard had taken his advice? Would other clever young men have followed his example? Might the whole political scene have been different?

And what did Maynard think himself? Did those Apostles inhibit his ambition? Did Strachey seduce him with his more exciting quests? Had worldly pursuits so fallen in his esteem that he really thought politics no more than a 'fairly adequate substitute for bridge'?

Or was it a rather different strain in his temperament that decided the matter? He lived very much in the present, his enthusiasms were usually directed to something here and now. He may have felt towards Trevelyan's long-range plan of action rather as he felt towards those beneficent economic forces which only yield their good results 'when we are all dead'.

In the Christmas vacation he went off with his old friends Dundas, Harold Butler and O. C. Williams[36] to Forest Row in Sussex, where they would be the neighbours of Humphrey Paul, to make up leeway in his mathematical studies.

In this last year before the Tripos there occurred an event which bade fair to be the beginning of one of his lifelong friendships. A new star had appeared at Trinity, acclaimed as such by Strachey and others. When Maynard met him he joined in the chorus of praise. This was Mr (now Sir) Arthur Hobhouse. Economists are aware of how excited Maynard became on the occasion of a new economic finding. In those young days these enthusiasms were directed to people. Mr Hobhouse had all the right qualities, intelligence, interest in intellectual matters, fine sensitivity and personal charm. There was a spirit in all the Strachey set of restless quest for those who had the wit and feeling to enter with sympathy

36. Orlando Cyprian Williams, Eton Scholar an election senior to Maynard, then at Balliol, since Clerk to the House of Commons and author under the name of Orlo Williams.

into their circle. Friendship, after all, was the most important thing in life.

Maynard saw a good deal of Hobhouse in these months. Their paths later were to lie apart. Hobhouse, like Swithinbank in the end, faded from the scene. He took up the law and later went into politics. But the traditions of his family were those of progressive public service, and, on the decline of the Liberal Party, he entered local government where he won for himself a position of high importance and esteem.

In the final vacation before the Tripos they were together working at Truro. Even Maynard had to make a spurt now. Had he failed to obtain a First, that would indeed have been a universal disappointment – and what of his future? It was a horrible gruelling interlude. He consoled himself with *cris du cœur* to his friends. Swithinbank had just obtained a first-class in honours moderations, and Maynard opened with a bloodthirsty paean of triumph over the Balliol dons, who, for some reason, seemed always a little unfriendly to Swithinbank.

## *J. M. Keynes to B. W. Swithinbank*, 18 April 1905. Truro

I want to see you; for the last three weeks I have been on the point of writing to you, and I have been filled with an affection for you – but I have not written.

I am still your friend – I hope you are mine; but I am slothful and we are at different Universities – what is to be done? In the meantime I am soddening my brain, destroying my intellect, souring my disposition in a panic-stricken attempt to acquire the rudiments of the Mathematics.

Heaven help the examinee where so ever he be found.

\*

What are you thinking and reading about? How is your health and your energy?

I find my chief comfort more and more in Messrs Plato and Shakespeare. Why is it so difficult to find a true combination of passion and intellect? My heroes must feel and feel passionately – but they must see too, everything and more than everything.

What is there worth anything except passionate perception.

Alas – as you see I am liable to blather. However, perhaps you see what I mean.

We have communicated so little lately that it scarcely seems possible or amusing to say anything about the details of one's existence. Hence these generalities.

All the same, I still feel as if I were intimate with you, and yet I do not know what, at this moment, you are really like.

Do you understand this letter? I wonder.

> Ever your affectionate,
> J. M. KEYNES

And then on his return to Cambridge:

*J. M. Keynes to G. L. Strachey*, 23 April 1905

I was working six hours a day at work which I was actively loathing almost the whole time I was at it.

He [Hobhouse] – without intermission – was ill in health and attempting to force himself to do more work than he was fit for.

However, it was – ethically – the most valuable three weeks I have ever spent. I am coming round more and more to your view of the appalling dangers of work. It is not merely that the more I do the less time I have for more respectable pursuits – but the less *desire* I have for anything that is decent. That is the horror. However – today being the Sabbath I haven't done a stroke – and I feel the better for it.

Ah, one might write like that; yet by his own free will and choice he was to live laborious days for the next forty years.

Next term he faced his ordeal.

*Mrs Keynes to J. M. Keynes*, 5 June 1905

. . . I must send a line of greeting. For half my life you have occupied a large place in my thoughts and affections and it is natural that I should think of you and hope for you today.

I hope for – and expect – success this time as so often before, but whatever the result may be next week, I shall be proud of your University career and satisfied that you have spent your time well.

In the examination list he was bracketed twelfth Wrangler. Some congratulated; some condoled. The result was respectable, but not triumphant. Mathematics were not his love – although he was to remain deeply interested in mathematical philosophy. Yet it is doubtful if he would have been much happier in any other prescribed course of study. He had already outgrown the examination phase. His mind was wandering in strange new fields of thought. He had to find out for himself where his life's work lay.

# [3]

# In Quest of a Way of Life

I

At about this time there were those who began to have an uneasy feeling that there was something subtly amiss in the way in which Maynard was developing. Was he not deviating from the high road so clearly marked out for him? Was he not becoming too much wrapped up in the psychology and personal interests of a particular set? After all, he was not destined to be a poet. He had great intellectual and practical gifts, which clearly suggested some kind of distinguished career of active service. A man with such a destiny may devote himself to things poetical and artistical at school, and perhaps for a year or two at the University. But he must not dwell amid these pleasant scenes too long. He must begin to get busy and devote all his energies to what is expedient and necessary for the harsh battle of life. Was there not something hot-house about the introspective interests of this circle, the intensive brooding upon the fine shades of some young man's character, to assess whether he corresponded with the utmost nicety to the ideal of Moore or the fastidious susceptibilities of Strachey? . . . It is impossible to legislate for genius. No doubt for one who had a definite ambition, to become Chancellor of the Exchequer or sit on the Woolsack, no time was to be lost. But Maynard's thoughts ranged further afield. If one believed that one might attain the discovery of new truth or might alter the course of events, then it might be needful for the time to lose oneself entirely, forget material aims and follow the immediate promptings of the spirit. The forty days in the wilderness are no doubt symbolic of a longer period of time. Five years, ten years, may well be sacrificed to the neglect of one's career, if these are necessary to penetrate below the surface of things and acquire depth of insight. How many eminent men of affairs there are, worldly wise, good judges of character, full of apt expedients to meet a particular situation, who, when taken outside their professional range, asked to judge in some human problem, are completely at a loss, embarrassed, out of their depth. Those who came into contact with Maynard had the strong sense that, admirably as he might discuss the gold question or the slump, he would be a guide no less admirable if the soul was in torment. He was a sage and a philosopher. There was layer below layer of insight and understanding; it would be a great man indeed who would plumb to the depths of him. Nor can it be doubted that this depth enhanced the influence of his economics, enabling him to appeal to the layman as well as the expert, to feeling as well as to thought.

Among those who were uneasy was his old friend, Mr Geoffrey Winthrop Young, whose temporary spell as master at Eton had overlapped Maynard's time there. Maynard had a high regard for Young, which he retained through life, and it was therefore a pleasure, as well as an honour, to be invited by this famous mountaineer to join him in a climbing expedition in the August following his Tripos. 'In Switzerland I spent some time with the superb Geoffrey Young', he afterwards wrote to Swithinbank.

Young had an ulterior motive. When he writes in the passage which I have quoted[1] that he took him climbing to redress the balance, this must be taken seriously. He felt that Maynard's interests were becoming too hot-house, and that the high altitudes and the perils of climbing would reduce his introspective tendency and revive his more adventurous and practical impulses, and when he 'watched him climbing over the very steep snow and ice slope of the summit with smooth security and fine nerve', he may have felt that he had achieved some success. 'Obviously he was revelling in every minute of it.'

1. See pp. 56–8.

*J. M. Keynes to G. L. Strachey*, 11 August 1905

We have made our way to Chamonix over passes; on Tuesday we climbed up to a hut (circ. 9000 feet) to sleep. After two and a half hours' sleep we set out in the dark with lanterns on to the glacier, crossed a pass, climbed a mountain and reached our destination after nineteen hours. The expedition was lengthened out to this untoward length by the incompetence of the guides who took us wrong at every crucial point. This is private, namely: – Robin[2] disappeared absolutely out of sight into a crevasse, but he was hauled out intact. (2) One of the guides lost his head on the mountain and went well nigh mad; according to G. W. Y. it was one of the most dangerous situations he had ever been in. (3) We had to cross a beastly bit of glacier in the dark. So much for Switzerland. I liked the excitement.

*

What rot all this is about nature; I have seen the superbest views and the wildest and most desolate expanses of snow and ice; there was even danger: but not for one single moment have I been moved with anything I can call violence. Feelings of course one gets and a kind of passion of calmness but the whole is on an altogether lower scale of merit.

He uses 'lower' by comparison with the joys of intellectual activity and friendship.

Geoffrey Young recalls how Strachey came to see him after a visit to Skye. This time too he had hopes that nature had made an impression. The tremendous peaks of the Coolin, their sombre outlines and sheer fall to the sea, their shadows and depths of colour – surely they had meant something to him?

Lytton Strachey: 'I thought them simply absurd.'

It was no use. They were, in those days, irretrievable intellectuals. It was impossible to shake the settled convictions of the two cleverest men that Beazley had ever met.[3]

2. Mr Robin Mayor.
3. This visit to Skye was in August 1908. Strachey wrote to Maynard. 'We're nine miles from Portree, the nearest centre of civilization (and beauty), and we're surrounded by deserts of green vagueness, multitudes of imbecile mountains and eternal rain.'

Between the Tripos and this holiday in Switzerland, the remainder of it spent with his family there, he had already found time to do some serious reading in economics.[4] The question was considered whether he should take a second Tripos (Part II) and the choice seemed to be between Moral Science and Economics. In the event he took neither.

### J. M. Keynes to G. L. Strachey, 8 July 1905

I have finished Wells's *Utopia*, which rather peters out. And masses of economics.

From the latter I have discovered someone whom I had not realized to be very good – namely Jevons. I am convinced that he was one of *the* minds of the century. He has the curiously exciting style of writing which one gets if one is good enough – particularly in the 'Investigations into Currency and Finance', a most thrilling volume. Moreover his letters and journal prove that he was probably apostolic. At the age of nineteen he had to earn his living and was accordingly sent to Australia, where he earned a respectable and assured income. But he seems to have spoken to no one and to have devoted the whole of his spare time to the study of meteorology.

However at the age of twenty one he came to the conclusion – although he had never been intimate with anyone in his life – that the only things really worth having were love and friendship (these are his words); sometimes he inclined to think intellectual insight to be a little use. At the age of twenty-two he came to himself and realized how eminent he was; he became quite clear that his brain was full of original thoughts. He threw up his post and all his cash and came back to England for further education: it was not long before he boomed: but he suffered from sleeplessness and depression, and was drowned while bathing at the age of forty odd . . .

In the autumn term he was back at Cambridge and attended Marshall's lectures. 'Maynard does a good deal of work for Marshall, who describes some of his answers as

4. Diary of Dr Keynes, 28 June: 'Maynard now working assiduously at Marshall's *Principles of Economics*.'

brilliant. I am afraid Marshall is endeavouring to persuade him to give up everything for Economics.'[5]

*Alfred Marshall to Dr J. N. Keynes, 3* December 1905

Your son is doing excellent work in Economics. I have told him that I should be greatly delighted if he should decide on the career of a professional economist. But of course I must not press him.

Pigou had him to breakfast once a week and gave him coaching in the subject. Towards the end of the year he was reading 'the superb Hume' and also works on psychology. His book-buying activities persisted unabated.

Meanwhile Strachey, after residing in Cambridge for six years, had at length gone down. For the biographer this event raises the curtain on the scene of Maynard's life. For, once parted, these two friends entered upon an almost daily correspondence of long letters, which lasted for a number of years and revealed their common interests. It is quite plain that we are in the middle of a scene, and that the discussions carried on with such assiduity in these pages had been proceeding with equal energy for a long time past. The evidence of these letters has helped me in the distribution of emphasis in the foregoing account of the undergraduate period.[6]

These letters have much to say, as is natural between

5. Dr Keynes's Diary, 26 November 1905.
6. Evidence coming from this and other sources makes it impossible to confirm the statement in Mr E. A. G. Robinson's interesting and valuable Memoir, that 'Keynes's absorbing interest at this stage of his life was politics' (*Economic Journal*, March 1947, p. 10). No doubt politics was an interest to which he devoted much·attention. And indeed, had he been a man of normal capacity, one might have been able to infer from his substantial volume of political activity that this was his 'absorbing' interest. It would be as though one who was unacquainted with his work in economics argued that, at the time he was composing *The General Theory of Employment, Money and Interest*, his principal interest in life was the theatre. His 'absorbing' interests as an undergraduate were philosophy, 'the Society', and the quest for perfection of mind and character among his contemporaries.

intimates, about passing moods and humours. The main
subjects of discussion are the characters, personal relations
and opinions of their friends. The discussion is always critical, judging by some ideal intellectual and moral standard,
which they shared. The letters are full of esoteric jokes and
allusions. I will only quote, by way of example, one letter
which is more straightforward than most. In reading it one
must bear in mind the intense interest which they both took
in the affairs of 'the Society' and the importance of choosing
the right men for election.

*J. M. Keynes to G. L. Strachey*, 15 October 1905

I have given way to unrestrained Fresher excitement ...
Hobby [Mr Arthur Hobhouse] gave a breakfast party this morning at which Norton and A burst into view. Never has a term
opened with so fair a prospect. I have formed an opinion, but it
is still a little incoherent. Norton is the more obvious – more
grown-up than I was on arrival, very Etonian and with that part
of Etonianism which is probably a little offensive. I am sure he
has a very good logical kind of mind and that is his strength; his
own view, however, is that he is cultured – and he is incredibly.
His whole person is girt about by a writhing mess of aesthetic
and literary appreciations, which I have – so far – discovered no
means of quelling. He's very proud of all this, but it is really
rather nonsense : what saves him is a strong comprehension – I
hardly ever caught him really stupid.

There is nothing to say about his appearance – ordinary public
school.

I am sure we shall elect him, and equally sure that we shall
elect A. He (A) is, I think, more attractive *qua* character – at any
rate as regards that part he shows first, for he is less self-conscious
than the other, a little wilder (Norton is not wild at all), and a
good deal vaguer. Artistic. He has had little conversation in the
past and was completely carried away by the sodden excitement
of the party. His appearance is very apostolic and so is his mind –
but I doubt whether he is as clever as Norton and he might be a
bore sometimes.

It is to be remembered that I have seen them once only and
not at all alone.

James[7] still eludes me. I have climbed the stairs three times but in vain. Today I have left a card asking him to come and see me. Yesterday I saw B and Lord C – also at Hobby's.

B is much more elementary, and possibly stupid – but I liked him : there is no mushiness.

C (*i.e.* Duke of D) is the pale, dull aristocrat; of the appearance bred by those who marry beauties.

Forster is up, and of course old McTaggart was at last night's supper.

Have you heard that Dickinson's horse bolted and threw him yesterday? He seems to have concussion and is attended by a nurse – but reports allege that it is not serious.

*

Sheppard is booming Knox but Hobby is against him.

I have private advice from Oxford that there is no small danger of Swithin's departure – another crisis is hatching. I have come to the conclusion that it does not much matter if he does. Of course it hastens the problem of what next: but as long as he is at Oxford he will be miserable and no better off —[8] when the end comes.

Hobby saw him into his cab; as he closed the door Swithin leant out, smiled, and said 'I am leaving Heaven'.

*

There was a wonderful interview with Swithin very late on his last evening – we got as far as it is possible for pure friendship.

I feel a little lost. I want to argue with you about these wretched Freshers.

Such letters passed almost daily. The analysis deepened and became more intricate. Many figures flit across these pages; those which appear most frequently are Mr (Sir Walter) Lamb,[9] Dilly Knox, Mr (Sir Arthur) Hobhouse, Mr James Strachey and H. T. Norton. Of these the last two

7. Mr James Strachey, Lytton's younger brother.
8. The word he uses here, denoting 'from a worldly point of view', was part of the secret language of the Society.
9. Secretary of the Royal Academy since 1913 and elder brother of Mr Henry Lamb, the well-known painter.

remained Maynard's close friends for many years. Norton won the highest regard both of Maynard and Strachey, and became, so to speak, a member of the family party. In this large portrait gallery the economists most frequently referred to were Hawtrey, who often came up to Cambridge from London, and Pigou. A very close watch was also kept on the development and troubles of Swithinbank, who was not happy at Oxford.

Maynard appears to have devoted a great deal of time to these questions. It was not merely that taken up in correspondence with Strachey and other friends about them; he took immense pains to get to know all these young men personally. It was as though he was conducting an oral examination of them, extending over many weeks and months. He made elaborate plans to introduce them to one another. In a carefully arranged setting X might be brought into contact with Y. If the meeting was not a success, the question arose whether it showed a lack of sensitivity in X in failing to appreciate the subtle character of Y, or showed that Y did indeed lack qualities which had been, perhaps over-hastily, assigned to him. To someone who did not know Maynard's capacity for work, it might appear that these personal investigations must have occupied all his time.

Strachey's letters reveal his own interests and inward life, and are often very moving. He was eager to know about the Cambridge young. Living now in London, he could not reciprocate in the offer of many new young acquaintances for analysis. But there was one old friend who began to assume importance. Duncan Grant had been, as we have seen, a companion of childhood. But now he was coming of age and had to be considered anew, weighed and judged on his own merits, no longer to be taken for granted. This was a great topic for consideration. It was indeed assumed from the beginning that he was 'perfect', but the precise shade of perfection had to be carefully defined.

### J. M. Keynes to G. L. Strachey, 18 October 1905

I am writing in the train and have seen Mr Shaw's . . . play. Is it monomania – this colossal moral superiority that we feel? I get the feeling that most of the rest never see anything at all – too stupid or too wicked. The contrast between you and Duncan, and Mr Shaw's view of the world has been too violent.

### G. L. Strachey to J. M. Keynes, 2 November 1905

Oxford Union Society

Here I am, a little shattered. Last night I spent with the Raleighs, partly at a rather dull concert, and partly listening to his consummate brilliance. It is so great that I think it practically amounts to a disease. But in any case he belongs to the age before the flood – the pre-Dickinsonian era[10] which is really fatal. He is not interested in the things which absorb us – result, dead silence on my part, and blank boredom on his – though of course there are compensating moments. He might be one's father.

### J. M. Keynes to G. L. Strachey, 12 November 1905

I forgot to tell you that I read my paper on Beauty at Dickinson's last Wednesday. It was too esoteric and I did not feel that it was much of a success. Knox (of course) was highly enraged at anybody's writing such rubbish. The discussion dull: Pigou subtle but not very relevant; Sheppard and Dickinson in practical agreement: and the rest quite foggy.

Don't fail to come up next week.

### J. M. Keynes to G. L. Strachey, 15 November 1905

I find Economics increasingly satisfactory, and I think I am rather good at it. I want to manage a railway or organize a Trust . . . It is so easy and fascinating to master the principles of these things.

### J. M. Keynes to G. L. Strachey, 23 November 1905

Marshall is continually pestering me to turn professional economist and writes flattering remarks on my papers to help on

10. This refers to G. Lowes Dickinson; the passing reference is a noteworthy tribute to the importance of his influence.

the good cause. Do you think there is anything in it? I doubt it. I could probably get employment here if I wanted to. But prolonging my existence in this place would be, I feel sure, death. The only question is whether a government office in London is not death equally.

I suppose I shall drift.

Later this term excitement was provided by the appearance of his brother Geoffrey, who came from Rugby to seek a scholarship at Pembroke College, which he obtained. At Rugby he had become great friends with Rupert Brooke. He brought Rupert and two other Rugby boys to stand for scholarships, and they were all put up in Harvey Road. Rupert obtained a scholarship at King's.

Geoffrey and Rupert were plunged into the Cambridge *milieu*.

### *J. M. Keynes to G. L. Strachey*, 7 December 1905

There has been a long party here this evening – five hours through which Hobby, Norton, Sheppard, Furness, Rupert, and my brother have floated for shorter or for longer periods.

Maynard was conscious that his brother Geoffrey was effacing himself in the extreme anxiety that Rupert should shine and do himself justice.

In the intervals of psychology and book-collecting, Maynard returned to his old love of genealogy and read out a history of the Keynes family in his home on Christmas Day.

During the autumn G. E. Moore read his paper on 'The Nature and Reality of Objects of Perception' to the Aristotelian Society.[11] This caused great excitement.

### *G. L. Strachey to J. M. Keynes*, 2 January 1906

Who d'you think – talking of intellects – has been here half today? Moore. He was really splendid. We talked about the Society and his Aristotelian paper from 2.30 to 4.30. Then he sang. Pippa[12] pronounced him the most charming person she

11. Republished in his *Philosophical Studies*, 1922.
12. Miss Philippa Strachey, Lytton's sister.

knew. He did not seem to understand the objection against electing Freshmen – said that if they were worth anything they'd stand up against us. I wonder. On the question of secondary qualities, etc., he was quite superb. He had used an argument in his paper about hens and eggs which Hawtrey said was 'too simple'. It was, that in order to know that hens laid eggs, *some-one* must have seen both a hen and an egg. Hawtrey denied this – because the fact that hens laid eggs determined your mental state, and therefore you could infer it from your mental state. Moore said he could only say such things because his head was full of philosophical notions. Quite magnificent! I was with him heart and soul. But I wish I could tell you more of what he said . . .

### *J. M. Keynes to G. L. Strachey,* 17 January 1906

Oh! I have undergone conversion. I am with Moore absolutely and on all things – even secondary qualities. It happened while arguing with Ernst[13] – who has read P. E.[14] seven times. – Something gave in my brain and I saw everything quite clearly in a flash. But as the whole thing depends on intuiting the Universe in a particular way – I see that now – there is no hope of converting the world except by Conversion, and that is pretty hopeless. It is not a question of argument; all depends upon a particular twist in the mind.

### *J. M. Keynes to G. L. Strachey,* 20 January 1906

I really believe I would leave Cambridge and come to London at once – but for one reason. I suppose the Society must be put on its legs again – or at any rate one has to try.

I labour for myself most of the time, but I am certainly labour-ing for future generations in this.

But I am really pretty cheerful – doing a little more work than you I expect, but very little – for Swithin has been here and I have hardly got started.

So zealous were they for the Society that Strachey wrote as follows from Mentone:[15]

13. P. E. Goldschmidt (Trinity), prominent member of the Biblio-graphical Society and author of *England's Service* by Sarpedon.

14. *Principia Ethica.*

15. Within eight years Keynes read twenty papers to the Society!

*G. L. Strachey to J. M. Keynes*, 21 February 1906

Did I tell you that I had a melancholy and very very Swithin-esque letter before I departed? He seemed to be pretty hopeless, but to be looking forward to a visit from you. Must you go on a Saturday? Why not in the middle of the week? Isn't it rather terrible to leave those children [i.e. new members of the Society] to the tender mercy of — and —! – Those infants in arms! – However, I hope you will manage to cheer him up when you do go, and try to persuade him to send something to the Inde-pendent.[16] It was really very wicked of him to have destroyed the paper on Virgil. But he is wicked – Never mind, though! He exists.

*J. M. Keynes to G. L. Strachey*, 21 February 1906

I am studying Ethics for my Civil Service.

It is *impossible* to exaggerate the wonder and *originality* of Moore; people are already beginning to talk as if he were only a kind of logic-chopping eclectic. Oh why can't they see!

How amazing to think that we and only we know the rudi-ments of a true theory of ethic; for nothing can be more certain than that the broad outline is true. What is the world doing? It does damned well bring it home to read books written before P. E. I even begin to agree with Moore about Sidgwick – that he was a wicked edifactious person.

Meanwhile he read a paper on 'Egoism' in Cambridge, and in Oxford he opened a 'sad discussion' at the Jowett Society after a paper on 'Time and the Absolute'. At about this time he read Moore's paper on the 'Objects of Percep-tion', and was deeply impressed.[17]

*J. M. Keynes to G. L. Strachey*, 5 March 1906

I have just come away from tea with Beazley and it is plain that he is really quite unspoilt . . .

16. *Independent Review*. See p. 73.
17. At one point he worked the doctrine of this paper into his argu-ment in the *Treatise on Probability*: but the relevance is not alto-gether clear!

A man called Flecker[18] was there and, according to Swithin, is always there ... I am not enthusiastic about Flecker, – semi-foreign, with a steady languid flow and, I am told, an equally steady production of poems and plays which are just not bad ...

### *G. L. Strachey to J. M. Keynes,* 11 March 1906

I am glad you are seeing a good deal of James and Norton; for I suppose that means you are at any rate en route to becoming intimate with the former as well as the latter ...

I suppose it really doesn't matter very much whether you get into the C. S. or not, does it? If you didn't, wouldn't you get a fellowship, and take rooms in the Temple? That you might do in any case – very charming. Oh dear me! When will my Heaven be realized? – My Castle in Spain? Rooms, you know, for you, Duncan and Swithin, as fixtures – Woolf of course, too, if we could lure him from Ceylon; and several suites for guests. Can you conceive anything more supreme! I should write tragedies; you would revolutionize political economy, Swithin would compose French poetry, Duncan would paint our portraits in every conceivable combination and permutation, and Woolf would criticize us and our works without remorse.

About this time Sidgwick's *Memoir* appeared. Maynard reacted strongly and immediately sent off his comments to Swithinbank and Strachey. I shall quote the letter to Swithinbank, because there can be no suspicion that his tone might have been influenced by the receiver. It is, so to speak, a key to his twentieth-century revolt against the accepted standards of the nineteenth. And indeed it may be regarded from a wider point of view. Does it not epitomize the general change in attitude among thinking people?

In reading his letter we may recall Strachey's book on *Eminent Victorians*, in which revered figures of the nineteenth century were pulled off their pedestals. Keynes's criticism is more decisive evidence of a revolution in thinking, because while Strachey's Victorians were persons of whose eminence there might have been two views even among

18. James Elroy Flecker, the poet.

contemporaries, the high integrity and moral nobility of Sidgwick were disputed by none. Again, in the case of Strachey there may be some doubt regarding the interpretation he put upon the course of events, while in the case of Sidgwick the facts were nowise in dispute. It is thus a pure case of revaluation; we consider those attitudes of mind which seemed so noble to his contemporaries and ask whether we do indeed regard them as noble.

A further point may be noted in this connection. Keynes's style of attack upon Woodrow Wilson and the other peace-makers has been thought to have been influenced by Strachey's method in *Eminent Victorians*, which had recently appeared. Keynes's reaction to the Sidgwick *Memoir* suggests that his mind had this bent twelve years earlier. There is no reason to suppose that in this he was influenced by Strachey rather than conversely. When Strachey received Keynes's letter he had not read the *Memoir*; after reading it he cordially agreed. It is to be noted that the point at issue is not the truth or falsity of certain theological dogmas, but the question of honesty with oneself.

And just because that was the question, it seems worth quoting tributes from two men who are diametrically opposed examples of the Victorian tradition. Bishop Gore was an Anglican churchman of rare quality, whose high spirituality made a deep impression on all who knew him. His tribute to the free-thinking Sidgwick is therefore particularly notable. Speaking at a meeting in Cambridge, after Sidgwick's death, he said:

> But, of course, it was impossible to know him without feeling that incomparably the most impressive thing about him was his character ... When I came away from the last interview with him ... there was only one thought which came to my mind, in which I seemed able to sum up and express the impression which was left upon me, and it was the most sacred of all promises – 'Blessed are the pure in heart; for they shall see God'.[19]

19. *Cambridge University Reporter*, 7 December 1900. Report of a meeting for promoting a memorial to the late Henry Sidgwick.

At the other extreme was Mr F. C. Schiller, pragmatist philosopher and of extreme modernity by the standards of the time. Indeed he was regarded as a dangerous character among Oxford philosophers well into the twentieth century.

After a few prefatory remarks, in which he deprecated the intention of merely dialectical refutation, Sidgwick read what seemed to me – perhaps because I felt a strange touch of solemnity which I could not account for – the most lucid, sincere and impressive piece of philosophic criticism which it had ever been my privilege to hear.[20]

## *J. M. Keynes to B. W. Swithinbank*, 27 March 1906

Have you read Sidgwick's Life? It seems to be the subject of conversation now. Very interesting and depressing and, the first part particularly, very important as an historical document dealing with the mind of the period. Really – but you must read it yourself. He never did anything but wonder whether Christianity was true and prove that it wasn't and hope that it was. He even learnt Arabic[21] in order to read Genesis in the original, not trusting the authorized translators, which does seem a little sceptical. And he went to Germany to see what Ewald had to say and fell in love with a professor's daughter, and wrote to his dearest friends about the American Civil War.

I wonder what he would have thought of us; and I wonder what we think of him. And then his conscience – incredible. There is no doubt about his moral goodness. And yet it is all so dreadfully depressing – no intimacy, no clear-cut crisp boldness. Oh, I suppose he was intimate but he didn't seem to have anything to be intimate about except his religious doubts. And he really ought to have got over that a little sooner; because he knew that the thing wasn't true perfectly well from the beginning. The last part is all about ghosts and Mr Balfour. I have never found so dull a book so absorbing.

It is clear that early in this year he abandoned the idea of taking a second Tripos and contented himself with working

20. *Henry Sidgwick: A Memoir*, p. 586.

21. He spent much time both on Hebrew and Arabic, the latter in order to study the origins of Mohammedanism for comparative purposes.

for the Civil Service examination. As late as 8 April Marshall was still anxious that he should take the Economics Tripos.[22] But Maynard was probably determined to sample life in London – continued residence in Cambridge would be too deadening. In his own person Marshall was not the man to tip the scales for Maynard. He belonged essentially to the Sidgwick era, and, although different in many ways, had the Victorian taint. Had Marshall combined his economic eminence with the personal qualities of G. E. Moore, Maynard might have been won over and have given his whole mind to economics at an earlier date. Yet that might not have been to the benefit of his economics in the long run.

## *J. M. Keynes to R. H. Dundas*, 13 September 1906

Amusing that you have met Marshall. A very great man, but I suppose rather a silly one in his private character. Mrs is charming, isn't she.[23]

Earlier in the year Mrs (Alys) Russell[24] had proposed that Maynard should join her sister (Mrs Berenson) in Italy

22. Dr Keynes's Diary.

23. I do not rely on this letter as sole evidence for his feeling about Marshall as a man. On more than one occasion in private conversation, when I assumed a tone of reverence due to a great one in speaking of Marshall, Maynard seemed anxious to correct any misapprehension. 'He was an utterly absurd person, you know.' The economic student, who gets to know Marshall's economic writings well, soon becomes unconscious of their intensely Victorian moral outlook. The point was brought home to me vividly, after many years of teaching Marshall, by a pupil from the Far West of the United States, a gifted Rhodes Scholar, who came to me and said: 'Surely you cannot expect me to read all that drivel.' I was duly horrified, and prepared myself to deliver a severe lecture on my pupil's total incapacity to pass judgement on this great economic classic, when I realized that it was not the economic aspects with which he was quarrelling, but the background of Victorian morality. He categorically refused to read the *Principles*, and I had to find other means for him to acquire economic wisdom.

24. Bertrand Russell's first wife and sister of the beautiful writer, Logan Pearsall Smith.

for Easter. Geoffrey Scott,[25] then an undergraduate at New College, would be of the party. This was arranged. Mrs Berenson took the two young men for a tour of Tuscan sightseeing.

### J. M. Keynes to G. L. Strachey, 2 April 1906

Mary[26] was just the person to travel with in a motor – for her incredible competence as hostess; all the arrangements for one's comfort were complete. She was full of Italian and money and which hotel was best and what food they could best cook. We must have cost her pints of gold – for everything down to entrance fees to galleries was paid.

\*

Also she roars with laughter the whole time, allows you to laugh at her, and never worries one. And when she journalized about the pictures, Scott was always there to make the appropriate remark. The Costelloe females, Ray and Karin, don't talk much. But they did very well.[27] Scott is dreadfully Oxford – a sort of aesthetic person; and of course his point of view always seems to me a little shocking; but we are quite happy together ... I have never seen the aesthetic point of view so close. I find I object to it on high moral grounds – though I hardly know why. It seems to trifle deliberately with sacred reality. But isn't this rather cant?

Maynard had prudently arranged with Geoffrey Scott to have a time working alone together at Siena. They then proceeded to stay with the Berensons at Settignano near Florence, where there was a large party of young ladies.

### J. M. Keynes to G. L. Strachey, 15 April 1906

I've no news unless I describe our way of life. I seem to have fallen in love with Ray a little bit ... The comfort here is of

25. The author of *The Architecture of Humanism* and *Zélide*.

26. Mrs Berenson.

27. Ray and Karin were the daughters of Mrs Berenson by her first husband. Ray afterwards married Oliver Strachey (Lytton's elder brother) and Karin married Adrian Stephen (Thoby's younger brother).

course incredible; the cypresses and sun and moon and the amazing gardens and villas in which we picnic every day high above Florence have reduced me to a lump of Italian idleness.

We go to bed later and later and gradually find methods of working fresh meals into the day. Last night it was nearly five before we retired.

*

Oh. Scott is very amusing but he makes me angry by plotting at the greatest inconvenience to himself never to leave me and Ray alone. Everybody tries to bring it about occasionally, but, no, he forbids ...

On his return journey he joined his brother Geoffrey in Germany amid mountain snows. Geoffrey, too, was acquiring an interest in high mountains, and, unlike Maynard, maintained climbing as a hobby. He became quite an expert rock climber, and sometimes went on expeditions with George Mallory.

One more term before the Civil Service examination. The cycle of studies had come round to history and political science. There were various distractions: sailing with Knox on the Ouse, playing golf at Royston, going to a farewell dinner for Robin Furness who was off to Egypt, theatres in London. And he still spent much time among his own friends at Cambridge. Even his mother, for all her wise patience, began to get anxious about his lack of application to work at this time.

For the examination, which spread itself out from 3 August to 25 August, she took a flat in London at 33 Coleherne Court. This time it was to his young friend James that he wrote a *cri du cœur*.

### J. M. Keynes to James Strachey, 2 August 1906

I was glad to get your letter this evening when I returned pale and dry in the pen from a three hours' disquisition on 'Drama, Melodrama and Opera'. They are rather a crew – my competitors; a few of the more presentable I knew, but good God! I trembled for our Indian Empire when I saw the bulk of them. It is rumoured that there are very few vacancies in the Home and none in the Treasury . . . Do come. I hope I shan't have quite sunk beneath the weight of my fate . . .

*J. M. Keynes to James Strachey, 6 August 1906*

I am doing my papers all right, but am feeling rather black and perfectly aimless . . .

I wonder why 'someone to talk to' is so comforting.

And how superb a 'happy marriage' would be, but might not one want to change sometimes? I doubt whether marriage by itself is a very ingenious institution. But marriage and divorce if necessary – that is from heaven.

Well perhaps it may happen to someone some day . . .

Unable to bear it any longer, he went, in the midst of the examination, to stay with the Strachey family at Betchworth, at a house they had taken within reach of London for the summer. Miss Philippa Strachey recalls his extreme insouciance and her taking him to task. 'Really, Mr Keynes, is this a pose, or don't you care whether you get into the Civil Service or not?' He reassured her; he had worked it all out; he was quite confident that he would be among the first ten; and, as he didn't mind whether he was first or tenth, why bother? Did this express his true mind? If it did, it was extremely characteristic – to come to a crisp decision about the whole matter and bother no more. Actually his position among the first ten was a very important question. The list of vacancies only appeared after the examination, and Maynard decided that there were only two that he would care to accept – the Treasury and the India Office. The result came out at the end of September – he was second. As his father wrote in his Diary, it was 'a wonderful achievement' considering how little work he had done in preparation. The first on the list (who had a long lead over Maynard) chose the Treasury, and thus Maynard had the India Office. Had he been first? That would indeed have required more than a little last-minute cramming at

Betchworth. Still, if he had worked really hard, he might have done it. And then what? Had he gone to the Treasury, he probably would not have come out after two years. Would he as a permanent, and not a temporary, Civil Servant have resigned at Paris in 1919? What would have been the balance of good? Rising towards the top of the Treasury in the inter-war period, would he have achieved a better conduct of British finances? We can hardly doubt that Mr Churchill, the innocent victim, as Chancellor of the Exchequer, in the crucial years (1925–9), of the old orthodox school at the Treasury and the Bank of England, would have found in Keynes a man after his heart's desire. We may guess that Keynes would have influenced the mind of Benjamin Strong of the Federal Reserve Bank of New York. Could he and Strong's successors between them have availed to mitigate the great slump of 1929–32? Then the Nazis would not have come into power. A fascinating speculation! But then, although no doubt he would have written books – and possibly on economics – they would inevitably have been of a different character. Valuable analyses we might have had, but the strong undercurrent of rebellion could hardly have been present, and, without that, would his works have had comparable influence? Miss Strachey evidently asked a very pertinent question. As she talked to Lytton's clever friend, it could not have crossed her mind that perhaps wars and horrors of untold dimensions hung upon the answer.

Before the result was known he gave himself a pleasant holiday visiting Mr Henry Hobhouse (Hobby's father) at Hadspen, his home in Somerset, and then going with Lytton and James and Norton to Scotland. A last wild excess, we may be sure, of talk upon the old subjects.

*J. M. Keynes to G. L. Strachey*, 4 October 1906

My marks have arrived and left me enraged. Really knowledge seems an absolute bar to success. I have done worst in the only two subjects of which I possessed a solid knowledge – Mathe-

matics and Economics. I scored more marks for English History
than for Mathematics – is it credible? For Economics I got a
relatively low percentage and was the eighth or ninth in order of
merit – whereas I knew the whole of both papers in a really
elaborate way. On the other hand, in Political Science, to which
I devoted less than a fortnight in all, I was easily first of everybody. I was also first in Logic and Psychology and in Essay.

His indignation was afterwards crystallized in the saying:
'I evidently knew more about Economics than my examiners'.[28]


2

For the next two years his life was divided into two compartments, work in the India Office and study of the theory
of probability. Of these the former was much the less important. When at the end of two years he resigned from the
India Office he told Page that all he had succeeded in

---

28. I am unable to agree with Professor E. A. G. Robinson, who puts
in a plea for the examiners in his fine memoir (*Economic Journal*,
March 1947). On the one hand, we have to consider Keynes absorbing
Economics through every pore at Harvey Road, correcting Sidgwick's
proofs, reading solidly for some months – and for him that would
mean massive reading – and receiving instruction from Marshall and
from Pigou at the weekly breakfasts. We have to think of his quick
absorptive capacity. When reading the *Principles*, he would not be
beguiled by its apparent facility; he would apprehend at once the
bare bones of the argument. In his papers he would no doubt have
discussed the difficult mathematical substratum, carried the analysis
further, raised abstruse difficulties. On the other side, we have to think
of the extraordinarily small number of people in England on whom
the Civil Service Commissioners had to draw, who were capable of
understanding such by-play with Marshall. I have the advantage over
Professor Robinson in having been at an eminent University (Oxford)
before Economics became the subject of an Honours examination
(1923), and I know what extraordinarily jejune stuff passed muster
with the authorities as economics (Professor Edgeworth standing
apart in glorious isolation); and, after all, Oxford was contributing
a fair proportion of those who sat for the Civil Service examination –
and perhaps even occasionally an examiner in economics!

achieving during that time was getting one pedigree bull shipped to Bombay. This was no doubt a Keynesian exaggeration. But there were frequent complaints of his having nothing to do during office hours. 'Business is very slack here. I did not do one minute's work yesterday.'[29] 'I have not averaged an hour's office work a day this week so that I am well up to date with the dissertation.'[30] He was initially posted to the Military Department. In November Dr Keynes notes that Maynard was 'getting into the habit of doing his own work in office hours'. None the less when he was offered a resident clerkship in the following February, he conscientiously refused in the interests of his own work, although assured by Sir Arthur Godley, the Permanent Secretary, that he should not overestimate the amount of evening work that there would be at the office!

In March he was transferred to the Revenue, Statistics and Commerce Department, where work became more interesting. He had to compile the annual report on 'The Moral and Material Progress of India'. He did not see eye to eye with the authorities on all questions of morality, but he pleased himself by translating these matters into 'beautiful curves'. He regretted that this part of his report would be for ever locked in secrecy.

*J. M. Keynes to G. L. Strachey,* 7 March 1907

I like my new Department. I have not much to write at present, but there is an excellent system by which everything comes to me to read, and I read it. In fact there is so much to read, that it takes me all my time. Some of it is quite absorbing – Foreign Office commercial negotiations with Germany, quarrels with Russia in the Persian Gulf, the regulation of opium in Central India, the Chinese opium proposals – I have had great files to read on all these in the last two days.

I lunched at the House of Lords today, and Gosse was at the next table; really he is purely a figure of fun, and the company

29. Letter to Mrs Keynes, 9 May 1907.
30. Ditto, 6 December 1907.

seemed to realize it. I felt very pompous smoking and drinking coffee in the Library afterwards.

Yesterday I attended my first Committee of Council. The thing is simply government by dotardry; at least half those present showed manifest signs of senile decay, and the rest didn't speak.

### *J. M. Keynes to G. L. Strachey,* 18 April 1907

I have really been almost overworked in this office. I really believe that I have written almost every despatch in the Department this week.

Dr Keynes notes in his Diary that 'he is liking his work much better, has much reading, as he sees all papers that come into the Department'.[31]

Somewhat later he wrote an interesting letter, summarizing his experiences as a Civil Servant. Something must be allowed for the frustration of youthful enthusiasm, something for his not yet seeing clearly the inherent limitations in any central department of government, discharging administrative duties under parliamentary control.

### *J. M. Keynes to G. L. Strachey,* 13 September 1907

I'm thoroughly sick of this place and would like to resign. Now the novelty has worn off, I am bored nine-tenths of the time and rather unreasonably irritated the other tenth whenever I can't have my own way. It's maddening to have thirty people who can reduce you to impotence when you're quite certain you are right. I am enraged just now over another memorial. A poor man has been censured for doing X, and after repeated memorials to the Government of India has now memorialized the Secretary of State, vehemently denying that he ever did anything of the kind. I have demonstrated quite clearly that he is wholly innocent of X, but that if he had been charged with a quite different offence Y, and if he had been allowed to reply and the thing had been investigated, he would probably have deserved censure for Y. But it seems to me that, whatever else is done, censure for doing X

31. Dr Keynes's Diary, 7 March 1907.

should be cancelled. They say – No, he deserves censure, and therefore censure must be maintained.

This theory that if even a tolerable face can be put on the matter Government never withdraws anything – even in matters of justice – seems to me quite wrong and very dangerous. It was just the same in the — affair. — is apparently censured for negligence in his laboratory. Of this he is demonstrably innocent. But Government maintain their position because an entirely different reason renders it undesirable to employ him again in his old position. It is quite clear to me that, whatever they do subsequently, censure for the thing of which he is innocent should be freely withdrawn first. (Don't mention this in public, please.)

Then the preoccupation, which seems characteristic of officials, to save their own skin, is fatal. Drake's dread of taking any responsibility is almost pathetic. And of course it prevents any original or sporting proposal ever being made. With this machine there is not the least chance of anything's being done rashly or precipitately; so that the risk to India of free speech in the India Office is nil. But you may be 'snubbed'. Lord!

Or again, the public write in to obtain information on some point. One has material which isn't in the least secret and which may prove most useful to them. But they mustn't have it unless it is *absolutely certain* that the information is correct in every detail – even if you add qualifications 'probably', 'as far as we know', 'without guaranteeing'. What 'absolutely certain' means is that somebody other than yourself is responsible for its accuracy.

The consequence is that although one is most careful to acknowledge letters by return of post and to spend an infinite amount of trouble finding out what is 'absolutely certain', your final letter to the public is not worth the postage, although as the result of your investigations you may be bubbling with information of ordinary reliability.

Like your impression of Hurst, this may be highly coloured; but I am sure it is substantially just, and the colouring, like that in the microscope slides of dissections, only put on to make it intelligible.

All my thoughts are on Probability . . .

He had a 'service' flat at 125B St James's Court. He had more than a fortnight's leave at Christmas and decided to go off with Lytton somewhere. Should it be Paris? Expense was a drawback; but they decided that the cost of the journey and a week in Paris might reasonably be kept down to £5 a head. Maynard had a slight qualm – it seemed rather 'wicked' to go off to Paris. In the event they went to Rye, and afterwards he spent Christmas at home.

Although Maynard was a humanist, and his sympathies comprehended the female sex, he did not show any marked leaning towards feminism and 'women's rights' in the narrower sense. But he was always ready to enter with enthusiasm into the affairs of his friends, and when Miss Philippa Strachey became deeply involved in organizing a great procession and demonstration on behalf of the Society for Women's Suffrage, his services were at her disposal. This was the first big public demonstration in the Women's Suffrage campaign and was a notable landmark. Three thousand women proceeded on a very wet day from Hyde Park Corner to Exeter Hall. This was afterwards known as the 'Mud March'. A band had to be found, and Maynard accompanied Miss Strachey on a dark and foggy winter's evening to Bermondsey, where the location of the band was only identified by strains of practising coming from behind a high bleak wall. On the day, he was put in charge of arrangements at the Exeter Hall. He arrived in good time to make the necessary plans for the reception, but he found the hall barred and bolted. Matters looked black. However, he managed to get it opened in the nick of time. A letter is extant from the Secretary, Miss Bompas, thanking him for his valuable services as steward.

In the Easter vacation he went to Paris and stayed with Duncan Grant, and afterwards to North Molton in Devon, where there was quite a party of Moore, Strachey, Bob Trevelyan, Sanger and others.

*G. L. Strachey to B. W. Swithinbank*, 31 March 1907

At this moment Keynes is lying on a rug beside me, turning over the leaves of a handbook on obstetrics which seems to keep him absorbed. Norton is next to him on a camp-stool, and it is he who is writing mathematics. Next to him is Bob Trevy, under an umbrella, very vague and contented, and planning out his next *chef-d'œuvre*. I should have mentioned that I am on a basket chair (with plenty of cushions in case of accidents), and that I am perfectly happy, as I am writing to you instead of doing what I ought to be doing, viz., composing a preface to Warren Hastings ...

... Oh dear! Keynes has deserted his obstetrics and become absorbed in Norton's mathematics. He declares that gamma is a function of theta, but Norton thinks that he is integrating PV and so none of it will do. How shocking ...

More holidays came in July, and he went off mountaineering, not with the superb Young this time, but with his father, his brother Geoffrey, and Fay, in the Pyrenees. Unfortunately Dr Keynes and Geoffrey had to return unexpectedly early; Maynard found his way down with Fay to the hotel at Biarritz.

## *J. M. Keynes to G. L. Strachey*, 13 July 1907

You would adore this place – so do I. The climate is absolute perfection – never a cloud, never hot, never cold. And the food – the food is divine. And the tea shops, not Rumpelmayer, but as good, I think. Yet there are two clouds. I lose the most appalling sums at *Petits Chevaux*, and it is doubtful whether I shall have enough money to provide any meals on the journey home. Last night, I finished up by losing forty times running; and I have had other spells almost as bad. [Fay recalls that Maynard did his utmost to replenish his funds for gambling by drawing on him, but met with no success!]

The other cloud is the ugliness of the people in these parts, including the visitors. I don't like the Basque type – in fact it is hideous.

*

But then I should add that I have left my heart in Aragon, the most beautiful country in the world, whence I have lately returned, having spent three days in a peasant's hut.

*

About a week ago I had a letter from Godley saying that he had thought it right to call Morley's[32] special attention to my Minute on the Madras Malikhana case, and enclosing an autograph letter of compliments for me from J. M. He did not say whether or not he had reversed the damned Committee and agreed with me.

Fay also recalls that at this period, when they had naturally discussed the great question of one's future, it never crossed his mind that Maynard would become a professional economist. He assumed that, were Maynard to return to academic life, it would be as a philosopher. In writing to Pigou in the following winter, Maynard said that, should he return to Cambridge, his field of study would be Logic and Statistical Theory.

Leave certainly seems to have been not inadequate, for in the middle of October we find him settling into some rooms in King's College to pursue his researches for a fortnight. There is no doubt that he was working very hard on Probability at this time – probably harder than he had worked for many years. He seems to have resisted the temptation, for which this residence in King's during the first fortnight of the Michaelmas term provided such a unique opportunity, of making a minute inspection of the new arrivals.

The culmination of his work on Probability was to be the submission of a dissertation as a candidate for a Fellowship at King's. Each year King's offers a small number of Prize Fellowships. Success would not necessarily mean abandoning one's career as a Civil Servant. It would simply be an honour and carry a very small stipend. On the other hand, it would clearly be an encouragement to return to Cambridge life, by its implication that one was of the necessary standard.

The College appointed as assessors W. E. Johnson, Maynard's old friend of childhood, and Alfred Whitehead. This seemed sufficiently propitious. But Maynard was not elected.

32. John Morley was at this time Secretary of State for India.

It was a great disappointment. Page, who had by this time become an eminently proficient mathematician, and Dobbs, a classic, were the successful candidates. The election was hotly contested; a Fellow of King's, writing the next day, said that he thought they must have voted about fifteen times.

### J. M. Keynes to G. L. Strachey, 23 March 1908

I have had a very interesting time at Cambridge and heard all about everything from Pigou. I really think it was sheer bad luck – a hair would have turned the balance; also a little wickedness on their part, for P. says that there was a solid block who voted against me from the beginning *on the express ground of seniority*, while admitting that on merits I was better ...

I was also damaged, I think, by Whitehead's report. He is a follower (an ardent follower) of Venn! and it seems to me from his criticisms, which are futile, that he can have understood very little of the philosophy. He praised the formal logic and the mathematics. Johnson's report is almost as favourable as it could possibly be. I spent most of Sunday talking to him, and he had made a great number of very important criticisms, which, with the exception of one fundamental point, are probably right, and practically presented me with the fruits of his own work on the subject which have extended over years. On the pure logic of it he is, I think, quite superb and immensely beyond anyone else.

Pigou seems to have struggled nobly on my behalf – but I will tell you details tomorrow. I still have the subject on the brain.

Please bring Darwin vol. ii.

Yr.

J. M. KEYNES

Really Whitehead's report was not competent. Of my two most important and original chapters, which, whatever their truth, are entirely novel, he says 'are really excellent discussions and expositions, but – as I suspect – contain little that is new to a fairly well instructed philosopher'. While Johnson says 'it is highly original, very neatly executed, and meets an urgent need in logical science', Whitehead ought not to have said it was old, unless he himself knew of some passage where it had been said before. It is no good 'suspecting' that it must have been said before, because it seems reasonable. [33]

The reports of Johnson and Whitehead were both very good, praising the dissertation as an important contribution to knowledge. It was indeed a lucky college to have two better men! Whitehead, it is true, dealt rather roughly with certain passages, but on being asked by Pigou to make a further statement, he said that his report as a whole had been intended as 'very favourable'. All his friends encouraged Maynard with rosy hopes of success in the following year.

Soon after this the question was mooted whether he should not return to Cambridge without a Fellowship. His father had had some doubts of the wisdom of his giving up the India Office, even with a Fellowship, and wrote in his Diary before the result of the election was known: 'He will be throwing up a certainty and taking risks. That fits in with his scheme of life, not with mine.'

Alfred Marshall had been in the habit of paying out of his private pocket two sums of £100 a year each in order to sustain lecturers for the new Economics Tripos at Cambridge, and in April, although soon about to retire from his Chair, he wrote to Keynes offering him a lectureship in Economics on these terms. Keynes was interested. The Economics Tripos, first established in 1903, had been looked after by the Special Board for Economics and Politics.

33. Keynes may well have been in the right in this criticism. It is possible that Whitehead was not widely read in philosophy outside his range at this period. I remember a remark which he made to me as late as some time shortly after World War I. He was not predisposed to expect good philosophy to emanate from Oxford, but he praised *Kant's Theory of Knowledge* by H. A. Prichard, on the ground that it made it unnecessary for one ever to think of reading Kant. Good Kantian scholars know that whatever the other virtues of Prichard's book – and it was a notable philosophical contribution – it did not have this one. Whitehead's reading in general philosophy became more extensive later. It was not his professional duty to have wide philosophical knowledge until he was appointed to the Chair at Harvard in 1924, at the age of sixty-three.

When this met on 3 June 1908, it had to face a minor crisis in its affairs. Pigou had just been elected to the professorship in place of Alfred Marshall. Marshall had at once withdrawn from Chairmanship of the Board, and on 3 June Dr J. N. Keynes (Maynard's father) was elected to the Chairmanship in his place, a position he was to hold until 1919; but at this particular meeting Professor James Ward, who had been Chairman of the Board in its early stages, resumed his place. Marshall's self-effacement went further. He had intimated that he did not intend to continue lecturing. This was to give Pigou, who was still only thirty-one, a fair chance to become established as the principal lecturer upon the subject, and to give himself the greatest possible amount of time to complete the volumes planned in succession to *The Principles of Economics*. Admirable although this policy was, it meant that the number of first-rate lecturers available to the Board was reduced by one. Meanwhile a letter was read from H. S. Foxwell, who was very sore at the election of Pigou, so much his junior, to the Chair, stating that he did not intend to continue lecturing. Furthermore, Mr D. H. MacGregor,[34] the other principal lecturer on Economics for the Tripos, had been appointed to the Chair, at Leeds. There was evidently sore need for replenishment. A letter was read from Pigou, generously offering to pay £200 from his private pocket for two lecturers, as Marshall had done. The Board decided to offer one of these lectureships to Walter Layton,[35] and the other to the young Keynes.

On 5 June Keynes resigned from the India Office.[36] His father made him an allowance of £100 a year; he was to have £100 a year from Pigou; that was all the certainty. He would undoubtedly earn money by lecturing and taking

34. Drummond Professor of Political Economy in Oxford, 1922–45.
35. Now Lord Layton, distinguished economist and authority on international affairs, and editor of the *Economist* newspaper from 1922 to 1938.
36. He was succeeded in his position there by Mr (now Sir Cecil) Kisch.

pupils, but the rates were low in those days and there were barely more than twenty men in the whole university reading for the Economics Tripos. Should he succeed in being elected to the King's Fellowship in the following March, he would get a stipend of £120 a year. It suited him to take the risk.

*J. M. Keynes to Dr J. N. Keynes,* 18 July 1908

I have finished up with a week of quite hard work, and have been in charge of the Department for the greater part of the last two days. It seems quite like dying – initiating stages in pieces of work which move heavily on, knowing that one will never see the outcome. I spent the morning mastering the arrangement of the Customs Department – the knowledge dies with me. But I have no regrets – not even now that it has come to it – not one.

In these two years, he had gained the knowledge of how a Government Department works. One might almost say that such knowledge should be regarded as an essential part of an economist's education! He had acquired an interest in Indian affairs; the problem of the rupee was the livest issue in the field of money in those days, and Keynes was to make his début as an economist by his treatment of that subject. His brief spell at the India Office had a consequence which was more important than either of these. He had made his abilities known to the officials of the Office. That knowledge was a necessary link in the chain of events which brought Keynes into prominence in public affairs fairly early in life. He might well have achieved prominence in other ways, but his path would necessarily have been more devious.

At about this time there occurred an event which was to have an important influence for many years in his private life. It may be defined as follows: for some years before this, his reply to the question 'Who is your greatest friend?' would undoubtedly have been 'Lytton Strachey'. From about this period until his death, the reply would have been 'Duncan Grant'. It was not a question of the one supplanting the other, for the relation to each was different. There was no break in his friendship with Strachey, and their correspondence continued for a number of years. There is a subtle question involved concerning the kind of friendship which satisfies one's innermost needs at various phases. In Strachey he had found a kindred spirit of rebellion against Victorian conventions; he had been able to learn from a somewhat older man; he had been fascinated by his genius; he had been succoured by his power of sympathetic understanding. They both had dominating personalities; they both had in some sense a mission. Is it putting it too simply to say that Keynes's mission was to make men think differently on important matters, Strachey's to make them feel differently? Strachey continued to be poor, having to eke out his livelihood by journalistic work; he only gained a good footing on the publication of *Eminent Victorians* (1918), at the age of thirty-eight. But all this time he was, within a circle of intellectual friends, establishing a kind of dominance. He was struggling to find self-expression, he was asserting himself, he was diffusing his influence.

Thus there was the possibility of an uneasy relation. Eager as Keynes had been to learn what Strachey had to offer, appreciative as he always was, it was clearly impossible for him to be one of a group of followers. He had his own far-reaching and commanding powers. Yet within this circle, to which Keynes freely chose to attach himself and with which some inner urge compelled him to maintain his intimacy, it was Strachey who had to be the leader by reason of the principal interests of the group. They were not mainly concerned with economics or logic or public affairs or University matters, but with art and literature. It was Keynes's great intimacy with Duncan Grant that gave him his special and congenial position in the circle, neither as leader nor follower.

Duncan Grant combined a delightful and winning personality with a very good intellect. In the correspondence between Keynes and Strachey there were recurrent references to Duncan's fine intelligence. By comparison with Strachey he was *rangé*. He had, of course, his periods of depression and he had a struggle to achieve his full potentiality in his painting, but that form of self-expression was less competitive in a social group than Strachey's, who felt an inner compulsion to gain acceptance for his points of view. Grant was less restless and volatile. Not that he was merely a passive figure; he was strongly original, and had abounding interests and an eager flow of spirit. Keynes found him an ideal companion.

After leaving the India Office he immediately went up to Cambridge, at which the Long Vacation period of residence was proceeding. We hear at once of new figures – Gerald Shove [37] and Hugh ('Daddy') Dalton.[38] Shove was destined to be on intimate terms with the Keynes–Strachey circle for many years; Dalton diverged on to a somewhat different path at an earlier date. Later in the year, when Keynes finally settled down at King's, we hear also of Francis ('Frankie') Birrell and George Mallory. The former of these remained an intimate until his death; the latter was a special friend of Geoffrey Keynes. Rupert Brooke was already an established figure in Cambridge.

Keynes got quickly to work upon Probability. He had had the benefit of comments and suggestions by W. E. Johnson. Whitehead also sent him an exposition of the points in which he was in incomplete sympathy. During the summer there was a joint discussion on Probability with Russell and Moore.

Early in August Keynes took Margaret, his sister, over to visit Mrs Berenson, then staying at Court Place, Iffley, near Oxford, where the company was gay and living very comfortable. 'In a few minutes we are going in the launch to Christ Church to see the pictures in the Library there.' [39]

37. The well-known economist.
38. Well known in due course as a leader of the Labour Party: Chancellor of the Exchequer, 1945 to 1947.
39. Letter to Duncan Grant, 8 August 1908.

What a delightful way of 'doing' Oxford! But the high point of the year was a stay for some two months with Duncan Grant in the Orkneys, Duncan being busy painting – his work including a portrait of Maynard – while Maynard was busy working on Probability. The result appears to have been successful.

*J. M. Keynes to Duncan Grant, 5* February 1909

I met Whitehead in the street today and he stopped me to speak about the Dissertation. He says that the new version has now convinced and converted him on the fundamental point on which he formerly disagreed with me. His conversation was due to the chapter which I wrote chiefly in the field above Stromness, and a reference to the argument brought back to me quite clearly the view of the harbour. He thinks I had better publish at once with a few minor alterations, without waiting to get the argument completely filled in regarding certain points which I have left so far in an unsatisfactory condition.

He came south at the end of October. He was invited to give advice on certain points in the next annual report on 'The Material and Moral Progress of India'. He had to dismantle his flat in London and, having had an attack of influenza, did not settle into College until the end of November. He retained a *pied-à-terre* in London by sharing with Duncan Grant accommodation in Belgrave Road. Meanwhile he was finishing off his dissertation. We may anticipate by saying that Johnson and Whitehead wrote still more favourable reports upon it when it was re-submitted; Whitehead explained that his doubts on certain points had been removed. In the following March, Keynes was elected a Fellow of King's, which he remained until the end of his life.

3

Between 1906 and 1911 Keynes was devoting all his spare time to the theory of Probability; indeed, we may state the matter more emphatically by saying that the main stream of his intellectual energy was flowing into this work; his other activities were comparatively easy for him, and he could take them in his stride. After his failure to be elected to the Fellowship in 1908, he attacked the problem with renewed zest for re-submission; after his election he read widely in the subject and greatly enlarged the book for publication.[40] In 1912 other work supervened, and his treatise had to be left on one side until 1920, when he polished it up before its appearance in 1921. Thus it was his main work from the age of twenty-three to twenty-nine.[41] In the case of some men of outstanding powers, their constitution or environment prevents full fruition until a later date. But Keynes developed early, and his environment was not such as to inhibit work of the best quality. Indeed we may believe that his intellectual powers at this period were at their height; his treatise must be regarded as embodying a substantial proportion of his best life-work. It would be quite wrong to think of it as a *jeu d'esprit* thrown off by an economist to show that he had some philosophical capacity also.

The task he set himself was a gigantic one. It was nothing less than to cover the whole field of empirical thinking, whether resulting in the widest and most abstruse generalizations of physics or in the commonplace knowledge about the facts of our everyday life. Thus Keynes set himself to examine the validity of the processes by which we obtain all the constructive knowledge that we have. He had to examine the principles of induction. Since no knowledge

40. There was during this period a review of *Éléments de la théorie des probabilités*, by Émile Boule, in the *Mathematical Gazette*, March 1910: and of *Wahrscheinlichkeitsrechnung*, vol. ii, by Emmanuel Czuber, ibid. October 1911.

41. J. M. Keynes to Dr Marshall, 13 September 1910: 'I have been spending all this Long on my Probability Treatise to the exclusion of everything else, and am glad to say that the end seems in sight. It has occupied all my spare time for the last 4 years, and I shall not be sorry to be free again for other things.' But more remained to be done.

acquired by inductive reasoning reaches the level of absolute certainty, he had to examine the theory of Probability. He set himself to weld the abstract theory of Probability to the theory of induction more closely than earlier writers had attempted, and to deduce all his principles from a minimum number of self-evident axioms, in the manner in which Whitehead and Russell had deduced the whole of mathematics from a minimum number of definitions and logical axioms. While there had been many treatises on probability and much writing about induction, it would be difficult to find a parallel for a comprehensive attack of this kind since the days of Aristotle. In Mill's treatise there is little serious tackling of the theory of probability.

It is usually maintained, and Keynes himself did not dissent, that these abstruse speculations about the validity of empirical knowledge are of merely academic interest, since the scientists will proceed with their good work without too much concern about its logical foundations. It is possible, however, that the position is now changing. The Quantum Theory has recently been taking a course which seems to run counter to normal scientific progress, in that it has to multiply (rather than reduce) the number of fundamental entities, the existence of which has to be assumed. And there are the puzzles connected with indeterminacy. It may well be that before we reach the next great simplifying synthesis, which will surely come in time, there will be some confluence between ordinary physical thinking and the philosophical theory of the relation between items of evidence and the facts which they are deemed to support. Thus these fundamental logical speculations cannot be ruled out as inevitably of no practical use. It must be emphasized that Keynes's work is concerned with the foundations of Probability, and not with the working mathematics of it. Statistical mechanics proceeds apace, using far more abstruse mathematical methods than are to be found in Keynes's treatise. That book, despite its ample display of mathematical symbolism, is not a contribution to the mathematical theory of Probability. It is concerned with the logical substructure of that theory.

What were the qualities displayed in the *Treatise on Probability*? First we may note the purely logical faculty, the power of distinguishing the finest shades of difference between arguments of deceptive similarity. This logical faculty is different from that of the pure mathematician. We have seen that Keynes did not attain the highest flight of mathematical proficiency. The mathematician is working at every point with symbols, which guide and govern him, although he has to become their master. The logician at certain points has to dispense with this guidance and depend upon intuition. In the intuitive perception of distinctions and of relevance, Keynes probably ranks with the greatest logicians.

Secondly, he displays a special kind of mathematical ability which is distinct from this logical ability. For the purpose of deducing the ordinary theorems of the mathematics of Probability from a few general logical propositions, a special kind of mathematical apparatus had to be used. Very few persons at that time, perhaps only two in England, were adept in this particular form of mathematics. Both have given their verdicts, in view of which we are able to give Keynes high marks for his proficiency in this very special and difficult field. In his report on Keynes's submission on the first occasion, Whitehead wrote:

Turning now to the mathematical division of the dissertation … His symbolism is excellent; it has the great merit that accompanies good symbolism, that essential points which without it are subtle and easily lost sight of, with it become simple and obvious. Also his axioms are good; they are simple and few and by the aid of the symbolism he deduces the whole subject from them by rigid reasoning. The very certainty and ease by which he is enabled to solve difficult questions and to detect ambiguities and errors in the work of his predecessors exemplifies and at the same time almost conceals the advance which he has made.

In his review of Keynes's book as it finally appeared, Bertrand Russell wrote:

> The mathematical calculus is astonishingly powerful, considering the very restricted premises which form its foundation . . . The book as a whole is one which it is impossible to praise too highly and it is to be hoped that it will stimulate further work on a most important subject which philosophers and logicians have unduly neglected.[42]

It should be noticed, however, that this praise was relative to a first attempt. I believe the expert view now to be that the mathematics are by no means impeccable.

Thirdly, there was his immense erudition in the history of thought. It may well be that Keynes had a wider knowledge of the literature of probability than he ever acquired in his chosen subject of economics. Complaints were made that his treatment of it was somewhat sporadic, and that he did not present the reader with a clear view of the general development of the subject. He might well have replied that he was using historical sources for their relevance to the central problems which he was endeavouring to solve. To have given an outline of the historical development of empirical logic would have required a separate volume.

Finally, we come to a quality which is more important than all these and more difficult to define. It is to be emphasized that his subject-matter was a vast one. In some parts of the field precise and rigid mathematical work had already been done; others had only been treated somewhat vaguely; all had been treated from various points of view and with conflicting conclusions. The authorities were numerous, and the subject no less than the whole of human knowledge itself, save for that part of it which is contained in purely deductive processes. Keynes displayed the most astonishing ease in moving about this tremendous field. He had a keen eye for the mutual relevance of apparently widely separated problems. Most important of all, he showed the quality of realism in a very high degree. One may proceed

42. *Mathematical Gazette*, vol. xi, July 1922.

from certain assumptions and develop an elegant theory of probability; Keynes was quick to reject theories which, however meritorious in themselves, did not apply exactly to the actual processes of thought which man uses in his scientific or general reasoning. The power of apprehending simultaneously in his mind widely disparate theories and facts, the fine judgement of relevance and intense realism – these are his great qualities. To them we must add his faculty for developing a chain of rigid logical reasoning, once he had assured himself that he had achieved relevant premises and was not merely spinning fine theories in the void.

It will at once occur to economists that these were the same qualities that marked his theoretical work in economics. He was second to none in his logical capacity for developing a fine-spun theory; but he was entirely averse from doing so save when he believed his premises to be realistic and his conclusions applicable to life. His realism was unsurpassed among economists of his calibre. He had an extraordinary capacity for going below the surface of things. This keen sense of reality, this power of visualizing how tendencies do in fact work themselves out in the market-place, is not often combined with first-class theoretical power.

In his biography of Alfred Marshall, Keynes emphasized the point that Marshall understood that the task of the economic theorist was something more extensive and more difficult than the development of a mathematical technique. He inserted the following footnote:

Professor Planck of Berlin, the famous originator of the Quantum Theory, once remarked to me that in early life he had thought of studying economics, but had found it too difficult! Professor Planck could easily master the whole corpus of mathematical economics in a few days. He did not mean that! But the amalgam of logic and intuition and the wide knowledge of facts, most of which are not precise, which is required for economic interpretation in its highest form, is, quite truly, overwhelmingly difficult for those whose gift mainly consists in the power to imagine and pursue to their furthermost points, the implications and prior conditions of comparatively simple facts, which are known with a high degree of precision.[43]

I happened to sit next to Keynes at the High Table of King's College a day or two after Planck had made this observation, and Keynes told me of it.[44] Lowes Dickinson was sitting opposite. 'That's funny,' he said, 'because Bertrand Russell once told me that in early life he had thought of studying economics, but had found it too easy!' Keynes did not reply. It was unlikely that Russell's remark was to be taken with the seriousness that Lowes Dickinson seemed naïvely disposed to attribute to it.

The *Treatise on Probability* did not appear until 1921. Bertrand Russell's review was full of high praise.[45] There was a favourable notice by Mr Harold Jeffreys,[46] who with Dr Dorothy Wrinch had already begun to work on similar lines, and who has since become the greatest expert on the subject. There were other good reviews, not all of which showed understanding of the purport of the work. There were some unfavourable reviews. Certain persons of actuarial training showed irritation, not realizing that they themselves had not the faintest idea what the philosophical problems were that Keynes was trying to solve. A full and favourable appreciation was given in *Mind* by Professor C. D. Broad, who had been through some of the proofs with the author and Russell in 1914. A year later, however, there appeared in *Mind* an article on the *Treatise* by H. W. B. Joseph, a philosopher of considerable reputation in his own University of Oxford. It can hardly be claimed that he had really tried to comprehend the central features of Keynes's thought. He and those who agreed with him at Oxford were extremely hostile to the ideas of Russell and Whitehead. Joseph was

43. *Economic Journal*, 1924, reprinted in *Memorials of Alfred Marshall*, p. 25.

44. He had just returned from Berlin, where he had been advising on the depreciation of the mark in November 1922.

45. op. cit. For some points raised in the review, see the note which is appended to this volume.

46. *Nature*, 2 February 1922.

alienated by their manifest influence upon Keynes, and used
his space rather for general skirmishing with the Russellian
presuppositions of the book – there is a contemptuous reference to Russell's 'lingo' – than for close grappling with
Keynes's original contributions. The review was hostile, and
at one point Joseph wrote that 'Mr Keynes is no safe guide
in fundamental logical problems'.[47]

Keynes was staying with me in Christ Church some time
after that, and I thought that it would be suitable to bring
these eminent persons together. Accordingly I invited
Joseph to breakfast – breakfast was still often made a social
occasion at Oxford in those days. When I told Keynes that
Joseph was coming to breakfast, I detected a look of pain on
his face. But I was not alarmed, because I thought that I had
provided adequately for his comfort by arranging that the
breakfast should be at 9.30 a.m. 'Breakfast is at 9.30,' I said.
But his pain was not much assuaged. 'It is a very long time
since I have got up as early as that,' he said, 'but if Joseph
is coming . . .'

Throughout his mature life, and long before his serious
illness in 1937, he made it a habit of lying late in bed, to
conserve his energies. His morning post was brought to him
and considered; the financial intelligence which he received
was carefully scrutinized; the decisions of the day were
taken; letters were dictated: in fact most of what might be
called his office work was conducted before he rose from
bed. Thus, when he did finally get up, he had a clear day
before him for seeing those whom he had to see, for his solid
work of writing, or for meeting his friends.[48]

47. On the appearance of Joseph's *Introduction to Logic* (1907) Dr
Keynes had written to his son: 'I began reading Joseph's *Logic*. I
thought that in the first chapter he put some points well: but in the
other chapters I have read it seems to me confusion of thought almost
from beginning to end. A good deal of it is not even worth serious
criticism. I agree with your pencilled comments.'

48. For an alternative way in which another great man, albeit of
far robuster constitution, conserved his energies, see *The Gathering
Storm*, by Mr Winston Churchill, p. 329.

Mr Duncan Grant recalls how, when he was sharing an apartment in London with Keynes, the telephone bell rang. He had a receiver by his bedside. It was still dark. He turned on the light and looked at his watch. It was 7 a.m. He took up the receiver.

VOICE: 'This is Margot Asquith. I want to speak to Mr Maynard Keynes.'

DUNCAN GRANT: 'I'm sorry; Maynard is still in bed; I do not think that I can disturb him.'

MARGOT ASQUITH: 'Well, tell Maynard Keynes from me that if he does not get up earlier than this, he will never get on in the world.'

On the occasion of the Oxford breakfast Keynes played his part and appeared punctually. A minute later Joseph came bustling into the room. 'I have been taking two pupils,' he said; 'I put on my nine o'clock pupils at 8.15, in order to breakfast here.'

But I had not the heart to raise the issue of Probability at the breakfast table. The conversation eventually turned towards the Social Credit theories of Major Douglas. Joseph gave an elaborate refutation. He, like Moore, had developed a style which purported to carry ordinary prose to the extreme limit of clarity and precision of expression. But there was a difference. Moore's style, for all its straining after precision, retains a certain flexibility and vitality, adapting itself to weak human nature, so that one can follow all the difficult twists and turns as they proceed. Joseph's style was more mechanical, and less thoughtful of his auditor. He had certainly, by long habit, acquired a facility for stating with a high degree of accuracy precisely what he meant to say. None the less, it was extremely difficult for the listener to apprehend what he meant. The sentences were often long and contained many subordinate clauses. They succeeded each other quickly. It was an astonishing *tour de force*. Polysyllables were avoided, and the sentences always seemed to end grammatically, as they should. One had the sense that, if only one could have each sentence before one and study it carefully for a long time, one would be able to apprehend its meaning, and that its meaning would be clear. But as his speech went rapidly forward, each sentence faded out into oblivion, and one realized that one would never grasp the thoughts that had been set before one. I do not know whether Keynes's abnormal powers of quick apprehension rose to this forbidding ordeal. At the end of Joseph's lengthy and elaborate refutation, Keynes summoned up his most gracious manner and leaning forward said: 'That is the most clear and admirable exposure of Major Douglas's fallacies that I have ever heard.'

Some time after that I met Alfred Whitehead. Keynes had been to him for advice. He had been hotly indignant at Joseph's article, and eager to rend him. Whitehead had strongly dissuaded him, on the ground that the article was so irrelevant as to be unworthy of his attention. No rejoinder was in fact written. Whitehead added that he had also had in mind that Joseph was 'really a silly man', and he recalled an incident which I knew already. When I was an undergraduate and secretary of a philosophical society,[49] I persuaded Whitehead, whom I had known since boyhood, to come up and read a paper to it. He consented with some reluctance, on the ground that the mocking atmosphere of Oxford disturbed those 'pieties' which he cherished. His paper gave rise to a discussion of 'relations'. A relation was one of those indefinables of which, according to Joseph, one had a direct understanding, and that understanding vouchsafed the information that a relation had two terms and two terms only. Whitehead insisted that a relation might have more than two terms. He cited the instance of the apices of a triangle. One could not specify the relation between two of the apices without also referring to the third apex, which thus constituted an essential ingredient in the relation. Joseph was obdurate. 'It was of the nature of a relation to have two terms only.' But why? 'If one understood what a

49. The Jowett Society.

relation was, one knew that it could only have two terms.'
Whitehead was disgusted. This was merely a 'silly man'.
Keynes was spared much trouble, for Joseph would undoubtedly have made a rejoinder, and, for all his failings,
had formidable powers as a controversialist. Thus Joseph's
obstinacy in regard to the two terms of a relation released a
considerable portion of Keynes's energies at his maturity for
the benefit of economics.

The only criticism which disturbed Keynes at this time
came from another quarter. There was an undergraduate at
Trinity, Cambridge, who had recently arrived from Winchester, the son, like Keynes, of a Cambridge don.[50] This
was Frank Ramsey.[51] Keynes quickly spotted him as a young
man of outstanding genius. Although he was still an undergraduate when the *Treatise* appeared, his criticism carried
more weight with Keynes than any other, and it is not clear
that Keynes felt that he had a satisfactory answer to it.[52]

After the publication of the *Treatise*, Keynes did not make
further contributions to logic. We may suppose that his interest continued. He proceeded to add the great classics of the
subject to his library, and he read more of what he bought
than most bibliophiles. I recall an incident towards the close
of his life. I was a member with him of an interdepartmental
committee on economic problems during World War II,
and had circulated a lengthy memorandum for the business of the day. He came into the room after I was seated,
and touched me on the shoulder as he passed my chair: 'I
am afraid that I have not had time to read your memorandum, but I have been reading your paper on Memory.'[53]

(A further account of the contents of the *Treatise* is given
in the Appendix to this volume.)

50. A. S. Ramsey, mathematician and Fellow of Magdalene College.
51. See Chapter 8 (5) below.
52. See Appendix to this volume.
53. This had recently appeared in *Mind*, January 1942.

# [4]

## Fellow of King's

### I

In 1908 economics at Cambridge had for long been dominated, and was for long to continue to be dominated, by the personality of Alfred Marshall. Keynes has himself supplied us with a brilliant account of his character, work and influence.[1] Marshall had qualities which fitted him for scientific leadership. His reading in his subject was very great, and the standard which he insisted upon for his own publications very high. His every sentence was carefully weighed and polished. He had a sense of responsibility and a consciousness of his own eminence, which made him give thorough judgement before pronouncing, as though he were indeed a wise monarch issuing decrees to his subjects. He was a fine theorist, and in his younger days spent much time in elaborating a mathematical framework; but, as we have seen, he did not confuse economic excellence with proficiency in manipulating symbols, and did full justice to the need for the study of institutions and to the difficulty of obtaining an understanding of their inner modes of operation. Hence his admiration for Keynes's early work in the field of money. Without sacrificing one scintilla of the requirement for truthful and impartial study, he was something of a diplomat in regard to the presentation of his work. He was anxious to make it acceptable to various types of reader, businessmen, labour leaders, etc., and, with this in view, at times

1. Obituary notice in the *Economic Journal*, September 1924, reprinted in *Memorials of Alfred Marshall*, edited by A. C. Pigou, publ. Macmillan, 1925: and in *Essays in Biography*, by J. M. Keynes, 1933.

tended to conceal the abstruse mathematics by which he achieved some of his results. For the general reader he made economics seem somewhat easier than it really was, although the students at Cambridge were made aware of the various pitfalls. Furthermore, he was extremely anxious to maintain the unity of the subject, both in time and place. He knew that economic controversies exposed it to the contempt of the ordinary man. He sought to find some good in various schools of thought and to preserve historical continuity, such as exists in the more developed sciences. In Cambridge, his leadership was paramount; on the whole his pre-eminence was recognized in Britain generally; and his reputation was worldwide. At Oxford, Professor F. Y. Edgeworth, an original economist of notable achievements, was his unqualified admirer.

While his work in pulling the subject together and establishing an authoritative text (his *Principles*) was of great value, his predominant position had disadvantages. In due course there became discernible some spirit of rebellion in London, or, one might say, of competition against his monopoly; this tradition may have accentuated controversy between Cambridge and London at a later date.

Marshall thought that the fundamental principles of the subject were now fixed beyond dispute, and that the next generation of economists would be free to concern themselves mainly with the application of these principles to all the bewildering variety of institutions and practices in the real world. On the whole, the Cambridge school, including Keynes, carried out this programme, Keynes devoting himself particularly to currency and banking questions. There were disadvantages in the Marshallian programme. The hold of a scientific system which consisted essentially of definitions and classifications, and contained no quantitative laws, was precarious. Such a system ought to be subjected to constant challenge, in the quest for still better classifications. There was something unnatural in the state of calm imposed by Marshall. The established system began to acquire an odour of sanctity, which was unhealthy. When Keynes, a quarter of a century later, proposed a reclassification in part of the field, he met with much opposition, not all of which was purely rational.

At the point of time with which we are concerned, Marshall had just been succeeded by Pigou. He withdrew from active participation in educational work at Cambridge; but his *Principles* and his monetary theories, embodied in evidence before successive Royal Commissions and in the lecture-notes of Cambridge pupils, continued to govern the thought of the place. Pigou was his disciple and favourite pupil. He was a man of wide interests, and had partaken in the keen discussions of the Dickinsonian circle about life and art and social welfare; he has to his credit publications on theism and on Browning. He had also been President of the Cambridge Union, where his speeches on the fiscal controversy were long remembered. There was more fire and passion in his oratory at this time than in that of Keynes, who tended to limit himself to the strict argument.

Pigou made a notable impression as professor. Tall, athletic, lucid and unadorned in his lecture manner, yet going very effectively to the heart of the subject, he created great confidence. What appealed above all were his simplicity and utter lack of affectation or of pomposity. He was friendly and talked with the young on terms of equality. He usually had some very close friends among the choice spirits, who would be taken with him during the vacations to share in the ardours of mountain climbing. In later years he gained the reputation among economists of being somewhat inaccessible. He was always ready to deal with specific difficulties, but did not much care for general economic discussion, still less for interviews with those who only came to him in a sightseeing spirit. I remember a letter from a Japanese student, whom I had permitted to attend my lectures. He had visited Cambridge with imperfect success. Pigou he had found away; the gate-keeper of Marshall's graveyard was also away, so that he could not obtain access to the grave;

but he had been lucky enough to have an hour's conversation with Mr D. H. Robertson. He was now on his way to Scotland, where he hoped to have better luck with Adam Smith than he had had with Marshall or Pigou. Pigou, had he been in Cambridge, would not have welcomed a visit of this character.

The first examination for the Economic Tripos (Part I) in Cambridge was in 1905; and the first Part II examination was in 1906. Numbers were small. Candidates for the two together rose from six in 1906 to twenty-five in 1910. W. E. Johnson lectured on advanced theory, Lowes Dickinson on political science, J. H. Clapham on the economic history of France and Germany, C. R. Fay on British economic history and general economics; H. O. Meredith was brought back to Cambridge, being given the Girdler's Lectureship in succession to Pigou, which he retained until he became professor at the Queen's University, Belfast, in 1911; Alston was then lecturing for those who took economics in the ordinary B.A. degree. A strong team, but a small one! To these were now added Walter Layton and Keynes. Layton lectured on the structure and problems of industry and on labour problems. His lectures were long remembered for their admirable grasp of actualities. In the Lent and Summer terms of 1909 Keynes lectured on Money, Credit and Prices, three times a week. He at once made a great impression. He was evidently a theorist; he expounded Marshallian monetary doctrine, which still had not much publicity outside the Cambridge classrooms. He was evidently also a realist. He abounded in the jargon of the market-place – arbitrage, backwardation, etc., but his explanations were in every case impeccably lucid. Theory was reinforced with massive illustrations. The question of gold production seemed then to be of the first importance, and most recondite information was brought forward on this topic. Even in his lectures on Principles, which he gave somewhat later, there was more factual illustration than is usual in such courses. He anticipated Schultz, although no doubt without his laborious research, by providing his class with the actual elasticity of the demand for sugar; he illustrated the theory of profit by detailed statistics from the cotton industry; copious figures were given on the export of capital. The lectures were animated and intriguing in their mode of delivery. He succeeded in conveying to his hearers that the theories he expounded really did apply to what was happening in the country. He seemed to be in close touch – although his contacts at this date were still slender – with business affairs. The outside world was brought vividly before the minds of the Cambridge class – and yet he was not merely a practical man; he was essentially a theorist manipulating Marshall's formulae on the blackboard.

All this was very exciting. Pigou, Layton, Keynes, supported on the peripheral subjects by the other distinguished men I have mentioned, certainly did succeed with their widely different styles of lecturing, in producing from this small class a notable group of economists who have become illustrious. The First Class lists in the Triposes in these years before 1914 included the names of D. H. Robertson, H. D. Henderson, G. Shove, F. Lavington, C. W. Guillebaud, P. Sargant-Florence, and – outside the ranks of professional economists – P. Noel-Baker.[2] Among those appearing in the first division of the Second Class was Hugh Dalton.

Keynes was a very busy lecturer throughout this period. During the last three years before 1914 he gave a course in every term twice a week on Principles. Pigou may have wished to give his young colleague a chance in this subject, or himself have become weary of repeating the same course year after year. We may give as an example of Keynes's activity his schedules in the two years 1911 to 1912 and 1913 to 1914; these were the busiest years, but the others little less so. In the Michaelmas term he lectured twice a week on

2. Professor of International Relations in the University of London from 1924 to 1929, Labour M.P. from 1929, Parliamentary Secretary to the Ministry of War Transport, 1942–5, and Cabinet Minister, 1945–50.

Principles, twice a week on the Theory of Money and once a week on Company Finance and the Stock Exchange; in the Easter (Summer) Term, he lectured twice a week on Principles, twice a week on Currency and Banking and once a week on the Money Market and the Foreign Exchanges. Earlier in 1911 he gave a course once a week on the currency and finance of India.

In this pre-war period he certainly went through the mill of hard university teaching.

2

By the end of November 1908 he had settled into his rooms in King's. He spent the first three weeks of December writing a paper on 'Recent Economic Events in India' for the *Economic Journal*.[3] This was a short time for the preparation of his first important appearance in print, but he was no doubt fortified by knowledge acquired at the India Office. The paper deals with the disturbances of 1907–8 and their relation to the management of the rupee. The reasoning was solid and the statistics used with caution. I do not think that there is anything in the paper of which he would have been ashamed thirty years later, although the technique of analysis is naturally different. Emphasis is placed on the inflationary effect of the inflow of foreign capital into India acting through the mechanism of the rupee issue. He regarded the currency system not as something that should be as automatic as possible, but as capable of being deliberately managed to obtain a desired result. 'The Indian Government have not yet hit on an ideal system, and they should not rest content with the knowledge that many of their newspaper critics are wide of the mark.' In the spring of 1909 he had a series of letters in the *Economist* of a statistical character, arguing that estimates of British investments in India were exaggerated, and that they were nearer £350 million than

3. March 1909.

the £500 million alleged.[4] He also had a letter in the *Economist* urging that even moderate tariff reform would involve a great loss to Britain in receipts from invisible exports.[5]

The social life of Cambridge proceeded.


### *J. M. Keynes to Duncan Grant*, 19 January 1909

... I delivered my lecture [his first lecture] this morning before an enormous and cosmopolitan audience – there must have been at least fifteen, I think, but a good many of them really had no business there, I am afraid, and I shall have to tell them that the lectures are not suitable to their needs ...

On Sunday at breakfast, Sheppard delivered an indictment on poor Rupert[6] for admiring Mr Wells and thinking truth beauty, beauty truth. Norton and Lytton took up the attack and even James and Gerald (who was there) stabbed him in the back. Finally Lytton, enraged at Rupert's defences, thoroughly lost his temper and delivered a violent personal attack.


### *J. M. Keynes to Duncan Grant*, 2 February 1909

What do you think – I have received today the offer of an appointment – to be representative of H.M.'s Government on the Permanent International Commission for Agriculture *at Rome*. Salary £500 increasing; duties practically *nil*. Shall I accept? Will you come with me if I do? Would *you* like the post? Nothing has happened today as I have been teaching the elements of economics since it began.

On Sunday Sheppard's salon continued until after 2 a.m. with himself, Gerald, Rupert, Master Birrell and me. An attack on Gerald, led by Rupert, for calling himself a Christian when he isn't one. Master B. had never seen a real set-to before and *loved* it, screaming with excitement.


4. The *Economist* newspaper, 27 February, 20 March, and 8 May 1909.

5. ibid. 2 February 1909.

6. Rupert Brooke.

*J. M. Keynes to Duncan Grant,* 10 February 1909

... The excitement of this place when combined with a good deal of work is enough to unhinge anyone and I really do not know how any of us last through the eight weeks of it ...

Last night MacCarthy appeared, bringing Hilaire Belloc with him, and Rupert gave a supper party from half-past ten to half-past one. The usual collection of people, Gerald, Master B., James, Daddy and me. Belloc is an astounding theatrical figure, and maintained a monologue for the whole three hours ...

In the Easter vacation he took fresh air with his family at Whitchurch, near Tavistock in Devon, playing golf with his father, and then had a fortnight at Versailles with Duncan Grant. In the course of this vacation he wrote an essay on Index Numbers, which won him the Adam Smith Prize. He may have felt that it was desirable to have some academic recognition of his skill as an economist, since he had not taken the Tripos. His work on Probability no doubt aided him in the Index Number problem.

*J. M. Keynes to Duncan Grant,* 10 May 1909

Oh, they've announced today that I have got the Adam Smith Prize, – £60 down, so Versailles more than paid its way ...

Tonight, instead of preparing a lecture I have been reading the examiners' criticisms on my essay. One of them, the Professor at Oxford,[7] and supposed to be the leading authority on the subject of the essay, seems to me *hopeless*. I feel *convinced* that I'm right on almost every point he attacks and that where my argument is novel he simply has not attended to it. His criticisms show a *closed* mind and I feel I could never convince him since he wouldn't ever properly attend to what I was saying ...

*J. M. Keynes to Duncan Grant,* 14 May 1909

Geoffrey [his brother] is an extraordinary fellow. The other day he wrote a very affectionate letter to Mr Henry James who's a total stranger to him, asking him to come and stay. Mr Henry James has accepted; in an enormous letter even more complicated

7. Professor F. Y. Edgeworth.

than a novel beginning 'Dear Geoffrey Keynes'. So he is coming
from a Friday to Tuesday at the end of the term.

My rooms are completely furnished now. The carpet is of a
delicious substance, but too pale perhaps – every mark is
shown . . .

*J. M. Keynes to Duncan Grant,* 24 May 1909

Mr Henry James has accepted my invitation to breakfast on
June 13th – he will be 'enchanted' to come . . .

Memories of that breakfast are rather painful. Norton,
James Strachey, Duncan Grant and Gerald Shove came and
talked volubly in their own idiom about their own subjects.
Henry James is said to have looked thoroughly flummoxed.[8]
When, after breakfast, Mr Desmond MacCarthy appeared
at the door his face lighted up with pleasure. Here at last
was someone who would have some contact with something
that he understood. He was anxious to know if Rupert
Brooke, the brilliant undergraduate, was a good poet and
consulted MacCarthy. The answer must have been rather
disparaging, for James is remembered to have said: 'Thank
goodness; if he looked like that and was a good poet too, I
do not know what I should do.'

In July Keynes was with his family again in the Pyrenees,
climbing. Then he took a house at Burford (Oxon), in order
to work peacefully on Probability. Friends came to stay in
relays – Swithinbank, James Strachey, Sheppard, Cecil
Taylor,[9] Humphrey Paul, Duncan Grant, his mother, and
his sister Margaret. He had this house again in the summer
of 1910.

8. An alternative version supplied by Mr MacCarthy from Henry
James's own account is that he, James, had to do all the talking,
while the young men showed no powers of response. 'It was like the
Meet of a Hunt, at which one had to provide the fox, the hounds and
the huntsman oneself.' By either account the breakfast was not a
success!

9. Subsequently a great schoolmaster, pillar of Clifton until 1948.

*J. M. Keynes to Duncan Grant*, 15 October 1909

... I seem to have spent most of my time seeing pupils. I have already got eighteen of these, which will be rather hard work, but ought to bring in nearly £60 ...

*J. M. Keynes to Duncan Grant*, 20 October 1909

... The work of the don is the hardest work in the world ...

*J. M. Keynes to Duncan Grant*, 24 October 1909

... The day before yesterday I founded a Political Economy Club for the undergraduates and am to give an opening presidential address on Wednesday week ... My private pupils have now risen to 24 in number. So work lies heavy on me ...

On 7 November 1909 he was able to tell his father that he was now drawing an income of £700 a year, including the £100 that his father gave him. In view of the small size of his basic salaries, and of the fees per pupil, he must have had to work extremely hard for this.

*J. M. Keynes to Duncan Grant*, 7 November 1909

... I shall probably examine the Mercers' Grammar School in Holborn in December ... It will take the whole of my time for five days, but will bring in £15 ...

In 1910 he was made Director of Studies for undergraduates reading economics in Trinity, and thereby became Mr D. H. Robertson's director.

In 1911 he was still grateful for small increments.

*J. M. Keynes to Dr J. N. Keynes*, 6 June 1911

I heard from Macaulay yesterday that the Council had appointed me to an annual lectureship in Economics with a stipend of £50. For this I am to lecture to members of the college free of charge and do any supervision if it is required. I think the terms are very generous.

The Political Economy Club referred to in the letter of 24 October developed into his Monday Evenings which became famous. They were already established in Robertson's undergraduate days and continued regularly every term, with an interruption for World War I, until 1937. By the advice of the directors of studies in economics in the various colleges, he selected from his own college and elsewhere a dozen or more undergraduates who were supposed to be the most promising. Other dons were also invited, but on a given evening there would not usually be more than one. A paper was read by one of the undergraduates. Lots were drawn and every member had to speak before the fireplace in the order determined by the drawing. Keynes himself summed up at the end. The use of lots appears to have had a vogue in Cambridge at this time. It was used at 'the Society' (which may have set the example), at Dickinson's Discussion Society, and at Keynes's Club. The practice is, I believe, unknown at Oxford. Does this indicate a greater cocksureness on the part of a typical Oxford undergraduate, always ready to get up on his legs? Or does it indicate a greater suavity of Oxford manners, a kind consideration for the shy man, who is allowed to remain shy until after a term or two he finds his feet without compulsion? [10] The following is Professor E. A. G. Robinson's account of the Club [11] in the period after World War I.

During those early post-war years it was through the Club that Keynes's influence was widest and most powerful. It was essentially an undergraduate club. Dons, both economist and others, who, like Richard Braithwaite or Frank Ramsey, were interested

10. This process of lot was even extended to a dining-club known as The Cranium, which met once a month between the two wars and consisted of 'Bloomsbury' (see below) and thereby mainly Cambridge men. Keynes was a member during the latter part of its existence. Lots were used to determine who should sit next to one another at dinner. I am informed, however, that it is no longer a common practice in Cambridge.

1. *Economic Journal*, March 1947.

in kindred problems, might come. If Keynes had a visitor, more particularly a visitor from abroad, he would bring him. But the papers in nine cases out of ten would be read by undergraduates or young research workers – in those days researchers in economics were few, their distinction from undergraduates unimportant, and the Ph.D. unknown. To the undergraduate of the early twenties, I can say from experience, Keynes's club was fascinating but alarming. Fascinating because here one heard Keynes, a large part of the Faculty, and all the best of one's rivals discussing in realistic detail all the real and most urgent problems of the world. Alarming because if one read a paper one was likely to find one's undergraduate efforts (I speak from painful memory) being dissected by a visiting Mr Hawtrey, destroyed by the full power of Frank Ramsey's dialectical analysis, and when one had maintained one's position to the best of one's ability, Keynes would sum up in friendly but utterly devastating fashion – I learned a certain sympathy with the prisoner waiting for the judge's black cap. Alarming also because if it was not one's turn to read the paper, one must draw a number from the hand of the Secretary, and take one's turn on the hearthrug to discuss a paper on a subject about which one might well feel an embarrassing ignorance in the presence of some of the most critical minds of Europe. But a wonderful training, because in Keynes's presence there were certain forms of nonsense that one did not enjoy perpetrating once, and remembered for life not to perpetrate a second time.

Through his Club, Keynes knew intimately right down to his illness in 1937 all the best of each generation of Cambridge economists, and exercised a more personal influence upon them than anyone else. The very great influence of Professor Pigou on the whole technique of Cambridge economic thought in our generation was of a rather different character – exercised less personally and more through his writings and lectures. And through the Club we insensibly acquired certain elements in Keynes's own approach to the problems of economics. In the early years his interests were almost wholly in the practical problems of economic policy. I can remember very few papers on purely theoretical issues, though we covered a very wide range of questions. The choice was mainly our own, made in consultation with the undergraduate Secretary, but our tastes were in some measure the consequence of his.

I will only add to this account two impressions of my own.[12] One must imagine Keynes very cosily arranged in the corner of the sofa beside the fireplace, his legs outstretched, his hands tucked into his cuffs, on his face an expression of kindly interest. One might know that ruthless criticism would come in due course; but for the time being one had the impression that he was eager to hear what one had concocted, and that he was essentially one's friend, covering one with his support and protection. Then in the summing up, it was not only the criticism – which might not always be fierce – that was 'devastating'; it was also the extraordinary range and variety of knowledge that he invariably displayed in relation to the subject of the paper. Here one had worked away for two or three weeks, studying the special literature, and then Keynes, without preparation and out of his own stock, seemed to know so very much more, whatever the subject might be. That set a standard, too high indeed for most of us.

In addition to these heavy teaching duties, he already had in this early period some administrative work. In 1910 he was elected to the 'Special Board for Economics and Politics', and in the autumn of that year he was made Secretary of the Board, which he remained until the end of 1914. Thus with his father in the Chair, the Keyneses might be said to have Cambridge Economics in their pocket!

His examining duties in Holborn in the following December[13] were the occasion of his making a better arrangement for a permanent footing in London. He took two rooms in 21 Fitzroy Square, which he shared with Duncan Grant, the latter using one room as a studio and Keynes the other for a bedroom when he wished to visit London. Duncan Grant lived with his family at Hampstead. During the examination Keynes had to work hard at the papers, but went one evening to a party.

12. Formed during my visit to Cambridge in 1922; cf. ch. 8, 5.
13. cf. p. 174 above.

*J. M. Keynes to Mrs Keynes*, 18 December 1909

At midnight yesterday I went with some friends to a fancy dress supper party (clad as a cook) – when who, to my immense surprise, should enter but Geoffrey! – clad as an ancient Briton. Then on the top of Max Beerbohm, Will Rothenstein, Wilson Steer, and all the other artists, in came a whole train of them – Gwen and Margaret Darwin,[14] Ka Cox,[15] Karin Costelloe, Justin,[16] Rupert, Jacques,[17] all in the most ornate garments. I was never more astonished. Had you heard anything about it? At two o'clock in the morning they were gallivanting in the streets of London as dead leaves before the West Wind.

This winter there was a General Election, consequent upon the rejection of Lloyd George's Budget by the House of Lords. Keynes wrote a long letter to the *Cambridge Daily News* on the Liberal side.[18] In January he went to support his old Eton and Cambridge friend, Edward Hilton Young (Lord Kennet, brother of Geoffrey Young), who was standing as a Liberal for East Worcester. Headquarters were in Birmingham.

*J. M. Keynes to Mrs Keynes*, 8 January 1910

It's a good thing that I came yesterday as on my arrival I found a note saying that I must at once make my way to The Shelter, Blackwell, about 12 miles from here and address a meeting. I got on all right, but shall feel more at home tonight, I expect.

J. M. Keynes
Fellow of King's College, Cambridge

is billed to speak somewhere every night.

The rural districts are solid Liberal, but are swamped unfortunately by the outlying parts of Birmingham.

I am going to enjoy myself very much, I think ...

14. Daughters of Sir George Darwin, afterwards Mrs Raverat and Mrs Geoffrey Keynes.
15. Afterwards Mrs Will Arnold-Forster.
16. Justin Brooke – no relation of Rupert, the poet.
17. Jacques Raverat.
18. 24 December 1909.

### J. M. Keynes to G. L. Strachey, 14 January 1910

I've been enjoying myself here enormously, but am leaving tomorrow. Life without a howling audience to address every evening will seem very dull. Have you any picture in your mind of Birmingham and its inhabitants?

The Easter Vacation brought very different scenes, when he visited Greece and Constantinople with Duncan Grant. In the summer, after a visit to Mrs Berenson at Oxford, with all the comfort and luxury of it, he had some money-making toil at Hammersmith in London:

### J. M. Keynes to Duncan Grant, 10 July 1910

There is an unexpected vacancy to do in Hammersmith what I did last December in Holborn, and for the sake of £15 I have agreed to go. As it's the largest centre in England, I shall get no times off and will have to sit there daily from 9.30 till 8 ...

Then more work on Probability at Burford. Some of last year's visitors reappeared, and also Daniel Macmillan and Frankie Birrell. In the midst of this, to refresh himself, he made a bicycling tour over the Berkshire downs and further westward.

In the later part of this year he became involved in a fierce controversy with Karl Pearson. He published the review of a study made by Miss Elderton, assisted by Karl Pearson, on the influence of parental alcoholism on offspring.[19]

The authors had inferred from a sample the absence of malign influence. Keynes questioned the sufficiency of the sample, and held that the logic of the arguments was imperfect. His mind was no doubt already full of the pitfalls of statistical inference. His review ended with the words: 'As a contribution to the solution of the general problem the memoir is almost valueless, and, from its failure to direct the reader's attention to essential facts, actually misleading. As a study in statistical method it is a salient example of the application of a needlessly complex mathematical apparatus

19. *Journal of the Royal Statistical Society*, July 1910.

to the initial data, of which the true character is insufficiently explained, and which are in fact unsuited to the problem in hand.' Meanwhile Alfred Marshall broke his 'almost absolute rule against controversial correspondence' by writing to *The Times*.[20] The persuasive power of Marshall's arguments is rather spoilt, for later readers, by his shocked tone. Pearson was stung, and replied in a pamphlet entitled *The Influence of Parental Alcoholism on the Physique and Ability of the Offspring: A Reply to the Cambridge Economists.* Keynes made a rejoinder in a letter which seemed devastating;[21] but Pearson had some defence,[22] and Keynes made a final reply,[23] more judicial now, in the grand manner, maintaining his original position that Pearson's sample and methods were inadequate.

The controversy meanwhile had become widespread. Dr Mary Sturge and Sir Victor Horsley produced a pamphlet. Keynes made a clever use of those of their arguments which were good. Pigou joined in the fray with a short article,[24] restating the main Cambridge position in most carefully worded sentences, as though cautiously picking his steps among burning cinders.

Keynes showed his brilliant powers as a controversialist; his style was delightful; he had rapier thrusts and plenty of jokes and nuances of phrase, making Pearson look very foolish, more foolish than he was. While Keynes had good points, it is not apparent that Pearson was completely in the wrong.[25]

In the issue of the *Journal of the Royal Statistical Society* in which Keynes's last letter appeared, there was also a note by him on 'The Principal Averages and the Laws of Error which lead to them'.

20. 7 July, 2 August, and 19 August 1910.
21. *Journal of the Royal Statistical Society*, December 1910.
22. ibid. January 1911.
23. ibid. February 1911.
24. *Westminster Gazette*, 2 February 1911.
25. Keynes made a very brusque attack in the *Treatise on Probability* on some of Pearson's work on Probability.

Keynes was also involved in the second General Election of 1910.

*J. M. Keynes to Duncan Grant,* 6 December 1910

Nothing has happened here except a General Election. It occupies our tongues appallingly and we go to the Union every night to cheer the results, – where it appears that all Tories have bass voices and all Liberals tenor. Last night I spoke at a very enthusiastic meeting for Montagu – at Histon, where Chivers makes his jams. The audience was entirely male and very much excited in our favour – so I found it most exciting to address them ...

He had maintained his interest in India. We find him writing a spirited letter in protest against disparaging remarks about the Indian students at Cambridge.[26]

*J. M. Keynes to Duncan Grant,* 24 October 1909

The reason I couldn't come this morning was the appearance of an embassy from the India Office to discuss Indian prices and currency. Professor Marshall and I and the ambassadors have just completed a six hours' discussion of the question. I found it extremely interesting, but it has left me rather exhausted ...

In 1910 he was writing to the India Office to point out errors in the statistics of the *Indian Trade Journal*. He maintained a correspondence with Mr Lionel Abrahams of the India Office with whom he saw eye to eye on many points concerning the rupee. In the spring of 1911, he wrote a paper on the Indian Currency Question, which is the first manifestation of his path-breaking capacity as an economist. It was read to the Royal Economic Society at its *quarterly* meeting – those were arduous days – on 9 May 1911; it was printed in India for circulation to those in the Government of India who were concerned, but it was not published. It contains the essence of the ideas that were developed in his volume published two years later.

26. *Cambridge Review*, 17 May 1909.

*Extract from Paper on the Indian Currency Question*

I will endeavour to give reasons for thinking that this existing system to which the name of *Gold Exchange Standard* has been given, is something much more civilized, much more economical and much more satisfactory than a gold currency. I should like to see it openly established in India on a permanent basis and all talk of an eventual gold currency definitely abandoned.

The Government of India has been the first to adopt the Gold Exchange Standard on a large scale. But every year there are fresh converts; nor will it be long before it becomes, in effect, the standard of half the world. And out of it, in my belief, will be evolved the ideal currency of the future . . .

The following is interesting in view of his subsequent opinions.

Time has dealt satisfactorily with what were originally the two principal grounds of criticism : – First, that the new system was unstable; and second, that a depreciating currency is advantageous to a country's trade.

The reasons for these opinions were marshalled with great clarity and succinctness.

His reputation as an economist was growing. In April 1911 his father, Dr Keynes, was elected to an Honorary Fellowship of his old college, Pembroke. Alfred Marshall wrote to congratulate him.

*Alfred Marshall to Dr J. N. Keynes,* 28 April 1911

Among your many honours, there is perhaps none greater than that of being the father of J. M. Keynes.

In the Easter Vacation he was with Duncan Grant in Tunis and Sicily, and paid a visit to Settignano on his way back. The house at Burford was not resumed that summer. For part of the vacation he was in Cambridge working hard at German treatises on Probability. He also went and spent some time under canvas near Moreton Hampstead in Devon in a camp organized by Justin Brooke, where the Olivier sisters,[27] Virginia Stephen, Rupert Brooke, Maynard's brother Geoffrey, and other congenial spirits were present.

In the second half of September he went on a grand Liberal tour of Ireland, organized by the 'Eighty Club' (15–30 September).

### J. M. Keynes to G. L. Strachey, 20 September 1911

This Irish affair is proving extraordinarily interesting – in Dublin, especially, it was an experience of another life. But they work us to death and my constitution has already completely crumbled . . .

### J. M. Keynes to Duncan Grant, 3 October 1911

It is now a week since I left the Eighty Club. The affair was very interesting, but a point came when I could support crowd life no longer and when I felt as if I should go mad if I heard another speech. So I left Gerald to whirl on with them and deserted. You have not, I suppose, ever mixed with politicians at close quarters. They are *awful*. I think some of these must have been dregs anyhow, but I have discovered, what previously I didn't believe possible, that politicians behave in private life and say exactly the same things as they do in public. Their stupidity is inhuman. The most decent people were the *Morning Post* reporter . . . and a charming old peer called Lord Saye and Sele. There were one or two others, whose characters were not particularly sympathetic to me, but were really all right. The rest of them had minds and opinions as deplorable as their characters . . . Oh, I forgot Mrs Max Muspratt, a middle-aged lady whom I found very sympathetic and who thoroughly agreed with me about the rest of the company. Our progress through Ireland was of the nature of a royal procession. We travelled in a private saloon train and were received everywhere with addresses (we must have received thirty or forty), illuminations, and bands playing 'Rule Britannia' and 'God save Ireland'. I'd a good many very interesting conversations with local notabilities . . .

Ireland is almost entirely made up of undulating grass lands, hedged and walled into small fields, and of a great deal of water, lakes and rivers. The fields are richly green, the air is soft and the

27. Daughters of Sir Sidney (Lord) Olivier.

whole thing very charming, especially in the evening light. The trees and the country have a much richer, warmer colour than in England, but there is no arable whatever. Yet I think England is preferable – a great part of Ireland seems to me unexpectedly to lack mystery and not to make up for this by peacefulness. Galway and Aran (and I dare say Connemara where I didn't go) are a great exception to this. Galway town is very romantic and the Aran Islands, though I didn't stay there long enough to get a quite clear impression, obviously wonderful. The coast and the sea reminded me both of Greece and of the Orkneys, and Aran itself is a bare stony upland of the same material as Syracuse. It was very strange and interesting and the people fine and healthy instead of rather mean looking as so many of the children and men of Ireland are ... Here [Glengarriff, County Cork] I am in the regular tourist part of the country. Islands, hills, sea, lakes, streams, woods and open country inextricably mixed up together, and I suppose it's beautiful. But this too seems quite lacking in mystery and is exactly what the hotel keeper, having the best taste of his class, would have created. Although the country is wild and almost uninhabited, I feel as if Queen Victoria and the Prince Consort must some time about 1850 have unveiled it and declared it open ...

## 3

Probability was nearing completion and events were drawing him inexorably away from logic to economics. In the autumn of this year he was offered, and accepted, the editorship of the *Economic Journal*, which his father had refused twenty-one years before. It was a great honour for one so young, who had published little. Marshall's strong support was no doubt crucial. An editorial committee was appointed, but it is not supposed that it had much occasion to interfere. He retained the editorship for thirty-three years, when he was succeeded by the author of this volume. But from 1919 onwards he had a joint editor.[28] In 1913 Keynes also became

28. Edgeworth, who had been editor from 1890 to 1911, was brought back to a joint-editorship in 1919, when Keynes was busy peacemaking. Edgeworth was succeeded as joint editor by Professor D. H. MacGregor in 1926 and he by Professor E. A. G. Robinson in 1934.

Secretary to the Royal Economic Society. And for a large part of thirty-three years he successfully managed its finances, with the goodwill of Mr Alfred Hoare, who was officially the Honorary Treasurer until 1937. The affairs of the Society prospered exceedingly.

On taking over, he discovered heavy arrears. Edgeworth often found it difficult to make up his mind. Among articles which had long been waiting for a verdict was one by the famous and formidable Archdeacon Cunningham. It was embarrassing for a young man to reject work by one so eminent, but he grasped the nettle firmly. Thereafter he would not allow any accumulation; if there was no more room in the next issue, he refused. He maintained the tradition of having some contributions from persons outside the academic field and of combining realistic with more theoretical studies. Indeed, Edgeworth, oddly enough, had been very inhospitable to purely theoretical work from any pen other than his own, and Keynes, with so many more contacts outside the academic world than Edgeworth ever had, judged it necessary to redress the balance in favour of academic theorists.

Keynes performed his duties with the minimum of fuss. On retiring he explained that his only apparatus was one drawer in his desk for his papers and some porcupine clips to hold them in bundles. Through this economy in overheads, the Society had flourished. But if he was economical in expenditure, he was lavish in the time that he devoted to contributors. He often sent comments of many pages on articles submitted, both when he accepted and when he rejected. In the latter case, especially with younger writers, he explained his objections at great length. In the former case he suggested improvements, and many articles were re-submitted several times before their final appearance. Authors were usually grateful in the end for this editorial insistence on their perfecting their work.[29] Great as the pressure of his

29. An egoistic footnote may perhaps be allowed to the author who was on one occasion injured by Keynes's zeal. During 1928 I sub-

other business finally became, Keynes maintained this habit. He esteemed his editorship as an occupation having the highest claim.

The Easter Vacation found him at Beaulieu, on the Riviera, with Gerald Shove. He also went on a riding expedition with Mr Archibald Rose, setting out from Salisbury. Mr Rose recalls how they arrived one Sunday morning at Wells, not too late for church. They entered the cathedral shyly, as they were much bespattered with mud, and, to their consternation, the verger showed them to a front pew. The preacher was Dr Hensley Henson.[30] The main theme of his discourse was that the resurrection of Jesus Christ was not a physical fact. There was much murmuring among the good ladies of Wells on the Green, and Rose himself was a little upset. He recalls how Keynes consoled him that evening. Settled in his easy chair, with his gentle smile and comforting expression, as of one who had knowledge of deep mysteries – 'You must not be upset,' he said; 'this fellow has thought deeply about these matters; he has been reading and studying all the time that you have been on the far

---

mitted a short article, setting out what I called the 'increment of aggregate demand curve'. Keynes showed this to F. P. Ramsey who raised objections. Being in poor health at the time, and heavily burdened with college duties, I was discouraged and put the article away in a drawer for eighteen months. I then took the matter up with Ramsey, who was an old friend, and he recanted. The article was re-submitted and appeared in June 1930. Mathematical demonstration was supplied in December 1931. Mrs Robinson, at the suggestion of Professor E. A. G. Robinson, rechristened the 'increment of aggregate demand curve' 'the marginal revenue curve'. This now appears in most textbooks of economics. Mrs Robinson gave recognition to my publication in the preface to her *Economics of Imperfect Competition*, and referred there to other economists who independently had the same idea. Study of her preface indicates that if Keynes had not listened so readily to Ramsey's criticisms and the article had appeared in 1928, my claim to have 'invented' this well-known tool of economics would be without challenge.

30. Afterwards the Bishop of Hereford, 1918–20, and Bishop of Durham, 1920–39.

frontiers of empire; he knows what he is talking about; you can trust him; it is quite all right.'

In the course of their riding they put in at the Crown Hotel, Everleigh, a delightful village on the edge of Salisbury Plain. Keynes was so pleased with it that he formed the plan of taking over the whole place for himself and his friends in the summer holidays. This was not possible in August, but he had the whole house for July and a number of rooms reserved for August. Thither many of his friends came – Duncan Grant, Sheppard, Gerald Shove, Frankie Birrell, Dilly Knox, Rupert Brooke, the Olivier sisters, Katherine Cox, Archibald Rose, Chester Purves, Justin Brooke, Ferenc Békássy, G. H. Luce, and Maynard's brother Geoffrey. Many looked back to this as a delightful holiday, a high spot in the days before 1914. Keynes preserved the collective poems and collective drawings composed during the evenings. Luce was a poet and a great friend during these years. Keynes afterwards financed the publication of his poems through Macmillan's. But Luce eventually followed Swithinbank eastwards and taught English at the University of Rangoon.

Békássy was an undergraduate of King's who made a mark in Cambridge. After Everleigh, Keynes paid a visit to his parents, who lived in feudal splendour near Budapest. On the way home he made a stay in Vienna, which was entirely to his taste.

In the autumn of this year we first hear of a figure, Keynes's interest in whom had far-reaching effects – Ludwig Wittgenstein, an Austrian philosopher of great genius. Having studied engineering for a period at Manchester, he came to Cambridge, where he was attracted to Bertrand Russell's lectures on Mathematical Logic. A great friendship eventually sprang up with Russell, but the friendship with Keynes was in some ways more important. Wittgenstein had something of the waywardness of genius, and was not naturally inclined to follow the conventional path of an academic career. Keynes was fascinated. His love of the unusual and the exciting, his sympathetic understanding and his capacity for friendship came into play. There was Keynes the thinker, the writer, the man of business, Keynes the omnicompetent; but there was also Keynes who was the student of character in all its forms, the undergraduate friend of Strachey and his friends, with his uncanny insight and sage sympathy. He was thus able to have some influence on Wittgenstein in his practical life, and he was always his advocate. He played some part in securing Wittgenstein's return to Cambridge after World War I, during which he had done duty in Austria as a soldier and a schoolteacher. At Cambridge he became a Fellow of Trinity and eventually Professor of Philosophy. He exerted a dominating influence over the younger generation of philosophers, and his influence even extended to Oxford, breaking down, from a distance, the entrenchments of the older schools of thought there.

### J. M. Keynes to Duncan Grant, 12 November 1912

Wittgenstein is a most wonderful character – what I said about him when I saw you last is quite untrue – and extraordinarily nice. I like enormously to be with him.

It was a satisfaction to Keynes to be able to settle the details of an allowance of £200 a year given anonymously by this new friend, Wittgenstein, to his old friend and philosophical mentor, W. E. Johnson, in order to enable the latter to cut down his teaching commitments and have more time for research.

It is normal for young fellows of colleges, after finding their feet, to feel growing discontent with the way in which their seniors manage affairs. And so it was at King's. A number of those, who had been elected recently, began to form a group in order to promote change. The principal members were F. E. Adcock, Charles Webster, Dillwyn Knox and A. E. Dobbs. They styled themselves the Young Turks, and it is even recalled that at a council of war held before a College meeting, one of them arrived masked, to underline the conspiratorial nature of the occasion. Keynes, who had begun to form his own opinions about the College finances, was glad to have the support of a semi-organized bloc of votes, while the group on its side welcomed the leadership of such an admirable spokesman. He felt that the College was not making the best use of its resources and that developments were held up through excessive conservatism. College bursars are apt to tuck away surpluses in order to obviate extravagant expenditure.

Although the revolt seemed to be running on normal lines, it was pregnant with great things; for Keynes was eventually to revolutionize the finances of the College. In 1911 he was made a member of the Estates Committee and an Elector to Fellowships. Matters remained on the boil for some time. The great explosion occurred in the autumn of 1912. Keynes moved three motions. One attacked the maintenance of large cash balances. This, although frowned upon by the authorities, was carried. The next asked for a Committee to consider the integration of the Kitchen, Buttery, and Combination Room departments in the matter of contracts and prices, and to inquire into the conditions of the employment of staff.[31] This too was carried and Keynes was appointed to the Committee. But it was the third motion which really shook the College. Keynes proposed an increase in Fellowship dividends from £120 to £130 a year. This was revolutionary indeed. It implied lack of confidence in the Bursar who advised the College as to the amount of Fellowship 'dividend' that could be paid. The motion was decisively beaten, but many were left wondering what might be in store. The older members were not completely obdurate. At the same meeting Keynes was elected to 'the Council' which in effect governed the College. And in the following year he was made a member of the committee to consider a letter of resignation from the Bursar. It was no doubt in consequence of the agitation that an assistant bursar was appointed in the following year.

31. cf. his concern for the staff at the Union seven years earlier.

Some time during the course of 1912 he began work on *Indian Currency and Finance*, which was completed early in 1913. This is, by common agreement, a work of first-rate quality. Those who were unconvinced by his later writings, all of which were controversial, like to acclaim it as his best book. The second chapter (on the Gold Exchange Standard) is of general interest, quite apart from the rupee problem, and has become a classic. The book well manifests Keynes's characteristic powers and tendencies. It is the work of a theorist, giving practical application to those esoteric monetary principles which Marshall had expounded and Keynes was explaining in the Cambridge classrooms, and at the same time it showed an outstanding gift for penetrating the secrets of how institutions actually work. His India Office experience and the contacts, which he had maintained, no doubt helped him; but these would have been of no value without his peculiar power of insight. It also displayed his thoroughness in amassing all available information.

Its main thesis was to develop the ideas in the paragraphs from his Royal Economic Society paper which I have cited. In this book, as in all his works, whether on domestic unemployment or international monetary institutions, Keynes appears as a man of expedients, full of plans for modifying arrangements in this way or that, in order to produce a better result; but, unlike most men of expedients, he always related his projects closely to the fundamental theory of the subject. It was not in vain that he had imbibed in his early youth the late Victorian respect for first principles.

In the past those who were keenly aware of the complexities of the economic system as a whole had tended to shun particular expedients and to incline towards *laissez-faire*. Keynes had the courage to go ahead, believing that despite the interlocked nature of the system and the ramifying effects of particular interferences, it was possible to make improvements. He was a currency expert, believing in the importance of the currency question. One feels in these pages his sense that currency reform could contribute much towards making India a happier country. And at the same time he had his eye upon wider questions. Might not Indian currency reform be an example for adoption elsewhere? Although a close adherent of traditional economic theory, he clearly thought that its proponents took too facile a view about how long-run beneficent forces operate through particular institutions. Having stated certain general monetary principles they would then cite the detailed working of the British Money Market and Foreign Exchange Market, to show how these forces worked in practice. But Keynes – and this kind of point reappears in other writings – argued that the British Gold Standard worked as smoothly as it did, not because of the very nature of a gold standard, but because of the unique position of the London Money Market in the world. This has now become a commonplace, but it was a novelty, anyhow among monetary theorists, at the time.

He was mainly concerned with advocating a gold exchange standard for India and similar countries. He opposed those who wished for a gold currency, the reactionaries, and brought to bear his powers of incisive argument and satire. In one passage (page 101) he hints that the time may not be far distant when we shall be ready to put something better in place of the Gold (including the Gold-Exchange) Standard itself.

He negotiated with Macmillan's for publication, at the same time transferring the *Treatise on Probability* from the Cambridge University Press to them. At this early period he began to work on lines which were afterwards to prove advantageous to him, by persuading Macmillan's to share profit with him in respect of both the volumes, on a fifty-fifty basis. *Indian Currency* continued to sell in good quantity for some ten years; about 4,900 copies had been sold by mid-1942, on which he realized £295. Before *Probability* appeared, he had, for reasons which will be described, gone over to a full profit basis; some 3,500 copies had been sold by mid-1942, and no less than £952 realized by him.

In the spring of 1913 came the pleasant news that his

sister Margaret was engaged to be married to Archibald Vivian Hill, Fellow of Trinity College and physiologist of rising repute. In the Easter Vacation Keynes took an even longer journey than usual and went off to visit his old friend Robin Furness in Egypt.

While there he received a communication of great interest. A Royal Commission had been appointed to inquire into Indian Finance and Currency and he was invited to be its secretary. His time in the India Office was yielding a dividend! But there was one difficulty. His book had not yet appeared. Would its publication be prejudiced? He telegraphed back to inquire. Lionel Abrahams had a proof and could show it to those concerned.

*Telegram from Sir William Holderness to J. M. Keynes,*
  3 April 1913

Am instructed to offer you seat on Commission. This is considered in view of book more suitable than secretaryship and will give greater scope. Hope you will accept.

This was a great honour for a young man of twenty-nine. He consented to serve, and wrote to Mr Austen Chamberlain, who was Chairman, to obtain an official clarification.

*Austen Chamberlain to J. M. Keynes,* 21 April 1913

... The selection of the Commission was entirely a matter for Lord Crewe. He knew before he proposed your name to the King that you were publishing this book and told me that he had seen the proofs and thought that the character of the book and its subject were a qualification and your method of treating the subject no bar to your appointment. In these circumstances, you are at liberty to publish it ... It is possible that you might wish to modify a phrase here or there, but of this, you should be the sole judge.

Very civilized!

Indian currency had been a vexed question ever since the world abandoned bimetallism in 1873. India left the Silver

Standard in 1893. The Fowler Commission, the second of two within a decade, reported in 1899 that the authorities should take orderly steps directed towards the eventual establishment in India of a gold standard of the British type, with gold currency. Actually, things did not so work out. A somewhat different system was evolved, by *ad hoc* administrative measures adapted to meet particular situations as they arose. The system, thus developed, resembled much more closely a plan put forward to the Fowler Commission by Mr A. M. Lindsay.

There had been a serious crisis in 1907–8. There were various uncertainties and ambiguities in the situation and, since the Fowler recommendations were clearly obsolete, the time seemed ripe for a new survey. Public opinion was more interested in the sale of some silver by the Government of India to a well-known firm of bankers, which was said, without foundation, to have been given the business through favouritism, and even through a family connection. This occurred in the autumn of 1912 and was clearly an admirable matter for Press comment and Parliamentary question. It probably precipitated the appointment of a new Commission.

Keynes had a twofold task. In the first place he had to convince the Commission of his view, already expressed in the paper to the Royal Economic Society and his book, that actual developments had been in the right direction and that the system, by now known as the gold exchange standard, was superior to an old-fashioned full gold standard. We do not know if this task was difficult; anyhow, it was successfully achieved. Chamberlain scrupulously refrained from reading Keynes's book, except for the first two chapters of it, since he wished to give an unbiased lead to the deliberations of the Commission. Only when the trend of opinion had become clear did he do so.

*Austen Chamberlain to J. M. Keynes*, 12 August 1913

I scarcely know whether to congratulate you on it or condole with myself! You will certainly be considered the author of the

Commission's report whenever that document sees the light. I am amazed to see how largely the views of the Commission as disclosed by our informal discussions are a mere repetition of the arguments and conclusions to which your study had previously led you . . .

Although there were difficulties ahead, the progress thus revealed seemed satisfactory.

Keynes's second task was to procure a distinct advance. The possibility of doing so seemed to him to be centred upon the establishment of what was called a State bank. (This must not be taken to be synonymous with a Nationalized bank.) Mr E. A. Hambro had added a note to the report of the Fowler Commission recommending this. His proposal had been favourably considered, both by the India Office and by the Government of India in the following years, but there were serious obstacles which inhibited action. In his annual speech to the Midland Bank, Sir Edward Holden, its Chairman, had reopened the question (24 January 1913). Later *The Times* had a weighty article on the subject (14 March 1913). Mr Lionel Abrahams, Keynes's India Office friend and correspondent, who had been head of the financial department and maintained his interest in its business when he was promoted to be Assistant Under-Secretary, put a memorandum before the Commission in favour of a State bank. The Commission assigned to Sir Ernest Cable and Keynes the holiday task of preparing a draft proposal. Keynes had some consultations with Cable, but it seems that he did the main part of the work himself. He did not succeed in persuading the Commission to incorporate it in its report. Important witnesses had already been examined and it was thus too late to get their views. Some felt that a visit to India would be necessary, if the Commission was to give its authority to such a far-reaching proposal. Although this draft was not incorporated, it was published as an annexe, and received a very good blessing in the report. The Secretary of State and the Government of India were urged to appoint a small, expert committee to inquire into the matter without delay and either reject the proposal or put forward a concrete scheme for the authorities to act upon.

This annexe by Keynes may well be deemed more interesting than the report itself. He had to tackle some very thorny problems. There was the question of the relation of the Government to the Bank. He was eager that the Bank should have a large measure of independence and envisaged its capital as private. But the Government was to have a part to play in making appointments and an eventual share of profits, when these exceeded a certain amount. More difficult was the possibility of jealousy and friction among the three great Presidency banks and the Exchange banks. Tact was necessary, and Keynes showed his cunning. There would be difficulties if one of the Presidency banks (presumably the Bank of Bengal) was elevated into being the State bank. Keynes hit upon a scheme not unlike the projected Federal Reserve System; there was to be a Central Board and the three Presidency banks were to become the three 'head offices' of the new Bank. It does not appear that Keynes looked to America for guidance – it was hardly a place to which one would look for banking wisdom at that time; there are signs that he made a closer study of Continental banking developments – but there is a footnote pointing out the parallel with American proposals. The annexe was not only concerned with constitutional matters but also gave him scope to elaborate more fully his ideas of currency management. He argued that in due course it would be desirable to develop in India a more extended money market and bank-rate control.

One certainly has the sense that in this fine essay Keynes was thinking not only in terms of immediate exigencies, but of a system that would slowly grow to maturity. This bank, in its initial form, would merely be a starting-point. By successive stages the Indian economy would surely develop into a more complex and mature organism. What is equally striking is the moderation of the young enthusiast as regards the immediate benefits he claimed for his system. This was no crank advocating a panacea. It was as though he already had the wisdom acquired by long experience of the intractable difficulties in human relations. There was a certain unity about his life's work. Here he was, just reaching thirty years of age, making the draft of a monetary plan that might be the beginning of a great advance in the development of the Indian economy. And there he was, thirty years later, doing similar work for a greater organism at Bretton Woods.

In fact, India only achieved her central bank (Reserve Bank of India) after the interruption of World War I and after two more Commissions had deliberated.

*Alfred Marshall to J. M. Keynes*, 3 March 1914

I dipped in here and there, and then read the conclusions: and finally turned negligently to the Annexe. But that held me. I had had no idea you had written it. Much of it, as of the Report itself, deals with matters beyond my knowledge and judgement. But there is quite enough of it within my understanding for me to have been entranced by it as a prodigy of constructive work. Verily, we old men will have to hang ourselves, if young people can cut their way so straight and with such apparent ease through such great difficulties ...

Meanwhile, after the summer there was still heavy work to be done. On the day after the last evidence was given Keynes had dinner with the Chamberlains.

*J. M. Keynes to Mrs Keynes*, 20 December 1913

The Commission is very nearly finished now, and most of the Report is in its final form. The last three days have been about the most exacting to character and intellect that I have ever been through and I feel rather a wreck, – wishing very much that I was off to the South of France for an immediate holiday. We sat for seven hours a day, and one had to be drafting amendments at top speed and perpetually deciding within thirty seconds whether other people's amendments were verbal and innocent or substantial and to be rejected. I must say that Austen came out

of the ordeal very well, and I believe he may yet be Prime Minister – I don't suppose on the purely intellectual score that he is
any stupider than Campbell-Bannerman ...

Before Christmas the Commission decided that only two
more days would be needed, and 12 and 13 January were
fixed. Keynes went off after Christmas with Duncan Grant
to stay at Roquebrune on the Riviera.

*J. M. Keynes to Mrs Keynes*, 3 January 1914

Just as I was to start yesterday for home I was smitten down by
a somewhat bad attack of tonsilitis – temperature 103° and so
forth. I am being very kindly nursed by Mrs Rendel, Madame
Bussy's sister. Today I had a French doctor from Mentone who
describes it as a bad 'quinsy' but certainly nothing worse and
thinks I may be able to travel in five days ... I feel very miserable
but the disease is going its normal course. It is particularly annoy-
ing because I am missing the final sittings of my Commission.

But it was something worse. It was diphtheria. He was sorely
ill, the more so no doubt for the wrong diagnosis at the outset. The truth was in due course discovered, he was given
the anti-toxin and removed to a nursing-home at Mentone.
His mother went out to him. It was a critical moment.

On the Agenda for 12/13 January were certain amendments over the names of R. W. Gillan and Keynes for making the note-issue more elastic. They hoped, even without
a central bank, to introduce a little management in place
of the pure automatisms of the existing system. The proposals, as stated by Gillan, seemed to the Commission to be
somewhat obscure, and too complicated. It would not accept
them.

Various members wrote to Keynes expressing sympathy
and regret that he was not at these last meetings. His guidance had been much missed. It was unfortunate that his
proposals had not been accepted, but they seemed too complicated. Even Gillan seemed doubtful in the face of the
arguments of the other side. There evidently was a feeling
that Keynes would be distressed. He wrote to inquire if

there could not be another meeting. But this was deemed to be altogether out of the question. The members were dispersed. It would not be possible to get more than two or three together. Austen Chamberlain wrote to him to express the hope that he would not feel obliged to add a minute of dissent. After all, the report so largely embodied his views; he had had great success; it would be a pity to spoil the unanimity (save for H. Begbie, who wrote a note in favour of a gold currency), on a comparatively minor point. It was taken for granted that Keynes would either add a note of dissent or acquiesce.

But that was not his way. Gathering together what remained of his strength after a severe illness, he penned a note of such consummate cogency that, despite the lack of another meeting, Chamberlain felt it necessary to authorize various changes.

The currency reserve requirements were exceedingly complicated, relating as they did to more than one reserve fund, and it would be needless to ask the reader to re-enter the old ground of debate. None the less, Keynes's note is such a good early example of his polemic style that it may be appropriate to quote an extract from it.

The Commission have retained without alteration a preamble (enlarging on the benefits and the need of elasticity) and a summary of advantages to be obtained from their proposals (paragraph 114), which were written for quite a different scheme. With reference to this previous scheme these passages were relevant and truthful; but with reference to the new scheme they are, in my opinion, neither the one nor the other. If the Commission believe that the disadvantages referred to in paragraph 105 can be cured, or the benefits (2) and (3) of paragraph 114 can be obtained, at any rate for some years to come, from the scheme they are now recommending, they are unquestionably deceived. If, as I presume, they only acquiesced in this scheme in the belief that advantages (2) and (3) would really accrue from it, they ought to reconsider the matter. The recommendations as they now stand are of a spurious character. They toy with the idea of temporary loans, even suggest to the ordinary reader that they

encourage them, and do this only to deceive. This make-believe
element in them is open, I think, to criticism of an exceedingly
damaging kind.

He proceeded to substantiate his case. Chamberlain could
not hold out against this sort of thing! And so changes
were made and the story ended happily.

The early months of 1914 were now beginning to slip by.
Keynes, professing to be well although not fully recovered,
was back at his heavy duties in Cambridge (which he had
had to sustain during the sittings of the Commission also).
What was to be the next call upon his powers?

His contacts with his old friends had been maintained.
Note must be taken of a more recent friend, Lady Ottoline
Morrell, niece of the Duke of Portland. She had a lovely
house, Garsington Manor, near Oxford; an early Tudor
stone frontage stood at the end of banks of clipped yew,
which overtopped the house; [32] beyond were descending ter-
races, a rectangular stone pond with baroque sculptures and
a wide view of southern Oxfordshire. It was a small house,
furnished by Lady Ottoline with exquisite taste, and adorned
with John drawings and other choice works. It was a favourite haunt of the talented youth of Oxford – poets and
others interested in all things artistic. She was herself a
lady of great presence, tall, with a certain aquiline beauty,
her face heavily made up, not always skilfully, her clothes
striking, not of the period – sometimes a crinoline and a
large straw hat with ribbons. She was seen – in the days
when motors had entirely displaced horse-drawn carriages
– driving about Oxford next her husband, perched high on
a gig. She spoke with a protracted drawl, which seemed to
emerge from a far remote recess of nose or throat. Behind
these eccentricities she had a certain flair for detecting and
encouraging early genius and a quality of mind which made
intelligent men of various types enjoy conversation with
her. It was not only the clever undergraduates who went to
Garsington. Famous poets and other distinguished men

32. These have since been cut down to a lower level.

were constantly in the house. They felt happy there. She had some of the attributes of those great French ladies who conducted a salon. Bertrand Russell was a close friend. It is even hinted that Lytton Strachey may have had some romantic feeling for her. She also had at this time a house in Bedford Square, which afterwards became the London residence of the Asquiths.

*J. M. Keynes to Mrs Keynes*, 2 July 1914

Tonight I am to go to a small dinner party at Lady Ottoline Morrell's to meet the Prime Minister.[33] She thinks it is time he broke out in a new direction and is asking no one but a few of my so-called 'Bloomsbury set!' Duncan was at a party at Downing Street last night! But I am afraid he won't like us much . . .

33. Mr H. H. Asquith (afterwards Lord Oxford and Asquith).

# [5]

## Bloomsbury

### I

On 22 February 1904 Leslie Stephen, illustrious Victorian man of letters, died, leaving four children by his second wife, Thoby, Adrian, Vanessa and Virginia. Stephen's contributions to thought and literary criticism are adequately recorded in history and lie outside our purview. We may notice, however, that early in life he had, like Sidgwick, resigned his tutorship at Trinity Hall, Cambridge, on grounds of religious disbelief; and he was much engaged during his career in championing the cause of agnosticism. Although there were many eminent agnostics at that epoch, none the less the maintenance of one's position as such appears to have imposed a certain strain. We have seen Maynard's impatience with Sidgwick's lifelong anxieties. The easy eighteenth-century scepticism of Hume and Gibbon seemed no longer possible, owing, perhaps, to the waves of religious revival that had swept over England from Wesley onwards. As a counterweight to their unorthodoxy, the free-thinkers seemed to need to build up defences; if one was an agnostic, it was difficult to be just an ordinary simple person; one had to be especially high-minded and moral.

Stephen had known many of the great thinkers of the Victorian age; there had been an element of intellectual excitement and ferment. Inevitably, as he grew older, the ferment died away, while he retained his position as an eminent, respected and important *philosophe*. Living must proceed; the movements of a Victorian household were somewhat starched; the thrill of old battles no doubt remained in Stephen's memories, but there was not much in what still went on in his house to provide intellectual excitement for the young people. The great men were dead, settled in the country, or themselves becoming a little starched.

The Stephen boys had their own careers and friends, but what of the young ladies? No doubt they 'came out' and had parties and balls, but these may not have been more interesting than the ordinary round of conventional Victorian society. Something of the atmosphere of this home is represented in Virginia Woolf's novel, *Night and Day*.

Stephen's second wife, mother of the four children, predeceased him by nine years. So there fell to the daughters housekeeping duties, which may have been sufficiently onerous. They were then entering upon their twenties, their minds alert and their imaginations seeking greater scope. Towards the end Stephen became very deaf, and in his last two years was ill with cancer.

When he died, the old house, 22 Hyde Park Gate, at the end of a cul-de-sac leading from Kensington Gore, was given up, and the four young people set up house at 46 Gordon Square (in which I am now writing these pages). Freedom had been found. At first the pattern of life may not have changed very much. Stephen's old friends found their way to the new establishment in Bloomsbury. Thoby had already been bringing his college friends to Hyde Park Gate, and their visits continued. Gradually the scene began to change, but there were interruptions. In 1905 Virginia had one of those periods of mental sickness, whose later renewal the selfless vigilance of her husband did so much to avert or mitigate. The trouble passed away, and the whole family decided in 1906 to take a holiday in Greece, for recovery and enjoyment. Life revived under the influence of the sun, the beauties of Greece, and their adventures.

But, alas, the shadow fell again. Thoby caught typhoid fever, from which he did not recover. Thoby! Handsome, gifted, winning, idolized by a group of the most brilliant youth of Cambridge, entirely unspoilt, taking all admiration with unselfconscious gracefulness, a man of affairs, one who might make a great mark in the world. He would have been in touch with the ideas of his clever friends, and his common sense and balance might have carried them forward into the world of high politics. His name deserves to be remembered, along with those others which appeared on a lengthening list eight years later, as one who might have contributed to the better guidance of Britain's affairs. Weep no more, woeful shepherds.

Early next year a pleasant event occurred, in the marriage of Vanessa to one of Thoby's best friends at Trinity, Mr Clive Bell. The married couple took over 46 Gordon Square, while Adrian and Virginia moved to 29 Fitzroy Square. And so now there were two establishments. Would the pulse of life begin to quicken after these times of trouble? Clive and Vanessa made a resolution that they would devote themselves solely to their work, Clive to his writing and Vanessa to her painting. Very soon, however, these two houses became focal points in a grouping of talented people who were to play a significant part in the cultural development of London at this time.

Chelsea is the name of a London postal district. It also has a connotation. Certain famous painters have had their studios there, a multitude of art students have lived there, and been seen in the streets clad unconventionally in a way that struck spectators more forcibly in the early years of the century than it would now. Thus Chelsea means essentially a place of art and of art students. The annual 'Chelsea Arts Ball' has nation-wide celebrity.

Bloomsbury also had a connotation, but this was of a different kind. For a number of years, if one used the word 'Bloomsbury', otherwise than as a postal address, one referred to a particular group of people. Lexicographers may have their qualms. The question turns on the consequence of the group and on how wide is the currency of the designation used with specific reference to it.

The difference between Chelsea and Bloomsbury was that the former referred to general qualities while the latter referred to particular people and through them to their point of view. One could live in the middle of Bloomsbury and yet say that one was very anti-Bloomsbury.[1]

Who were these people? In this matter of definition an element of snobbery may enter in. Some purists who refined and refined – 'X was not quite Bloomsbury because he lacked one quality, nor Y because he lacked another' – and who excluded brothers, sisters, husbands, wives, might reduce the membership so much that the number could be counted upon the fingers of one hand. Taking a more generous view, taking account of those who were on terms of close intimacy with the leading members of Bloomsbury at some time or other within the period from 1907 to 1930 and who partook of their general way of life, one might reach some such figure as twenty or thirty. One could certainly cast the net wider, and by accepting others, who might not have been intimate friends, but who acknowledged the leadership, were in some respects of the same way of thinking, and spoke with a 'Bloomsbury voice', one could reach a much larger number. However the argument may go, no one could deny that the Misses Stephen were part of the central core of Bloomsbury. How did it happen that they became such important figures in an intellectual group?

There may have been qualities which came by heredity

1. This matter is of some importance for the future student of Keynes's opinions. Recently the word Bloomsbury has come to be used in a very loose sense, quite unconnected with that defined in the text. For convenience I will call the latter its 'original' sense. It has been used for ill-defined groups of young intellectuals. There is danger of confusion, because this secondary use would not have arisen but for the prior existence of the 'original' Bloomsbury. Keynes was a member of the 'original' Bloomsbury, and is rightly believed to have shared many of its views. But he had no connection with this secondary Bloomsbury, and future students must beware of attributing to him views stated in current literature to be held by it. I may cite as examples a reference on page 28 of Professor Jewkes's notable book, entitled *Ordeal by Planning*, and an interesting leading article in *The Times Literary Supplement* of 17 July 1948. In neither case can I find any connection between the views and characteristics described as belonging to Bloomsbury and those of the 'original' Bloomsbury.

and upbringing. There was Stephen's free-thinking and there was the distinguished social position which he achieved in the Victorian period. Thus on the one hand there were the germs of rebellion, which might sprout into a new kind of free-thinking and a new kind of intellectual ferment. On the other hand there were the traditions of society, which imply certain amenities that are necessary, if a circle is to be held together in harmony, however unconventional and Bohemian that circle may seek to be.

In their own persons, they were beautiful and clever and had also a sense of fun and liveliness. They were very individual people, with complex characters which it was a pleasure to their clever men friends to unravel. Furthermore they had a particular quality which differentiated them from the majority of their sex and was essential for the purpose in hand – intellectual coolness. (One need not imply that in most women the absence of this trait is a deficiency; this turns on the function they are destined to perform.) With Virginia and Vanessa all the subjects under the sun could be equably discussed, all opinions, however outrageous, quietly assessed. The men who frequented their society knew that they were in no danger of hearing those rising, strident tones of emotion which must destroy good talk. They had no tendency, as an argument took this turn or that, to read into its bearing an affront to their class, their set, their sex, or themselves.

Another great asset was that there were two ladies with these notable attributes; and, already by 1907, there were two centres. One lady may by her outstanding attainments draw around her a circle of people; that is a *salon*; it is the Hôtel de Rambouillet. But if there are two centres, they may form the nucleus of a social group.

It may be thought that the characteristics enumerated were not enough by themselves. English society contains many clever, level-headed, witty women, who are good talkers and good friends, who have drawn round them a circle for a time, but none the less have not gone so far as to become the centre of an interesting community, have lost their friends with the passage of the years, are known to be interesting and delightful people, but in the long run become more or less isolated figures, seeing their friends occasionally and giving pleasure, but living rather lonely lives. Were the qualities that I have mentioned sufficient ingredients for the creation of a social nucleus?

The fact of the matter is that there was a third leading figure, who lived at home, with no independent establishment in London, one with tremendous resources of inner vitality, with a point of view to assert, with absurd mockery always lurking and awaiting its moment, with a zest for life and friendship, exclusive in the highest degree, cruelly crushing to alien intruders, galvanic, temperamental, dominating, even terrific. This was Lytton Strachey. By a most happy harmony the Misses Stephen and Lytton Strachey, whose families had been on cordial terms and had had common friends among distinguished Victorians,[2] found themselves in great sympathy on many matters of discourse, serious or gay. Between them, these three sufficed to make the coterie.

It was a piece of the greatest good luck for Strachey. We have seen how much 'the Society' and his group of Trinity friends meant to him at Cambridge, and how he tended to remain there after his proper period. These friends had lived together, pooling their ideas, impressions and experiences, building up a community of taste and of philosophy, and sharing their private jokes, whose meaning depended on their common experiences. It is very rare for such groups, formed at a University, to hold together. There some young men may seem to themselves to have constructed, out of the views they share on life and on art and out of their common idioms and interpretations, durable, spiritual habitations, in which they will be able to meet to-

2. Lady Ritchie, a daughter of Thackeray (Aunt Annie), was Stephen's sister-in-law by his first marriage. She was an intimate friend of Lady Strachey, and James's godmother.

gether for the rest of their days. They are but summer-houses, destined to be deserted and to fall into rapid disrepair. The man, when he has to face the battle of life, usually finds that he has to advance alone. He is always tending to fall away from his friends, to be pushed about hither and thither, moving in and out of different circles, in accordance with his shifting interests and fortune. Then, if he marries, it is the wife who builds anew for him, decides what is to be done, who has to be seen and what the pattern of life is to be. He may pay a visit to his old college, he may attend an annual reunion of his friends, reviving the old anecdotes, rehearsing the old jokes, living in the old atmosphere for a pleasant evening; but it is all a mere echo; the next day's work will go forward as usual.

With Lytton it was to be different. In Vanessa and Virginia he found two women who were Apostles to the finger-tips – no less for having had no university education. With their aid the old summer-houses could be kept in being, and enlarged into great mansions, into palaces. The old thoughts could continue to flow, the new impressions be shared and the jokes kept green and living.

To these we must add Duncan Grant. He was an important element. It may well be that he was a necessary element, not only on account of those qualities which had made him so much beloved, but on account of his steady intelligence and balanced judgement. After all, Strachey often let his imagination run away with him, adopting extreme and untenable positions. Duncan Grant had the brains to understand him, but could maintain his own view. He had the painter's intelligence, which has a peculiar quality of level-headedness. For an imaginative writer, a new idea, albeit fundamentally unsound and in fact false, may none the less have some ingredient which will be an indispensable aid to the work of creation. For the time being and provisionally, he must cling to it, and assert it. But the painter creates with his brush. In the world of ideas he has no axe to grind. And he can thus preserve his balance.

With these aids Strachey was to be able to keep his community alive. It was by a further piece of good fortune that the two young ladies elected to marry two of his intimate friends from Trinity. We have seen already Vanessa marrying Mr Clive Bell. Six years later Virginia married Mr Leonard Woolf, after his return from Ceylon. Thus the Trinity party was kept together, gaining strength from its new adherents.

When Maynard returned to Cambridge he retained a London *pied-à-terre* in Belgrave Road; a year later he took rooms in Fitzroy Square with Duncan Grant. In 1911 he made a change, taking a share in a house at 38 Brunswick Square, his fellow-tenants being Adrian and Virginia Stephen, Duncan Grant and, on his return from Ceylon, Leonard Woolf. (When Leonard and Virginia married in 1913 they went off to Clifford's Inn.) The act of leaving London for Cambridge made the whole question of London much more important to Maynard. When residing there he had been busy at the office and with his pen; the whole future lay before him. But when the future lay in Cambridge, he had to be careful not to let his connections with London decay. In due course, sharing houses, sometimes here, sometimes there, he became a member of the Bloomsbury family. He lived as a bachelor in college for part of the time; but Bloomsbury was in a very real sense his home, providing the feminine interest and the human interest which were the background of his daily work.

The question has been raised whether he can be considered as part of the innermost circle of Bloomsbury. Some high authorities would like to raise a doubt and stress certain differences. There were inevitably certain differences. Most of the others were devoting their lives to writing or to some form of artistic endeavour. Maynard was a don; his work in economics was more in the nature of science than of literature; in due course he became a man of business; and in part of the period he was in public life. The nature of the influence he strove to exert implied a difference in outlook. His friends sought to influence the world – in so far as they could be said to do that at all – through the perfection of their artistic achievement. He sought to exert a more direct influence, namely by persuasion and personal intervention. Thus his life was bound to be more littered up with the transaction of business and he had at times fairly close contacts with the great, whom Bloomsbury despised. In no other way could he have achieved his object.

What is so remarkable is that, despite the pressure of worldly interests which were the interests inherent in his profession, he preserved his inner self so untainted that he was always welcomed by the Bloomsbury friends as one of themselves. They felt that at heart he was their unqualified supporter. And so indeed he was. There is no doubt that in his own mind he believed that the work and the personalities of these friends mattered more than the eminent and famous persons with whom he came in contact. It was the friends who provided him with the specific image of what is meant by the idea of a good life. And it was their good opinion of him that he valued most.

It must not be supposed that there was a self-conscious attempt to form a group or that its members wished to be known by a collective name. The group grew up naturally and spontaneously. In the early days there were a number of young people, who were on friendly terms with the others; some of these eventually drifted away, and new friends were added. It turned out that a certain number desired to remain intimate and maintained continuous contact for a long period. With the passage of years these friendships became deep-rooted. To the emotional sympathy, which is present at the inception of a deep friendship, there was added something less usual, namely, the growing familiarity of daily intercourse, so that the friends became almost a family or clan.

What were the leading characteristics of this group? It would be beyond the scope of this volume to attempt a full analysis. There is no authoritative record, and it is to be feared that there may never be one; the student of this episode in the history of British culture will have to glean his information from bits and pieces. A few fragmentary notes that suffice in this place. They are necessary, since what so filled the mind of Keynes and furnished forth his idea of the kind of society which it was the economist's task to make possible must be of relevance to his history and to his economics.

As philosophical background, G. E. Moore's theories were translated from Cambridge to London and became *de rigueur* in Bloomsbury. The supreme values of life were the states of consciousness involved in human relations and in the appreciation of beauty. In a certain sense it may be said that Bloomsbury was a prolongation in London of that phase in the life of 'the Society' which was reached in the years immediately following 1900.

At Cambridge Strachey had laid an emphasis, unusual at a university, on the importance of the visual arts, in this ably supported by Clive Bell. This doctrine remained a central one. Maynard was infected by the enthusiasm, and, in due course, became a buyer of pictures as well as books. His flair for the subject is testified by the value of his collection of modern pictures (£30,000 at his death), which he bought, for the most part, at very modest prices. Some hold, perhaps correctly, that his success in this field was due to some uncanny extension of his intellectual power into the world of aesthetics, and that he was never deeply moved by visual, as he undoubtedly was by literary, beauty. Strachey, indeed, is said to have remarked when in a peevish mood, 'What irritates me so about Pozzo[3] is that he has no aesthetic sense'. Whatever may be the true view about his independent aesthetic judgement, there is no doubt that

3. For many years in Bloomsbury Keynes was familiarly known by the name Pozzo, having been so christened by Strachey after the Corsican diplomat, Pozzo di Borgo – not a diplomat of evil motive or base conduct, but certainly a schemer and man of many facets.

he shared the sentiment that the painter and the sculptor should be the most highly honoured among men. It must be mentioned that Roger Fry was from early days a great friend.

Much had been done, before Bloomsbury, to redeem English society from the deep philistinism of the mid-Victorian period. Indeed movement succeeded movement. Bloomsbury in turn made its contribution, notably at the period of the first French Post-Impressionist Exhibition in London, towards the wider education of public opinion. We shall see that later in his life Maynard endeavoured to carry this education further, by devising practical arrangements for making modern work better known to the general public.

Then there was the other ultimate good defined by G. E. Moore, the good to be found in personal relations. This raises wide questions. Conclusions might be reached which disturbed age-old moral conventions and codes. Leslie Stephen raised the banner of agnosticism concerning the date of the creation of the world. If the Misses Stephen disregarded established codes of everyday behaviour, this would be a revolution even more significant for ordinary people. They too would become pioneers in their day, no longer the daughters of the veteran rebel, going to conventional dances, but rebels on their own account, leaders in a new movement for emancipation.

It may well be said that Bloomsbury was but an eddy in a mighty stream carrying world-wide opinion far from the tenets of the Victorian era. None the less it had its specific characteristics. The first answer of many, in reply to the question who in England had been most responsible for a change of sentiment in these matters, would be Mr George Bernard Shaw. There is, however, considerable difference between his tone and temper on these subjects and that of Bloomsbury. The lessons to which the writings of Shaw appeared – to the young in the early years of this century – to point were that the Victorian codes were harsh and brutal and replete with hypocrisy, and that, if we brushed those cobwebs away, natural instinct, which was sound and healthy, could be trusted to secure the right arrangements. Shaw in this, as in other matters, seems to suggest that the final answer to these vexed questions is really simple and under our noses. If only we would all think with the clarity and boldness with which he seems to write, our affairs would fall into proper shape.

Bloomsbury cordially agreed that the Victorian codes were harsh and brutal and replete with hypocrisy, and that the cobwebs must be brushed away. But the answer did not seem so simple. When one examines with integrity and disinterestedness the phenomenon of love, taking Nature as we actually find her, we shall discover many curious and unexpected deviations, many twists and quirks. Nature must be examined fearlessly, without prejudice or inhibition. The human heart will be found to have many strange complexities. Bloomsbury would not presume to think that the problems were simple or that the solutions could be written into a modern textbook. Rather they felt that they were on the eve of a great awakening. But much would have to be thought, much tried, much experienced, before we should understand how to arrange affairs so that human relations could be harmonious and happy, and fulfil Moore's ideal of the good.

The debate which proceeded in this society, over the years, covered many matters which it was unusual at that time for women to discuss, matters that are dealt with in treatises on psychoanalysis. They were not discussed in the language of the clinic, but in the language of humanity and charity. Science might take many ages before it reached precise conclusions or formulated them in an intelligible way. Meanwhile these were human problems, demanding an answer if we were to advance to a better way of life. They were discussed in a spirit of humanity and charity, but also, when the occasion was suitable, in one of levity and frivolity. This was a very important point. In problems concerning sexual impulses, whether straightforward or abnormal, one was not likely to reach a sane and balanced judgement if the discussion was always in hushed tones and with solemn faces. What this subject needed, above all others, was far greater frankness and sincerity. And if the ice was really to be broken, laughter and jest must be introduced into the consideration of the matter. In politics or business it would be obvious enough that one could not achieve a realistic view of what was happening if one was debarred from discussing principles or acts save in terms of respectful solemnity. Fun and ridicule must be allowed to play their part in the analysis of the motives or characters or doings of the principal actors; otherwise political discussion would remain at an unrealistic level, and those who discussed them would have a sense of servitude. And so in these questions of sex.

At that time there were many who were shocked at these proceedings. But in this matter of being shocked it is expedient to demand the credentials of those who are shocked and of those at whom they are shocked. I suggest that there did not exist in England at that time any persons who had a moral claim to be shocked at the discussions in which these ladies thought fit to engage. Since this is but an opinion, it is proper to bring as evidence to the court of posterity the writings of Virginia Woolf. These contain passages showing the finest delicacy and sensitivity, deep psychology, great humanity. I suggest that the opposition will not be able to bring forward contemporary writings of greater spiritual quality, whether from pens of reverend persons, professors, philosophers or any other class of society, which would entitle their authors to censure the conversation of the author of *The Waves*; and what applies to Virginia Woolf applies to her sister also.

It may be that these controversies are dead and done with now, and that all these problems are freely and openly discussed, save, perhaps, in some very restricted circles. Has the Bloomsbury point of view in fact triumphed? The matter is not so certain. It may be that in the last resort what is important is not merely that certain matters shall be discussed fearlessly, but also the quality of mind and intention that is brought to the discussion, the high elevation of Moore, or the great tradition of 'the Society'. Has true emancipation even triumphed in what might be called 'highbrow' circles? One may go to a party of a younger generation in London. On the walls are pictures by Duncan Grant, Matisse, Chagall, on the tables books from the press embodying the current creative effort. The setting seems similar. And what of the conversation? Yes; these problems of human relations are being discussed in a spirit of frankness; the Bloomsbury emancipation has held its ground. But listen again. What is being said sounds, surely, very crude and callow. Surely one ought not to be allowed to say such things in public. One may imagine at this party a young man fresh from school, mature beyond his years, with his secret experiences and visions. He may resolve that when he goes to Cambridge, or it may be to Oxford, he will found a society whose main principle shall be that the tender and delicate affairs of the heart shall only be allowed, by a strict convention, to be discussed with a sole confidant, and that all this crude gossip and unfeeling comment should be most strictly ostracized. If such a man got, Strachey-wise, astride public opinion in the university, and later in a wider circle, the wheel might come full circle back to the Victorian conventions . . . The situation is perhaps not quite so parlous. The steady progress of professional psychology is a safeguard.

But there is another point that strikes us when we ask whether the humanizing influence of the Bloomsbury coterie is being more widely diffused in our society. If circumstances rivet the attention of thinking people upon the problems of Hitler, atomic warfare or the Police State, will they find a residue of intellectual energy to direct towards the problems of personal relationships? Do not these aspirations require those old presuppositions of Harvey Road – a stable

British Empire and assured material progress? May we have to face a period in which civilization slips back for a while, and the deeper human questions which intoxicated the mind of young Bloomsbury are neglected? Yet in the long run that period too will pass. It is a misfortune that the thoughts of these friends have not been better recorded for the consideration of coming generations.

Bloomsbury was something more than a discussion group, conducting its deliberations over a number of years. It also set out to achieve a way of life. The Cambridge ideals of unworldliness, pursuit of truth and other absolute values, were carried forward, and the group of friends attempted, in ways admittedly imperfect, to pursue them. In the past, idealists have gone forth to outlandish places to establish communities based on the principles of Robert Owen, Fourier, etc. Here was a village community, living in our midst, using the same shops, post offices, omnibuses as other people. It was sustained, no doubt, by certain elements of unearned income, and Maynard's un-Apostolic activities in financial speculation often led to his purchase of an object of visual art at a convenient moment. Bloomsbury would not presume to be proud of this achievement and was conscious of its own imperfections as well as those of the wider society within which it lived. Despite all these imperfections, it remained an experiment very sincere in its intentions, which is worthy of study as an episode in the history of culture.

*The Waves* gives a picture of certain elements of Bloomsbury. It is also coloured by the very individual personality of the authoress; and it is suffused with a certain melancholy. Bloomsbury consisted of sensitive people, who had their fair share of sadness and distress. But in its social aspect the keynote of Bloomsbury was its perpetual gaiety. How could it be otherwise, with Lytton Strachey setting the pace? Maynard's sparkling spirits and his impishness made their contribution. He might go forth into the grave world of high finance and politics; but he came back full of stories of how ludicrously and comically people were behaving, often parodying them, and exaggerating shamelessly. And the others too, plying their daily affairs, returned to the fold full of absurd anecdotes. If one listened to Bloomsbury conversation, one envied these people for finding in the course of what might seem to be a dull day's work so many incidents, which were fantastic in the telling. Why was one's own life not filled with diverting interludes of this kind? They had the seeing eye. Furthermore, if one rejects the presuppositions upon which ordinary people talk and act, and puts in their place other, perhaps juster, presuppositions, that serves to make ordinary sayings and doings seem highly ridiculous. It was impossible to be bored for a moment in Bloomsbury society. Each utterance was pointed.

The Bloomsbury voice was a distinct contribution. It was based on Lytton Strachey's, consisting not so much in a special pronunciation of words as in the cadences of sentences. These cadences could be used to express implications, additional to the formal meaning of the sentences. Many distinguished persons adopted these mannerisms, probably without knowing it. They were infectious. Maynard alone, among the men in the inner circle, was altogether immune; his soft, distinctive manner of speech remained unchanged from early years.

The voice was emphatic, but restrained. Certain syllables, or even letters, were rather strongly stressed, but not at all in the manner of a drawl. The presupposition of the cadence was that everything one said mattered. Emphasis had to be applied. In a subtle way this maintained the standard of conversation. For if one was on the verge of uttering something silly or flat, one perceived in advance that it would not bear the emphasis that the Bloomsbury manner required, and so it would be left unsaid, to the benefit of all.

The cadence was a trick by which one could produce various effects. A favourite word was 'really'. In ordinary speech the stress is on the first two vowels. In Bloomsbury speech it fell upon the ll's, which were rolled luxuriously, and followed by a sharp diminuendo. A stranger might utter a bromide. 'Really' – with great interest and surprise. The stranger felt flattered at the interest taken. These clever people evidently paid special attention to everything that was said. It was nice to have this considerate reception. After all, what he had said had not been so particularly interesting. But why the surprise? Surely his remark had expressed quite a commonplace truth. Its truth could not presumably be questioned. But wait! Could it be? Was it conceivable that these clever people took a different view? Was it really true? Then an abyss would open. Pausing to reflect, he realized that this old truism was in fact a piece of consummate balderdash. He had been horribly crushed by one word.

Another trick could be played with this 'really'. A philistine might say that X 'liked', 'was fond of', or 'was devoted to' Y, meaning little more than that if X and Y were placed next to one another at a dinner-party, they would get on very well together. He was confronted with 'Really', spoken again with great interest and surprise, the implication being that his harmless words referred to a scandalous intrigue or to a desperate and forlorn love. There were two distinct 'reallys' in this connection; one with a rising note on the '..all.', suggested that it was delightful news that a friend should be involved in this happy affair; the other, with a diminuendo on the '..all.', suggested disgust. This might be a mere tease. Or it might be a joke, if the idea of these two people being in love with one another was particularly incongruous. Or there might be a more subtle implication. Bloomsbury was deeply interested in all questions of love and wished to make it plain that in their view, if one could apply such a word as 'devotion' to X's attitude towards Y, that was a matter which must be taken seriously and had weighty implications. They were determined to maintain a heightened interest in human beings, and sustain an active-minded commentary; they were not content to have dry, colourless words applied to the motions of the heart; if people were so dull as to have no deep feelings, then at least these should be attributed to them.

2

Some reference should be made to the achievements of the group. One may cite examples, without claiming to provide an exhaustive list. Although Keynes drew spiritual sustenance from these friends, the main part of his work has, of course, quite different sources of inspiration. There are occasional traces of Bloomsbury influence in points of style and illustration. Monsieur Étienne Mantoux, whose criticism of Keynes will be discussed in the proper place, accuses him of dragging into his *Economic Consequences of the Peace* (1919) a mention of Freud in order to titillate the reader by this reference to a recent finding of psychology. The criticism is extremely wide of the mark. The kind of analysis which Keynes gives of President Wilson's character had been common form in his discussions with his friends for more than a dozen years. Of greater importance was his persistent tendency to ridicule those in authority. This was in part a native strain, but we may believe that it was encouraged – some may think unduly – by the persistently mocking vein of those among whom he spent his happiest hours. And then there was that vision of the good life, which animated his endeavours, of which his readers catch glimpses all through his works.

The achievements of those whose names I have mentioned are well known – Lytton Strachey, Virginia Woolf, Vanessa Bell, Duncan Grant, Clive Bell, Leonard Woolf, Roger Fry. To these we must add E. M. Forster and David (Bunny) Garnett. The latter was younger than the others; he became an intimate and devoted friend of them all, and of Maynard in particular. When the group was established, containing so many whom Lowes Dickinson had known as undergraduates, he was inevitably in some sense of it. Sheppard retained his links. There was another younger member, whose work may possibly survive that of all the others – Arthur Waley. Whatever the beauties of Lady Murasaki's novel in her native tongue, Waley's exquisite translation must long remain a classic, giving English readers their chance of comparing this great masterpiece with the finest products of Greece or France or Russia. James Strachey and W. J. H. ('Sebastian') Sprøtt have produced work in psychology. Gerald Shove, the economist, had close contact at a certain period. After World War I, marvellous to relate, a very small infiltration of Oxford men was permitted. Of these first mention should be made of Raymond Mortimer, a literary critic of great distinction, who has done much to kindle and sustain British appreciation of the civilization of France. He was fully adopted by Bloomsbury. With the advantage of years on his side, he has carried forward some of its traditions into a generation that knew it not. May it yet fall to this Oxford man to compose for posterity some record of what was in essence a Cambridge movement? Other Oxford figures were Stephen Tomlin,[4] Philip Ritchie, Roger Senhouse and Edward Sackville-West. The future will not have the chance of hearing Sackville-West's superb execution on the piano as a young man, but the novel entitled *Simpson* and the biography of De Quincey, entitled *A Flame in Sunlight*, will surely long be treasured. What strikes the eye, when it inspects this catalogue of work, is the great dissimilarity between the items. There is no case here of a literary school self-consciously imitating its master. It is quite a different kind of phenomenon – a grouping together of men of individual genius or talent, finding stimulus in the society of the others, finding a congenial way of life, but each pursuing his own bent and striving after his own unique form of expression.

It has been erroneously held that Bloomsbury was in the nature of a mutual admiration society. This is very far from the truth. No doubt as friends they would give each other

4. See also pp. 222–4 below.

a helping hand towards material advancement. But within the circle they were keenly critical of one another. There was no question of mollycoddling. A sharp, biting wind of criticism blew through all the recesses of their habitations. They did not give mercy nor expect it. Indeed, if you chanced to hear one member of Bloomsbury pull another to pieces, not leaving a shred, destroying him utterly, you might wonder what form their criticism would take when directed against an outsider. The fact of the matter is that, broadly, outsiders were neglected. It was a world within a world. By concentrating on the criticism of their friends, they focused their thoughts.

This concentration was not a device for self-advancement but for protection against all the irrelevant, distracting and disintegrating forces at play in our rather loosely connected modern society. It was a return to the Greek City State. No doubt there was a consciousness that other men of talent were also writing or painting. This might occasionally be denied in conversation – 'Really, you know, there isn't anyone else' – but this pleasant, whimsical conceit was not to be taken too seriously. Many other distinguished people were living in London at the time, and many of them were very anti-Bloomsbury. Action and reaction are said to be equal.

Although I have made no attempt at comprehensiveness, it would be very contrary to the canons of Bloomsbury if I mentioned only those who achieved successful work. It is fitting that I should name also two or three others whose membership was prized as highly as those better known.

We have had a glimpse of the arrival in Cambridge in 1905 of Harry Norton, and his early success there. He very quickly became a central figure and remained so for a dozen years. He adopted the creed of unworldliness and sometimes took his friends to task. He was a man of some means, and for a number of years made an allowance to Lytton Strachey, which was paid back in full after the publication of *Eminent*

*Victorians.* By profession he was a mathematician, and was elected to a Fellowship at Trinity in 1910, where he did pioneering work on the mathematical theory of genetics. Publication was delayed, but in a notable paper [5] he supplied rigorous proofs for a number of important theorems. Ill health prevented his achieving all that was hoped; he relapsed into a condition of inertia and sadness, and died at the age of fifty.

Then there was Francis Birrell. He went up to Cambridge in 1908 and Maynard became his staunch supporter and friend. He was one of the most delightful conversationalists of the group, very Bloomsbury, very light, a man of literary interests and wide reading and excellent judgement. He purveyed his learning and his thoughts with exquisite gracefulness and subtle, delicate wit, always with a slightly deprecatory note – 'Will this quite do?' 'Is it quite like this?' He was the most companionable of beings. He died of a tumour on the brain at the age of forty-five.

I once expressed a touch of envy at the lovely life he led in an endless round of discussion among intelligent and affectionate friends. 'Oh, no,' he said, 'it is not at all like that really. I spend most of my time with my father' (Augustine Birrell, the well-known Liberal Minister and man of letters); 'he is very lonely, he has no friends, he needs my society, I keep him company on most evenings.' 'Well,' I replied, to make the best of the situation, 'he must have an endless fund of reminiscences of those famous Victorians whom he knew.' 'Oh, no,' he replied, 'he does not at all like speaking of the past; what he likes is argument. As a matter of fact there is really only one argument, which goes on repeating itself.' *Harrod*: 'What is that argument about?' *Birrell*: 'Whether contraceptives are right or wrong.' [6]

5. *Transactions of the London Mathematical Society*, 1926.
6. In his Memoir Club paper ('Early Beliefs'), already cited (cf. p. 93 above), Maynard makes just points of criticism against early Bloomsbury philosophy. It is possible also to detect a slight change of feeling, leading to some lack of sympathy, which would have given

Mention should also be made of Miss Carrington, afterwards Mrs Ralph Partridge, always known as 'Carrington', a Slade student, with an attractive face and a straight fringe across her forehead.[7] During World War I she had chances of seeing Lytton Strachey, and they became fast friends. Lytton Strachey had not much to offer women by way of ordinary masculine blandishment. She had intellectual cravings and some subtlety of apprehension, and she achieved satisfaction in her ready appreciation of his fancies. He found her a sympathetic companion; in due course she came to idolize him. After the war she and her husband joined him in his house in Berkshire, and they remained with him till the end. When he died, the sun went out of her life; everything seemed savourless and purposeless. She did not long survive him.

Among the few who filtered in from Oxford, very soon after the war, was Stephen Tomlin ('Tommy'). He was rather nearer to Lytton than to Maynard, although he often came to the Maynard home. He was a man of extraordinarily versatile talent, classical scholar at New College, poet, brilliant actor, pianist, and, by profession, sculptor. Above all, he was a conversationalist whose assiduity was capable of exhausting even Bloomsbury. Not that he was for a moment a boring talker; on the contrary, some might rank him as

---

him great pain had he foreseen it when younger. In tracing his progress as an economist, the biographer must regard positions reached late in life as having greater validity than earlier doctrines. In matters of sentiment, he should regard earlier positions as having no less authority than later ones; there are disadvantages in growing old. Maynard applied the adjective 'brittle' to the friends, adding 'especially Frankie'. I do not know why he singled out Birrell in this way, nor, I believe, do his friends. The publication of the Memoir, without his having had the chance to revise it, may unduly enhance the importance of what may have been no more than a passing whim. Francis Birrell was a rare and beautiful spirit, whom they all loved dearly.

7. cf. also pp. 245, 255 below. Partridge was another notable Oxford accession to Bloomsbury.

the most interesting of them all. Although he was at Oxford (but only for three terms), he was just a little more serious in his tones than standard Bloomsbury. Some Bloomsbury mannerisms were superimposed on a beautiful, rich, mellow and appealing voice. His knowledge was considerable and his mind in incessant activity. He had a commanding intellectual power, so that the cleverest people were impressed by his judgement, even when he was very young. He acquired a great interest in psycho-analysis and was one of the few amateurs who made the more technical parts of Freud interesting and enticing. 'So-and-so, you see, has an anxiety'; the word 'anxiety' would be rather lengthily drawn out in the Bloomsbury manner; and then one knew that one might expect a fascinating diagnosis.

He was interested in these techniques; but, long before he knew about them, he had a natural power of psychological sympathy. Starting with some bits and pieces, some stray ends of foolish thoughts of a soul in distress, he could create for him a different view, illumine his path, give him new thoughts, new hopes, invest his life with a new interest and dignity. For anyone, however different – he need not be of Bloomsbury – talk with him was always exhilarating, leaving the soul replenished.

You might part company, grateful and pleased at having met him; there was a strong handshake and a winning smile. You might watch him walk away with a rather deliberate tread, his shoulders swinging with a suspicion of jauntiness that was not quite Bloomsbury. You saw him proceed, turn into a side street and disappear behind the railings. Then, if you reflected a moment, you knew that black and horrible despair and anguish seized and rent him; it was hardly possible to walk forward; he felt himself personally guilty of all the sufferings taking place in the world; was there not some sick person with whom he could exchange his life? How shuffle off these terrible mortal coils quickly?

In his conversation with others he brought good cheer; he seldom referred to the dark side. One asked him if he could not look at matters differently. He replied calmly that he supposed he must have a disease of the brain; that he must be a little mad really. His was a case in which it would seem that so much psychical force went into the understanding of others, interpreting life so as to create for their benefit something intelligible and hopeful, that there was no energy left for building up some kind of idea about his own life; when it came to that, he found himself stripped of all vitality, a poor dejected creature, a broken reed. He died of pneumonia at the age of thirty-five. There is a bust of Lytton Strachey by him in the Tate Gallery, one of Virginia Woolf in the possession of Mr David Garnett, one of Duncan Grant in the possession of Lady Keynes, and he did a number of other skilful portraits. There is a fine woman nude, on a large scale, in the grounds of Biddesden House, in Wiltshire.[8]

Such were Keynes's associates for more than a dozen years. Later, the pattern was to change somewhat. He found in a happy marriage the ideal background for the prolonged creative work that he had then to do. Meanwhile he profited much from the constant stimulus and affection of his Bloomsbury friends. And of course he gave much. They on their side were stimulated by his delightful company, his vitality and the impact of his abounding interests. And they gained, too, from his resources of knowledge and worldly contact. He was their main pillar of strength, their sage, their financial adviser, their patron. He was always ready to help, in one way or another, to promote their material interests. They also drew intellectual sustenance from him. Was he not a logician, a mathematician, a philosopher, an economist and an expert on many aspects of public affairs? They valued his judgement on all these topics. They were not flimsy *littérateurs*, content to take up philosophical or scientific ideas by hearsay or from inferior sources. One and all, they wished their work to be well based, if only it were possible, on a sound philosophy. 'Is it right, Maynard?' 'Is it

8. The property of Lord Moyne.

sound?' 'Is it logically tenable?' 'Are these really the facts?'

They were all people of strong individuality, and were strongly individualist in creed. And so was Maynard. He was an individualist to the finger-tips. For him those concerned with government were a lesser breed of men, whose role was essentially a subordinate one. The idea that a government, however popularly elected, should be entrusted to make certain value judgements on behalf of the community was anathema to him. He had no sympathy with the project of limiting consumers' freedom of choice for the sake of greater efficiency, mass production or standardization.

On the other hand, he was violently opposed to *laissez-faire*. Mr Sheppard recalls a speech which he made at a Liberal meeting when an undergraduate. He defined Conservatives and Liberals in this way: let there be a village whose inhabitants were living in conditions of penury and distress; the typical Conservative, when shown this village, said, 'It is very distressing, but, unfortunately, it cannot be helped'; the Liberal said, 'Something must be done about this.' That was why he was a Liberal. Sheppard was impressed with this simple statement of creed. Whether or not it can be regarded as an adequate and comprehensive definition of the philosophies of the two parties at that time, the view asserted to be Liberal was assuredly Maynard's throughout his life. He believed that distress in all its forms should not go unheeded. He believed that, by care and pains, all our social evils, distressed areas, unemployment and the rest, could be abolished. He believed in planning and contriving. A way could be found. That was his experience in his private life and in the affairs of his college, and the same maxim should be applied in public affairs. He always had a scheme. His mental energy and resources were limitless. If a thing could not be done in this way, it could be done in that.

How can one reconcile the adamant and uncompromising individualism which was at the centre of his being and his fervent belief in planning? Did he resolve what might seem on the surface to be a contradiction? – a question of no little interest, since its successful resolution may be the prerequisite for the maintenance of the kind of civilization we have known. In Keynes's economic writings is to be found his solution of this dilemma. It is one of the problems to which he applied his whole mind, a not inconsiderable one, and deep study of his conclusions will long remain worth while.

This problem is tied up with another, to which he gave less explicit thought. We have seen that he was strongly imbued with what I have called the presuppositions of Harvey Road. One of these presuppositions may perhaps be summarized in the idea that the government of Britain was and would continue to be in the hands of an intellectual aristocracy using the method of persuasion. If, owing to the needs of planning, the functions of government became very far-reaching and multifarious, would it be possible for the intellectual aristocracy to remain in essential control? Keynes tended till the end to think of the really important decisions being reached by a small group of intelligent people, like the group that fashioned the Bretton Woods plan. But would not a democratic government having a wide multiplicity of duties tend to get out of control and act in a way of which the intelligent would not approve? This is another dilemma – how to reconcile the functioning of a planning and interfering democracy with the requirement that in the last resort the best considered judgement should prevail. It may be that the presuppositions of Harvey Road were so much of a second nature to Keynes that he did not give this dilemma the full consideration which it deserves.

There is also the eternal question in economics of the relation of means to ends. Conscientious economists usually stress the point that their science is concerned with means only, and that it is for others to prescribe the ends. None the less it is hard to draw the line, especially when the economist concerns himself with practical issues. An idea as to what the appropriate ends are may lurk implicit in his recom-

mendation. Some economists are felt to have had too narrow
a view of the ends of society. Not so Keynes. His writings
are instinct with broad and generous views. We need not
attribute this to the influence of Bloomsbury; but we can
associate it with his being the kind of man who would enjoy
Bloomsbury society.

While he had his own inner vision, he was none the less
aware that economists as such must not overstep the mark.
He once defined his position in some words very carefully
chosen. It was at the end of his speech at a dinner given him
by the Council of the Royal Economic Society in 1945 on his
retirement from the Editorship of the *Economic Journal*
after thirty-three years. It had been a wonderful speech, easy,
pleasantly flowing, mellow, full of amusing anecdotes and
fascinating character sketches of Balfour, Haldane and other
eminent people, with whom he had had contact as secretary
of the Society. Finally he came to the toast. 'I give you the
toast of the Royal Economic Society, of economics and
economists, who are the trustees . . .' It would have been easy
to say 'the trustees of civilization', and to have sat down
amid appropriate applause. '. . . who are the trustees, not . . .'
One could not help having the idea – 'Why this pedantic
"not"?' Surely this was not the moment for academic qualifications, for ifs and buts. It was true that he was addressing
the members of the Council of the Royal Economic Society,
professors, men of learning. But still, we were also human.
It was a golden hour; our hearts had been touched; we had
drunk champagne. We had in fact each had one modest
glass of champagne, but had arranged that Maynard should
have champagne only, from the soup onwards through the
evening. Really there was something intolerable about the
donnish 'not' coming at this hour and place. It was so unlike
Maynard not to say a thing simply and boldly. But he was
choosing his words: '. . . and to economists, who are the
trustees, not of civilization, but of the possibility of civilization.' He had said what he wanted to say.

And what he had said was true, not something slipshod,

which might pass muster on such an occasion, but an accurate description, which would bear the test of close scrutiny in the clear light of day. And it did full justice to economics. When he came to the 'not', did there flit through his mind a vision of Lytton, of Duncan, of Virginia? They were the trustees of civilization. Economists had the humbler, but still quite indispensable, role; it was that to which he had devoted his own life.

# [6]

## World War I and the Paris Peace Conference

### I

It was Sunday, 2 August 1914. The day was dawning on a new and terrible world. The benignity of the sunshine had departed; and in its place was a harsh glare, as it might be on some strange planet, a place of unknown and nameless horrors. Britain was to be carried far from her moorings. Would she ever regain them? Civilization was to be disrupted. Would it ever be restored? What would become of poetry and painting and philosophy? What of old friends and friendships? And what, amid these stern and cruel events, of a group of sensitive and peace-loving people, who had aspired, in their quiet way, towards a more harmonious manner of living? All things would indeed be built anew, but by the blind force of circumstances, not by the mind and will.

When it was decided that it would be more appropriate for Keynes to serve as a full member of the Indian Currency Commission, Basil Blackett had been appointed to the vacant post of secretary. He was now in the Treasury, struggling with great issues and great events. Britain was on the brink of war. What of her gold standard? What of her financial leadership? During the preceding decades, stretching back for a century, she had in effect provided a stable currency for the whole world, and thereby contributed greatly to the growth of trade and production everywhere. It has since been a commonplace of the history books that this system was terminated by World War I, and that up to the present time no alternative system has been found to work so well to the satisfaction of all parties. But Britain did not abandon her responsibilities without some struggle. Basil Blackett, conscious of the momentous nature of the decisions which would be taken, took up his diarist's pen, which had been idle for some years. He was most anxious that, at this crucial moment, the right things should be done, and, at the time, the maintenance of specie payments seemed all-important. The Treasury was of one mind on this, and was supported by the Bank of England. But there were already present on the scene representatives of bankers, making sweeping demands for the creation of new assets and the suspension of liabilities – sinister presage of so much that was to follow. In Blackett's view the bankers must be defeated at all costs, and his mind reverted to Keynes, who had proved such a splendid warrior on the Indian Currency Commission.

Blackett's message reached Keynes in Cambridge on Sunday. The trains seemed unsatisfactory, and Keynes appealed to his brother-in-law, A. V. Hill, who was the proud possessor of a motor-bicycle and side-car. Hill made a trip to London in order to give Keynes a lift. As they drew near to Whitehall, they had an uneasy feeling that it would be incongruous to approach the august portals of the Treasury on a pre-war London Sunday afternoon in this conveyance. Keynes alighted at the end of the street.

### Extracts from Basil Blackett's Diary

*August 2nd:* Keynes turned up (I had tried to get at him to influence the Bankers on Friday night) and he, Hawtrey and I had tea at 6 p.m. (my first meal since breakfast) at the United Universities Club. Keynes is entirely with us, though (like me) he does not share in full Bradbury's detestation of the Joint Stock Banks' paying in gold to the Bank of England. We all agree that it would be better that they should use their gold to pay customers (and we are trying to say so in our reply to them), but if their gold is freely paid out by the Bank of England, no great harm arises, so Keynes and I think.

Blackett had serious misgivings about the capacity of Lloyd George (commonly known in Treasury circles as 'the

Goat'). *August 1st:* 'If Sir Edward Grey is indispensable at
the Foreign Office, the last few days suggest that Lloyd
George could be dispensed with at the Treasury.' *August
2nd:* 'There was imminent possibility of their' (Lloyd George
and some others) 'resigning forthwith, and being replaced by
Opposition members. This suggested Austen Chamberlain
for the Treasury and the financial situation saved.'

*August 3rd:* House rose about 10.15 p.m. Back to Treasury to
get memorandum by Keynes on disastrous character of any
policy leading to suspension of specie payments which he was
preparing at my instigation. Home reading it, arriving about
11.40 p.m. . . .

*August 4th:* Keynes's memorandum given by Hamilton to
Lloyd George, who asked who Keynes was, and on being told that
he was a friend of mine, expert in currency, said it was monstrous
that Treasury officials should call in outsiders on their own
responsibility. But he read the memorandum . . .

*August 5th:* Lloyd George has at last come down on the right
side and is in a fair way to becoming quite a currency expert. He
has clearly imbibed much of Keynes's memorandum and is
strong against suspension of specie payments . . . We are all in
high spirits at the prospect of victory for Treasury views . . .

*August 8th:* Lloyd George's conversion was a triumph, but he
himself is really a wonder. It took some time to teach him, but
he promises now to reach the front rank of financial experts, if
his present knowledge makes him retain a taste for the pure
finance side of the Treasury work which he has hitherto entirely
neglected.

No further services were required of Keynes for the time
being, and it was only early in 1915 that he entered the
Treasury 'for the duration'.

Apart from a holiday in a camp near Coverack, he was in
London during most of August and September and composed an article for the *Economic Journal* which appeared
in the September issue, under the title 'War and the Financial System, August 1914'. This was a description and analysis
of the tangled situation at the outbreak of the war. It was
written with his masterly clarity. He was widely congratu-

lated on it as a fine performance, although some, who were ignorant of the fierce battles which had raged in the first few days, thought that he had been rather too severe to the bankers. He softened his criticism in an article which appeared in the following (December) issue, probably less from any sense that his previous strictures were too strong, than from his general respect for the City and its ways, and his desire to maintain its prestige in these difficult times. He would not be likely to exaggerate in stating his views to Alfred Marshall.

*J. M. Keynes to Dr Marshall*, 10 October 1914

Thanks very much for your letter. It was impossible to do justice to the question of the behaviour of the banks in the early days of the war without going into personalities, which was not possible in the *Journal*. — and — were the spokesmen of the bankers and the men whom the Treasury looked to as their leaders. The one was cowardly and the other selfish. They unquestionably behaved badly, and it is not disputed that they pressed strongly for suspension of cash payments by the Bank of England. By no means all of the other bankers either trusted — and — or agreed with their immediate proposals; but they were timid, voiceless and leaderless and in the hurry of the times did not make themselves heard. I think, however, that, taking a long view, the banks themselves are to blame for this. They are too largely staffed, apart from the directors, on what in the Civil Service is called a second division basis. Half of their directors, on the other hand, are appointed on hereditary grounds and two-fifths, not on grounds of banking capacity, but because they are able, through their business connections, to bring to the bank a certain class of business. Naturally when the time comes they find themselves without a leader of the right kind. And no one but themselves is to blame. Parker, here, tells me that the meetings at the Treasury took place before the Board of Barclay's had an opportunity to meet. Of course they did. In crises you must have a few men at the top capable of taking wise decisions immediately. Fortunately we had a few such – but not amongst the Joint Stock Bankers.

At least that is my view of what happened.

The second *Journal* article carried on the story and gave a forward survey. Although it has been less read since, and described events of less crucial importance, it is in some respects more interesting than the first article. He made prognostications in regard to the future of the exchanges, and he predicted, correctly as it turned out, that gold would be released on a big scale from the reserves of the various belligerents and suffer a consequent decline of value in terms of commodities. This article is a most striking example of his skill in predicting likely future developments out of complicated situation.

And what would be the final upshot? The article contains a speculation of some interest.

It is, therefore, a possible consequence of the present war, more likely in proportion as the war is prolonged – I cannot say that I yet think it probable – that some international regulation of the standard will be forced on the principal countries of the world. If it prove one of the after-effects of the present struggle, that gold is at last deposed from its despotic control over us and reduced to the position of a constitutional monarch, a new chapter of history will be opened. Man will have made another step forward in the attainment of self-government, in the power to control his fortunes according to his own wishes. We shall then record the subtle, profound, unintended, and often unnoticed influences of the precious metals on past historical events as characteristic of an earlier period. A new dragon will have been set up at a new Colchis to guard the Golden Fleece from adventurers.

In the welter of confusion that followed World War I, nothing of this sort was thought of. It was only after the years had passed and another great catastrophe had befallen the world that such a plan began to take shape, with Keynes himself as the master mind. And even now we do not know if man will have sufficient resolution, amid the difficulties that have followed World War II, to bring the plan to fruition. Keynes foresaw at an early date what would be necessary; but blind forces have moved more quickly than wise planning, and the domain of Chaos continues to be extended. While Keynes has been so often criticized as a vacillator, I would stress the continuity through his life of his main ideas and plans.

Another example of this continuity is furnished at this time, although the matter was a less momentous one. Keynes's preference for maintaining men at work rather than in unemployment, which was to play such an important part in his later views, is seen in this letter to his mother, who had sought advice in her capacity of Guardian of the Poor.

*J. M. Keynes to Mrs Keynes*, 9 August 1914

. . . Where money can be usefully spent on capital improvements, a large part of it going in payment of labour which *might otherwise be unemployed*, the argument for spending it is very strong. It would, for example, be ridiculous for the guardians to contribute to the amount of unemployment in Cambridge by refraining from useful building, and then spend money, in order to give relief, to maintain men in idleness or in relatively useless occupations . . .

Keynes also published an article on 'The City of London and the Bank of England', in the November issue of the *Quarterly Journal of Economics*. His Treasury position prevented him from writing more for the rest of the war. He found time, however, to review the new edition of the *Works of Walter Bagehot*,[1] whose precepts he must have had in mind on the outbreak of war. He placed Bagehot very fairly, resisting the claim that he is to be taken seriously as a critic of Shakespeare or Milton. In the history of economics, Bagehot and Keynes are probably to be reckoned as the two economists most highly endowed with psychological insight. It is fascinating to read the comment of the one upon the other. While paying a tribute to Bagehot's subtlety, when analysing the minds of business men (not of poets – Keynes was not a member of Bloomsbury for nothing), and to

1. *Economic Journal*, September 1915.

Bagehot's many other fine qualities, he points out correctly that Bagehot had but small capacity for economic theory, which was a drawback.

The same issue of the *Economic Journal* contained a review article by Keynes on a number of German publications regarding the German war effort ('The Economics of War in Germany'); his appraisal was cool, without warlike passion or distortion, and praise was given where due. There was warning that the methods employed were likely to lead to very serious inflation. But when he came to deal with Professor Jaffé, expounding a social philosophy of strength for the sake of war, the venom of Keynes's attack was as potent as that of the most heated British patriot. Keynes thought it important to keep track of what the Germans themselves were thinking, and in collaboration with Mr Dudley Ward, by this time his colleague in the Treasury, he had a translation of some weighty articles in the *Frankfurter Zeitung* published by Macmillan (*England's Financial Supremacy*, 1917). This appeared anonymously. The opening preface of three pages is clearly from Keynes's pen.

Michaelmas Term (1914) saw him back at Cambridge at his normal duties. Sorrow lay heavily upon him, as on so many others.

### *J. M. Keynes to G. L. Strachey,* 27 November 1914

. . . For myself I am absolutely and completely desolated. It is utterly unbearable to see day by day the youths going away, first to boredom and discomfort, and then to slaughter. Five of this college, who are undergraduates or who have just gone down, are already killed, including, to my great grief, Freddie Hardman . . .

### *J. M. Keynes to Duncan Grant,* 25 April 1915

. . . This has been a horrible weekend, and I feel again, although I thought I should not, as I did after Freddie's death. Yesterday came the news that two of our undergraduates were killed, both of whom I knew, though not very well, and was fond of. And today, Rupert's death.[2] In spite of all one has ever said, I find myself crying for him. It is too horrible, a nightmare to be stopt anyhow. May no other generation live under the cloud we live under . . .

In December he went to visit his brother, Geoffrey, who was on medical duty at a hospital in Versailles. He took this opportunity of obtaining information about the French financial conduct of the war. Soon afterwards, when installed at the Treasury, he had to go on a deputation to Paris, which included the Chancellor of the Exchequer, Lloyd George. In the railway carriage, Lloyd George gave his exposition of the state of affairs in France. He called for comment. In due course Keynes was asked to speak. 'With the utmost respect, I must, if asked for my opinion, tell you that I regard your account as rubbish.' A couple of years later it happened that Bonar Law, when he had just succeeded McKenna in the Chancellorship, applied this same word to an exposition by Lloyd George at a Cabinet meeting. 'Ah,' said Lloyd George, 'I see you have learnt Treasury manners quickly.'[3]

Lloyd George liked to gather around him persons who were not of the official hierarchy but had full access to secret information, in order that they should give him independent advice as a check upon his officials.[4] He developed this policy on a large scale when he was Prime Minister, and his advisers of this class were known as 'the garden suburb'. As Chancellor he had one such adviser, Sir George Paish, who had to write him numerous memoranda on the various topics arising. Paish felt himself overburdened and asked for an assistant, and it was as such that Keynes, whom Blackett had been most anxious to get into the Treasury, was taken on in January 1915.

The situation soon changed. Lloyd George was succeeded

2. Rupert Brooke.
3. On his return to the Treasury that day Bonar Law asked his officials for an explanation of this *riposte*, and they remembered the railway carriage incident.
4. Mr Churchill had a similar plan in World War II, albeit on a less grandiose scale.

by McKenna in May 1915, and Keynes was incorporated as part of the regular staff of No. 1 Division, which was concerned with finance.

In the following June he had to accompany Mr McKenna to Nice in order to make financial arrangements with the Italians. He had several days of exceedingly hard work. He did not go to bed for three nights and on the final night had a race with time, labouring with Signor Nathan to get the agreement into order. He attributed it to the sudden strain of this highly responsible and fatiguing work that, when he got home, he had to have an emergency operation for appendicitis and was gravely ill. There were complications, which were to have serious consequences twenty-two years later.

*J. M. Keynes to Mrs Keynes,* 17 July 1915. Garsington Manor

I was none the worse for stepping briskly into the train yesterday. This is a most lovely place, but the weather is dreadful. At the present moment I am still lying in bed after breakfast and writing letters.

I couldn't say to you all I felt of gratitude and deep affection. It has really been very nice, in spite of the circumstances, to spend five weeks together.

I have been made very miserable this morning by hearing [from his brother] that Békássy has been killed. He fell in the Bukovina on June 25th after only four days' fighting. Of my party at Everleigh – it seems only the other day – three are now gone.

Thereafter he made rapid progress in the Treasury. Sir Otto Niemeyer and Sir Richard Hopkins contributed the following account to the obituary notice which was published in the *Proceedings of the British Academy*:

Once there, his quick mind and inexhaustible capacity for work rapidly marked out a kingdom for itself, and before long he was a leading authority on all questions of external, and particularly inter-allied, finance. It would be untrue to attribute to him the substitution of loans to the Allies for the time-honoured British practice of outright war subsidies: that had already been decided in the early days of the war in consequence of the special relations between the U.K. and the Dominions, who were the earliest borrowers, and of the pride of the main allied borrower, France. But it was Keynes who developed and applied the system of allied war loans, largely from the angle of control over the use of these borrowings and its relation to our own needs and orders for material. When America came into the war, the American Treasury found the system fully fledged and itself adopted a similar practice. Equally absorbing was his interest in the provision of foreign exchange resources for U.K. expenditure abroad. Keynes took an active part both inside the Treasury and in the periodical discussions on this subject with the Allies before the entrance of America into the war. Many stories are told of his resource in the frequent moments of stress. One may be repeated here. There was urgent need for Spanish pesetas. With difficulty a smallish sum was raked up. Keynes duly reported this, and a relieved Secretary to the Treasury remarked that at any rate for a short time we had a supply of pesetas. 'Oh no!' said Keynes. 'What!' said his horrified chief. 'I've sold them all again: I'm going to break the market.' And he did.

The point about the 'control over the use of these borrowings' should be noticed. This was a new departure. The historic loans by Britain to her Allies were spent by them at their own discretion. On this occasion the magnitude of the loans and Keynes's eye for detail combined to bring about new methods, whereby the items on which the money was spent were under observation and control. It was natural that, when in due course the United States proceeded to advance money to Britain, she should copy our system of control. Alas, the second world disaster has renewed the need for advances, subject to control, and they are still (1950) proceeding. Among his many contributions to practical economics it must unhappily be reckoned that he was the father of such systems of control.

In the early stages he was working in close collaboration with Blackett. He soon became the authority in chief for the matters referred to in the foregoing extract. The Treasury had a tradition of developing responsibility upon younger

men. Mr Dudley Ward, who was below Keynes in the hierarchy, recalls that at one time he was summoned by Robert
Chalmers, then Joint Secretary to the Treasury, who informed him that he was too busy to attend to all details and
would countersign Ward's decisions without study. If mistakes were made, Chalmers would take the blame. But if a
serious mistake was made, Ward would be assigned to
another department. Thus Keynes soon acquired ultimate
responsibility for these grave matters. He was allowed direct
access to the Chancellor of the Exchequer. Early in 1917 his
province was carved out of No. 1 Division and transformed
into a separate 'A' Division.

On the outbreak of World War II Keynes sent Sir
Frederick Phillips an interesting note on exchange policy
during the first:

> In the last war there was no exchange control as such, apart
> from import licences, restrictions on foreign investment, etc. The
> procedure adopted was analogous to that of the Exchange
> Equalisation Fund before the war. That is to say, there were free
> dealings over the exchange at a rate which was 'pegged' by the
> Treasury, unlimited dollars being supplied at this rate. The only
> difference was that the pegging was done in New York and not
> in London, the dollars being supplied by Morgans' as our agents.
> E. C. Grenfell would come round to the Treasury each morning
> with a pink cable in his hand, showing what had been paid out
> on the previous day.
>
> Complete control was so much against the spirit of the age
> that I doubt if it ever occurred to any of us that it was possible.
> But the absence of it made my task of preparing a monthly
> budget of the dollar position very precarious. I used to obtain
> each month an estimate from the various departments and from
> the allies both of their total outstanding dollar commitments
> and of the amounts which they expected to mature in each
> month. To this, if I remember rightly, I added my own estimate
> of the probable requirements of the 'free exchange'. On the other
> side, our dollar assets, actual and prospective, were set out in the
> shape of gold and securities and the proceeds of loans. But the
> requirements of the 'free exchange' would come irregularly in
> great rushes, just like the demands on the Equalization Fund,

largely depending on the nature of the war and political news. I remember in particular a terrific run at the end of 1916, when the daily requirement (if my memory is correct) ran for a short time in excess of $5,000,000, which in those days we considered simply terrific. Chalmers and Bradbury never fully confessed to Ministers the extent of our extremity when it was actually upon us, though of course they had warned them, fully but unavailingly, months beforehand of what was coming. This was because they feared that, if they emphasized the real position, the policy of the peg might be abandoned, which, they thought, would be disastrous. They had been brought up in the doctrine that in a run one must pay out one's gold reserve to the last bean. I thought then, and I still think, that in the circumstances they were right. To have abandoned the peg would have destroyed our credit and brought chaos to business; and would have done no real good. I recall an historic occasion a day or two after the formation of the second coalition government at the end of 1916. The position was very bad. We in the Treasury were all convinced that the only hope was to pay out and trust that the drain would suddenly dry up as it had on previous occasions. But we had no confidence in the understanding of Ministers. Chalmers went over to Carson's room (my memory tells me that it was in the War Office; was it?) to report to the newly formed War Cabinet. 'Well, Chalmers, what is the news?' said the Goat. 'Splendid,' Chalmers replied in his high quavering voice; 'two days ago we had to pay out $20,000,000; the next day it was $10,000,000; and yesterday only $5,000,000.' He did not add that a continuance at this rate for a week would clean us out completely, and that we considered that an average of $2,000,000 very heavy. I waited nervously in his room, until the old fox came back triumphant. In fact the drain did dry up almost immediately and we dragged along with a week or two's cash in hand until March 1917 when U.S.A. came in and that problem was over. So far as I know, the Germans were totally unaware of our financial difficulties. But the American Government, of course, knew them. It has been an important part of the case of the recent Nye Committee for denying credits to belligerents that Mr Page cabled to his government as follows on March 5th, 1917: 'I think that the pressure of this approaching crisis has gone beyond the ability of the Morgan financial agency for the British and French Governments. Perhaps our going to war is

the only way in which our present prominent trade position can
be maintained and panic averted.'

On the other hand, my monthly estimates were saved by the
fact that, as a result of delays in deliveries, the departments and
the Allies never succeeded anywhere near in spending up to their
forecasts. At the end of the war quite a significant part of the
orders placed by Ll. G. and Russia in the summer of 1915 were
still undelivered; and there were still hundreds of millions of
dollars of these old orders outstanding when we were cleaned out
in March 1917 and the American Treasury had to foot the bill.[5]

These reminiscences are not meant to be wholly irrelevant. It
is true that in one important respect our problem then was
different. Foreign balances in London were insignificant and were
greatly outweighed by what foreigners owed us on acceptance
credits. The financial crisis of 1914 was due, not to our being
unable to pay what we owed abroad, but to foreigners being
unable to pay us. It was not sterling which crashed in that month,
but the dollar (which went temporarily over 6 to the £). But by
1916 the difference between the position then and the position
now was not so fundamental.

It is, therefore, well to remember that we did get through after
a fashion without blocking the exchanges; and this policy was
not without considerable advantages of simplicity and efficiency.

The work was extremely exacting. It does not seem to
have given rise to major political or interdepartmental crises.
All went forward smoothly. It is a happy nation that has no
history. And if this was so, we may be justified in attributing
it to Keynes's commanding ability. The issues were all sorted
out in that clever brain of his, rather than at the committee
table. He always saw several moves ahead and thus prevented a crisis developing which might give rise to interdepartmental or political acrimony.

There have been men of ripe judgement who affirmed that
Keynes contributed more than any other person in civil life
to winning World War I. This proposition is carried easily
on a gust of enthusiasm, and it has been applied to more

5. I have depended wholly on my memory, unrefreshed by documents, in writing the above, and it is probably inaccurate in detail.
(Note by J. M. K.)

than one person. The fact remains that all who had any knowledge of these matters were united in praising Keynes's great efficiency; much as he has been criticized on other counts, I have found no criticism of this phase.

From one point of view this was the height of his career. Never again in his life did he occupy a position of major administrative responsibility. Some will value his thought and writing more highly. Those who have greater regard for practical ability and prefer action to theorizing should give Keynes the highest honours. He occupied the key position at what was without challenge the centre of the inter-allied economic effort, he thought out the policy, and in effect bore the ultimate responsibility for the decisions and carried the business forward with a success that was universally acclaimed.

After the war was over and he had resigned and written his polemic against the Peace Treaty, he was for a time in bad odour among grave persons. But his point of view gained ground quickly, and it began to be said that, after all, he was in the right. This gave rise to an uneasy attitude towards him. Accordingly a dictum was coined, which was passed from mouth to mouth at the club and the dinner-table and became the correct thing to say about him in a wide circle of people, who had no real knowledge of the matter. It became in fact a cliché. 'Keynes is, of course, a most brilliant man, and the right way to treat him is to pick his brains; then he can be most useful: but you must never put him in a responsible position, because he will let his enthusiasm carry him off the rails.' As is so often the case with sayings that become fashionable, this was the exact opposite of the truth. It was the symptom of an unresolved conflict in the minds of those who wished to give it currency. One had to condemn him for writing the book and yet applaud what was in it.

To pick his brains was by no means an easy matter, and the attempt to do so could easily lead to unfortunate consequences. On a great occasion, when he knew that he had to make his case and persuade his audience, he had an inexhaustible reserve of fluency, of apt illustration and varied argument, that placed him in the highest rank of advocates. But in the ordinary course of discussion he often attributed to his interlocutors his own quick powers of apprehension. If he put an argument in a form that was cogent and decisive, he thought no more need be said; he assumed that the point had been taken; he did not think it necessary to restate it in a number of different forms, embroider it, give it illustrations, restate it in a way that would appeal to prejudice. He used economy of utterance. If a statement was cogent in itself, it did not need further dressing. The best years of his own life had been given to the study of logic, and this was the consequence. Thus those pundits who talked with satisfaction of picking his brains were often quite incapable of doing so. They appreciated that what he was saying was clever, but often missed the essential logical link, and, when they came away from their dinner congratulating themselves on their evening – 'Keynes is a most interesting fellow' – they may have altogether failed to learn the lesson he desired to impart. Even in his elaborate writings he suffered much from misunderstanding.

But when he was in a position of responsibility himself, he had a superb capacity for picking the brains of others. When in the presence of one who knew his subject, he was completely modest. He sat watching with his steady, searching eyes; tentacles seemed to go out in quest of any weak spot, any falsity in his interlocutor, any axe he had to grind. He absorbed all good information readily, welcoming it from the humblest source, and knew how to reject the shoddy. In the quest for truth he was essentially judicial. There was none of the self-importance, of the reluctance to discard a view that has become associated with one's ego, of the terror of renouncing what one has committed oneself to in public, which are the besetting sins of great persons.

It was only in the case of theorists, whose logic he felt well able to judge for himself, or of pompous people, or of the self-opinionated, to whom we must in truth add the long-winded, that he became impatient and snapped them off with a sudden rudeness. Did not these rare qualities fit him for responsible positions and final decisions?

In the one great administrative position he held during his life there was no question of his being carried away by enthusiasm or of going off the rails. Clever as his diagnosis was, its value was greatly enhanced if he was in a position to put it into effect himself.

There is another piece of interesting evidence on this point. In the case of his financial activities, which developed when the war was over, whenever he was the sole autocrat, as in the case of his private investments and in that of the finances of King's College – where the Estates Committee gave him a fairly free hand – he achieved spectacular, almost magical, success. But when, as in certain companies, he had to carry partners or co-directors with him, results were sometimes unsatisfactory or doubtful.

It is to be feared that the English have some mistrust of clever people. By a happy chain of accidents this clever one was placed where he could render vital service in the first war. Some credit for his promotion must be given to the high traditions and intellectual eminence of the British Treasury at that time.

2

For Britain World War I was in some ways grimmer than the Second. There was not the danger from continuous air-raids, there did not seem to be so great a risk of defeat, and Kaiser Wilhelm was not such a black fiend as Adolf Hitler; there was not, at least until the last eighteen months, the same austerity of living; but there were more widows and mothers that lacked sons. Perils could be borne with courage; the long casualty lists were facts, and the burden of sorrow was heavy.

None the less, life had to proceed day by day, and its character was determined then, as always, by what was physically possible. In this case it was possible to maintain

many of the social amenities and amusements of peacetime. The black-out was sketchy, theatres were open till late,
and provisions remained in fair supply. Moreover, the fact
that the static front line was so deadly and so near at hand
made the constant return of troops on leave more charged
with emotion and a more prominent feature in daily life.
The home country had to maintain good cheer on their
account; they must be greeted with gaiety and dancing.
The hideous word 'goodby-ee' was invented to mask the
tragedy implicit in the simple 'goodbye'.

There were other reasons also why Keynes, despite his
heavy load of work at the Treasury, despite the exhaustion
which sometimes kept him for a day in bed, and despite his
keen sense of the horror and tragedy of it all, found social
life beginning to flow in new streams. He was now continuously in London for the first time since his brief sojourn
at the India Office. Bloomsbury was tending to break up
under the pressure of events; there are purists who say that
when the friends resumed the life of peace after 1918,
Bloomsbury, despite its greater renown at this later period,
never regained its pristine *élan*. Meanwhile in 1915 there
were new faces, new young ladies, younger young ladies.
There was Faith Bagenal, an ex-student of Newnham, who
was soon to marry Hubert Henderson, the economist. She
shared rooms with Barbara Hiles, a Slade student, who was a
little later to marry Faith's brother. There were Carrington
and Brett, Barbara's fellow-students at the Slade. Another
friend was Alix Sargant-Florence, who was in due course to
marry James Strachey and share in his psychological activities. These entered into the stream of Keynes's life. Barbara
was his favourite.

At the beginning of the war the establishment at Brunswick Square was broken up and Keynes moved to 10 Great
Ormond Street, and then to 3 Gower Street, which he shared
with Sheppard and, at first, with Gerald Shove. Sheppard
had come up to London to serve at the War Office. Carrington and Brett were for a time lodgers, and, further aloft,

Middleton Murry and Katharine Mansfield. Large supper parties were organized here. The very young flowed in and met the no longer quite so young. There was an atmosphere of excitement and exhilaration. There were feasting and dancing and brilliant conversation and the faint whiff of great events due to the presence of one who was known to be at the centre of the war effort. Barbara Hiles on her side organized parties in her studio at Hampstead, and Keynes gave little dinner-parties at the Café Royal.

The young women were struck by his extraordinary kindness and attentiveness; his brimming gaiety and optimism seemed magical in that grey world. There was that special characteristic of his, the gift of immersing himself completely in whatever happened to be engaging his attention at the moment, and if his attention was engaged upon making life more pleasant for these young people, how delightful for them! When he talked of their painting and their gossip, these became the things that mattered most in the world, and the war utterly unreal. It was delightful for him too; he was enjoying this new world.

The pattern of Keynes's life is clear. As an undergraduate his youthful friendships had been of supreme significance. It is natural, and indeed right, that a young don in his first years, if his studies do not exhaust all his energies, should look upon the undergraduates of the next generation as potential accessions to his circle of intimates. The gulf of years is not too great. We have seen how this happened. Norton, James Strachey, Frankie Birrell, and, in London, Duncan Grant, and later Bunny Garnett, became no less important than Lytton Strachey and Woolf. As the years proceeded the gulf widened, although the interest and the quest were maintained, and we hear of undergraduates 'whom I did not know very well, but was fond of'. Then there was his London life. But it was broken. He was there for two or three days, then gone. He entered into all the doings and projects and gossip of Bloomsbury, but he was not resident. He spent much of the vacations travelling abroad.

But now he was permanently resident in London, and his thoughts and feelings began to take a new turn. There was an element of romance. But he was not to meet his destiny for some years more.

There was another new strand in his social life. When Asquith formed the first coalition government in the spring of 1915, Reginald McKenna took Lloyd George's place as Chancellor of the Exchequer and thereby as Keynes's chief. McKenna was a man of considerable intelligence, and his good grasp of finance was manifested, not only in his work as Chancellor, but also in his subsequent speeches to the Midland Bank, which have an important place in the literature of the period and influenced thought on monetary policy. Keynes soon came to be on intimate terms with his chief. The McKennas were close friends of the Asquiths, with whom Keynes also had contact through Lady Ottoline Morrell. Her house at Garsington was not far from the country home of the Asquiths, The Wharf, Sutton Courtney. Before long we find Keynes frequently staying for weekends with the McKennas or the Asquiths, and he appears to have been adopted by them quickly as an intimate. This was another kind of intellectual circle, and it was a brilliant one. There was Asquith, a scholar as well as a statesman, with his fine level judgement, and there was his wife, Margot, with her quickly flowing stream of witty and whimsical talk. Keynes would certainly meet his match in the lightning speed of her rapier-like *ripostes*. Her fancies were often wild and wayward, but she was in a tradition of fine culture and had been a member of that earlier circle, the Souls, who were prominent in London in the 1890s. But she was not merely the relic of a bygone age. The Asquiths maintained a lively interest in the most modern literature and thought. Asquith's commendation of Strachey's *Eminent Victorians* in his Romanes Lectures (1918) contributed to its acceptance as a work of major importance among educated people far outside the influence of Bloomsbury. No longer was it necessary for Keynes to regard all politicians as people who talked in private life as though they were on a platform.

*J. M. Keynes to Mrs Keynes*, 26 March 1916

I have been leading such a giddy life lately that there has been no time to write letters, – only two evenings in the last fortnight when I haven't dined out.

This weekend I am staying with Lady Jekyll, the other guests being Mr and Mrs McKenna, and Mr and Mrs Runciman. Unfortunately McKenna has been taken rather badly with influenza and has retired to bed. Last weekend I went to Ottoline's at Garsington. Sir John Simon came to tea on Sunday . . . I've dined twice at Downing Str in the last fortnight, at a large dinner party of twenty on Friday and at a small one in the following week. Lord and Lady Waldstein asked me to dinner to meet the American Ambassador. I dined with Violet Asquith and her new husband in her new house, her first party in honour of Margot; I have delivered my evening lecture at the Admiralty;[6] and I have testified before the wicked leering faces of the Hampstead Tribunal to the genuineness of James's conscientious objections. Oh, and I have brought out the March *E.J.*[7] and entertained a Swedish Professor.[8] So this will be a sufficient catalogue, on the top of my work officially so called, to justify poor letter writing.

I thought the interview with yourself, which you sent me, very well done. Who wrote it?

I see that God has been striking dead several members of the Cambridge Tribunal . . . I hope public opinion is keeping them reasonably just. Lytton has got off altogether on grounds of health and James got 'non-combatant'. Duncan's case hasn't come on yet.

*J. M. Keynes to Mrs Keynes*, 27 May 1916

Walter[9] tapped me over, thinks there may perhaps be a slight adhesion to the scar and gave me a tonic.

6. An explanation of the financial situation given at Balfour's request, at the original suggestion of Sir Vincent Baddeley.

7. *Economic Journal*.

8. Knut Wicksell.

9. His uncle, Sir Walter Langdon-Brown, late Regius Professor of Physic at Cambridge.

This has been a most glorious and beautiful weekend, and also a very interesting one. Into a nest of rebels, Philip Snowden, Massingham, Bertie Russell, Lytton Strachey, the Morrells, two young ladies from the Slade and me, who are the house party, enter this afternoon the Prime Minister, Sir Matthew Nathan, Lady Robert Cecil and Lady Meux, – a queer mix-up.

### *J. M. Keynes to Mrs Keynes*, 17 November 1916

. . . Last Sunday evening a very bad feverish cold came on, which kept me in bed all Monday. The fever persisted all Monday night, but abated on Tuesday morning, so that I went to the office. Until today, however, I felt wretched and not able to work nearly fast enough to keep level with my papers. Short of not going to the office, I've taken great care of myself, sailing everywhere in taxis and taking to my bed when not at the office, with the result that today strength has re-entered my limbs.

The party was a great success, and we sat down thirty to supper without being overcrowded. I hope all looked cheerful when your ghost peeped in.

I shall not be at Cambridge this weekend as I am staying with Margot (Oxfordshire).

### *J. M. Keynes to Mrs Keynes*, 18 January 1917

Last week I stayed with the McKennas and the week before that with the Asquiths, – so I have been seeing my old friends again . . .

In January 1916 Asquith's Government introduced compulsory military service, with a conscience clause. It has to be recorded that many of Keynes's most intimate friends of the Bloomsbury circle were Conscientious Objectors. Their position was a difficult one. They did not belong to any religious sect with an injunction against taking life; it is not even clear that they had an objection to taking life in any circumstances. Their individual views differed from one another, but some rough outline may be attempted.

It will be remembered that they were people of serious purpose, who had set before themselves certain standards of behaviour. Precisely because they lacked any definite reli-

gious creed, they adhered with a certain intensity to their
own notions; the philosophy which each had formed for
himself called forth those urges which in other cases find
vent in religious observance. Thus they felt themselves
unable to fall into line with public opinion, as does the man
in the street, when an emergency occurs. Fighting was no
part of their creed. They had not taken much interest in
domestic politics, still less in the grimmer aspects of foreign
affairs. Their values were such as to make them distrust any
government. It may be said that the war took them by surprise. England had been at peace for a hundred years, save
for minor wars, which they would have condemned as manifestations of imperialism. War was a recrudescence of bar-
barism, which should surely be stopped at once. The affairs
of countries were conducted by men in whose aims they were
not interested, and for whom they had contempt. They were
prepared to obey the law within limits and comport themselves as well-conducted citizens, but they were not prepared
to be 'butchers'.

Lytton Strachey, carrying the matter further, is remembered to have said on more than one occasion: 'What difference would it make if the Germans *were* here?' This did
not imply that he did not prefer the British political system
to the German. But, it could be argued, the difference between the two régimes was not sufficient to justify such
fearful carnage, leading on to hatred and revenge and bitter
grievances and a desire for further revenge, and so from
tragedy to tragedy, the tale of which has not yet been told. Of
course, it may be said that this judgement was superficial, for
lack of the time dimension, that more regard should have
been paid to history. It was not only a question of the British
system as it was then and of the German system as it was
then, but of their roots and probable development in the
future. Had Strachey been alive twenty-three years later, it
would not have sounded so plausible had he asked, 'What
difference would it make if Hitler *were* here?' It should be
added that some members of Bloomsbury who were still

living at the time of World War II took a different attitude about it.

It may be right to go behind Strachey's *ad hoc* judgement and ask whether there was not a radical weakness in the philosophy of these friends that may be traced to G. E. Moore's teaching. We have seen how sadly his book was lacking in any adequate theory of moral obligation. His ideals, so persuasively set forth, floated in a void. One had to seek those ideals, but little attention was given to the more immediate principles which have to govern action in this troubled and irrational world. Other philosophers had laboured with these more proximate problems. Moore hardly appeared even to have considered that problem which obsessed Hobbes, namely, the inevitability of uncertainty and violence unless men subject themselves to social obligation which, from their own immediate point of view, may seem quite irrational. This problem has claimed the attention of moral philosophers ever since. In Moore there was little trace of thought about it. His personal authority, his great array of arguments, his finely wrought logic and his challenge to the philosophic notabilities of the past concealed from his disciples this great gap in his armoury. It is still for the future to decide whether it was right to be a Conscientious Objector in World War I, but it is clear that under Moore's guidance one might easily go wrong. The sincerity and courage of this group are not in question.

Keynes himself did not share their view. But it inevitably had an important influence on him. These were people whose opinions he valued and to whom he was attached by strong ties of affection. It pained him to be in imperfect agreement with them. They pressed him in argument, and, to meet their case, he made two gestures of appeasement. Of these, the first was a trivial one, which need not be taken very seriously. He announced for their benefit that, although he was not a Conscientious Objector, he would conscientiously object to compulsory service. Accordingly, when he received his calling-up notice, he replied on Treasury writing-paper that he was too busy to attend the summons. This appears to have quelled the authorities, for he was troubled by them no more. On the other hand, he did not carry this policy through to its final conclusion, for a year or two later the Treasury discovered a gap in its records. In the file there was no notice of exemption against his name. And so, to placate the Treasury Establishment Officer, he walked quietly round and went through the formalities of obtaining exemption.

His second method for meeting the views of his friends was a far more serious matter. 'We are in it now,' he argued, 'and we must go through with it; there is really no practicable alternative.' He could have shown that convincingly enough. 'But what we must do is to see that, when it is all over, we establish world affairs on a new and better basis, so that this shall not happen again. May no other generation live under the cloud we live under.' This was more than a gesture; it was a solemn pledge. How could he be sure that any such attempt would be made? Well, he was on intimate terms with the Prime Minister, Mr Asquith, on whose worthy motives and sage statesmanship he could implicitly rely. And was not Sir Edward Grey, the Foreign Secretary, a most high-minded man? He knew that in the minds of these Liberal leaders and in that of Lord Robert Cecil were germinating ideas which led eventually to the concept of the League of Nations, of which President Woodrow Wilson's admirers have no right to claim that he was the sole inventor. All this was in 1916. Keynes was deeply immersed in war-winning activities, but he was now solemnly pledged to do all that in him lay to secure a durable peace and a new pattern of international relations. And, while his condemnation in 1919 of the Treaty of Versailles was warranted by the plain logic of the facts, this implicit pledge contributed to his physical prostration when his hopes had been dashed in Paris, and to the passion and venom with which he penned his subsequent book.

Meanwhile he exerted himself to befriend those friends

who were in trouble. His mother wondered whether he was not too lenient to them.

### Mrs Keynes to J. M. Keynes, 29 March 1916

... I am very glad that Lytton's physical disabilities stood him in good stead for once in compensation for past trials – and I am glad that James is allowed non-combatant service. But what about his conscience? No doubt he could conscientiously say that he hated the whole business; most of us do. It seems to me that many of the people who have no conscience are now suffering so badly that I begin to doubt whether in the general torture that is going on conscience ought to put in a special claim for consideration. Don't you think it is being a little coddled? Once the voluntary principle has gone, I really don't see where one can honestly and reasonably draw the line ...

Is there any chance of your coming on Sunday week? You will see from the above that I really need a talk with you to bring me round to a proper attitude towards Conscientious Objectors. So you must not neglect me too long. Anyhow I should dearly love to see you.

Keynes knew that the objectors were sincere. He appeared on several occasions at the tribunals, and on days when his friends had been up he gave little dinner-parties at the Café Royal to restore shattered nerves.

At about this time he had a very lucky escape. Our financial relations with Russia were becoming involved, and it was thought that the Treasury should proceed to the scene of action. It was arranged that Keynes should go on the ship that carried Kitchener and was sunk. But at the last minute it seemed that he could not be spared from his heavy duties in London.

### Mrs Keynes to J. M. Keynes, 6 June 1916

It was a horrible shock to hear of the *Hampshire* disaster and to know that you missed it by so little! I could hardly breathe when I realized it first ... And it was your birthday. Oh – how thankful we are that you were celebrating it by making presents to those picturesque deputations.

Later in the year Gower Street was given up and Keynes moved into that 46 Gordon Square which had been taken by the Stephen family twelve years before. Clive and Vanessa Bell and Duncan Grant retained some accommodation in it, but were mainly absent during the war; Keynes brought Sheppard and Harry Norton to share it with him. This remained his London residence for the rest of his life.

Another domestic change occurred at this time, the acquisition of a house, Charleston, near Lewes in Sussex. It nestles under the northern slope of the South Downs in a rich, unspoiled country, with fine trees, pretty old villages and abundant agriculture. It was easily accessible for Londoners, being a few miles from Lewes, which was reached by the express from London in an hour. The Woolfs had already established themselves in the neighbourhood at a house called Asheham. Mr Leonard Woolf recalls how, when Keynes stayed with him at this time, the express train was sometimes stopped at Rodmell-Southease Halt to enable him to mount it. The primary purpose of Charleston was to provide a country home where Duncan Grant and David Garnett (who had done Friends' Ambulance work in France, along with Frankie Birrell, in the earlier part of the war) could discharge their obligations under the National Service Act by doing agricultural labour. This became Keynes's principal place of refuge in the country, both during the war and for some years afterwards, until, on his marriage, he found a house for himself (Tilton) a few hundred yards away. The Bells also took up residence at Charleston.

*J. M. Keynes to Mrs Keynes*, 29 October 1916

. . . I took the opportunity to come down to Duncan's new country house. It's a most lovely place, a farmhouse of very considerable size with a walled garden and a large pond on the edge of the downs which rise straight up to Firle Beacon. However the weather has been so abominable and the country so waterlogged, that I have scarcely taken the neighbourhood in yet. We're only a few miles from Lewes and from Asheham where I have stayed many times.

Last night Mrs Garnett was here. She told me that she last saw father when he was about my age. He had very blue eyes and was always smiling. You were 'serene'. When you became engaged people said that it was a great waste for two to marry who both had such perfectly good tempers, 'when they might have made two homes happy'.

## J. M. Keynes to Mrs Keynes, 6 May 1917

Last week I took Saturday off and spent a long weekend at Duncan's farm in Sussex, enjoying the weather immensely and even digging potatoes with a view to the improvement of my figure. This week I have stayed quietly here, giving a luncheon party today to Massingham, Dickinson and Sheppard.

Work has not been overwhelmingly heavy and the negotiations with the U.S., which occupy a good deal of my time, are going extremely well. If all happens as we wish, the Yanks ought to relieve me of some of the most troublesome of my work for the future. Relations with Russia on the other hand are not what they should be. That's a piece of diplomacy over which we have blundered hopelessly, with our ridiculous tears for the Tsar and the rest of it.

Another move may be mentioned. In the later part of 1917 a scheme was hatched for taking a house in the country, called Tidmarsh, near Pangbourne, to be a haven for war-weary workers at weekends. At the root of the project was the somewhat forlorn condition of Lytton Strachey, who was of precarious health and still very hard up. It was felt that he should have a comfortable place for continuous work. Carrington and Barbara Hiles threw themselves into this plan and undertook to look after the domestic side; they made Keynes promise to watch the finances. Lytton Strachey, Oliver Strachey, Harry Norton, Saxon Sydney-Turner and Keynes each put up £20 a year. This was in effect a subsidy to Lytton, since he was expected to be there all the time, while the others would go for occasional weekends. Carrington remained in residence to run the house, and this was the beginning of her association with Lytton Strachey, which was not broken by her marriage. She moved with him later to Hamspray, a house near Hungerford, in Wiltshire, and they remained together till their death.[10]

Lady Ottoline Morrell's house at Garsington was also a great haven during the war, and some Conscientious Objectors resided there for a period.

At the end of 1916 Lloyd George took Asquith's place as Prime Minister. This is not the place to discuss the manoeuvres by which that change was brought about. Keynes's work at the Treasury was not adversely affected by it; indeed it was shortly after this that 'A' Division was given a form which lasted till the end of the war.[11] But in a more general sense the change was a setback, since Keynes had established a close intellectual understanding with Asquith. His mind was not of a temper to be impressed by Lloyd George's wizard powers, which he recognized, and he felt the lack of Asquith's steady intellectual quality. Moreover, for one whose feelings, although not his thoughts, were centred on what was to come afterwards, the change was likely to arouse misgivings. He was always critical of the powers-that-be, but in the succeeding period his criticisms became more acid.

Not much importance need be attached to the following misadventure.

*J. M. Keynes to Mrs Keynes*, 11 February 1917

. . . I was approved and included in the final list to get a C.B. this honours list. But when Lloyd George saw it he took his pen and struck my name out, – an unheard of proceeding. Purely revenge for the McKenna War Council Memoranda against him, of which he knows I was the author. Chalmers is very angry and has been very nice about it. I can't say that I care appreciably. But you won't see my name in tomorrow's list. However (partly I suspect to cancel the above) I have got a much more solid

10. See above, p. 222.
11. See above, p. 239.

advantage in these last few days, having been properly constituted head of a new Dept., with a staff behind me, to deal with all
questions of External Finance. It will be an enormous advantage
to have a staff of my own, whom I can organize according to my
own ideas. I have been given some very good men and I hope
before long to devolve a great deal of work, which is now entirely
in my own hands, and to get much freer. I was told that I could
have more pay if I asked for it. But I didn't.

The C.B. came along in the Birthday Honours List in the following summer.

The Department referred to in this letter was the famous
'A' Division, which held together for the rest of the war.
Some of its members remained Keynes's close associates in
his subsequent business interests. Of the Civil Service proper
there were Mr (Sir Andrew) MacFadyean and Mr (Sir Frank)
Nixon. MacFadyean was later seconded to the Reparations
Commission in Berlin, and, still later, has played a prominent part in the Liberal Party. Nixon went to the League of
Nations for a time and, after important international experience, became head of the Credits Guarantee Department. Mr Dudley Ward, who had a common interest in
having been a great friend of Rupert Brooke, was a pillar
of strength and is referred to by Keynes in his 'Melchior' as
his chief of staff at the Paris Peace Conference. Mr (later
Sir Geoffrey) Fry was of the party and is named in 'Melchior'
as 'my private secretary'. A very able member was Mr
Rupert Trouton, aged eighteen, who asked to be transferred
from another department at the sacrifice of his salary. He
was young enough to become Keynes's pupil in Economics
in Cambridge when the war was over. They were closely
associated thereafter by common business interests.

In the course of 1917 there was a notable accession in the
person of Mr O. T. Falk, who was destined to have a considerable influence on Keynes's career. Keynes was struck
by the ability of a speech made by Falk on a question of
war finance and invited him to join the Division. Falk also
worked with Keynes at the Paris Peace Conference. He was

a man of wide culture and considerable intelligence and he had a flair for financial questions. He was interested in the theory of currency and exchange. Keynes used to call him one of 'Nature's economists', hinting that they were often better economists than those more learned in the lore of the subject. Falk was a collector of modern pictures, and this in future years was to be one of their many links. He was a friend of the Asquith family, so that there was also a social link.

In 1917 Falk began giving little dinner-parties for those who were interested in the problems of currency and finance. Inflation was proceeding at home (this was not Keynes's department!) and abroad; these problems were to outlast the war. This was the dawn of a new age of currency derangement and, according to pious hope, of new forms of currency management. The old economic textbooks did not give an adequate account of these matters. There was room for fresh thinking and analysis.

These dinners soon crystallized into 'The Tuesday Club', which was probably the most influential of such gatherings of practical economists in the twenties, and still exists. Its first meeting was on 19 July 1917. The Club dined monthly at the Café Royal, and after dinner a member raised a question for discussion. Guests were allowed, and an invitation was deemed a mark of distinction. There was an atmosphere of intellectual ferment. The Club felt that it was formulating new ideas to fit a changing world, and that its discussions might have an influence on events. Keynes read a number of papers in the years after the war. He regarded it as a fitting place in which to ventilate his latest views. It is interesting to notice that when he read on devaluation, on 10 November 1921, there were thirty persons present, as against an average of nineteen at the meetings during that half-year. Falk has expressed the opinion that whenever Keynes was there he easily dominated the Club.

*J. M. Keynes to Mrs Keynes,* 30 March 1917

I was immensely cheered and excited by the Russian news. It's the sole result of the war so far worth having. But they're not through their troubles yet. An acute and even struggle is now going on between the Socialists and the Milyukoff constitutionalists. I see not the remotest chance, however, of any pro-Tsar counter-revolution . . .

What sort of a wedding-present would G. like from me?

His brother Geoffrey had become engaged to Margaret Darwin, granddaughter of the great Charles, for whom Keynes had expressed such enthusiasm in his youth. Through him the Keynes line has been carried on. There have been four sons, one a Fellow of Trinity, Cambridge, another making strong progress in the medical profession. The former married the daughter of the renowned physiologist, Professor Adrian, O.M., Nobel Prizeman. A son (Geoffrey's grandson) was born on 21 April 1946, the day of Maynard's death, and christened Maynard. He now has a younger brother. In their veins runs the blood of Darwin, Adrian, Keynes and of David Hume's brother.

Maynard also had two nephews and two nieces through his sister Margaret, whose husband, A. V. Hill, was also a physiologist and Nobel Prizeman. Of these, David was, in due course, elected to a Fellowship at Trinity, Cambridge, and Maurice to a Fellowship of King's.

Keynes's work involved various trips to Paris, but in the autumn of 1917 he had to go further afield – to the United States. He accompanied Lord Reading on a mission to settle outstanding financial questions.

*J. M. Keynes to Mrs Keynes,* 11 September 1917

. . . The weather is mild and just warm enough to sit without coat or rug. I have seldom done so little, – conferences with Lord Reading for about two hours a day on the problems awaiting us on the other side being my whole work. My first three nights on board I slept for 12 hours, 10 hours and 11 hours and dozed a good deal during the day as well. Seasickness, by the way, by drawing the blood from the head promotes sleep in the most extraordinary way. [Is this correct? Its dogmatism is very characteristic.] . . . The only member of Reading's immediate entourage besides myself is Colonel Swinton, an Assistant Secretary of the War Cabinet, who during the first year of the war was 'Eye-Witness' at the front. I did not know him before; but he turns out a most attractive companion and very kind to me.

Please tell father that as a fruit of the early education received at his hands I have won £20 at piquet off a Polish Count, although we have played but little and not for very high points. As I hadn't played the game for years and as he plays it every day at one of the most expensive gaming clubs in London, this is very creditable, I think.

On his arrival at New York he found his old friend Blackett, who was acting as secretary to the Financial Secretary of the Treasury, then stationed on the other side. 'Keynes much excited with his first view of the U.S.A.'[12]

A loan of $50,000,000 for what is now known as an 'offshore' purchase of Canadian wheat was the first business to be transacted. More fundamental questions concerning inter-allied finance had to be discussed. Keynes got through his work with his usual rapidity and was on his way home a fortnight later, leaving Reading behind.

Writing to his mother from America, he said, 'I live in a small but comfortable private house with Lord and Lady Reading, both of whom I like immensely'. This statement should be set against what he says of Lord Reading in 'Melchior',[13] which was written when his feelings were at their most bitter.

### J. M. Keynes to Mrs Keynes, 15 October 1917

Before you get this letter you will have had my telegram to say that I am safely back . . . We are travelling one of a convoy with an escort, – it is a very beautiful sight, seven great liners, with a total population I suppose approaching 20,000, steaming in formation with a cruiser at their head and two destroyers on

12. Basil Blackett's Diary.
13. See *Two Memoirs*.

their flanks. Today we are in the extreme danger zone, and as it is a horribly clear afternoon we are looking out rather anxiously for the additional escort of destroyers and perhaps hydroplanes which was to have joined us last night but has not yet turned up . . . Lockhart's Life of Scott has been my chief solace; but that's now finished and I'm very much enjoying Dr Thorne . . . As I am carrying despatches and have the best cabin on board, I sit at meals next the Captain of the ship along with the American colonels. These are innocent middle-aged gentlemen from the Mexican border with whom I get on very well and spend unnumbered hours playing poker – at moderate expense to my pocket.

*J. M. Keynes to Mrs Keynes*, 6 December 1917

I got safely back on Wednesday [from Paris this time], after nearly a week's absence, travelling very comfortably by special trains and destroyer, by which latter 18 miles of the Channel was crossed in half an hour. I enjoyed Paris very much, but it was rather hard work with perpetual conferences and entertainments and by no means the amount of sleep I am accustomed to. On the last day I actually reached the point of talking French!

At the final Plenary Conference of the Dixhuit Pays Inter-Alliées I sat with Mr Balfour, Lord Reading and Lord North-cliffe (sitting between the two latter) representing the British Government!

*J. M. Keynes to Mrs Keynes*, 15 December 1917

I had thought of coming home this weekend, but I have had too much work to do and couldn't get away. It has been rather a bad week with endless hours absolutely wasted in a newly established monkey house called the Inter-Ally Council for War Purchases and for Finance. I should imagine the only possible analogy to Government by Inter-Ally Council is Government by Bolsheviks, though judging by results the latter are far the more efficient. I can't believe these things happen at Potsdam . . .

Next weekend I shall probably have to go to France again which is a great nuisance; the weekend after that to the McKennas; and the weekend after that to the Asquiths. For Christmas I hope to go to Charleston if, as I truly anticipate, I get back from France. But you may not unlikely see me on Jan. 12 or Jan. 19.

I was very glad to see Vivian's[14] name on the new Air Inventions Committee.

But despite these various excitements, there were black moments. During the last eighteen months losses had been gigantic. It was still obscure how it would all end.

### *J. M. Keynes to Mrs Keynes,* 24 December 1917

My Christmas thoughts are that a further prolongation of the war, with the turn things have now taken, probably means the disappearance of the social order we have known hitherto. With some regrets I think I am on the whole not sorry. The abolition of the rich will be rather a comfort and serve them right anyhow. What frightens me more is the prospect of *general* impoverishment. In another year's time we shall have forfeited the claim we had staked out in the New World and in exchange this country will be mortgaged to America.

Well, the only course open to me is to be buoyantly bolshevik; and as I lie in bed in the morning I reflect with a good deal of satisfaction that, because our rulers are as incompetent as they are mad and wicked, one particular era of a particular kind of civilization is very nearly over.

I wonder how long your Cambridge queues are. If we put prices low enough and wages high enough, we could achieve the most magnificent queues even in peace time. There never has been anything like enough caviare to go round. How soon do you expect piano queues? Length of queue $= \dfrac{\text{wages}}{\text{prices} \times \text{supplies}}$. If $w$ constantly increases while $p$ and $s$ diminish, $q$ tends towards infinity.

### *J. M. Keynes to Mrs Keynes,* 10 February 1918

Meanwhile I am terrified at the prospects of meat rationing and feel that I shall require frequent trips abroad to get a square meal. The proposed rules seem to me appalling – calculated to dry up the food supply on the one side and starve me on the other. Besides they will drive the population on to cereals which is at bottom a far more serious problem than the meat problem which latter by no means deserves to be treated so tragically.

14. A. V. Hill.

It is interesting to observe that meat rationing was only introduced after three and a half years of war.

### J. M. Keynes to Mrs Keynes, 22 February 1918

. . . Tomorrow I go down to the Asquiths for the weekend.

Oh! you'll be amused to hear that I was offered a Russian decoration yesterday, a belated one just arrived from the Provisional Government. Being a Bolshevik, however, I thought it more proper to refuse . . .

*

The course of politics at the beginning of the week was deeply shocking. Bonar could have become prime minister if he had liked, but funked it; and as no one else seemed inclined to take the job, the government struggled through, emerging however without many tail-feathers left.

### J. M. Keynes to Mrs Keynes, 3 March 1918

. . . I have followed my refusal of a Russian order by refusing this week a Belgian one. I consulted Chalmers about it and he thinks this the right course. If people come to you with a decoration in one hand and a request for a million pounds in the other, the position is a little delicate; and in the peculiar position in which I stand to the Allied gentlemen I must I think maintain perfect independence of them. Besides the whole thing is rather humbug.

I was very glad indeed to see that Vivian had been nominated F.R.S.

The distresses of war and politics were relieved at this time by a ray of sunlight. An auction was to be held in Paris of Degas's private collection, including some of his own work. Duncan Grant suggested that the National Gallery should be a buyer. Keynes took up the point with the Chancellor of the Exchequer. Our loans to France were running up and we did not know when we were likely to see them back. Why not help the French balance of payments by buying some of these pictures? Bonar Law was converted and Keynes was given £20,000 to take to Paris on one of his excursions on Treasury business. 'Bonar Law was very much amused at my wanting to buy pictures and eventually let me have my way as a sort of joke.' [15] Keynes was accompanied by Charles Holmes, the Director of the National Gallery.[16] Big Bertha was shelling Paris during the auction, and this is said to have depressed prices. Keynes also made some purchases on his own account, including Cézanne's 'Apples' and a drawing by Ingres. This event was really the beginning of his career as a collector of modern paintings.

## Duncan Grant to J. M. Keynes (*telegram*), 23 March 1918

Do buy Ingres Portrait of Self, Cézanne, Corot, even at cost of losing others.

## Vanessa Bell to J. M. Keynes

We are fearfully excited by your telegram and are longing to know more. This is a line to say do consult Roger[17] before you go, as he'll know who to get hold of in Paris. Duncan says be as professional as possible in the buying and get at the right people – otherwise some German or Scandinavian will trick you . . . We have great hopes of you and consider that your existence at the Treasury is at last justified.

I think a feast off our pig will be one of your rewards.

## David Garnett to J. M. Keynes

Nessa and Duncan . . . are very proud of you and eager to know how you did it. You have been given complete absolution and future crimes also forgiven.

But gloom descended again.

15. Letter to Mrs Keynes, 23 March 1918.
16. The pictures purchased for the National Gallery were: *Corot*: Claudian Aqueduct. *Delacroix*: Baron de Schwiter. *Delacroix*: Abel Widner. *Forain*: The Tribunal. *Gauguin*: Flower Piece. *Ingres*: Oedipus. *Ingres*: M. de Norvine. *Ingres*: Roger and Angelica. *Ingres*: Pindar offering his lyre to Homer. *Manet*: Execution of Maximilian. *Manet*: Lady with a cat. *Rousseau*: Vallée de S. Vincent. *Ricard*: Bust portrait of a Man. Also 8 Delacroix, 2 Ingres and 1 J.-L. David drawings.
17. Roger Fry.

*J. M. Keynes to Mrs Keynes*, 14 April 1918

The Wharf, Sutton Courtney.

. . . Politics and War are just as depressing or even more so, than they seem to be. If this Government were to beat the Germans, I should lose all faith for the future in the efficacy of intellectual processes; – but there doesn't seem much risk of it. Everything is always decided for some reason other than the real merits of the case, in the sphere with which I have contact. And I have no doubt that it is just the same with everything else.

Still and even more confidently I attribute all our misfortunes to George . . . In the meantime old Asquith who I believe might yet save us is more and more of a student and lover of slack country life and less and less inclined for the turmoil. Here he is, extremely well in health and full of wisdom and fit for anything in the world – except controversy. He finds, therefore, in patriotism an easy excuse for his natural disinclination to attack the Government. People say that the politician would attack, but the patriot refrain. I believe the opposite is true. The patriot would attack but the politician (and the sluggard) refrain.

*J. M. Keynes to Mrs Keynes*, 10 May 1918

The result of yesterday's debate was very disappointing. For a moment I entertained the hope that the Goat had been caught at last, but not he! However it means, I think, that the liberals have now gone definitely into opposition which is a great deal gained.

British letters owe a debt of gratitude to Sir Edward Marsh. He was zealous in his quest for young men of talent, and by his encouragement of poets did much to help them in the early years of the century. He was quick to appreciate Rupert Brooke. Deeply moved by his death, he wrote a Memoir. He portrayed Brooke as the type of poet and idealist who had given his life, and, partly through this memoir, Brooke came to symbolize for the whole nation the heroism and tragedy of the war. In this process something of the literal truth was lost. Brooke's friends felt that Marsh had given a sentimentalized version, which failed to convey the peculiar individuality of his hero. Keynes wrote to this effect to his mother: 'Most of the most intimate of Rupert's early friends are not so much as mentioned. Geoffrey [18] and the Oliviers, for example, not at all; James Strachey and Ka once each and casually. Whereas a weekend with George Wyndham figures.'

### J. M. Keynes to Mrs Keynes, 21 September 1918

. . . Duncan is with me having come up for his annual holiday. My drawing room is to be refurbished and decorated and is going to be, when finished, the flashiest room in London.

Work goes on now in a steady routine. I am again increasing my staff which will now number seventeen, and I hope soon to be in my new consolidated quarters. My most amusing job just lately has been to invent a new currency for Russia. Dudley Ward and I have been spending a great deal of time on the details, as we have had to design the notes, get them printed, choose the personnel, answer conundrums and do the whole thing from top to toe. We hope to have the plan launched on the world in two or three weeks' time.

There's a certain amount of talk been going on behind the scenes about the Provostship. I still think W. D.[19] most likely to be elected, but Raleigh may possibly be asked to stand. I have been flattered by several people (including Macaulay) saying that I would be their first choice. But of course this is out of the question, – in fact no one really thinks otherwise.

In the autumn of 1918, jaded, war-weary London had a most delightful interlude. The Diaghilev Ballet returned for the first time since before the war and had a season at the Coliseum. Bloomsbury and, indeed, all artistic and literary London were swept off their feet.

### J. M. Keynes to Mrs Keynes, 13 October 1918

I've stayed in London for the last two weekends, but have had a very gay life as Duncan and Vanessa have been staying here and it has been the height of the Russian Ballet season. Apart

18. Maynard's brother and Brooke's literary executor; editor of Brooke's *Poetical Works* (Faber, 1946), and *Democracy and the Arts* (Rupert Hart-Davis, 1947); also of *Letters* now in preparation.
19. Mr Walter Durnford, who was elected.

from the parties I've been to, this house has been perpetually full of people, with the result that my supply of sheets amongst other things has completely given out!

The Sitwells, now burgeoning into the fine bloom of their youthful period, were among the greatest enthusiasts, and a party for the Ballet was given in their house at Carlyle Square. Keynes was amongst the guests.

So also was the exquisite ballerina, Lydia Lopokova, who was enthralling London by her performances in *The Good-Humoured Ladies*. The eyes of those invited were attracted by a large number of many-coloured stuffed love-birds in a glass case – a characteristic Sitwell touch. It is recalled that Lydia threw up her arms in ardent appreciation and asked if she could not be given one of these love-birds. It is not recalled that her request was granted at this party.

### 3

In the autumn of 1918 it began to appear that victory was in sight. A matter with which the Treasury would be concerned was that of German reparations. A historical retrospect and statement of principles had been composed by Keynes and W. A. Ashley for the Board of Trade as early as 2 January 1916.

'A' Division now got busy on this topic. They worked hard and long, exploring the matter from every angle – Germany's pre-war foreign trade, her production, her foreign assets, the value of those territories (Alsace-Lorraine, a portion of Silesia, etc.) which she was likely to lose, and of her colonies, and the amount of all those forms of damage which, under the terms of the Armistice, were likely to give rise to claims. Information was assembled from every quarter. The team laboured under Keynes's guidance. He had an acknowledged flair for 'global' estimates of this kind. Indeed, among the many things that owe their origin to his influence may be listed the use of 'global' statistics in debate and decision concerning broad political issues. Before his day, even economists had tended to argue about political issues in qualitative terms only.

'A' Division had certain special qualifications for dealing with this problem. Their methods of handling inter-allied finance had brought them face to face with the problems of capacity to pay, estimates of probable deficiencies, priorities among the various items of trade, the capacity for expanding various kinds of production under pressure. Their knowledge of the details of world trade, which came to them from their day-to-day experience, must have been unrivalled at that time.

Their findings were before the Cabinet at the end of November. Biasing their estimate on the high side, they found that the bill against the enemy, in accordance with the Armistice terms, might be about £4,000 million. On an optimistic forecast they thought that Germany's capacity to pay might be £3,000 million, but that it would be more prudent to reckon on £2,000 million. This was a large sum. In order to bring it into focus, one may compare it with the indemnity exacted by the Germans after the Franco-Prussian war of £212 million. This French indemnity was always reckoned to be a heavy one. It would be impossible for Germany to hand over the proposed £2,000 million at once; at the then prevailing rate of interest of five per cent this sum would represent £100 million a year until it could be paid off. This was certainly a stiff proposal; yet, looking back, we may doubt whether it was the maximum obtainable. Keynes was no doubt biased on the side of leniency, and this may have influenced the Report. It should be noted, however, that the £100 million was to be the net payment recoverable and not the total burden on Germany. Before the war Germany had had a substantial adverse balance of trade, offset by invisible items which would now disappear. Furthermore, Germany was due to suffer loss of valuable income-earning territory and her mercantile marine. The Treasury appears to have been satisfied with the document, and it was presented.

There was at that time a member of the War Cabinet of forceful personality and ardent temperament – Hughes, the Australian Prime Minister. He had no qualifications especially entitling him to a judgement on these topics, but that did not deter him. He regarded the Report as chicken-feed, and affirmed that Germany should pay for the full amount that the Allies had spent upon the war. A new independent committee was set up, and, oddly enough, Hughes was made the chairman. The committee associated Lord Cunliffe, formerly Governor of the Bank of England, in its deliberations. It took the view that Germany should pay for the full cost of the war to the Allies and this was set down at £24,000 million. These gentlemen saw no reason why Germany should not pay five per cent on this sum, namely £1,200 million a year, until the capital could be paid off. No army of occupation would be needed to enforce these payments. Lloyd George was emphatic in laying down that any project should be based on this assumption, and the committee accepted this limitation. The figure was, of course, wholly fantastic. It was more than a hundred times the indemnity exacted by Germany. It has not been explained, to my knowledge, how a former Governor of the Bank of England could have lent himself to such a ludicrous proposition. It is interesting to compare the figure of £1,200 million per annum with the claim made by Britain in all good faith in 1931 that it was economically impossible for her to pay £35 million a year to the United States, although she had not recently lost her mercantile marine or a large part of her territories or just fought an expensive war, and although she had pledged herself to pay this amount by an agreement freely arrived at. No doubt one interprets possibly somewhat differently in the case of a friendly power and in that of a defeated foe. None the less, allowing most liberally for that, our claim in 1931 sufficiently exposes the Cunliffe figure.

It appears that this Report was written in total ignorance of the most elementary points. It was put to the authors that these heavy payments would surely compel Germany to compete strongly in British export markets. (In fact, if she captured half the British pre-war export markets and the whole of the French, she still would not be exporting enough goods to meet the bill.) Hughes denied the allegation. If Germany had to pay a large indemnity, she would have to impose heavy taxes, and these would raise her costs of production. Britain could remit taxes, and this would lower her costs. Thus the net effect would be to improve the British chances of competition against Germany! It is clear from this that he had no notion at all how the indemnity would have to be paid. If £1,200 million a year was actually to be delivered, Germany would have to secure that her exports exceeded her imports in value by that amount; if her taxes were heavy, wages would have to be reduced correspondingly, until German goods were so cheap that she could compete successfully and flood all markets with them. In this utter nescience Hughes may not have been different from many other politicians of the time, who conceived of the indemnity simply in terms of writing a cheque for that amount and levying it upon the citizens. The transfer problem was not envisaged. Keynes told them about it, but they turned a deaf ear.

While this Report was in progress, Lloyd George was conducting a General Election. He obtained advance figures from the committee and used them on a public platform. I shall have more to say of this election in the following chapter, where Keynes's views on the reparations clauses and other aspects of the peace treaty will be discussed.

The Cabinet left the matter undetermined. The British delegates went forth to Paris in January 1919 with the Treasury Report, a Board of Trade Report, which reached similar conclusions, and the Hughes Report in their pockets. Keynes, although anxious, was not yet desperate, since he was sure that Wilson would not agree to exacting the whole cost of the war from Germany.

He went to Paris as principal representative of the

Treasury, with power to speak, when necessary, for the
Chancellor of the Exchequer. Members of 'A' Division –
Dudley Ward, Falk, Geoffrey Fry – went with him. Later,
he also had the services of Mr Harry Siepmann,[20] who returned from active service.

### J. M. Keynes to Mrs Keynes, 14 January 1919

Majestic Hotel

At last on Friday I travelled over here with Lord Reading and
soon found myself in the full swing of affairs. I write in haste as
I am off to Germany for a few days in a quarter of an hour. But I
give you yesterday as a sample. 10 a.m. Armistice Committee to
settle the renewal terms with Germany, Foch presiding; after a
short time Bonar Law left me alone and I had to lift up my voice
loudly against the French; as a result deadlock and the matter
referred to the Supreme War Council in the afternoon. 12.30
Conference with the Americans. 1.15 report morning's results to
Bonar Law. Lunch with Lord Reading. 2.30 Supreme War
Council, which was extraordinarily interesting – Wilson, Clemenceau and all of them there; Bonar Law and Wilson strongly
supported my view and Klotz, speaking for the French, was
completely defeated. 4.30 Supreme Council of Relief and Supply
which lasted to dinner time; after dinner Treasury bag from
London and finally bridge.

These days in hot French rooms are very tiring.

As I am British Financial representative to go with Foch to
meet the Germans I am now off to Treves, to arrange amongst
other things the sale of food to them, where I expect to meet the
President of the Reichsbank.

There is an enormous crowd here and as you may imagine a
perpetual buzz of chatter, gossip and intrigue.

The Armistice terms stated that 'the Allies contemplated
the provisioning of Germany to the extent that shall be
deemed necessary'. This was taken to mean that the Allies
would relax the blockade to this extent, but not that they
would provide the food gratis. Germany must pay. But
how? She had at the moment no surplus of goods waiting at

20. Since 1945 a Director of the Bank of England.

the ports for exportation. In the immediate future, payment could only be made in gold or foreign securities. But this the French had not been willing to permit, since they regarded these assets as earmarked against the reparations account. So no food was going into Germany, and the position there seemed likely to deteriorate. The Armistice had to be renewed each month, and when Keynes wrote the letter quoted, Marshal Foch was about to mount his train for talks with Germans at the frontier regarding the second renewal. I will not give the details of these negotiations, as Keynes has himself supplied a sparkling account of them in the Memoir entitled 'Melchior'.[21] The delivery of food was not achieved for another two months, since the French remained unwilling for gold to be used in payment. This refusal, on technical grounds, for a period of four months, of the food promised at the Armistice was a graver wrong than the more commonly cited 'continuance of the blockade'. The British troops were sickened by the spectacle of ill and hungry children, and the wrath of Lloyd George at French obstruction was finally aroused. There was also the fear that Bolshevism might spread into Germany, and this was the political argument most frequently used in the interest of humane treatment. Keynes, critical as he was of Lloyd George on many counts, gives a fine description of his passionate onslaught on French obstruction at a meeting on 8 March. Even Clemenceau was overwhelmed by the fire and fury of it, and the main point was gained.

The French, however, still had one obstructive ruse in reserve. On the second occasion of the renewal of the Armistice, it was laid down that the Germans must hand over their mercantile marine, the need for ships to carry food to them being put in as a justification for adding this fresh demand. (Everyone knew that the terms of peace would include a surrender of the merchant fleet, but it was not included in the original armistice terms.) In January and February the Germans had delayed handing over, since, until they were

21. *Two Memoirs.*

allowed to use their gold to buy food, they saw no prospect of obtaining any. On 8 March the French insisted that the Germans should express unconditional willingness to hand over their merchant fleet, regardless of the food question, and that only after they had undertaken to do so, would they be told that they would be allowed to use their gold for food. The French may have reckoned that the Germans, not yet knowing the second branch of this double proposal, would refuse to comply with the first, so that there would be more delay. But Lloyd George was in earnest now. He informed the First Sea Lord, who represented Britain on this formal occasion of the final demand for the surrender of the German merchant fleet, that he must use all means necessary to see that the negotiations in regard to food went through successfully. The First Sea Lord's Chief of Staff sought the help of Keynes, who on a previous occasion had had some conversation on the side with Melchior, the principal German delegate. It was a satisfaction to him to be able, again on the side but this time in association with a representative of the British Navy, to tell the Germans that they could solidly count on a release of gold for food, if they first agreed to hand over the fleet. French obstructionism was at last overcome.

All those who met Melchior were impressed with his dignity and integrity. Although he eventually refused to be a party to the Treaty of Versailles and resigned, his bank in Germany did not dare allow his picture to remain on the walls of its parlour when the Nazis attained power. He happened to be a Jew. Keynes often told a story which is not included in the Memoir. Melchior was being particularly obstinate on a certain point, no doubt under instructions. 'If you go on like that, Melchior,' Keynes said, 'we shall think you are as difficult as an Ally.' The rage of his French colleagues may be imagined.

Shortly after the first negotiations in January, Keynes took to his bed with influenza. The epidemic raged furiously among the British delegates somewhat later; many left

Paris and did not return; it is conceivable that this thinning out was a source of weakness in the very critical days before and after the presentation of the peace terms, and that, but for the influenza, we might have had a slightly better Peace Treaty. Keynes tells us in his Memoir how he went off to recover at the house of his friend Madame Bussy, on the Riviera, where six years earlier he had been at the door of death. But he does not add that he was up to his old tricks again, and, having visited Monte Carlo, had to borrow from Madame Bussy the wherewithal to get him back to Paris.

From the end of December a body had been functioning in Paris, known as the Allied Supreme Council for Supply and Relief. On 8 February, this was transformed into the Supreme Economic Council. Keynes was the official Treasury representative. Lord Robert Cecil was the principal British representative and took the chair, *de jure* by rotation, but *de facto* at every meeting. This Council was concerned with transitional problems. Until peace was signed, inter-allied control of finance, shipping, food, materials, etc., had to be maintained. This was familiar territory for Keynes, and he was able to carry on in Paris with the good work of 'A' Division. Whatever else may have happened there, the Supreme Economic Council continued to function efficiently. Mr Baker wrote:[22]

Out of these, during the Peace Conference, developed the Supreme Economic Council, which became for a brief time a kind of economic world government: the greatest experiment ever made in the correlation, control, and direction, in time of peace, of international trade and finance. In some ways it was the most interesting and significant, because it was the newest, aspect of the Paris Conference. Military and political alliances and cooperation are not new in the world, but such a degree of economic cooperation never before existed.

It was a little nest of liberalism in the Paris wilderness. The principal French representative, M. Loucheur, was a much

22. *Woodrow Wilson and World Settlement*, vol. ii, p. 335.

more reasonable man that M. Klotz. Keynes had scope here for useful work.

*J. M. Keynes to Dr J. N. Keynes,* 16 March 1919

. . . I am Deputy for the Chancellor of the Exchequer on the Supreme Economic Council with full powers to take decisions; also one of the two British Empire representatives on the Financial Committee of the Peace Conference; chairman of the Inter-Allied Financial Delegates in Armistice Negotiations with Germany; and principal Treasury Representative in Paris. All of which sounds rather grander than it is, – but it's a full day's occupation.

On 23 January a Commission on Reparations was formally constituted with instruction to report on the amount which enemy countries ought to pay and on what they were capable of paying. The Great Powers each had three representatives. Keynes was not among the British; the British Treasury and Board of Trade were both unrepresented. This point has not been sufficiently stressed. It is one thing to resign, as Keynes ultimately did, but critics might hold that a great man should have been able to influence decisions so that he did not have to resign. It is important to emphasize, therefore, that Keynes was not on the body which was formally responsible for the matters in question. His official work in Paris was mainly concerned with the purely transitional matters looked after by the Supreme Economic Council, and with carrying out any other incidental Treasury business that might arise there. In regard to backstairs influence, it must be remembered that this was largely exerted by Lloyd George's 'garden suburb', and Keynes did not belong to that either. There Philip Kerr[23] ruled the roost.

Lloyd George's nominees to the Reparations Commission were Hughes, Cunliffe and Sumner. We have already had a glimpse at the mentality of Hughes and Cunliffe. In his

23. Later Lord Lothian, British Ambassador in Washington, 1939–40.

*Memoirs of the Peace Conference* (1939) Lloyd George writes as follows with reference to the Report of the Hughes-Cunliffe Committee in December 1918: [24]

> Mr Bonar Law and I regarded the conclusions of this Report as a wild and fantastic chimera. It was incredible that men of such position, experience and responsibility should have appended their names to it.

Why, if such was his view, did he appoint these same men only six weeks later to the Reparations Commission, to the exclusion of representatives of the British Treasury and the British Board of Trade? Lord Sumner was a judge of high repute, but of no financial knowledge. He appears to have been a man of narrow views and took the ordinary line that the Germans should be thoroughly trounced; he thought his duty well discharged in using his legal abilities in support of Cunliffe. In a note to Philip Kerr, dated 25 March, Keynes quoted the following trenchant observations upon them by Norman Davis, the American Treasury representative:

> If we can quiet down the Heavenly Twins [Lords Cunliffe and Sumner] by agreeing any fool report for the Three and then get rid of them by winding up the Commission, we can get around with some human beings and start quite afresh.

It was wrong that the British Treasury should not have been represented on the Commission. Lloyd George, who knew Keynes's views, no doubt had it in mind that if, in the course of his acrobatics, he began to wish to play down reparations, he could produce Keynes out of his hat. 'This is Mr Keynes; he is here representing the British Chancellor of the Exchequer, and what he says has the Chancellor's authority. I should feel the gravest difficulty in committing my country to a course of action flatly opposed to the express advice and considered conviction of my Chancellor of the Exchequer; I cannot do it. You must find me a new Chancellor, gentlemen.' But Lloyd George's thoughts did not take this turn.

24. p. 305.

As it turned out, the deliberations of the Reparations Committee, so far as any positive proposals were concerned, were futile. But the British members exerted a crucial influence at a certain point. I do not believe that the upshot would have been quite the same had Keynes been on the Commission representing the Chancellor of the Exchequer. Had he been a co-equal member with Sumner, speaking with the authority of the Chancellor, Sumner would have had to give close attention to his views and arguments.[25] Sumner may have been a bigot, but he was also a judge and thereby trained to listen to arguments when these are advanced in court. Keynes's arguments happen to have been quite impregnable, and he was a matchless advocate on occasion. This would have been his supreme hour. Before Lord Sumner he would have deployed argument upon argument with ice-cold logic and precision; no time for rudeness now, or for fancy; not the flicker of an eyebrow; just the unanswerable case. He would have been at the top of his bent, keyed up by his passionate intellectual contempt for the trash of Hughes and Cunliffe, and from far away, from some remote recesses of his being, would have come the distant, but distinct, voices of Duncan and the others – 'go on ... go on ... remember your pledge, remember that all that we hold dear and all that you hold dear is at stake, and that decent living for many generations will depend on how you state this case'.

But it was not like this at all. The opportunity did not arise. Keynes had to rely on unofficial methods for spreading his views, save for the occasions when it might be Lloyd George's whim to consult him. Readers of his book, who judge his stature by it, are in danger of overestimating his importance in Paris. His abilities were still unknown, except to the British Treasury and to some circles of London

25. Austen Chamberlain instructed that on the Supreme Economic Council Keynes should be received 'on the same footing as I should if I were present, namely that of a full member with full rights of speech and decision'.

society. The Treasury officials knew his capacity to handle matters entrusted to him. But it was not supposed by them or anyone else that he would play an important part in peacemaking. His youthfulness itself was a handicap in a gathering of the most famous statesmen of Europe. Did he make sufficient efforts to draw attention to his own existence? It has been suggested that he relied too much on the inherent soundness of the documents he wrote, and did not do sufficient 'lobbying' among other members of the British staff of his own standing. In the Civil Service it is important that members of different ministries should be aware of each other's views and play into each other's hands. It is interesting to notice that in the Diary of the Peace Conference which Mr Harold Nicolson has published, the first reference to Keynes is on 28 May, which was towards the end of the proceedings. He notes Keynes's views as though they were new to him.

### *Extract from Diary of Mr Harold Nicolson*

May 28. Lunch with Maynard Keynes. Discuss reparation chapter of the Austrian Treaty. We are fully agreed of the absurdity of applying to Austria the German reparation and indemnity clauses . . . Keynes is very pessimistic about the German Treaty. He considers it not only immoral but incompetent. The Germans can gain nothing by signing and lose nothing by refusing to sign.

### *Letter to Vita Sackville-West,* 28 May

. . . Keynes has been too splendid about the Austrian Treaty. He is going to fight. He says he will resign.

### *Mr Harold Nicolson to his father (Lord Carnock),* 8 June

. . . I have tried, with the help of the Treasury man, who is first-class, to water down the Austrian financial clauses, but was told by Sumner to mind my own business. Anyhow I think we shall, provided Lloyd George wins his battle, get the Germans to sign. God help us if we can't! They will have us at their mercy.

It is a well-established fact that there was insufficient getting together or pooling of ideas by the experts in Paris. All were working at full pressure, attending to day-by-day crises, as well as mapping out the future of Europe. Their various proposals were submitted and modified by the Big Three, no doubt usually in a sense hostile to the enemy. They knew little of what the others were doing. It came to them all as a great shock when they first saw the Treaty as a whole immediately before it was presented to the Germans. The cumulative effect of adverse decisions separately taken had produced a Treaty which, considered as a whole, was quite different from what any of the experts had envisaged. Thus Keynes was not alone in being in imperfect liaison with all the other experts.

He did what he could. Mr Alwyn Parker was private secretary to Lord Hardinge, and his wife produced some tea in the afternoon, at which Eyre Crowe, Tyrrell and others of the Foreign Office appeared. He recalls that Keynes was often there, and his views would thus be well known to the leading members of the Foreign Office. Parker kept a diary and noted down this portrait by Eyre Crowe, which, although inaccurate in some respects, gives a typical account of the impression made by Keynes upon an intelligent observer who did not know him well.

Then the Frenchman began talking about *ce drôle de corps Monsieur Keynes*, who always carries argument to a logical extreme and overworks self-determination to such a point, regardless of history, tradition, and geographical propinquity, that he would even bestow it on *Les Iles Sorlingues* or the Isle of Wight. Crowe said: 'Oh, you don't understand Keynes, and for that matter neither do I, but a great deal depends on his health. He is an artist and a bit of a genius who knows quite a lot about his own job and has picked up something all round. Put him in the Treasury and he has the horizon of a cupboard; but plant him in front of a large map and he has the range of an eagle, quicksighted and farsighted in his own purview, though in politics his illustrations are seldom closely related to the logic. That is because he has as little aptitude or taste for politics as you or I have for the refinements of economic speculation. But he is a very clever man and has the talent of the good learner. I am much more sanguine than I was that he will end by realizing what is possible and reasonable even in regard to self-determination. Then he will step forward with the convictions of a proselyte and the pretensions of a prophet. And he will do it very well, for when he is at his best every word tells and he has the gift of getting the greatest possible meaning into a small compass. Like Mme Du Deffand: *il dit d'un seul mot tout ce qu'un mot peut dire.* He is a truly remarkable man and has a kind of critical intuition only to be paralleled by that of some of our greatest historians and scientists. I cannot myself cross-examine him about his figures as to the level of Reparations, but there are people who will not admit them as accurate. The bent of his mind is of that peculiar type that he takes a positive delight in argument for its own sake. Many of us who had frequent contact with him during the War have learnt to our cost that he only sees, for the time being, the point he has set himself to prove, and regardless of the fact that he has proved something very different yesterday, and is very likely to prove something different still tomorrow. He can bring a converging series of arguments to bear upon a single point, so that he succeeds in making everything else seem to have a minor interest to other persons, and it is doubtful if it even has a subordinate interest for Keynes himself. His opinions are in a perpetual state of progress, and therefore of apparent flux. He never shrinks from paradox and sometimes seems to aim at it for its own sake. He has not much of the *suaviter in modo*, but he's a delightful companion and does some very kind acts by stealth.

On certain occasions Keynes was able to work closely with Lloyd George. Mr Dudley Ward recalls an episode. There was a very tangled question concerning shipping in the Adriatic, which had to be settled by the Council of Four one afternoon. Over lunch Keynes and Ward reached the conclusion that they had briefed Lloyd George for the meeting in a sense diametrically opposed to British interests. They rushed round to the meeting. Lloyd George was at his seat in the semicircle round the fire and already speaking to the

subject; Dudley Ward judged that, since the arguments were
so tangled and British self-interest must not be too blatantly
advanced, nothing could now be done. Keynes, however,
took up half a sheet of notepaper on which, having advised
Lloyd George to reverse the British demand, he summarized
with a brevity Ward would not have believed possible the
arguments supporting this change. Keynes passed the paper
to Lloyd George, who looked at it quickly and proceeded.
He continued on the same lines as before. Ward was confirmed in his idea that it was too late to do anything. But
gradually, as they listened, a gentle trickle of thought of a
new kind began to appear in Lloyd George's pleadings. And
then slowly, as he took plenty of time in making his case, the
whole trend was transformed, and he was soon using all
Keynes's arguments on the opposite side; he added an admirable one of his own. He carried the day, and Ward is sure
that the others did not perceive the change of front. It was
the finest example which he ever knew of cooperation between two master minds to achieve what at first seemed
quite impossible. If only there could have been like cooperation between them in the whole business of peacemaking!

During January and February little progress was made on
reparations (or on other questions). On the Commission
there was a complete deadlock. The Americans refused to
agree to the French and British demand that the Germans
should pay the full cost of the war, on the ground that it was
contrary to the terms of the Armistice. But already in
February the Americans were making certain approaches to
the French, which were to render the Sumner-Cunliffe policy
abortive. The Americans pointed out that, if the full cost of
the war was put into the bill, the French would get a much
smaller share than if the claim were confined to reparation
of damage proper. And as even the French may have had a
suspicion, in their heart of hearts, that the full amount would
never be paid, they saw that it might be against their interest
to be put down for a smaller share in a larger amount rather
than for a larger share in a smaller one. It was also hinted

to the French that it might be possible to persuade Wilson to agree to an affirmation of Germany's theoretical liability for the full cost of the war, so long as their contractual liability was limited to the amount authorized in the Armistice terms. Such an affirmation might appease popular clamour in France. This was the origin of the famous 'war-guilt' clause, which aroused such indignation in Germany in the inter-war period. It was not originally designed to humiliate the Germans but to reconcile the French and American points of view.[26]

At the outset the Reparations Commission appointed three sub-committees. No Power had more than one representative. The British appear to have managed things well, since Sumner, Cunliffe and Hughes were the chairmen of the three sub-committees. The deadlock continued on the main questions of what Germany was liable to pay and what she was able to pay.

There was an interlude in the last part of February and beginning of March, when Wilson, Lloyd George and Clemenceau were out of action for different reasons. When Lloyd George returned, full of zest for getting to grips, hope revived. It was decided, on 10 March, to set up a committee of three 'experts', to report directly to the Council of Four on reparations. These were Norman Davis (U.S.), Loucheur (France) and E. S. Montagu (Britain). This was the Montagu who was President of the Cambridge Union in Keynes's first term and had invited him to speak 'on the paper'; he was now Secretary of State for India and a good Liberal. His appointment was certainly hopeful, and he would take Keynes's advice. This committee soon got away from unrealities.

26. It is interesting to notice that Keynes, for all his prescience about so many matters, did not perceive that this clause would be a cause of trouble. With reference to it he wrote: 'So far, however, all this is only a matter of words, of virtuosity of draftsmanship, which does no one any harm, and which probably seemed much more important at the time than it ever will again between now and Judgement Day. For substance we must turn to Annex I' (*Economic Consequences of the Peace*, p. 141).

Montagu and Davis agreed upon £2,000 million (the figure of the original Treasury draft) as the amount that Germany would be able to pay and Loucheur is said to have admitted that he agreed privately, although he could not be so quoted.[27] A report was suddenly required of them on 15 March. They did not dare to present so low a figure, and, instead, put forward the figure of £3,000 million, with another £3,000 million to be paid in German currency, which should only be converted when conditions were favourable. In view of this last proviso, the proposal was not unreasonable. According to Mr Burnett, Lloyd George and Clemenceau were both convinced.[28]

But on 17 March a memorandum came to Lloyd George from Hughes, Cunliffe and Sumner proposing a payment to rise to £600 million a year in 1926 and to run for about thirty-five years thereafter.[29] Such figures were still not far from the realms of fantasy. On the next day the 'experts' were summoned back by the Council of Four and told by Lloyd George of the official British proposal. In these circumstances Lloyd George stated that he could not abide by the finding of the 'experts'.

At this point he invited Keynes to propose a scale of payments which would yield a total sum of £5,000 million. This must have been painful work for Keynes. But at least Lloyd George's tendency to break away from the 'Heavenly Twins' was welcome. He worked out a scheme, with the assistance of Mr R. H. Brand, which had rising annual payments, and reached a maximum of £400 million a year in 1951–60. Although this involved total payments of £11,000 million in all, at 5 per cent the present value was only £3,800 million.[30] This was unsatisfactory, since the figure of £3,800

27. *Reparation at the Peace Conference*, by P. M. Burnett, vol. i, p. 54. The statement is based on the authority of Mr Davis.

28. op. cit., p. 56.

29. Lloyd George's *Memoirs of the Peace Conference*, p. 334.

30. They accordingly felt it necessary to add a footnote showing a steeper graduation of payments, which would give a present value of about £4,800 million, but they deprecated this footnote.

million was deemed to be politically unacceptable. It seems strange that it was always taken for granted that the wrathful masses, whose profound ignorance on these economic topics has been so often cited as the main obstacle to a wise settlement, had a perfect understanding of the significance of these large figures and would at once judge that £3,800 million was a puny sum.

However, at this time, Lloyd George is said to have told the Americans that £5,000 million would be acceptable to him, if only they could get Sumner and Cunliffe to agree.[31] We see clearly the baleful influence of these two. They were associated in the public mind with stern treatment, and Lloyd George was not prepared to face his public on a settlement which lacked their blessing! It was at this time that he went to Fontainebleau, taking Philip Kerr and others of the 'garden suburb' with him, and composed a memorandum (25 March) which was liberal in sentiment. This did not move the French, however, and led to the interchange of sarcastic letters between him and Clemenceau. At the same time (25 March) a memorandum by Claude Lowther, to the effect that Germany should bear the whole cost of the war, was circulated to all members of Parliament and published in *The Times*. Lloyd George scented dangers at home.

Meanwhile two major developments were taking place in the reparations discussion which determined the final settlement. The first was the idea that no total figure for reparations payments should be mentioned in the Peace Treaty, that being left to be determined by a permanent Reparations Commission (to be distinguished from the Reparations Commission of the Conference). This plan has been severely criticized. It meant that Germany could not regain creditworthiness for a long period. No one knew whether those who sought for impracticable sums would not prevail on the Reparations Commission. The United States was at that time, as she has been once more, the main source of credit.

31. Burnett, vol. i, p. 59.

But it was perfectly clear then that this credit would have to come, not by way of government loans, but through the operations of private financiers. Therefore, to render Germany uncreditworthy for a long term of years was to make it impossible for her to find means of recovery or to pay substantial reparations. The whole of Europe would suffer accordingly.

It is easy to see why the plan was attractive at the time. Those who really hoped to exact very large sums were not being invited to surrender their claims. Those who only wanted to maintain the appearance of exacting large sums, to satisfy their constituents, had their faces saved. Genuine liberals could argue that, when passions had had time to cool, the Reparations Commission would abate its demands and had powers enough to wrangle a satisfactory settlement, despite the clauses of the Peace Treaty. Lloyd George has argued that such was his own view; that the American, British and Italian representatives would together have formed a majority on the Commission in favour of leniency; and that it was the defection of the Americans which upset the apple-cart.[32]

Between 25 and 28 March there was a last desperate attempt to reach an agreed figure, Sumner, Cunliffe and Keynes negotiating for the British! On 28 March the Council of Four decided that no figure should be inserted in the Treaty.

The second development was the British proposal that the value of separation allowances and pensions should be classed as damage inflicted upon the civilian population, in acordance with the Armistice terms, and added to the reparations bill. In regard to this Keynes wrote: 'If words have any meaning, or engagements any force, we had no more right to claim for those war expenses of the State, which arose out of Pensions and Separation Allowances, than for any other of the general costs of the war. And who is prepared to argue in detail that we were entitled to demand

32. *Memoirs of the Peace Conference*, p. 341.

the latter?'[33] Mr Burnett has indeed shown conclusively that the French and British understood quite well at the time of the Armistice that they were signing away their right to demand the full costs of the war.[34] But if Wilson could be persuaded that the inclusion of separation allowances and pensions was right, a compromise might be effected. Such a formula would yield a large enough total for the French realists to feel that it was as much as they were ever likely to get; it would satisfy the British. But at first Wilson held out. Oddly enough, he was finally convinced by a memorandum from General Smuts, the most enlightened of all the plenipotentiaries at Paris.

Smuts felt indignant that under the pure Wilsonian formula Britain would get so little by way of reparation. He had it in mind that she, and not France, had been bearing the main brunt of the war during the last two years, both in fighting manpower and in money. The device of including pensions and allowances would secure a larger share of payments for Britain. As, in Smuts's view, the bill, even without allowances and pensions, exceeded Germany's capacity to pay and would therefore not be demanded in full, Germany would not suffer from the inclusion of these items also. They would swell the theoretical total, but would not increase what was actually demanded, only altering its distribution among the Allies. It might have been possible to justify such a device if the Allied representatives had been sensible people working together in cordial amity, and had there been no question of asking Germany to pay more than she was really able to. In the actual conditions of Paris, it was ill-starred.

On 1 April Wilson agreed to the inclusion of pensions and allowances under the influence of Smuts's memorandum. But the battle was not yet lost, for one major point remained to be settled, and a right decision on this would render the inclusion of pensions and allowances nugatory.

33. *Economic Consequences of the Peace*, p. 144.
34. Burnett, op. cit., ch. 1.

This was the question of the time limit. Throughout these discussions Lloyd George emphasized that the bill against Germany should be cleared within the lifetime of the generation that made the war. This was usually taken to be thirty years. So long as this time limit was observed, it seemed clear that Germany could not be asked to do more in total than meet the bill as assessed before the inclusion of pensions and allowances. Thus, when, after three days of heated debate among the experts, the point about the time limit came for decision to the Council of Four on 5 April, Mr Davis was able to say that President Wilson *'had conceded pensions on the theory that this would not materially increase the actual amount Germany would have to pay, but would rather affect the method of distribution, because we regarded Germany's capacity as being agreed to as within the thirty-year limit.'* [35] This was the Smuts view. Wilson's decision about pensions was the one for which Keynes took him most severely to task. But it seems that the really operative decision was made by the Council of Four on 5 April (House then representing Wilson, who was unwell), when the proposal to insert a time limit in the Treaty was dropped. Thereafter it was no longer possible to argue that the Germans would not feel the full weight of the inclusion of pensions and allowances, and that this only affected the distribution of the spoils among the Allies. Here we have a striking example of how Wilson's position was whittled away.

It is interesting to observe that the major vital decisions (no fixed sum, inclusion of pensions and allowances, no time limit) were reached before the famous telegram from 380 Conservative members of Parliament arrived on 8 April. None the less the moral of those who stress the importance of this telegram is correct. Lloyd George's subservience to Sumner and Cunliffe reflected his fear of hostile Conservative criticism at home.

Thus Keynes's hopes were dashed and unreason prevailed.

35. Burnett, op. cit., vol. i, p. 829.

But it was difficult on this, as on other occasions, to cast him down. Defeated on one line, he sought another way out of the difficulties. He fell back on his position as chief British representative on the Supreme Economic Council. This was responsible for the actual economic conditions of the moment, which were, in all conscience, sufficiently deplorable. Help was given day by day, but this could not go on indefinitely. There was clearly a gap between the present time and that happy time when Germany could comfortably pay £500 million a year or whatever it might be. Was it not the duty of the Supreme Economic Council to endeavour to bridge this gap? Accordingly Keynes worked upon a scheme, which was known for a time as 'The Keynes Plan'. This was for an issue of £1,000 million bonds by the German Government (and proportionate issues by the other enemy governments), one-fifth to be used for the purchase of food and materials, and four-fifths to be payable on reparations account. Interest was to be guaranteed jointly and severally by the enemy states, with priority over Reparations payments, and to be underwritten by the Allied and Associated governments, as well as by the Scandinavian governments and Holland and Switzerland, in certain proportions. These bonds were to be acceptable as first-class collateral for loans by all central banks. The effect might be that Federal Reserve Banks of the United States would be asked to make a loan for the whole amount, or a great part of it, and this loan would temporarily finance not only the immediate payment of reparations by Germany, but also the immediate payment by the other Allies of the interest on their debt to the United States. It would prevent Germany being immediately stripped of all her working capital and would assist the European Allies to carry their heavy burden. It was indeed a sort of Marshall plan, albeit on a smaller scale. Europe would be screened from the immediate catastrophe which would take place when the reparation clauses of the Treaty came into operation. It would cover a period within which a change of heart might occur among the Allies, so that, after all, the European position might be saved.

He spent a week in England in the middle of April.

*J. M. Keynes to Mrs Keynes,* 17 April 1919

46 Gordon Square

I have been kept about here until today getting through the Cabinet a *grand scheme for the rehabilitation of Europe.*

Austen Chamberlain (Chancellor of the Exchequer) wrote to Lloyd George warmly supporting the Keynes Plan.

Lloyd George sponsored the scheme in Paris and wrote a fine covering letter to President Wilson. But this time it was the Americans who would not play. The U.S. Treasury affirmed that it was unthinkable that Congress would authorize an arrangement which might involve the Federal Reserve System in making a large loan of this kind. The U.S. Treasury argued that already since the Armistice they had authorized loans to Europe amounting to £600 million, a large sum for peacetime – their loans during the war had amounted to £1,400 million – and that Congress would go no further. Keynes's life repeated itself. Was not his last great work doing with success what he failed to do in 1919? The attitude of the Americans had changed meanwhile.

They had a good excuse in 1919 for rejecting this proposed liability. In replying to Lloyd George, President Wilson wrote: [36]

You have suggested that we all address ourselves to the problem of helping to put Germany on her feet, but how can your experts or ours be expected to work out a *new* plan to furnish working capital to Germany when we deliberately start out by taking away all Germany's *present* capital? How can anyone expect America to turn over to Germany in any considerable measure new working capital to take the place of that which the European nations have determined to take from her? Such questions would appear to answer themselves, but I cannot refrain

36. *Woodrow Wilson and World Settlement*, by R. S. Baker, vol. iii, p. 346.

from stating them, because they so essentially belong to a candid consideration of the whole difficult problem to which we are addressing ourselves, with as sincere a desire as that of their colleagues to reach a serviceable conclusion.

Commenting on this, Keynes wrote to Philip Kerr:

The President's letter, as it stands however, indicates a spirit far too harsh for the human situation facing us. In particular, it is surely impossible for the Americans to disclaim responsibility for the Peace Treaty to which, wisely or not, they have put their name equally with the other governments . . . It is also worth remembering that while the Americans greatly criticized the aggregate of the indemnity they did not, so far as I remember, oppose the initial £1,000 million.[37] Yet the force of the President's letter entirely turns on the inadvisability of exacting this sum of £1,000 million . . . Nevertheless controversy on the above lines would be vain. There is a substantial truth in the President's standpoint and we can only look for fruitful results out of the discussions of the new committee.

Despite this setback Keynes's initiative might have had some effect. On 9 May the Council of Four set up a Committee of Experts (with Lord Robert Cecil and Keynes for the British Empire) to deal with the problem. Their report was presented on 4 June. The trouble was that the Americans had been unable to offer much money. None the less, this Report, agreed by British, French and American delegates, grappled with the problems confronting Europe, and, if the discussions had been kept alive, the Americans might have been led on to a more helpful attitude. But the Council of Four had lost interest, and it never considered the Report. The labours of its collaborators had been in vain.

After his return from London in the third week of April, Keynes had found that Montagu, to whom he had been referring for ministerial decision, had left Paris. At the suggestion of the Chancellor of the Exchequer, an arrangement was now made by which, when he needed ministerial guidance on the spot, he should go to General Smuts. In April

37. This had to be paid by the Germans before 1 May 1921.

he was attending the Council of Four regularly when financial and reparations questions were discussed, often as the senior British official immediately behind Lloyd George. This was the phase of tidying up for presentation to the Germans. The clauses did not get more lenient in the process.

The Peace Treaty was presented on 7 May; German comments soon began to come in and their full-length reply was received on 29 May. Keynes in his book stressed the point that, while Lloyd George was now prepared to make concessions, Wilson's attitude stiffened. The latter had persuaded himself that the Treaty, as drafted, was in accordance with his principles, thereby greatly deceiving himself; to admit the German criticisms would imply that he had betrayed his own cause; this was psychologically impossible for him. It should be observed, however, that on the question of reparations he was in this phase still trying to get a more reasonable settlement, including the naming of a fixed sum.

Keynes made a last despairing attempt in a note handed to Lloyd George on 2 June, on the basis of the Germans undertaking the physical restoration of France and Belgium. In this note he estimated the total claims against Germany (including pensions and allowances) at £6,300 million.[38] He suggested a deduction from this sum, on the Austrian precedent, of a share of reparation attributable to territory to be ceded under the Peace Treaty. He suggested that this would leave £5,000 million – a convenient sum, as the draft Treaty had made specific provision for the payment of at least that amount. From this he deducted £2,000 million for the physical restoration and proposed that the Germans should be required to pay the balance of £3,000 million spread over a reasonable period, without interest. But it was all in vain. The American battle to get a fixed sum inserted failed.

The Treaty was signed on 28 June, but Keynes had already left Paris.

38. cf. the official finding of the Reparations Commission nearly two years later of £6,600 million.

## J. M. Keynes to Mrs Keynes, 14 May 1919

It must be weeks since I've written a letter to anyone, – but I've been utterly worn out, partly by work partly by depression at the evil round me. I've never been so miserable as for the last two or three weeks; the Peace is outrageous and impossible and can bring nothing but misfortune behind it. Personally I do not believe the Germans will sign, though the general view is to the contrary (i.e. that after a few moans and complaints they will sign anything). But if they do sign this will be in many ways the worse alternative; for it is out of the question that they should keep the terms (which are incapable of being kept) and nothing but general disorder and unrest could result. Certainly if I was in the Germans' place I'd rather die than sign such a Peace.

Well, I suppose I've been an accomplice in all this wickedness and folly, but the end is now at hand. I am writing to the Treasury to be relieved of my duties by June 1 if possible and not later than June 15 in any event. So I may just be back in time for the tail end of the May Term.

Apart from any other reasons, I am quite at the end of my tether and must have a holiday.

I've a letter lying unanswered inquiring if I will be a candidate for the Directorship of the London School of Economics, – pay £1,500 or perhaps more. I shall ask a few questions about it, but have no intention of accepting. I hope father agrees.

I am supposed to be sitting to John for my portrait for his Peace Conference set; but there has been no time so far.

## J. M. Keynes to Duncan Grant, 14 May 1919

. . . I have been as miserable for the last two or three weeks as a fellow could be. The Peace is outrageous . . . Meanwhile there is no food or employment anywhere, and the French and Italians are pouring munitions into Central Europe to arm everyone against everyone else. I sit in my room hour after hour receiving deputations from the new nations. All ask, not for food or raw materials, but primarily for instruments of war against their neighbours . . .

One most bitter disappointment was the collapse of my grand scheme for putting everyone on their legs. After getting it successfully through the Chancellor of the Exchequer and the Prime

Minister and seeing it formally handed to Wilson and Clemenceau, the American Treasury (from whom no more was asked than any one else) turns it formally down as a most immoral proposal which might cost them something and which senators from Illinois would not look at. They had a chance of taking a large, or at least a humane, view of the world, but unhesitatingly refused it. Wilson, of whom I have seen a good deal more lately, is the greatest fraud on earth.

The weather is very fine. I spent last weekend in Fontainebleau Forest and tried to get to Chartres, but was defeated by two punctures to my motor. Do write to me and remind me that there are still some decent people in the world. Here I could cry all day for rage and vexation. The world cannot be quite as bad as it looks from the Majestic.

A week or two ago I went to a Matisse exhibition and enclose the catalogue. I like the latest least. Am I right in thinking that he is becoming almost academic? ...

### *Austen Chamberlain to J. M. Keynes*, 21 May 1919

Bradbury has just shown me your letter of the 19th. I know how great a sacrifice of personal inclination, and even more, you have made in continuing your work for us in Paris. On your side I think you know how much I have valued and appreciated the enormous assistance which you have given us ...

Bradbury will write to you as to the other members of the staff but I could not leave to him the expression of my strong feeling that a continuation of your services for the present is of great importance in the public interest, nor can I refrain from making my personal appeal to you to continue your help until the situation is more clearly defined.

### *J. M. Keynes to Austen Chamberlain*, 26 May 1919

I appreciate your letter very much, just as I have had good reason to appreciate my treatment by the Treasury all through; and if my only grounds for leaving were the need of a rest and the desire to get back to my own work, I could not resist your appeal. But that is not the position. I was so anxious to leave this Conference on general grounds that I did not like to make too much fuss about my reasons arising out of my disagreement with the policy which is being pursued here. But I stated them in my previous letter and to me they are very real and important. We have presented a Draft Treaty to the Germans which contains in it much that is unjust and much more that is inexpedient. Until the last moment no one could appreciate its full bearing. It is now right and necessary to discuss it with the Germans and to be ready to make substantial concessions. If this policy is not pursued, the consequences will be disastrous in the extreme.

If, therefore, the decision is taken to discuss the Treaty with the Germans with a view to substantial changes and if our policy is such that it looks as if I can be of real use, I am ready to stay another two or three weeks. But if the decision is otherwise, I fear that I must resign immediately. I cannot express how strongly I feel as to the gravity of what is in front of us, and I must have my hands quite free. I wish I could talk to you about the whole miserable business. The Prime Minister is leading us all into a morass of destruction. The settlement which he is proposing for Europe disrupts it economically and must depopulate it by millions of persons. The New States we are setting up cannot survive in such surroundings. Nor can the peace be kept or the League of Nations live. How can you expect me to assist at this tragic farce any longer, seeking to lay the foundation, as a Frenchman puts it, 'd'une guerre juste et durable'.

The Prime Minister's present Austrian policy puts me in an equal difficulty. Lords Sumner and Cunliffe have produced a Reparation Draft of which I have already sent you a copy. Now General Smuts and I are invited to join their deliberations. But the British representation cannot be fundamentally divided against itself, and it is necessary to choose. I append a letter which General Smuts has written to the Prime Minister about this. [He refused to serve.] I also enclose two of Sir F. Oppenheimer's latest telegrams.


## *J. M. Keynes to Mrs Keynes*, 1 June 1919

Partly out of misery for all that's happening, and partly from prolonged overwork, I gave way last Friday and took to my bed suffering from sheer nervous exhaustion. There I've remained more or less ever since, rising only for really important interviews and for a daily stroll in the Bois, with the result that I'm already much better. My first idea was to return to England immediately, but General Smuts, with whom I've been working very intimately for changes in this damned Treaty, persuaded me that it was my duty to stay on and be available if necessary for the important discussions of these present days, declaring that one can only leave the field of battle *dead*. However the business will soon be determined and then, I hope in two or three days at latest, I return to England forever, – bar certain very improbable changes in the possibilities of the case.

I dragged myself out of bed on Friday to make a final protest before the Reparations Commission against murdering Vienna, and did achieve some improvement.

The German reply is of unequal merit but remains an unanswerable exposure of all our wickedness.

Don't think me more broken down than I am. I eat and sleep well and there's nothing whatever the matter except fatigue.

I have left the Majestic and am living in a flat on the edge of the Bois, which is quiet and where I am very well tended.

*J. M. Keynes to Mrs Keynes, 3 June 1919*

I am living alone in a flat, which has been lent to me, on the edge of the Bois with an excellent French cook and a soldier servant to valet me, and am getting on splendidly, – otherwise I would most certainly have sent for you at once. I spend more than half of my time in bed and only rise for interviews with the Chancellor of the Exchequer, Smuts, the Prime Minister and such. Dudley Ward comes down twice a day with the news. I am indeed so much better that only extreme prudence in matters of health keeps me secluded at all. But I distinctly looked over the edge last week, and, not liking the prospect at all, took to my bed instantly.

The P.M., poor man, would like now at the eleventh hour to alter the damned Treaty, for which no one has a word of defence, but it's too late in my belief and for all his wrigglings Fate must now march on to its conclusion. I feel it my duty to stay on here so long as there is any chance of a scheme for a real change being in demand. But I don't expect any such thing. Anyhow it will soon be settled and I bound for home.

### *J. M. Keynes to Norman Davis,* 5 June 1919

I am slipping away on Saturday from this scene of nightmare. I can do no more good here. You Americans are broken reeds, and I have no anticipation of any real improvement in the state of affairs.

### *J. M. Keynes to David Lloyd George,* 5 June 1919

I ought to let you know that on Saturday I am slipping away from this scene of nightmare. I can do no more good here. I've gone on hoping even through these last dreadful weeks that you'd find some way to make of the Treaty a just and expedient document. But now it's apparently too late. The battle is lost. I leave the twins to gloat over the devastation of Europe and to assess to taste what remains for the British taxpayer.

# [7]

## 'The Economic Consequences
of the Peace'

### I

WE have seen that in the later period at Paris, Keynes was in close consultation with General Smuts, who agreed with his opinions. Towards the end Keynes broached the project of writing a book to describe the whole sorry story; and Smuts strongly encouraged him.

*J. M. Keynes to O. T. Falk*, 25 June 1919

. . . On Monday I actually began writing a book about the economic condition of Europe, but may not persevere with it.

This was stage fright, which soon passed off. He had not yet matured his plan.

*The Economic Consequences of the Peace* was written during August and September at Charleston and appeared on the bookstalls in December. It made his name famous in many lands, and also infamous in many straitlaced circles. It was his deep anguish of soul that urged him to write and his utter fearlessness that carried the project forward. He did not hesitate to flout the mighty and to outrage prevailing opinion. He sought to change that opinion. In order to do so, he was ready to sacrifice his own worldly interests. In the event he did both. His influence on the British public was profound and rapid; in 1924 the French themselves became a party to a provisional reparations plan of a reasonable character; but he remained an outlaw from British official circles for many years afterwards.

In the following pages an attempt will be made to assess the value of this work as a contribution to the economics and politics of the day. We have the advantage of our acquaintance with subsequent events. Opinion has fluctuated in its judgement of the book, and even now the time may not yet be ripe for a final verdict. But however it be rated for political sagacity, it has another quality which entitles its author to the very highest rank. *The Economic Consequences of the Peace* takes its place as one of the finest pieces of polemic in the English language. The broad philosophical considerations, clearly marshalled, with which it opens; the fresh limpid style, the sparkling phrases, the sense of drama; the story unfolding stage by stage so that interest never flags; the comfortable authority of a man speaking with complete knowledge of his subject and clearly of intellectual eminence; the ruthless and terrible character sketches presented suddenly with great originality, invective of quite a different character from that found in the old masters, and hints that the author well understands his victims' good qualities also – hints which do not strike the reader as a mere ruse, but as reflecting a genuinely judicial quality; the arch-villain of the piece, Clemenceau, presented as a most lovable person; the story proceeding into elaborate statistics, which never weigh down the pages, but are welded into the irresistible logic of the argument; insensate folly leading to tragedy; a vision of the suffering victims, hungry, patient, not ready to revolt, but with a smouldering rage that may well work havoc; dark forebodings; a prophecy of woes to come which is vague in outline and thereby more convincing; the whole wrought into an artistic unity by an argument which moves breathlessly from first word to last – these qualities combine to create a great masterpiece.

The book is seldom read nowadays. People feel that they know what it says and have nothing to learn from it. They may be alarmed – needlessly – by the thought of statistics, now obsolete, concerning coal and gold and foreign trade. This is a mistake. There are a number of matters – the evils of inflation and price control – which continue to be of live interest. The German problem is still with us. But, beyond all this, there is the pleasure to be obtained from it as a work of art. We still read Pascal's *Provincial Letters* with delight, although not many still regard the distinction between efficacious and sufficient grace as a live issue.

The original manuscript included portraits of the Big Three. On consideration Keynes decided that, since he had so recently served Lloyd George, the main section about him should be omitted. It was shown to Asquith, who thought it a true portrait, and was subsequently published, along with a reprint of the description of the Council of Four, in *Essays in Biography* (1933). But one does not appreciate the full value of the portraits by reading them in isolation. Their interest is immensely enhanced when they are placed against the background of the European scene, as described in the original book. A reprint of this should be issued with the portrait of Lloyd George included. Keynes wrote another piece about the Paris Conference, his Memoir on Melchior (published 1949). Chronologically, the events described come at an early phase of the Peace Conference narrative. In a reprint of the book, however, it should not be placed at the beginning, but in an appendix. The tone and temper of much of it are totally different from those of the book itself, and its inclusion in the text would spoil the artistic unity. In 'Melchior' the personal comment is much more acid. Keynes wrote it at a time of extreme bitterness, to satisfy a personal impulse, and he was not restrained by the desire for a favourable verdict from all men of general good sense. Those who hold that the portraits in the *Economic Consequences* were heightened in order to titillate public opinion, should compare them with what he wrote when he was merely giving vent to his own private thoughts. One is struck at once with the restraint and dignity of the former.

It can seldom have happened that one, who had a month or two earlier been playing a notable part in a tense drama of great moment in world history, was able then to summarize it with the imaginative power shown in the following passage. This belongs to the Lloyd George section and was not printed in the original book. The 'King' is Clemenceau.

But it is not appropriate to apply to him [Lloyd George] the ordinary standards. How can I convey to the reader, who does not know him, any just impression of this extraordinary figure of our time, this syren, this goat-footed bard, this half-human visitor to our age from the hag-ridden magic and enchanted woods of Celtic antiquity? One catches in his company that flavour of final purposelessness, inner irresponsibility, existence outside or away from our Saxon good and evil, mixed with cunning, remorselessness, love of power, that lend fascination, enthralment, and terror to the fair-seeming magicians of North European folklore. Prince Wilson sailing out from the West in his barque *George Washington* sets foot in the enchanted castle of Paris to free from chains and oppression and an ancient curse the maid Europe, of eternal youth and beauty, his mother and his bride in one. There in the castle is the King with yellow parchment face, a million years old, and with him an enchantress with a harp singing in the Prince's own words to a magical tune. If only the Prince could cast off the paralysis which creeps on him and, crying to heaven, could make the Sign of the Cross, with a sound of thunder and crashing glass the castle would dissolve, the magicians vanish, and Europe leap to his arms. But in this fairy-tale the forces of the half-world win and the soul of Man is subordinated to the spirits of the earth.[1]

Of Clemenceau he wrote:

He felt about France what Pericles felt of Athens – unique value in her, nothing else mattering; but his theory of politics was Bismarck's. He had one illusion – France; and one disillusion – mankind, including Frenchmen, and his colleagues not least.[2]

And of Wilson:

At the crisis of his fortunes the President was a lonely man. Caught up in the toils of the Old World, he stood in great need of sympathy, of moral support, of the enthusiasm of the masses. But buried in the Conference, stifled in the hot and poisoned atmosphere of Paris, no echo reached him from the outer world, and no throb of passion, sympathy, or encouragement from his silent constituents in all countries. He felt that the blaze of

1. *Essays in Biography*, pp. 36–7.
2. *The Economic Consequences of the Peace*, p. 29.

popularity which had greeted his arrival in Europe was already dimmed; the Paris Press jeered at him openly; his political opponents at home were taking advantage of his absence to create an atmosphere against him; England was cold, critical, and unresponsive. He had so formed his *entourage* that he did not receive through private channels the current of faith and enthusiasm of which the public sources seemed dammed up. He needed, but lacked, the added strength of collective faith. The German terror still overhung us, and even the sympathetic public was very cautious; the enemy must not be encouraged, our friends must be supported, this was not the time for discord or agitations, the President must be trusted to do his best. And in this drought the flower of the President's faith withered and dried up.[3]

*

The President's attitude to his colleagues had now become: I want to meet you so far as I can; I see your difficulties and I should like to be able to agree to what you propose; but I can do nothing that is not just and right, and you must first of all show me that what you want does really fall within the words of the pronouncements which are binding on me. Then began the weaving of that web of sophistry and Jesuitical exegesis that was finally to clothe with insincerity the language and substance of the whole Treaty. The word was issued to the witches of all Paris:

> Fair is foul, and foul is fair,
> Hover through the fog and filthy air.

The subtlest sophisters and most hypocritical draftsmen were set to work, and produced many ingenious exercises which might have deceived for more than an hour a cleverer man than the President.[4]

*

At last the work was finished; and the President's conscience was still intact. In spite of everything I believe that his temperament allowed him to leave Paris a really sincere man; and it is probable that to this day he is genuinely convinced that the

3. ibid., pp. 44–5.
4. ibid., p. 47.

Treaty contains practically nothing inconsistent with his former professions.

But the work was too complete, and to this was due the last tragic episode of the drama. The reply of Brockdorff-Rantzau inevitably took the line that Germany had laid down her arms on the basis of certain assurances, and that the Treaty in many particulars was not consistent with these assurances. But this was exactly what the President could not admit; in the sweat of solitary contemplation and with prayers to God he had done *nothing* that was not just and right; for the President to admit that the German reply had force in it was to destroy his self-respect and to disrupt the inner equipoise of his soul; and every instinct of his stubborn nature rose in self-protection. In the language of medical psychology to suggest to the President that the Treaty was an abandonment of his professions was to touch on the raw a Freudian complex. It was a subject intolerable to discuss, and every subconscious instinct plotted to defeat its further exploration.

Thus it was that Clemenceau brought to success what had seemed to be, a few months before, the extraordinary and impossible proposal that the Germans should not be heard. If only the President had not been so conscientious, if only he had not concealed from himself what he had been doing, even at the last moment he was in a position to have recovered lost ground and to have achieved some very considerable successes. But the President was set. His arms and legs had been spliced by the surgeons to a certain posture, and they must be broken again before they could be altered. To his horror, Mr Lloyd George, desiring at the last moment all the moderation he dared, discovered that he could not in five days persuade the President of error in what it had taken five months to prove to him to be just and right. After all, it was harder to debamboozle this old Presbyterian than it had been to bamboozle him; for the former involved his belief in and respect for himself.

Thus in the last act the President stood for stubbornness and a refusal of conciliations.[5]

The book closes with the words:

We have been moved already beyond endurance, and need rest. Never in the lifetime of men now living has the universal element in the soul of man burnt so dimly.

5. *The Economic Consequences of the Peace*, pp. 49–50.

For these reasons the true voice of the new generation has not yet spoken, and silent opinion is not yet formed. To the formation of the general opinion of the future I dedicate this book.[6]

Before proceeding to our assessment, we may consider one criticism which has often been made. It is said that justice was not done to the Big Three, who were, after all, great men, giants in their age. If only comparable leaders, it is well argued, could have been found to guide our destinies in the twenty years which followed, what a much better place the world might have been. It is lacking in all sense of proportion to present them as evil or ridiculous figures.

The justice of the plea on behalf of these three may well be admitted. None the less, this criticism can be completely met. These sketches were not intended by their author as full-length portraits of his subjects to be hung in the shrine dedicated to our ancestors. The book was not written as a definitive history of the Peace Conference. It was quite intentionally designed as a polemic; it was composed in two months at a white heat of passion, immediately after the events. It sought to influence public opinion at once. Europe was disintegrating and must be saved. Keynes did not attempt to portray all the characteristics of his subjects, but only those relevant to the matter in hand, and in particular those which caused the mistakes to be made. He was telling his public that the Peace Treaty was an act of wickedness and folly. 'How can this be so?' they might reply. 'We do not know the facts and believe that you must have distorted them, since Wilson we know to be neither wicked nor foolish. And is not Lloyd George a life-long Liberal?' He did not distort the facts; the documents have on the whole confirmed his account. It was necessary for him to explain, therefore, how it could be that these two men, each trusted in their different ways, became parties to the transaction. To do so, he had to show certain weaknesses in sharp relief.

6. ibid., p. 279.

The sketches only give part of the truth; in this he carried out his own programme, clearly announced.

The disillusion was so complete, that some of those who had trusted most hardly dared speak of it. Could it be true? they asked of those who returned from Paris. Was the Treaty really as bad as it seemed? What had happened to the President? What weakness or what misfortune had led to so extraordinary, so unlooked-for a betrayal?

Yet the causes were very ordinary and human.[7]

These were his terms of reference. He was perfectly entitled to keep within them. Indeed, it would have been wrong to have done otherwise. It would have been irrelevant, and therefore injurious, and probably beyond his competence, to have given full-length portraits of these historic figures.

It is interesting to observe that M. Mantoux, arch-critic of the book, is satisfied with the portrait of his own countryman, which presumably he was better able to judge than those of the others:

His portrait of the old Tiger ... was masterly, and it is beyond anyone's power to excel it.[8]

It was not Clemenceau's backsliding that Keynes had to explain. The French attitude was well understood, and, it being what it was, the others would clearly have a very difficult task. He had to explain why they were unequal to it: 'But in such a test of character and method as Paris provided, the Prime Minister's naturally good instincts, his industry, his inexhaustible nervous vitality were not serviceable. In that furnace other qualities were called for – a policy deeply grounded in permanent principle, tenacity, fierce indignation, honesty, loyal leadership.'[9]

A slightly different criticism has been advanced. General Smuts remarked to me[10] that 'the portrait of Wilson was

7. *The Economic Consequences of the Peace*, p. 36.
8. *The Carthaginian Peace*, by Étienne Mantoux, p. 46.
9. *Essays in Biography*, p. 35.
10. Interview on 8 June 1948. See below, pp. 313–14.

absolutely truthful, but Keynes should not have written it;
after all Wilson was our friend'. This is a generous attitude,
but it may be difficult for General Smuts to judge the matter
aright. His immediate responsibilities were to lie elsewhere.
Keynes felt a personal obligation, after having partaken in,
and by his efficient services contributed to, the progress of
events at Paris, to do something at once towards rectifying
the situation. Wilson had spent his power and could no
longer help. That he was high-minded and well-intentioned
and had striven according to his lights for a good settlement
was now not relevant.[11] The public scarcely knew in what
respects the terms of peace were ill considered; what was
immediately required was elucidation. The sketch of Wilson
played an essential part in that. It would be for other hands
to write of all Wilson's good qualities and keep his memory
green.

But what may be deemed a misfortune befell Keynes's
work. The consummate artistry of his portraits has preserved them in our memories, and the notions entertained
by the subsequent generation about the characters of the
three great men have been largely influenced by Keynes.
He would, no doubt, have supposed, had it occurred to him
to think upon the matter, that others would arise to do
justice to these three in regard to all their manifold good
qualities and activities through long and illustrious careers.
The trouble in this matter has been that other pens of comparable power have not been found. Lloyd George gives an
excellent account, also critical, of Wilson, in manly, vigorous
prose; Lloyd George had some gift of words! Yet place it
beside the Keynes portrait, and you will at once feel it to be
the work of an amateur. Where are our great historians?
It is not enough to complain that Keynes did not do justice;
let them do justice themselves! Let them show these men
with all their vibrant powers. After all, they are good subjects. The fact of the matter is that the survival of these
portraits and the complaints against them are due to

11. See below, p. 344.

Keynes's greatness as a writer and not to any fault in his own intentions. It was the misfortune of these men to come across the path of one who had the divine gift of words.

> And he can spread thy name o'er lands and seas,
> Whatever clime the sun's bright circle warms.

Wood may have had many amiable qualities, but, unfortunately for his fame, he came across Swift's path.

### 2

Keynes attached great importance to two points, which need not be discussed at length. One was the fact that the Treaty was a violation of the Armistice terms, and the other its hypocrisy.

In regard to the former, Keynes was particularly interested in the inclusion of pensions and separation allowances in the claim for reparations from the enemy. This was a glaring breach. And what shall we say of the French and British delegates who, in the early stages of the discussion, advanced claims for the full costs of the war? It is clear that at the time of the Armistice they knew perfectly well that they were signing away the right to demand those costs. It is possible that Keynes was too ready to assume similar defalcations in regard to matters with the history of which he was less well acquainted.

There is some tendency to argue that the Armistice engagement had no great moral force, since the Allies were deceived as to the strength of the enemy, who might, after some more fighting, have agreed to unconditional surrender. Yet we must not altogether neglect the extra fighting, even although it might not have been severe. Each extra Englishman (or American or Frenchman) saved from carnage, each young man with his hopes and aspirations, his parents or wife or children who loved him, had his own unique value; it is not right to say, if these lives were saved, that there had been no *quid pro quo* for the concessions to the enemy con-

tained in the Armistice terms. Waiving this, there remains
the point of international law and morality. This was a moment at which the League of Nations was to be founded and
international law to be rebuilt on a secure basis. Those rules
which govern individual behaviour were to apply to the
nations also. How often does the private citizen, in the conduct of his ordinary business life, find that, after making a
contract, he could have got much better terms, had he
known all the circumstances of his competitor or his client.
It might seem that life would be easier if on all such occasions one could put an agreement into the wastepaper
basket. Not really so, because one might be the victim of
similar conduct. Were we not arraigning Germany because
she had treated the Belgian guarantee as a 'scrap of paper',
on the ground that circumstances had changed?

Keynes felt very strongly on the question of hypocrisy.
'The German delegation did not succeed in exposing in
burning and prophetic words the quality which distinguishes
this transaction from all its historical predecessors – its insincerity.' What he had in mind was that the Treaty was
couched in the language of idealism, justice and humane
consideration, derived from the great pronouncements of
President Wilson, while in its actual terms it was vindictive
on large issues and full of petty spite.

The distaste for hypocrisy is not peculiar to Keynes; I
believe that all the British dislike it. They are often accused
by foreigners of being a nation of hypocrites, but they deem
this accusation unjust; Dickens's castigation of Mr Peck-
sniff was one of his most popular excursions. Keynes's dislike of hypocrisy, however, exceeded the common measure;
we have seen this characteristic throughout. Long ago at the
India Office he was enraged that a man should be dismissed
for an offence of which he was innocent, although there
were other good reasons for dismissing him.[12] In undergraduate days his dislike of Victorian humbug was a point
of common sentiment with Strachey. Even at Eton we have

12. cf. pp. 143–4.

his reference to Mafeking – 'The papers call it a "fervent thanksgiving from the heart". I do not think that we are quite such hypocrites here.'

The main matters in the *Economic Consequences* which require discussion may be grouped under the heads of three propositions:

(1) It was right and expedient that the terms of peace should be magnanimous.

(2) The sums demanded in reparation were beyond the realms of practicability.

(3) The economic problems of Europe were much more important than the political questions of frontiers.

The first proposition was not argued at length, but is implicit throughout the book. The second was its main theme, but the third was also argued at length, and, if it is correct, it reinforces the importance of the second. It is natural that the ordinary man should associate the book above all with the first proposition, although it was not argued. It is the most controversial. After the second and third propositions had been widely accepted, doubts were still entertained about the first, and there was, not unnaturally, a revulsion from it during the Hitler period. In assessing Keynes's lasting influence on world affairs, it is necessary to come to grips with the first proposition, although we lack the benefit of his explicit defence of it.

It was the task of the Peace Conference to honour engagements and to satisfy justice; but not less to re-establish life and to heal wounds. These tasks were dictated as much by prudence as by the magnanimity which the wisdom of antiquity approved in victors.[13]

\*

Yet the financial problems which were about to exercise Europe could not be solved by greed. The possibility of *their* cure lay in magnanimity.[14]

\*

13. *The Economic Consequences of the Peace*, p. 23.
14. ibid., p. 135.

I cannot leave this subject as though its just treatment wholly depended either on our own pledges or on economic facts. The policy of reducing Germany to servitude for a generation, of degrading the lives of millions of human beings, and of depriving a whole nation of happiness should be abhorrent and detestable, – abhorrent and detestable, even if it were possible, even if it enriched ourselves, even if it did not sow the decay of the whole civilized life of Europe. Some preach it in the name of Justice. In the great events of man's history, in the unwinding of the complex fates of nations Justice is not so simple. And if it were, nations are not authorized, by religion or by natural morals, to visit on the children of their enemies the misdoings of parents or of rulers.[15]

Whatever may be said about the merits of magnanimity in the particular circumstances of the case, and about its relation to the French standpoint, it must be observed that Keynes's upbringing and environment made it utterly unthinkable that he should take any other view. He reminded English readers of what was bred in their bones, and scorned to develop the case further. High-minded Cambridge of the great Victorian era, 'the Society', the sage thinkers of refined feeling who were his immediate seniors, Whitehead, Trevelyan, Goldie Dickinson, all this world would accept the precept of magnanimity without question. There is no need in this connection to cite G. E. Moore and his Bloomsbury disciples, who may have carried their idealisms to unpractical extremes. Men of culture, in Cambridge, in London, throughout Britain, whose thoughts were conditioned by the reading of Shakespeare and other great masters, men rooted too, even when agnostic, in the ethics of Christianity, thought alike on this matter. This was Keynes's world. He was in it, of it. A trip to the Hotel Majestic could not change his nature. The question is not simply, Was Keynes wrong? but, Were the presuppositions of British civilization, as established during the Victorian period, impracticable in 1919? What was peculiar about Keynes was that he kept his

15. ibid., pp. 209–10.

head in the maelstrom, and voiced the sentiments of the civilization to which he belonged.

This way of thinking was not confined to scholarly and intellectual circles. Such thoughts were also in the minds of Asquith, Edward Grey, Robert Cecil and other eminent statesmen; from across the sea we had the imperial contributions which, if not specifically British, were derived from the same cultural roots – those of Botha and of Smuts. And in *The World Crisis* (vol. v) by Mr Winston Churchill, whose views will be considered presently, we find these moving words which relate to the evening of the day upon which the Armistice was signed : 'My own mood was divided between anxiety for the future and desire to help the fallen foe. The conversation ran on the great qualities of the German people, on the tremendous fight they had made against three-quarters of the world, on the impossibility of rebuilding Europe except with their aid.'[16]

We may go further and say that this mode of thought was not the exclusive property of deep thinkers or eminent statesmen, but was characteristic of the ordinary British citizen. It was part of the British way of life. History illustrates it. Indeed, old-time British statesmanship has been rebuked for carrying the leniency of peace treaties based upon hard-won victories to the point of folly. That the generous instincts, of which at the moment Keynes was the lonely spokesman, were really characteristic of the British is borne out by the fact that within a short space of time his had become the settled British view.

How came it then that Lloyd George, who was at times assailed by generous impulses in the course of the proceedings at Paris, felt that he must be harsh and even vindictive because of public opinion at home? That is a paradox which requires explanation.

Up to a point the explanation is simple. Human nature had been taxed beyond endurance. The horrors of the war were greater than had been known for many generations. It is

16. p. 20.

not surprising that primitive emotions had been roused. At the end of the war very decent people were talking of the Germans in language which four years earlier would have seemed unthinkable in any circumstances.

But over and above this, the general election of 1918 involved a vulgarization of British public life. That is really the gravamen of those who thought ill of Lloyd George's proceedings. The British constitution has drawn much of its virtue from the party system. Through the creeds of parties British citizens received political education. There were certain fixed principles. If new situations arose, the humble citizen who belonged to a party had some idea of the way in which those principles should be applied. The party, which as a social organism had some maturity, dispensed the individual member from the task, which might be beyond him, of creating a political philosophy for himself. The churches, established and dissenting, also had their fixed principles and made some contribution to the stability and coherence of political thinking.

As time went on, with the enlarged electorate, a fluid social and economic system and, it must be added, with the women – on whom party doctrine did not have so strong a hold – receiving a vote, there were growing numbers of the electors whose politics were not based on well-defined doctrines. It was these who were the ready prey of the vulgarizers in political journalism and, finally, in political leadership. They needed their clichés. Lacking settled principles, such slogans as 'Hang the Kaiser', or 'Squeeze the orange till the pips squeak' gave them convenient matter for private oratory. Such ideas had no relation to any fixed system of political morality. They responded to a transient emotion and were good matter for declamation.

In this vulgarization Lloyd George played his part. Unluckily at the time he was himself deracinated. At heart he was still a Liberal, but at the end of 1918 the solid phalanx of official Liberalism was opposed to him. He was not a Conservative. Somehow he must seek to win the greatest possible number of votes. It was an irresistible temptation to follow in the footsteps of the vulgarizing journalists and make a specious appeal to the momentary emotion of hatred for the Germans. Thus he collected his Parliament of what Keynes's 'conservative friend' (Mr Baldwin) called 'hard-faced men who look as if they have done very well out of the war'. This Parliament became his master.

It should be observed at this point that, in spite of the fierce anti-Germanism which was prevalent at this time, there was a strain of idealism in the thinking of the great majority of people. This opportunity should be taken to make the world a better place; peace must be ensured; international relations must in future be based on justice and conciliation. In the minds of many this idealism was canalized into support for the new League of Nations. This was pre-eminently so in the case of Woodrow Wilson. Was this the right answer? Men of genuine goodwill tended to turn away from the vexed problem of Germany, which aroused so much passion, and to concentrate their gaze upon the League, which might in the end harmonize conflicting interests and assuage national hatreds. The trouble was, however, that this was a new experiment; no one could say how it would function; paper constitutions are notorious for belying hopes. Keynes was naturally a supporter of the League. But I suspect that when this was presented to him as a panacea, he may have murmured to himself 'another monkey-house'.[17] He stated his views upon the League:

> The Assembly will meet more rarely and must become, as anyone with an experience of large Inter-Ally Conferences must know, an unwieldy polyglot debating society, in which the greatest resolution and the best management may fail altogether to bring issues to a head against an opposition in favour of the *status quo*.[18]

Not that he joined the cynics.

17. cf. p. 261 above.
18. *The Economic Consequences of the Peace*, pp. 243–4.

While it would be wrong and foolish to conceal from ourselves in the interests of 'idealism' the real difficulties of the position in the special matter of revising treaties, that is no reason for any of us to decry the League, which the wisdom of the world may yet transform into a powerful instrument of peace.

I suggest that Keynes's instinct was sound in not being led away by contemplation of the glorious possibilities of this new paper constitution from considering the immediate and actual human problem of the treatment of a fallen foe. One may dream dreams for the future. That does not exempt one from the painful task of doing what is right here and now to help one's neighbour or one's enemy. This League-worship involved a kind of escapism, of which Keynes was temporarily incapable.

The actual problem to be solved, with or without the help of the League, and the sooner the better, was the re-integration of Germany into the comity of Europe. I had the privilege of an interview with General Smuts on the subject of Keynes on 8 June 1948, and he stressed that this thought was the basis of their sympathetic cooperation at Paris in 1919. He had become well acquainted with Keynes during the war as the man to whom he went when difficulties arose in connection with the South African currency and who always seemed to have a ready solution. I listened to this revered philosopher statesman as he talked volubly and with full memory of the Peace Conference. He had found himself in agreement with Keynes and had urged him to write the book. He, Smuts, had at first refused to sign the Treaty, but had yielded to Lloyd George's strong pressure, with a reservation that he must be allowed to publish a criticism. He added that it had often been a consolation to him, as he discharged his responsibilities in a far-distant land, to think that Keynes was here in London exerting his influence at the centre of affairs. (Alas, for many years Keynes had less influence on the official world than Smuts may have supposed.) At one point his expression became troubled. He himself brought the question of pensions and allowances into the discussion and gave the version of his intention which I have quoted.[19] 'I got into hot water about that.' We have seen from the Minutes of the Council of Four that Wilson shared Smuts's interpretation, and, since it was to Wilson that the memorandum was primarily addressed, this is a strong point in favour of Smuts.

'The paramount task', he proceeded, 'was to bring Germany back into the fold. It was impossible to cut her out. One should think of it in physical terms. Here was a great mass of people in the centre of Europe, with outstanding qualities of industry, scientific ability and discipline. One could not just ignore them or ostracize them. Some means must be found for assimilating them. In 1919 the central problem was the reintegration of Germany, and' – his eyes flashed fire – 'that is the problem today. People should go back to Keynes.'

It is not enough for the purpose in hand to establish that Keynes really did represent his countrymen in his lone battle for magnanimous dealing. We have to ask the more exacting question whether this British instinct of generosity was an appropriate one in the world of 1919. In sharp contrast to the view I have outlined was Clemenceau's view as described by Keynes.

In the first place, he was a foremost believer in the view of German psychology that the German understands and can understand nothing but intimidation, that he is without generosity or remorse in negotiation, that there is no advantage he will not take of you, and no extent to which he will not demean himself for profit, that he is without honour, pride, or mercy. Therefore you must never negotiate with a German or conciliate him; you must dictate to him. On no other terms will he respect you, or will you prevent him from cheating you. But it is doubtful how far he thought these characteristics peculiar to Germany, or whether his candid view of some other nations was fundamentally different.[20]

19. See pp. 286–7 above.
20. *The Economic Consequences of the Peace*, p. 29.

Was that the view of German relations it would be wise and prudent to adopt in the period to come? This must be looked at.

The broad criticism of Keynes's view may be put as follows: After five years of tribulation, Germany obtained lenient terms in the Dawes Plan and promotion to an equal status in the Locarno Treaty. In the final upshot she obtained relief beyond the wildest dreams of Keynes, for, on her external account, loans from America exceeded her disbursements in reparations, so that she was a net receiver of money until the period of the world slump, when her obligations were suspended. With these advantages she enjoyed a period of comparative and not unsubstantial prosperity in the years from 1925 to 1929, so that Keynes's experiment was in the end tried. And what was the result of it? Hitler.

During the Nazi period there was a reaction against Keynes which embodied much muddled thinking. Mr Winston Churchill has, correctly in my judgement, gained wide acceptance for the proposition that World War II was an 'unnecessary' one. For many years after the first war we were in control of the situation and yet we allowed Germany to rebuild her armaments, so that she became far stronger than France, and perhaps stronger than France and Britain together. Was not this the utmost folly? Well then, had we not been too lenient to Germany? And was not this due in part to the influence of Keynes and his pleading in *The Economic Consequences of the Peace*?

Argument on these lines was often superficial. I recall that a Gallup Poll (or some similar inquiry) dealt with this problem by questions as follows: Was the Treaty of Versailles too lenient, or about right, or too severe? This is thinking at a very crude level. Severe in regard to what? There was another way of putting the matter, which has some truth, and yet does not really meet the case, namely, that the Treaty fell between two stools. This implies that all would have been well had it been either more severe or more lenient, and failed because it was middling in this regard. Such a formulation does not suffice either. Surely the right answer was that it was necessary to be severe in those matters in which severity is appropriate, and lenient in those matters in which leniency is appropriate. Severity was appropriate as regards allowing Germany to rebuild her armaments and renew aggression; leniency was appropriate in regard to allowing her, subject to suitable penalties, to resume a normal life of moderate prosperity, in conditions in which self-interest would promote progress, and to bringing her back into the comity of nations in the spirit of letting bygones be bygones.

There is no doubt that the French had a case which was intrinsically very strong. Was their just claim for security sufficiently met by the British and Americans? There was the League of Nations, an unknown quantity; there was the Anglo-American guarantee, which failed. (It must be remembered that Keynes's book was written before this failure was known.) Would these two have sufficed? It seems doubtful. Ought not the French plea to have been handled more sympathetically by the British and Americans? Ought not some further method of guarantee to have been hammered out?

Keynes is, I think, open to the criticism that he did not do justice to the problem of French security. To plead that this was outside his purview, since he was dealing with economics, is not perhaps sufficient, since his book was inevitably taken to have a wider application, with its plea for generosity as a general principle. We may admit that his work would have been strengthened if he had shown more recognition of the genuine character of the French fears and claims. However, where he erred, he did not err alone. It was not on this point that he distinguished himself from Lloyd George and those who were responsible on the British side for the Treaty. It might be held against Britain generally that she did not take the French case seriously enough. Where Keynes very distinctly joined issue was on the idea that a reparations plan should itself be part of the security programme. This was confusing two issues. This was applying severity where leniency was appropriate. Keynes never suggested that he would disapprove of military measures to prevent German rearmament. What he did undoubtedly hold was that it was a mistaken and hopeless and wrong policy to seek security against some future German aggression by crushing Germany economically. This was the French aim. Now on this point, which was Keynes's central point, it seems to me that the matter may be judged by reference to what has happened since, and that the judgement goes in favour of Keynes.

What was the object of these onerous financial obligations? The matter may be put quite simply in terms of two alternatives. Was it assumed that Germany would meet the obligations? Or was it assumed that she would not? Let us suppose that Germany, by a heroic effort of self-control, by hard work and living of an austerity unknown in any industrial society, and in a spirit of meek and mild compliance and honourable fulfilment of a treaty signed, achieved an export surplus of the required amount over the period in question. We have a picture of Germany building up a vast export industry, her workers producing and yet not consuming, with a self-discipline that would have been envied by Sparta, and, in this régime of fabulous austerity, her industrial strength being raised to a point exceeding anything that was achieved in Hitler's day. Meanwhile Britain and France would be living the life of lotus eaters, with taxation low, hours of work light, their markets gone, enjoying the well-earned fruits of victory for a period of thirty or forty years. Was it not obvious that, if this were actually to happen, at the end of the period France and Britain would be totally at the mercy of Germany? This clearly was not the way to provide the French with security.

What of the other alternative? German default, followed by sanctions. Was this a satisfactory method of achieving security for France? Did the French really desire to see a long series of German defaults, so that they might have the justification for continuous interference, occupying towns and districts, boycotting, interfering through the Reparations Commission and so forth? Thus would Germany be continually harassed and kept low. This is what actually happened for five years; but surely it should have been perfectly clear that such a régime would be unstable. One could not go on indefinitely with this restless intervention. This instability was bound to be terminated in one way or the other. Either the French would have to make up their minds to occupy the whole of Germany, or the clauses of the Treaty would have to be scrapped and a liberal solution put in their place. If the French had the former alternative in mind, this was clearly foolish. For the right time to have a plenary occupation of Germany, if ever, was in 1919. It was quite unrealistic to suppose that the French, who shrank from such a strenuous adventure then, would have the energy to embark upon it five or ten years later. Thus the whole thing would necessarily end in a liberal solution. And so it turned out. But the five intervening years were a period of tribulation for Germany, which had its effects.

During this period sanctions were applied against Germany for her failure to make payment. These culminated in the occupation of the Ruhr, and in sum proved a fiasco. The French were at length persuaded to change their policy and agreed to the Dawes Plan, which represented a liberal solution. But all these abortive attempts to enforce the financial clauses brought a certain discredit upon the whole policy of coercive intervention. The life passed out of this mode of procedure, and it became widely regarded as futile. Yet the time was to come when such intervention would be by no means futile. It was not on the reparations clauses but on the disarmament clauses that France should have relied principally for her own defence. Therefore, when a fiercely militarist party achieved supremacy in a resurgent Germany and rearmament began, it was highly desirable that the Treaty should be enforced, by military measures if necessary. This is the hub of Mr Churchill's contention. But military measures had been discredited by their premature use for an irrelevant purpose. The Ruhr fiasco in 1923 was an important contributory cause of the lack of support for the proposal to prevent by force of arms the German remilitarization of the Rhineland in 1936. How much better it would have been to have had a Treaty in which only the really vital security clauses, namely the disarmament clauses, would require military intervention, and to have conserved one's energies and will-power for that supreme purpose.

Meanwhile the question may be raised whether the severe economic terms did in the event matter so much, since all was changed five years later. To that extent it might be argued that Lloyd George's plea holds, namely that, when passions had cooled, common sense would find a better solution. This is entirely to neglect the importance of the intervening five years. For it was in that period, during which attempts were still being made to enforce the Peace Treaty reparations, that the social structure of Germany was undermined. Inflation persisted for five years, reducing the value of the mark to nothing. This cannot be done without gross injury to society. Keynes has a grave warning, of prophetic character, about the evils of inflation. Since in later days he was to be regarded as something of an inflationist – whether truly so depends on the definition of that term – it is interesting to observe that this picture of the evils of inflation is as vivid as can be found anywhere:

Lenin is said to have declared that the best way to destroy the Capitalist System was to debauch the currency. By a continuing process of inflation, governments can confiscate, secretly and unobserved, an important part of the wealth of their citizens. By this method they not only confiscate, but they confiscate *arbitrarily* ...

Lenin was certainly right. There is no subtler, no surer means of overturning the existing basis of society than to debauch the currency. The process engages all the hidden forces of economic law on the side of destruction, and does it in a manner which not one man in a million is able to diagnose.

... By combining a popular hatred of the class of entrepreneurs with the blow already given to social security by the violent and arbitrary disturbance of contract and of the established equilibrium of wealth which is the inevitable result of inflation, these governments are fast rendering impossible a continuance of the social and economic order of the nineteenth century. But they have no plan for replacing it.[21]

These words were written at a time when the German mark was 'worth less than 2d. on the exchanges'. It was to proceed through a long-drawn-out agony to zero. A vast disturbance in the German social order did in fact occur, and many stable elements belonging to the old régime disappeared. Furthermore, these events completely discredited the Weimar Republic. It may indeed be the case that the lamp of democracy always burns low in Germany. Still, it is incumbent on one to make the best use of what is there. If the Weimar Government was not nursed to strength, what should we have? It may well be that, if the German economy had not been overset in the period 1919–24, if more of the older order had been retained, if the Weimar Government had been allowed a successful first act, subject to the observance of the clauses of a more moderate treaty, then Germany would have stood up to the slump, like other nations, without a revolution. This is the gravamen. The reparations clauses doomed the youthful democratic government. It might not have succeeded in any case. But there was a hope, the only hope really, and it was wicked to destroy it – all to no purpose.

Thus I see no inherent conflict between the Keynes judgement on the reparations clauses of the Treaty and the view associated with Mr Churchill, that firmness on the part of the Allies could have prevented the second war. It is not of the laxity of the Treaty that Mr Churchill has complained, but of the lassitude and fecklessness ten years later. It may be noticed that Mr Churchill has expressed agreement with

21. *The Economic Consequences of the Peace*, pp. 220–22.

Keynes's view of the economic clauses both in *The World Crisis* and in *The Second World War*. In the former work [22] (1929) he made a reservation as regards Keynes which we shall presently consider.

... He showed in successive chapters of unanswerable good sense the monstrous character of the financial and economic clauses. On all these matters his opinion is good. Carried away, however, by his natural indignation at the economic terms which were to be solemnly enacted, he wrapped the whole structure of the Peace Treaties in one common condemnation. His qualifications to speak on the economic aspects were indisputable; but on the other and vastly more important side of the problem he could judge no better than many others.

It must in all fairness be admitted that the experiment of a more generous treaty might have failed, that the Weimar Republic might have proved a wolf in sheep's clothing. This merely points back to the question of military security. The economic clauses could give no security, whether they were enforced or not enforced. The French might well feel, however, that even with the new-born League and with the Anglo-American guarantee of their frontier, they could not feel safe. The French had waived demands, put forward strongly by Marshal Foch, for confining the German Reich to the right bank of the Rhine. They had done so with trepidation. When the Americans and British proceeded to default on the guarantee, they felt completely betrayed. It would seem that the British should have had the strongest sympathy for the French, alongside whom they had fought, in this dilemma. On the contrary, in the following period their belated impulses of generosity were gaining the upper hand, and, so far from being prompted by conscience to make some amends to the French, which were indeed due, they showed only mounting irritation. Thus these stupid reparations clauses were clouding the issue at a vital period.

22. Vol. v, p. 155.

The British deplored, and indeed were justified in deploring, the truculent attitude of the French in insisting on the letter of a financial settlement, which the British were coming to believe, partly in consequence of Keynes's advocacy, to be impossible of fulfilment. Yet this was no excuse for lack of sympathy for the new predicament of the French on the military side. The French were impelled to act on the reparations issue in isolation; they failed; they were humiliated; they felt alone and without bearings. This was the beginning of the disintegration of French morale and French policy, which had such disastrous effects in the thirties. Keynes's argument was not concerned with all this. The point remains that, since his book was not only an economic argument but also an appeal to magnanimous feelings, and thus had an influence on a wider field of policy, his failure to apply his mind to the problem of French security was a fault. This French problem was really one and the same as the problem of world peace; for, if France was attacked again, a general war would inevitably ensue.

3

Keynes insisted that the peace settlement was infected with unreality because the reparations clauses were impracticable. In a posthumous analysis of this proposition it may be expedient to define the word impracticable more closely than seemed necessary in the heat of advocacy. One may evisage a nation striving earnestly to make a payment, with all its citizens cooperating with the utmost goodwill, working hard and living austerely, and all the other nations making it as easy as possible for payments to be received. Alternatively, we may wish to consider what a reluctant, recalcitrant and aggrieved nation can be made to do under the threat of sanctions to be imposed at a distance or on its frontiers. Or we may consider what a nation would do under the lash of an occupying power. The third of these possibilities was ruled out from the beginning, and the first is not acceptable to common sense.

In a recently published book, entitled *The Carthaginian Peace, or The Economic Consequences of Mr Keynes* (1946), M. Étienne Mantoux has argued that Keynes's objections to the reparations clauses were grossly exaggerated and that payment of the full amount was a reasonable request to make. The author was the son of M. Paul Mantoux, official interpreter at the Paris Peace Conference and an economic historian of distinction. He was himself a young man of great promise, beloved by many; he was killed on active service on 29 April 1945. This book, written from the French standpoint, although fierce enough in its indictment of Keynes, is not extremist. It was composed when France was under the shadow of German occupation; such a time would not be a good one for perceiving the virtues of Keynes's plea for magnanimity. There are many moving passages in the book and much learning; the author's attempt was eminently patriotic and does him credit; his work has a power and range which suggest great promise.

Much of the book was concerned with those general questions of policy which have been discussed in the previous section. What has particularly attracted attention is that it set out to make a frontal attack on Keynes, on the ground on which he was supposed to be impregnable, namely, the feasibility of the reparations proposals. It is surprising, therefore, to find how small a portion of the book is devoted to argument on this particular topic. The challenge being so conspicuously daring, one would have supposed that the author would have been at special pains to substantiate it. Yet, in fact, there are only nine pages out of 203 devoted to the central part of the problem, namely, what is known as the 'transfer problem'. Another six pages are devoted to Germany's power to increase her income internally and six to the question whether other countries would gain or suffer by receiving German goods. The central question remains whether it was possible for Germany to pay out, by an excess of exports over imports, the sums demanded by the Allies. It must be said that the arguments put forward in this narrow compass of nine pages are feeble in the extreme. We are told that the transfer problem has been exaggerated, and M. Mantoux cites as a contrary instance the enormous sums transferred by Great Britain to her Allies and by the United States during World War I. This is clearly quite beside the point. In this case demand was ready-made. Here were allies requiring munitions, and the materials to make them, in amounts altogether beyond the ordinary. If the United States was able to supply those demands, it was naturally easy for her to have an excess of exports over imports of a large amount. It is surprising that M. Mantoux could advance such an argument seriously. His next instance is worse. He cites the enormous increase of production in Germany secured by the efforts of Adolf Hitler. Then, remembering that he is arguing in a section headed 'The Transfer Problem', he adds: 'It will, I presume, be argued that the case is irrelevant, and that the fifteen milliard marks spent annually by Germany on rearmament until 1939 are no measure of her capacity to pay, because the proceeds did not have to be *transferred abroad.*' Precisely! He then proceeds to a bitter, macabre joke. 'How interesting it would be to ask the citizens of Warsaw, of Rotterdam, of Belgrade, of London and Coventry ... what they think of this particular piece of argument! All have now tasted in a marked degree the quality of German products.' Then in what follows, it appears that this is not intended as a joke after all, on the ground that the production of these deadly weapons involved the same problem as an increase in exports, namely a big internal shift in German industry. But one may shift about one's industry without solving the transfer problem, since that requires finding foreign buyers for the new goods. The next instance is the transfer from the occupied territories to the German account during World War II. Here again two factors were present which do not apply to the situation that Keynes discussed, namely (1) an army of occupation to enforce payments, and (2) an abnormal demand for goods arising from Germany's war efforts. So ends this section. It is embroidered with a few cursory theoretical observations. Such being the contents of the part of M. Mantoux's work that directly challenges Keynes's main thesis, his claim cannot be taken seriously.

There is an earlier section, not germane to the central issue, in which he has some statistical criticisms that are more successful. He seems to convict Keynes of carelessness in failing to allow fully for the depreciation of the franc when holding up certain French estimates of damage to ridicule.[23] It is to be regretted that M. Mantoux himself makes mistakes in the opposite sense,[24] and the upshot ap-

23. pp. 102–8.

24. Later in this passage Mantoux compares the French claim before the Reparations Commission for 127 milliard francs, condemned by Keynes as a fantastic exaggeration, with the cost subsequently established in 1932 as 103 milliard francs. As the index number of French wholesale prices stood at 335 (base 1904–13) when the Commission reported, and then rose steadily to 784 between 1921 and 1926, which was presumably the most active period of reconstruction, and remained thereafter above 600 until the slump and above 400 until the end of 1931, the fact that the actual cost of reconstruction in this period of inflated prices was only 103 milliards shows that the estimate of 127 milliards in 1921 was indeed grossly exaggerated. Yet by a remarkable piece of jugglery, combining a coefficient for depreciation in terms of gold and one for that in terms of goods in an illegitimate way, Mantoux concludes that the actual cost of 103 milliards was 'almost exactly' equal to the estimate of 127 milliards made when prices were so much lower! In this passage Mantoux shows a high degree of irresponsibility.

Mr J. R. Sargent has made a careful statistical calculation, by applying successive price index numbers and weights, of the cost of French reparations, as established in 1932, in terms of pre-war gold francs, and arrived at the figure of 22.2 milliard. He checked this by taking the figure of 175 milliards of francs quoted in 1932 'as representing the capital value with regard to the gold value of the franc at the various dates of payment' (Mantoux, p. 106) and reached the figure of 23.5 milliard pre-war gold francs, which sufficiently confirms his other figure. The French claim (1921), allowing for the prices ruling when it was made, amounted to 36.8 milliards pre-war gold francs.

pears to be that, while the French estimates did not over-
state the damage as grossly as Keynes claims, they were by
no means all as reasonable as M. Mantoux claims.

In another passage M. Mantoux makes great play with
Keynes's predictions.[25] Keynes has rightly gained a reputation for a rather remarkable power of prediction. One would
hardly expect hints thrown out in a polemic written in a
period of confusion and uncertainty all to be correct. But
the main reason why M. Mantoux is able to make quite a
goodly collection of apparent mistakes is that he sometimes
relates Keynes's forecasts of what would happen, should an
attempt be made to carry out the reparation clauses, to conditions in Germany after the attempt had been abandoned.

Since this book was written, an event has occurred which
would have enabled M. Mantoux to replace his absurd
illustrations about transfer by a good one. During World
War II, Britain sold foreign investments and incurred heavy
war debts, while other factors also began to operate against
her trade balance, so that experts estimated that after the
war she would have to increase her exports by fifty per cent;
this estimate was soon revised to seventy-five per cent. By the
end of 1948 she had achieved the fifty per cent increase. If
Germany had made a proportionate achievement she would
have exceeded Keynes's estimate of her capacity. Yet, in
World War II, Britain underwent economic strain and loss
which far exceeded those which Germany suffered in World
War I. Germany escaped in the end without payment, but
Britain, who fought alone against tyranny in her finest
hour, is having to bear a reparations burden much greater
than Keynes's estimate for Germany, not for thirty or forty
years, but in perpetuity. This burden that Britain has to
carry corresponds more nearly to an indemnity than to
reparations; for it essentially consists in the main of a retrospective payment for part of the cost of the war to other
United Nations.

While Britain may claim credit for the uncomplaining

25. pp. 160–63.

courage with which she has faced this burden and for what she has already achieved, the illustration does not prove that Keynes was too lenient, for there are three important respects in which the situation differs. In the first place, Britain has had the advantage of assistance on a large scale towards recovery. There were the American and Canadian loans, amounting to £1,250 million, and there has been 'Marshall Aid'. The loans were similar to the assistance which Keynes proposed at the eleventh hour in order to retrieve the European situation, but which was not granted.[26] On the contrary, Germany was expected to pay no less than £1,000 million in the first two years. This proposal was an object of Keynes's special criticism.

Secondly, Britain has had an advantage, which would not have accrued to Germany, in having one of her principal competitors in foreign markets laid low. This time the victorious powers have adopted a policy diametrically opposed to that recommended to them by M. Mantoux, a kind of inverse reparations. Instead of making it incumbent upon Germany to increase her industrial capacity and compete furiously everywhere, we have reduced her industrial capacity and her power as a competitor.

The third and most important point relates to the will to achieve. This brings us back to the precise definition of what is practicable. If Britain had had to raise her exports, not in order to achieve balance and regain her fair prospects in the world, but in order to meet a levy imposed by victors, would it have been psychologically possible for her to make the tremendous effort which she has made in the last three years? Would she have done this, even if threatened with sanctions on her frontiers? Again, we might wonder if she would have achieved it, even if occupied by a victorious power. It remains doubtful what the Allies could have extracted, even had they embarked upon the heroic task of total occupation of Germany. We lack experience of what civilized white men will do under the lash. It must be remembered that the

26. cf. pp. 288–90 above.

proposed surpluses represent greater output per head than backward people ever produce at all. They could only be gained by the utmost exertion of skill, ingenuity and applied science. Thus the example is indecisive. It suggests that Keynes erred on the side of leniency; yet when psychological factors are taken into account, he may have been in the right.

Finally, we have to deal with the third proposition, namely that the economic issue was more important than the political questions that had to be decided. 'To what a different future Europe might have looked forward if either Mr Lloyd George or Mr Wilson had apprehended that the most serious of the problems which claimed their attention were not political or territorial but financial and economic.' [27] This opinion was supported by a review of the state of Europe in chapters 2 and 6.

The statement that economics was more important than politics was in itself a political judgement. We have seen that two distinguished authorities, Eyre Crowe, and Mr Churchill writing in 1929, had doubts about Keynes's qualifications in the political field. But it is necessary to distinguish. Crowe at least was probably thinking of politics in the narrow sense, namely, the ways and means of diplomacy. We may also think of political wisdom in a broader sense, namely, judgement about what forces are likely to rouse passions and sway men's minds towards revolution or war. In this broader sense Keynes's aptitude may not have been so deficient. Indeed, it may have been superior to that of many of his contemporaries.

He opened chapter 2 by stressing the precariousness of that European prosperity, which in the preceding decades we had come to take as a matter of course. 'After 1870 there was developed on a large scale an unprecedented situation, and the economic condition of Europe became during the next fifty years unstable and peculiar.' [28] This was a charac-

27. *The Economic Consequences of the Peace*, p. 134.
28. ibid., p. 7.

teristic vein of thought in Keynes, the idea that conditions which many accept as normal are in fact dependent on very special circumstances. We have seen it already in his account of the British Gold Standard in his book on Indian currency. The theme was to recur when he argued that full employment was not the inevitable consequence of the working of a free enterprise system, but had occurred before 1914 owing to a number of favourable factors. The precariousness of European prosperity was analysed under three heads – the pressure of population, entailing an abnormally large dependence on overseas supplies; the intense division of labour in Europe, which made the surrounding countries peculiarly dependent on German prosperity; and the insecurity of the psychological basis of capitalism. The second of these points was the most germane to his topic, and perhaps the most valid. In chapter 6 there was a fine account of how economic convulsion gives rise to inflation with all its concomitant evils.

It is not necessary to agree with Keynes in detail on all these points. In reading the book one feels that he was tentatively and no doubt hurriedly searching for arguments to support a conviction, which was itself more solidly based than the supports which he outlined. It was in fact what we have come to call a 'hunch'.

And now, as we look back over those twenty years between the wars, do we not find that it has indeed been economic disturbance that has been the main cause of our troubles? The great successive political crises have in fact been caused by economic disorders. It was economic turmoil that so inflamed the impatience of millions of Germans that they were willing to accept the Nazis as their leaders and saviours.

'If we aim deliberately at the impoverishment of Central Europe, vengeance, I dare predict, will not limp. Nothing can then delay for very long that final Civil War between the forces of Reaction and the despairing convulsions of Revolution, before which the horrors of the late German war will fade into nothing, and which will destroy, whoever is victor, the civilization and progress of our generation.'[29] The policy of impoverishment was called to a halt five years later, and the full effect of its initial enforcement was delayed for a period. Keynes's financial colleagues often noticed that he made predictions of remarkable accuracy regarding forces likely to affect the values of assets, but was at fault in the timing. He predicted that events would occur during the coming weeks that in fact occurred six months later, or predicted something in six months that occurred two or three years later.

I see in the passage I have quoted a dim presage of the Nazi violence which in due course developed with effects that are still unfolding. The prediction was not clothed with detail, but was justified in its trend. I see in it political wisdom of the higher kind. It has an uncanny insight into the kind of things which were to happen, and a modern flavour beside which the vaticinations of his contemporaries in that period seem stale and obsolete.

There is one final point which must be considered. Keynes has been taken to task on the ground that his book, with its discouraging picture of Europe, contributed towards driving the Americans into a policy of isolationism. This is clearly an important point and has damaged Keynes's reputation in the minds of some.

We may first consider the question of the rejection of the Peace Treaty by the United States. Upon this Keynes's book had no influence whatever. The decisive vote in the Senate occurred on 19 November 1919, when a resolution for unconditional ratification, requiring a two-thirds majority, was defeated by fifty-three votes to thirty-eight. *The Economic Consequences of the Peace* had not yet appeared. This vote was not affected by the economic clauses, which the Americans regarded as outside their province. The main issue was the League of Nations, and next in importance the Shantung settlement. Reservations were proposed which

29. *The Economic Consequences of the Peace*, p. 251.

Wilson could not accept. Of these the one bearing on reparations merely stipulated that the Reparations Commission should not regulate or interfere with exports from the
United States to Germany or from Germany to the United
States, save by means approved by a joint resolution of Congress. This reservation alone would not have killed the
Treaty, and it was certainly not inspired by Keynes.

It is true that negotiations proceeded until the following
February; and that, as soon as the book came out, passages
were quoted by Wilson's enemies. But throughout this
period the League of Nations was the principal obstacle to
acceptance, and there were no indications that this obstacle
could be overcome. *The Economic Consequences of the
Peace* was neither here nor there. Keynes can be entirely
exempted from any shadow of responsibility for the great
American decision, which was to have such a vast effect on
the working out of the European settlement.

The critic may return to the charge and urge that the book
reinforced the sentiment of isolationism in the following
years. It is incumbent on him to specify precisely how, but
for the book, the situation would have developed differently.
After all, it was not the book, but the actual course of events
in Europe, culminating in the fiasco of the Ruhr invasion,
that mainly swayed the Americans. The book did little more
than give pleasure to them by confirming their worst sus-
picions. Yet the Americans did not remain altogether aloof;
after the settlement devised by Dawes, himself an American,
their financiers lavished their money upon Europe. In so far
as the book, by its influence on British opinion, prepared the
way for such a settlement at an earlier date than might
otherwise have been possible, it expedited American assistance to Europe. No doubt any self-disparagement has unfortunate repercussions abroad. The allegations against
Keynes in this respect have been grossly exaggerated, and
without sense of proportion or regard for chronology.

And so he had said what he believed. He incurred great
odium in official circles and was for many years in the wil-

derness. This was a turning-point in his career. Hitherto, although spurning the India Office, he had been drawn more and more into consultation in official circles. His reputation steadily grew. His war work had been supremely efficient and was praised by all. His fertility of ideas seemed boundless. Knowledgeable persons before 1919 would have pointed to him as the man likely to have the biggest inside influence on the conduct of our financial affairs in the coming time. But now he had burnt his boats. He had appealed against the authorities to a wider public. The official world could no longer use him.

There was a compensation. In the period after 1919 his main energy was directed to guiding public opinion on current topics. But, as the years passed, his thought deepened and he began to suspect that our persistent troubles were not wholly due to mistakes and follies, but were largely caused by a deep-seated malady in the system of free exchange. He set himself to devise remedies which would enable that system to survive by curing it of its main defects. And so it happened that when the second great catastrophe came, he had armed himself to stand forward at the new dawn of things, not as a critic, but as a constructor. Is it an exaggeration to cast him for the role of the 'Prince' when the second war drew to its close? After all, the United Nations Organization does not contain new ideas of great import. Men had come to believe that the economic issue was the crucial one. Keynes was at hand now with his timely message that the system of free enterprise could be made to function better, that employment could be sustained at a high and stable level, that trade depression could be avoided, and that the nations could cooperate to ensure that these benefits were enjoyed on a world-wide scale. Keynes, more than any other man, seemed to be the bearer of doctrines which gave new hope. Three new personalities were now astride the world. American affairs were in the hands of one greater than Woodrow Wilson. In Britain was a man 'with a policy deeply grounded in permanent principle, tenacity, honesty, loyal leadership'.[30] But a happy ending was not to be achieved easily. Once again in the drama, as it unfolded, there were hints of tragedy. One great man was stricken down by death, another removed from power for the time being by the exigencies of party politics, and on the face of the third a hostile expression began to appear. And then – the 'Prince' himself was taken from us. Were 'the forces of the half-world' to triumph again on this second occasion? There was still a gleam of hope. 'Prince' Wilson had wielded his power by oratory and statesmanship; Keynes's strength lay in his ideas. Ideas do not die with the man. Thus it is still possible that the powers for good may regroup themselves, and the weary nations leap forward to new prosperity.

30. cf. p. 304 above.

# [8]

## Reconstruction

### I

ON 5 June 1919, while Keynes was spending his thirty-sixth birthday lying on his sick-bed in Paris, Clive Bell and his Bloomsbury friends were having an enjoyable and indeed a thrilling evening. It was one of those rare first nights when an English audience allows itself to be carried away on a great wave of enthusiasm – the first performance of the *Boutique Fantasque*. Every foot of standing room in the Alhambra was occupied. The *Oiseau de Feu* was given first and applauded; but it was plain that expectancy was concentrated on the new production that was to follow. Throughout the *Boutique* ripples of applause ran through the audience, and when the Can-Can dancers appeared, the house was drowned in a great roar of 'Massine! Lopokova!' Excitement continued to mount. Expectations were surpassed. All agreed that the performance was superb.

The whole season was one of great triumph for Diaghilev. In the reaction from the sorrows of war phlegmatic London was in a receptive mood, ready to entertain new experiences and appreciate new forms of expression. When the utterances of political leaders were reaching their lowest depths and the news from Paris was blurred and depressing, the voiceless beauties of the ballet seemed to bring a new message of hope. The world was going awry; but here before our eyes something was enacted which achieved perfection. We could console ourselves that man's powers were not decaying.

Bloomsbury shared in the enthusiasm; contacts made in 1918 were revived, and once again the painters and dancers flowed in and out of 46 Gordon Square. It was rather a strange confluence; for there on the one hand were Derain

334

and Picasso and these wonderful Russian dancers, and there on the other was a group of rather academic English folk, talking quietly, critically, intellectually, stretching out their hands with gestures of warm welcome from a background so very different. Under the stimulus of their appreciation for these great foreigners, they dissolved and became exuberant. Keynes arrived in the midst of all this on his return from Paris. What a change of atmosphere! Towards the end of the season he helped to organize a great party in Gordon Square, a culminating occasion of gaiety and revelry. Unhappily Lydia Lopokova, the brightest star, had temporarily withdrawn herself from the ballet and disappeared from the scene of action.

In these months of June and July Keynes divided his time between London, Cambridge and Charleston. Important decisions had to be taken. It was clear to him that he did not wish to return to the pattern of his pre-war life, in which he had had to work so hard at teaching, external examining and other minor chores in order to make a reasonable livelihood. He felt he had a vocation now to intervene actively in shaping public opinion. He had knowledge and experience and a clear vision of what ought, and what ought not, to be done. He must not become so cluttered up with routine work as to be unable to give his main energies to the salvation of Europe.

No doubt there was another strand in his thinking. Although he entered with zest into his teaching work, and enjoyed it thoroughly, he had never felt attracted by the prospect of the life of an ordinary college tutor. Something had always beckoned him to a wider field of action. Could he not find a way of combining his work for King's, which he loved, with other work in London, which might be more remunerative and would keep him in touch with the centre of affairs?

Money was certainly a problem. He had no inheritance, and, so far, had had no business connections. But he felt that his experience in the Treasury could be turned to good account; one who had managed the external finances of the nation during the war with acknowledged success would surely have some market value in the world of finance. He must look around. By temperament he was courageous and always ready to take risks. In June 1919 he decided to reduce his University and College commitments, in the hope that something would turn up.

Accordingly, he explained to his College that he did not wish to be too heavily burdened with pupils. He informed the University that he would lecture once a week only, namely on the 'Economic Aspects of the Peace Treaty'. (As a consequence of this he resigned his Girdler lectureship in May of the following year.) There was some discussion in June about bursarial matters at King's; a committee had already reported with the suggestion that Keynes be asked to undertake duties in connection with the College finances and accounts. No doubt the College wished to obtain the benefit of his expert knowledge, but it was not yet ready with a definite proposal. Only in the following November was he appointed Second Bursar. The stipend was £100 a year!

A proposal came to him during June to be Chairman of a foreign-owned bank at a salary of £2,000 a year. It was explained that the duties would not be such as to occupy him more than one day a week or interfere with his academic duties in Cambridge. A tempting offer for a man whose academic appointments were apt only to bring him in sums of the order of £100 or £200 a year. He consulted Sir Robert Kindersley, Mr Brand and Mr Falk. The Bank was concerned with the finances of Scandinavian trade, and Keynes had some doubt whether he would have effective control. There was also the idea that a foreign connection might jeopardize other appointments in the City. His friends advised him against accepting, and he took their advice.

*J. M. Keynes to Mrs Keynes*, 6 August 1919

Charleston.

After a very feverish ten days in London, I have settled down
here for the rest of the summer. The weekend before last I spent
at a rather amusing party at the Asquiths, – the Grand Duke
Michael and Countess Torby, Mrs Keppel, the Countess of
Crewe, etc. etc., old-world celebrities as you see, off whom I won
£22 at bridge. On the following Tuesday I gave a party at Gordon
Square to round up the season, which was judged a great success, – I was too much occupied with the strenuous staff work of
host to see much of it. We sat down thirty-three to supper shortly
before midnight and did not rise from table until half-past one.
It is astonishing what the resources of a household are, when
pushed. The next evening was amidst great excitement the last
night of the ballet, all of my various worlds being there. I also
kept various business appointments, gave evidence before the
Indian Currency Committee, addressed the Fight the Famine
Council, opened a discussion on the Peace Terms at a city Dining
Club, and lunched and dined out every day, – after which I was
quite ready for the country. It's amusing to pass from Cambridge,
where I'm a nonentity, to London, where I'm a celebrity.

I have arranged for my book [*Economic Consequences*] to be
published by Macmillans.

Here my breakfast comes at 8 and my book occupies me until
lunch, before which I am not seen in the public rooms. After
lunch *The Times* and after *The Times* gardening until tea time.
After tea my correspondence. All very regular. I have brought my
own servants down here, as the total party is large, and Gordon
Square is shut up.

Old Asquith, by the way, is coming to next King's Founder's
Day as my guest and will probably stay the weekend.

During August and September he was immersed in writing his famous book, but not so immersed that his mind
could not dwell on other matters also. Early in August he
began a new career, which he was not to relinquish for many
years, that of a speculator. Depositing a modest cover with
Mr Falk's firm, he began buying and selling foreign currencies forward in large quantities. His operations included
the rupee, the dollar, the French franc, the mark, the lira

and the Dutch florin. Broadly, he tended to be a bull of dollars and a bear of the European currencies. His trading was active and continuous, large amounts being bought and sold every few days, but it was always based on his judgement as an economist, and not on rumours of the marketplace. He soon found that he was making substantial profits.

### J. M. Keynes to Mrs Keynes, 3 September 1919

I haven't lived such a regular life for years and am very well.

My diversion, to avoid the possibility of tedium in a country life, is speculation in the foreign exchanges, which will shock father but out of which I hope to do very well.

At this time he entered deeply into certain plans of Mr Henry Strakosch for setting up a new company to sell South African gold. He and Strakosch were to be the managers. It was felt that existing marketing arrangements could be improved. There was active discussion throughout the autumn; there was a meeting with the Rothschilds and consultation with the South African Government. In the end it was decided that it would be undesirable to start operations until the South African Government had defined its currency policy more clearly. Early in 1920 General Smuts wrote to Keynes asking him to come out to South Africa for two months to define their currency policy for them, but the invitation was declined. He was all in the midst of laying the foundation of his career in the City of London, his book had just appeared and he ought to be ready to take part in any controversies arising out of it, and he did not wish to make a break in his College duties, so lately resumed.

Meanwhile another opening had occurred. In September, through the intervention of Mr Falk, he was invited to join the Board of the National Mutual Life Insurance Company, of which he became Chairman in 1921, a position which he retained until 1938. His financial career was beginning.

In the midst of writing and business, he was keeping his eye on developments in Europe. Early in October he was invited by Dr Vissering to attend a meeting of experts on international finance which was organized by the Bank of the Netherlands. The agenda was to consider how the creditworthiness of the principal nations could be revived and an international loan floated. Keynes was encouraged by the constructive attitude of the Dutch and went to another meeting later in the year.

Macmillan's were doing his book. He was anxious that the first edition should be a large one and consist of at least 5,000 copies. He had confidence that it would interest the public. After discussion, it was agreed that he should take the risk himself and pay for the publication, giving Macmillan's a royalty of ten per cent. (He had shared profits on *Indian Currency and Finance* on a fifty/fifty basis.) By paying for the publication he gave himself the prospect of much bigger profits should the sales prove large. In the long run this arrangement with Macmillans was highly advantageous for him, since his other books were published on the same basis, but misfortune dogged *The Economic Consequences of the Peace*, both as regards the 5,000 copies and, as we shall see presently, his profit on the book.

It was printed by Messrs. R. & R. Clark of Edinburgh and the sheets came to London by sea; a ship carrying 2,000 copies was driven eastwards by storm and finally wrecked; the copies were thrown overboard in order to lighten the load. Thus, after all, the book went out of print soon after it appeared. Meanwhile the kindly waves of the North Sea were carrying the precious sheets in an easterly direction, and, lapping gently upon the coast of Denmark, brought three large bales safely ashore. The pages had not been much injured by the water. Keynes first heard of this from an old Cambridge man, Mr David Pritchard. The sheets were sold by public auction in Denmark.

He was having trouble on the American side. He consulted Mr Felix Frankfurter, who passed through London on his way home from the Paris Peace Conference, where Keynes had made friends with him. Frankfurter offered to help and took a copy back with him. On the boat he showed it to two fellow passengers, Brandeis and Graham Wallas, who pronounced it to be a great work. On arrival he gave it to Mr Walter Lippmann, then a reader for the recently founded firm of Harcourt Brace & Co. Frankfurter wrote back explaining that this was a new firm, but that he had consulted people of judgement who thought that it would do well. Keynes characteristically replied that he had complete trust in Frankfurter's discretion; let him go ahead.[1] The early success of Harcourt Brace was not entirely unconnected with their publication of *The Economic Consequences of the Peace.* A year later Keynes persuaded Lytton Strachey to change his American firm and undertook all the negotiations with Harcourt Brace for the publication of *Queen Victoria* in America.

The *Economic Consequences* appeared in England at the end of December 1919, and a month later in the United States. Its impact on the public mind was immediate and its reception tremendous. Long reviews appeared in all the papers, in the United States sometimes with banner headlines. For a month it was the main topic of conversation.

Reviewers predisposed to agree with its opinions were lyrical in its praises. All used such phrases as 'a book that will have to be most seriously considered', 'the most important book which has appeared since the Armistice', 'more exciting than a novel'. Many reviews were hostile; but only a few very insignificant papers presumed to make light of the book. The rest, even when advancing what they deemed to be weighty criticisms, paid it the compliment of careful attention. They made it plain that an effective blow had been struck and that the reply must be well thought out. One has the impression that, even on the first round of discussion, most critics took defence of the economic clauses of the Treaty to be rather a forlorn hope; they made the

1. Frankfurter also arranged that extracts from the book should appear in the *New Republic*. For many years thereafter this journal provided an important outlet in the United States for Keynes's views.

most of the writer's lack of political experience and background. There was also much stern rebuke. An ex-member
of the Treasury, who had been at Paris, had no right to
make an attack on a treaty to which his country was party.
The portraits of the Big Three were said to be in bad taste.
Lacking good arguments, the critics took refuge in moral
censure. There was another sentiment, sometimes mounting
to passion, in the hostile reviews, which was more respectable than the moral reprobation, because more genuinely
felt, namely, violent displeasure at what one reviewer called
Keynes's 'fervent indifference to German criminality'. Lloyd
George was no doubt right in deeming that an intense hatred
of the Germans was still widespread, and Keynes's plea that
the terms were impracticable as well as unjust was brushed
aside by the torrent of hostility to the defeated enemy. This
choleric pugnacity outlasting the war makes curious reading for one who has lived through the aftermath of the
second war, in which the Germans displayed attributes much
more detestable. Is it that the British have grown too weary
to nurture lusty feelings of indignation? Or is it possible
that moral standards have risen since the close of the first
war? Is it possible, even, that Keynes's own influence has
altered the feelings of the younger generation about decent
behaviour in victory?

He was inundated with requests to write and speak, refusing most. In January 1920, however, he made a little tour and
addressed three meetings in Liverpool and Manchester. One
of these was organized by the League of Nations Union.
There were violent protests against that organization having
anything to do with such a man.

Yet, despite the vehement denunciations, the bluster and
the moral reprimands, Keynes's arguments quickly sank in.
Those of leftward opinions acclaimed a new leader; those of
the centre and right were deeply impressed, for Keynes had
certain qualities which sharply distinguished him from
other writers of the left. He had a strong vein of realism
which appealed to the type of mind that disliked Utopian

fervour. He appeared to be in touch with actuality, to understand how things worked, to be a connoisseur of the high
affairs of state beyond the grasp of ordinary folk; despite
his radicalism, he seemed to many on the Conservative side
to be one of themselves, because he spoke in terms of reality
and not vague aspiration. They looked one another in the
eye: 'I suppose this fellow is right; I suppose we have made
a most fearful hash of things'.

Keynes retained his poise. He paid no attention to personal
attacks; they were a matter for his own conscience, and that
was clear enough. Very soon he felt justified in taking the
view that his main battle was already won. All those of
reasonably good information had been convinced by his
arguments that the Treaty was unworkable; the only remaining difference of opinion was whether to have an outright revision or to trust that in the working the terms would
be changed out of recognition. Mr John Foster Dulles wrote
a long letter to *The Times* on 16 February defending the
American delegation at Paris, while admitting that he had
'reached the conclusion, although with considerable doubt,
that pensions and separation allowances were not properly
chargeable to Germany'. He placed his hopes on the wisdom
of the Reparations Commission in making an intelligent
alleviation of terms and modes of payment, 'in the event that
they should prove to be excessive'. Keynes made a long reply
on 19 February in a strain of confidence. 'It is more than two
months since my book was published, and it has attracted
much notice and many readers. I have been criticized on
various grounds, personal and otherwise. But no one has
made a serious attempt to traverse my main conclusions.
The illuminating influence of time has done its work, and
those conclusions no longer conflict with the instructed
opinion of the day.'

Reference may be made to another letter in *The Times*
on 27 February, since Keynes's answer to it (1 March) is
worth quoting as a fine example of economy in controversial
writing. The letter of Keynes's critic consisted of 259 lines in

the columns of *The Times*. Keynes's answer consisted of twenty-seven, as follows:

*Sir,*

　　On November 5th, 1918, the Allied Governments, subject to two qualifications, 'declared their willingness to make peace with the Government of Germany on the terms of peace laid down in the President's address to Congress of January 8, 1918, and the principles of settlement enunciated in his subsequent Addresses'. I have argued that this agreement was not kept, and that its breach is dishonourable to us.

　　—'s letter, which you publish today, is directed to the contention, not that the Treaty is in fact in accord with these terms and principles, but (1) that, as there was no independent authority in a position to endorse this agreement, it was not a 'contract', and (2) that some of the terms and principles in question were so lacking in legal precision that their interpretation 'might be argued for months without any irrelevance or waste of time'. What, for example – this philosopher asks – are 'rival States'? What is a 'group of nations'? What 'territorial settlements' were 'involved in this war'? It is an extraordinary commentary on the workings of the human mind that — should believe that he has thus contributed to the establishment of our good faith.

I am, Sir, your obedient servant,

J. M. KEYNES

　　In the United States there was less moral reprimand, and the anti-German fury seemed to have died down. There too, however, he had many critics. There was some exploitation of his book by the political opponents of the President, and Senator Borah read long quotations in a speech in Congress on 10 February. Some reviewers spotted that in the controversy about the League, which had been raging for six months, the Americans had been arguing off the point and were now being taught for the first time what the Treaty was all about. However, it was too late to change, and the Treaty was already doomed to defeat on account of arguments previously adduced. Friends of the Treaty pointed out that the economic plight of Europe, as shown in the book, made it all the more necessary for the Americans to play their part in the League and the Reparations Commission in getting wise and helpful decisions.

In his constructive proposals Keynes had voiced the view that the present governments of Europe were untrustworthy, and that a change was necessary if progress was to be made. 'If I had influence with the United States Treasury, I would not lend a penny to a single one of the present governments of Europe.'[2] This sentence was seized upon and given a banner headline in some American newspapers.

Professor Allyn Young, who had been an expert in the American delegation at Paris, had some correspondence with Keynes about the book and gave publicity[3] in America to the following passage in a letter which he received:

### J. M. Keynes to Professor Allyn Young, 28 February 1920

As regards my picture of the President, you must remember two things: one, that I wrote it in July immediately after I left Paris and before I had any knowledge of his illness, and, two, that although it is generally taken as an attack on him, I intended it not so much as an attack as an explanation. Many persons here believed that in spite of appearances the Treaty must be in accordance with our engagements, because the President had acquiesced in it. I thought it necessary therefore to give a human explanation of how it came about that this was not so. In spite of everything I say about him, and of all my disappointments, I still believe that essentially the President played a nobler part at Paris than any of his colleagues.

Keynes could feel satisfied with the effect that he had produced on opinion in England at the price of aspersions on his character. It is interesting to record that at this time, when many pompous persons were looking down their noses and reviling him as a backslider, he was by no means completely outcast. On 4 January Bonar Law had him to dinner. On 2 February Austen Chamberlain, then Chancellor of the Exchequer, wrote to him to obtain his personal opinion

2. *The Economic Consequences of the Peace*, p. 267.
3. *The Republican*, Springfield, Mass., 1 April 1920.

whether the recent rise in the Treasury bill rate had been a
wise move. While journalists castigated him for letting down
British Ministers, the Ministers in question were seeking
his advice. At that time he held the orthodox view that a
stiff rise in money rates was desirable in order to check
inflation.

He felt that things were very slowly beginning to move in
the right direction. In the Easter Vacation he went to Rome
with Duncan Grant and Vanessa Bell. These settled down
to painting, while Keynes spent much of his time in a social
round. He was fêted by Italian Liberals as a great man. He
found at the British Embassy an old King's man, Mr Haslam, and they had much to talk of. This revival of an
acquaintanceship had further consequences, for on Mr
Haslam's return to England a couple of years later he proposed to the Provincial Insurance Company that Keynes and
Mr Falk should be invited to act as economic advisers. In
1923 Keynes joined the Board and became President of their
Finance Committee, where he guided the investment policy
of the Company. He remained a member of the Board
throughout his life, and this was one of his city connections
which he valued most.

Good news came to Rome of his financial speculations.
Since leaving England he had made a profit on francs of
about £22,000 to set against losses on dollars of about £8,000.
He was 'indulging in an orgy of shopping of all kinds of
objects which in spite of the difficulty of getting them to
England are amazingly cheap. I should think we have
bought about a ton so far, including quantities of furniture.'[4] When tired of gaieties, he went with the others to the
Sabine Hills and thereafter proceeded to the Berensons.
Thus the ways of peace were revived, and his personal prospects seemed fair.

Soon after his return to England they became overcast.
His speculations were based on his judgement of economic
trends, but they were carried out in day-to-day operations

4. Letter to Mrs Keynes, 16 April.

with a very narrow margin of cover. This technique was not really suited to the basis on which his risks were taken. At least, he would require the most consummate skill if he was to match the one to the other. In the later days of May the dollar showed an obstinate refusal to appreciate, and the mark showed an obstinate refusal to depreciate. It was contrary to reason, but such was the case. The mark underwent a surprising and substantial revival.

Looking back, we may deem the rise of sterling against the dollar to have been not unnatural. The slump hit America first, and for some months she had been feeling her way towards a policy of deflation. But the Federal Reserve System moved slowly, and its influence on the market was always delayed; there were twelve Banks, each with some independence, and there were numerous Bank Rates, varying according to the class of paper. One could not say that a six per cent Bank Rate was generally established until June. The Bank of England retained some of its old skill; it put the Bank Rate up to seven per cent on 15 May, and that was effective. Although relative interest rates do not exert their normal effect on the foreign exchange when there is no par of exchange, we may suppose that they exert some effect, and that the more efficient deflation on the British side was responsible for the temporary strengthening of sterling. The strength of the mark is somewhat more difficult to explain; it was suggested at the time that American investors were having their first flirtation with German Municipal Bonds, the later development of which, after the new mark had been stabilized by Schacht in 1924, led to such wide-reaching effects. The movement of the mark at this time may merely have been a reaction from its earlier collapse; the other continental currencies also showed an upward tendency. All these movements were shortlived, and when another three months had elapsed the previous trends had been resumed.

Keynes could not wait for three months. As the later days of May ebbed away, it became clear that he was ruined. Between the beginning of April and the end of May he had lost £13,125. A small syndicate, for part of the resources of which he was morally responsible, also lost £8,498. Previous gains were wiped out, and his small cover. Sales had to be effected. His firm asked him to pay in £7,000 to keep the account open. They gave him favourable treatment, which helped to carry him through.

It is clear that, in the last resort, such a call was not beyond the means of his parents. Dr Keynes had capital and would be ready to help. Maynard Keynes himself argued in retrospect that at the worst point his own assets were just enough to meet his liabilities, on the assumption that he sold all his pictures, books and other possessions; there may have been a little wishful thinking here. However, the position was clearly not irretrievable. It would indeed have been a disaster if the man who had so recently set world opinion agog by claiming to know better than the mighty of the land had himself become involved in bankruptcy. One can imagine the banner headlines. He was never really near such complete disaster.

In the event the call of his firm was met in part by a loan of £5,000 from a famous financier, with whom he had no close personal relations, but who knew, through a third party, of his work at Paris and admired it greatly. This was repaid in December. For the rest he had another resource. There was *The Economic Consequences of the Peace*. He had already had large sales in England, and in the course of business Macmillans had advanced him £1,000. That had already gone. They would not ordinarily settle his account till after 1 July. He wrote to request an advance settlement in respect of what was due. They promptly sent him a cheque for £1,500. Did he finger it lovingly? This was the reward for his masterpiece, a work of passion and anguish of spirit. He had torn himself away from the hateful coils of Paris in order to drain all his resources of knowledge and skill and art into persuading the world to be more wise and generous. It was the great work of his life so far; perhaps he would not achieve such another. There was the £1,500 lying on his desk. It was a just reward. But it was no longer his. It would be paid into his bank and at once paid out again, to swell the balances of those sagacious persons who thought that the mark had a rosy future and the dollar a poor one.[5]

2

His parents, whom he took into his confidence about the setback, did not offer reproaches, but advised caution in the coming year. We may be confident that he had learnt his lesson. The intellectual apparatus would be brought to bear to make quite sure that this would not recur. To expect caution was perhaps asking too much; this was beyond his range; prudence he might conceivably achieve. The loan had sufficed to carry him through. Within a few weeks he was deeply in again, working on the same general lines. He was temperamentally daring and confident of his own reasoning. It would have been against his nature not to back it with all he had. Besides, this was his fight for freedom. He had no inheritance which he could enlarge by more orthodox financial methods. In the previous year there had been some hint that he might be offered a place on the board of one of the great British banks;[6] his book had made that quite out of the question now. He was determined not to relapse into salaried drudgery. He must be financially independent. He felt that he had that in him which would justify such independence. He had many things to tell the nation. And he wanted a sufficiency. He must be able to take stalls at the Russian Ballet whenever he wished – and entertain the dancers, if that struck his fancy. He must be able to buy friends' pictures – and pay them handsomely. These other

5. Mr Daniel Macmillan recalls meeting his old friend in the street in the autumn of 1919 and being warned by him not to follow the current fashion of buying German marks at low prices. Mr Macmillan was not inclined to indulge in speculation; had he been so, and disregarded Keynes's advice, Keynes could have settled his account on the book by returning Macmillan his own cheque!
6. Not to be confused with the firm offer by the Scandinavian Bank.

dealers in money merely squandered their earnings on banal conventional luxuries. He must use his brains to put some of their money into his pocket, where it would fructify, not only financially, but in supporting the arts, and people who really mattered, and in giving his own powers scope.

So he went deeply in. By the end of 1924 he reckoned that the value of his assets, after deducting his large overdrafts, and not counting pictures and books, was £57,797. By the beginning of 1937 it was £506,450. He died leaving about £450,000, if we include the value of pictures and books.

It is proper to mention that from time to time rumours have circulated among those who did not know Keynes well, that he made his fortune by using inside information when in the Treasury. Such rumours were especially apt to occur among those who disagreed with his opinions on political economy. They may be scotched by the facts.

He had no foot in the Treasury (or any other official position) between June 1919 and July 1940. The operations which he undertook within a year of leaving the Treasury in 1919 cost him the whole of his accumulated savings to date (about £6,000) and the main proceeds of the English sales of *The Economic Consequences of the Peace*. His speculative account opened on 14 August 1919, and his fortune reached its peak in 1937. To start with, in order to sustain his operations, he put in a modest cover of about £4,000 worth of securities. His firm required ten per cent. He borrowed small sums from certain members of his family, paying them a handsome rate of interest on the loans. He ploughed back his quick profits and was thus able to pyramid his holdings. Then came the reverse, when he lost all and went outside for help. From this time onwards his position was built up by a gradual process, of which he kept a record.

We may add that to those who knew him at all well the charge appears quite fantastic. He was punctiliously honourable in all financial matters. Not only would it have been entirely inconsistent with his character to have taken advantage of official information, but he had a certain idiosyncrasy, well known to those who worked closely with him, which made it extremely distasteful to him to use ordinary inside business information acquired in a straightforward manner. This was partly based on intellectual grounds. He believed that the safest way to earn was to consider a proposition in the light of the general economic situation and his own judgement as to how that would develop, and to back his judgement. He believed that 'inside information' more often than not led investors astray. It was a favourite dictum of his in the thirties that 'the dealers on Wall Street could make huge fortunes if only they had no inside information'!

There was also a moral side to this idiosyncrasy. He too had his puritan blood. Was there some obscure corner of his nature which evoked that sympathy, which his urbane style could not altogether conceal, for the poor Presbyterian President in his difficulties? There seemed to him to be something wrong in taking advantage of special knowledge, even when that knowledge had been gained in a thoroughly proper way in the ordinary course of business. It was not quite playing the game. The game was to pit one's intelligence against others who had the same public information at their disposal, so that the reward, when it came, would be, subject to the inevitable risks, the prize of superior judgement. These traits of his character are known to many, who can give the lie to malicious rumour-mongers.

It is convenient at this point to cast a forward glance over his financial dealings. He continued his daily intervention in the exchange markets. Towards the end of 1920 he began to take an interest in cotton, and at the beginning of 1921 he opened an account in this commodity and dealt heavily. Then his interests broadened, and we find him trading in lead, tin, copper, spelter, rubber, wheat, sugar, linseed oil and jute. All this dealing was based on a close study of general influences affecting the world markets in each of the commodities. He maintained this active interest until 1937, when he fell ill and decided to abandon it; it was one of the few sacrifices which he made to the clear need for conserving his energies. During the twenties his personal operations were highly speculative, being supported on narrow margins of cover.

He was also interested in securities, and participated in a number of syndicates. In the twenties he was very close to Mr Falk, and they often acted together in a professional way as occasional consultants to firms. In 1920 Debenham & Co. constituted an Economic Committee, on which he and Falk and one or two others served for a period of four years. In 1921 a small investment company was formed, consisting of Mr Falk, Sir Geoffrey Fry, Sir Frank Nixon, Mr Dudley Ward, Mr Trouton and Keynes. The names are familiar. The old 'A' Division of the Treasury had come together again, to pool their wisdom, and, to celebrate the fact, the company was christened 'A.D.' Somewhat later he and Falk took part in the formation of the Independent Investment Trust, which was on a somewhat larger scale. Then, later again, he participated in the formation of a very select company, called 'P.R.' ($\pi\acute{\alpha}\nu\tau\alpha$ $\dot{\rho}\epsilon\tilde{\iota}$). This was a channel contrived by Keynes to enable his close friends to increase their capital. It was, therefore, a matter of particular concern to him. When the slump of 1929–31 came there was a woeful depreciation, and Keynes had some difference of opinion with his associates. The rights and wrongs of this do not concern us, but Keynes felt it incumbent on him to have the capital divided into four parts, and by the clever manipulation of his fourth he was able to ensure that his friends regained their capital in full.

In the early period he had the idea, which was shared by Mr Falk, that it should be possible to turn an economist's understanding of the vagaries of the business cycle to profitable account. There should be appropriate movements between gilt-edged securities and equities, and between long-term and short-term securities. For this purpose it was more needful to study business barometers than the qualities and characteristics of any particular asset. It is possible that his services were sought partly because he was supposed to have special expertise in interpreting these mysteries. He hoped at one time to assist the fortunes of King's College by applying such methods in the investment of certain funds. It is not clear that this technique ever met with great success, save in one respect, namely, that his confidence in the early thirties that the rate of interest would fall and Stock Exchange values be restored to a due relation with the values of the physical assets which they represented, greatly assisted him and all the institutions which depended upon his advice. In due course he himself became sceptical of the practical value of business-cycle theory for the purpose of private gain, and concentrated on the careful choice of particular investments, mainly with a view to their long-term prospects. It is clear that in the early rapid build-up of his private fortune he cannot have relied upon long-term considerations or even upon business-cycle movements; in this case it was quicker changes that he had to take into account; he traded very actively, moving in and out continually.

In the management of his own capital and in these small companies, the aim in early days was to get a quick enlargement of capital, and the method one of extreme boldness, decisions being taken on an economic appraisal of the general situation. At the Bursary of King's College he had to look at matters very differently. Extremely long-term considerations were all-important. He soon acquired a dominating influence over investment policy there, becoming First Bursar in 1924.

In the case of the National Mutual and the Provincial Insurance Companies, he had a different problem again. As with the College, caution was necessary – he was prepared to cultivate this virtue when dealing with money not his own. But in the case of the insurance companies much greater stress had to be laid on liquidity. His success in increasing the revenues of King's was spectacular, and the insurance companies also prospered. It is fair to add that his own capital and that of the institutions whose investments he

managed felt the full brunt of the slump of 1929–31. In all
cases there were large advances thereafter beyond the pre-
slump positions.

Keynes gave zealous and unremitting attention to these
investment problems. He had the difficult intellectual task
of keeping distinct his three strands of thought, that relating
to his own affairs, that relating to the College, and that relating to the insurance companies. To most men this would
seem well-nigh impossible, and there were moments when
even Keynes complained that he had set himself too hard a
task. Yet we may be sure that basically this very difficulty
kept his interest alive in it. It afforded the kind of intellectual
conundrum which he thoroughly enjoyed. His work was
performed in bed in the morning. Financial intelligence
came to him from the various brokers and he assimilated the
information provided by the newspapers. He pondered upon
the implications of what he learnt and made his decisions.
He reckoned that the whole business took him about half an
hour each morning.

From an early date he had laid stress on the careful selection of long-term investments and adherence to them
through bad times. This aspect became, as time went on,
more important in the management of his own money. His
position had changed very considerably: he was no longer
a man trying to build up a capital out of practically nothing,
but a man of moderate substance who was trying to increase
it. This does not mean that in the following period his policy
was by any means orthodox. He was prepared to take considerable risks by buying securities of low market valuation.
Nor did the policy of relying for profit on one's selection of
particular securities imply adopting the common practice
of looking for inside information. His selection was based on
two main considerations, first, the prospects of the business
in the country in question, having regard to the general
economic circumstances, and, secondly, the balance-sheet
of the company. He laid great stress on the latter. Careful
scrutiny of the balance sheet was more valuable than all the

inside information in the world. The laws of arithmetic were more reliable than the winds of rumour. Having chosen his stocks carefully, he was entirely unwilling to be frightened out of them by short-term reverses. Nor did he take quick gains. Having convinced himself that the stock had a good long-term future, he waited patiently, through ups and downs, for the long-term potential to develop.

It is worth placing some emphasis on this characteristic of his later investment policy, which is well authenticated, because it is at variance with the commonly held view of him that he was an inveterate vacillator. One may beg to suggest that vacillation is not in itself a virtue or vice, but only so relatively to the matter in hand. Nothing is lost by changing one's allegiance in the realm of abstract doctrine as soon as one's assessment of the weight of argument changes. There is everything to be said for repeated changes of front when coping with a changing situation, or in the conduct of negotiations, as the strong and weak points of the opposition successively emerge. In other cases it may be vitally important to abide by one's original decision. Keynes showed his capacity for doing this in his investment policy; some have even thought that he carried his unwillingness to change his investments too far.

This shift of emphasis, which became marked in the early thirties, led to some disagreement with Mr Falk in connection with the Independent Investment Trust. They did not work together in financial matters subsequently, but their personal friendship was unimpaired.

There may have been a cause, other than the larger size of his own capital, for the shift of emphasis. Knowledge of his character suggests this, and the direct evidence of his associates corroborates it. His plans for private gain – including therein gain for the institutions with which he was concerned – were influenced by his abstract economic theory. He had been brought up in the traditional doctrine that successful speculation benefited the community. This was the view of Marshall and of the whole classical school. When in his letter to his mother, written in 1919,[7] he said that his father would be 'shocked' by his speculation, this did not refer to moral but to prudential considerations. His father was very strongly of the opinion that one should play for safety. As an economist, Keynes would, no doubt, have subscribed to the doctrine that wise speculation served a useful purpose. It tended to reduce market fluctuations; it provided a trustworthy finger-post for producers and consumers; it enabled the whole economic system to function more smoothly and efficiently. As regards the gains of the successful speculator, in the case of the foreign exchanges, this was solely at the expense of the unsuccessful, who, since he had voluntarily incurred the risk, had no legitimate hardship if the risk went wrong. In the case of commodities, the same argument largely applied; what speculator A gained, speculator B lost; the consumer, however, would find that there was charged into the price he had to pay a sufficient addition to give speculators the wherewithal to pay their staff expenses together with a prospective *average* private net income not greater than would afford a reasonable reward for their application to this profession; the ordinary processes of competition would prevent *average* rewards to speculators rising higher; and in effect the consumer would pay nothing at all, because the value of the speculator's services in reducing the costs of marketing would more than compensate for their rake-off. If a speculator, like Keynes, had no overhead expenses, he was being particularly helpful to the consumer. This was well-established doctrine. In the development of his own original theories, he became more doubtful about the beneficial effects of short-term speculation. This would not affect the value to the community of long-term speculative enterprise.

Speculators may do no harm as bubbles on a steady stream of enterprise. But the position is serious when enterprise becomes the bubble on a whirlpool of speculation. When the capital de-

7. cf. p. 338.

velopment of a country becomes a by-product of the activities of a casino, the job is likely to be ill-done.[8]

It is probable that there gradually settled upon him a reluctance to be part of the casino. Indeed he argued with friends to this effect. Thus the change in his speculative habit was in accord with the change in his economic doctrine. He was not inclined to put maxims of private conduct and maxims of social good into two separate compartments. His whole life was bound up in various ways with the promotion of what he deemed to be the general good; he would not have allowed his private quest for gain to be out of harmony.

### 3

His main intellectual task in 1920 was the preparation of the *Treatise on Probability* for the press. He found some difficulty in acclimatizing himself once more to the complicated mathematical language of his own devising. He had to go over the whole book, filling gaps and deciding points which had still been at issue in the summer of 1914.[9]

In the Easter Vacation of 1921 he took Mr J. H. ('Sebastian') Sprott on a holiday to Algeria and Tunisia, where they worked together on the index. Mr Sprott recalls an incident when a street-boy had polished their shoes. Keynes knew from his inner consciousness what should be paid, but this did not satisfy the requirements of the natives, and stones were thrown at them as they proceeded along the street. Sprott suggested that some further emolument might end their embarrassment, but Keynes was firm. 'I will not be a party to debasing the currency.' He was throughout his life careful about small money matters – but Sprott did not realize what good reason he had to be at this particular time.

As we move into that year, we get the sense of a great

8. *The General Theory of Employment, Interest and Money*, p. 159.
9. cf. chap. 3, p. 160.

crowding of duties, a multiplicity and variety of interests, which was to be a feature of his life until he fell ill in 1937. His primary duties remained those connected with his Fellowship at King's College, where he usually stayed from Friday until Tuesday. There he took pupils, sometimes one by one, gave lectures and held his Monday evening Club. His bursarial duties grew and he soon became mainly responsible for the College's investment policy. He maintained his interest in the quest for choice spirits in each new generation, for young men of intellect and sensibility, who would carry on the traditions of his own undergraduate days. The chosen ones became his friends, and he gave them an *entrée* into Bloomsbury. At this time these included Sebastian Sprott, Alec Penrose, Angus and Douglas Davidson. He took some interest also in University affairs and testified to the Royal Commission on Oxford and Cambridge, of which Mr Asquith was the Chairman. We find him writing a letter to the *Cambridge Review* upholding the cause of women.[10] He continued in his editorship of the *Economic Journal*, with his wonted careful consideration of articles submitted, whether he accepted or rejected them.

In London he had to think of his own intricate speculative dealings. These were vital, the foundation of his new way of life. He must not make a second mistake. His City interests were multiplying. He and Mr Falk were extending their operations as consultants. He never had any official connection with Mr Falk's firm of brokers, but he gave them the benefit of his opinions, while they stretched their facilities for dealing on his behalf to the utmost limit. He was in constant touch with them, and it was necessary for the success of his own undertakings and for maintaining the high quality of his advisory work that he should follow the financial situation closely from day to day. He was concerned with the status of currencies, the prospects of a number of commodities and the condition of the Stock

10. *Cambridge Review*, 25 February 1921 (vol. 42, pp. 273–4).

Exchange. Many would judge that his financial activities were enough to absorb all his time.

He had also to keep a careful watch on questions of high international politics. In these years there was a succession of conferences which produced constantly shifting reparations proposals. He had no intention of letting *The Economic Consequences of the Peace* be his last word, and he decided that, as soon as the *Treatise on Probability* was out of the way, he would write a new book on the reparations problem. He had a wide correspondence, in order to keep track as far as possible of the inner meaning of successive proposals. He studied the politicians in the attempt to plumb their motives; he must maintain the standard of psychological insight which he had set himself in the *Economic Consequences*.

All this was not only in preparation for the next book. He was writing all the time for the press, on the alert for any point which he thought the public should notice. Indeed he was developing quite a substantial journalistic activity. In the spring of 1921 he contributed regularly to the *Manchester Guardian*.[11]

Under the article of 27 April the subscript first appeared which is so familiar to his readers in later years: 'Copyright in the United States and translation rights reserved by the author'. Attempts to place some of these articles in the United States and elsewhere had been frustrated by the widespread quotation of extracts from the *Manchester Guardian* articles in foreign newspapers. He began to make it a habit, when he contributed an important article to the British press, to write round to half a dozen newspapers in various foreign countries offering it. He charged stiff prices, and his journalistic income was not inconsiderable. In the summer, seeking to vary his audience, he placed five four-columned articles in the *Sunday Times*. Meanwhile he was discussing a larger project with the *Manchester Guardian*.

11. See especially 1921 – 1 February, 5 March, 24 March, 27 April, 6 May, 13 May.

The plan was to issue a series of weighty supplements on European Reconstruction, with articles by the most distinguished authorities in each country, under Keynes's general editorship. During the autumn he was busy with preparations for this publication. He had time for various bits of voluntary work in good causes. He was a member of the Liberal Committee on Industrial Policy – rejecting, however, the idea that he should become a parliamentary candidate. He was thanked by Lord Robert Cecil for his work on the Disarmament Committee of the League of Nations Union.

All this many-sided activity did not lead him to neglect his old Bloomsbury friends. On the contrary, 46 Gordon Square was a great centre for parties and charades, or for pleasant intimate meetings and good talk. Bloomsbury had some revival after the dreary days of war. Lytton Strachey occasionally appeared from the country. There were the younger people coming into the circle. The work of members of the group was beginning to receive a wider recognition. Their ideas were assimilated by a larger number. There was a certain post-war excitement and effervescence. Keynes was quite at the centre of things in this period. He cast aside his public and financial preoccupations and sank himself in the old atmosphere, the talk about life and art, the gossip about friends. There was not any great change from pre-war days. Their habits of mind were too deeply engrained. The critical, amusing commentary on men and things proceeded. The curious idiosyncrasy of the group, the strong flavour, persisted.

An event occurred at this time which did much to enhance Keynes's reputation and instil a proper respect into his critics. On 1 May 1921 the Reparations Committee, in accordance with its instructions, published its assessment of the total liability of Germany under the Treaty. In his book Keynes had reckoned that this would be £7,120 million; he had rounded it up to £8,000 million in order to be on the safe side, since all the world seemed to be giving higher figures, and added a footnote prophesying that the result would lie between £6,400 million and £8,000 million. The figure provided by the Reparations Commission was £6,850 million.[12] Thus, his judgement was vindicated and, contrary to the expectation of his critics, his figure was found to err on the high side. He wrote a letter to *The Times* at once, in which he was able to cite other instances where his predictions were fulfilled by the Report of the Reparations Commission with remarkable accuracy.[13] What the critics had failed to appreciate was that it was Keynes alone (and other British Treasury officials who silently agreed with him) who had done the real work, and that the other experts had been lazily contenting themselves with dogmatic guesses. He politely suggested that, in view of this result, his critics might pause to reflect that his estimate of Germany's capacity to pay was also worthy of consideration.

In September three different newspapers to which Keynes had contributed, the *Manchester Guardian*, the *New York World* and the *Baltimore Sun*, had the same bright idea. Keynes should be their special representative at the Disarmament Conference, to be held at Washington. Although he was rather tempted – it would be pleasant to revisit the United States – he rejected the proposal. The Conference was likely to be mainly concerned with naval matters, on which he was not an expert. He wished to confine his journalistic output to subjects that he followed closely and not to become a journalist at large. There was a more specific reason for the refusal. The Government of India had invited him to become Vice-Chairman of a Fiscal Commission. He welcomed this revival of his connection with Indian problems. He would have to fit in a visit to India, and this certainly precluded his going to Washington also. In writing to Scott, editor of the *Manchester Guardian*, with reference to the Washington proposal, he pleaded his Indian commit-

12. viz. £6,600 (millions) + the £250 (millions) included in Keynes's estimate for redemption of Allied loans to Belgium.

13. *The Times*, 2 May 1921.

ment: 'The Commission will, I think, represent a last effort, almost certainly doomed to futility, to save India for modified Free Trade. But, though there is little hope of success, I expect you will agree that it is an enterprise which is worth while.' [14] Thus Washington had to give way to India. But the Indian visit did not come off either.

On 26 May 1921 Diaghilev opened a new season in London. It was marked by an event of considerable interest, the return to the company of Lydia Lopokova. Once again she did the Can-can Dancer in the *Boutique*, and she had the leading part in *Les Sylphides*. Once again she had tremendous ovations from the London audiences. For that autumn Diaghilev was planning something new, a production which some held to be the finest of all those he staged in London, *The Sleeping Princess*. Tchaikovsky and Bakst, Spessiva and Lopokova would their mixed power employ to enchant and captivate the spectators. The first performance on 2 November had the same kind of rapturous reception that had greeted the *Boutique Fantasque* two years before. But this time it was the seduction of pure loveliness. The part of the Princess was taken by Spessiva, great classical ballerina, while Lopokova danced the Lilac Fairy with all her sweet impulsiveness. Keynes went often.

In order to titillate his audience and maintain an excited interest, Diaghilev had the pleasant idea of varying the parts, and on certain nights Lopokova danced the Princess herself. Keynes made sure that he would see her thus. He was spellbound by this Princess, so light and quick, so charming and piquante, so coy and unexpected. As he watched, his whole being was filled with joy and exhilaration.

How he adored the Ballet! What a great man Diaghilev was! As these formulae came into his mind, he realized how utterly inadequate they were to describe what he now felt. Far away in some distant recess of his being a little idea took shape, which, travelling with the speed of light, gained

14. 14 September 1921.

possession of his whole mind and heart. This was a thought, new and strange, crisp and bold, daring ... Where would it lead him? He was daring by nature. It seemed hardly possible that it could lead to a good result. He was a contriver by nature too. His life was exciting and full, with all his new and varied interests, but he could see the danger that, when the novelty had worn off, he might be submerged in a multitude of activities which were a weariness of the flesh. He certainly lacked something to give personal significance to his multitudinous strivings. Some more vital motive was needed than the general good. This was certainly a very big idea. It was evidently much more important than Indian Free Trade.

He already knew Lydia. Bloomsbury had maintained its contacts with the Russian Ballet. He began to pay her attention. She was living at this time at the Waldorf Hotel, and he persuaded her to move to a flat at 41 Gordon Square, where she would be living below James and Alix Strachey and within easy reach of his Bloomsbury friends. He also discovered that she banked her earnings at the hotel. This was far from his idea of how to make the most profitable use of one's money, and he suggested that he might give her some advice on that topic. He would evidently have to proceed warily, for if the idea was new and strange to him, how much more so would it be to her! To abandon Diaghilev and become the wife of a Cambridge don! And then there would be another difficulty, since she was already married. She and her husband had parted and he was now in America. Keynes's utmost powers of contrivance would be taxed. He had clearly a long way to go before he could achieve what he wished. He decided to abandon the Indian project.

4

*A Revision of the Treaty*, Keynes's second book on the reparations problem, appeared at the beginning of 1922. It has the incisive and lively style of the earlier book, and

makes excellent reading. But it was more strictly addressed
to the economic issue and could not have as wide a public
as the book which analysed the inner motives of Wilson
and Clemenceau. Furthermore, it lacked the sense of impending doom that was present in the earlier work. Revolution and disaster had not come to Europe. Her peoples had
been patient, as he had admitted in the *Economic Consequences* that they might be; but, above all, despite fulmina-
tions and agitations, attempts to enforce the reparations
clauses of the Treaty had not achieved success, so that it
was natural that the disasters had not occurred. The book is
full of fire and epigrammatic denunciation of the circuitous
and dishonest methods of the politicians. One finds this kind
of footnote: 'If a partisan or a child wants a silly harmful
thing, it may be better to meet him with a silly harmless
thing, than with explanations he cannot understand. This
is the traditional wisdom of statesmen and nurserymaids.'

The book opens with a fine essay on the gulf between 'inside' and 'outside' opinion. This was Keynes's reaction to
the criticism that came to him from men of better judgement. 'Why make such a fuss? No one really intends to
do all these dreadful things that are talked about.' He
had for some time been convinced that this was true, but
the method of procedure shocked him. This opening chapter retains topical relevance and poses a fundamental question to the political philosopher. As the activity of the state
increases, will nominal democracy come to partake less and
less of the attributes of true democracy? Will the gulf between what really happens and what people are told and
believe about it ever widen?

Keynes proceeded to a very clear narrative of the successive results of the international conferences which had
been held since the Treaty. It was satisfactory to have the
story told so readably. He pointed out, without undue stress,
the fulfilment of some of his predictions. He returned to the
question of the legality of the demand for reparations on
account of pensions and allowances, pleading that it had

immediate practical relevance. The demand on this count roughly trebled the reparations bill; if it were removed, what Germany might rightly be deemed to owe under the Treaty was not far removed from what she was able to pay. Thus the excision of the pensions and allowances clause would bring the possibility of a satisfactory settlement into the foreground. The opposition had had two years in which to defend the legality of pensions and allowances, and no reasonable defence had been forthcoming.

In the original book Keynes had stressed the inability of the Germans to pay the sums demanded. The more popular argument against heavy reparations was the damage which British industrialists would suffer by competition if Germany was compelled to have a large excess of exports. This argument savoured of Protectionist fallacy; it could not possibly do harm to the economy as a whole to be the net recipient of something for nothing. None the less, Keynes recognized some force in the argument. The immediate effect of a large excess of German exports would clearly be detrimental to British producers of similar commodities. As against this, in the long run, after a period in which the country's economy could adjust itself to the new situation, there would be a clear gain. In the long run! That was the hub of the matter. If the reparations annuities continued in perpetuity, there would certainly be clear gain. But if they were to be paid for a limited time only, then, after a period of painful adjustment in our economy – during which we made way in our foreign markets for the excess of German goods, covering our adverse balance of trade by payments from Germany – the reparations annuities would come to an end, and we should have to recapture, perhaps with great difficulty, the markets which we had forgone during the interim. Thus, on the whole, he felt able to claim support from the arguments of those who disliked intensifying German competition.

Finally, he provided constructive proposals. He wished to go further now, suggesting that the British Empire should forgo all claim to share in reparations. At the same time inter-allied debts should be cancelled. Let Germany pay what the Allies were strictly entitled to demand under the terms of the Armistice and let the proceeds be divided between France and Belgium. He pointed out that this would give France a much more favourable settlement that she would get under the letter of the existing law, and *a fortiori* than she would get if attempts to enforce the existing settlement were imperfectly successful.

He had been warned that the American public was in no mood to waive the American claim for repayment of debt.

In their main substance, therefore, my suggestions are not novel. The now familiar project of the cancellation, in part or in their entirety, of the Reparation and Inter-Allied Debts, is a large and unavoidable feature of them. But those who are not prepared for these measures must not pretend to a serious interest in the Reconstruction of Europe.

In so far as such cancellation or abatement involves concessions by Great Britain, an Englishman can write without embarrassment and with some knowledge of the tendency of popular opinion in his own country. But where concessions by the United States are concerned he is in more difficulty. The attitude of a section of the American press furnishes an almost irresistible temptation to deal out the sort of humbug (or discreet half-truths) which are believed to promote cordiality between nations; it is easy and terribly respectable; and, what is much worse, it may even do good where frankness would do harm. I pursue the opposite course, with a doubting and uneasy conscience, yet supported (not only in this chapter but throughout my book) by the hope, possibly superstitious, that openness does good in the long run, even when it makes trouble at first.[15]

In a later passage he proceeded:

The average American, I fancy, would like to see the European nations approaching him with a pathetic light in their eyes and the cash in their hands, saying, 'America, we owe to you our liberty and our life; here we bring what we can in grateful thanks,

15. *A Revision of the Treaty*, p. 171.

money not wrung by grievous taxation from the widow and orphan, but saved, the best fruits of victory, out of the abolition of armaments, militarism, Empire, and internal strife, made possible by the help you freely gave us.' And then the average American would reply: 'I honour you for your integrity. It is what I expected. But I did not enter the war for profit or to invest my money well. I have had my reward in the words you have just uttered. The loans are forgiven. Return to your homes and use the resources I release to uplift the poor and the unfortunate.' And it would be an essential part of the little scene that his reply should come as a complete and overwhelming surprise.

Alas for the wickedness of the world! It is not in international affairs that we can secure the sentimental satisfactions which we all love. For only individuals are good, and all nations are dishonourable, cruel, and designing.[16]

Professor Allyn Young reviewed the book, and in a letter to Keynes confirmed the view set out above[17] that the arguments of the *Economic Consequences* were not responsible for the American rejection of the Treaty.

*Allyn A. Young to J. M. Keynes*, 7 February 1922

The difference between your position and mine is obvious. In England the practical problem was merely the revision of a Treaty which had already been accepted. Here the issue was whether the Treaty should be accepted or rejected. I believed, and still believe, that America should have accepted the Treaty and then should have done all that it could to secure its revision. We rejected on unworthy grounds; *not on your grounds* [italics mine]. Support of the Treaty means one thing in England, another thing in the United States.

During 1922 the great *Manchester Guardian* Supplements, twelve in number, were the main vehicle for the expression of Keynes's views. They were entitled *Reconstruction in Europe* and covered the whole field of finance, industry, trade and labour. Some of the issues were general, some

16. *A Revision of the Treaty*, p. 183.
17. Chapter 7, pp. 330–31.

specialized on some such topic as shipping or oil. To almost all Keynes contributed an introductory article, which summarized the subject and usually had some interesting ideas. In some issues he had two or three articles. In the first he had three articles of major importance, and his other contribution in chief occurred in the eleventh issue.

In the first issue there was a lengthy article on 'The Theory of Purchasing Power Parity', and another one on 'Forward Exchanges', which give a full account of the theory, which he subsequently summarized in his *Tract on Monetary Reform*. The leading article comprised proposals for dealing with the existing situation. He was tending now to shift his interest from the reparations problem proper; he had converted the world, and it was only a question of time before his ideas were put into effect. He turned his attention to the crumbling exchanges and bankrupt finances of the European countries. Stabilization of the currency should now be put in the forefront. He was in favour of a return to the Gold Standard, but not to a gold circulation. For the former he assumed that there would be general agreement. The vital issue was between a return to the old gold parities on the one hand, and all-round devaluation on the other. He strongly favoured devaluation. He considered the argument that it would enhance prestige for a country's currency to return to the pre-war gold value.

Where a country can reasonably hope to restore its pre-war gold parity soon, it is important. This might be said of Great Britain, Holland, Sweden, Switzerland, and Spain, but of no other European country. With the bankers of the city of London this argument, or rather this sentiment, is likely to weigh so heavily, even so much more heavily than it ought, that it will almost certainly prevail to the extent of giving the Bank of England at least a year's grace in which to try the policy of restoration. But if success is not attained within a year from now, arguments to the contrary may obtain a hearing. In the case of those countries, however, where the present exchange is very remote from its pre-war parity, this argument has little weight.

He proceeded to demolish the other arguments for a restoration of pre-war values.

He delivered a homily on lines that had long been familiar in Britain but were not so familiar abroad, that, to support the stabilization, countries must be prepared to use all the gold they had. A reserve was meant to be used. This was the doctrine which had established the financial supremacy of Britain, and Keynes continued to uphold it, as he had in 1914. He did not think that additional support for stabilization would be needed, but, further to underpin it, he proposed that the Federal Reserve Board might agree to make temporary loans at the penal rate of 10 per cent to an aggregate maximum of $500 million. The interest would be paid into a guarantee fund and all participating central banks would guarantee the Federal Reserve Board against ultimate loss. 'I do not think that such a plan would be contrary to the interests of the Federal Reserve Board or disagreeable to them, and they might find that on close analysis it presented more sound features than met the eye immediately.'

In the eleventh issue, which appeared eight months later, his tone had become more vehement. He made a frontal attack on deflation. The magnitude of the internal debt of most European countries was the main reason why it was impossible to restore the value of their currencies to their former level. But this was not the only reason. Deflation would cause business depression and unemployment. He cited an article by Professor Irving Fisher in the same issue 'written with overwhelming force and lucidity'. This article by Keynes was his first to sound a clear warning against the evils of deflation and may therefore be regarded as the preface to the work which was to absorb his interests for the next fifteen years and to lead him far from his original starting-point. In the *Economic Consequences* he had exposed the evils of inflation with consummate brilliance; but it was deflation that was to prove the main target of his attacks in future. I therefore quote a passage, in which he cites the policy of Czechoslovakia as an illustration.

Comparatively free from the burden of internal debt, and free also from any appreciable budgetary deficit, Czechoslovakia has been able, in pursuance of the policy of her Finance Minister, Dr Alois Rasin, to employ the proceeds of certain loans, which her credit enabled her to raise in London and New York, to improve the exchange value of the Czech crown to about double the level which seemed to me eight months ago, with reference to the circumstances existing at that time, a rate at which she could hope to stabilize the crown with advantage to herself. Owing to the rapidity with which under the above favourable conditions it has been possible to effect the improvement, the country has not suffered as severely as she would, if the change had been slower and more prolonged. But it has cost her an industrial crisis and serious unemployment. To what purpose? I do not know. Even now the Czech crown is only worth a sixth of its pre-war parity; and it remains unstabilized, fluttering before the breath of the seasons and the wind of politics. Is, therefore, the process of appreciation to continue indefinitely? If not, when and at what point is stabilization to be effected? Meanwhile the foreign resources, which might have been employed during the past six months to secure a definite stabilization, are no longer intact, and it will not prove easy to replenish them. Czechoslovakia was better placed than any country in Europe to establish her economic life on the basis of a sound and fixed currency. Her finances were in equilibrium, her credit good, her foreign resources adequate, and no one could have blamed her for devaluating the crown, ruined by no fault of hers and inherited from the Habsburg Empire. Pursuing a misguided policy in a spirit of stern virtue, she preferred the stagnation of her industries and a still fluctuating standard.

The Supplements, which ran to 810 large three-columned pages, contained expert information upon the whole field of economics. These were also published in French and German. Authors from many countries were brought into service and there were more foreign contributors than British. Keynes certainly laboured hard to attract authoritative writers, and I confess to finding fascination in the galaxy which appears in the list which I append in a footnote. This only constitutes about a third of all contributors, and I have no doubt that many of the foreign names which I have omitted were as illustrious in their own countries as the British names were in ours.[18]

Journalism was exerting a strong pull at this time. The third Supplement included treatment of the International Conference held at Genoa in April. The idea came forward that he should himself go to Genoa and, in addition to his contribution to the Supplement, write eleven major articles for the daily *Manchester Guardian*. The idea appealed to him. There was an arrangement with the *Daily Express* to publish some of this matter. He then approached, either by a direct letter or through an agency, numerous newspapers throughout the world. He had refusals, but was persistent, and finally got an arrangement with the *New York World* and with papers in France, Italy, Spain, Germany, Austria, Czechoslovakia, Holland and Sweden. The *Manchester Guardian* paid him £300, the *New York World* £350, and the other papers sums varying from £100 to £25. He stayed in Genoa for three weeks and wrote his contracted eleven articles. When the Conference bade fair to last considerably longer, he ruthlessly returned to Cambridge. It must have been a curious experience, having represented the Chancellor of the Exchequer at Paris – and he was destined to represent the Chancellor of the Exchequer many years later at another great international conference – to move about

18. Asquith, Ramsay MacDonald, Philip Snowden, Robert Cecil, Caillaux, Painlevé, Léon Blum, Herriot, Nitti, Beneš, Melchior, Dr Schacht, Sidney Webb, Walter Lippmann, Tawney, Maxim Gorky, Albert Thomas, Gustav Cassel, Croce, Ferrero, Rist, Gompers, Norman Angell, Henri Barbusse, Lowes Dickinson, Pigou, D. H. Robertson, Stamp, J. H. Clapham, L. B. Namier, Joseph Kitchin, Moritz Bonn, Schumacher, Andréadès, Einaudi, Paul Cravath, Bainville, De Jouvenel, Charles Hobhouse, Arthur Greenwood, Walter Layton, W. L. Hichens, Henry Clay, John Hilton, Henry Bell, Buckmaster, J. J. Mallon, R. Hilferding, R. C. Leffingwell, O. M. W. Sprague, Paul Warburg, J. H. Williams, Irving Fisher, Piero Sraffa, the Queen of Rumania, Georges Duhamel, H. N. Brailsford, G. D. H. Cole, H. Laski, T. E. Gregory, Parker Willis, Isserlis. In conclusion we may mention members of 'A' Division – O. T. Falk, Dudley Ward.

among familiar faces at Genoa in the capacity of newspaper man. He did not disdain the humbler role. He was
assisting his account with his brokers, while his great series
of articles in the *Manchester Guardian*, written with full
knowledge of what was proceeding, made an important contribution to the formation of opinion. He was invited by
members of the British Delegation to attend some of their
unofficial meetings after dinner and joined in their discussions. He took Mr Haslam with him [19] as his personal
assistant and, as his secretary, Mr Buttress, who had a long
career of service with him in King's College Bursary and
as Assistant Secretary to the Royal Economic Society. It
was Mr Buttress's first visit to the Continent. They all stayed
at Santa Margherita and in the evenings usually went to the
Casino at Rapallo. Keynes himself was no longer so much
tempted by the gaming tables as in former times; he had
bigger fish to fry now.

Later in the year he went abroad again. He received an
invitation over the signature of a number of distinguished
Germans to the 'Overseas Week' (17 to 27 August), an international gathering at Hamburg, to discuss the economic
situation. He attended the Conference and gave a public
address at the final meeting. He propounded a new reparations scheme by which the obligation to pay, which was
now pressing so heavily upon the German mark, should be
postponed to 1930, but an inducement to pay earlier, namely
six per cent compound interest, should be offered. He laid
great stress on the need for Germany to set her own house
in order and check inflation. She should be given a respite
in order to do this. The Hamburg correspondent of the
*Manchester Guardian* reported this as follows:

The brilliant contribution made by Mr Keynes, in giving his
personal view of a sensible settlement of the reparation problem,
was very warmly greeted. The Hamburg merchants, the descen-
dants of men who for centuries have had intimate relations with
England, did not regard Keynes as coming in the capacity of a

19. cf. p. 345.

friend of Germany. What they were prepared to value in the Englishman was his traditional business fairness. All the greater was the impression created by his address, and particularly his warning to avoid political Jeremiads and to work out practical and tangible proposals. For Germany has nothing to gain by a continuation of the morbid, spurious boom, with a continually sinking mark.[20]

The *Daily Telegraph* observed that 'his remarks are reported in the German press at a length and with a prominence which is usually reserved for the heads of governments'.


## 5

I had just finished my course of studies at Oxford in classics, philosophy and history.[21] Christ Church deemed this a good qualification for appointment to a post to teach economics. The first Honours examination in Oxford to include economics as a principal subject[22] was to be held a year later (June 1923). I was allowed two terms away, not so much in order that I should learn economics, as that I should broaden my mind by foreign travel. I took a different view. I happened to discuss my affairs with Mr Walter Runciman at this juncture; he advised me to get in touch with Keynes and offered me a letter of introduction. Naturally I welcomed the proposal.

I was bidden to lunch at 46 Gordon Square. I mounted the stairs to the drawing-room on the first floor, where the meal was served.[23] The room itself made a strong impres-

20. *Manchester Guardian Commercial*, 7 September 1922.
21. viz. *Lit. Hum.* and Modern History.
22. The Honour School of Philosophy, Politics and Economics.
23. Keynes later acquired the house next door, No. 47, of which he retained the large first-floor drawing-room for himself, letting out the remainder. This drawing-room was made accessible from the drawing-room of No. 46 by a small interconnecting door. In his preface to *Two Memoirs*, published 1949, Mr David Garnett errs when he asserts that Keynes constructed one large room out of the drawing-rooms of the two houses. The large room which he has in mind was simply the double drawing-room of No. 47.

sion. It seemed empty, devoid of the usual ornaments and
appendages, in a style that was rapidly to come into fashion,
but was strange to me. On the walls were two pictures only,
and these were very modern, perhaps by Matisse or Picasso.
The armchairs were exceedingly comfortable. There was
nothing else except the small table at which we were to
eat. This environment, with its assertion of modernity,
itself provided a slightly exciting background. Keynes came
quickly across to me and greeted the stranger with warmth.
There were two others at lunch, one of whom was a young
French economist on a brief visit.

The talk began without any pause; it was quick and
animated. Keynes was discussing with the Frenchman the
latest gossip about Continental statesmen, their mistresses,
their neuroses, as well as their political manoeuvres. These
seemed as exciting as fiction; I supposed they must be real.
There was financial talk of the latest movements in the exchanges, budgetary positions, the international movement
of money. This was still far beyond my ken. But then certain
more familiar strands began to come into the pattern, for
the three of them seemed able and ready to relate their
items of financial intelligence to theoretical doctrine, the
quantity theory of money, foreign exchange equilibrium.
There were passing references to the latest ideas of Cassel or
Fisher, and subtle points of criticism were made. Then I
realized that I was in the presence of something quite unusual
– this mixture of expertise in the latest theories with inside
knowledge of day-to-day events. The Frenchman must have
been in some sense a disciple of Keynes, for academic French
economists of that day did not normally move easily among
the latest ideas of Anglo-Saxon or Swedish theorists. The
excitement was almost unbearable.

Keynes propounded the view, of which Mr Colin Clark
has recently reminded us,[24] that no nation will endure paying more than a given percentage of its national income
in taxation, and if it has to carry a greater load it will almost

24. cf. *Economic Journal*, December 1945, p. 372.

automatically find escape from its plight by inflation. He ran over some French budgetary figures and concluded by prophesying that the French would not stabilize the franc until it had fallen below 100 to the £. The prophecy was fulfilled. He added that he would be willing to stake his whole fortune on that prophecy. I little thought at the time that it was quite possible that he was actually doing so!

After lunch he gave attention to the problems of the stranger. He made a fond reference to Mr Dundas and showed, with a few touches, that he knew something about current Oxford affairs. My problem was simple. I must undoubtedly come to Cambridge. That was the only place where they knew anything about economics. The London School of Economics – I had had some talk with Professor Cannan – was brushed aside. My College was very anxious that I should go abroad; was there not some foreign university? Certainly not; they knew nothing at all of economics on the Continent. Were his claims excessive? His whole exposition was so drenched in friendly feeling to myself that it was impossible to be critical. I must come to King's. He would see that I was made a member of the High Table and that everything was properly arranged. He already seemed to understand my sundry problems and difficulties perfectly. He had taken charge. He would manage my affairs for me – and I was certainly at a great loss at that phase how to manage them for myself.

It was four months later (October 1922) that I found myself among the Fellows of King's College, who were assembling in the Combination Room before dinner. Men of learning and reputation came into the room. The finely chiselled features and dignified bend of Macaulay seemed to symbolize pre-eminently the distinguished and scholarly character of those among whom I had come. Keynes entered with a brisk step. This was the first time that some of them had seen him since Hamburg. Old Dr Mann, the much beloved organist, who had been a member of High Table for many years, went up to him and, grasping his arm, said quietly, 'We are very proud of you.' It was characteristic that it should be the organist who gave this salutation, for the extreme reticence of academic persons militates against warmth of appreciation. Other Fellows contented themselves with explaining to me, almost in a whisper, that they thought highly of his economic work.

We proceeded into Hall in a dignified procession. I was all agog, since it was my first visit to Cambridge, save on a sightseeing trip. The procession came to a standstill before reaching its destination, and a young man, his hair very fair, exquisitely dressed in a double-breasted blue suit and red tie, stepped forward to read grace. He paused a moment, and his poise seemed perfect. In Oxford we prided ourselves on occasionally producing such types of elegant youth, but tended to assume that they were unknown in Cambridge. He gabbled through the grace very quickly in a manner that was usual in Oxford, and I was, therefore, rather surprised to hear Dr Clapham, who was next in front of me, murmur, 'Very blasphemous, very blasphemous.' This was Mr George (Dadie) Rylands, an undergraduate in his second year. I discovered that Keynes thought well of him, but he was then mainly under the tutelage and influence of Mr Sheppard. He was to be a figure of no little importance in Keynes's life. Already showing promise, and clearly a young man of sensibility and intelligence, he was likely to qualify for admission into the circle of chosen friends. He was prominent in the dramatic societies. Later, when he had become a Fellow of King's, he continued to act, and even to dance, upon the stage. This was something more than a mere hobby. His attainments were considerable. It was surely a crowning glory for a Cambridge don to be responsible, as eventually he was, for the production of John Gielgud in *Hamlet* at a London theatre. When Keynes became concerned with the foundation of the Arts Theatre at Cambridge, Mr Rylands was his right-hand man. He held various offices in the College, and, when World War II came, Keynes was able to entrust him with the bursarial duties, the College making him one of the Bursars (while he continued to serve as Steward); for, although his subject was English literature, and his great hobby stagecraft, he was also a 'hard-headed Cambridge man'.

Most notable of the undergraduates under Keynes's influence at this time was Frank Ramsey (see p. 164 and Appendix). He was a Trinity man, but there was plenty of intercourse between the two Colleges; his father was a mathematical tutor and, later, President of Magdalene.[25] The young Ramsey was a man of extreme brilliance and precocity. Now in his second year as an undergraduate, he was already correcting the proofs of Bertrand Russell's introduction to the second edition of *Principia Mathematica* and translating Wittgenstein's *Tractatus Logico-Philosophicus* from the German. Keynes gave him encouragement in the pursuit of these studies on the borderline between mathematics and logic, and it was partly through his influence that Ramsey was later offered a Fellowship of King's in mathematics. He was of large build, his forehead was broad and his face intellectual, but simply drawn. His character too was simple; kind and good-hearted, natural and unaffected, he was not in the least degree spoilt by his precocity or the admiration of his seniors. He had a beautiful laugh, not loud or hearty, but sudden, genuine and convulsive; it sounded as if his huge frame was cracking under the strain of it.

His main interests were in difficult and recondite reaches of logic, but he discussed philosophy in an extraordinarily easy style. Subtle thoughts were distilled into simple straightforward sentences. In an entirely effortless and almost gossipy way he set out the quintessentials of a problem. To me he was a tremendous stimulus, for, having studied

25. Not to be confused with Mr Ramsay, who was for part of the same period Master of Magdalene. The President was below him in the hierarchy.

philosophy as a schoolboy, I had met with much frustration and bitterness at Oxford, where, to my judgement, the true was often reckoned false and conversely. (The character of philosophical teaching at Oxford has entirely changed since then.) To my delight, this Cambridge undergraduate seemed to be saying that my truths might be true after all, more or less, and he had a genial contempt for the doctrines that had plagued me so much at Oxford; but he always gave the warning that it was necessary to understand mathematical logic, and he believed that, in order to do so, it was necessary to have advanced some way into mathematics. Was I to trust this consoling companion? Yes, surely, because although he was only nineteen, Bertrand Russell had given him his proofs to correct, and Keynes assured me that he was as good a philosopher as anyone living. It was at this time that Keynes was pondering on Ramsey's criticisms of his theory of Probability, which, as I have recounted elsewhere,[26] he took more seriously than any others. Alas, Ramsey died of jaundice at the age of twenty-seven.[27]

Another philosophical undergraduate of Keynes's circle was Mr Richard Braithwaite, a Kingsman and a year senior to Ramsey. He was temporarily a little overshadowed by his prodigious junior. Keynes told me of his high regard for Braithwaite's abilities; his intellectual interests were wide and active, and in general discussions he showed a versatility and agility which philosophical specialists are apt to lack. Mr Sprott (Clare College) was still up, debonair, dashing and an acknowledged leader. Adrian Bishop (King's) was the wittiest and most amusing, a little too flippant, perhaps, by the severe Cambridge tradition, a little Oxford

26. See Appendix.

27. For an obituary notice by Keynes, see *Economic Journal* and *Essays in Biography*. Ramsey published two important articles on economics, *Economic Journal*, March 1927 and December 1928; his philosophical papers were collected in a volume entitled *The Foundations of Mathematics*.

in fact, very polished and mature. Mr Steven Runciman, son of Walter Runciman, was a younger member of the group; he has since won a high reputation as a historian.

These were Keynes's particular friends outside the ranks of pupils and economists. After I had been in Cambridge for a short time I expressed one day my appreciation of the delightful company which I had got to know, and ventured to add that I would like them to introduce me to one or two others, as I wanted to acquire an extensive knowledge of Cambridge undergraduate life. The suggestion was not well received. 'But there isn't anyone else,' they said. (It must not be inferred that any of these men carried this exclusiveness into the rough and tumble of life – some of them were men of very broad sympathies – nor that all of them would even then have been as precious as my interlocutors on that particular occasion.)

On the words 'there isn't anyone else', there flashed into my mind Keynes's dictum that there wasn't any place but Cambridge where one could learn economics. It seemed clear that both statements were manifestations of the same strong tradition, which Keynes himself did something to foster. In retrospect one may trace a link with the Strachey circle twenty years earlier. For undergraduates there were advantages and disadvantages in this tradition. The chosen few could receive encouragement and stimulus from certain dons far exceeding what it was possible to mete out to the whole undergraduate body; they might be introduced to Bloomsbury. I contrasted their favoured state with the arduous competition at Oxford, where there had been many, perhaps more, talented aspirants of literary bent. Isolated dons might give encouragement, but there was not the same organized support for young men of promise. Was this a healthier condition? Or did some of the Oxonians, who might have made a mark, fall by the wayside for lack of timely support? A distinction must be drawn between literature and politics. At Oxford the avenues for the aspiring politician were probably wider than at Cambridge. Unhappily, the ablest men after World War I were not attracted by politics.

Keynes's attitude to Cambridge economics was another instance of this tradition of exclusiveness. It had some effect on the progress of economics in England at this period. The formation of a coterie may be valuable to sustain the courage of those whose work is in the realm of the imagination. Keynes may have tended to apply a helpful expedient in a sphere where it was inappropriate. He liked to think of a small band of economists who would be the pioneers; the rest would come along in due course. This idea, if only it were valid, could make possible an economy of effort. If one could carry with one, as well as learn from, Dennis Robertson, Hugh Henderson and a few others, and, in matters of high theory, Pigou, one could advance from strength to strength, confident that the broad ranks of other economists would follow. In the sphere of applied economics the counterpart of the advance guard in Cambridge might be found in London at the Tuesday Club. Blackett, Falk and its other members would be the spearhead of advance. For pushing some specific idea this method has advantages. But economics is many-sided. Keynes's attitude may have been partly responsible for the growth of a gulf between the thinking in Cambridge and at the London School of Economics, which was to prove detrimental in the coming years. There is also no doubt that Keynes made enemies among men who had established some reputation as practical economists before he was even heard of, by assuming that they were not worth consideration. Their hostility had ramifying effects and retarded the acceptance of Keynes's views.

We may well think, when we consider the enormous range of his work, that the concentration of intellectual discussion among a chosen few was a necessary economy. He was doing his best for a larger audience by his published work. He could not also give time and vital energy to maintaining good relations and entering into elaborate discussions with all the professional economists. It was not so much the practice, however, as its elevation into a doctrine which may have done harm. The other economists would have quite understood if Keynes himself was somewhat inaccessible, because so busy. The doctrine, which was not entirely secret, gave them the sense that they had been scorned.

I took my weekly essays to him alone. We sat in comfortable chairs in his rooms in Webb's Building. They were elegantly furnished, and one long wall had been adorned, shortly after the war, with frescoes of nude figures, flowers and fruit by Duncan Grant and Vanessa Bell. The essays were on such topics as rent and quasi-rent and covered the ground of Marshall's *Principles*. I recall an essay on 'The Real Terms of International Interchange'. Keynes characteristically gave me for my reading a letter which he had just received from his colleague Macaulay, whose subject was Mechanics. The letter was concerned with the effects of an agreement with the United States, should there be one, for paying off our war debt. Macaulay was asking Keynes to confirm his view that the burden for Britain would be considerably greater than that represented by the annual payments, since Britain would have to lower the prices of her exports in order to generate a sufficient export surplus. The letter was written in the language of a layman without economic terminology. I fear that when it came to the essay Keynes had to point out gently that I had not yet caught up with Macaulay in economic understanding.

It has been suggested that Keynes, who was such a great expert in the theory of money and business fluctuations, was not thoroughly grounded in the traditional theory of value. My recollection does not confirm this. It appeared to me that his knowledge of Marshall was very thorough and meticulous. He used to take the view at that time that the content of economic theory was extremely small and, although difficult to get right, could be mastered by an able man very quickly. He did not think that wide reading in economic theory was necessary. Following Marshall, he believed there was not much further work to be done in that field, and that progress in economics would lie in the application of theory to practical problems. His recipe for the young economist was to know his Marshall thoroughly and read his *Times* every day carefully, without bothering too much about the large mass of contemporary publication in book form. He was careful to add that one must read one's Pigou and anything that came from the pens of the chosen few. His own reading after 1914 was probably not much more extensive. He read what those near to him said he must. Contributions to the *Economic Journal* – he had to read about a hundred articles a year – gave him a fair sample of the refinements of contemporary thinking. When eventually he broke away from the Marshallian tradition and decided there was something new and important to be said about the fundamentals of theory, there were complaints in certain quarters that his work did not show evidence of wide reading in current periodical literature. There may have been truth in this. It does not follow that the gain to his thought from such erudition would have compensated for the reduction in his attention to current events that such study must have entailed.

He lectured once a week on Money. There was a foot-note to the notice of his lecture, stating that only those who had obtained a first class in Part I or were specially recommended could come. Thus the class was a small one. Each lecture was rigidly divided into two parts, the first half dealing with theory and the second with current events. In the first half he was expounding the 'Cambridge' doctrines on money for which Marshall was initially responsible. He wrote formulae upon the blackboard of the type used by Pigou in his well-known article,[28] and akin to those which he was shortly to publish in a greatly simplified form in his *Tract on Monetary Reform*. At this phase, however, the

28. *Quarterly Journal of Economics*, 1917: reprinted in *Essays in Applied Economics* under the title of 'The Value of Legal Tender Money'.

formulae were more, not less, complicated than those of Pigou. In the midst of one lecture, Frank Ramsey, who, being a mathematician, was present by invitation, interrupted with a criticism; Keynes was happy to receive it and embodied an amendment. Then, when half an hour was over, we were plunged into the story of what had been happening during the last week in the London money market and the foreign exchange markets. The account was lucid, but extremely technical and too quick to be easy to follow. We were greatly excited.

In the middle of this term he was invited to Berlin by the German Government to discuss measures for the stabilization of the mark. Mr Brand, Gustav Cassel, Vissering, Professor Jenks (of New York University) and Monsieur Dubois were also invited. The mark soared in the foreign exchanges on the news of this gathering. Keynes, Brand, Cassel and Jenks published a majority report. Keynes gave an account of the proceedings in the lecture on the following Friday. He had been deeply discouraged by the defeatism and apathy which he found in Berlin. It has often been said that the Germans deliberately destroyed the mark in order to evade reparations payments. If that was so, they paid a heavy price, since, along with the mark, they destroyed the whole social fabric. Keynes did not interpret events in this way. There had not been any deliberate attempt to destroy the mark. The point was that, owing to the severe pressure to which Germany was subject, manful action and a resolute will were needed to save it from destruction. Such a resolution he had not found in Berlin. There they seemed desirous of doing the right thing, but fearful of the consequences of the drastic lines of action that would be needful. They were timid, weak and without hope. It was quite clear to him that nothing adequate would be done and that the rot would continue. It did so until complete destruction occurred a year later.

He also hinted that part of the trouble was the absence on the Continent of the kind of economic analysis which he was giving us in these lectures. The quantity theory of money, suitably modified, must be the main instrument for a diagnosis of inflation. At the root of inflation was the budget deficit. Not that he agreed with those in England who thought it would be a simple matter to remove the German budget deficit. With galloping inflation, no lawful system of taxation would bring in enough money to do so, since by the time that taxes had been gathered, prices and government expenditure would have soared to new levels and the deficit would remain. Somehow the price movement must be stopped first. The proximate, as opposed to the ultimate, cause of the price movement was the collapsing exchange. Rising prices in Germany were chasing the falling exchange many laps behind. Therefore, stabilization of the exchange was the first step. This could only be achieved by a reparations moratorium. Once stabilization was accomplished, it would become technically possible to balance the budget. That must be done. If the budget was not balanced, the stabilization would be short-lived. He believed that with reparations demands out of the way for the moment, the balance of trade problem would not be intractable. Owing to the rapid movement of the mark, trade returns were chaotic. Keynes pointed out that the actual deficit in the preceding year could not have exceeded the sum-total of foreign bull speculation in the mark; and this could not have been very great. It is worth noting that the English, American and Swedish representatives agreed with Keynes. The report of the minority (which would not go the whole length with the majority on the Reparations moratorium) stressed Germany's balance of trade difficulties and her need for a foreign loan. For them, evidently, the trade disequilibrium was central to the problem, and external assistance the only remedy. And so it happened that Keynes and his friends proposed stiffer medicine for the Germans. If only reparations were temporarily pretermitted, the Germans could put their own house in order. Let them get the budget right, and the balance of trade would look after itself. Some may think that this has a moral for Europe after World War II, when the whole of Europe has had the kind of difficulties which weighed upon Germany after the first war.

Keynes's Political Economy Club was flourishing. Mr Austin Robinson, just a graduate, read a paper on Britain's Capital Exports, which was perhaps more intimidating to an Oxford man than the many-sided brilliance of the master. He had ransacked all sources for statistical information. He had constructed most beautiful diagrams, and discussed his results in the light of a refined theory of trade equilibrium. It was a highly polished performance, a fine example of Cambridge thoroughness, accuracy and theoretical expertise. At another meeting I read a paper on a methodological subject; this seemed safe for a beginner; my Oxford training enabled me at least to discourse fluently on questions of ethics and scientific method. The mischievous secretary, however, altered my title, when circulating the Club card, into '*Should Cambridge economists be read at Oxford?*' We had been discussing the list of prescribed textbooks for the new Honours School in Oxford, which consisted of Adam Smith, Ricardo, List, Jevons and Marx. There was nothing more modern. This was not the subject of my paper, as I was quite sure that Marshall, Pigou and Keynes ought to be read in my University. But Keynes had evidently been turning the matter over in his mind, for in his summing up he reverted to the question of Oxford reading and, to my surprise, made a delightful defence of the Oxford method. There, by deliberate policy and in accordance with their traditions, they liked to read the great old masters of ripe vintage, mellowed by time, survivors of the criticism of many generations, established, authenticated and indubitably worthy. It was on Plato and Aristotle that Oxford concentrated its mind. Their texts had been pondered upon by hundreds of scholars and their finest nuances of meaning analysed. This was the right way to introduce the young to knowledge. Let them study texts of which one knew that, whether they were true or false, they were the product of master minds. In economics the next best thing was to read Adam Smith and Ricardo. (Marx might certainly be discarded.) A hint could be dropped, of course, that to fill in gaps they should take a quick look at Alfred Marshall.

He himself read a paper on Malthus. This was Malthus in his aspect of population expert, the precursor of Darwin, not the initiator of the doctrine of effective demand; it was a delightful character sketch, glowing in praise; there was a passing reference to Ricardo as 'the most distinguished mind that had found economics worthy of its powers'. He also dwelt on modern conditions; the Malthusian devil was evidently still with us. In the discussion Mr Dennis Robertson produced some recent statistics; he was not sure about the Malthusian devil. Indeed he hinted that the modern danger might be the opposite one, a decline in numbers. Robertson seemed to know what he was talking about, and I had an uncomfortable feeling that it was he, and not my master, who was in the right on this occasion.

Somewhere on Keynes's stair there lived an undergraduate of sporting tastes, whose name escapes me. On some occasion when I was in Keynes's room he referred to the young man in an amused way, since thuds and crashes were heard, suggesting a fight and furniture being hurled around. To my surprise he was a member of the Political Economy Club, although his examination performance was expected to be very poor; he was the pupil of Keynes, who thought it a good idea to mix a hearty element into his highbrow group. In the Malthus paper there was a reference to contraception. Then, in 1922, this seemed startling and even shocking, so times have changed. The hearty undergraduate made a forthright protest; what he had heard was unseemly and immoral. Keynes was delighted by this intervention, and his handling of it was one of the most beautiful performances I have ever seen. He had a double objective. On the one hand, he wanted to make it absolutely plain to the group that the objector's criticism was foolish and untenable – for he, Keynes, was a profound believer in the need for birth control in the existing situation. On the other hand, he was obviously most anxious not to offend the objector's susceptibilities; the young man's academic pretensions were nil, and it was doubtful whether he would obtain his degree; there must, therefore, not be the faintest hint that Keynes was taking advantage of his slow-wittedness or scoring off him. It was his invariable rule never to be caustic at the expense of undergraduates.

He divided his rejoinder into two parts. First, there was the question of unseemliness. Keynes dealt with this in a few gossamer phrases; his easy power over words was beautifully displayed; one felt a sureness of touch and refinement of feeling. The objector must acknowledge, whether he agreed or not, that Keynes's philosophy paid due regard to the claims of sexual delicacy.

Then there was the question of immorality. Keynes argued that natural morals contained no principle which would stigmatize contraception. Therefore we must look to the morals of theology. This question of theology was important. Then suddenly he seemed to be speaking to the undergraduate directly, the room having vanished. He looked at him, with a twinkle in his eye, which appeared to plead with him. He was talking to him as man to man. There were a few words only. What they seemed to say was that he, the undergraduate, knew that Keynes respected his theological beliefs and also knew that he, Keynes, had no theology. They were both men of the world; they had regard for each other's convictions and experience; they could not discuss them in the presence of these people; it was the sort of thing that they would like to have a long talk about together. There was not the shadow of a hint that the man was lacking in intellectual acumen. He was treated with the greatest consideration, as an equal. All the same, the room made up its mind that it need not bother about this theological consideration. It was all over in a minute or two, but one felt that in those two minutes one had had a vision of the fine powers of this great man.

He has been criticized for the conduct of the Club on other occasions. I did not witness one of the kind in question and am informed that outside visitors were infrequent. He might have a businessman or banker to give an address, and demolish him with his well-known power of quick repartee. Having dazzled him with his superior knowledge, he proceeded to dissect the substance of his address and show that it made no sense at all. There was a silent communication between him and his pupils. You see, now, what frightful fools these bankers are, who are supposed to manage our affairs. Enemies were made, and perhaps not without just cause. There is no doubt that Keynes, while having a warmth of kindly feeling towards many different types, thought that all was fair in argument, and that a man should not have a grievance if he was refuted without mercy; if he was bold enough to advance an opinion, then he should not complain if he was shown to be an ass. If a man plays cricket, he has no grievance against the bowler who gets him out first ball. If sensitiveness was not in place in a game, still less was it so in the discussion of public affairs or economic problems. If one happened to be very good at the game, one did not expect jealousy and rancour.

To many of his own age he was somewhat awe-inspiring. The fact remains that people do not like to be bowled out first ball. Unless there was some link, some prior reason for friendliness, he did not melt on a first meeting. In so far as awe induced shyness in his interlocutor, that delayed the time for warmer relations. With the young friendliness came fairly easily. I have recollections of undergraduate evening parties with perhaps only one or two dons and some former undergraduates revisiting. He sat in an armchair with a glass in his hand; undergraduates were sitting on the arms of the chair, chaffing and joking; they were obviously on easy and intimate terms with him, treating him as a friend, as one of themselves. He chattered away, having plenty to say that amused them. As I left the room undergraduates were still chirruping around him – Maynard this, Maynard that; he had a heavy load of work the next morning, but this flow of intercourse with the young people was more important, and he looked quite prepared to outstay them all.

# [9]

# Return to the Gold Standard

I

HITHERTO Keynes's chief journalistic outlet had been in the *Manchester Guardian* and its great *Commercial Supplements*. In 1923 there was to be an important change. Then, and in the following years, those who wished to learn his most recent thoughts sought for them in the *Nation*, the Liberal weekly.

We may remember his early excursions in Liberal politics as an undergraduate at Cambridge in the Union, as a speaker at successive general elections, as a traveller with the Eighty Club in Ireland, as a member of the Liberal Financial Policy Committee after the war. By temperament and conviction he was certainly a Liberal throughout his life. During the twenties he hoped to see a working agreement between the Liberal Party and the Labour Party; in the thirties he may have nourished the hope that, when he had achieved the culminating expression of his own views, the cogency of his arguments would wean the Labour Party from State Socialism and make its members his own disciples. This final consummation was not achieved, however, and in the last year of his life he wrote to Lady Violet Bonham Carter with reference to the Liberal Party as follows:

I hope you are fairly cheerful about electoral prospects. All my good wishes are with you and the Party. I should view with great alarm a substantial victory by either of the major Parties.[1]

He was rather strongly opposed to the Conservative Party, although he had certain characteristics which normally incline men to cast their lot with the Conservatives. He valued institutions which had historic roots in the country;

1. 16 May 1945.

he was a great upholder of the virtues of the middle class which, in his view, had been responsible for all the good things that we now enjoy; he believed in the supreme value of intellectual leadership, in the wisdom of the chosen few; he was interested in showing how narrow was the circle of kinship from which the great British leaders in statesmanship and thinking had been drawn; [2] and he was an intense lover of his country. At times his instinctive belief in the superiority of the English made him utter sentiments that seemed quite reactionary. If he inveighed bitterly against his own country in connection with the Treaty of Versailles, it was partly because his very patriotism made him feel intensely the shame of what he regarded as dishonourable conduct.

All this, however, was overborne by other characteristics. He was keenly alive to great social evils and sensitive to suffering. He was by nature a progressive and a reformer. He believed that by thought and resolution things could be made much better, and that quickly. He was intensely impatient of obstruction in every form. Again and again he preached that the risk in taking what seemed daring action was much less than the risk of doing nothing. The over-cautious in high places appeared to him to be perilous liabilities to the nation.

In the years that were to follow, various troubles beset the country and he was quick and fertile in the suggestion of remedies. He was not author-proud or obstinate, and was always ready to modify his proposals in the light of valid objections. But as the years went on he found on successive occasions, not valid objections, but mere obstructionism alternating with condescending interest – and nothing done! The country seemed to be sinking in hopeless inertia and complacency; thus, naturally enough, he grew more and more anti-Conservative. The only remedy put forward by the Conservative Party was Protection, and that he continued for some time to believe to be based on a fallacy.

2. cf. *Essays in Biography*, pp. 79–83.

He had derived, as we have seen, partly from the gentleness of his own nature and partly from the philosophy of his dearest friends, a strong vein of pacifism. In the twenties he was prepared for Britain to go far in the direction of disarmament. In this field those on the extreme left were congenial to him. Furthermore his hostility to the Conservatives was enhanced by the Treaty of Versailles, of which they were the chief upholders. His bitterness about it was sharpened by his involuntary implication in drafting its terms. The fact that he had been a subordinate did not relieve his conscience, nor had his subsequent resignation completely assuaged its qualms.

On the other hand, he was not a Socialist. His regard for the middle-class, for artists, scientists and brain workers of all kinds made him dislike the class-conscious elements of Socialism. He had no egalitarian sentiment; if he wanted to improve the lot of the poor and that quickly – and he believed that far more progress was possible than was being made – that was not for the sake of equality, but in order to make their lives happier and better. In morals the first claim upon the national dividend was to furnish those few, who were capable of 'passionate perception',[3] with the ingredients of what modern civilization can provide by way of a 'good life'. He often explained that these could not yet be provided for all – though the day when they could be might come more quickly than some thought. The idea of destroying anything good in itself in the interest of equality was anathema to him.

He was not a great friend of the profit motive; he found something unsatisfactory in the quest for gain as such, and came to hope that an economic system might be evolved in which it was curtailed. But he did not think it would be beneficial for the State to run industry and trade. He considered the doctrine of State Socialism to be quite obsolete, the reaction from an environment which had now changed

3. See p. 119.

out of recognition. Thus both in temperament and doctrine he was opposed to many elements in the Labour Party.

On the other hand, the Liberal Party did not completely satisfy him. Although he worked actively for it from time to time, he was by no means a Party man. He held that the principles and platform programme of the Liberal Party needed complete refurbishing. Some Liberal causes – democratic enfranchisement, the abolition of tests, etc. – had triumphed so completely that nothing more had to be done. Social security also had triumphed in principle, although not yet fully in practice. Free Trade was of the utmost importance, but in this case the battle was a defensive one and was therefore not well suited to be the main engagement of a progressive party. How should the spirit of Liberalism cope with the new situation? How meet the new needs of the times? Too many Liberals were ready to pride themselves on past achievements and to suppose that there was a set of Liberal principles which could readily be applied to each successive situation without the need for new fundamental thinking. Keynes was not of that opinion. The spirit of Liberalism was living and imperishable, but in the year 1923 it appeared to him that a new programme would have to be devised, almost from beginning to end. Not that he supposed himself to have such a programme in his pocket. On the contrary, it could only be achieved by patient study of the ever-changing economic structure, and by the new idea that was apt to the situation.

His next years were spent in such thinking. He believed that Liberals should turn their backs on the old doctrine of *laissez-faire* which had served them in good stead in different circumstances. The State would have to intervene at many points. Yet the structure of a free economy with its scope for individual initiative must be preserved. Keynes remained essentially an individualist. In the twenty years that followed, many others have had the same idea; Keynes deserves study because he related it to the fundamental principles of economics and worked out its detailed applications. His work may still prove to be the foundation of a new kind of free economy, if freedom is indeed preserved.

There were other Liberals also who thought that the Liberal policy needed refurbishing, and some of these met together at Grasmere in the year 1921. The leading spirit among them was Ramsay Muir, who played a prominent part as an intellectual guide to the Liberal Party in the period between the wars. His mind was not a creative one in the highest sense, but he had enthusiasm, clarity, integrity and tireless industry. With him from Manchester was Mr E. D. Simon, a man of notable business achievement, then Lord Mayor of Manchester, and an authority on the housing question. There were Mr Walter Layton, Keynes's fellow-lecturer at Cambridge before the war, who had since proved himself an efficient public servant, and Sir William Beveridge, already famous for his work on Social Insurance. To cheer them all up was Philip Guedalla with his epigrammatic scintillations and coruscations. If we are not permitted to say that beneath this he was a 'hard-headed Oxford man', we may record that he had great intellectual ability and might have risen to political eminence had the fortunes of the Liberal Party at that time been different. There was also Ted Scott, son of the great editor of the *Manchester Guardian*. This group did not approach the economic problem in quite the same way as Keynes, but they were interested both in an active policy of industrial reconstruction and in providing the rank and file of labour with a status and dignity which should be as acceptable as the Utopian projects of Socialism – and more realizable.

One result of the Grasmere meeting was the establishment of the annual Liberal Summer Schools, the function of which was to consist in keeping Liberal enthusiasm alive, in educating a wide circle of Liberals in current problems, and in providing a forum for discussion. These 'Schools', which met in the following years alternately at Oxford and Cambridge for a week in August, were an unqualified success, and they still continue.

The group did not rest content with the Summer School. Their members came together for weekends during the winter to discuss each other's memoranda on current problems and projects of publication. One item in their discussion was the absence of a satisfactory Liberal weekly. It was true that there was the *Nation*. This was a most distinguished periodical which had been edited, since its foundation in 1907, by a great journalist, H. W. Massingham. He had a staff of able writers who were devoted to him. The impress of his personality upon the paper was marked; it had a distinction which appealed to intellectual people and has rarely been matched in weekly journalism. None the less from the point of view of the Grasmere group the *Nation* was not altogether satisfactory. It was not that it was insufficiently 'left wing'; on the contrary, in some respects it seemed further to the left than its contemporary, the *New Statesman*, which was by way of supporting the Labour Party. But its leftwardness was somewhat negative, consisting in sincere and passionate denunciations of the wicked things that went on in the world. It voiced the eternal protest of men of refined feeling against the obliquities and callousness and falseness of politicians. This was extreme Liberalism verging almost on the realm of revolutionary Liberalism, but it was not Liberalism with a 'new look'. The paper was not the vehicle of fresh practical ideas adapted to the requirements of 1923. Furthermore, the *Nation* was not a paying proposition; some thousands of pounds were lost every year, and the Rowntree family, which financed it, was becoming a little restive. As the result of certain discussions, it appeared that new money could be found to reduce the burden upon the Rowntrees if some change could be effected in the outlook of the paper.

Massingham decided at once that he would have nothing to do with all this. Great sympathy was felt for him after his many years of eminent work. But the facts could not be gainsaid. Keynes was already in a position to put up some money; others also came forward, the Rowntrees retaining a share. Keynes was to be Chairman of the new Board.

At first there was an idea that Ramsay Muir was the obvious man to be editor; but after some meetings it became clear that this would not work well. Although Keynes and Muir were alike in search of a new policy, their types of mind were somewhat different. In Keynes's view, they were starting with very little; it was needful to turn a penetrating gaze upon contemporary facts and glean from them, by science, by intuition, by political imagination, new types of remedies for new types of evils. It was a voyage of discovery on which they were embarked, to which Liberal principles could contribute little except that underlying spirit and temperament with which one approached the problems. Muir, on the other hand, tended to look inward to discover the truth. One had the feeling that locked within his breast was a sacred text in which the answers to all problems could be found. He was always ready with an answer, and that a sincere one; and this was a valuable gift in a politician. Keynes feared that these answers, derived from Muir's inner consciousness, might conflict with new ideas, hitherto unknown to Liberalism, which were derived from a study of the new situation. Muir was a modest man, but a stalwart crusader, with the pride of his own sincere beliefs. They both decided that there were possibilities of friction; Muir took on the editorship of the *Weekly Westminster*.

Mr Hubert Henderson, first class-man of the Cambridge Economics Tripos before the war, had done distinguished service on the Cotton Control Board and had since been lecturing on money and allied subjects in Cambridge. He was an outstanding member of that small band there who were setting themselves to apply the wisdom of Marshall to the post-war world. He was installed as editor of the *Nation* and held that position until 1929.

Keynes devoted much of his time to the affairs of the paper, especially during its first year under the new auspices. He hoped to make it a paying proposition, but in this, although there was some improvement, he did not succeed. The price was reduced from 9d. to 6d. He endeavoured to secure a balance by curtailing overhead expenses and by increasing the advertisements. He refused to countenance economies at the expense of the remuneration of contributors; on the contrary, he sought to attract writers of the first rank by paying them handsomely. Bloomsbury was roped in to assist. The first issue contained an article by Lytton Strachey on Sarah Bernhardt and one on Spain by Virginia Woolf. Other Bloomsbury names in due course appeared, as well as those of such distinguished writers as Augustine Birrell, Gilbert Murray, Maxim Gorky, Percy Lubbock, Osbert Sitwell, etc. At first it was hoped to secure Mr T. S. Eliot as Literary Editor, but he was not immediately available and the paper could not wait. Mr Leonard Woolf accepted that position; careful readers discerned that the literary part of the paper, in so far as it was political, was distinctly to the left of the political section where Mr Henderson reigned supreme.

Keynes made it a rule never to interfere with the editorial policy. He went each week to the office and had a long talk with Henderson on the significance of current events. They saw eye to eye on many questions, but there was never any discussion about what line the paper ought to take. That was left to the exclusive discretion of Mr Henderson. Keynes contributed nothing to the paper which was not signed or initialled, save for one note on Bonar Law. Henderson could on occasion write in a style of trenchant polemic. It was sometimes wrongly supposed that some of his admirably worded leaders were from the pen of Keynes.[4]

For a number of years Keynes contributed signed articles at intervals of about a month. For the first seven issues, and again for four weeks in July 1923, he also contributed the 'Notes on Finance and Investment'. His main articles often

4. cf. a number of anonymous articles wrongly attributed to Keynes on pp. 670–86 of the painstaking bibliography in *The New Economics* edited by Professor S. E. Harris.

aroused widespread interest, and on a number of occasions received notices – surely an unusual phenomenon in journalism – in the other important papers.

During 1923 most of his articles dealt with the development of the reparations problem, the subject on which he was an acknowledged expert. These were diversified by his address to the Liberal Summer School,[5] by a controversy with Sir William Beveridge on the population problem,[6] and by two articles on Free Trade, in connection with the General Election which took place in the autumn of 1923.

The Liberal Summer School met this year at Cambridge, where Keynes moved Mr Sheppard to produce his translation of the *Cyclops* for the benefit of a Liberal audience. Keynes's own address was mainly concerned with the evils of currency fluctuation and particularly of deflation. He thought that the Liberals ought to find in this currency question an important plank in their political platform. There were complaints that the currency question was difficult to follow, but Keynes insisted that the relevant arguments were no more complicated than those in favour of Free Trade. The general public had made the intellectual effort required to understand these arguments in the early Victorian period, to the lasting benefit of British politics and British prosperity. Why need it be assumed that they would be incapable of understanding the arguments in favour of a stable currency, which might well prove in the coming years to be an issue of as great moment for economic prosperity as the Free Trade versus Protection issue?

Keynes showed himself a convinced Free Trader in the two articles on that subject. One of them was specifically devoted to the fallacy of supposing that tariffs might be good for employment. During the General Election (1923) he

5. Issue of 11 August.
6. Issue of 26 October. Sir William Beveridge had given a presidential address to Section F of the British Association, to which Keynes made a more elaborate reply in the December issue of the *Economic Journal.*

made an important speech at Blackburn, in which he trounced the Protectionists and, striking at the left, attacked the proposal for a Capital Levy, of which he had been in favour immediately after the war. He criticized the inflexibility of the Labour leaders in not realizing that the arguments which had been valid then were no longer so at present.

2

On 7 July 1923 the Bank Rate was raised from three per cent to four per cent. Never, perhaps, was the decision of the Bank of England Court more fraught with far-reaching consequences; for it set Keynes's mind working upon a line of thought which has had a world-wide influence lasting until this day. He made a strong comment upon it in his 'Note on Finance and Investment' in the *Nation* of 14 July, and, contrary to the usual procedure when his contribution was merely a financial note, his name was billed on the cover of the paper. This rise in the Bank Rate was 'one of the most misguided movements of that indicator that has ever occurred ... The Bank of England acting under the influence of a narrow and obsolete doctrine has made a great mistake.'

Prices were falling and unemployment was severe, and it seemed clear that this change in the Bank Rate was not designed to adjust the internal credit situation, but was a step towards restoring sterling to its pre-war gold parity. What further steps would be required? Through what horrors of deflation might we be led?

During the winter of 1922–3 the centre of gravity of his interests shifted from the Reparations Problem to internal finance, and in November 1923 a book entitled *A Tract on Monetary Reform* appeared in the bookshops. This has an important place in economic history. Keynes wrote books of many different kinds, and a fascinating debate might be held about which had most ultimate significance. In the *Treatise on Probability* he explored the foundations of human knowledge in a work which, although not definitive, has continued to stimulate thought upon its deep problems. The *Economic Consequences* was his greatest masterpiece of polemic; it made his public reputation and had an important impact on foreign politics. The two large works, the *Treatise on Money* and *The General Theory of Employment, Interest and Money*, have had far-reaching effects on economic science and thereby indirectly on public policy. There are still purists who give the first prize to his book on *Indian Currency*. In spite of all this, a claim could be made on behalf of the *Tract on Monetary Reform*. For generations there had been economists who held that the Gold Standard was not the best possible form of money; recently a brilliant campaign had been conducted by the American economist, Irving Fisher. Yet on the whole it seemed that this sort of advocacy was confined to cranks and very academic economists. The Gold Standard – with the respectable alternatives of a Silver Standard or, now fading into the background, bi-metallism – was universally accepted. Its desirability was not a live issue. The *Tract on Monetary Reform* seemed to come near to making it one. Seemed – or had it really done so? At first this was in doubt, because, in spite of the book, Britain and most other countries returned to the Gold Standard shortly afterwards, and the matter appeared to be closed. However, the book caused a controversy which was sufficiently lively to be remembered for some years; the leading politicians and bankers took notice; the seeds of doubt had been sown among a wide public. For a year or two Keynes's view was in eclipse. But within a decade it had won the allegiance of at least half the world. Affection for the Gold Standard may yet revive. If it does not, the historian will record that Keynes, almost single-handed, killed that most ancient and venerable institution.

It was a notable achievement, because the Gold Standard was perhaps the most respected and sacrosanct of all the mechanisms of nineteenth-century Capitalism. If a Labour Party had gained power in the first quarter of the twentieth century on a programme for nationalizing the means of production and distribution, it would probably not have ventured to lay hands on the Gold Standard itself. Even Socialists claimed to respect the importance of a sound monetary system. It could, no doubt, be argued that it was World War I that really killed the Gold Standard, since thereafter it has proved difficult to make it work.

Yet in 1923 the vast majority were still striving after it. It was Keynes who first gained wide interest for the doctrine that it was not a good thing in itself. He did it very quietly and gently. It is interesting to compare the forceful and passionate polemic of the *Economic Consequences*, where he knew exactly what he wanted to say and said it with a vengeance, with the tentative and almost diffident tone of the last fifty pages of the *Tract*, where he was hardly doing more than thinking aloud. The reader feels that in Keynes's own mind the issue had for some time been in doubt. He finally reached his decision and explained in simple and unadorned language why he had done so.

The first section of the book does not carry a warning of momentous proposals to come. There is a thorough, and sometimes amusing, analysis of the evils resulting from an unstable currency. 'Thus Inflation is unjust and Deflation is inexpedient. Of the two perhaps Deflation is, if we rule out exaggerated inflations such as that of Germany, the worse; because it is worse, in an impoverished world, to provoke unemployment than to disappoint the *rentier*. But it is not necessary that we should weigh one evil against the other. It is easier to agree that both are evils to be shunned. The Individualistic Capitalism of today, precisely because it entrusts saving to the individual investor and production to the individual employer, *presumes* a stable measuring-rod of value, and cannot be efficient – perhaps cannot survive – without one.'

There were controversial sallies, to titillate the reader, and

Sir Josiah Stamp gave warning in an interesting review[7] that these might jeopardize its persuasive effect. There is a reference to 'many conservative bankers' who 'regard it as more consonant with their cloth, and also as economizing thought, to shift public discussion of financial topics off the logical on to an alleged "moral" plane, which means a realm of thought where vested interest can be triumphant over the common good without further debate. But it makes them untrustworthy guides in a perilous age of transition.' There is also in this section of the book an intriguing analysis of the rate at which a government can abstract purchasing power from the pockets of its citizens by means of inflation, the maximum possible rate tending to fall as inflation gets more rampant.

The middle part of the book has probably been the most widely read during the years since it appeared, as it has provided a convenient text for university teachers. Here Keynes re-entered the classroom and expounded the essential points of the 'Cambridge' monetary theory. For a wider public he greatly simplified the formulae which I had seen him place upon the blackboard a year earlier. The value of money was the consequence of the interaction of two decisions, the decision of the Central Bank as to how much credit to create and the decision of members of the public as to how much 'real' value, i.e. how much purchasing power over goods, they wished from time to time to hold by them in the forms of currency or a bank balance. Policies of the former had long been carefully studied, but insufficient attention had been paid to motives actuating the latter. He also dealt with the 'purchasing power parity theory' concerning foreign exchange rates, showing its usefulness and limitations; and he reproduced his account of the theory of forward foreign exchange rates from his *Manchester Guardian Supplement* article in a form useful for students. It is in the course of the academic section of the book that he used a phrase which we may now perhaps regard as proverbial in the English

7. *Journal of the Royal Statistical Society*, May 1924.

language. He spoke of the cruder form of the Quantity Theory of money as being valid only in the long run. 'But this *long run* is a misleading guide to current affairs. *In the long run* we are all dead. Economists set themselves too easy, too useless a task, if in tempestuous seasons they can only tell us that when the storm is long past the ocean is flat again.'

He moved quietly into the concluding explosive section of his book by presenting various alternatives. Should we prefer devaluation or deflation? The answer to that was easy. He reproduced material from his *Manchester Guardian* article in favour of devaluation. Then we come to something more exciting. Should we choose to have monetary stability – the early section of the book had argued its supreme importance – in the form of stable internal prices or a stable foreign exchange rate? This was a momentous question which has troubled the waters of opinion ever since. In the post-war world experts had been urging monetary stability, and it was generally assumed that this meant a return to the Gold Standard. Keynes thought the time had come to seek greater precision and to pose the alternatives.

The tacit assumption that gold would provide a régime of fairly stable prices, as well as stable exchanges, had to be reconsidered. In the nineteenth century it had served sufficiently well, partly because the expansion of output from the gold mines had kept fairly good pace with the expansion of general production. We could not rely on a succession of new gold discoveries on an ever-increasing scale. There was another even more important point. The essence of the situation in the nineteenth century was that the value of gold had been determined by a large number of independent forces, resulting from the policies of various nations and the behaviour of their citizens. The effects of changes in these often cancelled one another out. But now the situation was entirely altered, owing to the great absorption of gold by the United States of America. There was no longer any independent entity which one could call the Gold Standard; the

Gold Standard now simply meant the Dollar Standard.
Furthermore, the dollar was already a managed currency.
The Federal Reserve System had not been automatically
increasing the volume of currency or of credit in the U.S.A.
on the receipt of gold; had it done so, it would have produced a wild inflation there:

The theory on which the Federal Reserve Board is supposed to
govern its discount policy, by reference to the influx and efflux
of gold and the proportion of gold to liabilities, is as dead as mutton. It perished, and perished justly, as soon as the Federal
Reserve Board began to ignore its ratio and to accept gold without allowing it to exercise its full influence,[8] merely because an
expansion of credit and prices seemed at that moment undesirable. From that day gold was demonetized by almost the last
country which still continued to do it lip-service, and a dollar
standard was set up on the pedestal of the Golden Calf. For the
past two years the United States has pretended to maintain a
gold standard. In fact it has established a dollar standard; and,
instead of ensuring that the value of the dollar shall conform to
that of gold, it makes provision, at great expense, that the value
of gold shall conform to that of the dollar. This is the way by
which a rich country is able to combine new wisdom with old
prejudice. It can enjoy the latest scientific improvements, devised
in the economic laboratory of Harvard, whilst leaving Congress
to believe that no rash departure will be permitted from the hard
money consecrated by the wisdom and experience of Dungi,
Darius, Constantine, Lord Liverpool, and Senator Aldrich.

One might react to this by suggesting that to resume the
gold link would allow Britain to enjoy the benefit of this
currency management. Keynes saw objections:

It would be rash in present circumstances to surrender our
freedom of action to the Federal Reserve Board of the United

8. The influx of gold could not be prevented from having some
inflationary effect because its receipt automatically increased the
balances of the member banks. This uncontrollable element cannot
be avoided so long as the United States Mints are compelled to accept
gold. But the gold was not allowed to exercise the multiplied influence which the pre-war system presumed. (Note by J. M. K.)

States. We do not yet possess sufficient experience of its capacity to act in times of stress with courage and independence. The Federal Reserve Board is striving to free itself from the pressure of sectional interests; but we are not yet certain that it will wholly succeed. It is still liable to be overwhelmed by the impetuosity of a cheap money campaign. A suspicion of British influence would, so far from strengthening the Board, greatly weaken its resistance to popular clamour. Nor is it certain, quite apart from weakness or mistakes, that the simultaneous application of the same policy will always be in the interests of both countries. The development of the credit cycle and the state of business may sometimes be widely different on the two sides of the Atlantic.

It is important to observe that Keynes did not conceive the issue at stake to be whether we should have a managed or an automatic standard. An automatic standard had for some time ceased to exist in practice and was now no longer available. The question for him was whether our currency should be managed so as to secure stable external value, i.e. to maintain a fixed dollar parity (so-called Gold Standard), or whether it should be managed so as to secure a stable internal price level. His decision was in favour of the latter.

How then should we proceed? His answer was simple – 'By an adaptation of the actual system which has grown up half haphazardly since the war'. The adaptation should consist in a conscious quest for a stable internal price level. He referred to Irving Fisher's proposals, but doubted if they were adequate to cope with the short-period oscillations of the credit cycle. But he went some way with Fisher by allowing that 'the authority should adopt a composite commodity as their standard of value in the sense that they would employ all their resources to prevent a movement of its price by more than a certain percentage in either direction away from the normal, just as before the war they employed all their resources to prevent a movement in the price of gold by more than a certain percentage'. The actual movement of prices must not be the sole criterion, since action resulting therefrom might be unduly delayed.

Actual price-movements must of course provide the most important datum; but the state of employment, the volume of production, the effective demand for credit as felt by the banks, the rate of interest on investments of various types, the volume of new issues, the flow of cash into circulation, the statistics of foreign trade and the level of the exchanges must all be taken into account. The main point is that the objective of the authorities, pursued with such means as are at their command, should be the stability of prices.

He suggested a somewhat more formal arrangement than we actually had in 1923 (or in the period from 1931 to 1939). The Court of the Bank of England should fix the price of gold each Thursday, just as it fixed the Bank Rate. It should enlarge the margin between its buying and selling price. It should also offer to buy and sell forward exchange at fixed rates, thereby allowing the British to offer a higher (or lower) short-term rate of interest to foreign borrowers (or lenders) than obtained on domestic loans in London. The Bank would then have three levers to operate. On any Thursday it could alter its official discount rate, it could alter its spot buying and selling prices of gold and it could, simultaneously or independently, alter its forward buying and selling prices of gold. Here was a notable plan which he put forward for careful consideration, before we embarked upon the perilous course of fixing a parity with the dollar.

The book created a great flutter. On the whole the reception was hostile. People were profoundly shocked at the idea of abandoning the sheet anchor of stability constituted by the Gold Standard. Keynes could by no means carry all his Liberal friends with him. Indeed some Liberals were among those especially perturbed, since they intensely disliked handing over such an important subject to the discretion of the Government. They were not impressed by the argument that the currency was bound to be a 'managed' one in any case. The bogy of a great inflation was produced. To Keynes this seemed irrelevant. He deemed England a sufficiently mature country for it to be possible to assume that the authorities could be trusted to carry out a policy of monetary reform faithfully, and would not indulge in an orgy of feckless note issue. This was a notable mark of his respect for the Treasury and the Bank, despite the severe attacks he had felt bound to make upon them recently. It was one thing to accuse them of hopeless Conservatism, obscurantism, pigheadedness, failure to read the signs of the times, failure to introduce the reforms that were needed if Capitalism was to be saved, and quite another to assume that they were so irresponsible that, if only they were given the power, they would embark on a career of squandermania by printing bank-notes. Keynes believed that the old boys were fundamentally trustworthy and well-meaning; but they were blind and complacent, and greatly needed prodding. The old-fashioned Liberals ran away from his proposals on the dogma that Central Authorities can in no event be trusted; but these Liberals had no cure for the current ills. Thus Keynes had great initial difficulties in gaining acceptance for ideas which might provide the middle way between Socialism and a collapsing Capitalism. To him this currency reform was all-important, because it would be the basis for the other reforms that he was beginning to have in mind.

### 3

On 12 April 1924 no less a person than Lloyd George wrote to the *Nation* calling for a large-scale programme of public works. Unemployment figures had been for some time in the neighbourhood of a million. Lloyd George was the type of Liberal who was not averse from State intervention; he was temperamentally inclined to meet the manifest social evil of unemployment by positive action; the idea of a streamlined and up-to-date nationwide system of public utilities appealed to him; this seemed a fitting plan to offer in substitution for the inertia of the authorities. Lloyd George had been out of office for more than a year, and was seeking a policy both in agriculture and industry that would have some popular appeal. There followed a stream of letters from such authorities as Mr Walter Layton and Sir William Beveridge. Keynes allowed the correspondence to gather momentum, keeping his admirers in suspense about his own views, and finally intervened himself on 24 May: *Does Unemployment Need a Drastic Remedy?* Yes, it did. He proposed that the Treasury should use the Sinking Fund 'to spend up to, say, £100,000,000 per year on the construction of capital works at home, enlisting in various ways the aid of private genius, temperament and skill'. Housing was clearly a much-needed form of capital development, and he hinted at what we have come to know as 'prefabs', an idea to which his mind reverted in Washington in 1944. 'It should not be beyond the technical accomplishments of our engineers to devise a national scheme for the mass production of houses which would supplement the normal activities of the building industry and make up in five or ten years the deficiency with which the latter has proved unable to deal.' He also recommended the adaptation of our road system to the needs of modern transport, and a large scheme for the transmission of electric power. 'I look, then, for the ultimate cure of unemployment and for the stimulus which shall initiate a cumulative prosperity to monetary reform – which will remove fear – and to the diversion of the National Savings from relatively barren foreign investment into state-encouraged constructive enterprise at home, which will inspire confidence. That part of our recent unemployment which is not attributable to an ill-controlled credit cycle, has been largely due to the slump in our constructional industries. By conducting the national wealth into capital developments at home we may restore the balance of our economy. Let us experiment with boldness on such lines – even though some of the schemes may turn out to be failures, which is very likely.'

Two weeks later he replied to criticisms in an article which laid great stress on the diversion of savings from foreign investments.

In my opinion, there are many reasons for thinking that our present rate of foreign investment is excessive and undesirable. We are lending too cheaply resources which we can ill spare. Our traditional, conventional attitude towards foreign investment demands reconsideration; it is high time to give it a bad name and to call it 'the flight of capital'. But I must limit myself here to the single aspect which is relevant to the special problem of unemployment.

Some foreign investments lead directly to the placing of orders in this country which would not be so placed otherwise. Whether or not they are desirable on general grounds, such investments do no harm to employment. As a rule, however, this is not the case. A foreign loan does not, any more than a demand for Reparations, automatically create a corresponding flow of exports. Let us take a particular example. Last week New South Wales borrowed in the London market £5,500,000 new money 'for railways, tramways, harbours, rivers and bridges, water supply, irrigation, sewerage and other purposes'. A part of this may pay for orders placed here arising out of these undertakings. Probably the greater portion will not be used thus, but in paying labour on the spot, and importing supplies from elsewhere. That is to say, the resources will be transferred to Australia in roundabout ways. Sooner or later, the matter must be adjusted by increased British exports or diminished British imports. But this can only come about through the medium of a depreciation of the sterling exchange. Our exchanges have to depreciate so as to stimulate our export industries at the expense of our 'sheltered' non-export industries, and so redress the balance between the two. If the world demand for our exports at the present price level is inelastic, a considerable depreciation may be necessary to do the trick. Moreover, there may be violent resistances to the process of adjustment. The fall of the exchange tends to raise the 'cost of living', and 'sheltered' industries may struggle to avoid the reduction of real wages which this entails. Our economic structure is far from elastic, and much time may elapse and indirect loss result from the strains set up and the breakages incurred. Meanwhile, resources may lie idle and labour be out of employment.

The old principle of *laissez-faire* was to ignore these strains and to assume that capital and labour were fluid; it also assumed that, if investors choose to send their money abroad at 5 per cent, this must mean that there is nothing at home worth doing at 5

per cent. Fifty years ago, this may have been a closer approxima-
tion to the truth than it is now. With the existing rigidity of the
trade union organization of labour, with the undue preference
which the City organization of new issues and the Trustee Acts
afford to overseas investment, and with the caution which for
many reasons, some good and some bad, now oppresses the undertaking of new capital investment at home, it does not work.

Can I now carry my critics with me this far, – that, if in the
last six months, instead of £10,000,000 capital issues for new
home developments and £50,000,000 for new developments
abroad, the figures had been the other way round, this would
have been a change for the better, and favourable to employment? Surely they cannot maintain that England is a finished
job, and that there is nothing in it worth doing on a 5 per cent
basis. Then let them agree with me in wishing, if we could
manage it, to stimulate investment at home.

In considering how to do this, we are brought to my heresy –
if it is a heresy. I bring in the State; I abandon *laissez faire*, – not
enthusiastically, not from contempt of that good old doctrine,
but because, whether we like it or not, the conditions for its success have disappeared. It was a double doctrine, – it entrusted the
public weal to private enterprise *unchecked* and *unaided*. Private
enterprise is no longer unchecked, – it is checked and threatened
in many different ways. There is no going back on this. The
forces which press us may be blind, but they exist and are strong.
And if private enterprise is not unchecked, we cannot leave it
unaided.

For these reasons I claim to be nearer than Mr Brand to the
realities and possibilities of the modern world in repeating that
the next developments of politic-economic evolution will emerge
from new experiments directed towards determining the appropriate spheres of individual and governmental action. And proceeding to particulars, I suggest that the State encouragement of
new capital undertakings by employing the best technical advice
to lay the foundations of great schemes, and by lending the credit
and the guarantee of the Treasury to finance them more boldly
than hitherto, is becoming an inevitable policy. There is no
sphere where private initiative is so lacking – for quite intelligible
reasons – as in the conception and execution of very costly projects which may be expected to yield from 5 to 6 per cent. The
Trade Facilities Act continues to depend on private initiative, and

only such projects are helped by it as private enterprise is inclined to plan and to back. Mr Brand, the City Editor of *The Times*, and many others point to the unused balance of credit under this Act as convincing proof that there is nothing more to be done. I do not agree, because big new projects of a public character are not the kind of thing for which the Act is devised. Let me set against this the very recent report of the Chamber of Shipping Committee, which points out the urgent need of expensive developments in many of our great ports, as one proof amongst many that the equipment of this country is not complete and up-to-date in all respects. Indeed, it is a bold and hazardous saying of my critics that our savings must drift abroad at 5 per cent because there is simply nothing worth doing in England at that price.

We may ask ourselves what would have been the economic fortunes of Britain had she not returned to the Gold Standard in 1925, thus saving herself from the Coal Strike and the General Strike and other consequential industrial troubles, had she shaped a policy for maintaining the sterling price level when the world slump came in 1929, and had she executed a thorough reconstruction of her public utilities and basic industries in the twenties, when she had spare resources for the purpose. Such a reconstruction was found to be sadly overdue ten and twenty years later. In connection with this last point we may wonder if there were at the time youthful members of the Labour Party who judged that Keynes had more to offer than the stale old doctrines, and made mental notes of the plan for large-scale capital development, – only to have the opportunity to bring them out of their mental pigeon-holes at a period, of all periods in British history, the least suitable for such an undertaking, namely, 1945–50. The mind of the public was slow to move in 1924, and Keynes got little support for his double policy, which was planned to meet contemporary evils.

At the Liberal Summer School, in Oxford that year, Keynes returned to the charge upon the subject of foreign investment. He claimed that the Trustee Acts gave it undue preference; he put together a gloomy tale of how many of our past investments overseas had resulted in loss and default. Let the Trustee Acts be amended so as to give home requirements a better chance.

Keynes spoke with vehemence and a manifest desire to persuade. The matter clearly seemed to him to be one of the utmost importance. The audience was interested, but showed no signs of sharing his sense of urgency. I was there myself and watched its reaction closely. The feeling seemed to be that Keynes had made a case with his usual effectiveness for being somewhat more critical of foreign investment. This, however, appeared to be rather a specialized point, worth taking note of, but not apparently related to any big plank in the Liberal programme. Indeed, if one looked at his proposition from a political standpoint, it seemed somewhat anti-Liberal in tendency. Liberals had always stood for a large foreign trade and an international outlook. This preference for home projects seemed to be a little nationalistic in flavour. It might be wise, but was it specifically Liberal? Furthermore, from another point of view it was not very attractive, for many of the investments would be in our Dominions and Colonies, and so the proposition appeared to have a Little England flavour at a time when the Liberals had long ceased to think in Little England terms. Thus Keynes's address seemed rather to be fulfilling the educational function of the school than making a contribution to a fighting programme.

Yet Keynes himself clearly thought of it differently; to him what he had to say was obviously central and crucial. Why was this? Let it be granted that all that he said about the disappointments in past investments abroad was true; let it be granted that we should be more cautious in future; let it be granted that the Trustee Acts should be amended to give home development a better chance. Yet why was all this so crucial? In his mind it was clearly linked with the cure of unemployment. That certainly was crucial – but what exactly was the connection? Watching his enthusiasm on the one side and the comparative apathy of the audience on the other, I felt that there was some missing clue, something unexplained, that his statement needed amplification, that there was some message which he had failed to deliver.

There was indeed a missing clue. The task of discovering that clue was to occupy the next twelve years of his life. What was lacking was an explanation in terms of fundamental economic theory of the causes of unemployment. Orthodox theory did not appear to justify Keynes's contention that it could be reduced by diverting investment from foreign to home channels, and his own arguments seemed inconclusive.

Various interesting reflections occur in this connection. One is how early (1924) Keynes had completed the outline of the public policy which has since been specifically associated with his name – credit control to eliminate the credit cycle, State-sponsored capital development and, for a country in Britain's position, some check upon the outward flow of capital. The main framework was there in 1924. If Keynes put forward these proposals before being in a position to give a full theoretical justification of them, that was, no doubt, because he deemed it urgently needful for Britain to act with speed. It must not be inferred that they were thrown out at random.

In the last two years he had been actively working on the theory of credit and capital. He had been feeling his way forward. The processes of the mind are inscrutable. Did he in some primitive sense already know the theoretical conclusions that he was later to articulate? He had uncanny powers of intuition. Is it possible for the mind to jump from the data which are the premises of an argument to the practical conclusions, without being conscious oneself of the theoretical conclusions, which are none the less the necessary logical link between the premises and the practical conclusions?

It is desirable to give some example of the theoretical

dilemmas presented by his address. Why was he urging that a diversion from foreign to home investment would increase employment? He admitted that if foreign investment declined our exports would decline correspondingly, since our excess of exports would be equal in value to our foreign investment. Why therefore was not the loss of employment in the export trades due to the reduction of foreign investment equal to the gain of employment resulting from the additional investment at home? We may revert to his argument in the *Nation* article that, when a new foreign investment was undertaken, there was not an immediate adjustment, until in due course there had been a pressure upon the foreign-exchange rates necessary to promote the excess of exports required; but surely this maladjustment was 'short run' even by Keynes's standard, for he was arguing in terms of a programme for the next ten years. The reference to a consequential reduction in our standard of living would have been relevant, had he been arguing against an expansion of our foreign investment; but in fact he was arguing in favour of a reduction. Keynes tended to fall back upon his argument that so many of these foreign investments came to a bad end; but that was another point; it did not show that while they were going on they were any less good for employment than a corresponding value of investment at home. No really satisfactory explanation was offered.

Throughout the discussion Keynes seemed to have the idea that there was, so to speak, a lump of saving. He argued as follows. Let us suppose that the National Debt Commissioners contributed £100 million to the Sinking Fund. Holders of the Debt paid off would, by hypothesis, be either trustees or the type of investors who like trustee securities. They would then seek about for the next best thing, and find it, under the influence of the Trustee Act, in overseas investment. How much better, Keynes argued, if that £100 million went to home development. There was in his conception a definite amount of saving which could either be applied one way or the other. There was no hint of the notion that when, at a time of domestic unemployment, the authorities stimulated certain domestic capital developments, the additional activity and income-earning would themselves generate part or all of the savings required to finance the development. At this point Keynes was ill-equipped to combat what came to be called the Treasury view, which was that public works simply diverted savings from one outlet to another and failed to increase total activity. Mr Hawtrey himself, whose writings on credit and banking policy greatly influenced Keynes in other respects, subscribed to the Treasury view in this matter. According to him, if one expanded public works without expanding bank credit, one did not add to employment; if one expanded bank credit, one could add to employment without public works.

If one asked why, if payable projects existed at home, private enterprise had not found them out, Keynes offered an *ad hoc* and personal, rather than theoretical, answer. There was as yet no hint that 'liquidity preference' prevented the rate of interest falling to its proper level, which would render the projects in question payable. Instead we have the explanation that 'there is no sphere where private initiative is so lacking – for quite intelligible reasons – as in the conception and execution of very costly projects which may be expected to yield from five to six per cent'. (We need not, of course, reject this institutional explanation, even when we have the benefit of a theoretical one to reinforce it.)

When we have Keynes's *General Theory* (1936) in our hands, it is easy in retrospect to give a theoretical defence of the practical policy which he outlined in 1924. The Theory of the Multiplier gives the answer to the Treasury view, which is based on the idea of a lump of savings. The 'liquidity preference' theory of interest explains why payable domestic projects are not put in hand. Finally, the Multiplier theory explains both why domestic public works will give more employment than foreign investment, and also why – even when we have abandoned the lump of savings theory – some discouragement of foreign investment will be needed to make for home investment. If the economy passes from a state of considerable unemployment to one of much greater activity, imports will rise and, given the standard of living, the excess of exports over imports will be reduced. Thus the funds available for foreign investment will be reduced, not as Keynes seemed to imply at this early stage by the exact amount of the home investment, but by a different amount which depends on the marginal propensity to import. Thus a textbook explanation can now be given of the whole programme which Keynes propounded in 1924.

He did not give it himself at the time, and for that reason his plea lacked something in final potency. When Cobden and Bright undertook their great campaign, they could always reinforce their *ad hoc* platform arguments by the more fundamental reasoning to be derived from the pages of Adam Smith and Ricardo. Keynes was still lacking in the support of more fundamental modes of argument, and in due course had to forge them for himself. At the close of 1924 he was already planning in his head a treatise on the credit cycle. He did not then know how long and laborious the way was to be before his ideas took final shape – if indeed final is the right word, for there can be little doubt that with life and leisure Keynes would have reached a further stage in the development of his own thought.

Later in the year (October) he had another opportunity to ventilate his views about savings and investment. A Committee was sitting in order to report on Taxation and the National Debt (the Colwyn Committee). He made his point about the Trustee Act. He also departed from the austerity of orthodoxy by holding that it was not necessarily desirable to fund as much of the short-term debt as possible; the quantities of short-term debt and long-term debt available should be arranged to suit the taste of the market. While recognizing the value of a Sinking Fund, he did not subscribe to the virtues of a large one in the existing circumstances; the redemption of debt might mean taking money from the enterprising to put it into the hands of those who prefer gilt-edged security; they in their turn would lend abroad. A large Sinking Fund would be desirable if it were combined with a large programme of public works, which would provide the productive outlet at home for the capital made available by the Sinking Fund. He also proposed for the consideration of the Committee a scheme for State Bonds, which would have a guaranteed stable commodity value. This might attract certain investors and was in line with his general advocacy of a stable currency.[9] He gave evidence again in the following spring explaining why he was opposed to a Capital Levy in existing conditions.

His academic work gained recognition at this time by his being made a foreign member of the Swedish Academy of Science.

In the political world he returned to the charge in the General Election, making a speech at a big rally in Cambridge in support of the borough Liberal candidate. He criticized the Russian loan and continued to give warning against the dangers of Protection.

Meanwhile he had other intellectual tasks to perform in the course of 1924. On 13 July Alfred Marshall died, and Keynes set himself to compose the obituary notice for the *Economic Journal*.[10] Mary Marshall, the economist's widow, wrote to Keynes's mother, 'I am indeed glad that Maynard is writing it, for he will do it beautifully and Alfred was proud to count him among his pupils.' The note ran to sixty-two pages and is of permanent value, since it contains Keynes's summary of what he regarded as Marshall's principal original contributions to economics. It is also a fine

9. Some of his views appear in his review of the Report of the Committee in the *Economic Journal*, June 1927.

10. September 1924. The issue was somewhat delayed: his fellow-editor, F. Y. Edgeworth, informed me that he regarded the delay as amply justified by the superb notice. See footnote on p. 165.

example of the biographer's art. Keynes had shown his power
of portraying the weaknesses of his adversaries in vivid and
unforgettable touches; now he proved that he could do a
balanced portrait, fashioned with the loving care of a pupil,
but not omitting criticism. He made Marshall live for his
readers and endeared him to them; and his account of the
Cambridge background is also of abiding interest.

A little later he contributed to the *Nation* a short obituary
sketch of his old supporter at the Cambridge Union and
colleague in Paris, Edwin Montagu.[11]

The Sidney Ball Foundation invited him to give its annual
Lecture at Oxford. The title he chose was *The End of
Laissez-Faire*.[12] He was hot on the trail now. The foundations of old-fashioned Liberalism were to be finally de-
molished and a philosophical background provided for the
new policy. He knew that Oxford was well read in the great
thinkers of the past, and rightly judged that it would intrigue
his audience to hear his comments on them. His address was
an elegant performance; he leapt from idea to idea with
fascinating agility, picking up the various strands of thought
that contributed to the nineteenth-century doctrine of
*laissez-faire*. Although his presentation was witty and adroit,
it was not completely satisfying, since this part of his task
was destructive and the time at his disposal brief. His treatment of the great thinkers, whose first editions he was so
zealously collecting at this time, was inevitably somewhat
cavalier. He sought targets for attack, to the neglect of the
profound wisdom of the great men, Locke, Hume, Rousseau,
Bentham, Burke, Paley, Malthus, Darwin, whose names
bespeckled his pages.

The second part of his discourse was concerned with the

11. 29 November 1924. It was reprinted in *Essays in Biography*.

12. *The End of Laissez-Faire* was published by Leonard and Virginia Woolf at the Hogarth Press in 1926, being based on the Sidney
Ball lecture delivered before the University of Oxford in 1924, and a
lecture delivered before the University of Berlin in 1926. (See below,
p. 445.)

principles of policy in a society that had abandoned *laissez-faire*. In retrospect his proposals appear extraordinarily modest. In the first place, he cited what he called the 'self-socialization' of big concerns, of which the prime example was the Bank of England, whose policy was uninfluenced by the quest to maximize dividends and was solely governed by considerations of efficiency and public interest. This was a development to be encouraged. If it proceeded, as it was bidding fair to do, it would remove the necessity for State Socialism. 'There is, for instance, no so-called important political question so really unimportant, so irrelevant to the reorganization of the economic life of Great Britain, as the nationalization of the railways.'

Next he proceeded to policies where this solution did not apply.

I come next to a criterion of Agenda which is particularly relevant to what it is urgent and desirable to do in the near future. We must aim at separating those services which are technically social from those which are technically individual. The most important Agenda of the State relate not to those activities which private individuals are already fulfilling, but to those functions which fall outside the sphere of the individual, to those decisions which are made by no one if the State does not make them. The important thing for Government is not to do things which individuals are doing already, and to do them a little better or a little worse; but to do those things which at present are not done at all.

He proceeded to deal with managed currency, and then:

My second example relates to Savings and Investment. I believe that some coordinated act of intelligent judgement is required as to the scale on which it is desirable that the community as a whole should save, the scale on which these savings should go abroad in the form of foreign investments, and whether the present organization of the investment market distributes savings along the most nationally productive channels. I do not think that these matters should be left entirely to the chances of private judgement and private profits, as they are at present.

His third example concerned the need for a population policy.

In his final section he confessed discontent with the predominance of the money motive in the lives of many:

There is nothing in these reflections which is seriously incompatible with what seems to me to be the essential characteristic of Capitalism, namely the dependence upon an intense appeal to the money-making and money-loving instincts of individuals as the main motive force of the economic machine . . .

In Europe, or at least in some parts of Europe – but not, I think, in the United States of America – there is a latent reaction somewhat widespread, against basing Society to the extent that we do upon fostering, encouraging, and protecting the money-motives of individuals . . . Most religions and most philosophies deprecate, to say the least of it, a way of life mainly influenced by considerations of personal money profit. On the other hand, most men today reject ascetic notions and do not doubt the real advantages of wealth. Moreover, it seems obvious to them that one cannot do without the money-motive, and that, apart from certain admitted abuses, it does its job well . . . For my part, I think that Capitalism, wisely managed, can probably be made more efficient for attaining economic ends than any alternative system yet in sight, but that in itself it is in many ways extremely objectionable. Our problem is to work out a social organization which shall be as efficient as possible without offending our notions of a satisfactory way of life.

The next step forward must come, not from political agitation or premature experiments, but from thought. We need by an effort of the mind to elucidate our own feelings. At present our sympathy and our judgement are liable to be on different sides, which is a painful and paralysing state of mind . . . There is no party in the world at present which appears to me to be pursuing right aims by right methods. Material poverty provides the incentive to change precisely in situations where there is very little margin for experiments. Material prosperity removes the incentive just when it might be safe to take a chance. Europe lacks the means, America the will, to make a move. We need a new set of convictions which spring naturally from a candid examination of our own inner feelings in relation to the outside facts.[13]

13. All quotations taken from the pamphlet as it finally appeared.

There the matter rested. What then? He had not yet thought things through.

## 4

In the second half of 1924 sterling began to rise in a sinister manner in the foreign-exchange market. The originating impulse was obscure; it may have been connected with Federal Reserve policy; America had a minor trade recession in that year, and the Federal Reserve system, in accordance with its now well-established practice, proceeded to pump in credit in order to stimulate trade; this may have been the initial cause of the weakening of the dollar against sterling. Be that as it may, there is no doubt about what was responsible for the continuing major upward movement; a return to the old Gold Standard was definitely in the air now, and bulls were buying sterling at a discount in order to make a profit when the old parity should be re-established. The important thing to notice was that the rise in sterling did not reflect a reduction in British costs or a rise in American prices.

Keynes continued to hold that we should not return to the Gold Standard at all; as the months moved on, he seemed to be more and more isolated in this opinion. Even those, whose views on monetary policy were very near to his, thought that we should return. He was close in accord, for instance, with Mr R. G. Hawtrey on the subject of banking policy and owed much to his writing.[14] Mr Hawtrey hoped that under cover of the Gold Standard international cooperation in managing the value of money might be achieved on the lines of the resolutions of the Genoa Conference, in securing the adoption of which he had played a principal part. Reginald McKenna, now Chairman of the Midland Bank, was a fervent advocate of a managed currency on lines similar to those desired by Keynes. But he too thought that

14. In the autumn of 1922 he held Mr Hawtrey up to me as the best writer on currency and credit.

the thing could be done under the aegis of a Gold Standard. In the political world even his old friend Asquith (now Lord Oxford) felt it necessary to pronounce in favour of a return to gold at a meeting of the Cambridge University Liberal Club – a most unkind cut![15] Keynes was a voice in the wilderness. There hardly seemed now to be any respectable opinion on his side. It was a remarkable example of courage of conviction in a good cause. Only seven years later the great mass of opinion had come over, deeming that the return in 1925 to the pre-war parity had been a disastrous mistake. Keynes continued his advocacy by speaking and writing until the bitter end. He contributed two important articles to the *Nation* on 21 February and 7 March 1925. He caused some surprise in the latter by supporting the recent rise in the Bank Rate, as he deemed that the internal situation now justified it. This was not an inconsistency. If a currency is to be well managed, it does not follow that, if a rise in the Bank Rate was wrong in mid-1923, it was also necessarily wrong in 1925. On 18 March he delivered an address before the Commercial Committee of the House of Commons restating his views.

As the danger of the return became imminent, his interest naturally shifted from the superiority of a managed currency, as such, over a Gold Standard, to the error of re-establishing the Gold Standard at the pre-war parity. He contributed two articles to the *Nation* (4 and 18 April) on the over-valuation of sterling. It was difficult to prove the point precisely by means of index numbers, since, as he repeatedly pointed out, general index numbers of wholesale prices tend to move with the actual established rates of exchange and fail therefore to reflect internal prices and costs; but it is these latter that are relevant when we want to judge whether an actual rate of exchange is or is not at an equilibrium level. Keynes was on strong ground in holding that if the exchange was in equilibrium in mid-1924 it was certainly out of equilibrium in the spring of 1925, since the

15. 9 March 1925.

sterling exchange had moved up by some ten per cent, while British costs had not fallen nor American prices risen.

The now inevitable return to the Gold Standard occurred on 29 April. This was a bitter disappointment to Keynes. He saw in it the triumph of unreasoning prejudice. On the morrow he made a mistake, which was perhaps due to his ever buoyant optimism. He clung to the hope that things could not be as black as they seemed. By a misunderstanding of the legal position, he assumed too hastily we had only half gone back to the Gold Standard, that we had imposed a maximum but not a minimum price for gold, so that the foreign exchange would still be free to fluctuate in a range above the old parity; he welcomed this; things would not be too bad, if only an inflation developed in America raising prices there by the necessary ten per cent. He had to make a recantation in a letter to *The Times* [16] and in the following issue of the *Nation*. [17]

On 10 June of the preceding year (1924) Mr Philip Snowden (then Chancellor of the Exchequer) had appointed a strong committee to advise him on the amalgamation of the Treasury note issue with that of the Bank of England. This committee consisted of Lord Bradbury, Mr Gaspard Farrer, Sir Otto Niemeyer and Professor Pigou. Keynes gave evidence on this technical point. Some time afterwards the committee was evidently asked to divert its attention to the broader issue of the return to the Gold Standard. In his Budget speech announcing the return, Mr Churchill, who had become Chancellor, referred to the Report as containing a reasoned marshalling of the arguments. In fact the committee contented itself with a somewhat summary survey. It had not considered how the whole range of prices and wages in Britain were to be reduced, in order to bring the internal value of the currency into line with its enhanced external value, nor did it consider any of the major problems connected with the return. Keynes pitched into this re-

16. 6 May 1925.
17. 9 May 1925.

port with great ferocity in an article in the *Economic Journal*.[18] For him this was a grim moment. All his hopes for basing a new policy for capitalism on a managed currency were dashed. In view of the Chancellor's description, he argued, one might have expected a weighty document, comparable with the long chain of classic reports on British currency, or at least an 'armoury of up-to-date arguments in favour of old-fashioned expedients. But we find instead a few pages, indolent, jejune.'

In such a case it did not occur to him that asperity should be reduced in order to avoid hurting feelings. The committee included Professor Pigou. This was not an anonymous banker, but his very old friend, his colleague, his teacher, his benefactor. He may have judged, if he pondered upon the matter, that Professor Pigou had a certain grandeur of soul which would enable him to receive such knocks in good part, if he knew that they were actuated by sincere conviction. Not all his adversaries through life were of such temper. It has to be recorded that all seemed fair to him in controversial warfare, and that he seldom paused to consider whether what his cause gained by the insertion of an expression of obloquy was enough to justify the pain that it might give.

Inflation did not come in America; the Federal Reserve System kept business running in 1925 on a fairly even keel. To his horror, but not to his surprise, Keynes found that the British authorities were not putting in operation any plan to reduce costs in Britain and bring them into line with the new gold parity. It appeared that the first industry to suffer the full impact would be the coal industry, for this had a large export trade with many frontiers of keen competition, and wages constituted much the largest part of its cost of production. It was impossible for the coal industry to keep its export markets, save by exporting at a loss or by the reduction of wages. Accordingly it was decided that wages must be reduced, and a grave crisis

18. June 1925.

threatened. Keynes judged that this was the first instalment of troubles to come.

He got to work and composed three articles for the *Evening Standard* – which on the whole had been sound on the gold question – and these he published in a pamphlet with the Hogarth Press (Leonard and Virginia Woolf) under the title *The Economic Consequences of Mr Churchill*. Once thought of, such a title was irresistible, if one desired one's words to be read by as many as possible. It did not imply that Keynes felt that much personal blame should be attached to Mr Churchill. His attack was directed in part against popular clamour, but first and foremost against the experts who had advised the Chancellor. This was made plain in the pamphlet. Some years later Keynes wrote two reviews of Mr Churchill's *The World Crisis* (March 1927 and March 1929), which were reproduced in *Essays in Biography*. These show that Keynes had not only an intellectual appreciation of Mr Churchill's gifts, but also a certain warmth of sympathy for one whose type of mind was very different from his own. We may quote his concluding paragraph:

The chronicle is finished. With what feelings does one lay down Mr Churchill's two-thousandth page? Gratitude to one who can write with so much eloquence and feeling of things which are part of the lives of all of us of the war generation, but which he saw and knew much closer and clearer. Admiration for his energies of mind and his intense absorption of intellectual interest and elemental emotion in what is for the moment the matter in hand – which is his best quality. A little envy, perhaps, for his undoubting conviction that frontiers, races, patriotism, even wars if need be, are ultimate verities for mankind, which lends for him a kind of dignity and even nobility to events, which for others are only a nightmare interlude, something to be permanently avoided.

These words were written eleven years before the sublime apogee of Mr Churchill's great career.

Keynes's pamphlet was composed in his finest controversial

style. Every sentence told. The arguments were unanswerable, and the reviewers, mainly hostile, could only fume
and splutter. We had deliberately raised the external value
of the currency by ten per cent and had not planned for
adjusting internal values. Workers in export industries
would be required to reduce their wages; this would be quite
a reasonable proposition if there were any plan for reducing
all prices and wages in the country in similar proportion,
so that the money wage reductions would be only nominal
and not imply any loss in standards of living. If this was not
done – and there was no plan to do it – workers in the export trades would suffer gratuitous hardship. Or was there a
plan to do it? If there was, it apparently consisted in a deflationary policy, which meant in essence the creation of
sufficiently massive unemployment by the restriction of
credit to enable one to impose wage-cuts by *force majeure*
– a terrible process which it might take years to carry
through to the bitter end, and one not conducive to high
production or industrial progress in the interval. Meanwhile valued export markets would be lost, perhaps irretrievably.

A year before there had been no sufficient reason for a
reduction in the coalminers' wages. Now they were being
faced with the alternative of such a reduction or unemployment, and it would not be easy for them to find work elsewhere:

> On grounds of social justice, no case can be made out for re-
> ducing the wages of the miners. They are the victims of the
> economic Juggernaut. They represent in the flesh the 'funda-
> mental adjustments' engineered by the Treasury and the Bank
> of England to satisfy the impatience of the City fathers to bridge
> the 'moderate gap' between $4·40 and $4·86. They (and others to
> follow) are the 'moderate sacrifice' still necessary to ensure the
> stability of the gold standard.

He put forward a constructive proposal that the Government should take steps to negotiate an all-round five per
cent cut in wages and salaries, subject to a guarantee that

prices would fall correspondingly; to secure equity as between wage and salary earners on the one hand and property
owners on the other, he proposed the rough-and-ready
remedy of an increase in the Income Tax by 1s. in the
pound. The economic argument of the pamphlet was supplemented by an important letter to *The Times* on 4 September.

His words were unheeded. The coal industry was maintained in action by a subsidy during the winter, and the
nation then suffered the great disaster of the Coal Strike
and the General Strike. In the years between 1925 and 1929
Britain's industrial progress was markedly less than that in
other countries.

5

The Liberal Summer School at Cambridge no doubt expected to hear more about gold and coal. But he judged
that his readers had now been surfeited with this subject,
and instead he read a delightful paper entitled 'Am I a
Liberal?'[19] This set out in an amusing way the dilemma
of having to choose between the inadequacies of Conservatism and Socialism, and expressed his political point
of view which I have already outlined.[20] It may be of interest to quote one section of the address. Readers will not
have forgotten that all through those crowded years Keynes
was in intimate and daily contact with his Bloomsbury
friends. They were, in a sense, a different world. We may
remember their paramount interest in the subtler problems
of private life. We can imagine their chaffing him, and
saying, 'Why do you politicians never talk about anything
that really matters?' On this occasion he would take up the
challenge. Among the five topics that should be the main
concern of the Liberal Party in the future he included 'Sex
Questions'.

19. Reprinted in *Essays in Persuasion*, 1931.
20. See pp. 389–93.

The questions which I group together as Sex Questions have not been party questions in the past. But that was because they were never, or seldom, the subject for public discussion. All this is changed now. There are no subjects about which the big general public is more interested; few which are the subject of wider discussion. They are of the utmost social importance; they cannot help but provoke real and sincere differences of opinion. Some of them are deeply involved in the solution of certain economic questions. I cannot doubt that Sex Questions are about to enter the political arena. The very crude beginnings represented by the Suffrage Movement were only symptoms of deeper and more important issues below the surface.

Birth Control and the use of Contraceptives, Marriage Laws, the treatment of sexual offences and abnormalities, the economic position of women, the economic position of the family, – in all these matters the existing state of the Law and of orthodoxy is still medieval – altogether out of touch with civilized opinion and civilized practice and with what individuals, educated and uneducated alike, say to one another in private. Let no one deceive himself with the idea that the change of opinion on these matters is one which only affects a small educated class on the crust of the human boiling. Let no one suppose that it is the working women who are going to be shocked by ideas of Birth Control or of Divorce Reform. For them these things suggest new liberty, emancipation from the most intolerable of tyrannies. A party which would discuss these things openly and wisely at its meetings would discover a new and living interest in the electorate – because politics would be dealing once more with the matters about which everyone wants to know and which deeply affect everyone's own life.

These questions also interlock with economic issues which cannot be evaded. Birth Control touches on one side the liberties of women, and on the other side the duty of the State to concern itself with the size of the population just as much as with the size of the army or the amount of the Budget. The position of wage-earning women and the project of the Family Wage affect not only the status of women, the first in the performance of paid work, and the second in the performance of unpaid work, but also raise the whole question whether wages should be fixed by the forces of supply and demand in accordance with the orthodox theories of *laissez-faire*, or whether we should begin to limit the freedom of those forces by reference to what is 'fair' and 'reasonable' having regard to all circumstances.

There was much newspaper comment on this bold sally. Once again I was a member of the audience and once again I had the feeling that my neighbours did not think that he was giving them, in this part of his discourse, an important plank for the Liberal Party platform. Twenty-five years have passed since this oration, and much of what he said, which, it must be confessed, shocked some of those present, has passed into our common way of thinking.[21] In this field too he was a prophet of things to come, but the Liberal Party managers may have been wise in their generation in feeling that this line of thought was not well suited to retrieve the failing fortunes of the party.

6

The great production of *The Sleeping Princess* (1921) had over-strained Diaghilev's finances, and for a time he was unable to carry on. His company was in temporary dissolution. In 1922 Massine collected certain members of it, including Lopokova, and organized some productions at Covent Garden and later at the Coliseum. In the latter case the repertory included *The Masquerade*, by Vera Bowen, a great friend of Lydia. In 1924 elements of ballet with Lopokova were introduced into a revue called *You'd be Surprised* at Covent Garden; a little later she appeared again at the Coliseum. She also appeared in Paris in the *Soirées de Paris*, organized by Comte Étienne de Beaumont, and Keynes got over to see some performances. Only towards the end of 1924 did Diaghilev reappear in London, but Lopokova was not of the company on that occasion.

Meanwhile she was becoming a familiar figure in Bloomsbury. This was a strange new element in the circle of friends. They were delighted by the charming simplicity of her

21. Compare in this connection the tone and temper of the Report of the Royal Commission on Population (1949).

character, her gaiety, her jokes and sallies. Her struggles with English were the source of much fun in the early days. Her remark is remembered, 'I dislike being in the country in August, because my legs get so bitten by barristers'.

All were struck by her complete lack of vanity. There was no trace of the airs of the great ballerina. She took part in charades and similar amusements at 46 Gordon Square; she did not disdain to perform a *pas de deux* with Duncan Grant, until he missed his footing and went spinning to the ground, and all was dissolved in helpless laughter.

Some time during these years the great decision was taken; legal matters had to be settled up.

Meanwhile there were whispers and rumours and some uneasiness in Cambridge among the older generation. It was known that Keynes had strange artistic friends, but was not this going rather far? Perhaps some of the senior members at this time had culled most of their knowledge of the ways of London from their excursions there in the 1890s. 'Chorus girls' in those days were not considered highly eligible for matrimony. Did the prefix Russian make it any better? Or did it perhaps make it worse? They had not Sir Osbert Sitwell in their midst to explain to them about the highest achievement of twentieth-century art; if they had, they would probably not have believed him. There was distinct uneasiness. Keynes might be a great man, but Cambridge had its standards.

Signor Nitti, a Liberal statesman of Italy, and a former Prime Minister, was due to speak at the Liberal Summer School of 1925. Keynes issued a formal invitation to various pundits of the University to a luncheon in the Combination Room of King's College 'to meet Signor Nitti'. This was the ostensible purpose of the luncheon; the real purpose was to meet Lydia Lopokova. The old fogies might belong to the backwoods, but they were gentlepeople, highly trained in the art of discernment in such matters, and in two minutes they realized that Lydia was something totally different from what they had feared. All was well; Cambridge would be no problem; Lydia was accepted, and in due course won the hearts of the seniors in the University. Some years later I was seated next to Mrs Alfred Marshall at a luncheon, and our talk turned to Keynes's marriage. 'The best thing that Maynard ever did,' remarked that venerable lady.

The marriage took place on 4 August 1925 at the Saint Pancras Central Register Office in the presence of Dr and Mrs Keynes, Mrs A. V. Hill (his sister), Mr Duncan Grant and Mrs Harold Bowen. The married couple went off to Russia to meet Lydia's relations. Keynes wrote three delightful articles on Russia for the *Nation*. He was impressed by the 'religious' quality of the Communist experiment,[22] but found nothing of economic interest. The articles were published by the Hogarth Press under the title of *A Short View of Russia*.

To the majority of people this marriage appeared to be a crowning episode in Keynes's Bloomsbury life – and for a short time he may have thought that it would be. But it was not so in fact; indeed it was to prove to have been a turning away from Bloomsbury. At a deeper level Keynes probably knew this. The biographer must pause at the threshold and not seek to pry among the inner eddies of his subject's emotions. The secrets of the heart must remain secret. None the less there were certain salient facts in this connection which the reader should know for a proper understanding; a certain pattern may be detected and an interpretation ventured.

22. 'Now that the deeds are done and there is no going back, I should like to give Russia her chance; to help and not to hinder. For how much rather, even after allowing for everything, if I were a Russian, would I contribute my quota of activity to Soviet Russia than to Tsarist Russia! I could not subscribe to the new official faith any more than to the old. I should detest the actions of the new tyrants not less than those of the old. But I should feel that my eyes were turned towards, and no longer away from, the possibilities of things; that out of the cruelty and stupidity of Old Russia nothing could ever emerge, but that beneath the cruelty and stupidity of the New Russia some speck of the ideal may lie hid' (p. 28).

In his young days Keynes's contacts with the Lytton
Strachey circle, and above all with Lytton Strachey himself,
were a source of joy and exhilaration. The revolt, the adventure with ideas, the unknown territories to be explored,
the finer shades of feeling, the wit and the endless drolleries
fired his imagination and stimulated his thinking. Then
came the broadening out into the wider Bloomsbury circle,
in which miraculously the old atmosphere was preserved.
As individuals many of the Bloomsbury friends were creative
artists in the fullest sense. As a social group they were
essentially critical and gently mocking, not only *vis-à-vis*
the outer world, but *vis-à-vis* one another. They kept some
watch on Keynes, delighted with his sallies against the great
and pompous, heart and soul with him in his pleas for
justice, but ready to be doubtful when he consorted too
much with Prime Ministers, fearful lest he be tainted by
the vulgarities that are apt to be associated with public
renown. His relation with the friends was one of personal
affection; the intellectual community of interest was primarily in the world of letters and philosophy. While he interested himself in their opinions in the field of the visual
arts and was eager to be in the vanguard of their movement, it remains doubtful if his inner soul drew much sustenance from visual beauties.

He too, in his main life's work so far, was a critic, conducting his merciless onslaught on politicians and bankers.
Agile and ever active, darting now here, now there, his
rapier flashing, he inspired terror in a multitude of foes.
His friends sharpened their wits against society in their
drawing-rooms; he did so in a wider arena, while they
cheered him on. There was a certain restlessness in his life.
It is true that he focused his thoughts on a few fundamental
themes, Reparations and the restoration of Europe, Deflation, the Gold Standard, a programme for the Liberal Party;
but his mode of life with his journalistic enterprises, his
finance, his frequent excursions into the new fields of
political and economic controversy, was a little flurried. In

London he was at the centre of an intellectual movement; his friends were fulfilling themselves, realizing their capacities and achieving some renown individually and as a group; the atmosphere was exciting. In Cambridge his feelings might be steadied by the quiet rhythm of University life, but there too there was the ferment of youth, and his zeal in the quest for true spirits in each generation did not flag.

In the ten years to come the basic pattern was to be different. They were to be years, not primarily of criticism, but of creation. He was profoundly discontented with the current explanations of trade depression, he was confident that his fellow-economists had not thought matters through, and he set upon the task, not knowing at first how great it was to prove, of clarifying the issues. In the event he was to create an apparatus of thought for analysing our economy which was to be found useful by economists the world over. No light task! His apparatus has the appearance of beautiful simplicity, it seems the merest common sense, but the task of devising it was not so simple. What Adam Smith wrote in the *Wealth of Nations* seemed to be but common sense; but the world had had to wait for many generations before its economic affairs were sorted out and described by Adam Smith in a way which seemed so clear and obvious after it had been achieved. Keynes could not completely doff the role of critic; he had to give vent to barbed utterances – some thought needlessly – against the older school of economists. That, however, was not his main work. For his constructive task, cool, steady, continuous effort was needed. The seed of thought had to germinate and grow. During such an endeavour the basic tempo of the soul is different. By some mysterious process the thought gathers, forms itself, defines itself. It must be protected from too much dialectic and debate. Mr D. H. Robertson's subtle criticisms, which in the early days proved very stimulating to Keynes, seemed to become in the end an impediment to the final fruition of his ideas. All these fine points have their time and place. One is on the track of a great idea; one has almost seized it, but not quite; then it bursts upon one; but no, one is not at the goal yet; for is not this idea but one aspect of a still wider generalization not yet grasped? Creation is a subtle and precarious activity. The creator must be protected for the time from overmuch criticism, else the impulse will die. While he never lost his delight in the erosive and mocking comment on life of his Bloomsbury friends, it may be that he would not have prospered so well had their dialectic been the main background to his work.

The curve of the dancer's leap through the air, the tracing and interweaving of lines by motions perfectly designed, the pose of the figure come to rest, every inch of it controlled and carrying its meaning, these beauties of the ballet are not achieved without years of hard labour and experience, yet, when achieved, they are direct and unimpeded expression of emotion, an outflow of the soul into an appropriate form. There is a spontaneity, a joy of life, an assertion. We are far removed from the world of dialectic and debate, of criticism and second thoughts. The achievement is perfect – or perhaps it is not perfect – but it cannot be amended. 'Now, Lydia, if you would drop your arms a little more, that would express the feeling when love is on the one hand somewhat ...' All this is of no use. Lydia's droop of arms will express the finest possible shade, but it cannot be corrected in detail by discussion and analysis. This art achieves its purpose by a direct method; there may be trial and error; but each new trial is a new beginning and is not guided by reasoning on its path.

The emotion to be expressed is defined by the ballet itself; it must, in general, be a universal emotion, not idiosyncratic. But Lydia had a strongly individual character, to which, despite the rules, she gave vent, thus imparting an element of character-acting. This was not in the strict classical tradition, yet was so clearly inspired by the highest genius that it was allowed; the Diaghilev Ballet was great enough to assimilate it and was enhanced by it. And so the public saw this unique personality expressing something new and strange, something piquant and fascinating; those severe and hardly won techniques which the ballet taught were subjected to her individual creative impulse.

She was like that in private life also. The direct expression of feeling, the spontaneity, the inventiveness, the gaiety, the queer, unusual ideas, all flowed into her speech. Her aphorisms or comments, amusing, wise, or perhaps sheerly fantastic, were her offerings to the good cheer of the company. To Keynes they were meat and drink; his amusement and appreciation never flagged. Like the others, he was an aristocrat in his tastes, caring only for the best; subject to that, he was catholic. Was Bloomsbury becoming a little stereotyped? He at least delighted in novelty and freshness. His imagination was always ready to be stirred, even by the most absurd fancy.

Lydia's method was not really compatible with what were now the fixed habits of Bloomsbury. She might make a sally. 'Oh, Lydia, how fascinating; now do you suppose that ...' Here clearly was material for a delightful dissection, gentle mockery being piled on top of mockery, all in the greatest good humour; this should elicit some new defensive dictum, to be thrown into the cauldron and added to the excellent dish that was being cooked up, the final elucidation of all the fantastic consequences of her line of thought, the *reductio ad absurdum* achieved with great merriment. But Lydia had not the appetite for all this. She tripped on to another quite different comment, and another, and then, perhaps, relapsed into placidity, silently pursuing her own thread. This was frustrating to Bloomsbury; they felt cheated of their repast; it seemed that she must either spoil their flow of reason or be left out of it.

The flow did not appeal to her. The mordant irony of Virginia Woolf, her mocking comment, her remorselessness in defining exactly how things were, weighed on Lydia's spirits. She found these highbrows woefully depressing as a group.

Keynes had already had his little problems with his different 'worlds', but indeed the gulf between the Asquiths and Bloomsbury, or between the economists and Bloomsbury, or, for that matter, between Lydia and either, was far less wide than that between Lydia and Bloomsbury. The oil and water would not mix, and not all Keynes's alchemy could make them. Their temperament and attitude to life were utterly disparate.

This did not involve any breach. Many of the Bloomsbury friends were very fond of Lydia; they continued to be good friends, and were constantly in and out of the house. But for Keynes they had now become a delightful recreation, instead of being the main background of his life. It was a very great change in his mental environment, the greatest that had occurred since he left Eton for Cambridge. It may be surmised that, apart from the obvious blessings which flow from having a wife whom one loves, the change was an advantage to him in the kind of work he had now to do, first the great creative work of the mind, and then his public work, in which it was expedient that he should be mellow and comprehending, rather than critical and sceptical. For twenty years he had learnt all the tricks and twists and turns of the critical spirit. His education in that field was complete. What he now needed, when he rested from his tasks, was that repose which could be given by someone whose nature was fundamentally simple, affirmative, hopeful. All those who saw these two together in the years that followed will bear witness that his choice was triumphantly vindicated.

# [10]

## A Treatise on Money

### I

THE year 1925 had been full of events for Keynes; they took place against a background of continuing work as tutor in Cambridge, as Editor of the *Economic Journal*, as a financier, as Chairman of the Board of the *Nation*, as Bursar of King's College.[1] We see him in the last-mentioned capacity in a deputation to the Prime Minister on 15 June 1925 to make representations on the effects on college finances of the commutation of tithes – an intricate problem. Mr G. R. Y. Radcliffe planned that Keynes should cover the financial aspects and be followed by H. A. L. Fisher, then Warden of New College, who would deliver a well-rounded speech on the place of the two ancient Universities in our national life. We can imagine Mr Baldwin listening to the diverse fluencies of these two great pundits as he smoked his pipe.

There was also a background of thinking – or should we call this the mainstream of his existence? He had a book on hand in which he must dig deeper than in his recent publications. It must be the Keynes, this time, of the *Treatise on Probability*, unravelling the intricacies of the credit cycle. The country was dragging on in a condition of industrial depression and unemployment. He had proposed remedies. He had still to justify these by a deep analysis of the mechanism of our economic system, in order to satisfy himself and his economic colleagues, and to give firm ground to those who were minded to preach his doctrines. As his first thoughts developed, he needed a critic, and he found an excellent one in Mr D. H. Robertson. They had many a long talk, chasing the truth. Robertson himself had a book in gestation on

1. He became First Bursar in 1924.

this very topic. In part it was to bring up to date certain
ideas he had expressed in *A Study of Industrial Fluctuation*
(1915); but he was also to break new ground on the topic
of banking policy. His earlier work led him to hold that
fluctuation was not wholly due to monetary policy, but also
partly to shifts in certain broad categories of demand. He
held that such moderate fluctuation in output as was due
to these causes had the advantage of expediting economic
progress. He agreed with Keynes that monetary reform was
needed to check excessive fluctuation; and he was in favour
of currency 'management'. But if a modicum of fluctuation
in output was to be allowed, a moderate fluctuation in the
general price level would be a natural and desirable corollary; thus he did not wish price stabilization to be applied
too absolutely. In order to establish these points, he had
to embark on an intricate analysis of the processes of bank
lending, for which he invented his own vocabulary. The
analysis appeared exceedingly complicated, perhaps more
so than it really was. Keynes was never convinced on certain
points, and also held that further thought should enable
one to reduce the theory to much simpler terms.

These two minds had considerable influence on each other
at this time. Robertson inserted a generous expression in his
introduction to his book, which appeared under the title of
*Banking Policy and the Price Level* in January 1926. Robertson's own thinking led him to stress the importance of the
relation between saving and the demand for new capital
goods. He analysed minutely the problems arising from the
fact that the banks had a dual role which had to be carried
out in one and the same act. They had to provide the right
volume of circulating capital for industry and the right
volume of circulating medium for the general public (in the
form of bank deposits) to maintain prices at an appropriate
level. Both kinds of provision were made by extending loans
of various sorts. How were these two functions to be harmon-
ized? The following passage may be quoted as foreshadow-
ing Keynes's doctrine. Robertson was referring to a saver

who does not use his saved income for the purchase of an instrument of production or in making advances to productive workers. 'In this case he is from his own point of view saving, but is taking no steps to ensure the creation of capital. Unless others take such steps, the effect of his action, assuming equilibrium of production and sale to be preserved, is that the consumption of other persons is increased by as much as his own consumption is diminished.' [2]

On 13 February F. Y. Edgeworth, Keynes's collaborator in editorship of the *Economic Journal*, died, and Keynes wrote one of his charming obituary notices.[3] Despite his early rage at Edgeworth's obtuseness on the subject of index numbers,[4] he had come to appreciate the qualities of that great man. The appreciation was reciprocal. Edgeworth could not say too much in praise of Keynes. In old age his face was largely concealed in his beard, and his sunken eyes were not very expressive; but at a critical moment one could gauge that his feelings were overcoming him. One such was when, after many hours of lecturing and after many passages of digression with quotations from the classics and analogies from physics, he at last made the supply curve intersect the demand curve on the blackboard. One knew it was a great moment. He wagged his beard and muttered inaudible things into it. He seemed to be in a kind of ecstasy. And so it was on the mention of Keynes. I once told him that Keynes was staying in Christ Church. 'Ah,' he said, 'you have the pure milk of economics with you ...' and, flinging his arms above his head, he proceeded with an inarticulate eulogy.

It is a notable fact that those who were most eminent in

2. In this passage Robertson contrasts the purchase of an instrument or making advances to workers on the one hand, with hoarding the money on the other. He does not discuss whether saving necessarily leads to capital creation if the saver purchases securities on the Stock Exchange. Keynes later contended that in this case too the waste of savings, which Robertson noticed, might occur.

3. *Economic Journal*, March 1926. Reprinted in *Essays in Biography*.
4. cf. p. 172 above.

widely different walks of life – Lytton Strachey, Asquith, Edgeworth, Sir Richard Hopkins (of whom we shall hear later) – were not oppressed by Keynes's minor failings – impetuosity, changes of view, speaking beyond his book – but were more interested in his qualities of greatness.

Keynes was again writing at this time about Walter Bagehot; it was the hundredth anniversary of his birth, and he was thus Edgeworth's senior by only nineteen years![5] And, a very different kettle of fish, he contributed a review of a book by Trotsky, of which the concluding sentences are of interest:[6]

Trotsky's book must confirm us in our conviction of the uselessness, the muddle-headedness of Force at the present stage of human affairs. Force would settle nothing ... We lack more than usual a coherent scheme of progress, a tangible ideal. All the political Parties alike have their origin in past ideas and not in new ideas – and none more conspicuously so than the Marxists. It is not necessary to debate the subtleties of what justifies a man in promoting his gospel by force; for no one has a gospel. The next move is with the head, and fists must wait.

Public life, meanwhile, was proceeding. On his return from Russia he delivered an important speech in Manchester to a branch of the Federation of British Industries (which had viewed with doubt, although not with implacable opposition, the impending return to the Gold Standard). He surveyed the unhappy situation. He preached the stimulation of new capital developments, a 'prosperity policy', even if, in its early stages, it involved the loss of gold. The risk was worth taking. In the *Nation* (9 January), he reverted to his old theme of the French franc. The French should recognize openly that a restoration of the franc would unduly favour rentiers; they should stabilize the external value of the franc at about its existing level, using their gold reserves to support that level, and allow internal prices to rise into line. The French did not like this, and were par-

5. *The Banker*, March 1926.
6. The *Nation*, 27 March 1926. Reprinted in *Essays in Biography*.

ticularly hostile to the idea of using their gold reserve. But what is a gold reserve for, if it is not to be used on such an occasion? Keynes's prescription accords fairly closely with what was actually done by Poincaré later in the year.

In February he delivered a speech in Manchester, calling for a working agreement between the Liberal and Labour parties. Only thus, he felt, could the British voters overthrow the lifeless régime of the Conservatives. Britain wished a progressive policy, but neither Party could achieve this by itself. He knew that there were some who thought that the right solution was for the Liberal Party to fade out. He gave his reasons for unwillingness to trust the Labour Party alone. But the Liberals must be careful to restate their policy and adapt it to the needs of the times, so as to appeal to a sufficient number of moderate men in the Labour Party, to make a working agreement possible. Later in the year Keynes showed his open-mindedness by giving an address to the Summer School of the Independent Labour Party at Lady Warwick's house, Easton Lodge, in which he taxed John Wheatley (of the left wing) with being a Conservative! He refused, however, to take the chair at a Fabian meeting – that would be going too far!

In more orthodox circles he was giving evidence to the Indian Currency Commission and the Balfour Committee on Industry and Trade. He was an eminent public man now, and in that capacity allowed his name to be put forward for the Rectorship of Edinburgh University in what is essentially a political contest. He got more votes (568) than Mr Tawney (238), but less than Sir John Gilmour (1,027).

Meanwhile the coal crisis was unresolved. The industry had been carried through the winter by a subsidy. The men remained adamant in rejecting wage reduction, and in the spring the disastrous coal stoppage occurred, accompanied in its first ten days by the General Strike.

This led to an episode in Keynes's career which caused him much pain. Two years earlier Lloyd George had had a

formal reconciliation with Lord Oxford and the leaders of
the official Liberal Party. No one had greater reason to distrust Lloyd George than Keynes; but the deed was done;
what mattered now was the reconstruction of the Liberal
Party. It had no immediate prospect of accession to power,
and in this phase it seemed to Keynes that policy was all-
important, personalities much less so. Meanwhile Lloyd
George was making good showing. There had been his important pronouncement in the *Nation* on the question of
public works. He was supporting Keynes's views on the Gold
Standard in the House of Commons. He had a vigorous
policy for agriculture, which was not altogether acceptable
to the cooler heads, but displayed good intention, and now
he had come forward and made the Liberal Summer School
an offer of money to finance an independent committee of
experts who should formulate a programme of industrial
policy for the Liberal Party. He had solemnly undertaken
that he would use no veto, nor interfere in any way with
the impartial findings of the committee, so that the Summer
School could feel that its independence was not jeopardized;
but he asked to be allowed to take part in its deliberations.

Liberals of all complexions agreed that the General Strike
was not within the limits of constitutional action, that it
must be defeated and that it must be made plain that any
repetition was doomed to failure. But there could be
shades in one's attitude to the strikers. According to one
school of thought, all negotiations should be entirely held
up until 'unconditional surrender' had been secured. The
wisdom of such a formula as 'unconditional surrender' has
been queried by men of judgement, even when applied to
a nation that was giving its solid support to Hitler and his
gang. If it was open to reasonable doubt in such a case, how
much more so when applied to millions of fellow-countrymen acting according to their lights. Others thought that
negotiations should continue in some form, on the basis of
a return to the *status quo* before the strike began and of
letting bygones be bygones. No less a person than the Arch-

bishop of Canterbury organized a movement to influence opinion in this sense. We have seen that Keynes thought that there was no case in equity for requiring of the miners a reduction in wages, save as part of a treaty for a nation-wide reduction of money incomes, which would bring about a proportionate reduction in the cost of living. There was no prospect that, if the miners agreed to a reduction, the other reductions would follow; thus these men, who work in hard conditions, were being asked to make a one-sided sacrifice in their own living in order to satisfy the predilection of the financial pundits for the old gold parity. If the miners were in the right, what should one say of all the millions who came out on sympathetic strike? One might say that they were altogether in the wrong, but one would not be at all inclined to treat them as near-criminals. The breakdown in the negotiations had come suddenly. There had not been much time for cool thinking. The strikers were not revolutionaries, and were actuated by the motive of loyalty which is normally deemed praiseworthy. Consequently Keynes found himself on the same side as the Archbishop of Canterbury! And so did Lloyd George, an article from whose pen, written in this sense, appeared in an American newspaper on the first day of the strike.

On 26 May, when all was over, and the men, other than the mine-workers, were back at work, a letter from Lord Oxford to Lloyd George was published. He took him to task in a dignified and definite manner for having refused an invitation to attend the Liberal Shadow Cabinet at its second meeting during the strike on grounds of dissent from certain statements (on the lines of 'unconditional surrender') that had been made by Liberal leaders since the previous meeting. Lord Oxford included a reference to the American article. Lloyd George's reply was published at the same time; while protesting against the administration of the rebuke, in the language of one who thought consideration due to him, he defended himself in what was on the whole a conciliatory style. The *Nation* of 29 May carried a leader entitled 'Lord Oxford's Blunder' and a note affirming that Lloyd George was 'triumphantly and unmistakably in the right'. It made the case for Lloyd George's general attitude, and argued that, even if it was wrong, it was not so manifestly illiberal as to call for ostracism. The *Nation* erred perhaps in not in the first instance taking the charge for failing to attend the Shadow Cabinet more seriously. This was no doubt what mainly actuated Lord Oxford, since the refusal had the appearance of a monkey trick, a manoeuvre to secure freedom to adapt his line according to the success or failure of the General Strike, and to do so without the cooperation of, or in opposition to, his Party colleagues. The General Strike was a grave crisis in the history of the nation, and Lord Oxford judged that such a manoeuvre was beyond the pale of right conduct in a colleague.

The *Nation* received a mass of letters and defended its attitude in the following week. Keynes was in no way responsible for editorial policy and did not feel committed to opinions expressed by the paper. On this occasion it would have been possible for him, having regard to his long intimacy with Lord Oxford, to have lain low – but it would have been utterly unlike him. Accordingly on 19 June he wrote a letter to the *Nation* expressing his view. Liberals who were supporting Lord Oxford in this crisis made much of Lloyd George's past record – his treatment of the Liberal Party at the Coupon Election of 1918, his policy at the Paris Peace Conference and his use of the Black and Tans in Ireland. Keynes took the point that all these matters had nothing whatever to do with the case. They should have been examined, weighed and judged at the time of the reunion of the orthodox Liberals with the Lloyd George elements two years before. If it was a question of rejecting Lloyd George from the innermost councils of the Party now, that must be on the basis of what he had done since reunion, and Keynes was unable to find sufficient cause for such a drastic measure. He also hinted that, however highly one might regard Lord Oxford himself, one could not have a great opinion of many who were near him in the councils of the Party. Lord Oxford took this intervention much amiss, and they did not meet again.

In the complicated negotiations that followed, the elements in the House of Commons on which Lloyd George could rely were paradoxically those of the right wing of Liberalism, who had supported him in Coalition days and were prepared to be loyal, although they hated his action during the General Strike. Many who were loyal to Lord Oxford were further to the left, some calling themselves radicals. Among the rank and file in the country the division was somewhat different, since Lloyd George's energetic bid for a completely new programme was appealing to progressive forces. The Asquithians pleaded that Lord Oxford himself was perfectly ready to support the most radical proposals, when convinced of their soundness; but among others there was a feeling that he no longer had the energy to go forth and get people together or to insist, with all the drive that was needed, on having an up-to-date programme formulated and adopted.

Keynes was staying with me some months later on the occasion of a speech at the Oxford Union. He explained that he divided Liberals into two categories, the 'true' Liberals and the 'real' Liberals. The 'true' Liberals were men of high character, personal loyalty and unblemished record; they adhered unflinchingly to the old doctrines even, and not least, when it required courage to do so; they could be relied on unfailingly. The 'real' Liberals were more concerned with the future than the past and regarded personal questions as for the time being of secondary consideration; what they wanted above all was to have Liberalism applied to the existing situation, to have a new programme – it being the essence of Liberalism to adapt itself to changing circumstances – and to overcome, not after a passage of many years, but here and now, the crying evil of unemployment. He had to admit that he was a 'real' Liberal.

Later, when we were alone together, he told me that it

was with great grief and a sense of real personal loss that he had found himself divided from Lord Oxford and his family. As time went by, after Lord Oxford's death, he came once more to be on friendly and even affectionate terms with Margot Oxford, and other members of the family allowed this painful episode to be forgotten.

Immediately after the letter to the *Nation* he went off to a lecture engagement in Berlin, where he spoke on *The End of Laissez-Faire*.[7] Dr Moritz Bonn has told me that he went up to Keynes after the lecture and remarked that it was not necessary for him to have given that lecture in Berlin, since there in Germany they had never had anything remotely resembling the system of *laissez-faire* as he had described it. Keynes also gave a lecture on the General Strike. It was extremely difficult to explain to the astonished Germans that this had not been a symptom of revolution or sedition, but an example of loyal and well-disciplined Trade Union members doing their duty. Nor, he added, was the collapse mainly due to a stern assertion of authority by the State, but rather to the fact that the strikers had had time to think, and to reach the conclusion independently that what they were now doing went beyond the rules of that game which, as loyal Trade Unionists, they felt bound to play.

2

On 13 November 1926 Keynes published an article in the *Nation* on the Lancashire cotton trade; his remarks were confined to the American section of the spinning industry. Coal had been the first spectacular victim of the return to the Gold Standard; it was natural that his mind should turn to the industry which was next hardest hit, cotton. His main contention was that the practice of organized short time was a great mistake. He surmised that it sprang from a belief in Lancashire that the depression, which it had been ex-

7. cf. p. 417 above.

periencing for some six years, was transitional, a post-war maladjustment due to the disturbed condition of world markets. Keynes furnished figures to show that the world market was no longer in a depressed condition; from a world point of view the cotton trade was making normal progress; he cited the production of cotton piece-goods and the consumption of raw cotton; these were not declining; it was only Britain's share that was declining. The recipe of organized short time was injurious, because it increased overhead costs and thereby damaged Britain's power to compete. Lancashire would become involved in a vicious circle, since the more her sales contracted, the shorter the time required, and consequently the higher her costs would mount and the more rapid her loss of markets would be. Keynes went so far as to say that the rate at which she was losing business was only governed by the rate at which it was possible for her competitors to create additional spindle capacity.

The mishandling of currency and credit by the Bank of England since the war, the stiff-neckedness of the coal owners, the apparently suicidal behaviour of the leaders of Lancashire, raise the question of the suitability and adaptability of our Business Men to the modern age of mingled progress and retrogression. What has happened to them – the class in which a generation or two generations ago we could take a just and worthy pride? Are they too old or too obstinate? Or what? Is it that too many of them have risen not on their own legs, but on the shoulders of their fathers and grandfathers? Of the coal owners all these suggestions may be true. But what of our Lancashire lads, England's pride for shrewdness? What have they to say for themselves?

This issue of the *Nation* was dated 13 November, but so rapid was the reaction of Lancashire, that the evening papers of 12 November carried many columns of rejoinders from various eminent cotton men. A hornets' nest had been stirred. The comment was naturally hostile. What did this theorist know about the practical issues?

Such was the immediate press reaction. But on 16 November the *Manchester Guardian* carried the information that the Short Time Committee of the Federation of Master Cotton Spinners Associations had invited Keynes to come to Manchester. This was indeed astonishing news. That these shrewd practical men of long experience, hardened individualists, proud of their complete mastery of their own business, should invite an academic personage, on the strength of an *a priori* attack on their procedure, to come to discuss matters with them was a portent. In the *Manchester Guardian* of 19 November it was learnt that Keynes had accepted the invitation and was due at a meeting in Manchester on 22 November. The promptness of his reply and his courage in being willing to appear in person were much appreciated. Lancashire was greatly intrigued. There seemed to be a sporting element in this encounter; but the gravity of the matter to be discussed was recognized; the livelihood of thousands and the survival of Britain's greatest industry were at stake.

News soon came that responsibility for the meeting had been transferred from the Short Time Committee to the General Committee of the Federation. The discussion was private, but a communiqué was issued. Keynes had to explain himself on two points. He had never suggested that the recipe of short time was a mistake, when first adopted, namely in the depression following 1920. It was a reasonable remedy for what then seemed to be a transitional phase. The mistake had been to prolong the remedy after trade had recovered everywhere save in Britain. Nor had he implied, as comment had suggested, that the mills should all have worked full time; he agreed that that would have led to gross overproduction. Some other remedy should be sought. He advised some kind of compulsory cartel, to be enforced by the Federation and the Banks. This should adopt a system of transferable quotas, so that production might be concentrated in the most efficient mills. This cartel should be followed by the organization of holding companies which should provide finance for modernization and secure a rearrangement of the use of capacity.

Another article appeared in the *Nation*[8] to tidy up his proposals. He prophesied that short time would not last much longer. Actually it was terminated three weeks later, on the ground that lack of discipline had begun to make it ineffective. Admirers of Keynes might like to claim that he had killed short time. It is probable that its disadvantages had already become manifest and that its demise at this date contained an element of coincidence. It is possible, however, that Keynes's forthright attack precipitated action that would otherwise have been delayed.

There the matter might have rested, but for the existence of a Committee in Lancashire which had been formed to organize an American Cotton Yarn Association. The leaders felt that Keynes might be of assistance and made contact. On 10 December came the news that he had authorized the following statement:

Mr Keynes has expressed the view that the proposed Cotton Yarn Association is capable of modification and development in such a way as to achieve some of the objects which he had in view in suggesting a cartel. A meeting is being arranged between him and members of the Committee which is promoting the Association.

This meeting took place in London on 16 December and another article appeared in the *Nation* of 23 December.

It is not clear that what had been in the mind of the Committee was very close to the thought of Keynes. His enthusiasm was aroused, however, by the positive attitude of its members and their sense of the urgent need for action. A start might be made and the Association developed on sound lines. In the *Nation* article he enumerated certain points. The Association proposed to have a sanction to secure compliance – this was important.[9] Secondly, Keynes strongly supported the proposal that members should fur-

8. 27 November.

9. The method proposed was the assignment of £1 shares, a shilling to be paid up, with a right to call upon the remainder in the event of non-compliance.

nish prompt and complete statistics. Then came the question of price-fixing. Keynes stressed the importance that prices fixed should be protective minima, to prevent weak cut-throat selling, and not satisfactory prices. Then there was the project of quotas of output for each distinct section of the trade. The Association was to have a small capital and Keynes saw therein the possibility of working out a scheme of cooperative credit by which fresh working capital might be found. He thought the Association would provide a framework within which more fully developed cartel arrangements and amalgamations could be gradually organized, and adjured the banks to support it.

On 4 January 1927 Keynes addressed a large meeting in Manchester, organized by the Committee, with Lord Colwyn in the chair. A motion was put forward in support of the proposed Association, and carried with but one dissenter. The following notice appeared in the *Manchester City News* of 8 January 1927:

Mr J. M. Keynes is a famous economist. Whenever he rises to speak upon a specified subject he can be relied upon to provide new views and new or hitherto unsuspected economic facts. They may or may not be capable of contradiction; but at least he raises a controversy that compels attention to, and examination of, all sides of the given subject. His incursion into cotton was wholly unexpected. It says much for his personality and his capacity that he should have caused such a flutter in the dove-cote. His original attack – it was an attack – was necessarily received with much criticism and hostility, it naturally being supposed that those inside the cotton trade knew their own business best. At the same time Mr Keynes's articles were read for what they were worth. In them was found a directness that was stimulating and a knowledge of cotton that was most provoking to cotton traders . . .

Mr Keynes has an interesting presence. Of medium height [in fact, he was a tall man], dark, with a high forehead and deep-set eyes, when he stood up to address the meeting he immediately obtained close attention. His hands thrust into the pockets of his open jacket, he was not so much an aggressive figure as of rock-like steadiness. He had calmness and poise. He lacked affectation, and he had a message to impart – the truth of which he did not for a moment doubt. He spoke rapidly, but in a clear and cultured voice, making his points with admirable directness. In precise and direct tones he began swiftly to annihilate the various opposing schools of thought; and representatives of every business section listened intently to what he had to say.

It required courage thus to beard the lions in their den; courage to say that the banks were professional paralytics, and that the ignorance with which Lancashire carried on its trade was horrible . . .

In the course of this speech Keynes dealt rather fully with the proposed solution of widespread bankruptcy. Apart from the fact that this was likely to be a very slow and painful process, especially in view of the reluctance of the banks to take drastic action, he had a further criticism of the bankruptcy solution, where there was admittedly excess capacity. By itself it did not remove the capacity; the mills of bankrupt firms would still produce. 'If the Devil were left to take the hindmost, he would take everyone in turn . . . when the Devil took the hindmost what he did was to promote him to the top.' Bankruptcy might play a useful part in weeding out the inefficient in an industry that was on the whole expanding, but he did not believe that it provided a solution where the industry was due to have a contraction.

This conclusion, which was the fruit of careful thought about the problems of Lancashire, was to influence his thought in a wider sphere. It may be set alongside an opinion which he expressed about this time that schemes for organized contraction of the production of raw materials during a transition were not always to be condemned.[10] It does not follow that he approved of the cartelistic tendencies in British industries in the forms which they actually took in the inter-war period, for he emphasized that the primary objective in a contracting industry should be to concentrate production in the most efficient units. He had the awkward

10. Article in the *Nation* on 'Control of Raw Materials by Governments', 12 June 1926.

problem of reconciling the view that cartels and 'rationalization' schemes were sometimes desirable with the traditional Liberal policy of hostility to monopoly in all its forms. Many years later this considered opinion was to make itself felt in the Anglo-American discussions during World War II. While wholeheartedly working with the Americans upon schemes for removing currency restrictions and for expanding international trade on a multilateral basis, he could not subscribe to the full doctrine that pure competition would provide the right answer in every case. This was not an inconsistency, but intellectual honesty. He was not insincere in his advocacy of the greater freedom to be obtained through such agencies as the International Monetary Fund and the International Trade Organization; that did not mean that some central organization of an industry was in all cases undesirable; it was a question of reconciling these two objectives, not necessarily mutually inconsistent, and each justified by the needs of the modern world.

In the following months the Association came into being. It was claimed that the membership was some seventy-five per cent of the American section. During 1927 markets fell away; while seventy-five per cent might be sufficient for the achievement of objectives in good times, it was probably not so when trade was bad, for non-members took advantage of their freedom and the prices sustained by the Association, leaving members to bear the full brunt of reduced orders. Fears began to be entertained that the Association would not win through. On 27 August an article by Keynes appeared in the *Nation* sternly rebuking those who refused to come into the Association. 'I should like to offer a small prize for the best name to describe those who, in spite of the perilous position of a great industry to which they themselves belong, steal the advantages without joining in the subscription.' He hinted that there was a case for coercion by legislation. If not, there should be coercion by public opinion, and 'it is evident that the Banks could do a good deal if they chose'.

An official attempt was made to enlarge the membership at a rally in the Manchester Town Hall on 6 September, the Lord Mayor of Manchester himself presiding. Keynes was the principal speaker. 'I feel myself here today in a very delicate and unenviable position. I am not a cotton man. I am not a professional orator. The problem before us is a very broad one, where there is no need of the subtleties of an economist. I have nothing novel or sensational to propound to you. I am just an individual, bold enough, or foolish enough, to offer myself up for sacrifice, and in that spirit I hope you will accept me.' He made an urgent plea for the support of the Association, and also proposed that there should be 'what I might term an unofficial Royal Commission' to recommend action by the industry.

His plea was in vain and the Association had to abandon its main activities. Keynes wrote a bitter article in the *Nation* of 19 November:

I have paid several visits to Manchester in the past year in conditions where I have had exceptional opportunities of hearing opinions from all quarters; and I have always come away with a feeling of intense pessimism. I am not surprised at the break-down of the loyal efforts which have been made with so much ability and good temper by Mr Lincoln Tattersall and his efficient directors of the Yarn Association and Mr John Ryan, their Secretary. There is something desperately discouraging – insensitive, stale, unadaptable – in the atmosphere of Lancashire today towards any constructive effort – an atmosphere which is more ominous in my opinion than the statistical facts of the industry. It is hardly an exaggeration to say that the efforts of the Yarn Association have been watched even in more or less impartial quarters with a curious, half malicious hostility, which would scarcely be deserved even if the Association's ideas were intellectually misguided.

The reformers did not give up their efforts, and Keynes was always ready with his advice. In these years he devoted a considerable time to studying the intricacies of the cotton trade and conferring with the reformers. Keynes had always had the idea that the banks should intervene, a proposal most unacceptable both to the producers and the banks themselves! It turned out, however, that the next move was to come from that side. Keynes had many talks with his old friend Reginald McKenna, then Chairman of the Midland Bank; unhappily at this period the Midland Bank was not on terms of closest cooperation with the Bank of England. Finally Mr Montagu Norman's interest was aroused and the Bank of England decided to give aid. This time an attempt was to be made, not through a cartel, but through a large-scale amalgamation. Under the aegis of the Bank of England the Lancashire Cotton Corporation came into existence at the beginning of 1929, with the purpose of acquiring about one-third of the spindles in the American section. The capacity of weaker firms was to be bought up, and where they were unwilling legal proceedings were to be instituted by the banks. The Corporation itself was to concentrate output upon efficient units and aim at low cost production, which should set the rest of the industry on its toes. Keynes gave the project his blessing and had a word of 'unqualified praise' for Mr Montagu Norman's intervention.[11]

Keynes continued to follow the fortunes of the Corporation for some years. It had a difficult task. Apart from the inherent intractability of its problems, there were deep personal questions, issues of power politics, which were beyond the range of Keynes's cognizance and ability to judge. Subsequent developments lie outside our story; the impetus which Keynes gave was a distinct, although inevitably limited, contribution to the slow and painful process of readjustment.

### 3

It took Keynes five years to write *A Treatise on Money*. The history of his life in this period is principally the history of the inner workings of his mind. This intellectual task was

11. The *Nation*, 2 February 1929.

accomplished against the usual background of many varied duties, including that of keeping the public well informed on the progress of reparations, the return to the Gold Standard and his other special subjects. But, apart from his continuing interest in the programme of the Liberal Party, his interventions in public life were less important during this period, especially in the years 1927–9. On marriage he acquired the lease of a house, called Tilton, a few hundred yards away from Charleston; it had once been the property of the Keynes family. Later (in 1937) he also rented 300 acres (increased to 570), and secured the services of Mr Logan Thomson, who had been working on the King's College farms in Lincolnshire, to farm it; and, by the rule that he could not touch lightly on any subject without becoming deeply involved and expert in it, his farming activities at Tilton came, as the years went by, to be one of his major interests. From the time of his marriage he went to Tilton during vacations, while during term he spent the middle of the week in London and long weekends in King's College.

Although Lydia often came to Cambridge, these were essentially bachelor weekends. It was not until 1937 that he acquired a flat in Cambridge (opposite the Arts Theatre),[12] which constituted a permanent *pied-à-terre* for Lydia. During these weekends he immersed himself in all the affairs of the College. In the narrative that follows the reader should remember that Keynes's work in King's was continuing and constituted an important part of his active life.

We have seen that in the days before and after the first war he regarded the prospect of being a regular college don as too limited, and was anxious to establish strong links with London. There was also the converse side of this case. When his position in London as a financier and journalist was well established, he was equally anxious not to sever his connections with King's. On the contrary, his roots there grew ever deeper and firmer. His heavy work for King's was not merely a duty; as a source of private gain it had ceased to

12. See ch. 11, 3.

count; in 1920 he had become a Supernumerary Fellow without dividend. He continued with his labours for the College because they were a source of sheer joy and delight to him.

He used to philosophize about the matter sometimes. He held that one could find greater satisfaction in the affairs of what he called a 'closed system', in which one knew every detail about the personalities and modes of procedure, than in a larger organism. College business was more interesting than University business, and University business more interesting than national affairs. What would he say of international affairs? It may be that it was because he was able to import into the Anglo-American discussions (1941–6) on reconstruction an element of intimacy, because he eventually achieved a relation of real friendship with the American spokesmen, so that the international committees acquired something of the flavour of a college meeting, where everyone knew the character of the others well and understood each other's jokes, that he achieved the success he did. It was partly his fear that American notions would unduly formalize the international institutions and make these intimate mutual understandings impossible that led to his acute distress at the Savannah meeting in 1946.[13]

In the course of years his authority at King's naturally grew. Not that worldly fame counts for much in a university; he would remain a 'nonentity' there until his work in the place justified a different status. That work he did.

It was natural then that as Bursar in charge of successive and far-reaching alterations in College financial policy, and in the seeking of the 'unusual powers' without which they would have been virtually unworkable, he should have had his colleagues behind him; or that when he proposed amendments or motions in his own name as an individual Fellow, he was likely to carry the day. To the younger progressives, there was to hand an older authoritative progressive, on whose ideas they could hardly im-

13. See below, ch. 15, 1.

prove: with the older Fellows knowledge of the man and the logic of the argument prevailed over inherent apprehensions.[14]

His cognizance of College policy was by no means confined to bursarial matters. His love of detail was relentless and he kept track of every development. There were new building plans; there were new Fellowship elections. The latter were of no little moment for the well-being of the College. His versatility enabled him to play an unusually influential part in these elections. Normally an elector reports within his special field and assesses the reports of others on those competing outside it. Keynes was frequently able to base his judgement on the first-hand inspection of a candidate's work far outside the field of economics. When the Fellows were elected he soon became their friend.

He sat amongst them in his hour of relaxation in the Combination Room after dinner, playing patience and accessible to all. Since there were many – and the expansionist in him always wished that there were more – the variety of his discussions would have tired a normal man who had been working on his 'big stuff' almost all day. He had a great, an almost incredible power, of switch, from an abstruse economic point to the fine interpretation of a Statute or an estate matter, and he produced his opinion on the dot without taking his eye off the cards.[15]

In the Bursary, despite the growth of capital, he kept everything under his hand. Nothing was too small for his personal attention – the repair of a cottage or the personal problems of a tithe payer who was in arrears for £10. He sorted his correspondence himself, not allowing others to open his letters, and kept the bundles in his favourite porcupine clips on his own plan. Thus overhead costs were kept low.

Business barometers did not prove to be of much import-

14. Contribution by H. G. Durnford (p. 17), *John Maynard Keynes, 1883–1946, Fellow and Bursar, a Memoir*. Publ. King's College, Cambridge.

15. H. G. Durnford, ibid., p. 16.

ance in his investment policy. He selected investments with great care and boldly adhered to what he had chosen through evil days.

By 1924 he had already concentrated in one fund, which was called the Chest, various balances which represented past savings and accumulations over the disposal of which the College had complete discretion. These amounted to about £30,000. Unlike the original endowments of the College, and trusts constituted since its foundation, this 'free money' could be invested in ordinery shares. Keynes took advantage of this discretion, and by the time of his death capital appreciation on the original £30,000 amounted to about £380,000. This figure includes nothing for unspent income, and in fact the income of the Chest had been very largely spent as it was earned during Keynes's Bursarship on such things as improvements to College buildings and repayments of loans incurred in erecting new College buildings. It was out of the income of the Chest that the College was able to make donations of £1,000 to the Cambridge Preservation Society in connection with the preservation of the Grantchester Meadows, of £500 to the same Society for the preservation of the Gog Magog Hills and of £1,000 to a Newnham College building fund. The improvement which Keynes brought about in the value of the College capital was achieved entirely on capital account. Indeed, he always emphasized the importance of finding a wise use for current income, and showed his contempt for unnecessary miserliness by referring to some other Colleges as 'savings banks'. What has come to be called an 'active investment policy' has, after a considerable time-lag, been adopted by a number of other Colleges and similar institutions. We shall see that Keynes was himself able to introduce the principle at Eton much later.

In 1920 he had considerably increased the College income, at a time when it was most needful to do so, by selling land. Later this policy was reversed, and he became deeply interested in the problems of a landlord. The interest thus acquired in farming questions may have led him to take over the land at Tilton; his personal experience and his College experience in farming interacted.

Keynes was a Bursar long before he became a farmer. I do not think that he would ever have become a farmer but for the agricultural depression which set in about 1928 and compelled the College to set about farming some of its own land in Lincolnshire, bought only recently, lest worse befell. Here indeed was something new. If the dead Bursars may have turned slightly in their graves when the College sold half its land in 1920, they must have rolled right over at this latest development. But Keynes turned to his now flourishing Chest and persuaded the College to stock and nurse back the land. There was something expiatory in this. It was perhaps as far as Keynes was ever called to go in his relations with the College to retrieve a situation of his own choosing which had become rather desperate. Now he asked them to ride out the storm.

Thus it was that the Bursar who had hitherto judged farms and farmers by their showing in Valuers' reports or in the College accounts, began to go several better than his predecessors in his nearer acquaintance with the land. On his visits there was nothing perfunctory or superficial or merely social. Inappropriately dressed – the familiar blue serge and brown shoes – he was to be seen in his new element, in labourers' cottages or studying the points of stock or attending pig sales on the College farms. When he had mastered the dietetics of pigs, he began breeding them privately. His dairy herd soon followed. His contact with men of the soil seemed at that time to have a wider repercussion. It was as if something which had been latent now burgeoned and that he was glad of it – a something of additional softness in his relations with men of ordinary but genuine mould. From now on it was a pleasure to him rather than a duty to sit next to a tenant at the College Audit feast. They could talk each other's language. He supported a motion to hang the portrait of a grand old yeoman of 50 years' tenure in the Combination Rooms – at the same time he was preaching that bad pictures, no matter of how great past dignitaries, should go forthwith from prominence to some passage or room where they might no more be publicly seen.

He enjoyed seeing about the place College servants who, if

they were of no great value, had become traditional or were venerable to look on. He was sad to see the peacock and its octogenarian keeper, who had started life as a groom to some previous Provost, pass finally from the Courts and lawns. As warden of the Pension Fund he relished exhibiting mock depression over the longevity of certain of the sturdier pensioners. Alas that his actuarial optimism over the increasing span of human life should have been belied in his own case.[16]

All this zealous activity not only redounded to the interest of King's and to his own personal satisfaction, but also had a subtle influence on his attitude in public life. His administrative triumph in the first war had been on an exalted plane, where he could operate by convincing a small number of highly intellectual Treasury officials by good arguments. Now he had to cope with dons, who can be extremely obstinate and pernickety, with bailiffs, with farmers, with servants. By patient contriving, and after overcoming many obstacles and suffering frustrations, he saw his various projects come to fruition. He became philosophical about minor setbacks. The continuity in the development of his work over so many years had an integrating effect upon his character. When he turned back in the second war to the storms and stresses of public life, he was more patient, more forbearing – in fine, mellower.

Meanwhile there was another kind of life proceeding at 46 Gordon Square, which also had its continuity. Bloomsbury still frequented the house; with some of them Lydia achieved a happy intimacy. The circle tended to widen: it was reinforced by Lydia's friends and her capacity for new friendships; it remained predominantly artistic in tone. Individual politicians, financiers, economists might come to the great parties, but were conscious of not belonging to the nucleus.

Keynes was fond of giving parties, large and small. There continued to be charades and similar forms of entertainment. There was one great occasion when some of the *Bou-*

16. H. G. Durnford, ibid., p. 18.

*tique Fantasque* was performed and Maynard and Lydia
did the Can-can Dancers together. I inquired of one who saw
it whether he excelled in the role of ballet dancer also; the
reply was that at least he did it 'with great energy'.

A favourite item was Lydia's rendering of Victorian songs
to the accompaniment of Mr Basil Maine at the piano.
Nothing could have been more to Bloomsbury's taste than
listening to the luscious sentiments of the songs, while nur-
turing an ironic sense of their absurdity; each new extravagance heightened the enjoyment. Infinitely agreeable!
Lydia fully appreciated the grotesque quality of the ballads,
but in a slightly different way, a Russian way. She went a
little further than any member of Bloomsbury could have
succeeded in doing towards entering into their spirit. At
moments there was a full-throated quality in her emotion.
Bloomsbury found it not only absurd but also fabulous that
these moods and sentiments could have been seriously regarded as an appropriate expression of true feeling, implying
that they too had their emotions, but on a different plane. It
was evident enough that Lydia also found the ballads rather
ludicrous – but was not life like that? Was not life itself
absurd? This kind of emotion was a matter for amusement,
yet it was an essential part of life and it had its charm and
its meaning. We may ask ourselves which was the deeper
comment on those ballads. Bloomsbury fully appreciated
that her interpretation was subtly different from their own,
and this made the performance all the more enjoyable. It
was an extra flavour added to the dish. And Lydia's art was
perfect.

Maynard was the impresario. He busied himself finding
the music; he knew where it was and what he wanted. He
laid it out caressingly on the piano and bade Basil Maine
proceed. He retired to his chair and stretched out his legs.
On his face was an expression of benignant pleasure, a hint
of a smile, and just a faint hint too of possessiveness. See
what I am providing for you! And what was his interpretation? Did he too lose his detachment? Did that man of

rapier-like intellect travel away into a strange country where
the sentimental, while remaining absurd, acquired a certain
reality and beauty? Such an experience was not beyond his
range.

This social activity at Gordon Square, which also had continuity and development, may be reckoned an ingredient in
Keynes's life no less important than his work at King's
College or his campaigns to influence public opinion. His
feelings for things artistic was maturing; he was educating
himself all the while. When he made his great broadcast on
the Arts Council in 1945,[17] a wide public felt that his words
were inspired and that he spoke from a deep understanding
of the subject. They began to think of him as cast for the
role of leadership in the encouragement and dissemination
of the arts in this austere post-war Britain. He was something
more than an economist; he had a vision of what the good
life should be. His address was entirely different from that
of a man of ready fluency speaking some well-chosen words
appropriate to the subject. Such understanding cannot be
achieved save by a slow process of evolution. He threw himself with his wonted zest into appreciating the thoughts and
feelings of his artistic friends. This was an abiding interest;
it was an integral part of his total activity, and without it his
spirit would have languished.

4

During 1927 the Liberal Committee was making progress
with *Britain's Industrial Future*, commonly known afterwards as the 'Liberal Yellow Book'. Keynes was an active
member of the Committee, which often met for a weekend
at Lloyd George's country home (Churt). This book was a
much weightier document than is usually produced by a
political party; it might almost be said to be a treatise on
political science, written in popular style. It has often since
been used as a textbook in universities, and been widely

17 See ch. 12, 4, below.

studied as affording the best extant programme of action for those who seek the middle way; its ideas have been freely adopted by the parties on either wing.

Keynes's contributions were of central importance. He was able to get endorsement for his ideas on currency management, the stimulation of domestic investment programmes, a public investment board, which would also have regard to the scale of foreign investments, an economic General Staff, greater publicity for the finance of companies, and the encouragement of the semi-public concern as an agency of industrial operation intermediate between the state and private enterprise. While all sections of the book were the product of cooperative work and the committees played their usual role of amending texts line by line, it may be said that Keynes was primarily responsible for the composition of Book II ('The Organization of Business') and of Book V, chapters 28 and 29 ('Currency and Banking and the Reform of the National Accounts'). The Yellow Book appeared in January 1928.

He ventilated some of the proposals embodied in Book II at the Liberal Summer School (Cambridge) in July 1927. The subject was a tricky one. On the one hand he sought to develop the idea, which he had outlined three years earlier in *The End of Laissez-Faire*, that many large-scale undertakings were already semi-socialized in the sense that they paid little regard to maximizing profit and thought mainly of the efficient discharge of a public service. He was in favour, too, of 'rationalization', as in the case of cotton, where there was excess capacity; cartels and trade associations had a useful part to play in the organization of industry. On the other hand there was the evil of monopoly, against which Liberals above all were anxious to be on their guard. How reconcile these apparently conflicting objectives? His main solution for this problem was in publicity. In the case of firms above a certain size the State should have special rights of inquiry into the details of their finance.

He engaged in a certain amount of skirmishing. In November we find him hitting hard in his best polemic style against the Labour Party's proposal for a 'surtax'.[18] At the beginning of 1928 we find him writing, at Lloyd George's request, a confidential forecast of likely economic developments during 1928 for his guidance as a politician.

During 1927 he was much worried about Britain's external balance – a tiny foretaste of what was to come eighteen years later – and he feared that we were increasing our long-term investments abroad largely at the expense of our net liquid position. He wrote an important article on this subject for the *Economic Journal*.[19] He was following the policy of the Federal Reserve System closely and was in correspondence with Mr Bullock, among others, of the Harvard Economic Service.

In January 1928 his old friend Lord Oxford died and he wrote a notice in the *Nation*.[20] In March we find him delighting Winchester schoolboys by an essay on a future, not, he judged, so far distant, when the economic problem would be solved.[21] In the Easter Vacation he went with Lydia to see her relations in Leningrad.

Britain was at this time preparing to reabsorb the Currency notes, first issued by the Treasury in 1914, in the Bank of England. Keynes was disturbed at the official conservatism, which deemed it important to lock up much of the country's gold reserve as a backing for her notes. This was based on obsolete ideas. Control of the monetary system was now essentially control of credit; the legal restriction of the note issue would operate far too late, if considered as a check upon inflation; tying up the gold in this way might

18. This was to be a special tax on unearned income and is not to be confused with the super-tax, which had already been in existence since 1909 and was at that time, to make confusion worse confounded (deliberately?) re-christened surtax. See *Evening Standard*, 22 November 1927.
19. 'The British Balance of Trade 1925–1927', *Economic Journal*, December 1927. See also note in *Economic Journal*, March 1928.
20. 25 February 1928. This was reprinted in *Essays in Biography*.
21. cf. p. 469 below.

impede its use for its proper purpose of evening out discrepancies in the international balance of trade. Meanwhile
the other nations of Europe were being encouraged, in the
supposed interests of the efficient working of the Gold Standard, to have legal reserve requirements against their note
issues. This served to intensify the shortage of gold in the
world, which was already apparent and tending to maintain
deflationary influences. On his way back from Leningrad,
Keynes had talks with Melchior and Dr Schacht on this
subject, and found that they agreed with his views; back in
England he wrote of this to Sir Richard Hopkins, who had
become the fountain-head of Treasury policy, and gave
him a stern warning. He wrote a long article for *The Times*
on this topic,[22] and a note in the *Economic Journal*.[23] Meanwhile, across the Channel the French were recognizing a *fait
accompli* by formal stabilization of the franc. Keynes's prediction had come true.

It is interesting to compare the several fortunes of France and
Great Britain over the post-war period. In Great Britain our
authorities have never talked such rubbish as their French colleagues or offended so grossly against all sound principles of
finance. But Great Britain has come out of the transitional period
with the weight of the war debt aggravated, her obligations to
the United States unabated, and deflationary finance still in the
ascendant, with the heavy burden of taxes appropriate to the
former and a million unemployed as the outcome of the latter.
France, on the other hand, has written down her internal war
debt by four-fifths, and has persuaded her Allies to let her off
more than half of her external debt; and now she is avoiding the
sacrifices of deflation. Yet she has contrived to do this without
the slightest loss of reputation for conservative finance and capitalist principles. The Bank of France emerges much stronger
than the Bank of England; and everyone still feels that France

22. 12 May 1928.
23. June 1928. See also his article in the *Nation*, 19 January 1929,
on the task set the Finance Committee of the League of Nations of
assessing the adequacy of world gold stocks.

is the last stronghold of tenacious saving and the *rentier* mentality. Assuredly it does not pay to be good.

Perhaps we deserve what we have got. France has abandoned principle and consistency alike; but she has always refused sacrifices which were avoidable and has obeyed in the end the teachings of experience. We in England have not submitted either to the warnings of theory or to the pressure of facts, obstinately obedient to conventions.[24]

He was continuing to advocate a policy of capital spending on public account.[25] During the winter the Liberal Party was preparing for the General Election expected in the following spring. The Liberal Committee in Cambridge invited Keynes to stand as a Liberal for the University, and their invitation was supported by a personal plea from Sir Herbert Samuel. Keynes did not feel that this would be a wise course for him. In March the Liberals issued a pamphlet entitled *We Can Conquer Unemployment*, which gave the specific details of a Keynesian programme of public works and pledged the Party to carry it through. Keynes wrote articles in the *Evening Standard*[26] in support of Lloyd George, and finally issued a pamphlet in conjunction with Mr Hubert Henderson entitled *Can Lloyd George Do It?* The answer was naturally in the affirmative. The pamphlet was hailed as a model of lucid persuasion. Keynes composed it himself, but embodied large extracts from the fine leaders which Mr Henderson had written in the *Nation* on this subject. Keynes also presented himself to a crowded meeting of businessmen at the Cannon Street Hotel to be cross-questioned on the finance of the proposals for conquering unemployment. Mr A. M. Asquith (Lord Oxford's son) was in the chair. One question and answer may be quoted.

Q. Has Mr Keynes's opinion of Mr Lloyd George's character changed since 1918? Does he stand by his *Economic Conse-*

24. The *Nation*, 30 June 1928.
25. cf. article on 'How to Organize a Wave of Prosperity', *Evening Standard*, 31 July 1928.
26. 19 March and 19 April 1929.

*quences of the Peace* and hold that all the trouble is the fault
of Mr Lloyd George as the author of the peace?
A. The difference between me and some other people is that I
oppose Mr Lloyd George when he is wrong and support him
when he is right.
This reply was received with loud applause.[27]

In alarm at the gathering support of Lloyd George, the
Government took the unprecedented step of replying to his
proposals in a White Paper. This consisted of memoranda
by Ministers over their initials and an unsigned memorandum entitled 'Memorandum Prepared by the Treasury
under the Direction of the Chancellor of the Exchequer on
the Financial Effect of a Development Loan Programme'.
The *Nation* [28] carried a leader entitled 'A New Sort of White
Paper', while Keynes in his own contribution dealt with the
points of substance in it.

Alas, the hopes of the Liberals were dashed, and only
fifty-nine members were returned. This really marked the
end of Keynes's active public life as a party politician. He
was a member of a brilliant dining-club, consisting mainly of
politicians, not all from one party, and also of men eminent
in other professions. It was a place of good talk and pleasant
intimacy, more worldly in tone than the Bloomsbury gatherings in which he usually found recreation. He made a bet
with Mr Winston Churchill on the outcome of the election,
the consequence of which was the transfer of £20 from the
pocket of Mr Churchill to his. While it may be interesting
to record that our hero's forecast of the election result was
more accurate than that of Mr Churchill, it is disappointing
to find that on the same event he lost £160 to the Stock
Exchange.

Amid these excitements Keynes found time to write an
article on 'The Economic Chaos of Europe, 1919–1922' for a
publication entitled *The Universal History of the World*.[29]

27. *Manchester Guardian*, 29 May 1929.
28. 18 May 1929.
29. Published by the Amalgamated Press Ltd.

Of greater importance was his article in the *Economic Journal* on the German transfer problem.[30] This led to a controversy with Professor Ohlin which ran through the following issues, M. Rueff also contributing. Keynes argued against Ohlin that the burden of such a payment was not measured by the cash involved, but was augmented by the effect of the payment in turning the terms of trade against the paying country. He was interested in this problem not only on account of Germany, but because the arguments were relevant to the effects of undertaking foreign investments upon a country's standard of living. I was reminded of Macaulay's letter, which we had discussed seven years before. He contributed an article to the *Nation*[31] on the report of the Young Committee on a reparations plan to supersede the Dawes plan. 'I am not sure, therefore, that the Young scheme, regarded from a limited technical standpoint, is worth the pains it has cost.' But he threw out the hope that there was just a possibility that the Bank for International Settlements might provide the nucleus 'for the Super-National Currency Authority which will be necessary if the world is ever to enjoy a rational monetary system'.

In the summer of 1929 he was able to get abroad to Geneva, where he gave some lectures to the Geneva School of International Studies. At this time he was honoured by being made Fellow of the British Academy. Somewhat later in the year honours came to him entailing more onerous duties. On 4 November Mr Snowden, the Labour Chancellor of the Exchequer, announced the appointment of a Committee of Inquiry into Finance and Industry, with Lord Macmillan in the chair. Keynes was a member. On 22 January 1930 the Prime Minister announced his decision to set up an Economic Advisory Council as a standing body to report to the Cabinet on economic policy. Keynes was a member of this also. Mr Henderson was appointed to its staff, which involved his giving up the editorship of the

30. March 1929.
31. 15 June 1929.

*Nation*. He was succeeded by Mr Wright; but a year later this paper, which had never achieved solvency, was amalgamated with the *New Statesman*. Keynes came on to the board of the joint paper, and he was delighted to welcome Mr Kingsley Martin as its Editor; his connection with it, however, was much less intimate than that with the *Nation*, and, as the years went on, he fell out of sympathy with its policy.

At this time he lost two dear friends, one of the older generation, C. P. Sanger, who evoked memories of McTaggart and the early days of his membership of the Society, and one of the younger, Frank Ramsey, who, more than any others of the post-war vintage, seemed to embody the intellectual and personal ideals that were cherished in Cambridge at the opening of the century. Keynes contributed an appreciation of Sanger to *The Times* [32] and obituary notices of both to the *Economic Journal*.[33] A longer notice of Ramsey was included in *Essays in Biography*.

Meanwhile a momentous event had occurred, heavy with doom. The collapse of the Stock Exchange in Wall Street not only ruined many Americans; it sent out ripples over the wide world, which did not presently subside, but seemed to grow and gather, as time passed, into mighty waves. The bodies politic and economic of all nations experienced their fury, and there were few events in the following decade which may not be in some part attributed to them, including the rise of the Nazis to power and World War II. Altogether new problems were presented to the contriver of economic welfare. In particular the failure of the Federal Reserve System to check the gathering depression made some monetary reformers wonder whether a wisely managed Central Bank could be as potent for good as they had hoped.

It was to take time, however, for the full tragedy to develop; still longer for the mind to grasp its implications. In

32. 22 February 1930.
33. March 1930.

England experts were slow to diagnose the situation, and many were happy to attribute the evils which began to come upon us in 1930 to the incompetence of a Labour Government. Keynes, however, was quick to see what was happening. On 10 May 1930 he was writing in the *Nation*:

The fact is – a fact not yet recognized by the great public – that we are now in the depths of a very severe international slump, a slump which will take its place in history amongst the most acute ever experienced. It will require not merely passive movements of bank rates to lift us out of a depression of this order, but a very active and determined policy.

He was extremely busy all through this year, as a member of the Macmillan Committee and Economic Advisory Council, endeavouring to guide the nation.

The gathering gloom of the national and world economic situation was relieved by various pleasant events of a more personal character. In the summer he went off to give a lecture in Madrid, and, in order to lift his audience out of the prevailing depression, he took up the thread of his discourse to the Winchester schoolboys and delivered the address which he afterwards published in *Essays in Persuasion*, entitled 'Economic Possibilities for Our Grandchildren'.[34] Another important lecture at this time was that delivered on the Ludwig Mond Foundation at the University of Manchester,[35] on 'The Advisability of Methods other than High Wages as a Means of Improving the Conditions of the Working Class'; he felt that an increase in social services rather than a rise of wages should be the next step in advance. Most important of his contributions during this year was his article in the September issue of the *Svenska Handelsbanken Index* on the future of the rate of interest. He had become convinced that the time was ripe for a large and permanent reduction throughout the world. This was to be the basis of all his future thinking on economic policy;

34. This also appeared in the *Nation* of 11 and 18 October 1930.
35. 7 November 1930.

it also determined his investment policy on his own behalf and that of the institutions which he advised.

Another pleasant event was the announcement in the autumn by the Arts Theatre Club of nine performances to take place in December, starring Lydia Lopokova in *A Masque of Poetry and Music*. On her marriage Lydia did not completely give up dancing. She was appearing in Diaghilev's Ballet in the November season, 1925, and again from time to time in the June–July season of 1926 – she danced in *La Boutique* on the last night. In 1927 she appeared once only, at a gala performance in honour of the King of Spain (15 July). It was impossible to reconcile full membership of the Diaghilev company with her new way of life. A professional must never relax, and she would have had to wander round the world. Who knows whether, if the Vic-Wells Ballet had been in existence and reached some maturity, she would not have continued with full-time dancing in London? But the profession was an extremely laborious one, and her soul may have craved for some rest. She continued with her exercises. I well remember staying at Tilton in those days. There were great thuds and the house shook. What could be happening? It was too continuous for an earthquake, too violent for the pumping of water or other domestic machinery. I came out of my bedroom in alarm. It was Lydia doing her exercises at the top of the staircase.

While Lydia threw herself fully into all her wifely duties, got to know Maynard's friends in his different 'worlds', partook in the gaieties, or sat silent in contented placidity listening to endless conversation with economists, Keynes had the thought that she needed some more positive interest of her own, and at one period a tentative idea began to take shape that she might find her way on to the legitimate English stage. She was an excellent character actress. Language was the main difficulty, since she continued to have a distinctly foreign accent. Out of the charades and other nonsense at the parties at Gordon Square something a little more serious began to emerge. English poetry was sometimes recited. Keynes took infinite pains to coach her in pronunciation and scholarly rendering.

Lydia's friend, Mrs Harold Bowen, issued a piece of pasteboard inviting her friends to an At Home on 9 July 1926, consisting of a supper at 11 p.m. 'followed at midnight by a Tragedy'. This was *L'Amour africain* by Prosper Mérimée, with Lydia in the principal part. Keynes was much excited; he announced that Lydia was about to speak her 'first words on the English stage'. There was a hint that this evening might lead to great developments. But the performance, although enjoyable, did not proceed quite as it should. It was a hot evening; the craftsmanship of the make-up was imperfect; a large false nose worn by Mr Steven Runciman began to melt and had to be cast into the wings; other noses followed. Lydia was dissolved in laughter, and, when it came to her 'first words', she was unable for the moment to proceed.

It was in Dadie Rylands's rooms at Cambridge that a performance of *Comus* was first given, with Rylands and Lydia in the principal parts. This was repeated at an exceptionally grand party one evening in Gordon Square. Lydia had also played in Calderon's *Life's a Dream* at the Cambridge A.D.C. – her first appearance as an actress before a general audience. 'Her performance will remain an exquisite memory for those who have seen it. The precision and point of her gestures, the lithe grace with which every syllable of a delicate voice was subtly accentuated by her whole attitude, are things that deserve to be rescued from devouring Time.'[36] Later she appeared at the A.D.C. in *A Lover's Complaint*. This and *Comus* and some other pieces, including *Dances on a Scotch Theme*, were in the Arts Theatre Club programme. 'Producer: George Rylands. Ballets composed by Frederick Ashton. Music arranged and composed by Constant Lambert.' The audiences had the feeling that they were witnessing something rare and exquisite, graceful and gossamer. Her delicate but lively acting seemed almost

36. *Cambridge Daily News*, 5 November 1929.

to overcome the defects of her English diction. Might she not go forward?

Another interesting event in 1930 was the first performance of the Camargo Ballet Society. A large dinner was given in February to inaugurate the Society, at which Lydia proposed the toast of 'The Guests'. A letter from Mr Bernard Shaw denouncing the party was read aloud:

These people are idiots in business . . . the notion that a dinner can act as a send-off to a ballet season unless they can make the Lord Mayor drunk enough to dance a horn-pipe on the table among the nut-shells is beyond my patience. Intimate the same as violently as you can.

Lydia joined the committee – although she never loved the work.

The first Camargo Society production was in October at the Cambridge Theatre in London. Lydia did not perform but made a graceful speech from the stage, declaring that this was the birth of the British Ballet. The Society planned to give some four productions each year.

Early in 1931 it underwent a financial crisis and – inevitable development – Keynes was asked to take on the treasurership. This he did, and, although there were successive crises, solvency was maintained, and at the end of four years, when the Society ceased to undertake production, valuable assets as well as profits were handed over to the Vic-Wells Ballet, which was now forging ahead. Once an official, Keynes characteristically took a great interest in every detail. Mr Montagu Nathan, the Secretary, recalls an occasion when a performer insisted that her name should be 'billed' at the top of the list. What had he better do? The obvious thing was to consult Keynes. Should they set up a standing 'Billing Committee'? Or should they leave it to the cast to settle these matters among themselves? 'That will be all right,' Keynes replied, 'if you will provide the ambulance.'

Among the productions of the Camargo Society it is

proper to mention that of *Job* by Geoffrey Keynes, May-nard's brother. He had now become a surgeon of the first rank; but he too had time for many things and, among his various literary interests, had made himself our foremost Blake scholar. It occurred to him that Blake's conceptions would form a good setting for a ballet. The décor was executed by the artist Gwen Raverat (*née* Darwin, Mrs Geoffrey Keynes's sister and a friend of the Keyneses from early years), the music was by Vaughan Williams [37] and the choreography by Ninette de Valois. *Job* was subse-quently produced again by the Vic-Wells Ballet.

The final effort of Camargo consisted in two gala per-formances at Covent Garden, on 27 and 29 June 1933, in honour of the World Economic Conference which was tak-ing place at that time, and in the presence of the Queen and other Royalties, Lydia performed in *Coppelia*.

Keynes's efforts to help the arts were not confined to the ballet. Ever since the Degas sale (1917) he had gone from strength to strength as a private collector; he spent much time at sales, concentrating, on the whole, on modern French work. He acquired important paintings and drawings by Cézanne, Seurat, Derain, Picasso. At his death his col-lection was valued at £31,419.

He was responsible for the formation of the London Artists Association. The idea of this was to provide a regular annual income for painters of merit who had not yet achieved sufficient renown to be free from money worries. It also organized one-man shows or mixed exhibitions. If the proceeds exceeded the guaranteed income of members, they obtained the benefit. Keynes himself contributed to the guarantee fund, and also roped in Mr Hindley Smith, Mr Leo Myers the writer, who was a familiar figure in Blooms-bury, and Mr Samuel Courtauld. The last-mentioned was a great friend of Keynes; they had many interests in common, not only in the patronage of the arts, but also in economic matters, sharing as they did a progressive outlook, a belief

37. A cousin of the Darwins.

in the virtues of private initiative, and an acceptance of the fact that the State would have to play a much larger part in the general guidance of the national economy.

5

*A Treatise on Money* appeared in two volumes in December 1930. This great work embodied Keynes's gathered learning and wisdom on the subject of money, which was pre-eminently his own special field. It is rightly called a treatise. It comprises definitions, classifications, long passages of theoretical analysis, historical retrospect, statistical calculations relating to the recent period, and practical recommendations. In part it was the fruit of his thinking in the last five years, but it was more than this, for he had deliberately tried to bring together in these volumes the whole of his wider experience and knowledge in this field. It was the work of a lifetime, not of five years only. It is his most mature work. There is no doubt that, when he wrote it, he hoped that it would remain for long a standard treatise on the subject. It is written in a style appropriate to that view – lucid, sober, judicial. Although there are many amusing touches and his imagination occasionally took flight, as in his famous chapter on '*Auri Sacra Fames*', on the whole he eschewed polemic and wrote in the weighty and dignified manner of an assured master of his subject. The passages which are critical of the work of others have an unwonted suavity. He let his considered words stand with all the weight that was given to them by his unrivalled experience and intellectual power.

This treatise has had bad luck. Since it was published it has been much less widely read than he would have supposed when he wrote it. Keynes's thought about money had two dimensions. He was always widening his scope and bringing more phenomena into relation with his central doctrines; in this respect the *Treatise* is comprehensive. At the same time those doctrines were undergoing a continuous evolution.

From this point of view the book could not give a whole picture of his thought, but only a cross-section of it as it happened to be in 1930. It had not ceased its movement at that date, and indeed never did until he died. It was really impossible for such a man to write a definitive treatise. There is, however, something to be said for the view that the student of the future, if he had to choose among Keynes's works, would get the best picture of his total contribution to economics in the *Treatise*. It is not his last word on his central theme, but it supports that theme by a whole host of characteristic views about all the details of the complex subject of money which are only to be found in this volume. *The General Theory of Employment, Interest and Money*, which he published six years later, carried his thought forward and was concerned not only with money but with wider economic problems, and it adopted a wholly new terminology.

The appearance of the *General Theory* greatly militated against the reading of the *Treatise*. Few have time to read two large works by the same author which cover partly the same ground. Everyone wished to learn his latest thought and not something that was already superseded. The attack in the *General Theory* on certain economic doctrines which lie outside the technical field of money gave it an interest to a wider public. Age-old theories were being overthrown, so it was said; that was an exciting matter. Finally, since both sets of terminology were difficult to understand, many readers, including many serious students, felt dismayed at the idea of reading both books, since they feared getting thereby into a terminological muddle beyond repair. The fact remains that the future student who wishes to get the full measure of Keynes's importance and influence as an economist will not do so unless he reads the *Treatise*.

No attempt will be made here to summarize its contents since that would mean covering the whole field of money in all its rich detail. The book does not lend itself to summary, as its author does not waste words. Attention will be confined to the central point of doctrine, which he claimed to be a novelty, and to the practical proposals.

The central doctrine rested upon a distinction between what he called Investment, the meaning of which is equivalent to what is usually called capital outlay, on the one hand, and Saving on the other. The decisions to undertake capital outlay are made by one vast class of people in the community and the decisions to save by another. Saving provides the wherewithal of capital outlay, and the old doctrine undoubtedly has it that the savings of individuals will normally find their way into capital outlay, so that the total volume of capital outlay will be equal to that of saving. Keynes held that these two need not be equal, that if Investment was running ahead of Saving, conditions of boom or inflation would supervene, while, conversely, if Saving was running ahead of Investment there would be depression and unemployment.

An objector might raise the point that the old school did not necessarily hold that all saving would flow into capital outlay, since some of it may be put away in a stocking. If this was done, saving would exceed capital outlay. It was Keynes's contention, which was both a novelty and source of endless confusion among commentators, that a tendency for saving to exceed investment had nothing whatever to do with people putting money into a stocking or even with their leaving it idle in a bank account. Saving might exceed investment even if all savers immediately invested their money in industrial securities, and investment might exceed saving even if a great many savers were putting their money into stockings.

That sounds surprising. For a demonstration of the proposition readers must go to the *Treatise*. After it was published there were many who, thinking that they were expounding the wisdom of Keynes himself, explained how savings might run to waste by people putting them into a stocking or holding them idle at the bank instead of investing them. All that, right or wrong, had nothing what-

ever to do with Keynes's doctrine. In his view, the total of
investment and the total of savings were respectively the
effects of the decisions of different groups of people and
there was nothing to bring them into line. If investment
exceeded saving, we should have an inflationary tendency,
and conversely. Here was a conclusion which, if correct, had
an immediate bearing on practice. If the community was
suffering from depression and unemployment, this must
be due to an excess of saving and it would be expedient
to encourage investment or discourage saving; and again
conversely. This opened up quite new lines of thought.
Hitherto the economist, as such, had tended to encourage
economy and thrift in all circumstances. If Keynes's doctrine
was correct, it was most desirable to do so in times of in-
cipient inflation – but not at all times. On the contrary, in
times of depression and unemployment it was desirable to
encourage spending and lavishness. This clearly implied a
radical change of outlook. It was of no little relevance in
1930, when the world was suffering from unprecedented depression and unemployment. The old-fashioned reaction to
hard times – and depression was certainly a form of hard
times – was an increased dose of virtue, namely, more thrift
and economy. This was the attitude which the authorities
were still likely to take, and did take shortly after the book
was published. If Keynes's analysis was correct, this was
bound to intensify the depression and make matters worse.

We must pursue the analysis further. If investment was
running ahead of saving, prices would tend to rise, and
again conversely. This must be briefly explained. Money
income is earned by those who produce consumer goods
and those who produce capital goods. Only the former
goods come forward for purchase by consumers. If all who
earned money spent all they had, savings then being nil,
all the money earned, whether from the production of consumer goods or that of capital goods, would be applied to
the purchase of consumer goods; thus more money would
be applied in their purchase than had been earned in their

production and their prices would rise accordingly, standing above their costs of production by an amount equal to the whole cost of the capital goods. The same would be true, in less degree, if all earners together spent more in sum total than what had been earned in the production of consumer goods, which would mean that they saved less than the cost of the investment goods. This is more clearly seen in the case of war, where production of the sinews of war is analogous to the production of capital goods, since those who produce them earn money, but no corresponding set of goods comes on to the market for them to spend their earnings on. When there is over-saving, prices fall, and the excess savings of the thrifty, instead of finding vent in capital outlay, merely serve – by bringing about a fall of prices – to enlarge the consumption of those less thrifty.

Thus thrift may be a virtue or a vice according to whether the society is tending towards inflation or depression and unemployment. Broadly through history Keynes did not think that thrift had been the major virtue.

It has been usual to think of the accumulated wealth of the world as having been painfully built up out of that voluntary abstinence of individuals from the immediate enjoyment of consumption, which we call Thrift. But it should be obvious that mere abstinence is not enough by itself to build cities or drain fens. The abstinence of individuals need not increase accumulated wealth; – it may serve instead to increase the current consumption of other individuals. Thus the thrift of a man may lead either to an increase of capital-wealth or to consumers getting better value for their money. There is no telling which, until we have examined another economic factor.

Namely, Enterprise. It is enterprise which builds and improves the world's possessions. Now, just as the fruits of thrift may go to provide either capital accumulation or an enhanced value of money-income for the consumer, so the outgoings of enterprise may be found either out of thrift or at the expense of the consumption of the average consumer. Worse still; – not only may thrift exist without enterprise, but as soon as thrift gets ahead of enterprise, it positively discourages the recovery of enterprise and sets up a vicious circle by its adverse effect on profits. If Enterprise is afoot, wealth accumulates whatever may be happening to Thrift; and if Enterprise is asleep, wealth decays whatever Thrift may be doing.

Thus, Thrift may be the handmaid and nurse of Enterprise. But equally she may not. And, perhaps, even usually she is not. For enterprise is connected with thrift not directly but at one remove; and the link which should join them is frequently missing. For the engine which drives Enterprise is not Thrift, but Profit.

This analysis, in its broadest terms, was not very difficult to grasp, and has since been widely understood throughout the world. I believe that most people understand the terminology of the *Treatise* better than that of the *General Theory*, the idea of investment running ahead of savings or savings running ahead of investment being readily intelligible, and also their application to practice. It is necessary, however, that we should dwell on the definitions of saving and investment more carefully. There are, unhappily, pitfalls. The plain man may raise the question, What happens to the savings? If they are put in a stocking he can understand that; but he is expressly told that that was not what Keynes meant and that a depression would occur even if the excess savings were invested in industrial securities. Where do these excess savings get to?

Now it has to be admitted that in the pure book-keeping sense, from the point of view of one who keeps the national accounts, total capital outlay must be equal to total savings. This is the standpoint adopted by Keynes himself in the later volume. He recognized this book-keeping truism in the earlier volume also, and he came to the idea of a possible divergence between the total volume of investment and the total volume of savings by providing a rather fanciful definition of saving. Or is it the book-keeping definition that is really fanciful? He excluded from saving what may be called excess profit and did not deduct from it business losses. Excess profit is defined as such profit as causes the producer to increase output, and loss is defined as the difference between what he actually gets and what he would have to get in order to make him willing not to decrease output; if loss in this sense occurs, he decreases his operations in the next round. Thus if we add excess profit to saving, we get the book-keeping identity that investment is equal to saving, and if we deduct realized loss from saving the remainder is equal to investment. Keynes's reason for segregating this particular item of income (or loss) is that it is the dynamic element which causes the economy to move towards expansion and inflation on the one hand or depression and deflation on the other. It seems quite reasonable to distinguish between savings which arise in the ordinary prudent conduct of business life by an individual or a company and those savings which are windfall, unexpected, and the result of a disequilibrium in the economy. The notion of a discrepancy between the volume of investment and the volume of savings undertaken from ordinary motives in the ordinary way may be defended as valid and valuable; to those interested in book-keeping it can be pointed out that the deficiency of saving, as compared with capital outlay, is made up from another source, viz. windfall savings.

This analysis should make it plain why the question of whether individual savers invest their savings in securities or leave them idle at the bank (or in a stocking) is irrelevant. Taking the deflationary case, businesses will be making losses and these must entail a reduction in their cash balances or their portfolio of securities. (It is part of the doctrine that businessmen cannot make good such losses by cutting down consumption, for if some of them do this, it will merely lead to a corresponding increase in the aggregate of business losses, owing to this additional withdrawal of purchasing power from the market for consumption goods. The loss which has to be made good by the reduction of bank balances or the sale of securities remains equal – whatever the entrepreneurs may do about their private consumption

– to the difference between investment and saving in the whole economy.) Thus if the savers buy securities, this does not ensure that real capital outlay will be undertaken, since their action will be counteracted by the sale of securities of an equivalent amount by businesses which are making losses. It is not necessary to go into a minute examination of whether individual excess savers divide their savings between bank balances and the purchase of securities in the same proportion that businesses making losses divide those losses between a reduction of cash holdings and a sale of securities.[38] Keynes made the supremely important point that the effect of any discrepancy here will be swamped by the fact that the whole body of capitalists, all the savers of the past as well as the new savers, are continually adjusting their holding of securities of different types, equity and fixed interest, long and short, and the sizes of their bank balances, by reference to market conditions. In view of the large size of the total market by comparison with the size of new savings, what the new savers choose to do with their money is a relatively unimportant point, making but a negligible contribution to the total result. This is a key matter in Keynes's theory: the way that shifts in the desires of the whole body of capitalists, in regard to the kinds of assets they wish to hold, influence market valuations is analysed in lengthy passages. It is true that the reader may have some uneasiness as to whether Keynes did in the *Treatise* completely clear up discrepancies between the passage in which he analyses the forces determining the value of securities and that in which he analyses the forces determining the value of physical capital goods. This is a matter dealt with in important sections of the *General Theory*, in relation to what in that volume he names the theory of liquidity preference; it is more convenient to leave the discussion of this topic until we come to the *General Theory*. It should be

38. Some critics attempted to do this and became involved in sophistications about who got through to their brokers on the telephone first.

noted, however, that the greater part of the doctrine of the *General Theory* on liquidity preference is to be found quite clearly set out in the *Treatise*.[39]

This account has constituted but the barest summary of the quintessence of a doctrine, which is developed in great detail, and with regard to a large variety of possible circumstances, over hundreds of pages. Keynes was fully alive to the subtle complications of the real world. Comment tended too much to concentrate upon the spot-lit formula without having mastered fully the lengthy analysis which followed it. Keynes provided a much more extensive discussion of the applications and limitations of his doctrine in the *Treatise* than he gave in the *General Theory*.

It is beyond the scope of this work to assess the amount of originality that may be claimed for the central doctrine of the *Treatise*. Students of the trade cycle had long attributed causal significance to fluctuations in 'investment'. There had been theories of over-investment, under-consumption, under-saving. Keynes claimed that his theory was radically different from those, in that it made the crucial influence the *disparity* between investment and saving; for this he claimed originality. In this matter Knut Wicksell, to whom he paid tribute, came nearest to him; there is no doubt that the process of thought by which Keynes reached his conclusions was independent, and not derived from the study of Wicksell. To Mr D. H. Robertson, on the other hand, he was definitely in debt. In *The Banking Policy and the Price Level* there is an analysis of precisely this point, the discrepancy between capital outlay and saving, or, as Robertson called it, 'lacking'. Robertson, however, was not able to accept the full *Treatise* doctrine.[40]

It clearly followed from the theory that the objective of

39. Very clearly also in his rejoinder to Mr D. H. Robertson's article on the *Treatise*, *Economic Journal*, September 1931.

40. Keynes knew (cf. *Treatise*, p. 171, n.) of *The Final Buyer*, 1928, by A. H. Abbati, which contained similar ideas (cf. also *Unclaimed Wealth*, 1924, by this interesting pioneer).

policy should be to ensure that investment was kept as nearly equal to saving as possible; this would entail a stable price-level. Keynes had a soft spot for the idea that, in order that the economy should be progressive, there is something to be said for a slight excess of investment with a corresponding gentle upward trend of prices. None the less, in view of the great difficulties of getting any good policy adopted and of the need for having definite rules of action for the various authorities concerned, he deemed it better to keep to the clear objective of a stable price-level. A single nation may have great difficulty in doing this, if the rest of the world is not converted, and indeed even if it is. Changes affecting the natural flow of investment and saving may differ widely from country to country, and this will make it difficult to harmonize the maintenance of a single world-wide standard of value with the various policies required in different places to keep investment and saving level. He still thought that in existing circumstances the attempt to maintain an international standard was too ambitious, and he summarized the arguments in much the same way as in the *Tract*.

It is evident that the main effect of an international gold standard (or any other international standard) is to secure *uniformity* of movement in different countries – everyone must conform to the average behaviour of everyone else. The advantage of this is that it prevents individual follies and eccentricities. The disadvantage is that it hampers each Central Bank in tackling its own national problems, interferes with pioneer improvements of policy the wisdom of which is ahead of average wisdom, and does nothing to secure either the short-period or the long-period optimum if the average behaviour is governed by blind forces such as the total quantity of gold, or is haphazard and without any concerted or deliberate policy behind it on the part of the Central Banks as a body.

Since the publication of the *Tract* most of the world had returned to the Gold Standard and in the *Treatise* Keynes accordingly wrote as follows:

On a balance of these various considerations, it seemed, before the *de facto* return to the Gold Standard, that there were better prospects for the management of a national currency on progressive lines, if it were to be freed from the inconvenient and sometimes dangerous obligation of being tied to an unmanaged international system; that the evolution of independent national systems with fluctuating exchange rates would be the next step to work for; and that the linking up of these again into a managed international system would probably come as the last stage of all.

Today the reasons seem stronger – in spite of the disastrous inefficiency with which the international gold standard has worked since its restoration five years ago (fulfilling the worst fears and gloomiest prognostications of its opponents), and the economic losses, second only in amount to those of a great war, which it has brought upon the world – to reverse the order of procedure; to accept, substantially, the *fait accompli* of an international standard; and to hope for progress from that starting-point towards a scientific management of the central controls – for that is what our monetary system surely is – of our economic life. For to seek the ultimate good *via* an autonomous national system would mean not only a frontal attack on the forces of conservatism, entrenched with all the advantages of possession, but it would divide the forces of intelligence and goodwill and separate the interests of nations.

I am disposed to conclude, therefore, that if the various difficulties in the way of an internationally managed Gold Standard – to which the Resolutions of the Genoa Conference of 1922 first pointed the way – could be overcome within a reasonable period of time, then the best practical objective might be the management of the value of gold by a Supernational Authority, with a number of national monetary systems clustering round it, each with a discretion to vary the value of its local money in terms of gold within a range of (say) 2 per cent.

Some local freedom of action must be allowed.

It is on some such assumptions as these as to what the International Gold Standard ought to mean, that accusations are sometimes made against the United States or against France, that they are breaking the rules of the 'Gold Standard game', when in recent times they have, for purely local and domestic reasons, chosen to pursue a credit policy which attracted large quantities of gold to their vaults without allowing this influx materially to modify their policy. Yet it may be too much to expect that these countries will voluntarily sacrifice what they believe to be their own interests, in order to pursue a credit policy which would suit certain other countries better. I shall argue, therefore, in what follows, that the solution is to be sought, not by making such demands, but by arranging some compromise in virtue of which adherence to an international standard is combined in a regular and legitimate way with a reasonable measure of local autonomy over the rate of foreign lending. To this objective – which is one that each country must work out in detail for itself – we will now direct our attention.

In order to secure some freedom of movement he reverted to his plan outlined in the *Tract* of widening the margin between the gold points. This would make it possible to maintain the Gold Standard while having different effective rates of interest in the different countries, in accordance with what was required in each to balance saving and investment.

By the time that the *Treatise* was published he had already reached his view that the rate of interest was due to have a worldwide decline. In the *Treatise* he used the expression 'natural' rate of interest – which he later rejected – to designate that rate which would keep investment level with saving.

Thus I am lured on to the rash course of giving an opinion on contemporary events which are too near to be visible distinctly; namely, my view of the root causes of what has happened, which is as follows.

The most striking change in the investment factors of the postwar world compared with the pre-war world is to be found in the high level of the market-rate of interest. As a rough generalization one may say that the long-term rate of interest is nearly 50 per cent higher today than twenty years ago. Yet the population of the industrial countries is not increasing as fast as formerly, and is a good deal better equipped per head than it was with housing, transport and machines. On the other hand, the volume of lending to the less advanced parts of the world is not markedly large – indeed the contrary, since Russia, China and India, which include within their borders a substantial proportion of the population of the world, are able, for one reason or another, to borrow next to nothing on the international markets; whilst the United States has converted itself from a borrowing to a lending country. Why, then, should the rate of interest be so high?

The answer is, I suggest, that for some years after the war sundry causes, to be enumerated, interposed to maintain the natural-rate of interest at a high level; that these, more recently, have ceased to operate; that sundry other causes have nevertheless maintained the market-rate of interest; and that, consequently, there has now developed, somewhat suddenly, an unusually wide gap between the ideas of borrowers and those of lenders, that is, between the natural-rate of interest and the market-rate.

. . . I am bold to predict, therefore, that to the economic historians of the future the slump of 1930 may present itself as the death struggle of the war-rates of interest and the re-emergence of the pre-war rates.

There is a long passage discussing whether Central Banks alone could achieve the objective of a stable price-level (i.e. an equality of saving and investment). He had doubts, and quoted with respect the testimony of Governor Strong of the Federal Reserve Bank of New York to a Congressional Committee which was considering a project for making the Federal Reserve System legally responsible for keeping prices stable. On the whole he was more optimistic than Strong, but fully appreciated the magnitude of the difficulties.

This was a treatise on money and banking policy and not, therefore, the proper place for a full discussion of Public Works and the direct Government stimulation of capital outlay, which, however, got a passing mention on page 376, as a 'weapon by which a country can partially rescue itself when its international disequilibrium is involving it in severe unemployment . . . In such a case it is not sufficient for the Central Authority to stand ready to lend . . . the Government must itself promote a programme of domestic investment.'

The *Treatise* is capped by a proposal for a Supernational Central Bank.[41] This is somewhat more ambitious than the institution which he succeeded in getting approved at Bretton Woods fourteen years later.

## 6

Keynes had luck with his official commissions. He was invited to serve on the Indian Currency Commission immediately after completing his book on that topic. And now he had to serve on the Macmillan Committee on Finance and Industry after four years of intensive work on the central problems of money and finance and when his large treatise was about to appear. Thus in each case he had a great initial advantage. The discussions of the Macmillan Committee, which proceeded during 1930, reached a high intellectual level. It had distinguished members, such as Reginald McKenna, a progressive, whose own views were close to those of Keynes and who gave him constant support; Mr Brand, a little more cautious, but with an intellectual apprehension unusual in a banker; Professor T. E. Gregory, not prepared to accept Keynesian doctrine, but finding much common ground as a scientific student of money and finance; the Chairman himself, Lord Macmillan, a distinguished and thoughtful lawyer; and Mr Ernest Bevin, who brought his great sagacity and wide experience to the deliberations and played an important part. The others, too, made valuable contributions to the debate. They were able men; none the less, the fact that they went so deeply into their problem, seeming to transform themselves at times into a university seminar, was partly due to Keynes's extraordinary easy manner of clothing recondite theory in language intelligible to the layman, and his pleasant, intimate way of coaxing them into intricate discussions, appealing to their best faculties, treating them as his equals and making them feel at home in the world of academic subtleties. It was the ob-

41. cf p. 484 above.

verse of his power of making university students feel at home amid the arcana of practical finance.

The outstanding point that must be noted about these deliberations, which led to publication in June 1931, was that it did not seem worth considering at any length the alternative of abandoning the Gold Standard – so great was the awful respect in which it was held. Yet only three months later it was in fact abandoned. Keynes, if anyone, would have pushed for this solution, if there had been the remotest chance of its acceptance in practice; he did not lack courage; he had devoted several years to strenuous opposition to our return to it. Other venerable institutions, as we shall see, were questioned by this Committee, but not the Gold Standard! It is fair to add that Keynes held that there were reasons of substance, quite apart from public opinion, for adhering to the standard once we had returned to it. There was the question of world-wide confidence in the London market, and the implicit pledge that the balances held there were redeemable at par in gold.

Public proceedings opened with the examination of the Chairmen of the Joint Stock Banks and other banking experts. It was a dreary business. It was not only that these eminent practical men could not debate Keynes's latest theories; they seemed to be unaware of elementary textbook doctrines about banking which had been current for decades and were familiar to the merest tyro in economics or journalism. They took a narrow view of their duties and had no conception of their relation to wider questions of economic policy.

After a good deal of this sort of thing, it appeared to the Committee that Keynes, who had been sounding them in language sometimes lucid and clearly to the point, at other times full of mysterious and recondite hints, should be given the opportunity to state his views at leisure. The Committee arranged that he should do so at a series of informal private meetings. His evidence went on for five days.[42] It was one

42. 20, 21, 28 February, 6 and 7 March 1930.

of his great occasions, and may remind us of that other allocution, delivered fifteen years later, when he was pleading with the Americans for a loan. On both occasions he was speaking from very full knowledge, and on both it seemed to him to be of crucial importance that he should carry his point. In 1930 he had been for some six years trying to persuade the country to adopt a certain line of policy, and so far he had made no headway. If this distinguished Committee reported more or less in his sense, it might make all the difference. He was not unsuccessful. The following interchange occurred at the close of the fourth day:

MR KEYNES. I am afraid that a discussion of this sixth class of remedy has led me over a somewhat wide field. I still have my seventh class, which I have not reached, but it might be well to break off what I have to say to you at this point.

CHAIRMAN. We hardly notice the lapse of time when you are speaking.

MR MCKENNA. Extraordinarily interesting!

CHAIRMAN. We must not put too much strain upon you.

On the first day he developed his central theme within what might be called the limits of orthodoxy. The prime weapon in monetary management was the Bank Rate – and the rates in interest associated with it – and this had a short-term and a long-term effect. Its short-term effect in redressing a disequilibrium of foreign payments had been tested in practical experience and had been triumphantly successful. It operated through its influence on short-term international lending. But this only produced a temporary remedy; if the country's external trade was tending to be permanently out of balance, some further remedy was needful. This too came through the Bank Rate. It was a beautiful mechanism with its double working. It promoted long-run equilibrium by causing a rise or fall of prices at home, thus stimulating imports and discouraging exports, or conversely, as the case might be. Not enough attention, however, had been paid to precisely how this came about. He took the case of an adverse balance of trade. High interest rates led to a contraction of credit, the restriction of capital outlay, a consequent falling off in buying power and a fall in prices; for a time some businesses could carry on at a loss, but a real adjustment could not come until costs had been reduced into line with prices. Unemployment would continue to grow, until employers could secure a general reduction of money wage rates. But wages were very sticky, and severe unemployment and disequilibrium might remain for a long time. This long-term effect of the rate of interest worked quite smoothly when it was a question of a favourable balance and an upward adjustment of prices and costs; difficulties arose when a downward adjustment of costs was needed; owing to our position in the world and the general expansion, during the last eighty years no big downward adjustment had been required, save for the altogether exceptional occasion of the end of World War I; it was important for them to understand that the mechanism on which we had come to place our exclusive reliance could only produce a downward adjustment through severe unemployment leading to cuts in money wages. The ten per cent reduction in costs required by our return to the old gold parity in 1925 had itself put an intolerable strain on the system and now, with the world slump in prices, worse was to come.

On the second day he expounded to the Committee his doctrine of saving and investment. Applying that to existing circumstances, he explained that interest rates in Britain could not fall below the world level. If we reduced our rates, more capital would be tempted abroad than could be financed by our excess of exports over imports, we should be subjected to a drain of gold, and the gold standard would be in jeopardy. Thus a certain rate of interest was required to maintain external equilibrium, and that was higher than that rate which was needed to provoke sufficient investment in Britain, to make home investment, when added to foreign investment, equal to saving. That was the impasse for which the Committee had to find remedies.

It is to be observed that Keynes laid all his stress on the reason for the high domestic rate being because we had to keep in line with the world rate. There was no hint that it was kept too high by those forces which he afterwards summarized in what he called the 'liquidity preference', in spite of the fact that his theory of liquidity preference received a fully fledged exposition (in substance though not in name) in the *Treatise*. He had propounded the theory but he had not yet tumbled to its full implications; in the following testimony he ignored it:

If we were an isolated community, the rate of interest would always tend to fall to the yield of the next thing which was worth doing. If new investments could afford to pay a rate which was 3 per cent on the cost of production, then 3 per cent would become the prevailing rate for money; but if we are not in the closed system, then we are in a dilemma, because we must keep our rate of interest at a figure which prevents our foreign lending from exceeding our available balance of exports.

It is to be observed also that he propounded to the Committee what is known as the 'pump-priming' theory of public works. He did not envisage a chronic tendency for investment to fall below saving.

Government investment will break the vicious circle. If you can do that for a couple of years, it will have the effect, if my diagnosis is right, of restoring business profits more nearly to normal, and if that can be achieved, then private enterprise will be revived. I believe you have first of all to do something to restore profits and then rely on private enterprise to carry the thing along.

Towards the end of the second day the Chairman remarked that a cure, rather than a palliative, was needed. Was there any cure on the economic side? 'You are keeping us in suspense; you are a complete dramatist. At the moment the remedies have not been unfolded; I suppose they will be on Friday next?'

On the Friday and two later days he proceeded with the remedies, which it is convenient to leave over for a moment.

Shortly after that, they had a witness of greater distinction and power than the Bank Chairmen, the Governor of the Bank of England, Mr Montagu Norman. Now at last they had someone who could discuss their problems in an intelligent way. He had finesse and polish and a much higher level of understanding of general problems than the Joint Stock bankers.

At an early stage the Committee subjected him to criticism for the return to the Gold Standard at the high parity. Keynes could afford to sit back now; the others were making his case admirably. He reserved his fire. Although Mr Norman made a good defence, Keynes was sure that he was not convincing his listeners. Keynes's chief intervention came later and concerned the *modus operandi* of the Bank Rate. He briefly recapitulated what he had told the Committee, setting out with stark brutality the view that the long-period effect could only be achieved by creating unemployment. Mr Norman was more concerned with the short effect and the international relation of rates. Keynes pressed him on the long effect, and Norman replied, 'I should imagine that, as you have stated it, that is the orthodox theory',[43] and again, 'Applied to a long period, I should agree with it.' *Keynes*: 'So it is of the essence of the case that the Bank Rate should have an important effect; that when it is raised it should have an effect in the direction of unemployment. That is what you want. Am I right?' *Mr Norman*: 'Yes, I should think it was. . . .' There was a certain aloofness in the answers and an implication that this long effect was not his business. Keynes, when inveighing against our system, as he often did, on the ground that, on the orthodox view of it, it could only work by creating unemployment from time to time, could

43. *Minutes of Evidence*, vol. i, p. 216.

now bear it in mind that no less a man than Mr Norman
had endorsed this view of orthodoxy.

Mr Bevin took up the attack. He had listened to Keynes's
proposed remedies, which involved using various devices to
maintain a stiff rate for foreign borrowers and lenders, while
making a lower effective rate available for domestic borrowers. He asked Mr Norman if something of this sort could
be done. Mr Norman was intransigent. 'I believe it is absolutely impossible to have two separate policies. I can see no
practical way in which that could be done.'[44] Thus, this way
out of the unemployment problem was blocked. Mr Norman
did not seem apologetic for having to sponsor such a ruthless
system; he showed no sympathy for what Mr Bevin was
driving at. He had stated how things were, and that was
that.

On a later occasion he appeared before the Committee to
explain the activities of the Bankers' Industrial Development Company and the Securities Management Trust. He
hoped that these would do useful work in helping us through
our present difficulties; he conceived that their work should
be accomplished within five years. The Macmillan Committee had heard expressions of opinions from its own members and from witnesses that existing facilities for capital
issues were inadequate to meet the needs of small businesses
or new businesses. Eventually it devoted a chapter of its
Report to this subject, and existing inadequacies were thereafter often referred to as 'the Macmillan gap.' Mr Norman
gave no support to this view. In this matter he was quite
complacent, claiming that the vast resources of the City
were adequate; if the capital required was too small for an
established issue house, it could be obtained through brokers.
Nothing was to be gained by the recommendations that the
Committee had in mind. Thus, this door too was closed.
With reference to the Bankers' Industrial Development
Company, Mr Bevin asked whether, in the case of rationalization schemes, they had expert guidance on the labour

44. ibid., p. 217.

problems involved. No; that was not their business; they looked to private enterprise to deal with that. Mr Bevin pointed out that great upheavals of labour might be required. Mr Norman did not contemplate any trouble under this head. Mr Bevin, speaking from his wide experience, affirmed knowledge of cases where rationalization had been rendered nugatory by insufficient regard for the labour problem. It had been Mr Bevin's experience in both the schemes he had had to deal with. Mr Norman contented himself with monosyllables: 'It has not been mine.' So much for Mr Bevin.

In giving evidence on international cooperation and the early work of the Bank for International Settlements, Mr Norman showed his best powers. He gave a sophisticated and convincing account of what was on foot. He appeared to be genuinely enthusiastic for international cooperation, while evincing a statesmanlike appreciation of the difficulties and the need for slow progress. The Committee had been hoping that a remedy for the slump might be found in concerted action by the Central Banks designed to raise the world price-level. Mr Norman gave a warning; considerations of the general price-level were not yet within the philosophy of the Central Bankers who met. Their objective would be more restricted. Thus Mr Norman closed all the doors. It did not seem to occur to him that, considering existing levels of unemployment, this amounted to a damning indictment of the system for which he was responsible.

His object appeared to be to prevent the Committee from recommending novelties. He knew quite well that he could do nothing with Keynes. He may have hoped that his urbanity and his sophisticated and polished exposition would deter the others. His *insouciant* treatment of Mr Bevin showed that he did not appreciate the strength of the forces which would in due course be too powerful to be resisted by the complacent conservatism of international bankers. To the tough logic of Mr Bevin's mind it appeared clear that the Gold Standard was doomed. Although he signed the majority report, which implied its continuance, he made a reservation, greatly daring as an amateur, along with Sir Thomas Allen, which clearly showed the direction of his thought. His experience on that Committee made him an implacable opponent of the Gold Standard thereafter, and wary even of the compromise effected at Bretton Woods. Keynes, for the moment, had the harder task of trying to prise open all those doors which, according to Mr Norman, were firmly bolted, so that the Committee could make recommendations for reviving employment without jeopardizing the Gold Standard.

In the long column of witnesses who came before the Committee Keynes was confronted with an adversary who was a greater man than Mr Montagu Norman. It was needful for the Committee to obtain the views of the British Treasury itself; in particular it sought elucidation of the alleged Treasury view that public works – for which Keynes was pressing hard – merely diverted capital which would otherwise have given employment through private channels. Sir Richard Hopkins was the Treasury spokesman. The reader will remember the White Paper issued as a counterblast to Lloyd George's programme and the fact that it contained an unsigned Treasury memorandum. A reference was made to this. Sir Richard Hopkins assured the Committee that the Treasury had never had a hard and fast dogma on this subject; the memorandum had been addressed to the criticism of a particular scheme. But he also made it plain that he was opposed to the kind of large scheme which Keynes was known to be advocating.

Sir Richard's testimony was a great masterpiece. As a loyal Civil Servant he had to tread warily. He must not let down the former Chancellor who had authorized the memorandum; he must not let down the existing Chancellor who was responsible for a strictly limited scheme of public works, by which the existing Labour Government was going a certain way along the road, although not so fast as the dynamic Sir Oswald Mosley was trying to push them. He was speaking for the Treasury in words destined for publication, an unwonted role. The Treasury was a favourite subject of obloquy, and the public would seize on any scrap of evidence to justify its hostility. Sir Richard hinted at this jungle of limitations under which he gave evidence, not by any elaborate clauses or circumlocutions, but quite without fuss, by a word or a nuance. And, in spite of all these limitations, he gave the Committee the impression, which was no doubt a true one, that he was saying precisely and exactly what he himself thought, neither more nor less.

Mr Norman's negatives were cold, aloof and relentless; if Sir Richard took a negative line, he did so ruefully and under the impelling dictate of practical experience and hard thinking. Mr Norman's negatives appeared final, Sir Richard's provisional; one had the sense that the latter's mind was alive to the issues, ready to be convinced in due course, if possible, although not likely to be in the least impressed by the dialectics of a committee meeting.

Keynes and Hopkins soon became locked in a tense combat. Every muscle was taut, every move guarded against; displacement by an inch might give victory to one side or the other. Their styles of debate could not have been more contrasted. Keynes was ever agile, seeking one method of attack after another, driving his arguments to their logical conclusion, endeavouring to impale his adversary on the horns of a dilemma; Hopkins stood firm upon his sense of the practical, crisp in his vocabulary, not taking his listeners along a chain of reasoning, insisting on the multitude of relevant imponderables and the unfitness of logical deduction to determine the issue. He admitted that his position was incapable of formal definition. Keynes complained of the Treasury view that 'it bends so much that I find difficulty in getting hold of it'. Yet I think that Hopkins had made his audience understand his position exactly. At one stage he appealed to the Chairman for protection; he probably did not lose a point thereby, for he chose a moment when the audience would be feeling that Keynes was pressing him unfairly.

In due course they came apart, and Lord Macmillan gave his judicial summary – 'I think we may characterize it as a drawn battle'. It is always rash to indulge in a negative generalization, but I do not recall another occasion on which Keynes, in the plenitude of his power, arguing on his own chosen subject, was not deemed by a good judge to have had somewhat the better of the argument. If this is so, Hopkins has a unique distinction in his generation.

In one respect Keynes was labouring under a handicap – or perhaps it is fair to say that they both were. Keynes could not deploy his full case in the argument; he could not repeat to Hopkins the explanation of his theory of saving and investment which he had already furnished to the Committee; the *Treatise* had not yet appeared. Hopkins promised to read it when it did. In doubting the wisdom of a large-scale programme, Hopkins laid emphasis on two things. One was that, if the scheme was generally judged to be uneconomic and unsound, confidence in Britain would flag, domestic private capital outlay would be reduced, and more capital would tend to flow abroad. His other main point was concerned with the immobility of labour and materials; a scheme might give considerable employment to certain specific types of labour, create labour shortages at certain points while producing relatively minor effects elsewhere; it would also cause shortages of specific materials and bottle-necks. But he did also admit that another consideration weighed with him. If these works were not to divert capital from private employment, where was the extra capital to come from? He ungrudgingly conceded Keynes's favourite points about the saving on the unemployment dole, the transfer of idle deposits into activity, the gain to the Exchequer from a higher level of income, etc. Some part of the extra capital needed would no doubt be forthcoming in this way, but he remained anxious as to whether all this added up to enough. In Keynes's mind this addition sum left out the principal contribution, namely, that which would come from the reduction of business losses consequent upon the extra investment. He could not throw this into the argument. It would be of no use to assure Hopkins in the Committee at that juncture that the release of extra capital by the reduction of business losses would, nay, by his theory, must, make the total enough to finance public works to the extent he desired. Hopkins could not be expected to understand about the business losses or to have any notion as to whether a reduction in them – which he would no doubt have been prepared to admit – would have been sufficient in quantity to make a material difference. He certainly could not have admitted there and then that they *must* be of sufficient quantity. If it would have been in vain to bring in such an argument *ad hoc* in order to convince Hopkins, *a fortiori* it would be in vain to use it to convince a well-informed public pending the publication of the *Treatise*. Thus, this classic debate with Hopkins brings out in a very clear way how needful those five years' work upon the *Treatise* had been, both to clarify Keynes's own ideas and to convince others.

Later in the year Keynes was again asked to state his views. He developed further the proposals which he had made earlier, having regard to what had been learnt meanwhile, but confining himself this time to the strict terms of reference of the Committee – that is, excluding public works and such matters. Most of his proposals were adopted by the Committee, and it may perhaps be added that its most interesting proposals were in his evidence. He does not appear, however, to have convinced his colleagues of the need for a larger spread between the gold points and for fixing official forward rates. He laid great stress on the need for the banks to exert influence on the long-term rate of interest, and in this connection stated his 'liquidity preference theory' very clearly.[45] He was anxious that the Bank

45. See p. 540 below.

should strengthen its reserve, and proposed a substantial credit from the Federal Reserve System for this purpose.

He played a big part in the drafting of the Report. His scheme for its general structure was adopted with modifications. He wrote large sections of it, and his style is clearly visible in certain passages. Though the Report bears marks of compromise, it may be said to be broadly on Keynesian lines. It takes its place in the great historic line of British Currency Reports, and there is a certain sense in which it can be said that the views therein embodied became the orthodox views from that day forward.

Currency should be managed with a view to stability of output and employment at a high level. (Note the official recognition of the connection between currency and employment.) Central Banks were to secure this objective by influencing the flow of saving into investment at home and abroad. The monetary authorities should concern themselves more with the long-term investment market in future. The Central Banks of the world were to cooperate, first to get a lift of prices above their existing low level and then to maintain them at a stable level. They should confer together regularly, so as to concert measures to this end. Legal requirements for gold reserves should be relaxed, and balances with other countries and the Bank for International Settlement treated as gold. Some of the Committee thought that the stimulus of Government investment was needed to get a rise of prices in existing circumstances, and that there should be an international conference on reorganizing foreign lending.

For Britain certain changes were recommended. The Issue Department and Banking Department of the Bank of England should be amalgamated; there should be a fixed maximum fiduciary issue and a fixed minimum gold reserve, the size of the gold reserve no longer being related to the notes. Joint Stock Banks should pay notes held in excess of requirements into the Bank of England. The gold reserve of the Bank of England should be strengthened, but wide variations in it should be contemplated as normal. There should be closer cooperation between the Bank of England and the Joint Stock Banks. There was a chapter on the need for new modes of providing capital for small or new firms, and another on publicity and statistics.

The Committee as a whole was unwilling to express a view upon the wider question of public works. In Keynes's opinion this was an indispensable supplement to good monetary management. The more progressive members of the Committee, however (six, including Keynes, out of fourteen), joined with him in a supplementary report in favour of a public works programme.[46]

During the course of his five days' evidence on the earlier occasion (28 February) Keynes made a momentous proposal. He suggested that in the existing impasse some measure of Protection might be desirable, as a temporary remedy. Hitherto his record as a Free Trader had been without blemish; indeed the fallacies of Protection had aroused his especial fury. Now he argued that the Free Trade doctrine, like the Bank Rate doctrine, implied a fluidity of money wage rates that did not exist. In existing circumstances he no longer held that it was a fallacy to suppose that a measure of Protection could increase employment. No doubt, in the end, the rank and file would have a better standard of living, if they consented to a reduction in money wage rates and thus ensured that the resources of the country should be employed to the best advantage as between various industries, and as between exports and production for the home market. If money wage rates were not adjusted, there would be unemployment. Protection would undoubtedly reduce real wages and cause a less satisfactory distribution of productive resources; but it would ensure larger employment, and that for the moment was the supreme objective. It must be added that he was rather dubious about the policy of reducing money wage rates, even

46. Sir Thomas Allen, Mr Bevin, Mr Keynes, Mr R. McKenna, Mr J. Frater Taylor, Mr A. A. G. Tulloch.

if it were practical – first, because it would increase the burden of the National Debt, and, secondly, because the whole world might get into the vicious circle of competitive wage-rate reductions. It was one thing to have money wage-rate reductions when the trouble was that one's own nation was out of equilibrium in a world otherwise prosperous, quite another thing to have it when, in addition to that trouble, the whole world was suffering from a slump. The reduction of money wage rates in a particular country would bring that country into equilibrium, by allowing it to capture a larger proportion of world trade. If there was a disequilibrium consisting of an excess of saving over investment, a reduction of money wage rates would not tend to cure the disequilibrium in the country in which that excess obtained, or in the world as a whole if there was a world-wide excess. Wage reductions in Britain and elsewhere would do nothing to remedy the slump considered as a world phenomenon and would add to the burden of fixed charges throughout the world. His confidence in taking a new line about the effect of Protection on unemployment was due to his sense that he was on sure ground in his savings and investment analysis of unemployment. Protection would tend, assuming British money wage rates and costs to be fixed, to improve our balance of trade; it would thus increase our foreign investment and this would have the same effect on the unemployment situation as increasing investment at home (which was his principal remedy).

The virtue of Free Trade is that it does bring money wages down and it does not bring real wages down, whereas Protection is not so likely to bring down money wages, it is much more likely to bring down real wages. But the virtue of Protection is that it does the trick, whereas in present conditions Free Trade does not. Therefore the question is, how far one is prepared to be governed by short considerations, and it seems to me, when one has by virtue of Mr McKenna got some duties, it would be a very strange act to aggravate the position by removing them. When it is a question of putting on new duties it is a much more difficult question, and it also depends on what alternative remedies there are and how long the present situation is to last. If we are jammed for some time I think we should get some immediate relief by well adjusted tariffs . . . I want to link up what I have said about Protection to my general analysis. We have seen that Protection is another way of increasing the amount of our foreign investment and that is how it profoundly works in with my argument . . . If it is essential for equilibrium that we should invest abroad on a larger scale than at present, he protectionist way of doing it may be the method of least resistance, because it does not require reduction of money wages and it has less effect, for reasons that some of the members have been suggesting, in turning the terms of trade against us.

He added that one had to admit in favour of Protection that it would increase business confidence, and that, too, would make for a higher level of investment at home.

He put forward these views with diffidence. He hoped that the experiment would only be a temporary one, although that veteran Free Trader, McKenna, warned him that a guarantee of more than five years would be needed if investment in the iron and steel industry was to be stimulated. The proposal went into the addendum of the 'progressive' party in rather general terms. There was a suggestion that tariffs on imports should be accompanied by bounties on exports, to prevent distortion in the structure of industry, so that the effect of the proposals on foreign trade would be identical with a devaluation of sterling.

While these matters were on foot, the Prime Minister appointed a Committee of the Economic Advisory Council (24 July 1930), consisting of Keynes as Chairman, Mr Henderson, Professor Pigou, Professor Robbins and Sir Josiah Stamp, 'to review the present economic condition of Great Britain, to examine the causes which are responsible for it and to indicate conditions of recovery'. Keynes had by this time already had the advantage of much of the discussion in the Macmillan Committee, and the slump was getting continually more severe. The smaller committee went over

some of the same ground and came up against similar obstacles. It had wider terms of reference and could go further
afield in recommendations. On the Protection issue, while
three of the members were not in complete agreement and
had their own reservations, their minds were moving in the
same direction as that of Keynes. Professor Lionel Robbins,
however, took an entirely different view. He was a convinced
Free Trader, and his ardent, youthful spirit rose up in passionate protest against any proposals of this kind. In his
mind far more was at stake than the mere question of
whether a little extra employment could be given here and
now by means of import duties, although this, too, he questioned. He saw in the proposals a turning away from the
ancient traditions which made Britain great, and a devastating blow at the all-too-tender plant of internationalism.
He felt that it was a dire mistake, that we were selling our
birthright and at the same time giving a most shocking
example to the rest of the world. He was against it for
economic reasons and against it for political reasons, and
he felt that he must devote the whole of his strength to
resisting it. He refused to have anything to do with the
majority report, although he was not necessarily in disagreement with all of it, in order to mark clearly the far-reaching
nature of his dissent. Proceedings at times became somewhat
acrimonious. Keynes at first challenged the right of a single
individual to put in a minority report. It was not an easy
task for a young man to assert his view in a minority of one
against distinguished and famous seniors. He was no
doubt 'difficult', and Keynes felt this. Later he was to come to
think very differently of him, for they worked in beautiful
harmony in the Anglo-American negotiations of World
War II, and Keynes was particularly appreciative of Professor Robbins's mellowness and urbanity.

Keynes came during this year to address an undergraduate economic society in Oxford and stayed with me. I knew
nothing of the inner proceedings of the Macmillan Committee and the Economic Advisory Council. He told me that

he intended to give us an address in favour of a revenue tariff. My face fell, and I uttered some words of deprecation. He made haste to console me. It would be quite all right, he assured me, because when the present phase had passed, we should return to Free Trade. But I was not to be consoled. On learning that it was a rather large meeting – he had supposed a small group – he agreed not to deliver the intended address, and held forth instead on the doctrine of saving and investment, the *Treatise* not yet being out.

It seemed to me then, and still seems so, that he was relying too much on public opinion being amenable to his reasoning – he had bitter experience enough to the contrary – in holding that, once the great established entrenchment of the British Free Trade position had been scaled by the Protectionists, it would be at all easy to remove Protection when revival came. But, as we shall see, at heart he may not have thought this. Was he a little too ready to be an iconoclast? Was this tendency in part responsible for his turning against his old love? In his iconoclastic assault upon the Gold Standard I had been heart and soul with him from the beginning, because there it seemed clear that what he wanted to put in its place, a stable currency, was manifestly altogether superior; it was something to which the world, if it continued to be progressive, would certainly move. This piece of iconoclasm, on the other hand, represented a move towards something less good in itself, for the sake of temporary expediency. But then I had not had the advantage of seeing all the other exits from our present woeful prison bolted and barred by the inexorable logic of Hopkins and the other experts. It was a nice question.

These views did not become public until the following year. On 7 March 1931 Keynes published in the second issue of the new joint *New Statesman and Nation* a plea for a revenue tariff.

Yet the objections to the expansionist remedy – the instability of our international position, the state of the Budget and the want of confidence – cannot be thus disposed of. Two years ago there was no need to be frightened. Today it is a different matter. It would not be wise to frighten the penguins and arouse these frigid creatures to flap away from our shores with their golden eggs inside them. A policy of expansion sufficiently drastic to be useful might drive us off the gold standard. Moreover, two years ago the problem was mainly a British problem; today it is mainly international. No domestic cure today can be adequate by itself. An international cure is essential; and I see the best hope of remedying the international slump in the leadership of Great Britain. And if Great Britain is to resume leadership, she must be strong and believed to be strong. It is of paramount importance, therefore, to restore full confidence in London. I do not believe that this is difficult; for the real strength of London is being under-estimated today by foreign opinion, and the position is ripe for a sudden reversal of sentiment. For these reasons, I, who opposed our return to the gold standard and can claim, unfortunately, that my Cassandra utterances have been partly fulfilled, believe that our exchange position should be relentlessly defended today, in order, above all, that we may resume the vacant financial leadership of the world, which no one else has the experience or the public spirit to occupy, speaking out of acknowledged strength and not out of weakness.

\*

Free Traders may, consistently with their faith, regard a revenue tariff as our iron ration, which can be used once only in emergency. The emergency has arrived. Under cover of the breathing space and the margin of financial strength thus afforded us, we could frame a policy and a plan, both domestic and international, for marching to the assault against the spirit of contractionism and fear.

If, on the other hand, Free Traders reject these counsels of expediency, the certain result will be to break the present Government and to substitute for it, in the confusion of a Crisis of Confidence, a Cabinet pledged to a full protectionist programme. I am not unaccustomed to being in a minority. But on this occasion I believe that 90 per cent of my countrymen will agree with me.

In the following issue there appeared a spate of letters, headed by Sir William Beveridge. There was a certain tendency to concentrate criticism on Keynes's estimate of the yield of the proposed duties. In the next issue (21 March), he suggested that this might be caused by the lack of good logical arguments.

I am more nearly touched by Professor Robbins' contention, that a tariff, once put on, will never be taken off when the special circumstances that called for it have passed away. I know there is a risk that this may be so, but it is a risk that circumstances demand that we should take. Nor do I rate the risk as high as he does ...

He quoted instances of tariffs being taken off; he thought that when prices began to rise, people would wish to be rid of them.

If prices rise to their former level, and if unqualified Free Trade turns out to be as much in the interests of this country in the condition of the twentieth century as it certainly was in the conditions of the nineteenth century, then I believe that the tariff will be taken off again. But, if I look into the bottom of my own heart, the feeling which I find there is, rather, that a tariff is a crude departure from *laissez-faire*, which we have to adopt because we have at present no better weapon in our hands, but that it will be superseded in time, not by a return to *laissez-faire*, but by some more comprehensive scheme of national planning.

*

Professor Robbins taunts me in conclusion with abandoning 'the service of high and worthy ideals in international relations' for 'the service of the mean and petty devices of economic nationalism'. I know that he sincerely feels this, and that for him, as for many others, Free Trade stands as a banner and as a symbol of fundamental reason and decency between nations. Free Trade unbesmirched invokes old loyalties and recalls one of the greatest triumphs of reason in politics which adorns our history. It is a poor retort, perhaps, to this, to say that one must not let one's sense of the past grow stronger than one's sense of the present and of the future, or sacrifice the substance to the symbol. But I can at least say that my practical aims are to avoid a disastrous process of competitive international wage-cutting, and the social strife which this would bring; to enable this country to resume the financial leadership of the world which we alone are capable of using in the general interest; and to prevent a domestic political reaction which might delay progress towards international peace and interrupt our policy in India.

He followed this by a series of three articles on various aspects of the problem.[47]

*28 March.* I have reached my own conclusion as the result of continuous reflection over many months, without enthusiasm, as the result of the gradual elimination of the practical alternatives as being more undesirable. Nor do I suppose for one moment that a revenue tariff by itself will see us out of our trouble. Indeed, I mainly support it because it will give us a margin of resources and a breathing space, under cover of which we can do other things.

*4 April.* May I also register a mild complaint against the undercurrent of moral reprobation which I detect in some quarters? I seem to see the elder parrots sitting round and saying: 'You can *rely* on us. Every day for thirty years, regardless of the weather, we have said "What a lovely morning!" But this is a bad bird. He says one thing one day, and something else the next.'

*11 April.* Perhaps controversy with one's friends and colleagues is an essentially barren thing. But I come to the end of my attempt to deal with the controversy which I have provoked in the pages of the *New Statesman and Nation* with an unusually acrid[48] flavour in my mouth. There is a great deal to be said on both sides about this tariff question. It is a difficult decision. But in this discussion we have not been reaching more than the fringe of what are for me the real problems. As Professor Bellerby pointed out in his letter last week, my critics have not taken any notice of, or shown the slightest interest in, the analysis of our present state, which occupied most of my original article and led up to my tariff proposal in the last paragraph. Is it the fault of the *odium theologicum* attaching to Free Trade? Is it that Economics is a queer subject or in a queer state? Whatever may

47. 28 March, 4 and 11 April.
48. In the *New Statesman* this word actually appears as 'arid'. I owe the emendation, which is clearly correct, to Mrs J. N. Keynes.

be the reason, new paths of thought have no appeal to the fundamentalists of Free Trade. They have been forcing me to chew over again a lot of stale mutton, dragging me along a route I have known all about as long as I have known anything, which cannot, as I have discovered by many attempts, lead one to a solution of our present difficulties – a peregrination of the catacombs with a guttering candle.

Keynes's conversion on this point had wide influence. Perhaps it was merely that, with his uncanny sensitivity to the significance of current events, he reached a conclusion a year earlier which others of like training and opinion were bound to arrive at in due course, as the storm grew more ferocious. Was it inevitable? No one was braver than Keynes in standing alone for an unpopular course, if only it was a practical one, but he was not addicted to the pursuit of what was Utopian and unrealizable. If the Gold Standard had broken down early in 1930, I have no doubt that Keynes would have remained a Free Trader, and immediately after the suspension he wrote to *The Times*, urging that consideration of the tariff question should be deferred.[49] For another year, however, the Gold Standard was to appear quite unassailable. Did he have enough regard for the appalling repercussions of our *volte-face* on world opinion? He may have been right in feeling that if Britain declined into greater weakness and still more widespread unemployment, she would have to do things still more shocking. This was, in his mind, a case of *reculer pour mieux sauter*. Britain must at all costs be strengthened at this juncture, and thereby be enabled to give a lead towards international reconstruction, which the United States appeared to be in no mind to give. In the event Britain went off the Gold Standard, which removed the need for Protection, and had Protection also, and then failed to give any lead to international reconstruction.

49. *The Times*, 29 September 1931. Later, however, he moved somewhat further towards a Protectionist position; see p. 526 below.

# [11]

## 'The General Theory of
Employment, Interest and Money'

### I

It was during the time when Keynes was composing the *Treatise* that his most outstanding pupil of the inter-war period came upon the scene – Mr Richard Kahn. Keynes at once perceived his quality, and before long had roped him in to advise him and help him in his major tasks. The preface to the *Treatise* contains an expression of indebtedness. It was no doubt through Keynes's influence that Mr Kahn was made a joint secretary to the 'Committee of Economists' which was working for the Economic Advisory Council.[1] He was elected to a Fellowship at King's in 1930. In the following years he was in close contact with Keynes, and available for consultation on all difficult points. Mr Kahn was not only clear-headed and thorough; he had a penetrating mind and originality; he must be reckoned with those whom Professor Pigou has classified as tool-makers; he had the power of framing a new concept which would clarify the point at issue; that done, much antiquated conceptual lumber could be cleared away. While he followed and accepted the development of Keynes's thought, his writings, all too sparse, make it clear that his thinking has a distinctive quality which is different from that of his master. It was a happy alliance. Keynes brought him into the bursarial work at King's; he was made Second Bursar in 1935. Unhappily, during the war his work lay in a somewhat different field, and, although they were in constant communication, Mr Kahn lacked the benefit of intimate association in the work which was to make great changes in Keynes's notions about

1. cf. p. 502.

what was possible and desirable, and about what was impossible, in international economic relations. On Keynes's death Mr Kahn succeeded him as First Bursar of King's College and became his joint executor with Mr Geoffrey Keynes.

In his biographical study of Keynes Mr Austin Robinson describes the excitement in Cambridge on the publication of the *Treatise*.

It so happened that the publication of the *Treatise* coincided in time with a remarkable younger generation in Cambridge. R. F. Kahn had just been made a Fellow of King's; J. E. Meade was spending a year in Trinity before returning to Oxford; they with P. Sraffa, C. H. P. Gifford, A. E. W. Plumptre, L. Tarshis, Joan Robinson and several others of us formed a 'circus' which met weekly for the discussion of the *Treatise*, and R. F. Kahn retailed to Keynes the results of our deliberations.

Mrs (Joan) Robinson, who afterwards achieved international fame, deserves mention as an ardent disciple of Keynes; he had high regard for her intellectual powers. Mr Robinson mentions as an important point which arose in these discussions that Keynes 'visualized too simple and direct a mechanism whereby changes of investment were supposed to react on prices, and that in a strictly formal sense some of his conclusions required the assumption that output was fixed and not variable'. It must not be supposed that Keynes had not variations of output in mind; indeed the *Treatise* concentrates upon an analysis of the causes which make output vary, and of the consequences of that variation. In some respects the *Treatise* is more 'dynamic' than the later volume. The matter at issue may be put simply thus. Keynes's general treatment, and especially his 'fundamental equation' designed to show the essence of his theory, point to an excess of investment over saving causing a rise of prices and thereby stimulating an increase of output; and conversely. The question was raised whether an increase of investment might not operate directly upon output, and not via a rise of prices. The rise of prices might come later as a consequence of the increase of output and not conversely. While the thinking of the *Treatise* does not exclude this possibility, the 'fundamental equation' certainly does not provide a means for showing this alternative.[2] There was a further point. While a discrepancy between saving and investment is deemed in the *Treatise* to provoke a change of output, there is nothing to show what reaction this change will have on the discrepancy.

Mr Kahn got to work upon these problems and an article

2. This criticism, that Keynes's equation does not bring out the direct effect of an increase of investment upon output, is not to be confused with a technical error which also came to light at that time in the equation itself. By a curious mischance he made an elementary mistake in algebra. He used variables, some of which stood for money aggregates and others for aggregates of goods, and there are notorious pitfalls in manipulating equations embodying such disparate items. The consequence was that his 'fundamental equation' was formally incorrect save on the assumption that the ratio of output of consumer goods to the total output of the economy was constant. This error did not affect the main argument of the text and may easily be corrected.

In Keynes's first fundamental equation, $P$ stands for the price-level of consumption goods, $R$ for the volume of consumption goods, $E$ for total earnings (less windfall profits set aside), $S$ for the part of $E$ not spent on consumption goods, $O$ for the volume of output (consumption goods and additions to capital) and $I'$ for the cost (including normal profit) of additions to capital.

He writes (correctly) $PR = E - S$ and deduces that $P = \dfrac{E}{O} + \dfrac{I' - S}{R}$. The latter equation is incorrect save on the assumption that $O/R$ is constant.

This may be put right by writing $E_r$ for 'earnings' derived from the output of consumption goods and $E_c$ for 'earnings' derived from the output of additions to capital ($= I'$).

Then $PR = E - S = E_r + E_c - S$ and $P = \dfrac{E_r}{R} + \dfrac{I' - S}{R}$. The second term on the right hand of the revised formula is identical with that in the original and summarizes the forces making for what Keynes calls a 'profit inflation' (or deflation). The first term on the right in the revised formula has less scope than that in the original, but serves equally well to summarize the forces making for what Keynes calls an 'income inflation'.

from his pen, entitled 'Home Investment and Unemployment', appeared in the *Economic Journal* for June 1931. The ideas in this article had a crucial influence on Keynes's subsequent thinking. Mr Kahn shows the direct effect of an increase of investment upon the level of output by a device which came to be known as 'the multiplier'. The consequent rise of prices, if any, appears as a secondary phenomenon, not dependent (as it appears to be in Keynes's 'fundamental equation') upon the size of the gap between investment and saving, still less on such purely monetary factors as increase of bank credit or of velocity of circulation, but on the rise in money costs of production,[3] if any, consequent upon the increase of output. Furthermore, windfall profit ceases to play a crucial role in financing an excess of investment over saving, and similarly with 'losses' in the opposite situation; variations in investment are matched by variations in voluntary saving, of which the windfall profits, plus or minus, would only be a part. Further discussion of these matters may be postponed until we come to Keynes's later volume.

All this stimulated Keynes's mind to move forward. He received a different kind of stimulus from the reviews of professionals – for example, that of his old friend Mr D. H. Robertson in the *Economic Journal* and that of Professor F. A. von Hayek, who had lately come to London from Vienna, in *Economica*.[4] What Keynes felt about these reviews, and others, was that the authors had not in the least understood what he had tried to say. This was depressing, especially as he had hitherto had a reputation for clear writing. In his own view he had advanced a novel theory of the cause of oscillation, this consisting in divergences between investment and saving. While he fully recognized and discussed at length the causal relations, both simple

3. More strictly, on the slope of the supply schedule of goods in general.

4. See *Economic Journal*, September 1931, for a review by Robertson and rejoinder by Keynes; and *Economica*, August to November 1931 and February 1932, for controversy with Professor von Hayek.

and complex, between the divergence of investment from saving on the one hand, and changes in the quantity of money and velocity of its circulation on the other, he had emphatically denied that an inflationary or deflationary movement was normally caused or necessarily accompanied by the latter kinds of changes. His complaint of the reviewers was that, instead of considering the grounds and justification for this denial, they tacitly ignored it. They assumed that monetary theories of the old kind must be right; on this assumption it was easy to find all sorts of contradictions and inconsistencies in the *Treatise*. Keynes could only conclude that the minds of his reviewers had simply failed to grasp what it was that he was denying. If they had made a frontal attack upon that denial upon its merits, he could have encountered their arguments or, if necessary, made concessions to them. As things were, his rejoinders were displays of shadow fencing.

The controversy with Professor von Hayek was a sharp one. The latter, newly arrived in England, found himself terribly buffeted at this period. His book on *Prices and Production* had received a review of unusual acidity in the *Economic Journal* from the pen of Mr P. Sraffra, who had come from Italy somewhat earlier and won Keynes's highest esteem. In replying to Professor von Hayek's review of his own book, Keynes went out of his way to refer to *Prices and Production*. 'The book, as it stands, seems to me to be one of the most frightful muddles I have ever read ... and yet it remains a book of some interest, which is likely to leave its mark on the mind of the reader. It is an extraordinary example of how, starting with a mistake, a remorseless logician can end up in Bedlam.' Professor von Hayek replied with a powerful and dignified protest against this kind of behaviour. These polemics temporarily caused a widening of the gulf between Cambridge and London. It may be recorded, however, that at a later date Keynes and Professor von Hayek achieved a happy relation of friendship. During the second war Professor von Hayek turned his attention away from the technicalities of banking and capital theory and wrote a book on political economy which, despite certain exaggerations that it may contain, will remain a classic – *The Road to Serfdom*. This is a convenient point at which to record Keynes's reaction, which throws light on some of his views on ultimate questions at that time.

*J. M. Keynes to Professor F. A. Hayek*, 28 June 1944

The voyage has given me the chance to read your book properly. In my opinion it is a grand book. We all have the greatest reason to be grateful to you for saying so well what needs so much to be said. You will not expect me to accept quite all the economic dicta in it. But morally and philosophically I find myself in agreement with virtually the whole of it; and not only in agreement with it, but in a deeply moved agreement.

Turning to a few special points . . .

I should therefore conclude your theme rather differently. I should say that what we want is not no planning, or even less planning, indeed I should say that we almost certainly want more. But the planning should take place in a community in which as many people as possible, both leaders and followers, wholly share your own moral position. Moderate planning will be safe if those carrying it out are rightly orientated in their own minds and hearts to the moral issue. This is in fact already true of some of them. But the curse is that there is also an important section who could almost be said to want planning not in order to enjoy its fruits but because morally they hold ideas exactly the opposite of yours, and wish to serve not God but the devil. Reading the *New Statesman and Nation* one sometimes feels that those who write there, while they cannot safely oppose moderate planning, are really hoping in their hearts that it will not succeed; and so prejudice more violent action. They fear that if moderate measures are sufficiently successful, this will allow a reaction in what you think the right and they think the wrong moral direction. Perhaps I do them an injustice; but perhaps I do not.

What we need, therefore, in my opinion, is not a change in our economic programmes, which would only lead in practice to disillusion with the results of your philosophy; but perhaps even the contrary, namely, an enlargement of them. Your greatest danger ahead is the probable practical failure of the application of your philosophy in the U.S. in a fairly extreme form. No, what we need is the restoration of right moral thinking – a return to proper moral values in our social philosophy. If only you could turn your crusade in that direction you would not look or feel quite so much like Don Quixote. I accuse you of perhaps confusing a little bit the moral and the material issues. Dangerous acts can be done safely in a community which thinks and feels rightly, which would be the way to hell if they were executed by those who think and feel wrongly.

If Keynes had only had to cope with the stimulus of his critics, it would no doubt have been incumbent upon him to redraft certain portions of the *Treatise* in order to make his points more abundantly clear. But meanwhile his mind was moving forward. He was in search of simplification and a wider generalization. Once more he went into a great tunnel, from which he was to emerge with *The General Theory of Employment, Interest and Money* (1936). This was his main interest in the following years. His vast range of duties continued to occupy him and his correspondence was large, but his important public appearances were few.

Immediately after the Macmillan Committee concluded its proceedings at the end of May 1931, he went on a trip to America, his first since the expedition with Lord Reading in 1917. He had been invited by the University of Chicago to give a lecture on the Harris foundation, which was later published, along with other lectures, under the title *Unemployment as a World Problem*.[5] His main object, however, was to make a personal investigation into economic conditions. He had in recent months been sending regular appreciations on financial prospects to Mr Walter Case for the use of Case Pomeroy Inc. Through Mr Case he was brought into contact with knowledgeable men of business in New York. He had interviews with the leading persons in the Federal Reserve

5. Quincy Wright, editor. University of Chicago Press (Cambridge University Press), 1931.

System, and also with President Hoover. This was at the time of the 'Hoover Moratorium'. On his return he submitted a lengthy report on American conditions to the Prime Minister, Mr Ramsay MacDonald, who circulated it as a Cabinet Paper. The attitude of mind of the Federal Reserve authorities was thoroughly satisfactory; they would do their best to promote expansion. The condition of the member banks was deplorable. The slump in America was essentially a slump in construction; contrary to general belief, wage rates had not been much reduced – this was a satisfactory point; he took the gloomiest view of the prospects of an early recovery in the United States; he thought that recovery would come in other parts of the world first; the Hoover Moratorium had been thoroughly popular.

At this time we find him writing detailed comments on the proofs of Mr H. G. Wells's *Work, Wealth and Happiness of Mankind*. These notes contain the first record I have discovered of the *riposte* he was in the habit of using when addressed as a Professor – 'I do not enjoy suffering the indignity without the emoluments'.

He was still standing firm in the view that the Gold Standard must not be abandoned, but the economy campaign, which was gathering momentum, was not at all to his way of thinking. Of the Economy Report of the famous May Committee he wrote: 'The Committee show no evidence of having given a moment's thought to the possible repercussions of their programme either on the volume of employment or on the receipts of taxation.'[6] He is reported as having referred to it a little later at a House of Commons Committee as 'the most foolish document I have ever had the misfortune to read'.[7] He made a fierce attack on the Budget produced by the National Government, which Mr Ramsay MacDonald had now formed. 'The Budget and the Economy Bill are replete with folly and injustice.' It was monstrous to reduce the wages of school-teachers, just because they hap-

6. *New Statesman and Nation*, 15 August 1931.
7. *Daily Herald*, 17 September 1931.

pened to be the easiest target. The reduction in the road-building and housing programmes were a 'triumph of the Treasury view in its narrowest form' – the qualifying phrase was no doubt due to Hopkins's evidence to the Macmillan Committee. 'To raid the Road Fund in order to maintain the Sinking Fund is in present circumstances a policy of Bedlam.'[8] He warned a Committee of the House of Commons that the Budget was likely to accentuate deflation and unemployment, and pleaded for an international conference on gold.

And then on 21 September Britain left the Gold Standard. All these years of travail had been in vain. If only they had taken his advice in 1925! After they had failed to do so, he remained loyal to the established fact of a Gold Standard until the end. But now his spirits rose. Great new vistas were opened.

Yet would we take advantage of them? The drift in politics was profoundly unsatisfactory. He made a personal plea to Mr Ramsay MacDonald not to have a General Election. The problems that now had to be tackled were clear; there was no need of a mandate. The election was held, however, and the forces of progress suffered a complete eclipse until World War II. The economy campaign, which he believed to be folly, proceeded.

At first he thought that he might galvanize the Labour Party into constructive opposition on the basis of a programme for expansion. He saw much of Mr Kingsley Martin at this period and hoped that the *New Statesman and Nation* might become the vehicle for a balanced policy ultimately based upon his views. But the Labour Party had been greatly humiliated by the defection of their leaders and the smashing defeat at the polls. They had been represented, in part unfairly, as having played havoc with the nation's finances, used Post Office savings to pay the unemployment dole and endangered an inflationary orgy. It was perhaps human that Labour should react by moving rather distinctly to the left;

8. *New Statesman and Nation*, 19 September 1931.

Keynes's moderate statesmanship did not appeal to them; the *New Statesman* carried a foolish article suggesting the nationalization of the Joint Stock Banks – as though that could possibly do any good at this juncture! Labour did not take its defeat as an opportunity for showing its mettle and devising a realistic programme to cope with the facts as they were in the worst phase of the slump, but tended to move away towards its age-old panaceas; it might not be helpful to utter the old formulae, but it soothed the nerves. Keynes expressed his difficulties in regard to Socialism in an article in the *Political Quarterly*.[9] He had been concerned with the foundation of this journal, was on its editorial board and always maintained some interest in its progress. At about this time a volume appeared containing his Halley-Stewart lecture on the crisis.[10]

While mainly unsympathetic to the National Government, he warmly applauded Mr Neville Chamberlain's conversion operation.[11]

Reference may be made here to the publication of his two volumes *Essays in Persuasion* (1931) and *Essays in Biography* (1933). From the former, which appeared in the depth of the slump, after the collapse of the Gold Standard, the public did begin to appreciate that he had been prophesying correctly and advising wisely all these last twelve years. The *Essays in Biography* may be recommended to readers who wish to sample his prose style without having to follow an economic argument. These biographical sketches included his portraits of Wilson and Clemenceau at the Paris Peace Conference, and also the portrait of Lloyd George, which 'a certain compunction' had made him suppress in 1919. On the day of publication Lloyd George happened to be making

9. 'Dilemma of Modern Socialism', *Political Quarterly*, April–June 1932.

10. *The World's Economic Crisis and the Way of Escape*, by Sir Arthur Salter, Sir Josiah Stamp, Mr J. M. Keynes, Sir Basil Blackett, Professor Henry Clay and Sir William Beveridge (Allen & Unwin). All the pundits, in fact!

11. *Economic Journal*, September 1932.

a speech in Sheffield, in which he strongly supported an article that had appeared that morning in *The Times*[12] 'by a great friend of mine, Mr J. M. Keynes'. A *Daily Mail* reporter at Sheffield drew his attention to the book. 'That was written in 1919,' Mr Lloyd George replied, and dismissed the matter with a gesture of scorn.[13] But did he know what was in it, or was he merely thinking of the shorter sketch which appeared in the *Economic Consequences*?

Mr Lloyd George is rooted in nothing; he is void and without content; he lives and feeds on his immediate surroundings . . . this syren, this goat-footed bard, this half-human visitor to our age from the hag-ridden magic and enchanted woods of Celtic antiquity. One catches in his company that flavour of final purposelessness, inner irresponsibility, existence outside or away from our Saxon good and evil, mixed with cunning, remorselessness, love of power . . .

Mr Lloyd George could hardly be expected to take all this in a kindly spirit. In the second volume of his *War Memoirs*, which appeared in the following November, there was a strong attack on Keynes. It was based on an extract from a secret Cabinet Paper, from which Keynes was not allowed to quote. He wrote to *The Times* explaining his position in this regard and added:

Mr Lloyd George would, perhaps, defend his action on the ground that I had recently made so bold as to publish a character sketch of him. Regarded thus, as a competition in personalities, I make no complaint of what, indeed, any prudent persons would have expected from the subject in question. But I hope that the history and criticism of our financial policy during the war, a chronicle of high interest which still remains to be written, will not be confused by these polite exchanges, perhaps as inexcusable on the one side as on the other.[14]

The days of close collaboration within the Liberal Party were

12. See p. 520 below.
13. *Daily Mail*, 14 March 1933.
14. *The Times*, 28 November 1933.

evidently over. Was the spirit of Lord Oxford appeared? I think it had long since forgiven Keynes.

In 1932 there were faint signs of recovery in Britain, but hardly any in the world generally. It was decided at long last to hold a full-scale international economic conference in London during the course of 1933. With this in mind, Keynes wrote four 'turnover' articles in *The Times*,[15] which were reprinted in an expanded form in a pamphlet entitled *The Means to Prosperity*. On the domestic side he was still pressing those remedies which he had begun to urge in 1924 – large-scale public works on loan account. The most widespread criticism of Keynes during his life was that he was inconsistent. There was certainly no inconsistency in the dogged pertinacity with which he advocated this cure for unemployment over so many years. Indeed, the commentators on *The Means to Prosperity* complained this time of his consistency. Was he not offering the same old remedies which he had put forward in association with Mr Lloyd George in the election of 1929? What was right then, the critics implied, could not be right now.

*The Means to Prosperity*, however, contained a more satisfactory fundamental analysis than his earlier pamphlet, being based on the *Treatise* and subsequent thought. Keynes referred to Mr Kahn's *Economic Journal* article[16] and used the technique of 'the multiplier'.[17] He also gave his support to the idea of a double budget, one for current expenditure and the other for capital expenditure, which should be manipulated in accordance with the trade cycle. We begin here to get the first inkling of an idea, more radical than anything recommended so far, that the Chancellor of the Exchequer should pump in additional purchasing power, not only by financing public works through loans, but also by

15. ibid., 13–16 March 1933.

16. cf. p. 512.

17. Keynes followed up the pamphlet by a lengthy article in the *New Statesman* headed 'The Multiplier', an unusual title, as Mr Kingsley Martin observed to me, for an article in a popular weekly journal (*New Statesman and Nation*, 1 April 1933).

remitting taxation without reducing current expenditure. This is almost 'deficit finance' in the full sense. Keynes proposed to raise a loan of £60 million to finance public works on the one hand, and on the other to remit £50 million of taxation at the expense of the Sinking Fund. This reference to the Sinking Fund just – only just – made the project appear respectable.

In preparation for the World Economic Conference, he had something to say about external measures. He was sceptical of the feasibility of old-style foreign loans on a large scale.

Those countries which are best able to make them are least likely to do so. Nor is it reasonable to expect private investors to accept new risks of this kind when those they have already assumed are turning out so badly.

Additional domestic loan expenditure by strong countries would itself help the foreign situation, by leading to increased imports.

It may be better, therefore, to use our available resources to finance the additional imports, to which a bold policy of loan expenditure at home is likely to lead, than to make foreign loans. This will be just as beneficial to the outside world, and decidedly more healthy than further additions to international indebtedness . . .[18]

For the Conference [he went on] to occupy itself with pious resolutions concerning the abatement of tariffs, quotas and exchange restrictions will be a waste of time in so far as these things are not the expression of deliberate national or imperial policies; they have been adopted reluctantly as a means of self-protection and are symptoms, not causes, of the tension on the foreign exchanges. It is dear to the heart of conferences to pass pious resolutions deploring symptoms whilst leaving the disease untouched.

What he really wanted was to get worldwide, concerted

18. cf. letter to the *Economist*, 4 June 1932, by R. F. Harrod, of which he approved.

capital expenditure. Unfortunately each country separately would be reluctant to embark upon such a programme for fear of the repercussions on its external balance of payments. Therefore, some mechanism was required to assure them of some margin of international resources with which they could take some risks. If only the gold which existed could be scattered evenly throughout the world, that itself might be a solution. With adequate gold reserves the countries would not be afraid to go ahead. But that was an impossibility. The United States and France would not give it all away. His mind reverted to the possibility of a world Central Bank. Could not this, like any other bank, create liquid assets? He proposed that an international agency should print gold notes up to a maximum of $5,000 million and distribute them in proportions based on the 1928 distribution of gold with a maximum to any one country of $450 million. This project bears a remarkable resemblance to the International Monetary Fund with its quotas. The resemblance was not accidental! Here again we have an example of Keynes pursuing the same idea with dogged persistency through many years.

This proposal, although receiving ample comment, did not have a strong appeal. To the ordinary man it seemed unconvincing to say that by printing bits of paper and saying that they were worth $5,000 million, anything could be changed. The fundamental facts of production and trade would not be altered by this procedure. Mr Roy Glenday, Secretary to the Federation of British Industries, bluntly called it 'a confidence trick'.[19] It was no doubt to guard against aspersions of this type that the International Monetary Fund was drafted in a more restrictive way. Yet there was logic in Keynes's point of view. No one would think it a confidence trick if all these nations discovered an equivalent amount of gold in local mines and were encouraged to go forward by the reserves thereby acquired. Why should not gold certificates play a similar role? Internally in any national

19. *Economist*, 1 April 1933.

economy no one thought it a confidence trick to supplement gold supplies by printing more notes than there was gold to back them. Why not do so internationally? The real reason was an inveterately nationalist point of view in relation to these problems, and it was basically the existence of such a point of view that made Keynes sceptical about the outcome of the Conference. It was quite true, of course, that the gold certificates might all have drifted to the United States; but the trend of trade in the nineteen-thirties did not suggest that that was likely to happen.

Keynes was quite willing that strings should be attached to the use of this international medium. The following conditions should be complied with by any nation wishing to draw upon the fund:

Exchange restrictions should be abolished. Standstill agreements and the immobilization of foreign balances should be replaced by definitive schemes for gradual liquidation. Tariffs and quotas imposed to protect the foreign balance, and not in pursuance of permanent national policies, should be removed. The stronger financial centres should re-open their money markets to foreign loans. Defaults on public debts held abroad should be terminated, with the aid of the postponement of sinking funds and some writing down of interest or principal, perhaps based on an index number of prices, where incapacity, even in the new circumstances, is proved to the satisfaction of an independent expert body.

Thus it was not an invention of the Americans that strings should be attached, when nations sought to derive benefits from some newly devised international arrangements. The American negotiators of the British Loan in 1945 could simply have cut the relevant sentences out of *The Means to Prosperity* and handed them across the table to Keynes and the other British representatives!

If this scheme was adopted, Keynes was prepared to re-establish gold parities provisionally. He insisted, however, that there should be a still wider spread between the gold points than he had proposed before, namely five per cent.

The *de facto* parity should be alterable, if necessary, from time to time if circumstances were to require, just like bank rate, – though by small degrees one would hope. An unchangeable parity would be unwise until we know much more about the future course of international prices, and the success of the board of the new international authority in influencing it; and it would, moreover, be desirable to maintain permanently some power of gradual adjustment between national and international conditions. In addition the governing board should have some discretionary power to deal with emergencies and exceptional cases.

In fact, many of the essential features of the International Monetary Fund were there!

Whilst there were complaints that he was too consistent in continuing to advocate public works, there were also complaints that he was inconsistent in now recommending a modified Gold Standard. There were also complaints at the time of Bretton Woods that he was abandoning the progressive cause by soiling his fingers with a scheme involving gold. The following letter to the *Economist* is of interest not only as showing the consistency of his past attitude, but also because it gives a proleptic justification of the line he was to take at Bretton Woods:

I do not know that what you call 'the evolution of my ideas' is particularly important. But for the sake of accuracy I should like, in thanking you for your leading article of March 18th, to remind you that my recent advocacy of gold as an international standard is nothing new.

At all stages of the post-war developments the concrete proposals which I have brought forward from time to time have been based on the use of gold as an international standard, whilst discarding it as a rigid national standard. The qualifications which I have added to this have been always the same, though the precise details have varied; namely, (1) that the parities between national standards and gold should not be rigid, (2) that there should be a wider margin than in the past between the gold points, and (3) that if possible some international control should be formed with a view to regulating the commodity value of gold within certain limits.

You will find that this was my opinion in 1923 when I published my *Tract on Monetary Reform* (see chapter 5) and again in 1930 when I published my *Treatise on Money* (see chapters 36 and 38), just as it is today, as set forth in my articles in *The Times* and in my pamphlet *The Means to Prosperity*.

I apologize for occupying your space. But since there are people who deem it creditable if one does not change one's mind, I should like to get what *kudos* I can from not having done so on this occasion![20]

In preparation for the World Economic Conference the BBC arranged a transatlantic conversation between Keynes and Mr Walter Lippmann.[21] This was stated to be the first broadcast of a conversation between two individuals across the Atlantic.

It would be wrong to say that the World Economic Conference disappointed him, since he expected little. He covered it in a series of articles in the *Daily Mail*.[22] When President Roosevelt fired his well-known torpedo – he would not agree to stabilizing the gold value of the dollar – Keynes's *Daily Mail* article carried the headline, 'President Roosevelt is Magnificently Right'.

It is a long time since a statesman has cut through the cobwebs as boldly as the President of the United States cut through them yesterday. He has told us where he stands, and he invited the Conference to proceed to substantial business. But he is prepared to act alone if necessary; and he is strong enough to do so . . . The President's message has an importance which transcends its origins. It is, in substance, a challenge to us to decide whether we propose to tread the old, unfortunate ways, or to explore new paths; paths new to statesmen and to bankers, but not new to thought. For they lead to the managed currency of the future, the examination of which has been the prime topic of post-war economics.

The article created a stir, because it was the fashion at that moment to be very indignant with the President. It was

20. 20 March 1933.
21. *Listener*, 14 June 1933.
22. 8, 20, 27 June, 4 July 1933.

therefore noticed with interest that on the day on which it
appeared Keynes was lunching alone with the Prime Minister at the Athenaeum Club.

It may have been partly by revulsion from the futilities
of the Conference that he composed two elaborate articles
for the *New Statesman*, which carried his reaction from
Free Trade one stage further.[23] His orientation of mind
had changed. 'Partly, indeed, my background of economic
theory is modified. I should not charge Mr Baldwin, as I
did then, with being "a victim of the Protectionist fallacy
in its crudest form", because he believed that, in the existing circumstances, a tariff might do something to diminish
British unemployment.' There were broader reasons. He
had come to think that the quest for markets and investment opportunities abroad was inimical to peace.

I sympathize, therefore, with those who would minimize,
rather than those who would maximize, economic entanglement
between nations. Ideas, knowledge, art, hospitality, travel – these
are things which should of their nature be international. But let
goods be home-spun whenever it is reasonably and conveniently
possible; and, above all, let finance be primarily national. Yet, at
the same time, those who seek to disembarrass a country of its
entanglements should be very slow and wary. It should not be a
matter of tearing up roots, but of slowly training a plant to grow
in a different direction.

There is no doubt that what he mainly had in mind was
that he wanted Britain, sooner or later, to make a bold
experiment in achieving full employment by the methods
that he advocated; in order that the experiment should be
successful, British dependence on foreign conditions should
be limited. The International Conference made it abundantly
clear, if Mr Montagu Norman had not done so in his
evidence three years earlier, that the world was not ripe
for Keynesian experiments. So let us cultivate our own
garden; it was the best we could do. The articles lacked his

23. 8 and 15 July 1933.

usual precision of thought; they were a little rambling; it was perhaps proper that they should be, since what he sought to do was to bring about a change in mental atmosphere rather than press any particular doctrine.

If he was depressed by the gathered wisdom of the nations, and still more by the assertion of the British Government spokesman, Mr Runciman, that our experience refuted the idea that public works were conducive to employment,[24] he was greatly encouraged by the activities of President Roosevelt across the water. Here was someone who was interpreting the duty of the Government in the kind of way he had in mind. Not that he approved of all that was done. The spirit was right, but the actual content of the New Deal was a mixture of good and bad. Accordingly, he composed his thoughts and contributed a lengthy article to the *New York Times* in the form of an Open Letter to the President.[25]

You have made yourself the trustee for those in every country who seek to mend the evils of our condition by reasoned experiment within the framework of the existing social system. If you fail, rational change will be gravely prejudiced throughout the world, leaving orthodoxy and revolution to fight it out. But, if you succeed, new and bolder methods will be tried everywhere, and we may date the first chapter of a new economic era from your accession to office.

The President had a double task, recovery and reform. Keynes sympathized with both, but the former was more urgent, and it was important that it should not be prejudiced by undue haste in the reform programme. He did not judge that the NRA had made a contribution to recovery. 'As the prime mover in the first stage in the technique of recovery, I lay overwhelming emphasis on the increase of national purchasing power resulting from governmental

24. See letter to *The Times*, 17 July 1933.
25. *New York Times*, 31 December 1933. This appeared, subject to variation of form, in the London *Times* of 2 January 1934. He did a broadcast on similar lines: see the *Listener*, 17 January 1934.

expenditure, which is financed by loans and is not merely a transfer through taxation from existing incomes. Nothing else counts in comparison with this.' He feared that the devaluation experiment had been unduly influenced by a crude version of the quantity theory of money. He proposed stabilization of the dollar with the right to shift the parity at any time, but a declared intention only to do so either to correct a serious want of balance in America's international receipts and payments, or to meet a shift in the American domestic price-level relative to price levels abroad. There should be plenty of cheap credit, and there was no reason why the rate of interest on long-term Government bonds should not be reduced to 2½ per cent.[26]

In the course of the spring he had the honour of receiving an invitation to attend Commencement Day (5 June 1934) at Columbia University in order that he might receive the Honorary Degree of Doctor of Laws. His fellow-honorands were Mr James Aloysius Foley and Mr Cordell Hull. He made this an opportunity for taking a closer view of the American scene and for reviving and strengthening his financial contacts. He had remained in frequent correspondence with his friend Walter Case, who on this occasion gave him a great banquet to meet many influential people. Keynes had in his own mind complete confidence that interest rates would be permanently established at a low level in the United States, holding that many sound securities there had not recovered from the shock of the great depression and were due to have large increases in value. He paid special attention to public utilities, which, in his view, were suffering from vague fears induced by the New Deal, taking trouble to enlarge his knowledge of particular bonds and stocks. And then he went deeply in, following his maxim now of taking long views as an investor. His American public utility holdings made the most important contribution to

26. It may be of interest to record that a group of Oxford economists had submitted a memorandum to the President on similar lines through private channels two months earlier.

the great increase of his fortune in the thirties. In this connection mention should also be made of his heavy investment in Hector Whaling, to which he adhered through evil
days, in support of Mr Rupert Trouton, member of his staff
in 'A' Division and subsequently his pupil at Cambridge.
In the end the investment brought large profits.

Another old friend, Mr Felix Frankfurter, gave him a
batch of letters of introduction to personages in Washington who had important influence in the New Deal, members
of the 'Brain Trust', as it was then called. He had an interview with President Roosevelt – the one in which he was so
much preoccupied with the shape of the President's hands.[27]

*President F. D. Roosevelt to Mr Felix Frankfurter*, 11 June
1934

I had a grand talk with K and liked him immensely . . .

This interview has been the subject of much discussion.
The popular imagination was ready to seize upon the idea
that the President was learning his business from a foreign
economist. In wide circles in the United States the name
of Keynes became a hated one. There were many who, not
ready, and indeed not in a position, to discriminate those
aspects of the New Deal which were Keynesian in character from those which were not, laid at his door all that they
most hated in the bureaucratic activities that seemed to be
springing up like mushrooms on all sides. Advocates of
*laissez-faire* of the old-fashioned type were entitled to denounce Keynes, as he denounced them. To such apostles
of the old gospel, and there are still many in the United
States, almost all British economists and public men and
many American economists must seem black; if Keynes
figured more vividly in their imagination as an evil spirit,
it was because he was more potent. From the days of the
*Economic Consequences*, however, Keynes had been highly
esteemed by a large number of Americans. It is important

27. cf. pp. 23–4 above.

that still a larger number should think well of him, since it may well be in the United States that the most active steps will be taken to introduce such measures of central planning as are needed in the modern world to make free enterprise a viable system. Keynes, more than any of the modern planners, had a strain of passionate individualism, which should make him seem a kindred spirit to many Americans.

I have been at special pains to find out whether it is true that the President was profoundly influenced by this interview and guided his policy thereafter to some extent in the light of Keynes's theories. The evidence is conflicting. The preponderating opinion among those in a good position to know is that the influence of Keynes was not great. There need be no doubt that the President had the highest regard for Keynes; condemned by many economists in his own country, it may have pleased him to recall that this illustrious British economist was in sympathy with some of his economic experiments. That is very different from being deeply influenced by him. It is not clear that the President took a Keynesian view of loan expenditure. It is more probable that he sought to provide jobs on a great scale because men were jobless, and endeavoured to meet as much of the cost as possible by taxation. If there was a deficit, that was just too bad; it could be remedied later. It is not clear that he acted on the principle that it was the deficit, rather than the public works themselves, that was the potent agency in reducing unemployment. It has been suggested that Keynes gave him the courage to conduct his operations on a great scale. Keynes would certainly have urged that; yet it may be thought that the President's own instincts would lead him in the same direction, and that Keynes's advice was not the actuating factor. It seems likely that such influence as Keynes had on American developments came in a somewhat different way. His books were avidly read by those seriously interested in economics. The American mind is perhaps a little quicker than the English to welcome the new prophet. Keynes soon had followers in America who

meant business, and by the time that the slump of 1937–8
came, some of these were already in positions where they
could exert influence on presidential policy. Even in 1934
his views may have affected the course of events in the
United States, not through the President, but through the
clever back-room boys who had their ears to the ground.

*Walter Lippmann to J. M. Keynes,* 17 April 1934

. . . I do not know whether you realize how great an effect that
letter [viz. that in the *New York Times*] had, but I am told that
it was chiefly responsible for the policy which the Treasury is
now quietly but effectively pursuing of purchasing long-term
government bonds with a view to making a strong bond market
and to reducing the long-term rate of interest.

At the conclusion of his stay, he wrote a summary of his
impressions in a further article in the *New York Times*
(reproduced in the London *Times*), entitled 'Agenda for
the President'. He was now able to take a more optimistic
view of the American situation.

It is expedient to think much of the United States, but
an occasional thought may be given to Russia. On 27 October the *New Statesman and Nation* reproduced the verbatim
record of a conversation between Stalin and H. G. Wells
during the latter's visit to Moscow. This was followed by
comments by Mr Bernard Shaw, Mr Ernst Toller and
Keynes. These were bound up with some further letters in
a slim volume entitled *Stalin–Wells Talks*. Keynes's contribution was a brilliant affair and seemed to hit the nail
on the head more truly than the comments of his famous
seniors. In all this period he was quite clear that he had no
love whatever for Communism. But as the years wore on,
especially at the time of the Spanish Civil War, he could
not but observe the tendency towards Communism among
the young at Cambridge, and most markedly among the
choice spirits, those whom thirty years before he would
have wished to consider for membership of 'the Society'.

He attributed it to a recrudescence of the ancient strain of Puritanism in our blood, the zest to adopt a painful solution because of its painfulness. But he found it depressing.


2


By the end of 1934 the first draft of *The General Theory of Employment, Interest and Money* was complete. The following year was spent in revision and the conduct of correspondence with commentators. Keynes strove for perfection and was anxious to get as much agreement as possible from those whom he respected. He showed considerable readiness to accept suggestions. He took pains to reply in detail on all points raised, and, where there was disagreement, endeavoured by lengthy argument to bring his critics round.

In all this task, and indeed in the writing of the book itself, his main pillar of support was Mr Richard Kahn. Mention should also be made of Mrs (Joan) Robinson. With these two he could feel complete confidence that they understood what he was driving at. That was a great boon, for the old trouble, which he had had with the *Treatise*, began to recur. It was a sorry state of affairs. His main difficulty was not that his critics disagreed with his position, still less that they brought good arguments against it, but that he simply could not make them understand what the position was that he was taking up. Their ears seemed closed. It was indeed tantalizing.

It has been said, with some show of justice, that in this volume he went out of his way to stress differences from and find weaknesses in traditional economic theory. Would it not have been wiser to stress his own contribution and leave it to others to decide how much scrapping of established doctrine was entailed? To some he seemed to take a mischievous pleasure – perhaps he did – in criticizing revered names. In fact this was done of set purpose. It was his deliberate reaction to the frustrations he had felt, and was still feeling, as the result of the persistent tendency to ignore what was novel in his contribution. He felt he would get nowhere if he did not raise the dust. He must ram in the point that what he was saying was inconsistent with certain lines of classical thought, and that those who continued to argue that he was merely embroidering old themes had not understood his meaning.

The first proofs were sent to Mr D. H. Robertson, his old friend, whose critical acumen, if only it could be brought into service, would be of the utmost value to him. The gulf was now too wide. Robertson was frankly unsympathetic. He disliked the new concepts that Keynes employed in his analysis. He held that some of the propositions masquerading under a new guise were merely reformulations of what had been already said, reformulations which sometimes tended to allow a dangerous element of fallacy to creep in; that others, for which novelty might be allowed, could equally well have been stated in the old language; that others again were indeed fallacies. The Keynesian reconstruction was ill-judged because it made an unnecessary disturbance to well-tried modes of thought and opened the door to propositions the fallacious character of which the old terminology would have revealed. All these points Robertson made plain quite frankly, although the way in which he put his criticism confirmed Keynes's suspicion that Robertson was not really understanding what he intended to say.

The second set of proofs came along in June, and were dispatched to Mr Hawtrey and to me. Mr Hawtrey showed himself a true friend in the amount of trouble he took. The correspondence was voluminous and outlasted the publication of the book (February 1936). He made acceptable criticisms of detail and also criticisms of principle. At first it seemed to Keynes that they were not far apart on the issues where they disagreed. Most patient efforts were made by each to convert the other. They did not come nearer. Towards the close of the correspondence it was borne in upon Keynes with a force that he could not resist that Hawtrey, brilliant mind that he was, had also misconceived the main purpose of the arguments. It was a severe disappointment.

I too subjected him to a heavy bombardment. The pile of notes and letters is before me. I had forgotten how large it was. My comments poured in from Oxford, from London, from St Ives (Cornwall), from Land's End, and again from London, and again from Oxford. These comments were composed with fervour, in a strain of ardent admiration and with a sense of his mighty achievement, but also with a persistent and implacable zeal to convert him on certain points. Numerous detailed amendments were proposed. There was one main line of attack, the vehemence of which must have sorely tried his patience. There was a dreadful moment when he wrote to say that he suspected I had not understood. I set to work with the utmost speed – I knew how much his spirit had been tried by repeated misunderstandings – and wrote a précis of his main theory in my own language, which won an immediate withdrawal of his charge.

My main endeavour was to mitigate his attack on the 'classical' school. I agreed with him that there was a woeful gap in the traditional theory of unemployment and that the root of the matter was an incorrect theory of interest; where I differed was in regard to his allegation that the traditional theory of interest did not make sense. It seemed to me that this was pushing his criticism too far, would make too much dust and would give rise to irrelevant controversies. I supplied a diagram purporting to reconcile the classical theory with his theory, and he incorporated this in the volume – the only diagram in it! While he agreed with the traditional view that there was a tendency for 'the marginal efficiency of capital' to be equal to the rate of interest, he thought that in some way the classical writers had shown confusion by treating the marginal efficiency of capital and the rate of interest as one and the same thing.

It seemed to me then – and still seems so – that he was himself in some confusion about what the classical position really was; that he had not fully thought it through. He had propounded the old doctrine in successive courses of lectures in Cambridge before 1914, but there may have been a gap in his armoury. He used to ask for chapter and verse for adequate classical expositions of the subject, and these were hard to find; in a well-established system of thought certain things are taken for granted. I believe that this confusion can still be traced in certain passages in the *General Theory*, where he criticizes the views of the classical school, and claims for his definition of the marginal efficiency of capital more originality than can be accorded to it. His stress on the importance of expectations in this connection is, of course, wholly praiseworthy.

The *General Theory*, as its name implies, is basically an analysis, in terms of fundamental economic principle, of the causes of unemployment.[28] It was difficult to find in the standard treatises an explicit account of what determined the general level of employment, as distinct from the relative amount of employment provided by particular trades. He was concerned with unemployment over and above what may be called 'frictional' unemployment, viz. that due to the passage of men from job to job or from industry to industry. It can be said, however, that there was, in the traditional theory, an implicit doctrine of employment, namely, that in the case of the labour market, as in that of other markets, the price of labour tended to be adjusted to a level at which all labour would find employment. It was recognized by the classical writers, as by everyone, that the price of labour might not be freely adjustable. The logical corollary of the classical position was that, if there

28. I wrote a summary account of the doctrines of the *General Theory*, for consideration by professional economists, in an article entitled 'Keynes and Traditional Theory' (*Econometrica*, January 1937). This was reprinted in *The New Economics* edited by Professor S. E. Harris. Keynes gave this article his blessing.

was unemployment (other than frictional, transitional, etc.), that was a sure sign that labour, organized in Trade Unions or otherwise, was refusing to accept a wage sufficiently low to secure full employment. Classical writers might admit that in some cases labour was well advised to do this, since it might be better to have a fringe of unemployed than a reduction in the general standard of living; nonetheless, fundamentally, a refusal to accept lower wages was the cause of the excess unemployment. The further corollary was that, if labour consented to reduce wages sufficiently, employment would rise to the level of full employment. Keynes disagreed all along the line. He did not think that the high wage was the cause of unemployment or that lowering the wage would – subject to what is said below – increase employment. Thus the implicit classical diagnosis was wrong about a most important matter, and pointed to wrong policy. It is quite true that economists of the traditional school might agree that at a particular juncture it would be impolitic or even undesirable to press for a fall in wages, and be prepared to consider all sorts of other temporary expedients for stimulating employment. Yet at the back of their minds they would always have the thought that they were dealing in palliatives and not with the real evil, and this was bound to colour their proposals. Keynes denied that an attempt to reduce wages was dealing with the real evil at all.

In modification of this, he fully recognized that a particular country with a substantial foreign trade could gain employment by reducing wages and costs, always provided that other countries did not follow suit; thereby it would be able to underbid foreign producers and capture markets at their expense. In this he agreed with classical thought; but he disagreed in that he held that this manoeuvre would not tend to add anything to employment in the world as a whole. Secondly, he held that a fall in wages might stimulate employment, if it was expected to be followed by a rise in wages; for this would stimulate some to make hay while the sun shone. As against this, however, a reduction in wages under pressure, which most believed to be but the first step in a long grinding process of wage reduction, would increase unemployment. Thirdly, his own doctrine entailed that in the long run a wage reduction might increase employment by a roundabout process, viz. by the fall in wages and prices leading to surplus cash holding, which, in turn, might stimulate a rise of prices on the Stock Exchange, which, in turn, might, through the reduction in the effective rate of interest, stimulate capital outlay. This was a different line of thought from that of the old orthodoxy. He pointed out that precisely the same end result could be achieved much more easily by the banking system providing a little extra cash. He had some further minor concessions to the view that a wage reduction might increase employment, which were not of quantitative importance. His mode of refuting the classical view on this point was to establish his own positive theory. This was that if, in a state of full employment and of the full income-earning associated therewith, the total saving of the community would be greater than the capital outlay desired, there would not be full employment. Employment, and thereby total income-earning, would be established at a level at which the amount saved did not exceed desired capital outlay.

It is necessary to make a brief digression on his change of terminology. He abandoned the definitions which he had supplied in the *Treatise*, whereby one might talk of saving as exceeding or falling short of investment, and insisted on the book-keeping identity of the two. This represented what I believe to have been, on the whole, an unhappy victory of professional economists over laymen. The layman, in my judgement, understood well enough what Keynes meant when he said that saving might exceed investment, but professional economists had misunderstood him hopelessly. They thought that this excess entailed an increased propensity to hoard money in idle balances, or that the excess of investment, if there was one, could only occur through the creation of additional credit by the banks. All this had nothing to do with Keynes's *Treatise* doctrine and hopelessly confused the issue. Economists, long used to seeking for causal factors in changes in the volume of bank credit or velocity of circulation, would not open their minds to the fact that someone might really want to look at the matter in a different way. Keynes pointed out that extra credit created by the banks must be exactly equal to the extra hoarding of bank balances – so that these two forces cancelled each other out. One might meet Keynes's point by raising the question whether people would have wished to add to their balances if the banks had not provided extra credit, and so on, into a hopeless maze of hypotheticals and sophistications. 'The wild duck has dived down to the bottom – as deep as she can get – and bitten fast hold of the weed and tangle and all the rubbish that is down there, and it would need an extraordinarily clever dog to dive after and fish her up again.'[29]

Since there was a marked reluctance to adopt his own definitions of income and saving, which made sense of his *Treatise* theory, he thought that the only way to extricate himself from the tangle was to revert to the plain, straightforward book-keeping usage, by which saving and investment must necessarily be equal. Consequently, he could no longer say that in any circumstances saving would be unequal to investment. What happened then if producers, blindly disregarding the fact that at full employment saving would be greater than desired investment, chose to produce so much as to give full employment? Saving would in fact still be equal to investment. But the excessive propensity to save, in relation to investment opportunities, would compel producers either to accumulate unwanted stocks or sell at prices which they deemed inadequate. The unwanted stocks would constitute investment; if prices were so low as to entail losses, these would have to be deducted from the

29. *The General Theory of Employment, Interest and Money*, p. 183.

savings of the community at large; on this basis investment would be equal to saving. But the position would clearly be one of disequilibrium; it was the kind of position investigated in the *Treatise*; accumulating stocks and inadequate prices would lead to a reduction of orders and growing unemployment, and this process would continue until stocks ceased to accumulate and marginal production received an adequate remuneration. An equilibrium would be reached at which saving would balance investment without avoidable loss having to be subtracted from the former, or unwanted accretions of stock to be added into the latter. This equilibrium was of supreme importance. In the *Treatise* we only get an analysis of the economy when it is out of equilibrium and in a state of movement; the excess of saving gives a downward propulsion, the excess of investment an upward one. It is implied that there will be an equilibrium at a point where there is not an excess of either; but nothing is stated about what the relation of this equilibrium would be to a condition of full employment. There is no analysis – although hints may be found – of a condition of equilibrium with persistent unemployment. This is where the *General Theory* breaks new ground; it is an analysis of the possibility of stable equilibrium with high unemployment and no natural forces tending to redress it; a fall in wages will not avail. Employment is determined by total 'effective demand', depending on the propensity to consume and the propensity to invest. From the propensity to consume the 'multiplier' is derived; there is a certain amount of investment which the economy wishes to undertake, and this, together with the multiplier, determines how much employment there will be, which may be 100 per cent of full employment, 50 per cent, or any other figure. Only an increase of investment or an increase in the propensity to consume can raise the level. All alleged cures for unemployment can be judged exclusively by their effect on the propensity to invest or the propensity to consume.

We have not yet reached the heart of Keynes's quarrel

with traditional theory. In that theory there is an important equilibrating mechanism, namely, the rate of interest. If at full employment there is any tendency for voluntary saving to exceed voluntary investment, the rate of interest will decline and thus sufficiently stimulate investment (and perhaps discourage saving) to close the gap. It was Keynes's central contention that the rate of interest does not do this trick. At this point Keynes introduced the concept of liquidity preference. Wealthy owners always have a choice among the assets which they can hold; not only new savers, but also all the savers of the past, can review their position every day and decide to rearrange their assets. Some assets, such as wheat, have a disadvantage in that substantial storage costs are entailed; others, machines or houses, have the manifest advantage of providing, with luck, an annual yield; others have the advantage of liquidity, namely, that there is always a ready market for them. Money (cash or bank balances) has a low storage cost; [30] it has no yield, but very good liquidity. Now the rate of interest on bonds, on which the risk of non-payment is negligible, serves as an exact measure of the market's evaluation of the advantage to be derived from the liquidity of money compared with that of a bond. The bond, which is a promise to pay money, differs from money itself solely in its lower degree of liquidity, and the premium it carries must therefore measure its defect in that regard, since money and bonds are freely exchangeable for one another. If the rate of interest rose above the level thus determined, holders of money would demand bonds in exchange for it, causing the price of bonds to move up and the rate of interest to move down, until it reached that level. Whatever the propensity of the community to save may be, no one will create new assets of which it is reckoned that their prospective advantages, measured in money, add up to less than the yield of bonds. An increased propensity to save will have no tendency in itself to alter

30. In a community with a banking system this may be reckoned as nil.

the relative advantage of holding money as compared with the holding of a promise to pay money; therefore it will not alter the yield of bonds (which is the rate of interest). But since before this change of propensity, men of enterprise would have decided to create all the physical assets, whose prospective net advantages were not less than the yield of bonds, the increased propensity to save will have no tendency to stimulate capital outlay. Thus the decreased propensity to consume will not be balanced by an increased propensity to invest. Rather the other way; for the lower consumption may reduce the prospective net yield of physical assets which previously seemed just worth ordering and tilt the case against them, thus reducing the propensity to invest.

This liquidity advantage of money is not the same in the minds of all individuals; it depends for each on his particular prospects; it also depends on the judgement of each about the prospective selling value of bonds at future dates. Consequently liquidity preference cannot be set down as one definite value for all, but must be regarded as a 'schedule', showing the different prices that various individuals set upon having a little more liquidity; this schedule is analogous to the 'demand curve', which shows the different prices that various individuals are prepared to pay for extra motor-cars or for extra wireless sets. In this market for bonds, which is the reverse side of the market for money, as in other markets, the marginal buyer or holder is all-important. If the quantity of money is increased, a larger number of those who have strong liquidity preference can be satisfied and the preference of the marginal holder will be less strong; the rate of interest corresponds to the preference of the marginal holder. This shows very clearly how the banking system can affect the rate of interest; by providing more, or less, money, it can shift the margin. Thus, according to this doctrine, the rate of interest is not directly affected by the balance between savers and those who want to make capital outlay; it is affected by the balance of advantage in holding money as compared with other assets.

Yet there must be something which secures a balance between the desired volume of capital outlay and the volume of savings. According to Keynes, the equilibrating mechanism is the level of employment. If under the influence of liquidity preference the rate of interest is such that, when there is full employment, the amount which people will desire to save exceeds the amount which entrepreneurs of one kind or another desire for their capital outlay, redundant stocks will appear and profits will be inadequate, and the consequent reduction of orders will drive the level of employment downwards until a level of relative poverty is reached, at which the totality of what individuals desire to save no longer exceeds the amount for which business has a desired outlay. This is the central doctrine of employment. I cannot at all agree with those who suggest that it is the old story with minor modifications. To my judgement it is quite a new story.

It would seem from the foregoing that money is the nigger in the wood-pile. The idea has suggested itself that, if only the beautiful liquidity of money could somehow be destroyed and the advantage of holding it thus reduced, the rate of interest on bonds would fall to a lower level, so that wealth holders would be more ready to hold or create other assets with a lower net yield. Keynes accordingly had a good word for Gesell and his proposal for a stamped money which would depreciate over a period of time. He thought that this proposal should be taken seriously. He pointed out, however, that the root problem could not be solved in this way, since other assets, such as jewels and land, might be found to have good liquidity value, and these in their turn would compete as assets with motor factories or power stations and prevent investment in the latter, if their prospective marginal yield was below a certain level.

One by-product of these doctrines was the reintegration of the general theory of economics with monetary theory. Prior to this publication it seemed that those who discussed general economic theory, namely the supply of and demand for commodities and factors of production and their particular prices, were living in a different world from those who discussed banking policy and the general level of prices.

We have all of us become used to finding ourselves sometimes on the one side of the moon and sometimes on the other, without knowing what route or journey connects them, related, apparently, after the fashion of our waking and our dreaming lives.

One of the objects of the foregoing chapters has been to escape from this double life and to bring the theory of prices as a whole back to close contact with the theory of value. The division of Economics between the Theory of Value and Distribution on the one hand and the Theory of Money on the other hand, is, I think, a false division. The right dichotomy is, I suggest, between the Theory of the Individual Industry or Firm and of the rewards and the distribution between different uses of a *given* quantity of resources on the one hand, and the Theory of Output and Employment *as a whole* on the other hand.[31]

The book is mainly concerned with the development of these central ideas. Parts of it are taken up with the elaboration of some rather rigorous definitions (as, for instance, that of income) appropriate to a work designed to be a statement of first principles.[32] In the later portion Keynes indulged in some reflections prompted by his new findings. In these he may have allowed himself to be carried too far by the exhilaration due to emancipation from old fetters. He finds, for instance, in Malthus a precursor of his own theory of 'effective demand'. I cannot believe that Malthus, splendid as he was as a population theorist, contributed much of value to economics, in which he was always muddled. Again, in Keynes's handling of the mercantilists, he appears to me to have seized on isolated passages to find wisdom that was not really there. 'Roy strongly objects to Chapter 26',[33] he wrote to Mrs Robinson, 'as a tendentious

31. *The General Theory of Employment, Interest and Money*, pp. 292–3.

32. The definition of 'user cost' set out in this passage does not appear to have become popular.

33. Ultimately chapter 23.

attempt to glorify imbeciles'.[34] 'I have been occupied for several weeks,' his letter to Mrs Robinson proceeded, 'in somewhat rewriting Book I and completely rewriting Book II. In the case of Book II practically not a word of the version you have read has been left standing.' He worked hard in response to criticisms!

The practical policy which flowed from the theory was clearly that the banks should supply a sufficient quantity of money and influence interest rates by all means at their disposal, in such wise that they would stand at a level that would stimulate as much new capital outlay as was required to absorb the savings that would occur when the economy was fully employed. He did not, however, suppose that a solution of the unemployment problem could be achieved by banking policy alone. That weapon would not be powerful enough by itself to overcome the tendency of the economy to oscillate. He therefore held, pushing further forward his earlier views as to the expediency of public works, that the central authority must also have ancillary means of controlling the total volume of investment. Since public utilities and housing were the large users of capital, if the central authority could sufficiently influence the pace of investment in these, it could probably allow freedom in the main run of industry; and even where there had to be supervision over the volume of capital outlay, he always preached that this should be done in such a way as to exploit individual initiative to the full. If, as time went on, it proved difficult to find sufficient outlets for capital, the propensity to consume should be stimulated by distributing incomes more equally. Subject to these qualifications, he was in favour of the greatest possible freedom and furnished a notable reminder of the advantages of individualism.[35]

His aim in writing this book, many passages of which are difficult, was to convert his professional colleagues. He

34. Letter from J. M. Keynes to Mrs (Joan) Robinson, 3 September 1935.
35. ibid., pp. 380–81.

judged that a direct appeal to the people would be in vain, unless it could be reinforced by the majority of economists speaking with one voice. Despite all the trials he had endured, he remained confident of his ultimate power to convert the world to his way of thinking. He believed, furthermore, that, when this conversion was effected, there would be a great revival of courage and faith in the possibility of realizing ultimate social values. Men would rejoice in the prospect of being able, after all, to cure the great social evils of unemployment and poverty without having to endure the oppressive alternative of state socialism. The trend of thought of progressives would be strongly affected, and the old dogmas abandoned.

### J. M. Keynes to Mr George Bernard Shaw, 1 January 1935

Thank you for your letter. I will try to take your words to heart. There must be *something* in what you say, because there generally is. But I've made another shot at old K. M. last week, reading the Marx-Engels correspondence just published, without making much progress. I prefer Engels of the two. I can see that they invented a certain method of carrying on and a vile manner of writing, both of which their successors have maintained with fidelity. But if you tell me that they discovered a clue to the economic riddle, still I am beaten – I can discover nothing but out-of-date controversializing.

To understand *my* state of mind, however, you have to know that I believe myself to be writing a book on economic theory which will largely revolutionize – not, I suppose, at once but in the course of the next ten years – the way the world thinks about economic problems. When my new theory has been duly assimilated and mixed with politics and feelings and passions, I can't predict what the final upshot will be in its effect on action and affairs. But there will be a great change, and, in particular, the Ricardian foundations of Marxism will be knocked away.

I can't expect you, or anyone else, to believe this at the present stage. But for myself I don't merely hope what I say, – in my own mind I'm quite sure.

More than ten years have passed. The influence of the

book has been great. But its effect on feelings and passions has inevitably been somewhat different from what might have been anticipated in 1935. Then the doctrine pointed to measures of expansion, to boldness and daring in expenditure upon many things that would improve the lot of the people – but there has been the war. Since its outbreak the doctrines have pointed in the opposite way, namely, towards economy and a cutting down of all inessential investment programmes.

Keynes certainly claimed to be promoting a revolution of thought. The more comprehending critics have had some doubt, on the ground that his main work did no more than substitute one system of concepts for another. In the physical sciences some crucial test is usually available to decide between conflicting theories. If Keynes was really to be successful, he should have been able, it is argued, to refute, say, Mr D. H. Robertson, by showing a set of facts which the Keynesian doctrine would fit, while the older would not. Unhappily the state of economics is not so advanced. It is true to say that the Keynesian scheme consisted in essence in a set of new definitions and a reclassification. He asked us to look upon the multifarious phenomena of business life, and order them in our minds in a different way. In a certain sense one cannot dogmatically affirm one way to be right and the other to be wrong. Unless there is a logical flaw in one classification or another, it should be possible to sort out the facts so that they fit into either. Each classification must be judged by the ease with which the facts can be fitted and by the illumination one receives when examining the facts thus classified. One can only judge the alternative systems by using them in relation to various problems and situations. It is by actual use and application, not by logic, that Keynes has been, and will, I am confident, continue to be, triumphantly vindicated. The real defect of the classical system was that it deflected attention from what most needed attention. It was Keynes's extraordinarily powerful intuitive sense of what was important that convinced him that the old classification was inadequate. It was his highly developed logical capacity that enabled him to construct a new classification of his own. It took him ten years to do so.

The lack of appreciation by some of the older school of economists may have followed naturally from their method of approach.[36] They turned over his pages in a somewhat critical spirit, seeking aspects of the truth which they had neglected. They found that Keynes made certain points very effectively. He stressed the importance of expectation in determining present values. Yes; this was a point which had always been in their minds, but which he was probably quite right in saying that they had not stressed sufficiently. A mental note was made. Then again, there was his elaborate analysis of liquidity preference. Here certainly was something interesting. Reference to what he had in mind had sometimes been made in the discussion of velocity of circulation. But he was certainly right in holding that all this should be much more heavily stressed. These points might be jotted down for incorporation in the relevant sections of next year's lecture notes. Generous recognition should be accorded to Keynes for 'illuminating with strong light certain aspects of economic analysis whose vital significance for practice had not been seen before'.[37] These were perhaps the principal novelties they found, along with a host of detailed matters. Now these points, interesting and illuminating as they were in the relevant context, could by no means be deemed to overthrow that great structure of economic analysis, which had been refined and improved upon and

36. Professor Pigou's appreciation of Keynes in the King's College brochure is a notable and generous contribution from a slightly older economist of great eminence. Yet, in my judgement, it falls far short of giving Keynes his due rank as an economist. Pigou has since delivered two lectures on Keynes (published by Messrs Macmillan & Co., 1950), which withdraw a criticism made earlier, but still lack a real understanding of what may be called Keynes's methodological revolution.

37. Pigou, *John Maynard Keynes* (King's College), p. 22.

taught for a century. It was altogether lacking in proportion to claim for them that they constituted a revolution. I suspect that it was in some such way that the minds of the older school worked.

This inevitably entailed too low an estimate of his work. It is quite true that in themselves and in a given context the theories mentioned may be regarded merely as special improvements of the established corpus of doctrine. But that is not the point. Keynes deemed – and the whole issue turns on this – that by taking up these special points, he could completely reorganize the whole system of economic concepts required for the consideration of the level of output as a whole. A small clue made possible a mighty revolution in all our terms of thought about this subject. Classification in economics, as in biology, is crucial to the scientific structure. It is not by the intrinsic importance of the considerations which gave him his points of departure that he must be judged, but by what he achieved when he made the departure. The older school were concerned to argue that these new considerations could perfectly well be accommodated within the old conceptual framework. Of course they could be. These critics inferred that a new conceptual framework was uncalled for. Such an inference was fallacious. The splendid thing about these new considerations, it matters not whether we consider them as minor or major, was that they suggested a new conceptual framework, which has enabled us to transform all our thinking about the level of output as a whole.

The history of economic science, which is still in an early phase of development, has largely been the history of the formation of appropriate concepts. Our thinking about economic matters was revolutionized, for instance, when it was pointed out that all the multifarious costs of production could be grouped exhaustively under the three heads of land, labour, and capital. This made immense progress possible, and the whole of classical economics was based upon this classificatory improvement. Keynes's classification provides a new method of classifying the forces determining the level of output as a whole. In the old system, thought about this, when it was fundamental, consisted in applying to the general equilibrium of output concepts such as marginal costs and marginal utility, which were well-tried tools for analysing the levels of output in particular industries or firms. Instead Keynes provided the concepts of propensity to consume and propensity to invest and schedules of effective demand based upon them. The idea that supply creates its own demand disappeared; so also did the idea that unemployment is primarily due to unwillingness to work for sufficiently low wage rewards.

Keynes's classification has now been tested in use for a number of years. I am confident that those who have become accustomed to it will never wish to give it up for the old scheme of thought. It gives a sense of immense release. Of course, it has many serious pitfalls; but so has the old scheme. Where, so it seems to me, the older generation has been at fault has been in not judging the new system primarily by the test of using it. It may both be true that many things said by Keynes had been said, or could have been said, in the old terminology, and that his scheme has tempted its users into certain errors, and yet remain also true that, on the whole and on balance, his scheme is far superior. The older generation of economists looked at the new model car from the kerb of the pavement and pointed out all sorts of features which they thought unsatisfactory; but they lacked the courage to get into it and drive away in it; had they done so, they would not have wished to return to the old make.

Thus the real test of the *General Theory*, although this may seem odd to students of other branches of science, is neither logic nor fact, but convenience in use. It may be taken for granted that the logical structure is correct. It has now been used for teaching in universities in many parts of the world, and this is a searching test, as those who conduct seminars know well. Distinguished economists have continued to use it in their thinking. It has been proved viable. Even opponents have also, in some measure, slipped into using it. 'Those of us who disagreed in part with his analysis have, nevertheless, undoubtedly been affected by it in our own thinking; and it is very hard to remember exactly where we stood before. Not a little of what we now believe ourselves to have known all along, it may well be we really owe to him' (Professor Pigou).[38]

In public life it has played an even more important part. It is implicit in the thought of those who have to plan or assess tendencies towards an increase or decrease of employment, inflation or deflation, whether they be the advisers to the President of the United States, or the authors of the British *Economic Survey*. It is implicit in these studies on both sides of the Atlantic that employment will depend on an effective demand, springing from propensity to consume, propensity to invest, and Government expenditure. These reports do not use this division merely for purposes of statistical classification of past facts, but as a mode of gauging the forces making for employment. Had they used twenty-five years ago the language which they now boldly use, economists, one and all, would have assumed a supercilious smile and insisted that their diagnosis was entirely superficial. 'If you increase investment or Government expenditure, that can only be at the expense of something else. If there is unemployment, you must consider a reduction of wages; otherwise you will merely make confusion worse confounded. As an ancillary measure you should encourage all-round economy by precept and example, as that will always help to tone up the economic system.' It is sometimes claimed that economists of the traditional school were already moving away from these old practical maxims; in so far as they did so, it was really against their own doctrines.

It is fitting to draw attention to the tremendous intellectual feat involved in achieving a new workable classification.

38. op. cit., p. 22.

How many economists have tried and failed! To put the matter quite bluntly, I believe that the future historian of economic thought will regard the assistance rendered by Keynes on the road of progress as far more important than that of his revered master, Alfred Marshall. He seems, to my judgement, to stand rather in the same class as Adam Smith and Ricardo. In logical precision and penetration he was much superior to Adam Smith, in lucidity of writing to Ricardo. It must be confessed, however, that he did not produce a book which will survive as well as the *Wealth of Nations*. Many of his passages should be as durable as anything in Adam Smith, but they are scattered among works, no one of which gives a complete rendering of his mind, and parts of each of which will seem to the future student out of date for diverse reasons. This presents a difficult problem for a scholarly editor. There should, in due course, be a complete edition of the works. In addition there is needed a very clever selection, bringing into one or two volumes what it is essential to the student to know. It would be a great loss if Keynes's ideas were only studied at second-hand through their expositors, not only because he had a highly individual and elegant style as an economist – different from his popular style – which it is a pleasure for the professional to read, but also because his writing has a depth and recognition of the qualifications pertaining to any abstract doctrine, which nothing but the original text itself can convey.

Keynes loved the truth and hated the slipshod, and it would be unbecoming in a biographer to use exaggerated terms of praise. While, therefore, I put him in a class with Adam Smith and Ricardo, I express doubt whether his star, as an economist, was quite of their magnitude. Yet perhaps that is not the last word that can be said. One may go further, not in assertion, but in raising a question for the future to decide. Considering his great range of powers outside economics, his distinguished performance in logic, his depth of psychological insight, his literary power and his great versatility, may we not take his own dictum that 'Ricardo was the greatest mind that found economics worthy of its powers', and substitute for the word Ricardo the word Keynes?

By way of reaction from such thoughts, this may be the appropriate place to consider the failing for which he has been most widely criticized – that of inconsistency. It must be placed on record that this charge has been brought not merely by a rabble of detractors, but by many men of judgement, who were in a good position to know. The evidence is both extensive and weighty. As against this, I am bound to add that I cannot confirm the charge from my own experience, which consists of fairly regular contacts with him during twenty-four years and exhaustive research into his papers and published works. My own impression is quite the contrary. I detect a most remarkable consistency in the development of his theories and practical proposals, from his early studies in the Indian currency to the *General Theory* and Bretton Woods. It is, of course, true that during all this time his thought was undergoing an evolution. If it is deemed inconsistent in Darwin to have thought differently about the origin of species when a schoolboy and in his mature years, *cadit quaestio*. Considerable periods often elapsed between my opportunities of seeing Keynes, and in the interval important books might appear or public events take place. I almost always found that I knew quite well what his view would be, and did not have to write and ask him. In reading his published works I often had the feeling that I already knew what he was saying, although the reviewers sometimes displayed astonishment; this was simply because I knew his earlier views well, and what followed was a natural development from them.[39] His con-

39. This is confirmed by Mr Kahn's experience, who informs me that in practical questions relating to the bursarship of King's, he was usually able to predict correctly what Keynes would think about some new development or item of news before he had had the opportunity of consulting him.

sistency, it is true, was that of an original mind moving rapidly forward, and, therefore, has a different character from the consistency of one who is content to go through life propounding an established orthodoxy. To be consistent when one is striking out on new paths is a rare gift and implies a double dose of the virtue. I do not recall within my experience any notable instances of Keynes's inconsistency. There are, however, aspects of his life with which I was not in touch, and the charge is too widespread to be neglected.

It may, however, be to some extent explained – and perhaps explained away. In the first place, he certainly had a tendency in general conversation to *épater le bourgeois*. He liked to take an opposite point of view, in order to provoke discussion. He often pushed certain theories to a point of extravagance. Another failing may be mentioned in this connection. He cultivated the appearance of omniscience. He held forth on a great range of topics, on some of which he was thoroughly expert, but on others of which he may have derived his views from the few pages of a book at which he had happened to glance. The air of authority was the same in both cases.

A second cause of the criticism is, without doubt, that many who listened to his quick and clever talk on economic subjects were wrong in supposing that they understood his drift. Or they may have understood the actual content of his pronouncements without understanding his grounds for them. Then, some months later, they might meet him again, and his drift might seem to be in the opposite direction. Since, especially in the period from 1926 to 1935, there were only a few experts who understood his deeper thoughts on economic topics, it would not be surprising that many should attribute to inconsistency seeming contradictions, which were really due to their own failure to understand him.

Thirdly, in most controversial matters he was keenly alive to the arguments on both sides of the question. He might put the argument now on one side and now on the other to correct the bias of his interlocutor. Yet, a third party listening on two occasions might attribute this variation to inconsistency. When I first received my appointment at Oxford, a sage senior informed me that the most important function of a don was to make his pupil see that there were two sides to every question. Keynes was also a don.

Fourthly, he was essentially practical, and when convinced that the door was firmly barred against the best solution of a problem, he readily sought another one. It might be a *pis aller*, but that was better than a stalemate. For some, consistency involves pressing the same solution through thick and thin, just because it is the best solution, whether there is any hope of its being adopted or not. To go over to a less good solution, which may be accepted, seems a betrayal. A notable instance of this was Keynes's veer towards Protection in and after 1930. Free Trade, he continued to think, would have been better if only certain remedies could be applied to the unemployment problem. But when he was denied one after another of these remedies, he went over to an inferior alternative.

Another instance is his reversion towards Free Trade at the end of his life. From 1930 onwards he had become more and more convinced of the impossibility of adequate international planning, and accordingly moved further towards the view that a national full employment policy would require some measure of planned foreign trade. In itself this was not desirable; it was an instance of a *pis aller*. It was his actual experience of the cooperative spirit of the Americans, whose attitude was of no little importance in this connection, and their willingness to temper their principle of non-discrimination by all manner of safeguarding expedients, that made him veer back to favouring an open international system. So it came that we had the paradox of his rebuking me, who had been far 'sounder' on the open trading system than he during the intervening years, for not giving enough stress in my pamphlet (1946) to the principles underlying the International Trade Organization.[40] His American negotiations persuaded him that the better way was open to us, and he accordingly reverted to the advocacy of it. Such practical inconsistencies, if that is the right word for them, do not imply inconsistency of mind.

He was very quick to grasp the import of moving events in this changing world of ours. Some bits of news might make him despair of a particular recipe. His speed of thought and adaptation was so great as to seem unnatural, and others who could not keep pace or understand what was going on attributed them to an intellectual or a moral defect.

Fifthly, it must be admitted that Keynes himself might not have wished to rebut the charge of inconsistency.[41] He was in pursuit of truth. The traditions of 'the Society' and his own personal courage tended in the same direction. He was entirely free from the anxiety, which is a besetting sin of statesmen and scholars alike, not to be detected in contradicting what he had said on some previous occasion. 'Every morning', he used to say in this connection, 'I wake up as innocent as a new-born babe.' This does not, of course, mean that he was less consistent in his thinking than anyone else, but only that he was prepared to be inconsistent in utterance, if his thought required it, and that he did not modify his thought, either deliberately or by self-deception, to make it square with earlier recorded statements.

A sixth point is connected with his optimism and his pessimism. By nature he was always buoyant; his natural tendency was to take the brighter view. His intellect, however, discerned more keenly than many others the ghastly mistakes that were constantly being made. He may have exaggerated, owing to his remorseless logic, their evil effects. Thus an interlocutor might find him in his natural mood of optimism, or, alternatively, suffering from the shock caused by a vital error on the part of the authorities. As the years

40. See p. 734 below.
41. cf. the wording of his letter on pp. 524–5.

wore on, he learnt from experience that nature is strong, and that society somehow survives a series of abysmal errors, which logically should lead to perdition; thus his native optimism was confirmed by experience, and in later days he was more criticized for being too optimistic than too pessimistic. There is no doubt that he was sometimes one and sometimes the other. I do not know if this should properly be regarded as an instance of inconsistency. Every man may be allowed his moods. And, once again, we have the point that he may have sought to correct the bias of his interlocutor. Sir Hubert Henderson, a consistent pessimist in later years, is of the opinion that Keynes erred on the side of optimism in this period. Yet Keynes devoted tireless energy to explaining to the British Civil Service (and the Americans) that Britain would by no means be able to afford to behave as a rich uncle when the war was over, and that her trading difficulties would be immense; indeed he literally wore his heart out during his last years in devising means for solving our problems and persuading others how grave they would be. His sense of their gravity spurred him on anew to endeavours that were beyond his physical powers. A witness recalls that when staying with Mr Churchill during the war, he explained that the post-war problems would be quite soluble with a little wise management; Mr Churchill need not suppose that the nation would be overborne by them. Was he wrong to present this brave face to our leader? With wise management, indeed, things might not have turned out so badly as in fact they have done. But in private life he was in the habit of saying, when people complained of war-time austerities, that these were nothing to what we should have to suffer when the war was over. Was all this inconsistent?

He displayed certain traits of inconsistency in his attitude to people – but this is probably not what his critics have in mind. He used to make sharply adverse judgements rather quickly, and then a little later, after another interview, come out strongly on the other side. He attached more significance to casual remarks than they would truly bear, probably in consequence of his early training in 'the Society'. He overestimated the intellectuality of others, as he himself recognized in the Memoir Club paper.[42] Thus a stranger might express an opinion which seemed incompatible with having a nice nature or good sense, and he would be condemned in a flash of scorn. When Keynes met him again, he found no vice, and perhaps much virtue, and readily revised his judgement. Most opinions expressed by most people do not have the significance that Keynes was disposed to attach to them; they are mere flotsam and jetsam, giving little more indication of character than 'it is a fine day'.

I put on the record, with a considerable sense of responsibility, that a large number of good witnesses have testified to inconsistency. I am the channel between the witnesses and the student of Keynes, and it is right that I should transmit the messages. I confess that I retain my own opinion, and even venture to state the view that we may have here one of those cases where a popular saying, often repeated, is the opposite of the truth. I believe that Keynes was quite unusually consistent, and that this unusual quality made a disturbing impression on the minds of ordinary mortals, implanting an uneasiness which they assuaged by charging him with the opposite quality. The dictum gained support from those superficial manifestations of inconsistency, and those phenomena which seemed to be manifestations of inconsistency, but were not really so, which I have described. Thus the counterfeit coin remained in circulation.

Be that as it may, the careful student is able to trace a natural evolution of ideas from his early writings to the great system set out in the *General Theory*. Keynes had no inkling at the outset of what was to come; he approached certain technological problems in a modest and sober spirit; he had great regard for British monetary tradition and for the efficiency of our methods. But he was deeply impressed

42. See pp. 93–4 above.

by the amount of development there had been in a short space of time in the Indian system, which, although in a certain sense automatic, contained automatisms which had been introduced by a process of conscious adaptation. This might be carried further, and maxims of practical expediency might be married to those ideals for a stable currency which hitherto had been largely academic. He reacted to the great post-war inflations in a way natural to an economist, adding some points of his own but in substantial agreement with orthodoxy. Then came the deflations, opposite evils. Again he applied traditional wisdom, but this problem of deflation seemed more intractable. It was accompanied by the social evil of unemployment. One might urge the authorities not to deflate, and attack them for doing so. An economy that had been deflated seemed to need reviving. How was this to be done? He brought out his own proposals, to which orthodox economists raised objections. How were the objections to be met? Gradually it was borne in upon him that our understanding of the way in which deflation operates was inadequate. More understanding – that was the key to the matter; more thorough-going analysis. So we get those long struggles to clarify his own thought. In the end he found that the analysis of deflation required a completely new analysis of the forces governing unemployment: that is, of the forces governing employment itself. His progress was fairly steady. He published his results quickly. It is remarkable how little of his old thought had to be scrapped. The new thought took it up and placed it in a wider setting. The special law was generalized to cover a larger variety of cases. There is little doubt that he would not have rested content with the position that he had achieved in 1936 any more than Ricardo, whose mind was also continually moving forward, would have rested content with the last edition of his *Principles*. But, if Keynes's achievement was not final, it was sufficient to enable those who follow to advance to new positions. If he had stopped short at the *Treatise*, this might not have been so. Study of the *General Theory* enlarges our sense of how much there is in the *Treatise*. Yet, the fundamental concepts of the *Treatise* were not likely to prove acceptable and useful for other professional economists. Looking back upon his struggles with the *General Theory*, we may see them as a race with time. In his own mind he was quite sure that it would revolutionize thinking. But if this was to be so, he must state his position with absolute clarity; he must hear all objections, he must revise, refine, rewrite. It was a herculean labour, making a greater call upon the vital energies than his more spectacular work in the second war. It was only achieved in the nick of time.

### 3

1935 was mainly occupied with rewriting sections of the *General Theory* and corresponding with his friends about it; but there was also a strongly competing interest, the building of a new theatre in Cambridge. Keynes was in every sense responsible – for the idea, for the execution, and for the finance. Cambridge lacked at this time a high-class theatre, although there was a steady and ever-growing demand for one. The principal ingredients in this adventure were as follows. King's College owned land behind King's Parade, where rebuilding was due. Thus Keynes, as First Bursar, could represent the landlord's interest in the matter. He was prepared to make a substantial investment in the project with his own money. Mr Norman Higgins, who was known in Cambridge from his admirable management of the Cosmopolitan Cinema, was available to run the theatre. Mr George Rylands, Fellow of King's, could assist in supervising, knowing as he did the ideas that Keynes had in mind. Mr George Kennedy was chosen to be the architect; he had done important work in King's – the new Bodley's Building, the new Provost's Lodge – and he had shown his ingenuity in solving awkward problems of securing maximum accommodation within strict limitations.

Oxford men know his marvellous contrivance in converting a jumble of old buildings into the elegant Holywell Manor for Balliol. In the case of the theatre also the site was cramped, and great dexterity was required. Last, but not least, there was Lydia, who would not only be interested in visits of the Vic-Wells Ballet and in other matters connected with the programmes, but also might find opportunities herself to appear on the stage there.

Building proceeded during 1935, and the theatre opened on 3 February 1936. The cost of construction had originally been estimated at £18,000, and the company started with a registered capital of £20,000. Of this some £2,500 of preference shares were taken up by well-wishers in Cambridge. These were subsequently bought in. Keynes took all the ordinary shares at £12,500 and later £5,000 of preference shares. Between the original conception and the completion the scheme was constantly expanded and a restaurant was added. Eventually the cost proved to be £36,000, and a mortgage had to be taken out. This was paid off in five years. Losses were incurred in the first two years, but each year showed an improvement. The theatre held six hundred, and, to be profitable, had to be quite full. In order to attract first-class performances, visiting companies were sometimes offered more favourable terms than the true earning capacity of the theatre justified. Thus, in the early stages there was an element of considerable financial anxiety.

By 1938 the finances appeared to be in balance. Then Keynes formed a trust. He would probably have continued his private responsibility for a longer period, but he had become seriously ill, and the future was in doubt. The trustees were to consist of five *ex-officio* members, two representatives of the Town, two representatives of the University, and the Provost of King's, together with himself and Mr Rylands as 'representing the active management of the theatre'. In effect the management was little changed, and he continued to devote much time to the affairs of the theatre until the end. In his letter to the Mayor, he expressed his desire that 'the establishment of the Trust, with its potentiality of equal services to the University and town, should be in some sense a memorial to his parents and their devoted services to Cambridge over half a century'. In forming this trust, he was handing over an asset, which had cost £36,000, out of which he had personally provided the £17,500 of capital remaining after repayment of the mortgage. This idea of a trust, to be administered by a joint body for the artistic enrichment of the community, foreshadowed developments on a national scale, for which he was to be responsible as Chairman of the Arts Council.

The theatre, finally christened, after much debate, The Arts Theatre, was not a repertory one. It would provide a stage for the Marlowe Society, the Greek Play Committee, and any other suitable undergraduate enterprises. For the rest, it would depend on visiting companies of high quality. The standards set were principally governed by the judgement of Keynes and his wife. It was not intended to confine the theatre to 'high-brow' productions; their interests were more catholic, and comprehended popular works; a place would even be given to farce, if it was first-rate farce. The idea was that all the productions should be good of their kind; box-office considerations were never allowed to cause any deviation from this ideal.

The theatre opened with a Vic-Wells Ballet. The first plays presented were a cycle of four by Ibsen, Lydia taking the chief part in *A Doll's House* and *The Master Builder*, while Jean Forbes-Robertson performed in *Hedda Gabler* and *Rosmersholm*. Lydia had made occasional appearances as an actress since the *Masque of Poetry and Music*. She had played at the Old Vic as Olivia in *Twelfth Night* 'before a gala audience of 2,500, which she held spellbound'. She was 'a delight to the eye and to the ear' in the Ibsen plays, and, to her husband's great joy, this cycle subsequently had a run of eighty days at the Criterion Theatre in London. Another of Lydia's notable performances at the Arts Theatre was as Célimène in *The Misanthrope*.

When the Vic-Wells Ballet or any company in which Keynes had a special interest was visiting the theatre, he had a habit of giving a large party, at which the youth of Cambridge made acquaintance with illustrious performers. These parties became a notable feature of Cambridge life.

Keynes was often at the theatre, not only for his own pleasure, but also because he was determined that the finances should not be endangered by lack of attention to detail. Nothing was too trivial for him. By a happy and successful idea, a restaurant was attached to the theatre, and I recall receiving a letter from him asking me to write a testimonial for a chef. There was even an occasion when, by some mishap, the box-office clerk failed to appear and Keynes himself went into the box-office to issue tickets.

He was deeply interested in the programmes and spent many long hours discussing these matters with Mr Higgins. He was deeply interested also in the character of the audiences and in the kind of people who were attracted by the various productions. He sat in his office brooding upon them. 'Who are these people? Where do they come from? It is very queer; I do not know half a dozen people in the whole theatre.' He was as curious about the occupants of the cheap seats as about those in the expensive ones. Favourable terms were given for organized parties from factories in the neighbourhood. He caused a graph of the receipts at the bar to be made, to correlate the amount spent there with the various types of programme. He studied the stock book at regular intervals, deeply fascinated by it, pondering upon the variations in the consumption of liquor.

He was anxious to encourage expenditure upon wine in the restaurant rather than upon cocktails and spirits. His mind reverted to the admirable qualities of champagne. He gave an instruction that, instead of the usual addition of fifty per cent to the cost price, only 2s. 6d. should be added in the case of champagne, with the consequence that profits on that item actually rose!

In the matters connected with the artistic side he knew

that he was a learner. All trace of his habitual dogmatism and barbed repartee disappeared when he entered this world. In the world of finance he worked with the advantage of his vast experience and deep understanding; in most arguments he had an inner certainty of being in the right, and felt that it was due to the truth to enforce his opinion, however sharply. Where he knew that he had no certainty, he adapted his controversial methods accordingly. Mr Higgins recalls his beautiful tact. When they disagreed and Keynes had his way and it proved a mistake, the formula always was, 'You were right.' But when Mr Higgins had his way and it proved mistaken, the formula was, 'We were wrong.'

He was only able to maintain his active interest in these absorbing matters by his extraordinary power of switching his mind from one subject to another. Mr Higgins might have an appointment at 4.20 p.m. and find someone with him discussing a bursarial matter, who was dismissed promptly; Keynes talked on theatre matters as though he had been thinking of them all day; but at 5 o'clock a pupil appeared, and Mr Higgins in turn was expected to leave promptly.

At one period there was a regular routine of luncheon on Tuesday before Keynes caught the 3.15 to London. Talk on theatre matters proceeded apace. At 3 o'clock a man announced that the car was at the Lodge. Keynes then moved about the room selecting bundles of papers, which he put into his pouch. All proceeded in a leisurely manner. Mr Higgins went with him to the Lodge talking, drove to the station talking, and proceeded up the platform, when there was now less than a minute before the train departed, still talking. Higgins watched him settle into his corner; the pouch was opened and, before the train departed, Keynes was deeply immersed in the study of his documents.

4

The clouds were gathering. Keynes, like others, felt the terrible anxieties of those days. Taking refuge in academic work and returning to an old love after the appearance of the *General Theory*, he wrote an elaborate centenary memoir on Jevons for the *Journal of the Royal Statistical Society*.[43] A little later he burst into a great controversy on foreign policy in the *New Statesman and Nation*. In the twenties he had favoured disarmament, but now he wished the nation to be strong. He was sickened by views which appeared from time to time in the columns of that paper. All expenditure on defence should be resisted, it was contended, on the ground that the Government could not be trusted to make good use of the weapons. These writers were all in favour of resistance to Fascism; they held, however, that, because the Government had not entered into far-reaching commitments for military action, it must be at heart pro-Fascist and, therefore, must not be trusted with arms. As though the military strength of Britain could be turned on and off in accordance with each shift in British party politics! Keynes was very scathing in his exposure of these views. 'Surely it is impossible that there can really be such a person as "A Socialist"! I disbelieve in his existence.' Severely as he condemned our attitude in the Abyssinian affair, he was not altogether sure that Mr Baldwin's subsequent conduct of the foreign situation was wrong. 'You complain against Mr Baldwin's Government for not aligning itself definitely against the dictatorships. But Mr Baldwin is perhaps wiser than you are. He may be hesitating because he knows that *nothing* is certain. It may conceivably prove to have been right on our part not to clinch the situation, not to crystallize the fatal alignment of forces. No state of mind is more painful than a state of continuing doubt. But the ability to main-

43. Read before the Royal Statistical Society, 21 April 1936.

tain it may be a mark of statesmanship.'[44] In this agony of
continuing doubt Keynes, with his keen sensitivity to current events and regular habit of foresight, must have suffered
severely from the strain, despite his native optimism. I
should not be surprised if this was an important cause of his
collapse, now soon to come.

In the summer he visited Russia. On his way he stayed in
Stockholm and gave a lecture, which was arranged by
Professor Ohlin. He gave an important broadcast for the
BBC on the relationship between Art and the State; this
problem was coming to the forefront of his mind.[45] He
wrote an article on the gold supply, which was on the whole
optimistic in relation to the possibility of maintaining low
interest rates.[46] Somewhat later, he had a series of three
articles in *The Times* entitled 'How to Avoid a Slump'.[47]
Dear money during the present comparatively favourable
period was to be avoided at all costs. A Board of Public
Investment should be ready with plans to be put into execution when the slump should come. It came later in the year,
but by then rearmament was becoming an important influence. Turning back to another field of interest, he gave a
lecture at the Galton Anniversary dinner,[48] entitled 'Some
Economic Consequences of a Declining Population'. *The
Times* seems now to have become his regular vehicle for
expressing his views. The boom had not yet come to an end
and he thought it needful to consider whether the Chancellor's plan to borrow for defence might have inflationary
consequences. It need not; but careful planning would be
necessary.

I remember asking him during this period, when the
Arts Theatre had become an important preoccupation,

44. *New Statesman and Nation*, 18 July, 8, 15, 29 August and 12
September 1936.
45. *The Listener*, 26 August 1936.
46. *Economic Journal*, September 1936.
47. *The Times*, 12–14 January 1937.
48. The Eugenics Society, 16 February 1937.

whether he did not find that he had too much to do. He was always contemptuous of the idea of over-work. Referring to a well-known economist and man of affairs, who was popularly supposed to be very busy, 'I cannot think how X manages to fill up his time,' he observed. But on this occasion he made a concession. He did think that during term he had a little too much to do for comfort. I regarded the concession as ominous.

The crisis came during the summer term in 1937, when he had made an unusually long visit to Cambridge 'to escape the Coronation crowds'. His severe attack of appendicitis in 1915[49] had been complicated by a pulmonary embolus. This resulted in some physical derangement, which existed through all his busy years, and put an additional strain upon his heart. He fell gravely ill in Cambridge with heart disease due to thrombosis of a coronary artery. The situation seemed extremely serious, and after some weeks he was removed to Ruthin Castle in Wales. Friends awaited news anxiously. Would he recover? Would he, if he did, ever be the same man again? Alas, he never made a complete recovery, although, by a mighty victory of mind over body, he was able for a number of years to equal, and exceed, a normal man's output of work.

In the course of this illness he was brought into touch with Dr Plesch, who was as successful in his treatment as the condition allowed. Keynes had implicit confidence in him and sought his advice and followed it – to the extent that his nature would permit – until the end. Dr Plesch was a man of temperament and originality; he found himself in natural sympathy with his patient and ultimately became not only his doctor, but his very good friend.

Keynes was never completely out of action. Although he was perilously ill in Cambridge and his troubles were not yet thoroughly diagnosed, he insisted on Mr Kahn's keeping him well informed on College matters. Kahn visited him several times each day. With his assistance he wrote a

49. See p. 237 above.

lengthy letter to *The Times*[50] on the gold scare and appropriate Treasury policy. At Ruthin he had perforce to
acquiesce in inaction, since he had not the benefit of Kahn's
presence. But his mind strained after intellectual activity.
For a period he was allowed a ration of two hours' work a
day. He maintained contact with the King's Bursary, the
*Economic Journal* and other routine interests. There was
at length sufficient business for his secretary, Mrs Stephens,
to be summoned to Ruthin. Then he was transferred to Tilton, and by slow stages picked up the threads again.

In consequence of this great crisis, Lydia became a paramount figure. She had been a good and faithful wife in
happy days. Now she had to face a long-drawn-out ordeal.
For nine years his life hung by a thread. For her these were
years of unremitting anxiety and ceaseless vigilance. She
never flinched or faltered. This creature of air, so full of
fun and temperament, entered upon the stern path of duty
as might one trained from girlhood in conventual rigours.
Was there some deep inner Russian calm of soul which enabled her to carry her heavy burden through a long stretch
of time in patience and serenity. Her gaiety was undimmed;
her spirits remained high. Youth passed. Self was effaced.
No one has ever heard any word of self-pity from Lydia on
this score – not a word, not a whisper, not a breath. It is
hard not to be tarnished by self-sacrifice. Gradually, drop by
drop, a little pool of bitterness usually begins to form. It
was not so in her case. What she had to give she gave gladly
from natural goodness and true love.

In the course of 1938 he was in London for periods and
received visitors. Meetings of committees were arranged
at Gordon Square. Lydia became a familiar figure. A certain
ration of time was allowed. If he talked or debated for too
long, he would suffer afterwards. The Council of the Royal
Economic Society had its meetings at his house. When the
right time had elapsed, Lydia put her head round the door.
'Time, gentlemen!' Her rule was absolute. If items on the

50. 10 June.

agenda remained undiscussed, they must be left until the next meeting. It had been worth while for us to have our Secretary with us at the price of a shorter meeting. And so it went on; the ration allowed increased gradually, but discipline had to be maintained. Not that it was always easy to enforce discipline on the patient himself. Maynard tugged at the leash, impatient of all restraint. Lydia had to summon up all her fire and fury sometimes, in the good cause, and there were stormy conflicts of will.

In the later years of the war Keynes was doing full duty. At Bretton Woods and, still more, in the American Loan negotiations, he took part in exertions which left his healthy colleagues exhausted. He seemed to have limitless vitality. It did not mean that he was a sound man. As soon as he returned to his room at the end of the day's work, whether it was short or long, he became the invalid at once, and Lydia assumed her nursing duties. He had to go to bed, and she applied an ice-pack to his chest. Thus he was devoting himself to his duties even more exhaustively than appeared on the surface. His life was one of work and no play. He could only retire to the repose of his sick-room. There he might find solace in reading the works of Elizabethan authors. But he was not to be pitied, for he enjoyed his work. His intellectual temperament made it exciting for himself, as well as for those who had to work with him. It was a fascinating game. It was good to be alive and doing all these things.

In his time of convalescence and partial recovery he had more leisure to cultivate old interests and develop new ones before the full strain of his Treasury work came upon him during the war. His interest in his farm at Tilton grew, and would no doubt have become a main preoccupation, had he survived to the age of retirement. When he was able to get back to Cambridge, he continued to enjoy his Arts Theatre hobby.

His first public appearance after his illness was at the Annual General Meeting of the National Mutual Life

Assurance Society.[51] He made a speech of considerable importance; he had evidently been watching events with all his wonted insight from his sick bed. His speeches as Chairman of this company had long come to be regarded as notable events in the City. They were couched in the language of a businessman, and may have given financiers a better understanding of his views than they would derive from his books and articles. These addresses to the members received wide attention in the press – as much as, and perhaps more than, the annual speeches of the Chairmen of the Joint Stock Banks. On this occasion he had an important point to make. The gilt-edged market had weakened during the year, and this was commonly attributed to the general slump, which was now under way. In his view it was due to the method by which the Exchange Equalization Account had handled the inflow of gold. It was the recognized duty of the Account to sterilize incoming gold when it was undesirable that it should lead to an expansion of credit; in Keynes's view, the Account had gone beyond this and caused deflation. Normally when it absorbed gold, an equivalent value of Treasury Bills was released to the market. On this occasion the totality of National Debt operations had so worked together that the market was given an extra dose, not of Treasury Bills but of long-dated Debt. Meanwhile the foreigners, who brought in the gold, would be holding balances or Bills. Thus the net effect was that the quantity of bank money and liquid assets was reduced, while, at the same time, the market had been asked to absorb an extra volume of long-dated securities. This was certainly deflationary. Exchange Account policy should be corrected. In general he struck a note of moderate optimism, not thinking that the recession would go further. He ended with an impassioned plea to the Government to add 'to our knowledge of the actual facts and figures which alone can make the working of the economic system intelligible and distinguish true theories from false by the test of results.

51. 23 February 1938.

A great deal is at stake . . . we have to show that a free system can be made to work. To favour what is known as planning and management does not mean a falling away from the moral principles of liberty, which could formerly be embodied in a simpler system. On the contrary, we have learnt that freedom of economic life is more bound up than we previously knew with the deeper freedoms – freedom of person, of thought, and of faith.[52]

Meanwhile, he returned to the charge on the question of foreign policy in an article which contained a word of praise for Mr Churchill.[53]

His enforced abstention from many active pursuits caused a revival of interest in his earliest hobby of all, book-collecting. It had never been in abeyance. From his schoolboy visits to David's and the foundation of the Baskerville Club he had gone forward as an active collector, enlarging his scope as his income increased. Moving away from early printed editions of the classics, he concentrated his attention upon the first editions of the great English thinkers – Newton, F. D. Maurice, Hume, Berkeley, Bentham, Mandeville, Wordsworth and Coleridge. In 1934 he went to the sale of Gibbon's Lausanne library at Sotheby's and bought about sixty of Gibbon's books at the sale and subsequently. In 1936 he was at the sale of Lord Lymington's Newton papers at Sotheby's and bought about forty lots, and he followed up many of the lots purchased by the book trade and succeeded in buying a number of them. 1938 marked a great expansion in his activities. He had more leisure. It may be that in bed in the morning he began to pay less attention to brokers' reports and concentrated his mind on catalogues.

He was still primarily interested in the great thinkers and extended his attention to those of the Continent. He also began to branch out into English literature of the sixteenth and seventeenth centuries. 'He had a theory that the books of the Elizabethans were much rarer than most

52. cf. also letter to the *Economist*, 5 March 1938.
53. *New Statesman and Nation*, 25 March 1938.

people realized and that his was the last generation that would have a chance of acquiring many of them at any price at all.'[54] The rate of expansion in his library was truly remarkable in the final period, and might well have provided the full-time occupation of an ordinary man. 'At his death the rare-book collection, as opposed to the extensive general library, comprised perhaps 4,000 volumes and about 300 manuscripts and autograph letters.' This collection was bequeathed to King's College. 'There was also a large working collection of books on economics, the subject of a separate bequest to the Marshall Library at Cambridge.'[55] He kept a notebook with a page for each of his chosen authors. 'Booksellers' catalogues, English, Continental and American, were carefully read and marked, and there was hardly an auction sale of importance to which he did not send commissions. Whenever possible he viewed the books himself; only when pressure of work made this increasingly difficult did he delegate this to the booksellers. Buying for him at auction was entrusted to one of the leading London firms, but Keynes was far too independent a collector to place himself unreservedly in the hands of any one member of the trade; and it gave him particular pleasure to buy an expensive book (if the price were a fair one) from one of the smaller dealers.'[56] He had a copy of the *Short Title Catalogue of Books printed in England, Scotland and Ireland, 1475–1640*, in which he marked the prices realized at sales for items which he coveted, and it is clear that he often did not buy until he had formed an opinion, by successive entries, as to what a good price would be.

His brother, Geoffrey, was also a notable collector, and he made a present to Maynard of an acquisition which was a

54. 'Lord Keynes and His Books', by A. N. L. Munby, *The Times Literary Supplement*, 19 October 1946. For a fuller account of Keynes's activities as a book-collector, see contribution by Mr Munby to *John Maynard Keynes* (King's College), pp. 29–36.

55. ibid.
56. ibid.

little outside his field of interest, a rare eighteenth-century pamphlet, of which in 1938 only two other copies had been located, namely, an *Abstract of Hume's Treatise of Human Nature*, published in 1740. It had been supposed that Adam Smith in his boyhood at Glasgow had made an Abstract of Hume's *Treatise*. And now here was such an Abstract. Keynes sought the assistance of Mr P. Sraffa in examining it. They were able to show that the evidence for Smith's having written an Abstract was extremely flimsy, and that, on the contrary, internal evidence, derived from a comparison of the *Treatise*, the *Abstract* and the Appendix to the *Treatise* subsequently published, proved that the Abstract was by Hume himself! Hume had in fact written a puff of his own book, which so far (1740) had sold very badly. While Keynes and Sraffa proved their point by the collation of passages with scholarly conscientiousness, the general reader may well think that no mind yet born into this world, save that of Hume himself, could have written with the easy flow and relentless logic of the author of the *Abstract*. Keynes published it in 1938, writing an introduction jointly with Sraffa. It was indeed a crowning glory to have been able to give the world, with adequate proofs appended, a hitherto unknown work from the pen of 'the superb Hume'.[57]

Of his Newton collection Mr Munby writes that it 'is probably the finest ever put together by a private individual'. Browsing among these possessions, Keynes was led to some reflections which he embodied in an article. He stressed Newton's alchemical interests, and argued that in a certain sense his bent of mind gave him closer kinship with the preceding age than with the science of the future. This paper, entitled 'Newton the Man', was read after his death by his brother Geoffrey at the Newton Tercentenary celebrations on 15 July 1946 in Trinity College, Cambridge.

Unlike many collectors, he almost invariably read what

57. cf. p. 125 above.

he purchased. He found time for much correspondence with other scholars and always gave them ready access to his books. At the time of his death his entire collection of Hume, some 175 volumes, was on loan.

It fell to me to preside over Section F of the British Association at its Cambridge meeting in 1938, and I asked Keynes to contribute to our proceedings. He was not able to come in person, but furnished a paper, which was read aloud by his old pupil and friend, Gerald Shove. The subject was 'The Policy of Government Storage of Food Stuffs and Raw Materials'. He argued that the risk of holding surplus stocks until they should be wanted was beyond the scope of private enterprise, while the fluctuations in the prices of commodities were too violent to serve any good economic purpose. He proposed, therefore, official stocks, both to fulfil the function of making prices more stable for the benefit of producers and also to have an effect on the general trade cycle. This paper was the basis of proposals which he elaborated in greater detail during the war, to be a subject for Anglo-American discussions on post-war reconstruction. During the year which followed he carried on a correspondence with appropriate persons on the policy of 'stock piling', as it is now called, with a view to the possibility of war.

The ghastly ordeal of Munich came and went. In an article in the *New Statesman* [58] he attributed to Mr Chamberlain a Machiavellian policy. 'Neither the Prime Minister nor Herr Hitler ever intended for one moment that the play-acting should devolve into reality.' In effect, in his view, Britain was acquiescing in Germany's taking the safeguards she deemed necessary before launching an attack on the East. I suspect that the convalescent had resort to a little wishful thinking in this horrible period. He could not bear to suppose that British policy was quite as futile as it seemed to be. I had a talk with him at this time; he was lying on his sick-couch; he said what pain it gave him to think that a

58. 8 October 1938.

Government of Britain could comport itself in this appallingly inefficient manner. At this time he wrote a letter to *The Times*, the purport of which is indicated by its last sentence: 'We can no longer afford to leave the barter aspect of foreign trade to look after itself.' [59]

This was a time of great stress. He could find enjoyment by seeing Lydia act in *On the Frontier*, by Messrs Auden and Isherwood. He made a present to the Vic-Wells of the scenery and costumes by Derain for a new ballet, *Harlequin in the Street*.

Early in 1939 Sir Stafford Cripps started a campaign, which was eventually to lead him temporarily into the wilderness, to organize a united front of progressives in opposition to the policy of Munich. 'I am all for Sir Stafford Cripps, and I would join his movement, if he is successful in getting it launched. But I should like the movement all the better if Mr Herbert Morrison and all the others would join it too.'[60] He made a contribution to Sir Stafford Cripps's fund.

Thoughts inevitably turned to war finance. He contributed two important articles to *The Times*.[61] The point of greatest moment was his strong plea that the rate of interest should be maintained at a low level. This policy was carried out during the war to the immense benefit of our war effort and our post-war finances. He urged that the export of capital should now be controlled, that a Department of Co-ordination with an economic general staff should be set up. He spoke on the air about the conditions of full employment which would follow rearmament.[62] He returned to the charge with two more articles in *The Times*,[63] elaborating the technique of a low interest policy.

In the summer he and Lydia went off to Royat for a holiday. It was his last trip to the Continent of Europe.

59. 7 October 1938.
60. *New Statesman and Nation*, 28 January 1939.
61. 17 and 18 April 1939.
62. *Listener*, 1 June 1939.
63. *The Times*, 24 and 25 July 1939.

# [12]

## Into World War II

### I

AND so we were back where we had been twenty-five years ago. This time there were no qualms or doubts whether the cause justified the carnage. Germany, risen from her ashes, had assumed a mien so hideous and evil that no parallel could be found in the era of recorded history. Entire self-immolation was required and given. In other wars beloved sons had gone away to do their duty. Now the whole people would give battle rather than submit. All other hopes and prospects were blotted out. When in due course it fell to Mr Churchill to speak in sublime language of fighting in the streets, he expressed what was already in the hearts of the great majority of the people. There was a hatchet behind the cottage door; and it was meant to be used.

The dedication to the cause was so complete that a strange calm ensued. If one was still walking in the sunshine, enjoying good sleep or eating one's dinner, albeit on a reduced scale, these seemed to be gifts of providence unexpectedly thrown in, a pleasant epilogue to the happy drama of one's life which had ended when Hitler invaded Poland. And so it came about that British morale remained at the highest level as the long-drawn-out years proceeded. Keynes's congenital optimism asserted itself, and he was able to see good points in the military news. Really, it was possible to be quite cheerful.

What was to be done? Did he dream sometimes of 'A' Division? Ought he not to reassemble his staff to pick up the threads where they had left them? Where were Falk and Dudley Ward and Trouton? But, no. His juniors of those days were now in charge of the Treasury and had their own

575

ideas. Besides, he was still a sick man. 'My plan is to come up here [King's College] to run a good part of the bursary of the college, the *Economic Journal*, and teaching in the Economics Faculty, which in due course will release more active people.'[1] 'Committee work, which would involve quiet drafting in my own room and occasional visits to London, would be the sort of thing I might be fit for.'[2] In the following months he remained in Cambridge, going down to London for two or three nights in the middle of each week.

Inevitably his mind got to work on the problems of war economics. He was in occasional correspondence with Sir Richard Hopkins and Sir Frederick Phillips, the two pillars of the Treasury. On 15 September he sent in a memorandum urging that a moderate rise in controlled British prices should be tolerated, in order that they should not be too far away from the world level. He recommended long-term bulk purchases from the Commonwealth and Empire. On 24 September he sent in a paper on exchange control. He wrote to *The Times*, criticizing the budget, urging the supreme importance of borrowing at two and a half per cent and hinting at the desirability of new ways of raising money.[3]

The *New Statesman and Nation* was being troublesome again, and Keynes was stirred to writing the following letter:

The intelligentsia of the Left were the loudest in demanding that the Nazi aggression should be resisted at all costs. When it comes to a showdown, scarce four weeks have passed before they remember that they are pacifists and write defeatist letters to your columns, leaving the defence of freedom and of civilization to Colonel Blimp and the Old School Tie, for whom Three Cheers.[4]

1. Letter to R. F. Harrod, 7 September 1939.
2. Letter to Lord Stamp, 15 September 1939.
3. *The Times*, 29 September and 4 October.
4. 14 October 1939.

The illness of Sir John Withers, who was one of the two Members of Parliament for Cambridge University, made an early by-election likely. The Master of Magdalene College, Mr A. B. Ramsay, who had been a master at Eton when Keynes was a boy there, was now Chairman of the University Conservative Committee. This Committee instructed him to approach Keynes to stand for Cambridge. In view of the party truce that had been declared, it was the Conservative Committee which had the right to nomination, but it was understood that Keynes would be an Independent and that members of all parties would sign his nomination paper. It was practically certain that there would be no contest. Mr Ramsay used friendly persuasion; he explained that the Committee was fully aware of the limitations imposed by the state of his health and would not expect him to do more than use the House of Commons as a place for advocating his ideas when he felt moved to do so. Keynes was tempted; he consulted Dr Plesch. In the end he refused.

After what you told me [he wrote to his doctor], I am not taking this decision on grounds of health. It has been a tormenting decision to make, but gradually a clear and final conclusion has risen to the surface. I am, as you know, a pretty active publicist, but it appears to me rather definitely that I can only operate usefully and for my full influence on my own peculiar lines, if I am aloof from the day-to-day life of Westminster.[5]

At 46 Gordon Square he acted as host to regular meetings of the 'Old Dogs'. These were distinguished persons, who, like himself, had played a notable part in World War I, but had not yet been invited to serve in this one – Sir William Beveridge, Sir Walter Layton and Sir Arthur Salter. Mr Hubert Henderson, who already had a desk in the Treasury, also came. It was inevitable that the idea should occasionally crop up in such an assembly that things were being woefully mismanaged. Instances could be picked up in

5. 24 November 1939.

abundance. ARP, dispersion, the blockade, were among the topics discussed. Beveridge was playing a part in the Federal Union movement, and raised the question of war aims. Keynes drafted a memorandum which included the idea of a Reconstruction Fund to be supported by the United States, on terms of unprecedented generosity, as soon as Hitler was overthrown, to prevent the spread of Communism to Germany.

Gradually, however, as the autumn wore on, his mind became focused upon the central problems of internal war finance. He matured his plan for 'compulsory saving', which was explained in *The Times* in two long articles on 14 and 15 November. (By some mysterious leakage they appeared in the *Frankfurter Zeitung* on 7 November. That distinguished journal was much quicker off the mark in presenting Keynes's views to the German public in 1939 than he had been in presenting theirs to the British public in 1915!)[6]

*The Times* articles led to a voluminous correspondence, public and private, to editorial and Parliamentary comment, and to numerous cartoons by Low.[7] Meanwhile he was at work on a lengthier exposition of his ideas in the form of a small book, which appeared under the title of *How to Pay for the War*, in February 1940.[8] This was followed by vigorous propaganda. He presented the scheme over the air in a dialogue with Mr Donald Tyerman. He addressed a TUC group, the National Trade Union Club, the Fabian Society and a gathering of some 250 Members of Parliament of all parties. He interviewed numerous financiers of eminence, including the Governor of the Bank

6. cf. Chapter 6, p. 235.

7. See especially further articles by Keynes in *The Times*, 28 November 1939, letters of 1 and 6 December 1939, and 5 February, 15 March, 10 and 25 April 1940; letters in *Financial News*, 3 and 5 January and a controversy with Mr J. R. Hicks in the *Manchester Guardian*, 27–9 February.

8. 35,000 copies were sold in the U.K.

of England, 'who says he thinks it is the only solution, and with whom, after a long estrangement, this scheme has brought a personal reconciliation'.[9]

This little book is of great theoretical as well as practical interest. Complaints have been made that, in the elaboration of his *General Theory*, Keynes dwelt to a preponderating extent on the problems of unemployment. Deficient demand was the prevailing malady of the inter-war period, and Keynes kept his eye on the practical situation. In *How to Pay for the War* Keynes applied his technique of analysis to the economics of excessive demand. The book thus fills a gap.

The problems of war finance centre upon the question of inflation. As Keynes remarked, he had been cognizant of all the discussions of wartime inflation that took place in Britain during World War I, and never was it discussed in terms remotely resembling those in which he now presented the problem. Yet now, in 1940, his method of analysis was accepted both by those who were willing and by those who were not willing to support his practical proposals. Thus he had indeed the right to claim that his theoretical work between the wars had revolutionized the modes of thinking of economists upon inflation. They had long ceased to regard inflation primarily as an over-issue of notes or even an over-expansion of bank credits. The older school still clung to the idea that there would be no inflation if the budget deficit was financed by 'voluntary lending'. Keynes's central point was that the voluntariness of the lending was no criterion. Whatever the degree of inflation, the Government would always find voluntary lenders. Such ease of borrowing would not be a guarantee that inflation was not taking place, but, on the contrary, its consequence. For Keynes, borrowing was essentially inflationary whenever it exceeded the amount that people would have been willing to lend *in the absence of a rise of prices*. If the Government

9. Letter to Mr Geoffrey Dawson, 11 March 1940.

had to borrow more than that amount, a rise of prices would come as a consequence. In the inflationary process the role of money was secondary.

Shortly after the publication of the book, Keynes printed a *Budget of National Resources* for private circulation. This was an essay in national-income accountancy. In this trial balance-sheet there occurs in the first table a key item, namely, 'The increased value of output through rise of prices'. This was, so to speak, his index of the amount of inflation that had occurred. The problem of policy was so to increase other sources of revenue as to reduce this item to zero. It did not prove practicable to include any such key item in the subsequent official publications.

As it seemed evident to Keynes that the volume of voluntary saving forthcoming at the existing price level would be insufficient to fill the gap between tax revenue and expenditure, he proposed that voluntary saving should be supplemented by 'compulsory saving', or, as it came to be called, 'deferred pay'. A full war effort could not be deployed without some levy upon the wage-earning classes. He agreed that consumption by the lowest income group should not be reduced, but pointed out that, if output was to be increased, as was hoped, weekly wage packets would rise, even if wage rates did not. If prices did not rise, the higher pay packets would entitle wage-earners to larger consumption; such an increase of consumption would be quite inconsistent with a full war effort.

The problem might be solved by imposing sufficient direct taxes on wage earners. These would encounter serious political difficulty and provoke demands for wage increases. It was still uncertain whether we should maintain the normal system of determining wages by free bargaining during the war; in the event we did so, under the wise guidance of Mr Bevin, and the result was not unsatisfactory. Keynes now hoped that he could persuade the Trade Union world to accept, in the form of a compulsory saving or deferred pay scheme, what it would not have accepted in the form of direct taxation or taxes on standard articles of consumption. Thus the scheme was in essence an attempt to woo Labour to accept voluntarily an ordered plan for preventing a rise in purchasing power in lieu of the disorderly and unjust method of open inflation, which would undoubtedly ensue if something like his scheme were not accepted. Thus, at the outset, it was in essence a political device.

As time proceeded, however, he fell in love with his own scheme as a method of social reform. His advocacy of it on those grounds to workers' representatives was perfectly sincere. Reflecting upon the normal course of inflation, it occurred to him that what really happened was that the capitalist class enriched itself by the rise of prices, and emerged from the war the better off by the amount of the increase in the National Debt, to which they were enabled by the inflation to subscribe. His plan of compulsory saving would secure that a substantial part of the deficit was financed not by inflation-borrowing, but by a levy upon wage packets in return for an undertaking to repay later. Thus it would be the wage earners, and not the profit takers, who would emerge from the war as the main holders (in the form of deferred pay claims) of the newly created National Debt. Thus, by a process most conducive to the smooth working of the war economy, a wider diffusion of property, which had been the dream of social reformers, could be secured. This was a characteristically Keynesian invention, and we need not wonder that he harnessed all his enthusiasm to its advocacy.

We may pause to consider the extent of Keynes's influence on internal financial policy in World War II. First and foremost we must rank the influence due, not to this book, but to his previous work as an economist. Experts had absorbed his doctrine that inflation was not primarily a matter of the volume of bank deposits, but of the relation between the propensity to save and capital (or war) outlay. The problem was how to prevent the total stream of effective demand, viz.

that part of private income directed to consumption plus government expenditure, exceeding the resources available to meet it at existing prices. The inflationary 'gap' was the difference between the streams of total demand and of total supply; the money question occupied a second place. This kind of thinking had begun to permeate official quarters. As a consequence of this general approach, and also of Keynes's specific pleading, it was not thought desirable or indeed possible to check inflation by high interest rates. It would be quite safe to flood the market with liquid paper and keep the government interest rate at a low level. Although World War II entailed a much greater strain on our resources than the First, the long-term rate in the Second was about three per cent compared with five per cent in the First. Although the National Debt in 1945 stood at more than three times its level in 1919, the total interest charge in 1945 was only fifty-six per cent higher than in 1919. This economy, for which Keynes has far the major share of responsibility, has made our post-war problems much easier than they would otherwise have been. The United States adopted a similar policy. Their technicians were already imbued with Keynesian doctrine. If Americans wish to assess Keynes's influence in their country, they should think, not of the New Deal, but of the low rates at which they were able to finance World War II. That was Keynes's personal contribution to American prosperity – one of no little moment.

Thus Keynes's most potent aid to British success was not, this time, by administrative action at the Treasury, but by what he had achieved in earlier years at his desk in Cambridge or Sussex. Some admirers have suggested that *How to Pay for the War* provided a blue-print for what followed. It is true that his idea of 'deferred pay' was in fact adopted in the scheme of 'post-war credits'. The prices of basic necessities were maintained at a stable level by subsidies, as he recommended. (It must be added, however, that the policy of subsidies was begun before Keynes published his views.)

His scheme for the family allowance of 5s. per child was also adopted, but only at the end of the war.[10]

None the less, it is difficult to hold that the main idea in *How to Pay for the War* was put into effect. He pointed out that there were only three logical solutions to the war problem, namely, his scheme, sufficient taxation, or inflation. Sufficient taxation was impractical, and he feared inflation. But he recognized that there was also what he called a pseudo-remedy, namely widespread rationing and price controls. (He was, of course, in favour of rationing basic necessities in short supply.) This pseudo-remedy would lead to shortages and queues everywhere. He thought that, with the outlook prevailing, this, rather than open inflation, was the most likely outcome of the lack of an orderly plan. And he dreaded it. He was appalled by the waste and inefficiency of shortages and queues. His scheme was designed to avoid them. But, in the event, we had them! He proposed to raise £550 million a year by the deferred pay scheme; in fact he raised £121 million (annual average). Furthermore, his figure was geared to an increase in government expenditure of only £1,950 million. Our effort exceeded expectations, and, to achieve his desired effect, the amount taken in deferred pay would have had to be stepped up beyond his initial figure.[11] For him this plan was to be the centre-piece of war finance. In effect the post-war credit scheme was an interesting experiment, but only played a minor part in the whole situation. The larger diffusion of property which he hoped to bring about painlessly has not taken place.

10. It had by then been sponsored by Sir William Beveridge, who proposed 8s. – prices were then higher – in his famous report on Social Security. The main credit for this reform must be accorded to the tireless advocacy by Miss Eleanor Rathbone over many years.

11. To find out what would have been required one cannot simply do a sum in proportion by taking Government expenditure as it actually was, since, if his scheme had been implemented, the rise of prices and the increase of Government expenditure (in money) would not have been so great as it was.

2

On 20 March he gave an address to the House of Commons Currency Committee, of which Mr W. Craven-Ellis was the moving spirit. Giving 'Deferred Pay' a rest, he chose to speak on the rate of interest, and felt justified in doing so with some satisfaction. The Government appeared to be entirely converted to his view that the war could be financed at a low rate; he told the M.P.s that on this front all that need be done was to see that the position was held. But in the later part of his address he was impelled to proceed to a topic outside his terms of reference, namely, external finance. He professed himself much worried. The exchange control seemed to be confused in purpose and lax in operation. In the weeks that followed he gave all his attention to this problem, and indeed the question of external finance was to occupy the main part of his thoughts for the rest of his life.

### J. M. Keynes to R. F. Kahn, 16 March 1940

The more I think about it and the more extensive the information which reaches me, the more convinced I am that you are quite right about the lunacy of the present exchange control, and particularly about the level of the black rate. Indeed, I wrote to Dennis a few days ago saying how comforted I feel by its decline and pointing out that its previous high rate was symptomatic of the large amount which we must have been losing previously.[12]

All the same, I am much perplexed as to how best to attack it

12. The demand for foreign currency arose from those endeavouring to convert their sterling assets, while the supply consisted largely of the proceeds of British exports, which the exchange control was failing to net. In fact part of our exports was going to enable foreigners to convert their sterling assets. The decline in the black market rate was satisfactory, as being a sign that sterling was less in demand, i.e. that a smaller part of our exports was being lost to the use for which it was so much needed, the purchase of imports.

controversially. The matter is frightfully technical, of a kind which you cannot possibly expect the public to understand or form a judgement on. I should think there are hardly more than half a dozen people in the country whose opinion is worth having. Also, in matters of detail, it is extraordinarily difficult to be quite sure of one's facts. And I have learned to be cautious about public controversy unless I feel that I know the other fellow's case beforehand better than he knows it himself.

The concluding aphorism may be the key to his success in many controversies. He observed it consistently and not only in the latter end of his life. In the following months he was busy composing successive memoranda, which he sent to Sir Frederick Phillips in the Treasury. On 9 April the Chancellor of the Exchequer made an unsatisfactory statement, and Keynes was in correspondence with Mr P. C. Loftus and Mr R. Boothby with a view to their bringing further pressure in the House of Commons.

In his note of the previous September he had not shown himself in favour of blocking sterling completely. He clung to the hope that it might be possible to preserve some vestige of our international financial position during the war, and that this might stand us in good stead. He concentrated on the point that foreigners ought not to be allowed to sell sterling securities for freely convertible sterling. He also pressed very strongly for a unification of controls, as soon as practicable, to include not only the sterling area, but also France, Holland and Belgium. On 4 June he lunched with the Chancellor of the Exchequer to discuss these matters. On 7 June he had a good report from Dr Plesch, who pronounced him 'fit for any moderate activity'. On 10 June he submitted to the Chancellor a memorandum on integrating our external finance with that of France. He was also pressing the desirability of setting up a new department to deal with these matters.

Amid all the stress and strain of those anxious months an event occurred which gave him the greatest satisfaction. The masters at Eton have one representative on the Governing Body, who is supposed to pay special attention to their interests. Keynes was their choice on this occasion. He threw himself into his duties with great energy, and attended meetings regularly during the next six years, save when he was in the United States.

'I find that by now I have no modesty when on my legs, even before a strange audience', he had written as an Eton schoolboy. In the course of years he had made himself a supreme master of debate. That fine command of prose, manifested in his writings, was no less evident in oral discussion. Indeed, it was more spectacular, for his lightning speed of thought enabled him to improvise the just word and phrase. This gift was to serve us in good stead in the great negotiations with the United States. As a master of words Keynes was without peer in Washington or Bretton Woods.

But on the Governing Body of Eton he met his match. The Provost of Eton, Lord Quickswood (formerly Lord Hugh Cecil), had a command of the English language which was no less perfect. Elegant and epigrammatic, he was ever ready to hurl devastating insults in the most finely polished phrases. He had been a member of the House of Commons for thirty-eight years. Margot Oxford, with memories stretching back to her girlhood of Gladstone and other great English speakers, once accorded the palm of oratory among those of the younger generation to Hugh Cecil. He was viewy, with a tendency to adhere obstinately to rather a large number of principles, and he showed distinct signs of taking pleasure in argument for its own sake. The result of Keynes's appointment was a series of most scintillating displays in the Governing Body. The rapiers flashed. The other Governors were men who could appreciate the fine points of the cut and thrust. We must envy them. What would the boys playing cricket in the sunshine outside have thought of this battle of Titans over the precise regulations concerning attendance at School Chapel during an air-raid? Keynes himself enjoyed it thoroughly.

He was especially well qualified to make important con-

tributions at Eton at this juncture. A reorganization of the
Bursary was required. As in other academic institutions, an
efficient and conscientious Bursar was becoming so hard
pressed by the great mass of detail, that he had not time
for raising and considering questions of principle. Large
problems concerning estates belonging to the School also
arose at that time, and Keynes persuaded the Governing
Body to adopt a bolder policy of investment, in the manner
of King's, and to hold a proportion of their capital in town
properties and ordinary shares. He interested himself also
in all manner of details, such as a pension scheme for the
'dames'. These activities were a source of pleasure to him.
He had reached a time of life when it is agreeable to revive
schoolboy associations; the radical had mellowed somewhat, and in these years, when all around was crashing
down, he was anxious that those good things that he had
known as a boy should be preserved for another generation.

When France fell there was a round-up of enemy aliens,
who were shipped to the Isle of Man. These included distinguished refugee scholars, who yielded to none in hating
the Nazi régime. Those of good repute were released in due
course, but there were delays and red tape. The old fire and
fury flared up in his comments on the authorities. 'Our
behaviour towards refugees is the most disgraceful and
humiliating thing which has happened for a long time. Also
rather disconcerting to find that we have such obvious fat-
heads still in charge ... if there are any Nazi sympathizers
still at large in this country, we should look in the War
Office and our Secret Service, not in the internment camps.' [13]
'I can remember nothing equal to what is going on for
stupidity and callousness.' [14] He busied himself on behalf
of certain economists, notably Mr P. Sraffa, Mr E. Roth-
barth, Mr H. W. Singer and Mr E. Rosenbaum. A vast
correspondence piled up. There were various authorities,

13. Letter to Mr F. C. Scott, 23 July 1940.
14. Letter to Mr Leonard Elmhirst, 17 July 1940.

both governmental and academic, which professed to be dealing with the problem. Keynes, determined to leave no stone unturned, wrote to them all, and persisted until the matter was put right.[15]

In the month of June he received a second invitation, which was not so obviously attractive, because its import was obscure. The Chancellor of the Exchequer was forming a Consultative Council of eminent authorities to advise him on questions of policy, and Keynes was asked to join. In the month of July he was already submitting to the Council memoranda on such topics as 'War Damage' and the 'Prices of Equities'. These were business-like and relevant and far removed from academic impracticability. It occurred at once to Sir Richard Hopkins that more adequate arrangements should be made to enable the Treasury to pick this very remarkable brain. (This was the same Hopkins who had represented the Treasury before the Macmillan Committee.) Accordingly a room was provided. Keynes found himself in the neighbourhood of Lord Catto,[16] and, after the change in Treasury quarters due to the Blitz, next door to him;[17] their relations were always happy. This was the capacity in which Keynes re-entered the Treasury, and this was the capacity in which he remained there till the end. He was not a civil servant and drew no salary.

15. It is interesting to notice that Professor S. E. Harris, who has done so much to spread a knowledge of Keynes's doctrines in the United States, proposed that the emolument for his article on 'American Gold Policy and Allied War Economics' in the *Economic Journal* of June–September 1940, should be applied to a good cause in Britain. On Keynes's suggestion, he agreed that it should be given to one of the economist refugees, who had suffered financially from his internment.

16. Director of the Bank of England, and Governor 1944–9. Lord Catto had recently come into the Treasury in the high-sounding but indeterminate position of 'Economic Adviser to the Chancellor of the Exchequer'.

17. By consequence he was sometimes known as Doggo – especially when he was more reticent than usual about certain post-war reconstruction schemes.

Once he had obtained a room, it was inevitable that his influence should be felt. He had many ideas that he wished to bring forward, while the Treasury had much on which it wished to consult him. He spent most of his time in London now, going only for weekends during term to Cambridge and during the vacation to Tilton.

In the autumn of 1940 the exchange control problem, on which he had done so much work in the preceding months, had largely been sorted out. A system had been improvised which must be judged eminently successful by its results. During the course of the war we obtained credits from various external countries (excluding the United States and Canada), not all of them completely friendly, of no less an amount than £3,187 million.

In that same autumn we were faced with a truly appalling problem in external finance, which was vividly described by the expression 'scraping the bottom of the barrel'. Our gold and dollar reserves were rapidly running out. France had fallen and Britain was fighting alone now. At all costs our powers of equipping ourselves must be reinforced by American production. But there was no money to buy it. Clauses of the Neutrality Act and the Johnson Act still stood in the way of American aid, and Mr Morgenthau had been forced to make a pledge to Congress (in September 1939) that no United States Treasury money should be used to assist a belligerent. None the less, we decided during that autumn to place vast orders for aircraft and tanks in the United States, for the payment of which no means were in sight. It was a gigantic gamble. The Treasury carried a terrible strain and screened the public from knowledge of our position. The word went out that we must order to the full limit of our needs and of the productive resources available. Finance must be regarded as a secondary matter, and must not be allowed to stand in the way of our ordering programmes. Yet finance was not in fact secondary, and, had it not been that events moved in our favour in the United States, the programmes would have crashed in ruins.

Those were anxious months as we waited for the Presidential election and for action to be taken thereafter.

Something, indeed, had been already done by the Americans to help. There was the exchange of destroyers for bases. On the collapse of France, French orders were smoothly transferred to British account. The US War Department conveniently consented to state needs for weapons in excess of their true requirements, so that the Reconstruction Finance Corporation could furnish sufficient capital to firms to build factories on a corresponding scale. The British could then buy the output unwanted by the Americans, and thus be spared the capital outlay on the plant. Mr Morgenthau obligingly told a press conference in September 1940 that British orders had run into colossal figures, and that they were not worrying about any lack of funds, since they had plenty of money! All these helps and aids did not alter the fact that we were ordering tanks and aeroplanes for which we had no money in sight to pay.

We still had, it is true, certain foreign investments, and had arranged for a regular sale of these at an early date. They put us in a dilemma. Some of the investments consisted of marketable securities, the prices of which tended to collapse if one endeavoured to unload them upon the New York market at more than a certain rate. They produced a monthly trickle of dollars, but not more. Many of the investments were direct investments, the value of which, in one way or another, was tied up with British management, and it was extremely difficult to obtain anything like their true value for these by ordinary commercial sales. On the other hand, large figures had been quoted as estimates of the value of our foreign investments, and even our best friends in America suspected that we were not making an all-out effort to sell them.

Towards the end of October, at the request of an interdepartmental meeting, Keynes prepared a memorandum on the relation of our assets to our post-war position, which was his first essay in stating the case that he was to have to argue to the Americans during the next five years. The difficulties of selling investments, save at a heavy loss, were pointed out. The cases where the value depended on individual management were discussed. He acknowledged that it might be possible to sell our rubber and tin interests *en bloc* for an agreed sum to the American Government, but argued that we should not do this unless the Americans were prepared to take over the political responsibility for governing the regions in question. He argued the need of a minimum gold reserve of £150 million, to shield us from recurrent crises. Meanwhile Sir Frederick Phillips had proceeded to the United States, where he at once began his valiant work, which continued for some three years, of building up in American minds a knowledge of the British position.

### *J. M. Keynes to Mrs J. M. Keynes,* 6 September 1940

Last night I went to my Other Club and was put next Winston, so that I had some two or three hours conversation with him and listening to him. I found him in absolutely perfect condition, extremely well, serene, full of normal human feelings and completely un-inflated. Perhaps this moment is the height of his power and glory, but I have never seen anyone less infected with dictatorial airs or hubris. There was not the faintest trace of the insolence which Ll. G., for example, so quickly acquired. As perhaps you saw, he placed my new war damage scheme in his speech in the afternoon, so that I am now hopeful that that will really go through.

During September the Blitz was at its height. On 18 September Keynes's niece, Polly Hill, and his secretary, Mrs Stephens, were having dinner with him in the kitchen. A land-mine fell in Gordon Street at the other end of the Square; the doors and windows of No. 46 were smashed and the glass was strewn around and upon them. They slept in the passage that night. It was only next morning that they were informed that there was an unexploded bomb in the neighbourhood. This entailed evacuation from Gordon

Square for three weeks. During this period Keynes went to Tilton each night.

I have breakfast every morning at 7 a.m. [he wrote to Dr Plesch], leave the house before 8 a.m. and do not get back until about 8.30 p.m.; whilst my day at the Treasury, which is now my headquarters for all purposes, gets fuller and fuller every week. Nevertheless, all this and the suppressed strain of the Blitzkrieg seems to do my health nothing but good. I get reasonably tired, but no distressing symptoms.

In the autumn of 1939 Lord Stamp, assisted by Sir Henry Clay and Sir Hubert Henderson, was charged with the duty of securing economic coordination. They had a slender staff, which was joined by Mr Austin Robinson and Professor Jewkes on 1 January 1940. When the Churchill Government was formed in May, Mr Arthur Greenwood, Minister without Portfolio, had the duty of coordinating the work of the various Ministries concerned with our economic effort. His principal civil servant, Mr Francis Hemming, with wise foresight and commendable respect for economics, moved quickly and mustered a large team of professional economists. Although it was not clear at the outset that adequate work was available for them, this nucleus proved to be of great value as the war proceeded. The country owes much to Mr Hemming's initiative, for it alone prevented the dispersal of these economists, who would have been hard to recapture. Their close association had some importance for the future of economics. The association was by night as well as by day, for during the Blitz many of them slept in a basement below the massive structure of Scotland Yard, sharing it with the Metropolitan Flying Squad. There they could pursue their economic discussions removed from the din. Post-war research revealed that the innermost and apparently most secure sanctum was immediately below the pavement of the Thames Embankment. It is not surprising that they were severely shaken when a land-mine fell upon the County Hall opposite.

They were all surprised at the large measure of agreement they found with each other, on the basis of their economic science, despite political differences and adherence to rival schools of thought. Of special interest was the close association which grew up between Mr James Meade, a convinced Keynesian and moderate Socialist, and Professor Lionel Robbins, who had been a strong individualist and not entirely convinced of Keynes's doctrines. These two were to prove able to cooperate in the closest harmony in the heavy work of planning ahead for post-war economic policy, external and internal.

Mr Austin Robinson, who had followed with interest Keynes's study on *How to Pay for the War*, pressed the need for official work on the kind of statistics which Keynes employed in that book, and informed Mr Hemming that Mr Richard Stone was the ideal man for the purpose. He was accordingly brought into the party, and in the autumn of 1940 he and Mr James Meade worked hard on an analysis of the national income and expenditure. Seeking further authority and guidance in their efforts, they naturally found their way to the room of Keynes, who gave them the utmost encouragement and help. In full collaboration with him, they got out an account that winter. Keynes pressed the importance of such statistics on the authorities. He won the support of the cautious Sir Richard Hopkins, whose instinct was to be extremely sceptical of calculations of this kind; once convinced, however, he valiantly championed them and in his turn had difficulty in persuading the Chancellor of the Exchequer that the account should be published at the time of the 1941 Budget.[18] This was indeed a great revolution. The Treasury had hitherto confined itself to figures for actual, known transactions. This account included estimates, and certain figures had to be obtained by the method of difference from other estimates – all of which was very dangerous. Yet this kind of national income ac-

18. *An Analysis of the Sources of War Finance and an Estimate of the National Income and Expenditure in 1938 and 1940.*

counting has come to be regarded as the essential tool of any economic planning, whether of an Individualist or Socialist variety, and other nations have followed Britain in presenting such accounts. The initiative must be attributed to Keynes, but for whose active interest the compilation would not have been made and published at that time.

Mr Stone felt that the 1941 paper was only a beginning and that much further work was desirable. Meanwhile Mr Hemming's group of economists had been divided into two quite distinct sections. It was thought to be desirable to make a sharp division between the economists who were engaged in compiling statistics relating to the war effort and those whose duty it was to comment upon them for the benefit of Cabinet Ministers; the latter, if they were to be of any use, would naturally be expected to have strong views of their own, and there was the human danger that such views might influence the form in which the statistics were presented. The former group, namely, the compilers of statistics, became the Central Statistical Office, under Mr Campion; while the latter became the Economic Section of the War Cabinet Secretariat, under Professor Jewkes, and later under Professor Lionel Robbins. Mr Stone went into the Central Statistical Office. He felt doubtful whether his authorities there would allow him sufficient time for work upon the national income, and he approached Keynes for further support. A plan was accordingly drawn up, by which, while retaining his position in the Central Statistical Office, he was attached to Keynes as his personal assistant in the Treasury. The work on the national income went ahead. Three or four times each week Mr Stone visited Keynes, who took a meticulous interest in every detail.

In September Keynes did a broadcast on *British Finance After a Year of War*. He struck a note of optimism, appropriate to a time in which the Battle of Britain was waging but undecided. Seen in a broad perspective, our losses so far had not been great. But he gave a warning that severer sacrifices would be required. Two months later a further request came. There had recently been a campaign of propaganda in Europe based on Funk's 'New Order', which was to bring prosperity to the European peoples. The Ministry of Information suggested that Keynes might do a broadcast to counteract this, and asked for his comments on some notes which had been prepared by the Ministry for use as British propaganda. Keynes at once spotted that the line proposed was not likely to be effective. It sought to discredit the 'New Order' by contrasting it with the advantages of private enterprise and the Gold Standard, as we had known them before the war. Keynes pointed out that this pre-war régime had entailed severe unemployment and certain other features not wholly satisfactory. Might not listeners think that they would prefer to give the 'New Order' a trial? He urged, on the contrary, that the 'New Order' should be attacked, not for what it set out to do, but for being a fraudulent offer. The British, too, had in mind something of a new order, but whereas the German 'New Order' would be based on the mark and be a means for the further exploitation of adjacent peoples, the British new order would be based on sterling and the wide resources of the Commonwealth and Empire. The British could implement, in a way that the Germans could not, an offer of greater prosperity for Europe. If he was to broadcast on these lines, the matter would have to have interdepartmental consideration. There were counter-memoranda and meetings, and Keynes's draft began to assume greater importance than the script of a personal broadcast. Might it perhaps be expedient to submit it to the Americans for comment, especially as Keynes had reverted to his idea of a post-war reconstruction fund? The matter remained in suspense for the time being.

Two pieces of great good news came in the winter, the re-election of President Roosevelt in November and the announcement of Lend-Lease in January. Our worst financial perils were past. Good fortune, however, is soon taken for granted; our expenditure was rising and our solvency remained in doubt. Now all thought was concentrated on the details of Lend-Lease. Was it too narrowly drawn? Would it cover British as well as common-type munitions, tools for Canadian munition production, oil, food for the troops, food for civilians, tobacco, disbursements of British ships? These questions loomed into major importance. Then, what of the contracts for future delivery that we had already made, quite beyond our means? If these could be met, was there any chance of getting reimbursement of payments already made on capital account for United States plants? Meanwhile, there was a decline of prices in Wall Street in February, which further impeded the sale of our assets. Memoranda on these topics piled up, and there was a flurry of interdepartmental meetings. The question whether we should have to use our last ounce of gold before getting any Lend-Lease aid became insistent.

In March an exploratory visit to London was made by Mr Ben Cohen, who had an office in the White House; he was a man of wide vision and had a genius for tactful negotiation. Keynes put all the British troubles very frankly to him.

On the next day bad news came. Mr Harold Smith, the Director of the Budget, had pledged himself in Congress not to use Lend-Lease appropriations for back commitments. This was something of a disaster, for the commitments were truly more than Britain had the means to meet. Keynes got instantly to work on a new scheme, the essential idea of which was that a block of British securities should be handed over to the Reconstruction Finance Corporation as security for an outright dollar loan, to be redeemed over a term of years. The present owners would receive, in lieu of a dollar income, sterling from the British Treasury, and the managements would not be broken up. This was substantially the scheme that was finally adopted. Keynes had a further talk with Mr Cohen and with Mr Butterworth, who was returning to America to join the Reconstruction Finance Corporation. As the result of these talks, Mr Cohen conceived the idea, which he communicated to Mr Winant, the Ambassador, who cordially agreed, that it would be a good thing for Keynes to make a personal visit to the United States and explain the British situation in detail on the spot. This visit was presently arranged.

## 3

In May he flew to Lisbon. Lydia accompanied him. He took the opportunity to interest himself in the negotiations for a monetary agreement with Portugal which were then proceeding. Having stayed at Estoril several days, waiting for the Clipper, he and Lydia flew to New York on 8 May and proceeded to Washington on 10 May. Mr Lucius Thompson (afterwards Thompson-McCausland) accompanied him as an assistant. This was the first of six visits which he paid to the United States in the years 1941–6, all of great importance. He had old friends in the United States, such as Mr Walter Stewart, Mr Felix Frankfurter and Mr Walter Lippmann; he made many new ones. The recurrence of the visits was valuable, since the Americans with whom he had to deal came to know him well, to understand his idiosyncrasies and to feel the tie of personal affection for him.

This first visit was an exploratory one; he had a roving mission. He was empowered to discuss various points outstanding and to explain the British attitude in full. The main matters for discussion were the scope of Lend-Lease, the question of the British commitments prior to Lend-Lease, the problem of British exports in relation to goods acquired by Lend-Lease (the subject of the subsequent famous 'Export White Paper' of September 1941), the sale of British overseas investments and Britain's need to maintain a minimum basic gold reserve of at least £150 million. It was thought that he might also discuss with the Americans their domestic problem of mobilizing resources for war production, in the light of British experience, and the dangers of inflation. Then he also had in his pocket that draft for a broadcast talk on 'a new order', which might form the agenda for a discussion of post-war aims.

In considering Keynes's contribution to Anglo-American understanding, it is proper to refer to the work that had already been done. First and foremost there was the great series of telegrams from Mr Churchill to the President, which described with matchless lucidity and logic Britain's need. Free from all trace of the mendicant or the preacher, they set forth the common purpose of Britain and the United States, namely, the overthrow of Hitler, and what would have to be done for Britain, if that purpose was to be achieved. On a less exalted plane, mention must be made of Mr Arthur Purvis, head of the British Purchasing Commission, whose pioneer work in assembling British requirements and placing orders in 1940 is agreed by all to have been of the highest efficiency. He laid the foundations on which Lend-Lease was built. Splendid work was also done by M. Monnet, who remained in the United States after the fall of France as a member of the British Supply Council.

In 1941 Keynes's business mainly lay with the U.S. Treasury. Sir Frederick Phillips was already on the scene and had established excellent working relations. Steady and level-headed, of plain downright speech and palpable integrity, he won complete confidence. He became a familiar figure in Washington; sometimes unconventionally clad, resolutely plying his business, gaining the reputation eventually of being something of 'a character', he seemed to be a symbol of Britain's rock-like will and dogged imperturbability. He established a particularly good relation with Mr Morgenthau. When he died in 1943, the Treasury, after an interval, appointed Lord Brand as its principal representative. To him also Britain owes much. Bringing different qualities to the task, polished, intellectual, wise, with many long-standing connections in the United States, of vast experience as a banker, and thereby cautious, reticent, conveying by fine touches the kindliness and loyalty of his nature, he made a notable contribution to Anglo-American relations.

The following pages are concerned only with the achievements of Keynes. The reader will not forget that there were other British citizens, from Lord Halifax downwards, who laboured effectively in the good cause, toiling hard through the sweltering summers of Washington, full of anxieties for their friends and loved ones at home, often unable to form a precise idea of what London was suffering from the Blitz or the flying bomb. Their work must be recorded elsewhere.

It was Keynes's task to explain both in broad outline and minute detail the facts of Britain's financial position. His peculiar idiosyncrasies made him well fitted for the task.

Phillips had not been able to supply quite all that was needed. He had the traditional British reserve. He was temperamentally averse from expatiating beyond his terms of reference and what was obviously relevant to the particular point at issue. He had a civil servant's proper caution, and he was not inclined to trust to or impart figures which had not been precisely verified. Thus equipped, he had success up to a point. But the Americans needed something more. They thirsted for full and detailed knowledge, they wanted a background of general information, and, above all, they liked figures. In some cases they may not even have known precisely what it was they wanted to know, but were aware that they did not completely understand the situation for the lack of some clue. Keynes was ideally fitted to provide precisely all this. He gave the background; he explained the why and wherefore and the ins and outs. He expatiated at large on motives, policies, alternative possibilities. That was his *métier*. Above all, he was always ready to guess a figure in order to illustrate a point. He made no claim to having more knowledge than was available. When he provided private estimates, he admitted that they might be wrong. He explained that he was doing his best with imperfect data. Everything was explained in full. All these efforts were most gratefully accepted, and the consequence was that from that time forward there was a much more intelligent appraisal of British problems on the American side.

Keynes established a close contact with Mr Oscar Cox, who had a great hand in the original devising of the Lend-Lease scheme and played a vital part throughout the war, and he got to know many other officials in the Treasury. Later in the year he told the British that Harry White was 'a constructive mind'. And then there was Mr Morgenthau. Except for the President himself, Mr Morgenthau had done more than any other American to help the British in the dark days of 1940. He had had his hand in those favourable agreements which have already been referred to. It was not only in general measures of policy, but in all the detailed administration, that a friend could be of service. He exerted the utmost pressure to get supplies for Britain moving, often going far outside his proper ambit as Secretary to the Treasury. All this was not well understood in the British Treasury at the time, where he was still regarded as somewhat enigmatic.

Acute observers had some doubt whether the first impact of Keynes on Mr Morgenthau was a happy one. He delivered a homily on Britain's case, which was no doubt fine and tactful, but perhaps not quite what one would have addressed to a man whom one knew to be already quite convinced on that score. Mr Morgenthau was of an essentially cautious temperament and likely to be on his guard against people who seemed to be over-clever. Thus in the first phase he may not have been altogether favourably impressed.[19] Be that as it may, in due course they became great friends, each understanding the subtler points in the character of the other. This friendship was an important factor in the development of financial relations between the countries during the later period of the war.

Mr Morgenthau, rather reserved in manner, addressed

19. Mr Morgenthau does not confirm this himself.

me in carefully chosen words; fixing me in his kindly regard, he began his character sketch of Keynes: 'He was a
gentle soul ...' This is what Fay had so soon discovered;
this is the trait which dominates the memories of Sheppard
after forty-four years of intimate friendship; Lytton, too,
had been a gentle soul. Mr Morgenthau evidently had the
root of the matter in him. When he opened with these
words, I had a vivid sense that we belonged to one civilization, the wide waters over which I had travelled to him
making no difference.

'He was a very fine and pertinacious negotiator,' Mr Morgenthau proceeded; 'every visit he paid advanced the British
cause. He was the best emissary they could have chosen;
they were not always so happy in their choice.' Mr Morgenthau did not think that Keynes's sarcasm and barbed
utterances did any harm. His sharp repartees were good
rather than bad for personal relationships, because they
were stimulating and made one feel at the top of one's
form, and one valued the person responsible for the stimulus. 'He had a very fine intellect, but, unlike many intellectuals, was never cold, so that one always had a feeling of
intimacy with him.'

One evening early in June a dinner was given at the
National Press Club for Keynes to meet Mr Leon Henderson and about a dozen others responsible for policy in the
office of Price Administration and Civilian Supply. Keynes
urged that a more repressive fiscal policy was needed to
prevent the American economy falling victim to inflation.
A correspondence with Mr Walter S. Salant followed about
the figures and basic assumptions. Mr Salant explained that
they were taking into account not only the 'multipliers' but
also the 'acceleration' effect of defence expenditure. It was
satisfactory to Keynes to find that his own 'multiplier' tool
was being used by those responsible for framing policy with
characteristic American statistical thoroughness.

*J. M. Keynes to Walter S. Salant,* 27 July 1941

There is too wide a gap between the intellectual outlook of the older people and that of the younger. I have been greatly struck during my visit by the quality of the younger economists and civil servants in the Administration. I am sure that the best hope for good government of America is to be found there. The war will be a great sifter and will bring the right people to the top. We have a few good people in London, but nothing like the *numbers* you can produce here.

Soon after his arrival Keynes had a discussion with Lord Halifax about his 'New Order' draft. On 28 May he and Lord Halifax had an interview with President Roosevelt on this topic. The President expressed great satisfaction. He agreed with the line of thought, while expressing reluctance to enter yet into detailed plans for the post-war situation. This point of view accorded with British thinking. He had one or two criticisms of the draft. Being designed as a counter-blast to Funk, it was concerned with European reconstruction. The President felt that any important statement concerning war aims should take the whole world for its province. It was not only in Europe that a great reconstructive effort would be required. Furthermore, he noted that a British policy was being offered for the consideration of the nations as giving better promise of genuine advancement than anything that the Germans could offer. But, he pointed out, the United States was also standing by. If the British could offer more than the Germans, how much more could the British and Americans together offer. If an alternative was to be presented to the world, let it be not on a British but on a joint British and American initiative. This interview was before his Atlantic meeting with Mr Churchill. No doubt his mind was moving in that direction, and he may have felt that an important British declaration of aims might spoil the market for what he hoped to bring about on a joint basis. Thus, although the interview was satisfactory in showing agreement of general attitude between the President and Keynes, it was discouraging as regards any immediate action on the 'draft'. Meanwhile things were taking their own course on the other side of the Atlantic. There the Keynes draft had been in active circulation. On 29 May, the day after the interview with the President, Mr Anthony Eden made an important speech on war aims; the economic section of this was based upon Keynes's draft. The speech was welcomed in the press of America, which had long thirsted for more information on British intentions, although, unlike the President, it desired still more detail. Thus Keynes's work on this draft had borne good fruit.

Already in America there had been much thinking in official circles about the final outcome of Lend-Lease. It was generally agreed that the post-war world ought not to be burdened with a large money debt, and that repayments in kind of a multitude of Lend-Lease articles, from service aircraft to tobacco, would be impracticable. The idea germinated that claims in respect of Lend-Lease might be waived, not in return for tangible goods, but for a British undertaking to pursue a policy, in cooperation with the United States, that would be helpful for world recovery and prosperity and the consolidation of peace. Upon what such a policy should be based there were many ideas.

The several Ministries in the United States have been likened to independent sovereign powers. The sharp separation of the legislature from the executive and the absence of a Cabinet system on the British model have the effect of allowing each Department to develop its own policy and to go far in executing it without ensuring that the other Ministries are completely in line. There is, no doubt, the same tendency on the British side also, but the checks are stronger. The American system has its disadvantages, but it may afford better protection to the liberty of the subject. There is something to be said for dissipation of power at the centre.

Dominating the scene, so far as external relations are

concerned, is the State Department. Mr Cordell Hull, an eminent personage and much loved, had at this time been Secretary of State for many years. He had done splendid work with his Trade Agreements in a world of growing economic nationalism. He had played a lone hand in the international scene, but he did not lose courage. It occurred to him that this Lend-Lease situation might be an opportunity to secure British cooperation in his tasks, and to inaugurate a bold move to reduce trade obstacles. It was paradoxical that the Government of the United States, traditionally a highly protectionist country, should be taking the lead towards greater freedom of trade. While a general reduction of tariffs was considered desirable, Mr Cordell Hull's particular bugbear – and this was in line with State Department tradition – was 'discrimination'. Discrimination occurs when country A fixes a higher tariff on imports from country B than on those from country C or in other ways treats B and C unequally. The Ottawa Agreements had been particularly offensive to him. It was a natural and proper tradition of the State Department to oppose any arrangements whereby American exporters were given less favourable tariff terms than exporters from other countries. Meanwhile the situation had become more complicated. The trading policy of Germany, with Herr Schacht as the master mind, had been shaped to secure the economic exploitation of weaker foreign countries and to promote the political aims of Germany. It seemed perfectly obvious to the State Department that all right-thinking people would desire, after the war, to extirpate these forms of trade policy from the world for ever. Some might even feel that this was one of the most important war aims.

Mr Hull's ideas were reflected in the mind of his able lieutenant, Mr Leo Pasvolsky. At the outbreak of the war the British Embassy in Washington was lucky enough to be able to attach to its staff the British economist, Mr Redvers Opie, who happened to be on the spot. It was his duty, as economic adviser on Anglo-American relations, to regard the State Department as the supreme authority on the American side. He soon established good relations with Mr Pasvolsky. The consequence was that the State Department had an excellent channel for ensuring that its views were known to Britain. This was most valuable. There is no doubt that British policy in relation to the United States was, and still is, gravely handicapped by the existence of the Atlantic Ocean. It appears to be extraordinarily difficult to comprehend in London the thinking that is proceeding on the other side. Even a personal visit is inadequate; the British emissary returns with a clear mental vision of the American attitude; but after a month or two the vision usually seems to fade, and American attitudes sometimes change quickly. Lord Halifax used Mr Opie's advice freely and embodied it in dispatches which had influence in the highest quarters in London.

The consequence of Mr Opie's activities was undoubtedly to bring home forcefully to the British mind that the American attitude about 'discrimination' was not a chance foible of Mr Hull, but had full State Department backing and would continue to be a leading influence in American foreign policy. The British attitude on this would undoubtedly have a most serious influence in determining whether the settlement of Lend-Lease would be satisfactory or not. It was important that the British should understand this.

The State Department, working quickly, drafted a clause, to be inserted in the definitive Lend-Lease Agreement, which was shown to Keynes. This was known as the 'consideration', and was the first version of what ultimately became the famous Article VII of the Mutual Aid Agreement (February 1942). It was not, however, when first presented, identical with this article; in its original stripped form the only 'consideration' was the elimination of 'discrimination'. Now this word included not merely Imperial Preference, but all the Schachtian devilries. None the less, it might be regarded as a request by the Americans that we should abandon Imperial Preference in return for being let off the repayment of Lend-Lease goods.[20]

Keynes, as may be expected, reacted unfavourably. He, too, had had the idea that the Lend-Lease commitments might somehow be tied up with a big programme of collaboration in world reconstruction. What he had in mind was the application with American assistance of Keynesian remedies for unemployment and trade depression on a world scale. He was not averse from breaking down the barriers to trade, but thought that the necessary precondition was a much more thoroughgoing policy of reconstruction. He had also in the forefront of his mind the appalling problems that Britain would face after the war in the matter of her own trade balance. It was, therefore, far from his thought that all could be set right by the mere elimination of 'discriminatory' practices from trade policy. Mr Opie affirms that he referred to this first draft of Article VII as 'the lunatic proposals of Mr Hull'. He had to bring them back to England.

The word was passed around in certain British official quarters that Keynes had created an unhappy impression in the United States by insisting that after the war Britain would have to adopt bilateral methods in her trade policy. When the matter came to his ears, he strongly denied that he had advocated such a policy. He had in fact only had one talk about such matters in the State Department. In this he had taken the line that Britain would be driven willy-nilly to such a policy, unless there was a determined effort to reconstruct world trade and finance after the war, an effort which presupposed generous support from the United States. This single talk had been interrupted in the midst by the

20. Critics of Article VII have wrongly represented it as a concession wrung from us by Americans in our hour of need in return for supplies; this view is quite without foundation; the article is concerned not with the provision, but with the post-war settlement, of Lend-Lease; the supplies would have come just the same, had we refused to sign; but we should not then have been able to proceed to joint discussions on post-war reconstruction.

other engagements of his interlocutors. It was quite monstrous to charge him with having spread the doctrine of bilateralism on the strength of it.

Mr Harry Hawkins recalls the occasion; he had been the spokesman of the State Department. Keynes had indeed warned his audience that Britain would have to employ all the weapons of Dr Schacht, unless there was a large joint Anglo-American effort to restore equilibrium of trade and thus make such devices unnecessary. Mr Hawkins had not come briefed to make any adequate reply, and they had been pressed for time. He had confined himself to giving a counter-warning. Should Britain indeed feel compelled to adopt such measures, the United States would be driven, not out of ill-will, but by the inevitable logic of events, to adopt a similar policy herself. She would have to do so to protect and enforce the just claims of her own citizens. In this economic warfare, he pointed out, it was only too probable that the United States would be the victor. If Britain was hard driven and seriously attempted to employ Schachtian tactics, she must remember that she would not gain the benefits of a Power who did this alone, but would lead all others, including the United States, to similar ways, and the law of the jungle would rule in foreign trade. Weighty words!

Opinions may differ whether it was wise at this juncture to suggest that Britain might feel impelled to employ Schachtian methods when the war was over; it was certainly imperative that the Americans should recognize as early as possible the full magnitude of her prospective problems; was it not expedient to be forthright at the very outset in unfolding their possible consequences? Be that as it may, Keynes's principal work had been in the U.S. Treasury, where this first visit was deemed highly successful. In some respects it might be regarded as the most important of all his visits. By his full statement of the British position on the lines I have already described, he laid the foundation of all that was to follow. He gave the Americans the kind of information which made them feel able to gauge requests for assistance in all its various forms in subsequent years by reference to their own knowledge of the facts. That made all the difference. It is hinted that the State Department may have been a little jealous at being excluded from the Keynes conversations. It was his work in the Treasury that mattered, for it was that which provided us with the sinews of war.

4

As he flew home, he could feel that something had been achieved. The scope of Lend-Lease aid had been broadly defined; the project for a loan against the deposit of British securities was well in hand; by legal devices, such as the taking over by the U.S. Services of British orders and the subsequent release of the products for the benefit of Britain, it appeared that the Americans would carry a substantial part of pre-Lend-Lease commitments; he felt that his arguments on the need for Britain to be allowed to retain some basic gold reserve had, at least, made some impression, and he could tell the Treasury that Mr Morgenthau was a solid friend.

Scarcely had he landed in England when all went amiss. On the vital point of pre-Lend-Lease commitments Congress passed legislation which made the means that had been devised impracticable. The War Department appropriations had been severely cut, so that it would no longer be able to take over the old British orders. The unlimited contract authorization for certain supplies for the armed forces was repealed. The power to lend-lease vessels under the Maritime Commission was reduced to the power to lease them. Meanwhile the date of the next authorization of Lend-Lease funds had been postponed, so that there was a prospect of the money available for certain categories of supplies running out before new money was provided. The formulation of principles (the Export White Paper) to ensure that Lend-Lease goods were not re-exported by Britain, and that Britain did not embody in her exports Lend-Lease materials of a kind that were scarce in America, was proving difficult. Meanwhile, from every side there was news of delays in Lend-Lease deliveries. In a pessimistic moment Keynes minuted that 'if we are to be honest with ourselves, we must admit that the switch over from cash purchase to Lend-Lease has retarded the war effort by six months'. No doubt such teething troubles were inevitable; as the months passed these difficulties were adjusted, and the machine soon began to run much more smoothly.

A minute which Keynes wrote on 22 August about the disappointing Congressional legislation has a general interest:

Nevertheless, it is a good example of what I previously emphasized, namely, that one can take nothing whatever for settled in U.S.A., for the sufficient reason that the Administration, not being in control of Congress, is not in a position to enter into commitments on anything. We shall have to bear this in mind in all the negotiations for Anglo-American economic cooperation. What our representatives say binds the British Government. What the State Department or the Treasury or the Departments of Commerce or Agriculture may intimate in the course of our conversations with them can and does bind no one. Thus every bargain can, and very likely will, be overthrown by Congress. It is one thing to make concessions for a definite *quid pro quo*, another one to make them for promises which evaporate in practice. We shall, therefore, have to be very careful in tying up our side of the bargain with theirs and making the one definitely contingent on the other.

There was trouble, too, about 'the consideration'. It was good news that Britain might be able to get quit of all Lend-Lease obligations in return for a declaration of policy. But the high protectionists were up in arms. Imperial Preference was threatened. On this topic strands of thought became tangled in both countries. In Britain some resented the idea mainly on sentimental grounds that we should be asked to abrogate this valuable symbol of Commonwealth and Empire unity. Others, who were reasonable men, held that Britain, faced with appalling prospects on her trade balance after the war through the loss of her overseas investments, could not afford to abandon any device that might assist her to retain or enlarge her export trade. Such motives were honourable and not fundamentally inconsistent with what the State Department had in mind. Most of those who held such opinions would not have deemed it a wise long-run policy to push the system of Imperial Preference further and build up a self-supporting British Empire bloc. But there was a small minority which did hold this view; and these were the real enemies of the State Department doctrine. It must be emphasized that this minority was much too small to influence British policy, if the issue had been clearly put. The unfortunate thing was that the State Department had drafted its 'consideration' in such a form as to enlist on the side of the narrow group of British Schachtians the far larger and more influential numbers who were wedded to a moderate measure of Imperial Preference on grounds of sentiment or cautious prudence.

Opinions of Ministers were collected. Some saw great possibilities in this new search for a basis of Anglo-American cooperation; the majority, as is normally the case, fastened their attention on the objections. Keynes saw the importance of meeting this generous gesture of the Americans in a welcoming and constructive spirit. He continued to search about for a formula which should make the commitment to abandon 'discrimination' conditional upon the joint Anglo-American effort having created a sufficiently prosperous world to make such discrimination no longer necessary. He was ready to fall in with the State Department, always provided that the whole problem of international economic reconstruction was tackled by the two nations in an able and imaginative way.

Meanwhile the narrow formula of the 'consideration' was

far from giving satisfaction to many bold thinkers in the American Administration. In fact there were heated inter-departmental disputes. Even in the stronghold of the State Department itself there was dissentient opinion. On two afternoons in August a new form of words, on the lines of the published version of Article VII, was hammered out there by Mr Dean Acheson, Mr Herbert Feis, Lord Halifax and Mr Opie.

None the less, the matter dragged on. The calamity of Pearl Harbour took place. Some thought that the Americans would forget for a while about the 'non-discrimination'. But the State Department was adamant. The matter came finally to an interchange of communications between President Roosevelt and Mr Churchill early in 1942. These have not been published. The Mutual Aid Agreement, including the 'consideration' in the form of Article VII, was signed in February.

Mr Churchill was able to give comfort to his protectionist supporters. The fact that the problem of eliminating dis-crimination was to be discussed, without prejudice, in rela-tion to the whole problem of world economic reconstruction, was emphasized. The commitment was subject to certain safeguarding expressions. Conditions must be such as to promote 'mutually advantageous economic relations'; the objectives were to be obtained 'in the light of governing economic conditions'. Britain could not be asked to abandon defences that were vital to her position. However, it would clearly be quite wrong to suppose she retained as great a freedom to determine her own economic policy as she would have had if the Article had never been signed. American opinion considered it a great step forward, and it was widely acclaimed by the American press; it was felt that Britain had pledged herself to eschew unneighbourly policy. One cannot argue that signing the Agreement was merely put-ting one's name to empty words. Britain was pledged not to go forward on the lines of building up a self-sufficient bloc in contradistinction to America, on the one hand, and to

Russia, on the other. She was pledged to move away from discriminatory policy, so far as governing economic conditions allowed. Keynes fully understood this and accepted its implications. All turned on whether adequate measures could be devised under the other clauses of the Article to create a prosperous world, in which discrimination could be dispensed with.

Keynes meanwhile retained his other interests. In October he received an invitation to join the Board of Trustees of the National Gallery, a fitting tribute to his long-standing study and patronage of the art of painting. It was nearly a quarter of a century since the Degas sale.

In the same month he was elected to the Court of the Bank of England. This created quite a stir. Had not Keynes been the foremost assailant of the policy of the Bank for twenty years? The formula which he used in replying to friends who wrote to him in a congratulatory and sometimes chaffing vein, was – 'which will make an honest woman of the other is anyone's guess'. The sober historian has to record that no great change in either resulted. Keynes soon discovered that a Director, as such, played little part in shaping Bank policy. This was done mainly by the higher staff, and by one or two Directors, who gave their whole attention. Characteristically he took an active interest in the institutional side. New Directors by custom served on the Staff Committee, and he threw himself into discussions on conditions of service of junior ranks and the investment policy of the Superannuation Fund. He enjoyed making a close scrutiny of how policy decisions were given practical implementation, and, of course, he was intensely interested in the historical trappings of the Bank.

Thus duties multiplied. After his homeward flight from America he had a bad turn and took a rest in the country. But on the whole his health was remarkably improved. Lydia maintained her ceaseless vigilance. The pressures from which she had to protect him were multifarious. He was still Bursar of King's, a Director of the Provincial Insurance Company, an ardent book-collector, a Governor of Eton, Editor of the *Economic Journal*, and he kept a watchful eye on his farm in Sussex.

Before we proceed to the great drama of the Anglo-American negotiations, we may cast our view forward to another invitation, which came to him in February 1942, and led to a wide range of new activity. Mr Tom Jones, once a secretary of Lloyd George's Cabinet, a man behind the scenes, famous among those who knew for doing his best to avoid fame, had been the inspirer of a multitude of projects to bring sweetness and light. To the war, with its Blitz and bleakness and impending catastrophe, he reacted in a characteristic way; he thought this would be a good moment to get together a 'Committee for the Encouragement of Music and the Arts'. As Secretary of the Pilgrim Trust, which administered money supplied by the American, Mr Harkness, for good purposes in Britain, he was able to allot funds for the purpose of this Committee. Its object was to make the best kind of artistic production available up and down the country to a large number of people engaged upon their several tasks in the untoward circumstances of war. The project had already achieved some success when Keynes was invited to become Chairman. He hesitated. His work at the Treasury was now heavy, and he had to think of what his physical condition would stand. But the proposal was extraordinarily tempting. It would be a joy to be in close contact with artistic enterprises, when his soul was weighed down by his heavy and anxious Treasury work. There was something more important. He had long been of the opinion that in the modern world art required a new kind of support to take the place of the patronage of affluent classes in earlier times. This idea had been in his mind in his work for the London Artists' Association, for the Camargo Ballet Society, and for the Cambridge Arts Theatre. There was another idea. In the time to come the mass of people should be able to enjoy the delights of fine art which in the past had been reserved for the favoured

few. At the moment economic prospects were black, but
there was always running in his mind the theme of 'Economic Possibilities for our Grandchildren'. In the long run,
after this setback, the economic problem would be 'solved'.
It was not too soon to prepare the ground. He saw in CEMA
the germ of a great idea.

He accepted the invitation. He threw himself with zest
into his task, and showed all his wonted interest in minute
detail. He brought to this work his unusual combination of
administrative efficiency with understanding of the artistic
temperament. It was a great thing for CEMA to have a
man with these qualities to guide its affairs in the early
days. He maintained a great correspondence with the Secretary, Miss Mary Glasgow, both from his desk in the
Treasury and from the United States. He required minutes
of all the meetings to be sent to him when he was abroad.
The activities of the Committee were of many varied kinds.
One of his letters, for instance, contains detailed suggestions
concerning music travellers, symphony orchestras, the Vic-
Wells Ballet, Regional Organizers, the Mercury Players,
Cambridge Regional poetry readings, the British Institute
of Adult Education, and the Theatre Royal, Bristol. The
reconstruction and reopening of the charming eighteenth-
century Bristol theatre was a notable achievement.

CEMA was concerned with high art – the task of bringing popular music and plays to the forces and canteens was
left to the ENSA organization – and Keynes insisted on
the maintenance of its standards. At the same time, he
believed that in the long run this high art should be self-
supporting. One experiment after another was tried, but he
became a little suspicious when a particular line showed
persistent losses. His ideal for CEMA was that at the final
stage, no doubt not to be reached for a long time, it should
have no disbursements except the cost of administration.
He did not usually favour a simple grant for a particular
project, but preferred a complicated division between grant,
loan and guarantee, as in the prospectus of a new company;

and he expected projects to furnish him with very detailed financial statements. CEMA was essentially for the support of professional art; he frowned upon amateurs, thereby sometimes being in conflict with other members of the Committee. The organization soon became very complicated, with panels for each branch of art and local committees. He always sought to bring the artists themselves into the conduct of affairs, trusting the experts. He was especially good at keeping the staff fully apprised of all that was happening. They found it a pleasure to work with him. But he could be severe. He wrote from America, 'I was, therefore, considerably shocked by the light-heartedly enthusiastic way in which the Council gave the Executive Committee authority without, so far as I can see, any of the necessary information before then ... no doubt you will be able to assure me that it is not quite so irresponsible as it looks from the Minutes which have reached me. There is rather too much of an air of "warm endorsement" of half-baked ideas in these Minutes to leave me quite happy.'

As the war proceeded and austerities increased, the pleasure to be derived from things artistic was heightened. The following extract from his preface to the catalogue of a CEMA exhibition [21] of French book illustrations is characteristic:

Some may feel envious of such magnificence ... when the cry for austerity here is having the unfortunate result of making those wretches, who like it as such, appear virtuous. But the sight of these books will at least encourage us to insist that we should forget austerity and 'war emergency arrangements' at the earliest possible moment, and that there are such things as false economies in knowledge and the civilizing arts, which in fact use up an infinitesimal quantity of materials in relation to their importance in the national life and the comfort they can give to the individual spirit.

Before the war was over, it was decided to put CEMA

21. 1945.

upon a permanent basis with the title of the 'Arts Council of Great Britain'. At this point Keynes arranged that responsibility for the public grant should be transferred from the Ministry of Education to the Treasury. This brought the Arts Council into line with the universities and was designed to ensure that in times to come government interference should be kept down to a minimum.

This brief account does not reflect the importance of the place in his thoughts occupied by CEMA and the Arts Council until the time of his death. On the occasion of the formation of the Arts Council Keynes gave a broadcast talk,[22] extracts from which may better serve to explain the ideal for which he was working.

In the early days of the war, when all sources of comfort to our spirits were at a low ebb, there came into existence, with the aid of the Pilgrim Trust, a body officially styled the 'Council for the Encouragement of Music and the Arts', but commonly known from its initial letters as CEMA. It was the task of CEMA to carry music, drama and pictures to places which otherwise would be cut off from all contact with the masterpieces of happier days and times; to air-raid shelters, to wartime hostels, to factories, to mining villages. ENSA was charged with the entertainment of the Services; the British Council kept contact with other countries overseas; the duty of CEMA was to maintain the opportunities of artistic performance for the hard-pressed and often exiled civilians.

With experience our ambitions and our scope increased. I should explain that whilst CEMA was started by private aid, the time soon came when it was sponsored by the Board of Education and entirely supported by a Treasury grant. We were never given much money, but by care and good housekeeping we made it go a long way. At the start our aim was to replace what war had taken away; but we soon found that we were providing what had never existed even in peacetime. That is why one of the last acts of the Coalition Government was to decide that CEMA with a new name and wider opportunities should be continued into time of peace. Henceforward we are to be a permanent body, independent in constitution, free from red tape,

22. *Listener*, 12 July 1945.

but financed by the Treasury and ultimately responsible to Parliament, which will have to be satisfied with what we are doing when from time to time it votes us money. If we behave foolishly any Member of Parliament will be able to question the Chancellor of the Exchequer and ask why. Our name is to be the Arts Council of Great Britain. I hope you will call us the Arts Council for short, and not try to turn our initials into a false, invented word. We have carefully selected initials which we hope are unpronounceable.

I do not believe it is yet realized what an important thing has happened. State patronage of the arts has crept in. It has happened in a very English, informal, unostentatious way – half-baked if you like. A semi-independent body is provided with modest funds to stimulate, comfort and support any societies or bodies brought together on private or local initiative which are striving with serious purpose and a reasonable prospect of success to present for public enjoyment the arts of drama, music and painting.

At last the public exchequer has recognized the support and encouragement of the civilizing arts of life as a part of their duty. But we do not intend to socialize this side of social endeavour. Whatever views may be held by the lately warring parties, whom you have been hearing every evening at this hour, about socializing industry, everyone, I fancy, recognizes that the work of the artist in all its aspects is, of its nature, individual and free, undisciplined, unregimented, uncontrolled. The artist walks where the breath of the spirit blows him. He cannot be told his direction; he does not know it himself. But he leads the rest of us into fresh pastures and teaches us to love and to enjoy what we often begin by rejecting, enlarging our sensibility and purifying our instincts. The task of an official body is not to teach or to censor, but to give courage, confidence and opportunity. Artists depend on the world they live in and the spirit of the age. There is no reason to suppose that less native genius is born into the world in the ages empty of achievement than in those brief periods when nearly all we most value has been brought to birth. New work will spring up more abundantly in unexpected quarters and in unforeseen shapes when there is a universal opportunity for contact with traditional and contemporary arts in their noblest forms.

But we do not think of the Arts Council as a schoolmaster.

Your enjoyment will be our first aim. We have but little money to spill, and it will be you yourselves who will by your patronage decide in the long run what you get. In so far as we instruct, it is a new game we are teaching you to play – and to watch. Our wartime experience has led us already to one clear discovery: the unsatisfied demand and the enormous public for serious and fine entertainment. This certainly did not exist a few years ago. I do not believe that it is merely a wartime phenomenon. I fancy that the B.B.C. has played a big part, the predominant part, in creating this public demand, by bringing to everybody in the country the possibility of learning these new games which only the few used to play, and by forming new tastes and habits and thus enlarging the desires of the listener and his capacity for enjoyment. I am told that today when a good symphony concert is broadcast as many as five million people may listen to it. Their ears become trained. With what anticipation many of them look forward if a chance comes their way to hear a living orchestra and to experience the enhanced excitement and concentration of attention and emotion, which flows from being one of a great audience all moved together by the surge and glory of an orchestra in being, beating in on the sensibilities of every organ of the body and of the apprehension. The result is that half the world is being taught to approach with a livelier appetite the living performer and the work of the artist as it comes from his own hand and body, with the added subtlety of actual flesh and blood.

*

We of the Arts Council are greatly concerned to decentralize and disperse the dramatic and musical and artistic life of the country, to build up provincial centres and to promote corporate life in these matters in every town and county. It is not our intention to act on our own where we can avoid it. We want to collaborate with local authorities and to encourage local institutions and societies and local enterprise to take the lead. We already have regional offices in Birmingham, Cambridge, Manchester, Nottingham, Bristol, Leeds, Newcastle-on-Tyne, Cardiff and Edinburgh. For Scotland and for Wales special committees have been established . . . Certainly in every blitzed town in this country one hopes that the local authority will make provision for a central group of buildings for drama and music and art. There could be no better memorial of a war to save the freedom of the spirit of the individual. We look forward to the time when the theatre and the concert-hall and the gallery will be a living element in everyone's upbringing, and regular attendance at the theatre and at concerts a part of organized education.

*

But it is also our business to make London a great artistic metropolis, a place to visit and to wonder at. For this purpose London today is half a ruin. With the loss of the Queen's Hall there is no proper place for concerts. The Royal Opera House at Covent Garden has been diverted for other purposes throughout the war. The Crystal Palace has been burnt to the ground. We hope that Covent Garden will be re-opened early next year as the home of opera and ballet. The London County Council has already allotted a site for a National Theatre. The Arts Council has joined with the Trustees of the Crystal Palace in the preparation of plans to make that once again a great People's Palace.

No one can yet say where the tides of the times will carry our new-found ship. The purpose of the Arts Council of Great Britain is to create an environment, to breed a spirit, to cultivate an opinion, to offer a stimulus to such purpose that the artist and the public can each sustain and live on the other in that union which has occasionally existed in the past at the great ages of a communal civilized life.

This broadcast gained widespread attention. Keynes was acquiring a new place in the popular imagination. The great mass of people, who are not economists, had had to take his economic excellence on trust. Now he was speaking to them about things which they understood. His personality began to be seen more clearly. From his mouth came words of wisdom and of inspiration. Who else was there in Britain now who could speak to the people with winged words of things of beauty, who could point the way in these dreadful times to more hopeful prospects? It seemed indeed that he might yet become a prophet in his generation, a leader, a friend to the millions who listened from afar. He had not yet achieved the full span of life; he had not yet given expression to that fund of thought and feeling, which underlay his economic specialism. Might there yet be time for him to do so in the years that remained? Meanwhile he had to go back into his tunnel and grapple with the appalling problems of Britain's post-war economy. The end came too soon.

# [13]

## Bretton Woods

### I

THE autumn of 1941 was for Keynes a time of deep reflection and heart searching. Then, as afterwards, he was acutely conscious of how great Britain's balance of trade difficulties would be when the war was over. He never minimized these. He knew that we should have a hard battle. Furthermore, he had no illusions about our being able to keep afloat by prolonging our wartime arrangements for obtaining goods on credit. The German submarine, the British convoy system and the absence of markets elsewhere were of much assistance in directing supplies to our shores in wartime; they would not continue to do so. How should we then proceed? He was advised on every side that it would be needful to maintain something like the wartime system, suitably modified, of tight controls, of blocked accounts and bilateral bargains; the various recipes devised by Dr Schacht for Germany would have to be applied by Britain, it was hoped with greater skill. There was no other way of survival.

Yet he revolted against all this. He, like the Americans, disliked reverting to the law of the jungle. His instincts were for international cooperation. If these instincts had been dormant in the years before the war, that was because such cooperation seemed impracticable; the internationalists tended to be those who had not accepted Keynesian economics, and to hand international arrangements over to them would, in his judgement, be fatal. Until the world should be converted to his views, one must aim at trying them out in Britain, even if this meant some insulation. But was the world changing now? He certainly had supporters for his views in the United States. Indeed he is remembered to have chaffed a group of experts assembled to meet him on his first visit for being more Keynesian than he was himself. Perhaps the time was almost ripe to attempt to apply Keynesian thought on a world scale; that would be much better than doing so on a national scale only.

Meanwhile the nationalistic alternative was being withdrawn from us. This 'consideration', about which argument was proceeding, must be taken seriously. He remembered Mr Harry Hawkins's warning. Mr Opie was over on a visit, emphasizing that we must accept the State Department doctrine, if we wanted favourable treatment by America – and we should sorely need it – when the war was over. If we engaged in Schachtian tactics, the Americans would follow suit and beat us at the game.

I ran into him about this time in a Treasury corridor; he was leaning against a door-post. 'You must give up the bilateralist approach,' I said, 'and come down on the American side.' 'No,' he said, 'I must pursue both lines of thought ... *both*.' His expression was enigmatic. He seemed to be transfixed with a curious immobility that was unlike him. Some deep inscrutable thoughts were proceeding. Even his great brain was baffled by this problem.

He was soon busy on his first draft of an international 'Clearing Union'. This may be regarded as the introduction to an attempt to meet the views of the State Department. The Clearing Union embodied the minimum terms on which we should find it possible to put our authority behind, and participate in, a movement for greater freedom of international trade. If internationalism was to be reborn, we must think of world reconstruction on a big scale.

It is not necessary to recapitulate the contents of this project, which was later published.[1] The purpose of the plan was set out as follows:

We need an instrument of international currency having general acceptability between nations, so that blocked balances and bilateral clearings are unnecessary ...

1. April 1943.

We need an orderly and agreed method of determining the relative exchange values of national currency units, so that unilateral action and competitive exchange depreciations are prevented.

We need a *quantum* of international currency, which is neither determined in an unpredictable and irrelevant manner as, for example, by the technical progress of the gold industry, nor subject to large variations depending on the gold reserve policies of individual countries; but is governed by the actual current requirements of world commerce, and is also capable of deliberate expansion and contraction to offset deflationary and inflationary tendencies in effective world demand.

We need a system possessed of an internal stabilizing mechanism, by which pressure is exercised on any country whose balance of payments with the rest of the world is departing from equilibrium *in either direction*, so as to prevent movements which must create for its neighbours an equal but opposite want of balance.

We need an agreed plan for starting off every country after the war with a stock of reserves appropriate to its importance in world commerce, so that without undue anxiety it can set its house in order during the transitional period to full peacetime conditions.

We need a central institution, of a purely technical and non-political character, to aid and support other international institutions concerned with the planning and regulation of the world's economic life.

More generally, we need a means of reassurance to a troubled world, by which any country whose own affairs are conducted with due prudence is relieved of anxiety for causes which are not of its own making, concerning its ability to meet its international liabilities; and which will, therefore, make unnecessary those methods of restriction and discrimination which countries have adopted hitherto, not on their merits, but as measures of self-protection from disruptive outside forces.

The document was at once subjected to close scrutiny in the Treasury, and it went through many drafts. The obvious criticism was that it was too grandiose; it was thought to be almost Utopian. Keynes bided his time in regard to this view. He must first get the scheme into good order.

At this period there occurred a useful visit by Professor Alvin Hansen, the well-known economist, and Mr Gulick, a consultant of the National Planning Board and expert on the T.V.A. Although sponsored by the State Department, the nature of their mandate was obscure. They advocated Anglo-American cooperation to prevent world depression, and proposed the establishment of an International Economic Board to advise collaborating governments with respect to internal policy designed to promote full employment, economic stability and world trade. This Board should have research staffs in Washington, in London and in Ottawa, and ultimately in other centres, with provision for interchange of personnel. They also advocated an International Resources Survey and an International Development Corporation, with a view to promoting wise development overseas. These proposals were cordially welcomed; the doctrine seemed to belong to a different world of thought from that which took the elimination of discrimination in foreign trade to be a panacea for the world's ills. The idea that Americans would welcome advice by an International Board in respect to internal policy seemed surprising. But the emissaries argued stoutly for their proposals. Even Sir Hubert Henderson, who tended to be cautious in regard to post-war plans, was impressed.

Somewhat later a stimulus of a different kind came across the waters, in the form of a very able memorandum by Mr Pasvolsky, which pointed out how fatal it would be for Britain to abandon her traditional policy of open trade. Keynes was critical of it; he deemed Mr Pasvolsky a Rip van Winkle, who knew nought of the stresses and strains to which trade had been subjected in the thirties or of modern diagnoses of those maladies; none the less, he admitted that the document was convincing within the limits of its own thinking and should be taken seriously as evidence of the American point of view. Another reason for pushing on with the Clearing Union!

Meanwhile Keynes's mind was not the only one in the

Treasury to devote itself to these problems. The experts plied their pens, and a thick volume of memoranda and proposals regarding the post-war situation was produced. Most of this material elaborated the alternative to the Clearing Union approach. The latter, having achieved the status of a Cabinet paper, was printed on green and appeared in the middle of a large wad which was commonly known as the Treasury sandwich. In committee, discussion was apt to revert to the excellent caviare in this sandwich, to the neglect of the outer layers; the coherence and lucidity of this section drew attention to it; the excitement of something really great and novel began to filter through into the minds of the various officials, however staid; there was something irresistible about it. At first the Green Paper was indeed regarded as impractical, a sketch of something one might achieve in a world not realized, while a practical agenda should be sought in the other section. But in the course of discussion, comment and redrafting, gradually, over a period of many months, by an imperceptible process, it came to be recognized as the main Treasury plan.

The most potent influence in the Treasury at this time was Sir Richard Hopkins ('Hoppy'), Second Secretary, in charge of all external finance.[2] Short and slight of build, he had a bloodless, wrinkled face and a kindly expression. He weighed his words, speaking slowly, briefly and to the point, in Anglo-Saxon English. He had a great sense of humour and often ended his remarks by an amusing twist which showed how thoroughly sceptical he was about the subject under discussion. He was indeed deeply cynical about the ways of men, having little faith in international committees, pious resolutions or grandiose projects; he had too much experience of how things worked out in practice. Not that he was in the faintest degree cynical about his own duties. It went without saying that he would labour unremittingly for the general good, advancing cautiously step

2. cf. pp. 495–8 and p. 588 above.

by step, making sure of each foothold. One might take him for an ancient sage of China, who had somehow been wafted through the centuries to give wise counsel to a half-baked generation. His integrity was absolute. Lobbyists and pressure groups would spend their fury upon him in vain.

In the following years he did not go to the United States. 'He had always been lucky enough to find someone else to do his commercial travelling for him.' That may have been a pity. Britain had good representatives. It would have added something if the Americans could have met in the daily intimacy of a conference this embodiment of all that is best in the great traditions of the British Civil Service; typically British, too, in being a unique character. Those Americans, and there were many, who thought that the British were over-clever and ever ready to put across a quick one, would have had to think again when confronted with Sir Richard Hopkins.

He had, however, one chink in his armour, and that was a fervent and unqualified admiration for Keynes. He had provided him with a room in the Treasury. He had pressed the White Paper on National Income upon the Chancellor of the Exchequer. And now, marvellous to relate, this hardened empiricist was in the end prepared to give his weighty support – with all due qualifications and reservations – to the ambitious and far-reaching scheme of international co-operation represented by the Clearing Union. This was quite crucial. Despite his influence with Ministers, Keynes would have found it difficult, in those hectic days of belligerency, to get his scheme adopted against the opposition of the Treasury. If Hopkins thought it was all right, the official world would accept it.

The Bank of England was never sympathetic. It was natural for it to be more concerned with immediate post-war problems than with far-reaching schemes. It may have fallen a little too much in love with the system of controls which it was so efficiently working during wartime. And it would not be human if its approach was not influenced, even if unconsciously, by some degree of jealousy of a rival central banking institution, which might, in certain circumstances, poach upon its domain. But the Bank of England was not yet nationalized, and, while its criticisms were always heard with great respect, in the last resort its influence on policy was not decisive.

There were other advisers in the Treasury. Sir Hubert Henderson had been installed before Keynes and had influence. He had become with the years ever more cautious and pragmatic in his approach and distrusted large schemes. He was absolutely convinced that, as a matter of hard fact, we should have to resort to every conceivable device after the war to protect our balance of trade. We must not deceive ourselves. He advocated this view with tireless fluency. Indeed, he imported into his opposition to any nostrums the kind of dialectical ardour which is more often associated with the academic advocacy of a nostrum. Since the appearance of the *General Theory*, Henderson had aligned himself with the opponents of Keynesian doctrine, and any hint that this had now received official approbation goaded him to violent protest. Although the Clearing Union was not altogether to his taste, he did not regard it as a great evil and made certain constructive suggestions; his special fury was reserved for his opposition to a more liberal commercial policy. Henderson was a man of great ability and shrewdness, and Keynes, while somewhat rueful at the lapse of an old disciple, knew that his criticisms deserved attention.

Then there was Professor Dennis Robertson. Keenly sensitive to all the horrors that were unfolding, he threw himself into the routine of his daily duties, and overtaxed himself – in expiation, as it were. He was assigned the task of keeping track of the British balance of payments, and this he did without staff, in his own fair hand. It was only later in the war that he had the opportunity to apply his mind fully to the major problems of policy. His first-rate intellect and his proficiency and subtlety as an economist were to be of much value. Although, like Henderson, he had fallen away from the Keynesian fold, he was by no means out of sympathy with this new approach. Indeed, he welcomed it as a reversion from the nationalistic tendencies in the pre-war Keynes.

### D. H. Robertson to J. M. Keynes, 27 November 1941

I sat up late last night reading your revised 'proposals' with great excitement, – and a growing hope that the spirit of Burke and Adam Smith is on earth again . . .
And then also a growing hope that we shall choose the right things and not the wrong ones to have such rows with the Americans about as we must have.

Support was also available on the flank from Professor Lionel Robbins and his team of economists in the Economic Section.

Now that Keynes's enthusiasm was harnessed to his own scheme, his ambivalence on the main issue of an inter-nationalist as against a Schachtian policy in the field of money and foreign exchange faded out. His own natural internationalism came to the surface. There had been a consistent thread running through all his work on public policy from the *Tract* to the *Means to Prosperity*, advocating an international handling of the monetary problem as the correct solution for our troubles.[3] It must be recorded however, that he continued to have grave doubts until a very late stage of the feasibility of a return to an open non-discriminatory system in commercial policy.

In the autumn of 1941 I subjected him to a bombard-ment of memoranda in favour of cooperation with the Americans, of a world bank, etc. In one of these I ventured to draw his attention to the paper which he had presented to the Economic Section of the British Association at Cam-bridge in 1938 advocating buffer stocks of commodities. The

3. cf. p. 524 above.

Clearing Union would be part of an apparatus for international cooperation, not the whole of it. Keynes took up the
idea with zest and produced a full Memorandum on Buffer
Stocks. He had not cared for the Wheat Agreement, which
had just been negotiated – a shameless example of 'discrimination' against countries which were not parties to it,
as he pointed out in his comment on a State Department
document; there was danger that producers of other primary
products would successively get together and drive a hard
bargain with us to the further detriment of our post-war
balance of trade. It had to be recognized, however, that the
producers of primary products had a grievance, as he had
shown in his Cambridge paper; price oscillations had been
excessive in relation to the proper economic functions of
price movements. The idea of the Buffer Stock plan was to
meet the legitimate requirements of primary producers for
greater stability, while ensuring that, in the long run, prices
should move downwards, in accordance with the economic
forces. Thus, if Britain had to suffer somewhat by higher
prices during depressions, she would be sure of getting the
benefits of the long-run trend. Restriction, to which, failing
a Buffer Stock scheme, producers would inevitably resort,
should be outlawed. If long-run demand was falling, this
should be met, not by organized restriction, but by eliminating high-cost producers with due notice and in an orderly
manner. Furthermore the Buffer Stock plan had a cardinal
merit, not present in restriction schemes or plans of the
Wheat Agreement type, that it would tend to iron out the
cycle in general business. Stock-piling would have an ex-
pansive effect in slumps, and releases a damping effect in
booms.

Like the Clearing Union, the Buffer Stock scheme had to
run the gauntlet of interdepartmental discussions. It was not
popular with the Ministry of Agriculture, which claimed
that all other Ministries of Agriculture desired planned output (a euphemism for organized restriction), quotas and
fixed prices. 'All Departments of Agriculture are rackets',

Keynes threw out at one of the Committees. It was claimed by the agricultural experts that, if the Stock was open to buy unlimited quantities of a commodity at a price which only moved downwards slowly, supplies of products of all kinds would be tendered in such vast quantities as to overwhelm the Authorities. The scheme was, in fact, quite impracticable on this account. There was something a trifle absurd in the agriculturists' arguments – if the world's powers of production were really so great, we ought to be very happy – but concessions had to be made to it. It was agreed that in the case of particular commodities, of which large surpluses were mounting up, restriction might have to be allowed for a limited period; but it should only be permitted on condition that the nations resorting to it produced a plan which would soon render it unnecessary, and reported to the Buffer Stock on the progress of the plan. In all the discussions on his various schemes Keynes showed himself extraordinarily open-minded and ready to receive suggestions, however tentative. He drafted and re-drafted in an attempt to satisfy every point of view. He was entirely lacking in the kind of obstinacy which so often results from pride of authorship.

At the same time there were more general discussions concerning what the British should put forward at the conversations due to take place under Article VII, concerning modes of international cooperation. It was agreed that there were four main heads. One was currency and foreign exchanges; this was under active discussion in the Treasury. A second was commodity policy; on this there was the Keynes draft. A third was the question of international investment, and the fourth commercial policy.

In regard to international investment, it was agreed that the British ought not to take an initiative, on the ground that they would not be in a position in the period immediately following the war to contribute substantial sums towards it. It was for the Americans to take the initiative in this part of the field.

On the subject of commercial policy Mr James Meade took the initiative in the Economic Section of the War Cabinet office. He produced a memorandum, won the interest of the Board of Trade, met objections with characteristic courtesy, but pursued his idea with relentless persistence. His drafts gave the British good standing in their subsequent meetings with the Americans and contributed notably to the Charter of the International Trade Organization.

Keynes was by no means wholly absorbed in these schemes. He followed the daily twists and turns in the development of Lend-Lease, and was ready with his advice. Then, there were the early plans for relief, which in due course crystallized in UNRRA. In September 1941 he wrote a long draft on this topic, which was circulated as an official Treasury document. Relief became the special province of Sir Frederick Leith-Ross, whose generous impulses made it congenial to him. Keynes did not lack a sense of the urgent importance of assisting a stricken world to recover, but he had his weather eye on Britain's post-war balance of payments, and had to give repeated and scathing warnings that we must not plan to behave like a 'rich uncle'. In the early days thought was governed by the existence of large surpluses, which would be very handy for this problem. But in due course the surpluses evaporated. On the whole, Keynes leant towards giving relief in money rather than in kind, so that nations could use it in the most economical way. The problem was constantly assuming new aspects, as the world situation changed, and gave Keynes much trouble for several years.

There were problems on the home front too. In the spring of 1942, his old friend, Sir William Beveridge, was requested by the Government to examine the fuel situation, and he put forward a scheme for rationing. This gave Keynes an opportunity to show that he had lost nothing in the art of rudeness. Beveridge no doubt took it in the spirit in which it was intended. The rationing scheme was dropped.

Meanwhile, Beveridge had also been engaged on a greater enterprise. He had been asked by Mr Greenwood to preside over a committee for reviewing the various forms of social insurance. It was intended that the committee should consider how the existing arrangements were working, what gaps ought to be filled and what reforms were needed. Beveridge interpreted his mandate in a broad spirit. He felt that the time was ripe for a big advance, and that it was due to the people that they should have something to look forward to after their gruelling ordeal. He had been associated with social insurance from its first beginnings, and it was appropriate that he should sponsor a large new development. He was a man of humane feeling, and the spirit moved him to take this opportunity to give a lead. When it appeared that he was determined to make rather far-reaching proposals, the Civil Service became somewhat vexed. Whether his proposals themselves were right or wrong, the fact remained that the Cabinet had had no opportunity to consider the matter, although a large advance of this kind was a political measure upon which, by our constitution, only the Cabinet could decide. Accordingly, it seemed necessary to alter the nature of the committee, to ensure that its report should not have Ministerial authority. The departmental representatives on it were all told that they could no longer regard themselves as members of the committee, but merely as assessors to Sir William Beveridge, and that the report would appear, not as a document sponsored by the departments, but as the recommendations of a particular individual.

Even so, there was anxiety about it. Some took the view that it was the wrong kind of approach to post-war reconstruction to hand out a large part of the national cake before we knew how big that cake would be. It would be better to face our post-war troubles with grim determination, and provide better social services as and when recovery proceeded.

Keynes was brought into the discussion. He was indeed

uneasy about the post-war situation and would have preferred a position in which commitments were not so definite,
but the general philosophy of the Beveridge Report
accorded with his views. He was not prepared to join with
those who were filled with alarm. On the contrary, he pointed
out that, if the Report won general favour, its implementation would be extraordinarily economical from the taxpayers' point of view. Family allowances and other expan-
sions of social benefit would be called for, in any case, by
the social conscience, and would be supported by all parties,
but it would not be so easy to impose upon employees the
large contributions which the Beveridge Report recommended.

Expert discussion turned on how large the national cake
would in fact be, and Keynes had resort to Mr Stone to
throw light upon this matter. An attempt was made to ex-
trapolate the National Income figures. Sir Hubert Henderson intervened with his pessimistic prognostications and
produced much lower figures.[4] Keynes gave warm general
support to the Beveridge proposals, but he consented at a
late stage to act as a spokesman in persuading Sir William
to scale down the commitments. He, Keynes, was quite confident that the nation would be able to afford the scheme
in the long run; but he asked Sir William to reduce the
additional burden on the taxpayer to £100 million a year
in the first five years.[5] It was this intervention that caused
Beveridge to postpone the right to higher old-age pension
scales until such time as a certain number of contributions
had accumulated.

Before this controversy arose in the summer of 1942, the

4. Mr Richard Stone has given me his opinion that, in the event,
the post-war national income (1949) has had a size about midway
between that predicted by the optimists and that predicted by Sir
Hubert Henderson.

5. In assessing this the cost of the National Health Service was to
be reckoned as the excess of public and private expenditure on health
after the inauguration of the scheme over public and private expenditure on health before the inauguration.

Economic Section, under the inspiration of Mr James Meade, had produced a scheme for reducing future slumps by varying employers' and employees' contributions to social insurance. As unemployment grew, the size of the contributions would be reduced automatically and purchasing power increased. At first blush it might be thought that such a variation would have but a small effect in the event of a large industrial depression; but Mr Meade was able to show that, even if one supposed that the reduction of employers' contributions caused no substantial increase of purchasing power, the increased spending by workers would be quite large in quantity relatively to the forces operating in a depression. In fact, it should have a strongly curative effect. Keynes was quite convinced and took up the scheme with enthusiasm. It was eventually given a prominent place in the White Paper on Employment Policy,[6] which appeared two years later.

The narrative of these pages will be mainly concerned with Britain's external finances and international reconstruction projects. Keynes's work was by no means confined to such matters. Most of the important Treasury papers came to him for comment, and he felt it his duty to inquire into any matter where he suspected that action had been lacking or inadequate. He had some notions about most important things that were going on, and his advice was always welcome. At times his passion for detail seized him, he became determined to know the ins and outs of a particular problem, and he went off burrowing into 'low level' committees to find out how the matter was really being handled. Perhaps the Chancellor of the Exchequer wanted a word with him. Where was he? It was discovered that he was in the Board of Trade, attending a committee which no one had ever heard of, chasing up some detailed question. Keynes had more contacts than the high ranking officials, both with those above and those below him. It was natural that he should be able to talk to Ministers as an equal; and

6. Cmd 6527.

he knew that the real truth could often only be discovered from backroom boys, with whom he was on easy terms, ever ready to learn from them.[7]

In May 1942 Keynes was made an Honorary Doctor of Laws by Manchester University. In the following month his name appeared in the Birthday Honours list with the award of a peerage. The old rebel, who had been the victim of so many aspersions by pompous, self-important people in 1919, was now being re-admitted into high official places. He valued the links. His historic sense and his love of England and her traditions came into play. He had some pride of ancestry. That old William de Keynes of 1066 might have been pleased to think that his descendant would enter the ancient Council Chamber in a time of deepest national peril. He was to be Baron Keynes of Tilton, the property of his forbears.

The view commonly expressed was that the feather in the cap of the House of Lords was larger than that in his. All welcomed the opportunity that it would give him to contribute his wise counsel. The opportunity was to prove fruitful. There were those among his old Radical friends who were still disposed to look down their noses. With them he sometimes used the formula – 'I had to do it in order to get servants'. This defence was soon to become anachronistic, as the households of peers as well as commoners were stripped of domestic staff.

7. For a brilliant account of Keynes's position in the Treasury see Mr D. Proctor's contribution to the King's College brochure. This treats its subject with sympathy and affection; but it would be possible for a reader to get a wrong impression of Keynes's stature. Some of his shortcomings therein set out may have been the result of placing a man of great critical faculty and omnivorous interests in a purely advisory position without authority. One who read only this account would not readily guess that the same man had himself been responsible for conducting the whole of Britain's external finances in the first war with supreme efficiency.

*J. M. Keynes to Lord Samuel,* 24 June 1942

Sincere thanks for your letter, which is much appreciated. I am rather hoping to take my seat on July 8th. But it may be that the Letters Patent will not be through in time, in which case I shall have to put off for another fortnight. I have been giving a little thought as to where I should sit. I do not think my position at the Treasury need necessarily require me to sit on the cross benches. I must be regarded, I suppose – and indeed I should like to be – as an Independent. But, in truth, I am still a Liberal, and, if you will agree, I should like to indicate that by sitting on your benches.

2

On the other side of the water consideration of post-war problems was not confined to the disciples of Mr Cordell Hull. There was active discussion in many quarters, indeed quite an intellectual ferment. In this the central figure was undoubtedly Harry White. In Britain he is too often thought of as some dim scribe, some kind of robot, who wrote at the behest of that vaguely conceived entity, the American Treasury, an inferior version of the Keynes plan – mainly to vex the British! Far different was the real man. He was a very remarkable figure, who should be accorded an honourable place in British annals. Having been educated at Harvard, where he was somewhat above the average age of undergraduates and the father of children, he taught economics there for some years, and then obtained a chair at Lawrence College, Appleton, Wisconsin.[8] When Mr Morgenthau became Secretary of the Treasury in 1934 he asked Professor Viner to undertake a survey of Treasury problems. Among the economists whom Viner brought in was Harry White. During the years that followed White showed a marked capacity for applying economic doctrine to practical problems. He won the confidence of Mr Morgenthau.

8. Professor Taussig expresses gratitude to him in the preface to his book on *International Trade* (1927). He published a work on *French International Accounts, 1880–1913* (Harvard University Press).

His influence in the Treasury was always more important than the post which he held. He did valuable work on the Tripartite Agreement, and was concerned with the operations of the U.S. Stabilization Fund in support of the Brazilian and Chinese currencies. Thus he had practical experience of foreign-exchange problems. During the second war he became the leading figure in the Treasury.

He had very solid intellectual quality and was an ardent admirer of Keynes's economic work; he also had great practical energy and a forceful personality, which could readily dominate a committee. He was blunt and downright in speech, and also fervent. As his argument gathered momentum, he clutched his chair, his excitement mounted and his whole frame seemed to reinforce the thoughts of his mind. He had no particular felicity of prose style, but he had considerable fluency, and his earnestness and passion, supporting sound reason, made a strong impression on his auditors. His influence came to extend beyond the Treasury. He made enemies. In his determination to get his way, he adopted methods which might be labelled those of an intriguer. He was distrusted in the banking world, and also by some seasoned public servants. He gained the reputation of being a difficult person to deal with. But he was single-minded in the pursuit of his aims. He was a reformer of genuine conviction. It is to his credit that he won the devoted loyalty of such subordinates as Messrs E. M. Bernstein, F. Coe and A. F. Luxford. He was also able to count on support from higher officials of the Treasury, such as Mr Edward Foley and Mr Herbert Gaston, and he was in good liaison during the war with Mr Oscar Cox and Mr Lauchlin Currie. It is probably true to say that but for White's assiduity and galvanic personality a large scheme of the kind for which Keynes was working in Britain would never have come to birth at Bretton Woods.

White also worked strenuously to promote Lend-Lease and give strength to Hitler's enemy. He may, however, have been to some extent the victim of current American mythology about British Imperialism. Who shall describe the British? In this connection it may suffice to point out that they are a tough and obstinate people, with a love of travel and a spice of adventure, who have picked up an Empire more or less by accident. They have an easy knack of administration and are not corrupt, with the result that they have had marked success in introducing order and justice into this planless agglomeration. They are humane and tolerant. They are also law-abiding and have a definite tendency to conscientiousness. Thus, if anyone persuades them that it is really their duty to part with all or sections of this empire, they show a readiness to do so. But is it really their duty? How different is the American myth, based, we must suppose, on an ill-timed, but transitory, fit of British obstinacy, which was based on muddled thought. Americans seem to forget that it is not only in American textbooks that George III and Lord North appear as the villains in that particular drama; they do so in most British textbooks also. According to this myth, the British are a wily and cunning people, diabolically astute in international finance, the British Empire always occupying the first place in their thoughts and plans, determined at all costs to advance its interests, and easily able to make rings round anyone who would oppose their Machiavellian projects. This mythology exerted some influence during World War II, and continues to do so.

In 1938–9 White was concerned with the Project for an All-American Bank, which was, however, killed by Congress. During the later part of 1941 there were discussions, in which Professor Alvin Hansen and Mr Adolf Berle took part, for extending these ideas. In January 1942 the third Pan-American meeting of Secretaries for Foreign Affairs took place in Rio. White was there with a project for an International Stabilization Fund, and a resolution was adopted in favour of a conference to deal with it. In the early part of 1942 White devoted himself to working out more thorough-going international schemes. Thus he was some months

behind Keynes! There was no communication between
them at this stage. Mr Bernstein gave White invaluable
technical assistance. This American group also produced a
bulky volume, which, however, was not a sandwich with a
thin layer of internationalism in the midst of it, but all solid
internationalism. It contained projects for a Stabilization
Fund and an International Bank. The International Bank
was ambitious; it was to be a genuine international 'Central
Bank', with a right to issue notes and hold the deposits of
other Central Banks. Keynes later said that the International Monetary Fund ought to be called a bank and the
International Bank a fund; the origin of the terminology
we have is to be found in White's original plan. The Fund
had a limited objective of dealing with foreign-exchange and
balance-of-payments problems; it was a fund in the sense in
which the British Exchange Equalization Fund and the
American Stabilization Fund had been funds. The Bank
on the other hand, was to have been a Central Bank; its
objectives were described on bolder lines than anything
achieved at Bretton Woods. It was to eliminate the danger
of world-wide crises that are financial in origin, and reduce
the likelihood, intensity and duration of world-wide economic depressions. It already had in it the clause, which was
deemed so valuable in subsequent discussions, that the
Bank should impose no condition, upon an extension of
credit or loan, as to the particular country in which the
proceeds of the loan must be spent. It should organize and
finance an International Commodity Stabilization Corporation for the purpose of stabilizing the prices of important
commodities. It should buy and sell and hold gold and the
obligations and securities of participating governments, act
as a clearing-house of funds, balances, cheques, drafts and
acceptances on account of participating governments or
their fiscal agencies, and accept demand, time and custody
deposits and accounts from participating governments and
their fiscal agencies and Central Banks; it should discount
and rediscount bills and acceptances, and issue debentures.

It should make loans for the purpose of providing nations with metallic reserves with longer terms of repayment than loans for other purposes. It should have the power to issue notes and do its business in a new gold unit. Alas, all these splendid features were in due course to be removed.

Mr Adolf Berle, Under-Secretary of State in the State Department, was associated with Harry White in these early drafts. He had come into the State Department two years before the war and played some part in advising the President on means to combat the depression of 1937–8. He had some reputation in London for being a believer in the American myth about the British. He did not work in completely harmonious cooperation with Mr Dean Acheson, the most important other Assistant Under-Secretary of State. But, at this juncture, he played a key part of some moment. He used his influence with Mr Cordell Hull to persuade him that, if he was to achieve his ideal of non-discriminatory foreign trade, it was necessary that the United States should interest herself in financial props for the international economy. Cooperation must be extended to foreign exchange questions, international credits and international investment. Mr Cordell Hull assented. Without this assent it would have been impossible to proceed with Article VII discussions along the lines that led to Bretton Woods.

Sir Frederick Phillips and Mr Opie attended some of the meetings which discussed the White draft. On 8 July 1942 Sir Frederick Phillips was authorized by White to let London see it, and he sent a copy to Sir Richard Hopkins with an instruction that he should show it to Keynes only. Meanwhile, the Clearing Union had been got ready for dispatch. It was sent across late in August for the information of the US Treasury, and on 10 September there was a meeting there with White, Berle, Pasvolsky, Phillips and Opie present. When White saw a copy of the Clearing Union – 'Is is not a lucky thing,' he remarked, 'that we have been working on a Stabilization Fund?' Phillips asked White if they could not proceed to detailed discussions on the American proposal for an International Bank. White was unwilling, his fear being that, if this discussion was general, the British might offer to accept his bank scheme if he accepted the Clearing Union, and he saw grave difficulties in the Clearing Union.

Meanwhile in London, in October, a meeting of Dominions representatives was taking place, at which Keynes's ideas were expounded. It was judged to be a useful meeting. The Canadians were keen that the British and Americans should think alike on post-war topics; in these talks and throughout the subsequent negotiations the Canadians continued to make valuable contributions. They were represented on successive occasions by able men, including Messrs Rasminsky, Towers, MacIntosh and Pearson. Almost alone, outside the ranks of British and Americans, the Canadians seemed capable of understanding the international monetary problem as a whole. Their suggestions were intelligent and constructive, and the British and Americans were always anxious to have them. At this meeting the Australians began to take up what was their characteristic attitude. They were anxious not to commit themselves to multilateral arrangements on the side of money or commerce, unless there was some international guarantee that world-wide effective demand and full employment would be sustained.

When the Americans studied the Clearing Union, what struck them most forcibly was that Congress would never agree to the 'unlimited liability' implied in it. This expression, although commonly used, was not strictly correct. There was a limit to the liability, namely, the sum total of all the rights of all nations to draw upon the Fund; when they had all exhausted their quotas, the Americans – assuming them to be in a creditor position *vis-à-vis* the rest of the world – would have no obligation to provide anything more. But this total was a very large one, and it was not altogether misleading to call the liability 'unlimited'. There were various other points of difficulty to the Americans, but this was the central issue. Now, it was evident from Keynes's draft that the British were greatly exercised, and justifiably so, about the undue burden which has always fallen upon a debtor country, when disequilibrium in the balance of trade arises. If trade was unequal, should not creditor countries also play a part in curing the maladjustment? Keynes had introduced some devices for this purpose. When credits rose above a certain level, interest should be charged. A paradox, to pay interest on your deposit as well as on your overdraft! I was never convinced that this provision was practicable. There had been lengthy discussion as to whether some sharper form of sanction should not be applied to creditor countries. I pointed out to Keynes that, in the long run, his Clearing Union did not provide an automatic mechanism for redressing the balance; if all the debtor countries exhausted all their quotas, the creditor countries would have run up huge balances, and we should then be where we were before. He seemed only to have provided a temporary easement – albeit a very large one – not a permanent cure. Would it not be possible to divide debtor countries into those whose indebtedness was no greater than the average, and what might be called excess debtor countries? Only the latter should lose their drawing rights, while the condition of the former might be regarded merely as a reflection of the misdemeanour of the creditor countries in not redressing their own position. It seemed impossible to find a satisfactory formula, although the matter was much debated. As subsequently appeared, any formula of this kind would have been totally unacceptable to the Americans, as it would have imposed upon them an unlimited liability in the literal sense of the word. Keynes recognized that the problem was not completely solved in his Clearing Union; he hoped that the Fund was so large that within the period of easement provided by it the creditor nation or nations, in consultation with the debtor nations on the Board, would find means of adjusting their position.

In the Clearing Union, as presented, apart from the fancy

proposal about an interest charge, the real sanction against
the creditor country lay precisely in the large credit that it
would pile up in due course. The idea was, that when it saw
this credit grow, it would feel forced to take remedial
measures. Consequently, it was plain to the Americans that,
if they merely removed the 'unlimited' liability and sub-
stituted a limited liability, they would be removing from the
scheme the one genuine, albeit somewhat weak, sanction
against creditor countries which it contained. Something
would have to be done about this to satisfy the British.

Something was done. During the autumn of 1942 the
Stabilization Fund was got into a shape for formal presentation. Re-draft after re-draft appeared. The draft of 11
December still contained no 'scarce currency' clause. In the
draft of 16 December it was there. This was the American
answer to the problem. If debtor countries increased indebtedness beyond a certain level, they would lose their
drawing rights; if creditor countries increased their credit
beyond a corresponding level, their currencies would be
declared 'scarce' and would be allotted under a scheme, and
thus debtor nations would have a fully authorized right to
discriminate against the exports of the creditor countries.
Thus there was to be discrimination, not unilaterally at the
mere whim of the importing country, but only when the
condition of the Stabilization Fund showed that it was justified, namely, when a creditor country was allowing an un-
corrected favourable balance to continue indefinitely. This
was a very remarkable concession. If the United States was
really to maintain over a term of years the oppressive role of
creditor, which all predicted for her, it would mean that she
was by this clause authorizing other nations to discriminate
against the purchase of American goods, to take in each
other's washing and to maintain their own full employment
in the presence of an American depression.

It was not, of course, expected that matters would be
allowed to come to such a pass. Rather than have American
exporters faced with the consequences of the 'scarce cur-

rency' clause in operation, the Administration, it was expected, would take pains to prevent its ever coming into
operation. This could be done by encouraging long-term
loans abroad, stimulating domestic purchasing power by
appropriate means or reducing American tariffs. The important point was, however, that the Administration, instead
of being able to consider such recipes at leisure, and perhaps
postpone them for 'political' reasons till Doomsday, would
be under compulsion to adopt immediate and effective
measures, in order to prevent the scarce currency clause
coming into operation.

The draft of the Fund came over to London in February
1943. I did not hear of its arrival for some weeks. I acquired
it one day when I had to travel to Oxford by the train leaving
London at midnight. It was a characteristic wartime journey. The light was very dim; the carriage was crowded with
soldiers returning from leave. I was tightly wedged into a
corner. In my hand I had the Fund draft, a vile production
of British Treasury economy, single spaced, printed on both
sides of flimsy sheets, the ink showing through. The document was exceedingly difficult to read in the dim light, and
it was written in that tortuous language, later christened
Cherokee by Keynes, which was quite new to me. The
thought itself seemed contorted. Having read some paragraphs, I deemed it impossible to proceed, but the fascination was so great that I struggled on, painfully piecing
together the sense of it. I read on into it, through the scarce
currency clause and onwards. I could not believe my eyes or
my brain. I read it again and again. I studied some notes by
Keynes which I had with me. They did not seem helpful. I
was transfixed. This, then, was the big thing. For years we
had complained of the United States' attitude as a creditor.
For months we had struggled in vain to find some formula
which would pin them down to a share of responsibility.
Now they had come forward and offered a solution of their
own, gratuitously. This was certainly a great event. For it
was the first time that they had said in a document, un-

official, it was true, and non-committal, but still in a considered Treasury document, that they would come in and
accept their full share of responsibility when there was a
fundamental disequilibrium of trade. As I sat huddled in
my corner, I felt an exhilaration such as only comes once or
twice in a lifetime. There were the dishevelled soldiers
sprawling over one another in sleep; and here was I, tightly
pressed into my corner, holding these little flimsy sheets. One
had the urge to wake them all up. 'Here, boys, is great news.
Here is an offer, which can make things very different for
you when the war is over; your lords and masters do not
seem to have realized it yet; but they soon will; see for yourselves this paragraph 7; read what it says. I know that you set
great store by the Beveridge scheme; but that is only written
on a bit of paper; it will all fall to pieces, if this country has
a bad slump and trade difficulties. Here is the real thing,
because it will save us from a slump and make all those
Beveridge plans lastingly possible.' Was I too enthusiastic?
It does not seem so, because, whether the International
Monetary Fund proves able to play a leading role in world
affairs or not, the Americans were admitting the principle
of joint responsibility for disequilibrium, which has actuated
their policy ever since. Marshall Aid was reaffirmation of
the principle in different circumstances.

When I arrived in Oxford at 2 a.m. there was no question
of going home to bed. Instead I went to my rooms in College
and wrote the following letter to Keynes:

*R. F. Harrod to J. M. Keynes,* 2 March 1943

I have been reading your notes on the S.F.[9] with great interest. I have only just had the opportunity of seeing the two
documents this evening. I agree with most of what you say save
in your comment 7 (on S.F. 7)[10] and in your last sentence of 9.

Here I find myself in disagreement with your tone and nuance.
You point out that S.F. 7 creates difficulties for the credit coun-

9. viz. the Stabilization Fund.
10. viz. the Scarce Currency Clause.

tries, are on the whole disparaging, but suggest we might in certain circumstances make concessions to the American point of view.

I submit on the other hand that S.F. 7 is most highly advantageous for us and gives us what we should never have dared to ask for or hoped to get.

It embraces two possibilities. One, only lightly touched on, is that the credit country would provide extra emergency credit when its quota was exhausted. This does not seem to be looked on with much favour by them. It might be argued that this is none the less how the thing would work out in practice. If that were so, we should be in exactly the same position as under the C.U.[11]

The other possibility, the main one presented, is a rationing of the scarce currency (we need not bother about the proposals seeming 'unworkable'; something could no doubt be worked out). Under this there are two alternatives. Either free dealing in foreign exchange would be allowed and the scarce currency would go to a premium in the free market. Or other countries would have to ration purchases from the scarce currency country. Either of these alternatives gives us a more favourable solution than the proposals of the C.U. The wording of the last sentence of 7 indicates that it is the latter they have in mind.

The main objective of an expansionist policy aiming at the maximum of trade is to secure that the tendency of certain countries to build up large credit positions does not compel other countries to deflate or raise trade barriers. Either of the alternatives set out in the last paragraph would protect the debtor countries from this more adequately than the C.U. proposals. Either appreciation of the particular credit country's currency in the free market, if any, or the rationing of purchases from it, would deflect purchasing power from the market of that country to the market of other foreign countries or the home market. No deflation or general protection in the debit countries would be required. There would, if purchases were rationed, be discrimination against a particular country, but this would be discrimination according to an orderly and agreed plan, and confined to the occasions where it was really justified.

The cardinal point is that the Americans offer us in this what we could never have asked of them in the negotiations, especially

11. viz. the Clearing Union.

after signing Article VII, namely, that we (and other countries) should be allowed to discriminate against American goods if dollars are running short.

It is definitely better than the C.U. proposal. I think we agreed that under that proposal there was always the danger – in my judgement a very threatening one – that some countries would build up such large credit positions that the general run of debit countries would in due course exceed their quotas and that thus the general system would break down. Under the American system the check imposed on the countries tending to excess credit safeguards the debit countries. It means that the situation could not arise in which the general run of debit countries tended to exceed their quotas. Some might of course do so – but to these we want in any case to apply special correctives. Indeed the American plan provides a mechanism, which we never succeeded in finding, for automatically sorting out what in some of my earlier notes I called 'excess' debit countries from the general run of debit countries. This in itself is an advantage in their scheme.

It is no discredit, if I may say so, to the author of the C.U. that he did not find this satisfactory solution. The Americans have, happily, played a card which according to the rules of the game we could not play.

I infer from all this that our main object from now on should be to hold the Americans to S.F. 7. How this had better be done, in terms of tact and tactics, I will not presume to say. Clearly we must not underline the difficulties (e.g. about rationing) but on the contrary do our utmost to find a way out of them. We must not raise objections to any part of S.F. which is logically linked to S.F. 7.

It seems to me that if we can hold the Americans to S.F. 7 the main battle of long-range economic planning is thereby won. This is the crucial point. All the other points are of comparatively small importance.

I should like to suggest that a cable ought to be sent to Phillips and anyone else involved in discussions formal or informal on this paper, stating explicitly that from now on our main object should be to hold the Americans to the principles of S.F. 7.

### J. M. Keynes to R. F. Harrod, 4 March 1943

Your letter of March 2nd about S.F. and C.U. gives food for thought...

I agree that, read literally, the interpretation you give to this is the only one which makes any sense. Perhaps I ought to have attached more importance to it. I interpreted it as a half-baked suggestion, not fully thought through, which was certain to be dropped as soon as its full consequences were appreciated. I cannot imagine that the State Department really would put forward as their own solution the rationing of purchases from a scarce currency country. You must remember that the evidence as to the extent to which the State Department have actually accepted this document of Harry White's is somewhat flimsy. I should expect that the moment emphatic attention was drawn to this alternative, it would be withdrawn.

Nevertheless, I agree with you that it needs careful consideration and good handling. I will see that this is brought to Phillips' attention. But I should hesitate, as at present advised, to make the assumption that this alternative is really open to us as the basis of our future policy and instruction to Phillips.

### R. F. Harrod to J. M. Keynes, 6 March 1943

Many thanks for your letter of March 4. I appreciate your point about the probability that the Americans may run out if the State Department has not yet appreciated the full consequences of the proposal. I rather guessed it was what you would say!

On the other hand the State Department has in public utterances shown itself alive to the troubles caused to the rest of the world by the persistent U.S. credit position in the thirties. They must be well aware of the internal obstacles to radical tariff reduction. It is just possible that they are prepared to make an honest attempt to solve this problem on lines that they can get across at home. It would probably be easier for them to launch this rather complicated currency plan than a very drastic tariff reduction plan. Instead of having to present a highbrow economic argument to Congress in favour of free-er trade they could in the last resort use an honest-to-God type of argument – Well, they cannot buy our goods if they have not the money to pay for them, can they? ...

The Americans did not run out. The scarce-currency clause was incorporated, in a much stronger form than it had in the original draft, in the Bretton Woods Act passed by Congress in July 1945. In my recent researches I have asked on separate occasions several of those who were close to White about the origin of this clause. Witnesses agreed in affirming that it was put in quite deliberately, with eyes open, as the American contribution towards solving the problem of trade disequilibrium.

Neither Keynes nor the other British experts were at once convinced of the value of the clause. It only came to acquire cardinal importance when it became clear that the main structure of the White plan would have to be accepted by the British; it then became a sort of consolation prize. Meanwhile attention was focussed upon the drawbacks of the White scheme, which were indeed great.

In the first place, it was conceived on a niggardly scale. The credits that would be available under the Keynes scheme were calculated at approximately $25 billion; the White plan offered $5 billion (the Final Act of Bretton Woods contained a compromise figure of $8·8 billion, to which the quotas of those joining subsequently could be added). This quantitative difference in fact amounted to one of quality. Keynes wanted a Fund so large as to give governments the confidence necessary to relax unneighbourly restrictions; $25 billion might have achieved that; $5 billion certainly would not. Was this Fund really to be the foundation for the building of a better world? Or was it to be merely a modest subscription towards meeting some of the needs of poorer countries? Contemporary and subsequent opinions outside the United States have on the whole agreed in holding that Keynes was right. One could only console oneself by hoping that, should the Americans prove obdurate now, the Fund might be enlarged in the course of its operation.

Keynes's Clearing Union did not need initial assets of any magnitude; the assets would be built up in the course of working. The White scheme required gold subscriptions and a deposit of collateral. This was tiresome, and it would be necessary to scale down the proposed gold subscriptions.

Quotas and voting rights under the British scheme were to be related to foreign trade, since it was with this that the Clearing Union was concerned. This formula would have given Britain a position comparable to that of the United States. The White scheme made them depend not only on foreign trade but also on the size of their gold holdings and national income; this would greatly enlarge the Americans' share. The White scheme was interspersed with provisions for a four-fifths majority. The Americans were evidently more concerned to ensure an American veto against undesirable action than they were to ensure that a group of other nations would be unable to block progress.

There was an objection to the American scheme, which was more important than all these and which the course of events may yet show to have been fatal. This is somewhat difficult to describe briefly – a difficulty which proved to be a hindrance in the negotiations that followed. The objection was no less real for being difficult to expound. The structure of the American scheme was entirely different from that of the British, one might even say its converse. Keynes had the intuition that his form of structure was essential, if the Fund was to develop into a great institution of world-wide importance. The arguments in its favour were somewhat elusive and hard to keep in the forefront of a debate, in which many complex issues had to be discussed simultaneously among many experts of widely different points of view.

The Clearing Union was essentially a Central Bank, using a medium of exchange (Bancor) provided by itself (as a Central Bank provides its banknotes). Nations with favourable balances of foreign payments would acquire Bancor deposits, and those with unfavourable balances would be overdrawn in terms of Bancor.

The idea underlying such a Union is simple, namely, to generalize the essential principle of banking as it is exhibited within any closed system. This principle is the necessary equality of credits and debits. If no credits can be removed outside the clearing system, but only transferred within it, the Union can never be in any difficulty as regards the honouring of cheques drawn upon it. It can make what advances it wishes to any of its members with the assurance that the proceeds can only be transferred to the clearing account of another member.

It is true that Keynes's scheme did not make any special provision for 'advances'; but he certainly had it in mind that, if international plans for investment, commodity stabilization, etc., were developed, the Union would be able to help. Such projects were outlined in bold strokes in his Section IX. For instance, the Union 'might finance stocks of commodities held by such bodies, allowing them overdraft facilities on their accounts up to an agreed maximum. By this means the financial problem of Buffer Stocks and "ever-normal granaries" could be effectively attacked'. A World Central Bank would be in an extremely powerful position owing to its ability to 'create credit'. The Union was based on the central banking principle.

White's Stabilization Fund, on the other hand, was based on such precedents as the British Exchange Equalization Fund and the American Stabilization Fund. Its total assets were governed once and for all by the amounts voted to it in the first instance. The countries with unfavourable balances would be allowed to draw on this Fund of predetermined size. By contrast with the Clearing Union, no expansion would be possible save by the painful process of going to the taxpayers of the various nations and asking for more. In the course of all the prolonged discussions the point was constantly put that whatever one proposed to do by the Clearing Union scheme could be done, under different nomenclature and by a different technique, but with the same effect, by the Stabilization Fund. So long as one kept one's gaze fixed on the immediate concrete proposals in the Clearing Union plan, one could use this argument with some force. It was only when one turned one's gaze away and looked at the future vista, when one thought of international investment, commodity schemes, a super-national policing body, an international economic board to combat the trade cycle, etc., that one realized that there were great possibilities present in the Keynes plan that were absent in that of White. While it was right and wise to think forward to larger projects, albeit as yet but dimly conceived, it was difficult to sustain a detailed argument against the White plan on the ground that it could not achieve certain objectives, so long as those objectives were not specified in detail.

One has to remember that White originally conceived his Fund in conjunction with an extremely ambitious International Bank. The fresh vigour of those original plans had been lost through the normal attrition of inter-departmental discussion. It is extraordinarily difficult, in one's zeal to save something of one's original idea, to make a fair assessment of the value of a scheme that has been grievously pared down. Could White have gone back to his original point of view, would he really have thought that the Fund, taken in conjunction with an Investment Bank of a conventional pattern, would suffice to achieve the objectives which he had originally had in view?

One could always hope that both schemes could be enlarged and improved in the working. But one ought always to have had fixed in one's mind the important words penned by Keynes in his Clearing Union draft:

It may be doubted whether a comprehensive scheme will ever in fact be worked out, unless it can come into existence through a single act of creation, made possible by the unity of purpose and energy of hope for better things to come, spring from the victory of the United Nations, when they have attained it, over immediate evil.

During these crucial months, each nation had its characteristic failing. The British, painfully and correctly aware of their enormous prospective balance of trade difficulties, may have tended to stress them too much, and thus have given the impression that plans, which they had really designed for wider purposes, had been thought of in the first instance primarily as means for helping Britain in her immediate post-war difficulties. The Americans, on their side, tended to think of any assets they might contribute to or acquire in the Fund, as a charitable 'hand-out' to help their poor benighted neighbours. But this was a fundamentally wrong approach to the foundation of an International Monetary Agency. To regard one's deposit at such an Agency, before it had even opened, as a worthless piece of paper, and write it off in one's mind as a gift to others, showed a lack of confidence in the viability of the institution planned, which must fatally handicap its proper planning. The Americans might claim that post-war events have vindicated their fear that they would be called upon to make 'hand-outs' without end; and they have shown no lack of generosity in doing so. None the less, it was wrong to mix the two streams of thought. If the Fund was to be a success, all nations in it, the Americans not least, would have to regard their rights to draw upon it as first-class assets.

The two schemes were published in April. Press comment was not profound. Opinion in Britain and in other countries greatly preferred the Keynes version, although it is not quite clear how far this was due to his superior writing and draftsmanship. In the popular mind the big difference appeared to be that the White scheme more closely resembled a normal gold standard; this interpretation was based on some small points, which Keynes himself did not feel to be of importance.

Within Whitehall there was, as may be imagined, a meticulous comparison of the two schemes. Consideration was given to the points which could be most advantageously conceded. Keynes upheld the essential point in the following letter to Phillips:

*J. M. Keynes to Sir Frederick Phillips*, 27 May 1943

One can yield on the question of asking security and on the question of limited liability to the creditor without yielding on the main structure. I should much prefer to make both the former concessions and yield on the main structure only in the last resort. While in essence this is mainly a question of appearance, I fancy it comes to much more than that, if one looks forward into future developments and the use of the Union for various general international purposes.

The last sentence here is of importance. It was, therefore, a great disappointment when in June the Canadians put forward their own alternative, which, while more favourable in certain respects, was fundamentally modelled on the American pattern. Mr Rasminsky wrote:

You will note that we have worked on the principle of a Fund rather than adopt the Banking principle . . . As I see it, there is really no very important difference other than an aesthetic difference, between the two methods. In the one case all the resources you need are created at once whereas in the other case they are created only as they are needed. If one assumes, as one must, that the United States will insist on a limit on the amount of resources she is willing to put through the new institution, then the banking principle is not in itself necessarily more expansionist than the Fund principle. In either case the consent of a given country would be required for that country to provide additional resources to the institution.

But this was to neglect future possibilities.

During 1942 the British expected an early eventuation of the discussions referred to in Article VII on the Mutual Aid Agreement. Before that was signed, the Americans had appeared anxious to press on. Then there seemed to be a pause. This was, no doubt, when the White schemes were undergoing the process of attrition. The British at this time thought they detected some change of view in the United States. In the minds of some, including Keynes, there was the hope that in the hard intellectual work of hammering out the principles of the post-war economy and the structure of the international institutions that would be required, Britain and the United States would operate in bilateral discussions, and there was the further hope that, in the early stages of these new perilous ventures, the two countries would take sole responsibility for initiating the projects. Keynes's original draft of the Clearing Union contained the following words:

It is proposed that the Currency Union should be founded by the United States and the United Kingdom, which would be designated Founder States and given a special position.

These words contained the idea of an Anglo-American leadership, and in that respect, although not in others, his ideas bear some family resemblance to the key currencies approach proposed by Professor J. H. Williams, and supported by American bankers, which emphasized the importance of Anglo-American currency cooperation as a precondition for a wider scheme. But in the course of 1942 the Americans seemed to come round to the view that all schemes of this sort must be fully international from the beginning and that Britain should have no special status.

In February 1943 President Roosevelt surprised the world by summoning the nations to confer together upon the post-war food problem. This led to the meeting at Hot Springs, Virginia. The British were somewhat perturbed, as this initiative seemed to be a departure from the path of steady, albeit somewhat slow, progress in planning the discussions under Article VII. Those plans comprised the commodity, and thereby the food, question. The notice was short, and there was some consternation in Whitehall. However, under the able leadership of Mr Richard Law, assisted by Mr John Maud and Professor Lionel Robbins, the British acquitted themselves well at Hot Springs.

On his homeward journey through Washington, Professor Robbins was waylaid, in order that he might partake in discussions about the Stabilization Fund in the American Treasury. As soon as the White scheme was published, the Americans set about conducting informal discussions with other nations [12] to the greatest extent possible. The British Dominions were among those consulted, and Keynes at home was becoming anxious lest they should suppose that the Stabilization Fund was the sole candidate for consideration, to the exclusion of the Clearing Union. The Americans organized an informal international conference which Sir Frederick Phillips, Professor Robertson and Mr Opie attended. Professor Robbins was roped in. The Federal Reserve Board had recently produced a variant of the Stabilization Fund with a fifty per cent gold subscription; it feared that the White proposal would have inflationary effects in America. This variant found no favour with the assembled nations. There were some direct talks between the British and Americans, at which the difficulty the latter found in 'unlimited' liability was plainly put. Sir Frederick also organized a meeting with the other nations one afternoon at the British Embassy.

These British representatives, with the exception of Sir Frederick Phillips, who unhappily died later in the year, were all to play a notable part in the series of negotiations which followed. Professor Robbins proved a highly skilled negotiator and won great esteem in the United States. Keynes came to rely on him and to value his judgement. Robbins often played the role of conciliator; when Keynes had said something too sharp, Robbins was ready with his grave and well-reasoned fluency to put the matter in a slightly different light and to prove that what Keynes had said, when viewed from another angle, could be seen to embody the American point of view. His well-rounded

12. Australia, Belgium, Brazil, Canada, China, Czechoslovakia, Ecuador, Egypt, France, Luxemburg, Norway, Paraguay, the Philippine Islands, Poland, Venezuela.

phrases and weighty manner seemed to the Americans to reflect, as indeed they did, a mellow philosophy and ripe judgement. His learning in general economics, as well as Keynesian economics, served him in good stead.

Professor Robertson was at this time resident in Washington on Treasury business, and he continued to play an important part in these discussions until their culmination at Bretton Woods. He was well known on the other side to be one of the two or three foremost British economists. He was in sympathy with the American desire for a more liberal international economy, while fully cognizant of the complex system of controls that had grown up on the British side, and not prone to take an optimistic view about prospective British difficulties. He was not by nature inclined to enjoy the rough and tumble of hard bargaining, but his subtle mind moved easily among all the complexities of the proposed plans, and his comprehension of every detail of the clauses was unsurpassed. In due course he came to collaborate very closely with Mr Bernstein; it was recognized that no problem was so knotty but that these two could succeed in achieving an agreed solution.

While the Americans were now fully engaged upon the task of winning agreement for the Stabilization Fund, they were nervous of having a meeting that would attract the attention of the press. The British participants in these preliminary discussions all happened to be in the United States on other business. The meetings were semi-secret. Clearly the time had come when no further headway could be made until the authors of the Clearing Union and the Stabilization Fund should confront one another directly.

### 3

The meeting took place at Washington in September 1943. This was the second visit of Keynes's series. He was beginning to feel quite at home in Washington. He became an intimate member of a social circle. The Walter Lippmanns, the Frankfurters, the Achesons, the Chatfield-Taylors, Mr Archibald McLeish, were among his close friends. Lydia was always with him. He was still a sick man; and she never relaxed her vigilance. 'How are you, Lydia?' – 'I am very well. When Maynard is well, I am well; when he is ill, I am ill.' She became in due course almost a legendary figure. Her boundless gaiety, her manifest devotion, her resourcefulness in providing comfort on the most unpromising occasions with all sorts of queer contrivances, her shopping expeditions, her infinite sweetness with all his associates, her quips and sallies, unconventional and personal, but always acceptable, suffused with some unique quality of simplicity and thereby of dignity, endeared her to American hearts. To be a friend of the great British economist – that was something to be proud of; but to be a friend of Lydia – that was the supreme glory.

They used to stay at the Mayflower or the Statler, Keynes finally acquiring a preference for the latter, where he liked to take a light meal in the relative peacefulness of the Coffee Shop. Quentin Keynes, Geoffrey's son, had a post in Washington and was sometimes mobilized on these visits to act as aide-de-camp. He used to drive his uncle for weekends to the Sky-line Hotel, overlooking the Shenandoah Valley. On one occasion they stayed at the Mimslyn Hotel, and without flinching Keynes did the tour among the stalactites of the Luray caverns, although once started one is irretrievably committed to a two-hour walk. He went to the films and, when in New York, to the ballet and the play. He enjoyed visiting the Museum of Modern Art, perhaps to get some hints for his Arts Council work.

He carried his interests across the Atlantic with him. There was all the business of the Arts Council to be attended to; there might be articles for the *Economic Journal* to be read. Above all, the book catalogues continued to come and unintermittent buying by cable proceeded. I was in the Folger Library in December 1943. The Librarian asked me if I knew a fellow-countryman, Lord Keynes. 'Quite well.'

'We are not pleased with him. He was in here a couple of months ago and told us he had acquired a first edition of Spenser's *Complaints*,[13] which we bid for.' The Librarian then recalled this dialogue: '"How did you obtain information about it?" I asked him. "From the catalogue. How else?" "So did we; how did you order it?" "By cable." "So did we. How did you obtain the catalogue?" Lord Keynes looked a little guilty – "Well, as a matter of fact, it came over in the Foreign Office bag".' The Folger Librarian could not compete against the possessor of such privileges!

Now, at last, Keynes and White were confronted with one another in an open clash of will and personality. Keynes was not yet a British delegate in the full sense, as he was to be on subsequent visits, since these conversations were only informal and exploratory. But still he was a negotiator, fighting for a principle which might make things easier for Britain while establishing a basis for world prosperity. He was amply backed, or impeded, by telegrams from the Treasury. He was assisted by Sir David Waley, Mr Opie and Mr Thompson-McCausland. Mr Liesching of the Board of Trade was also there, and, ably seconded by Mr Shackle and reinforced by the economic wisdom of Mr James Meade, was conducting parallel negotiations about a 'Commercial Union'. Professor Lionel Robbins was at hand, with an interest in both sides of the negotiations; and he was also responsible, along with Mr Frank Lee, for the commodity discussions. The Foreign Office was represented by Mr Nigel Ronald.

The British delegation was officially led by Mr Richard Law, who opened with a powerful and moving speech. Of all the British Ministers at that time, Mr Law took the liveliest interest in international reconstruction. Such authority as was obtained from the British Cabinet from time to time

13. Edmund Spenser. *Complaints. Containing sundrie small Poems of the World's Vanitie.* 4to. London. Imprinted for William Ponsonbie, 1591. First edition: bought from Maggs Bros., £175.

for the continuance of the discussions was partly due to his untiring efforts.

More than one witness has said to me, 'You know, the fact of the matter was that Keynes had no love for White, and White had no love for Keynes.' I can affirm that the former proposition was not true, and those close to White deny the latter also. Keynes soon came to have a great respect for White's abilities; in these Washington talks he was still sorely tried by White's rasping truculence; but in the course of subsequent visits he also came to have a real affection for him. White was difficult, there was no doubt; Keynes, although not sparing him in verbal debate, exercised tact and forbearance. White's own feelings were more subtle. Only a few years ago, before his star had risen, he had revered Keynes as the greatest living economist. Now he was confronting him as a negotiator on an equal footing – or rather, on an unequal footing, for he himself represented the stronger power. There was inevitably something a little awkward in that relation. (This was true also of the other United States officials who had been brought up on Keynes's works.) White had to keep his end up as an economist among his colleagues. Keynes, it has to be confessed, was his superior, not only in pure economic theory, but also in his understanding of the techniques of the money and foreign-exchange markets. 'Do not let that clever fellow throw dust in your eyes,' White used to tell his American associates, hinting that he, White, was quite capable of seeing through it. They sometimes felt that he went out of his way to cast doubt on Keynes's motives or find fault in his reasoning when there was none. These were but superficial manifestations. At heart he admired and trusted Keynes. For diplomatic reasons a certain air of belligerency had to be maintained in public; it must at all costs not be said that he had been nobbled by Keynes. Behind the scenes they ultimately became great cronies, going off to the baseball game together and having plenty of fun.

Their modes of debate were diametrically opposed. White

was full of vigour and manful thrust. He could be wrathful
and rude. His earnestness carried him forward in a torrent
of words, which sometimes outstripped his grammatical
powers. Keynes, we know, was different; he was always ready
with his beautifully polished sentences; he detected any
inconsistency in the opposition, even in the most abstruse
matter, with lightning celerity, and pointed it out with seeming gentleness in barbed and sometimes offensive sentences.
He could always coin an epigram on the spur of the moment.
On the subject of the Fund's right to use its gold subscriptions to replenish, by purchase, its holdings of a scarce currency – 'You Americans,' he said, 'not content with having
sucked all the gold out of all the debtor countries in the
world, have now invented a scheme for sucking all the gold
out of all the creditor countries as well.'

It was not only at White that Keynes aimed his swift rapier
thrusts. The question has been raised whether his unconventional methods, his barbed utterances, his tendency to
rag the Americans and expose their foibles by jests which
became almost intimate, and his exploitation of every
resource of dialectic, were of advantage to the British cause.
Upon Americans confronting him for the first time the effect
may have been unfavourable, tending to confirm their
'mythology'. Had they not always known that the British
were diabolically clever and would put rings round the
simple-hearted Americans? Here, sure enough, was an example in the flesh. This impression soon wore off. They could
not succeed with a fallacious argument – that they had to recognize; they were put on their mettle. But when, as sometimes happened, Keynes took an unfair advantage in a debate,
exploiting some faulty expression on the other side and
securing a quick triumph, he made no attempt to hold the
position thus won. On the next day no more would be heard
of it. With a little experience the Americans came to appreciate this. They realized that he was a man of absolute intellectual integrity, and that his methods were designed to
elicit the truth and not to steal an advantage.

His sallies and his intimacies had a good and a bad side. They served to break through the formal considerations, which occupy so much time at international meetings, and to focus the attention of the committee upon the underlying realities. But they also had their perils. His rudeness was sometimes carried to an indefensible length and feelings were ruffled; there might even be rather hot resentment. It was the old story; he was too ready to assume that his adversaries in debate would take all as fair. But if it was brought to his attention that he had inflicted a wound, he would make amends by a most beautiful apology; and then the last state might be better than the first. The case was the same as with Dundas's home truths; a personal relation was established at a more intimate level.

On balance, his methods probably did injury at first, the dividend coming in after a time-lag. In due course the American negotiators learnt the true nature of the man; they came to understand that he was kindly at heart and fully appreciative of their own good qualities. The first and second rudeness might be taken amiss; but when it came to the third and fourth, they merely thought, as did his English friends, that he was being true to form, and were able to enjoy the fun of the game. Once one had given up taking offence, one was drawn into an atmosphere of good fellowship. Eventually, indeed, the Americans began to take a positive delight in his sharp sallies, even although they might be directed against one of their number; they enjoyed the privilege of being there on intimate terms with a world-famous wit. Harry White himself became mellow under this influence.

The vital elixir of friendship is of some use in overcoming national prejudices. The meeting of delegates at Washington was transformed, not merely into a group of honest technicians trying to solve problems on their merits, but into a group of friends working together for a common cause. If these discussions attained a level of objectivity unequalled in international negotiations, as those who partook in them testify, we may attribute it, not only to the earnestness and honourable purposes of the British and Americans, but also to that something extra, the personal magnetism of Keynes.

While his quick recognition of the validity of his opponent's reasoning, when it was valid, inspired American confidence, it was sometimes a trial to his British colleagues in this and subsequent negotiations. Keynes refused to maintain a position, when he was convinced that its only support was a shoddy argument. The minds of most men do not move so quickly. These British had set out from Whitehall with certain instructions and certain arguments in their bags, and here was Keynes letting them down completely on some particular point. He had been convinced that it was wrong, and that was that. Behind the scenes he castigated his colleagues for adhering to it. If he had a fault, it was in a tendency to imply that he had never in his life entertained such a fallacy, let alone only yesterday.

These talks covered a wide range of highly technical matters. Only the main trend can be indicated. White rested his case largely on his assertion, which was supported by his colleagues, concerning what Congress would tolerate. It was felt that, if the British Cabinet endorsed a scheme, Parliament would accept it. The relation of the President to Congress was entirely different. Of no scheme could it be said that it would certainly go through, while some schemes were manifestly without hope; White claimed to speak on this topic with authority. It would be far better to agree upon a scheme which might not be the ideal, but which had a reasonably good chance of acceptance. As White once put it, he regarded himself as a middleman between two sovereign powers, the American Congress on the one hand and the British Cabinet on the other. The British team made the most of Parliamentary difficulties, but this did not carry the same conviction.

Already before this meeting, the British had agreed

among themselves that they would have to yield to the American desire for limited liability, and also to their insistence that the Agency should have initial assets in the form of gold and local currencies. About the nature and proportion of these assets there was much argument.

Then there was the question of the structure of the Agency. Should it be based upon the banking or upon the fund principle? The Americans tended to take the line that it would be impossible to secure limited liability on the banking principle. If this position was not completely tenable, they could fall back on the contention that it would be impossible to convince Congress. Meanwhile, the stock argument was produced that everything which the Union could achieve could be done equally well by the alternative technical device of the Fund. So why quarrel if one was acceptable to Congress and the other not? Keynes, on his side, urged that much depended on the nations placing confidence in the institution; after all, it was their tendency to excessive nationalism that had to be broken down, and, if they lacked confidence, they would not play the required game. Even if the same things could in fact be done by the Fund as by the Union, the nations would not understand this. It was essential that the agreed scheme should be lucid and comprehensible. He inveighed against the jargon which the American technicians loved. He called it Cherokee, contrasting it with the Christian English of the Clearing Union. At one point, to secure an accurate comparison, Keynes translated the main principles of the Stabilization Fund into 'Christian English', and, when this was done, it was found that the two schemes looked remarkably similar. If the ear of Congress was soothed by the intoning of Cherokee – well, it was the master of the situation.

We may be sure that it was with a heavy heart that Keynes abandoned his structure. Mr Ben Cohen, whose wise insight observed its long-run advantages, approached him during the negotiations. Could he not re-dress the Clearing Union, so as to embody the limited liability principle with an explicitness that no one could gainsay? Keynes was already moving towards the conclusion that the forces against him were too strong. The trouble was that the important advantages of the Clearing Union principle lay in the long-distant future and related to uses of the Union that might in due course develop but were not yet specified or specifiable. It was difficult to argue against determined men, who had a rival scheme, alleged to be far more acceptable to Congress, for which they claimed that it could achieve all the prescribed objectives as effectively as the Union.

Meanwhile support for the Union principle was supplied from a different point of view. The Bank of England feared that the Fund arrangement would give the Agency powers of interfering on lines that had nothing to do with the general purposes of the scheme. Under the Union plan, nations would have deposits of Bancor (the new currency), over which they had control. Under the Fund arrangement the Agency would itself hold accounts at the Bank of England (and other central banks) which it could dispose of at its own will and pleasure. It might be able to instruct the Bank of England to hand the sterling which it held to some other foreign account. Still more alarming it would be if it had the power to sell British securities in the open market, thus depressing their price at a time most inconvenient to the British Government or the British monetary authority. In other words, the Fund seemed to be in a position to interfere in day-to-day matters that were the proper concern of the individual central banks and were not related to the long-run objectives of securing equilibrium in foreign trade. It was undesirable that an international Agency should have such power. According to this view, then, Britain should absolutely refuse to agree to the American plan unless it was made quite certain that the Fund would be 'passive' in these day-to-day matters. At this juncture it was for the Americans to show that the Fund could, by suitable provisions, be rendered 'passive'.

It was the British understanding that the Americans accepted the principle of 'passivity'; the doubt was whether their scheme would succeed in securing it in practice. Now just as the Keynes plan contained a new international unit of account, called Bancor, the White plan, too, had its international unit, called Unitas. In the White plan, as first presented to the British, Unitas played a part of negligible importance. It was a mere cloakroom ticket given to any nation which deposited gold, and could only be realized by the withdrawal of gold. As Keynes observed, its appearance in the Stabilization Fund plan was a 'vestigial survival of some much larger part it had once played'. A great effort was now made to revive the status of this Unitas, in order to secure 'passivity'. The plan was to accept White's language, the principle of limited liability, and the other points by which the Americans set store, but to arrange that, instead of the Fund having a mixed bag of currencies, in the form of disposal over deposit accounts in the various banks of the world, those banks should hold accounts at the Fund in the form of Unitas. This was known as the plan to 'monetize Unitas'. Only by so doing, the British argued, could the 'passivity' of the Fund in day-to-day matters be ensured. The battle for the monetization of Unitas went on after this meeting through the winter. The Americans made great efforts to show that 'passivity' could be ensured without the monetization of Unitas, but some doubt must remain in one's mind whether the British and the Americans ever came, even at Bretton Woods, to interpret 'passivity' in quite the same way.

Another important topic discussed in Washington was the gold standard question. Popular ideas about this were wide of the mark. Keynes and White agreed that it was desirable to have a fixed rate of exchange in the short run, with flexibility in the long run. Thus, on the central issue, neither side in these discussions was closer to the gold standard idea than the other. In the White plan the consent of the Fund would be needed for an exchange adjustment; in the

Keynes plan the consent of the Fund would be needed for any adjustment of more than five per cent away from the original par. But certain elements in the British Treasury had now come to take an altogether different view of the matter and began pressing that the British should preserve the right of each nation to devalue its currency without the consent of the Fund. This was as widely removed from the Clearing Union idea as it was from that of the Americans; and, in retrospect, one may perhaps say, quite frankly, that it was absurd. How could there be an international currency plan, if every nation retained full liberty to depreciate its own currency at its will and pleasure? Furthermore, as was pointed out at the time, such an arrangement might have been particularly unfavourable for Britain, for it was felt that Britain, as a principal architect and main support of the International Fund, would conscientiously carry out the principle of not depreciating except when in fundamental disequilibrium, while other nations might not be so conscientious in abstaining from cut-throat competitive depreciation. It must be added that the Treasury was not unanimous in favouring liberty to depreciate; none the less, the telegrams which it sent caused Keynes much trouble at Washington.

It may seem surprising that Keynes thought it worth while to insert in his original plan the right to depreciate without leave by such a small amount as five per cent once and for ever. It is seldom that a fundamental disequilibrium could be cured by so fine an adjustment. The fact of the matter is that this five per cent was also vestigial, for in the early drafts of the Clearing Union nations were to be allowed to depreciate without permission by not more than five per cent *in a single year*. This is a totally different matter! Under that original plan the safeguard against wanton depreciation lay, not in the necessity to go to the Union for leave, but in the necessity to carry out the redress of disequilibrium in an orderly, because slow and gradual, manner. The idea was that, if a maladjustment occurred suddenly, it would be unneighbourly to make a sudden adjustment; the Union was there precisely to carry a nation through the period of an adverse balance of payments, due to some sudden derangement. The adjustment of exchange rates was only designed to correct a tendency towards long-run disequilibrium due, for instance, to secular changes in the rates of interchange of goods between nations or to gradual divergences in the rates of increase of efficiency of labour. Short-run upsets were to be catered for, not by exchange adjustment, but by drafts upon the Union. This all-important 'in a single year' was rubbed out of the Clearing Union during the process of departmental attrition. The moral seems to be that a much better scheme would have been put to the assembled nations at Bretton Woods, if only Keynes and White had been allowed to meet together and given a completely free hand to devise an agreed scheme as soon as the 'consideration' was signed. The native ideas of both men had been sicklied over by departmental discussions long before they ever met.

I believe that the best solution of the exchange problem was that embodied in the original draft of the Clearing Union, namely, that the nations should have the right to depreciate by not more than five per cent in a single year without the leave of the Fund; but that solution did not come up for international discussion. To leave the nations an unlimited right of depreciation would clearly have been entirely contrary to the whole idea of international co-operation. A compromise was reached, that nations should have a once-over right to depreciate by ten per cent without leave, with special facilities accorded for getting leave for another ten per cent.[14] Larger depreciations were allowed, but subject to agreement by the Fund.

One point at issue in these discussions was the right of withdrawal from the Fund. The British were thinking not only for themselves, but for all countries likely to have a parlous trade balance, in seeking a safe escape from the

14. See Final Act of Bretton Woods, Article IV, Section 5.

commitments of the Fund, should their difficulties prove insuperable; they, therefore, wished to insert the right of immediate resignation without penalty. White was at first inclined to take a firm stand; having once embarked upon this brave undertaking, nations should not be allowed to wriggle out too easily. After he had stated this high principle with his accustomed vigour, Bernstein whispered to him: 'You know, this may mean a lot of trouble for us in Congress.' White withdrew his opposition, and the British point was won.

Once it appeared that the Keynes scheme was likely to be unacceptable, the importance of the 'scarce currency clause' came into prominence. The Amerians took the initiative in proposing that the wording should be greatly strengthened by comparison with that in the original Stabilization Fund scheme.

In due course it was decided that this combined group in Washington would be able to reach a substantial measure of agreement, and that a document could be prepared. The procedure actually adopted was that White's Stabilization Fund was taken as the basis for the agreed draft, and Keynes was asked to erase all that he objected to and to add what he wished. The resulting document was then discussed paragraph by paragraph in great detail. It was accepted by the experts on both sides, and published, after further modifications during the winter, in April 1944, under the title 'Joint Statement by Experts on the Establishment of an International Monetary Fund'. It was in this clause-by-clause discussion that the meeting reached its highest point of goodwill and fair give and take.

When the statement had attained its final form, a somewhat larger meeting was held, with members of other departments present. White meanwhile had conceived the idea that all the features of the Stabilization Fund which had not been agreed upon should be grouped together at length in an Appendix under the title 'Minutes of Evidence'. This Appendix was produced at the meeting. Keynes was lost for a few minutes in study of it; when he discovered what it was, he was furious and tossed it to the ground. They both blazed up. White is remembered to have referred to him with bitter irony as 'Your Royal Highness'. The visitors who witnessed the scene may have contributed to the rumours which floated round that Keynes and White were at daggers drawn. During the lunch hour Bernstein persuaded White to confine his Appendix to two or three points of crucial importance, and in the afternoon all was peace.

The Washington Conference did not limit itself to discussion of the monetary project. Keynes's plan for Buffer Stocks was considered. The American team was sharply divided into two opposing schools of thought. Messrs Wheeler and Appleby desired a wide adoption of restrictionist schemes; Mr Clayton was a firm believer in the workings of a free market. The Americans were united only in opposing the British scheme. The British, however, were able to make some headway. A report was drafted and agreed upon, in which the restrictionist element was narrowly curtailed and the need to eliminate high-cost in favour of low-cost producers emphasized. The matter was referred for further discussion.

The British plan was not put forward in subsequent negotiations during the war, although it had a direct influence on the chapter on commodities in the International Trade Charter. This was partly due to further difficulties encountered in discussions with the Dominions,[15] especially in regard to the finance of Buffer Stocks. Partly also, it must be admitted, it was due to a general weakening in the British initiative in regard to post-war plans. Some Ministers were hesitant about these, thinking it wiser to advance warily. Thought at the highest level was heavily preoccupied with preparations for D-Day; the time was inopportune for lengthy discussions in the Cabinet on post-war projects.

International investment was also discussed at the Washington meeting. Keynes is remembered to have adopted

15. See 679 below.

an attitude which seemed to be a mixture of levity and cynicism. He had long held the doctrine that nations which invest their savings abroad are never likely to recoup them in total; they are only able to keep the borrowing nations in play by always re-lending in the form of new investments what is due to be repaid upon the old, and it may be, by re-lending much of the interest and dividends also. An exception is when such a nation goes to war, as it may then be able to realize some portion of its foreign investments at a knock-down price. This does not mean that the borrowers need always be expected to default on any of the particular loans; investors may expect repayment, as and when due, always provided that the nation to which they belong is re-lending an equivalent amount of money for some other project. Keynes put his view forcibly, because it appeared to him that the Americans were still suffering from dangerous illusions, and were likely to expect a degree of security for their international projects which was unobtainable in the nature of the case. It was part of his natural frankness and essential integrity to put the matter very baldly. That does not mean that he had given up the hope that the Americans would undertake the role of international investors in a big way, or deemed it a matter of indifference whether they did so. Professor Robbins sought to soften the effect of Keynes's bluntness by a timely intervention. An International Bank would be valuable in stimulating less developed countries to focus their thoughts upon their investment problems and develop plans into a form that could be put forward for international consideration.

Finally, commercial policy was discussed more fully than the commodity and investment problems. The views of the State Department were already well known; Mr James Meade had worked out a comprehensive scheme on the British side, containing safeguards for nations likely to be in a debtor position. Keynes was not yet convinced of the feasibility of a large move in this direction. He never lost sight of Britain's prospective difficulties. His Clearing Union

project, which had stood in his mind as the minimum terms
on which Britain could cooperate 'to mutual advantage' in
a liberal commercial policy, had been woefully cut down.
His realism compelled him to remain uneasy. The following
note will not be taken *au grand sérieux* by those who knew
Keynes well. It was partly meant to tease. It must, however,
be admitted that Mr Pasvolsky, had he seen it, would have
been deeply shocked.

### J. M. Keynes to P. Liesching, 8 October 1943

Thanks for your note on State trading. If in this matter you
leave loop-holes in your scheme, it will not upset *me*. Indeed, the
more loop-holes you leave the wiser you will be in my opinion.

As you know, I am, I am afraid, a hopeless sceptic about this
return to nineteenth century *laissez faire*, for which you and the
State Department seem to have such a nostalgia.

I believe that the future lies with –

  (i)  State trading for commodities;

 (ii)  International cartels for necessary manufactures; and

(iii)  Quantitative import restrictions for non-essential manu-
       factures.

Yet all these future instrumentalities for orderly economic life
in the future you seek to outlaw.

The reader may remember my conversation with him in
the Treasury corridor two years earlier, when he referred to
the need to continue to think along 'both' lines. So far as
the monetary question was concerned, he was now fully
convinced of the virtues of a multilateral system and free
dealing. He was not yet convinced on the commercial side;
that was to come later. His mind still remained ambivalent.
In the preceding ten years he had gone far in reconciling
himself to a policy of planned trade; these ideas had sunk
deeply in. Even for him, with his readiness to follow where
an argument led and his power of quick adaptation, it was
difficult to unlearn so much. The memorandum to Liesching
states one extreme view provocatively. He was to continue
for some time to display impatience at the initiative taken

by the Board of Trade in developing proposals for an open
trading system.[16]

Besides the four main topics, there was also some discussion on the point in which the Australians were known to be
especially interested, namely, international cooperation for
sustaining full employment. It was thought that this was not
an objective, like orderly currency or international investment, for which a specialized agency was appropriate.
There was no given set of measures which would secure
full employment; rather, full employment depended on the
success of all the separate measures under their several head-
ings. It appeared, therefore, that there should be some International Economic Board, which would secure co-
ordination among the policies of the various Agencies,
having special regard to their success in maintaining a
high level of employment. This matter should be referred to
those who would be responsible for the general organization of the United Nations. This subsequently happened;
and the United Nations Commission and Sub-Commission
on Employment and Economic Stability were brought to
birth.

Keynes next spent some days in New York, where he
attempted the hard task of converting the bankers to the
desirability of an International Fund. His old friend, Mr
Russell Leffingwell, provided him with a room to himself
in the offices of J. P. Morgan.

On his way back to England he could reflect with some
satisfaction on what had been achieved. He had not floated
his own scheme; he had hardly hoped for that. But the
White scheme had been considerably liberalized. The spirit
of the meetings had been excellent, and close Anglo-
American cooperation was an established fact. This would
surely continue. If that really happened, then this meeting,
which he had just attended, was an important milestone in
twentieth-century history.

16. For his ultimate conversion to the Board of Trade point of view,
see below, pp. 721–2.

All the relevant American Departments [he wrote to the Chancellor of the Exchequer] were present at the conversations and were satisfied with the result, in particular the State Department and the Federal Reserve Board. We could never have got so far if there had not been a marked will to agree. The debates were extremely strenuous, since Harry White gives nothing away except after a rasping battle, even when he has really made up his mind from the beginning that he is not going to fight to the end. In spite of some sharp passages, particularly the last lap of all when there seemed to be a risk of their wanting to re-open a wide part of the field, good humour prevailed.

On the Saturday Harry White proposed that we should mutually initial the final document and exchange letters. On the Monday I carried out my part. But he made excuses why he should not initial or confirm anything. I was much annoyed for a moment. During the war I have altogether spent five months in close negotiation with the United States Treasury and on no single occasion have they answered any communication of mine in writing, or confirmed in writing anything which has passed in conversation. In this my experience is not unusual. I doubt if anyone has seen Harry White's initials . . . All this does not matter two pins. It is just an interesting illustration of the American way of doing, or not doing, business.

\*

. . . We are all of us agreed that the atmosphere could not have been better and the progress far in excess of our best expectations. The American Departments, and particularly the State Department, were exceedingly coy and slow in accepting the necessity of primary Anglo-American cooperation. But after a little experience of it they have embraced it with both hands. There is no risk, I should say, of the old stand-offish attitude. All the committees have worked together constructively and fruitfully, and it is most unlikely that the civil servants, whatever the politicians may feel, will want to return either to isolationism on the one hand, or to the method of the grand monkey house on the other. Apart from questions of method, both sides have discovered a far wider range of common thought than had been expected.

He felt that the Agreed Statement of Principles would set

forth the project to the world in terms inspiring greater confidence than the Stabilization Fund draft. The gold subscriptions had been reduced, exchange elasticity ensured and the right of withdrawal recognized. The monetization of Unitas was still under discussion, but he doubted if great principles were involved. An important point was that the principle of the passivity of the Fund had been accepted.

... Here the Americans started with a totally different point of view. They thought of the Fund as an active, benevolent institution which would study the advisability of every transaction and O.K. it or not as a faithful schoolmistress. What they had in view would clearly cut right across international banking arrangements as they have existed hitherto. It was a very great concession on their part to come round to our view of the Fund as a reserve resource, entirely passive, except in the more extreme contingencies where countries were running towards the limit of the facilities of the Fund in one direction or another.

The wording shows that Keynes had no doubt that the Americans had conceded the passivity principle. To points where there was still room for doubt, e.g. on the Scarce Currency clause (see below), Keynes was careful to draw attention. Their plea that passivity could be ensured equally well under the Fund principle as under the banking principle was the main consideration which induced the British to abandon the banking principle in the last round. But did the Americans in their hearts fully accept the principle of 'passivity'? Was there a residue of misunderstanding? This point became important again later.

There is a deep paradox involved in the conflict between Keynes and the Americans on this topic, which continued to the end. The Americans are in the habit of praising private initiative and inveighing against paternalistic socialism. In the minds of many Americans who do not specialize in these subjects, Keynes has been thought to be a sort of high priest of the paternalism they so much dislike. Yet, when the Americans turn their eyes away from their own rights under the Constitution towards the international sphere, it is they who have recently tended to be the chief advocates of paternalism. It was Keynes who had to fight the battle of liberalism against the voracious appetite of the Americans for paternalistic interference. Keynes thought of the international institutions as setting up a framework within which individual initiative could flourish; they were to settle certain broad principles of action; the Fund, in particular, would establish certain drawing rights, but only interfere in their exercise on most exceptional occasions. The Americans wanted to give meticulous scrutiny to each individual transaction. In all this long-drawn-out conflict it appears that Keynes was fighting for the philosophy of freedom against the philosophy of regimentation.

### *J. M. Keynes to the Chancellor of the Exchequer*, 16 October 1943

There is one point of some importance that I forgot to emphasize in my letter to you of October 14 reporting the outcome of our conversations.

In addition to the chief objects we had in view as catalogued in that letter, I forgot to add a sixth object, which is by no means the least important, namely, to get the principles so drafted that one of the prime purposes of the Clearing Union, namely, to put pressure on creditor as well as debtor countries to restore equilibrium, should not wholly disappear. We have in fact got this back in an extremely drastic form. Clause 10 of the Statement of Principles, which deals with the apportionment of scarce currencies, puts the creditor country on the spot so acutely that in the view of us all, the creditor country simply cannot afford to let such a situation arise.

*

We, in fact, suggested something rather milder. For we had doubts, and in fact still have doubts, whether Congress can be expected, if they understand it, to swallow anything so extreme. Nevertheless, the U.S. Treasury, the State Department and the Federal Reserve Board quite deliberately prefer this ruthless provision, since in their view it is essential, if the U.S. is to be brought to do what it should, to create a really serious crisis.

They think that this clause will make it necessary to find some way of preventing it coming into effect. If the Americans really live up to their present proposals it will be the U.S.A. and not the rest of us which will get into real trouble, if U.S.A. develops a favourable balance which is not adequately disposed of by foreign lending or in some way.

The clause was safely passed by Congress in the summer of 1945.[17]

On his return to England, he was plunged once more in the day-to-day business of the Treasury. Progress with the international schemes seemed slow. On the one side, certain outstanding questions had to be settled with the Americans through normal channels; on the other side, British Cabinet authority had to be obtained for further progress. On the home front Mr Richard Law took a vigorous initiative. A statement was drafted and the views of Ministers collected. When real need arose, as now, Keynes allowed his argumentative power to be enlisted on behalf of commercial liberalism. Ministers' chief anxieties were, as was to be expected, on the side of commercial policy. Some were worried about the gold implications of the International Monetary Fund. Keynes had a heavy task in providing explanations on all the intricate points that were raised. In the statement for Ministers great stress was laid on the scarce-currency clause.

The offer [viz. the scarce-currency clause] is a signal mark of their courage, of their fair-mindedness and of their sense of responsibility to the other nations of the world.

This proposal represents, therefore, a revolutionary change for the better compared with the position in the inter-war period. The Americans offer voluntarily to abjure their former stranglehold on the world's economy and never again to allow their hoarding propensities to force deflation on others. Moreover, this particular provision has been published and Congress is aware of

17. I may be allowed some satisfaction in observing that the views which I had so strongly pressed in my letter written in the early hours of the morning of 2 March 1943, were fully vindicated by the course of events. (See p. 645 above.)

it; yet, so far, it has not been the target of any particular criticism. It would seem rash on our part to reject so fair an offer and to prefer to return to the chaos and irresponsibility of the former lack of system.

The problems of the transition period had been somewhat neglected in the September discussions, and these became the subject of an interchange of views between the British and Americans. One last attempt was made to save the banking principle by the 'monetization of Unitas'. American resistance stiffened. A consideration of some weight in this connection was the representation of the Federal Reserve Board that the banking principle by which it would probably have to hold a large account with the International Monetary Fund would set up an uncontrollable inflation in the U.S., of the danger of which after the war they were, in any case, very much afraid. At this juncture the Americans also stressed the argument that the introduction of a new international unit of account might prejudice the acceptance of the scheme by Congress. 'Unitas', or whatever new name might be devised, would sound far-fetched and crackpot in congressional ears. It was hard for the British to judge the validity of this argument. It had been suggested earlier that the proposal for a new international currency unit might make an idealistic appeal to certain members. Some wished at this time that it were possible to get the verdict of President Roosevelt himself. Might he not find in a new international currency matter for an imaginative appeal to the nations? Certainly there was little in the *Agreed Statement of Principles* to fire the imagination of mankind. It would hardly have been possible for the British to appeal against the United States Treasury to the President. Mr Churchill could not be expected to give prolonged attention to such a matter at such a time. Keynes was half convinced, perhaps against his better judgement, that all things which could be achieved under the banking system could be achieved under the Fund system also. Unitas was in due course dropped.

During the autumn White's proposal for an International Bank for Reconstruction and Development arrived in England. Stripped, as it long since had been, of all the exciting features, this document was an uninspiring one. The Bank had been dressed, with an eye to Congress, to look as orthodox as possible.

In March 1944 there was another series of meetings with the Dominions, which Keynes was unable to attend, being for a period under doctor's orders. The *Agreed Statement of Principles* was published in April, and received a very favourable press. Keynes expounded the theme to his old friends of the Craven-Ellis group in the House of Commons and also to another group of Conservative M.P.s. Apart from some rumblings from Mr Boothby, these meetings did not lead him to anticipate opposition. But the debate in the House of Commons in May was a bitter disappointment. 'I spent seven hours in the accursed Gallery, lacerated in mind and body.' Apart from an admirable statement by the Chancellor of the Exchequer, Mr Pethick-Lawrence's contribution was the only one of value. This was the first symptom of a trend in British feeling which was to cause Keynes considerable distress until his death. There seemed to be an extremely strong undercurrent of anti-Americanism. Members gave no signs of having studied the plan, but seemed to come violently prejudiced against it for no other reason than that the Americans had agreed to it. This development was curious, and perhaps psychopathical. It was in complete contrast with the splendidly cordial co-operation in the Services. Is it fair to suggest that those who formed opinion in the lobbies concerning post-war plans consisted mainly of persons who were taking no very active part in the war effort, and found compensation in cultivating anti-American feelings? These cavillers failed to notice the fact that the Americans had made great concessions to the British point of view, and also the remarkable combination of boldness with technical detail exhibited in the *Statement*. It should have been obvious that such conclusions could only have been achieved by goodwill and hard work without precedent in international relations. All this was completely ignored.

Quite a different atmosphere prevailed in the House of Lords, where the debate was free from the pettiness displayed in the Lower House. Keynes himself made an admirable speech, which no doubt contributed to a better understanding. The Barony of Tilton was proving its usefulness.

In the spring of 1944 Keynes's mind reverted to Britain's immediate post-war position. Debts, in the form of 'sterling balances', were growing at an alarming rate, and the prospect was truly appalling. Should some scaling down be attempted? Should they be blocked, or funded? The problem was an exceedingly complex one, since the holdings of the various countries differed both in their origin and in the form in which they were held. The Indian holdings were concentrated in the Reserve Bank of India, and formed the reserve behind the rupee circulation. In other cases the indebtedness was privately held by a large number of individuals. Part originated in the normal sales of goods to Britain, part (within the sterling area) from the turning in of dollars, earned by exports to the dollar area. Part was due to the expenditure of British troops overseas. Some of the debt was incurred by sales to the British authorities at normal prices, some by sales at highly inflated prices in local currencies, which were then converted into sterling at the old, and thereby obsolete, rates of exchange. Thus the sterling liability incurred was sometimes greatly in excess of the value of the services received in exchange for it. In regard to the debt held by each country, there was a large number of diverse special considerations. In fact there was a terrible tangle. Keynes drafted a memorandum on the subject for interdepartmental consideration. It was his misfortune to be concerned with a department of our war effort in which prospects grew ever darker as the military prospects became brighter.

Happily he had other interests to sweeten his days. CEMA grew and prospered. Lydia struggled buoyantly with the growing hardships of living. He had weekends at Tilton, where the farm was flourishing under the careful direction of Mr Logan Thomson. He had occasional glimpses of Duncan and Clive and Vanessa. In February, there was a pleasant ceremony. He gave a luncheon party, which included the Kenneth Clarks and Duncan Grant's mother, to celebrate the unveiling of mural decorations of Cinderella by Duncan Grant and Vanessa Bell, which were handed to the Tottenham Town Council for use in the Children's Restaurant. As he drew the curtain from each picture, he gave his own amusing version of the story of Cinderella. Thus he had reminders of those really important things, for the sake of which this terrible struggle was being waged, with all its sacrifices, and its heroisms, and the threat – could he avert it? – of financial ruin for Britain.

## 4

In the third week of June Keynes and his wife were on board the *Queen Mary* bound for Bretton Woods. These voyages were pleasant interludes, despite the spice of danger. Life-belts were worn continuously. It was somehow extraordinarily impressive to meet them pacing the deck in this garb. They were not Lord and Lady Keynes, conventionally dressed for a reception or the opera; they were just two human beings fitted out as was needful for the emergency – but two great human beings. One felt that one had been brought into closer contact with the pure essences of these blithe spirits. To have seen them thus was a precious and unforgettable memory.

On some of the trips it was possible to have leisure and do some reading. On one occasion a friend commented on the interesting company they had on board. 'I prefer Trevelyan,' Keynes replied curtly. But this time there was to be hard work. A number of delegates from the nations which had headquarters in London were present. It was decided to have meetings on the subject of the International Bank, which had hitherto been somewhat neglected. Keynes's enthusiasm was fired. A draft was prepared.

On arrival in New York on 23 June they were met by Mr Brand; he had been in Washington for some years as head of the British Food Mission, but had recently been transferred to be the Treasury Representative and was to play an important part, not only at Bretton Woods, but also in the Lend-Lease and Loan negotiations of the following eighteen months. Other members of the British team were Sir Wilfrid Eady from the Treasury, Mr Ronald from the Foreign Office, Professor Robbins, Professor Robertson and Mr Opie.

They went straight on to Atlantic City, in order to have discussions with the Americans and a few other delegates concerning outstanding points to be settled before the larger meeting. There were also some Dominion representatives with whom separate discussions took place.

*Extract from Professor Robbins's Journal*, 24 June 1944

In the late afternoon we had a joint session with the Americans, at which Keynes expounded our views on the Bank. This went very well indeed. Keynes was in his most lucid and persuasive mood: and the effect was irresistible. At such moments, I often find myself thinking that Keynes must be one of the most remarkable men that have ever lived – the quick logic, the birdlike swoop of intuition, the vivid fancy, the wide vision, above all the incomparable sense of the fitness of words, all combine to make something several degrees beyond the limit of ordinary human achievement. Certainly, in our own age, only the Prime Minister is of comparable stature. He, of course, surpasses him. But the greatness of the Prime Minister is something much easier to understand than the genius of Keynes. For, in the last analysis, the special qualities of the Prime Minister are the traditional qualities of our race raised to the scale of grandeur. Whereas the special qualities of Keynes are something outside all that. He uses the classical style of our life and language, it is true, but it is shot through with something which is not traditional, a unique unearthly quality of which one can only say that it is pure genius. The Americans sat entranced as the God-like visitor sang and the golden light played around. When it was all over there was very little discussion . . . But, so far as the Bank is concerned, I am clear that we are off with a flying start.

Dinner with the Pasvolskys. Leo declared himself very gratified at the line Keynes had taken.

In regard to the Fund, there were three main matters on which it was desirable to reach agreement before meeting the great concourse of nations – exchange flexibility, the 'repurchase'[18] provisions and the transitional period. In regard to the first mentioned, the British had continued during the winter, against the force of all argument, to hanker after more liberty of action. It proved possible now to make some concession to them. It was agreed that, should a nation alter its par of exchange in conditions when leave from the Fund was required, and that leave was refused, the nation should not automatically forfeit membership of the Fund, but merely lose its drawing rights. There would then be a period for further discussion and, if all went well, ultimate reconciliation without any lapse from membership. The British were again assisted by reluctant American recognition that an easement of strict discipline might make the Fund more acceptable to Congress.

The meetings, which lasted a week, were deemed to be highly successful, and Harry White's masterly conduct of the Chair greatly enhanced his reputation.

And now, on the night of 30 June, they mounted their train to proceed to Bretton Woods and face the vast assembly of forty-four nations, all with large delegations and staffs.[19] It was a spot of extraordinary beauty, of woods and green meadows, surrounded by low mountains.

Proceedings were opened by a dignified speech by Mr

18. Final Act of Bretton Woods, Article 5, Section 7.
19. Professor Robbins informs me that the Chinese Government alone was represented by no less than forty-seven persons.

Morgenthau, who, as Secretary of the Treasury, was in the Chair. That evening Keynes gave a dinner-party.

*Extract from Professor Robbins's Journal,* 1 July 1944

This evening, I participated in a particularly *recherché* celebration. Today is the 500th anniversary of the Concordat between King's College, Cambridge, and New College, Oxford, and to commemorate the occasion, Keynes gave a small banquet in his room consisting of himself representing King's, me representing New College, Nigel Ronald representing Winchester, a sister foundation, Dennis Robertson representing Eton, which was closely linked to King's, and Dean Acheson, Oscar Cox and His Excellency, the Leader of the Chinese Delegation, representing Yale, with whom there exists a much more recent concordat. Keynes, who had been looking forward to the event for weeks as excitedly as a schoolboy, was at his most charming. He delivered an exquisite allocution explaining to his guests from Yale the nature of the celebration, and drawing the moral that the academic corporations coming down from the ancient past constituted, in all our countries, the centre and core of much that is most precious in the world's civilization. It was an interesting example of the curiously complex nature of this extraordinary man. So radical in outlook in matters purely intellectual, in matters of culture he is a true Burkean conservative. It was all very pianissimo, as befitting the occasion, but his emotion when he spoke of our debt to the past was truly moving.

There was a tremendous Agenda. White was scrupulous in his insistence that all the amendments proposed by all the nations should be carefully considered. The United States delegation was broadly based. Members of Congress were there, including two Republicans, Senator C. W. Tobey and Mr J. P. Wolcott, and Mr E. E. Brown, President of the First National Bank of Chicago, to represent a banking point of view. Three main Commissions were set up, one to deal with the Fund, one for the Bank, and one for residual questions. White took the Chair at the Fund Commission, and Keynes at the Bank Commission. These Commissions, however, met but rarely, and the main work was done in com-

mittees. Keynes and White did not partake in these
committees, but each sat apart in his own room, available
for reference on the controversial points that arose. Their
labours were ceaseless. Meanwhile, Professor Robertson and
Mr Bernstein re-entered their close collaboration; it was
they who distilled the multifarious committee decisions
into the agreed text that finally emerged. 'Dennis Robertson', Keynes wrote to his mother, 'is perhaps the most useful
of all – absolutely first-class brains do help!' [20]

### J. M. Keynes to Sir Richard Hopkins, 22 July 1944

Everyone in our team has played together splendidly. If anyone is picked out, I think it would have to be Dennis, whose help
has been absolutely indispensable. He alone had the intellectual
subtlety and patience of mind and tenacity of character to grasp
and hold on to all details and fight them through Bernstein, so
that I, frequently occupied otherwise, could feel completely
happy about the situation.

It has to be said that, on the whole, the other nations did
not contribute ideas of novelty or importance. The International Monetary Fund and the International Bank were
the product of English and American brains, with valuable
assistance from the Canadians. The other nations were
greatly interested, however, in the size of their quotas. The
Russians, in particular, insisted on their right to a large
one. The Chinese quota was somewhat inflated by American
ideology, and the Indians complained bitterly that their
own was derisory by comparison with it. The British exerted
their influence on behalf of the Indians, whose quota was
raised in consequence. Mr F. M. Vinson, of whom we shall
hear more, was present in his capacity of Director of the
Office of Economic Stabilization, and was Vice-Chairman
of the United States Delegates. He was mobilized to deal
with this question of quotas, which was indeed the thorniest
of the Conference, and his handling of it, which was force-

20. Letter written from Montreal on 25 July 1944.

ful, but at the same time tactful, helped to bring matters to a peaceful issue.

Another vexed question was the location of the Agencies. The British disliked the idea of location in America, which would reinforce the arguments of critics that the Agencies would be entirely dominated by the Americans. However, facts had to be recognized. The United States was the most powerful party; large sums of money would have to be spent, and the British had repeatedly affirmed that they would have little money to spare after the war. Mr Dean Acheson, with his charming easy manner, remarked on the side, 'You fellows will have to give way on this matter, you know, if the Fund is to get through.' Accordingly, Article XIII, Section 1, provided that 'the principal office of the Fund shall be located in the territory of the member having the largest quota'. The British reserved their position on this.

The first meeting of the Bank Commission was on 3 July, when Keynes introduced the subject in a fluent and persuasive speech. Committees were set up, but their meetings were delayed, as the more complex and novel constitution of the Fund continued to receive greater attention. Then a spurt was made. The Charter of the Bank was drawn up, not by the formal committees, but by Professor J. W. Angell and Mr E. G. Collado, working on successive days into the small hours; they referred difficult points to Mr Dean Acheson and sometimes to Mr E. E. Brown, prior to assimilation by the British. The principal basis for their work was 'the boat draft', which consisted mainly of a set of principles. Keynes was deeply immersed in Fund questions, but kept his eye on what they were doing.

The size of the Bank was one of the points at issue. The American experts wanted to have a high ratio of loans to assets, but their bankers would not agree; Keynes, whose natural tendency would have been to favour a large size, could not give vein to this impulse owing to Britain's prospective difficulty in finding money. The biggest question at issue was never fully discussed, namely, whether the Bank should be a sound conservative institution on normal lines, or depart from orthodox caution in the direction of greater venturesomeness. Keynes had a dictum that the Bank would not have discharged its duty if it had not dissipated its assets within ten years; this caused consternation among the United States Treasury officials. But on the whole he was content that the Bank should have a fairly orthodox structure. It was in the Fund that new ideas would be tried out.

On the Bank, too, the Russians gave trouble. They had wanted a large quota in the Fund, $1,200 million, but refused to offer more than $900 million for the Bank. In the case of other nations, their quotas, which they tended to regard rather as drawing rights than contributions, tended to be of the same order of magnitude as their subscriptions to the Bank. The Russian insistence on a large quota and small subscription was felt to be rather shameless; Keynes and Vinson both exerted to the full their very different types of oratorical appeal in urging the Russians to come into line. At the last meeting of the Commission the Russians were still obdurate. But at the final Plenary Meeting of all the Bretton Woods Delegations, the Russians announced at the outset that they would raise their subscription to the Bank to the full $1,200 million. Delegates jumped to their feet and cheered wildly. 'There is more joy in the kingdom of Heaven over one sinner . . .', Professor Robertson remarked. Yet, looking back, we may share in the emotion; under the influence of the meeting, the Russians had moved towards an international point of view. Might this portend a change of heart?

After three weeks of tremendous labour, the proceedings drew to their close.

*J. M. Keynes to Sir John Anderson,* 21 July 1944

The pressure of work here has been quite unbelievable. It is as though, in the course of three or four weeks, one had to accomplish the preliminary work of many interdepartmental and Cabinet committees, the job of the Parliamentary draftsmen, and the passage through several Houses of Parliament of two intricate legislative measures of major dimensions, all this carried on in committees and commissions, numbering anything up to 200 persons in rooms with bad acoustics, shouting through microphones, many of those present, often including the Chairman, with an imperfect knowledge of English, each wanting to get something on the record which would look well in the Press down at home, and one of the most important Delegations, namely the Russians, only understanding what was afoot with the utmost difficulty and expense of time. On the top of this the Press, which is here in full force, has had to be continually fed and guided. And each of the Delegations expects some measure of social and personal consideration. Well, I need hardly say more. We have all of us worked every minute of our waking hours practically without intermission for what is now four weeks. I have come off best because under the iron rule of my medical attendant I have resolutely refused to go to any committees after dinner (except once only against orders which promptly led to a heart attack, so that I suffered from guilt not less than from bodily discomfort!); whereas the others have been sitting in committees night after night up to 3.30 a.m., starting again in the committee at 9.30 a.m. next morning. How people have stood it at all is a miracle. At one moment Harry White told me that at last even he was all in, not having been in bed for more than five hours a night for four consecutive weeks. The climate has, however, been on the whole excellent and there is something in the air here that allows one, most dangerously in the long run, to use up one's reserves. So no one has actually broken down. But all of us from the top to the bottom, not least the secretaries and Gambling and his staff, are all in. You provided us with a magnificent team and everyone has played his or her part. Typing and mimeographing half through the night has been all in the order of the day. The official papers of the Conference, some of them of great length, number nearly 500; and in addition much written matter has passed between ourselves, not to mention telegrams to and from home.

Our personal relations with the Russians have been very cordial and we have seen quite a lot of them socially. We like them exceedingly and, I think, they like us. Given time, we should, I believe, gain their confidence and would then be able to help them a good deal. They *want* to thaw and collaborate. But the linguistic difficulties and very poor interpretation are a dreadful obstacle. Above all, they are put in a most awkward, and sometimes humiliating, position by the lack both of suitable instructions and of suitable discretion from Moscow.

Well, we have survived. In my opinion the final products are clear and even aesthetic in presentation. I hope you will like the substance and will feel that we have protected your position not too badly. I have never forgotten your Parliamentary difficulties and in every little detail of phrasing have tried to take care of that aspect of the problem as much as was possible without becoming unreasonable or tiresome.

The heart attack referred to occurred on 19 July, when Keynes, having dined with Mr Morgenthau and tarried rather long, ran upstairs to reach his Committee. The attack was not a serious one, but there were press notices and anxieties in England.

The proceedings on the final day ended with a speech by Keynes. He chose to treat his subject in a light vein.

Mr President,

I feel it a signal honour that I am asked to move the acceptance of the Final Act at this memorable Conference.

We, the Delegates of this Conference, Mr President, have been trying to accomplish something very difficult to accomplish. We have not been trying, each one to please himself, and to find the solution most acceptable in our own particular situation. That would have been easy. It has been our task to find a common measure, a common standard, a common rule applicable to each and not irksome to any. We have been operating, moreover, in a field of great intellectual and technical difficulty. We have had to perform at one and the same time the tasks appropriate to the economist, to the financier, to the politician, to the journalist, to the propagandist, to the lawyer, to the statesman – even, I think, to the prophet and to the soothsayer. Nor has the magic of the microphone been able, silently and swiftly perambulant at the hands of our attendant sprites, the faithful Scouts, Puck coming to the aid of Bottom, to undo all the mischief first wrought in the Tower of Babel.

And I make bold to say, Mr President, that under your wise

and kindly guidance we have been successful. International conferences have not a good record. I am certain that no similar conference within memory has achieved such a bulk of lucid, solid construction. We owe this not least to the indomitable will and energy, always governed by good temper and humour, of Harry White. But this has been as far removed as can be imagined from a one-man or two-man or three-man conference. It has been teamwork, teamwork such as I have seldom experienced. And for my own part, I should like to pay a particular tribute to our lawyers. All the more so because I have to confess that, generally speaking, I do not like lawyers. I have been known to complain that, to judge from results in this lawyer-ridden land, the *Mayflower*, when she sailed from Plymouth, must have been entirely filled with lawyers. When I first visited Mr Morgenthau in Washington some three years ago accompanied only by my secretary, the boys in your Treasury curiously inquired of him – where is your lawyer? When it was explained that I had none, – 'Who then does your thinking for you?' was the rejoinder. That is not my idea of a lawyer. I want him to tell me how to do what *I* think sensible, and, above all, to devise means by which it will be lawful for me to go on being sensible in unforeseen conditions some years hence. Too often lawyers busy themselves to make common sense illegal. Too often lawyers are men who turn poetry into prose and prose into jargon. Not so our lawyers here in Bretton Woods. On the contrary, they have turned our jargon into prose and our prose into poetry. And only too often they have had to do our thinking for us. We owe a great debt of gratitude to Dean Acheson, Oscar Cox, Luxford, Brenner, Collado, Arnold, Chang, Broches and our own Beckett of the British Delegation. I have only one complaint against them which I ventured to voice yesterday in Commission II. I wish they had not covered so large a part of our birth certificate with such very detailed provisions for our burial service, hymns and lessons and all.

Mr President, we have reached this evening a decisive point. But it is only a beginning. We have to go from here as missionaries, inspired by zeal and faith. We have sold all this to ourselves. But the world at large still needs to be persuaded.

I am greatly encouraged, I confess, by the critical, sceptical and even carping spirit in which our proceedings have been watched and welcomed in the outside world. How much better that our projects should *begin* in disillusion than that they should *end* in it! We perhaps are too near to our own work to see its outlines clearly. But I am hopeful that when the critics and the sceptics look more closely the plans will turn out to be so much better than they expected, that the very criticism and scepticism which we have suffered will turn things in our favour.

Finally, we have perhaps accomplished here in Bretton Woods something more significant than what is embodied in this Final Act. We have shown that a concourse of 44 nations are actually able to work together at a constructive task in amity and un-broken concord. Few believed it possible. If we can continue in a larger task as we have begun in this limited task, there is hope for the world. At any rate we shall now disperse to our several homes with new friendships sealed and new intimacies formed. We have been learning to work together. If we can so continue, this nightmare, in which most of us here present have spent too much of our lives, will be over. The brotherhood of man will have become more than a phrase.

Mr President, I move to accept the Final Act.

Delegates paid tribute by rising and applauding again and again. 'In a way, this is one of the greatest triumphs of his life. Scrupulously obedient to his instructions, battling against fatigue and weakness, he has throughout dominated the Conference.'[21] As he moved towards the door to leave the meeting, the Delegates rose again and sang, 'For He's a Jolly Good Fellow'.

He proceeded from Bretton Woods to Canada, for some discussions on the general financial position. In Ottawa he gave a dinner-party to celebrate the 250th anniversary of the Bank of England.

And so homewards. What did he think of his achievement? His original plan, with its broad scope, had been sadly whittled down. He could hardly have expected otherwise. Indeed, in the early days of the Treasury talks, two and a half years ago, those who sat round the table would have been amazed to learn that anything nearly so like the original scheme would be accepted by forty-four nations.

21. Professor Robbins's Journal.

There had been general enthusiasm. Above all, the sustained and active cooperation of the Americans was heartening. So long as that cooperation continued, the schemes ought not to fail.

To have devised in the quiet of one's study a new economic theory which determined the nature of the economic thinking of the younger generation in two great nations, to have gone further and devised practical proposals for international cooperation to implement that theory, to have gone still further and won acceptance for those proposals by persuasion, first among officials and politicians at home and then in a wide international arena, was surely an accomplishment for which it would be difficult to find a parallel. The combination of the purely scientific aptitude for intellectual construction with a keen sense of realities and power of adapting theory to practice, and the combination of these again with persuasive and diplomatic faculties, were surely unique. We may be confident, however, that, as he journeyed home, he was not thinking mainly of his own accomplishment, but of the next thing that had to be done. He must turn his thoughts to Britain's immediate financial prospects, which were exceedingly grim.

# [14]

## The U.S. Loan to Britain

### I

KEYNES had to return to the United States almost immediately for a much longer visit. He spent more than two months in Washington, and it was probably on this occasion that he cemented his friendships, and acquired that detailed knowledge of the American scene, which stood him in good stead when he had to plead for a large loan to Britain a year later. This was his fourth wartime visit. It was a very important one, although less has been heard of it than of the others. The official purpose was the formulation of a programme of Lend-Lease assistance during the time in which we should be fighting the Japanese, but not the Germans. In the jargon of the period this was known as 'Stage II' (in the United States as 'Phase II'). The issues involved were exceedingly complex. In theory and according to public pronouncements both nations would continue to make an all-out war effort until the Japanese were defeated. In practice this would not be strictly the case; the limitation on shipping alone precluded the mobilization in the Far East of manpower and materials on the scale used against Germany. None the less, a very great effort would have to be made. It was clearly an intricate problem to determine the scale on which it would be fair and useful for the United States to contribute Lend-Lease assistance in these circumstances. But the meeting was not only to discuss general principles. All the various items, aircraft, bombs, guns, ships, raw materials, food, had to be surveyed in detail. Every tree in the wood had to be scrutinized, yet the wood as a whole must not be lost sight of. Keynes had to turn his mind from the general principles and technicalities of international finance to a serried mass of statistical estimates of the needs and supplies of all the various materials and finished products required for the war effort and for civilians. He kept track of every detail in these negotiations, involving, as they did, so many specialized interests. Those who are sceptical of economics and long-range plans may like to think of this negotiation as one of his finest achievements.

At the same time, through all these weeks of detailed work, he never lost sight of the sinister problem of Stage III – that happy period when we should be fighting neither Germans nor Japanese, and merely facing economic ruin. He took every opportunity to drive home our difficulties to the Americans. The position had changed vastly since his preliminary essay in the art of expounding this subject in 1941. Our external indebtedness had reached gigantic dimensions. Throughout the war we had worked on the principle that finance should be no obstacle either to the use of our own resources or to the inducement of others, by means of promises to pay, to use theirs in the common effort. Our exports, whereby we normally pay our way, had been allowed to decline to about one-third of their previous level in order to release manpower and productive capacity at home for the war effort. We only exported those goods which could be shown to be helping others to make their contribution to the war. Our reserve position was better than it had been in 1941, owing to the large out-of-pocket expenditure by American troops in Britain. While this gave us a little cushion, small indeed in relation to the shock that would come to us when the war was over, it added to the difficulty of expounding our case. There was always the tendency to say, 'First use up your reserves, and then we shall see what we can do for you.' During this visit Keynes delivered a lecture to a large gathering of officials in the State Department on the sterling area, about which the Americans had many misconceptions. The lecture was deemed a success.

The Stage II negotiations in Washington followed immediately upon a meeting between President Roosevelt, Mr Churchill and the Chiefs of Staffs at Quebec ('Octagon'). Mr Churchill had gallantly offered a full British effort. It was not for President Roosevelt, responsible for the lives of American citizens, to refuse that offer. But the Washington negotiations were immensely complicated by the fact that the United States Naval Authorities took a slightly different view. The American Navy had already achieved glorious things in the Pacific; it was going from strength to strength; it felt that it had the matter well in hand; the fighting spirit was ambitious for a single-handed victory – all honour to it; a Blücher was deemed unnecessary. This ardour of heroism was reinforced by a technical argument. If products of American factories were consigned to Britain to be absorbed in British formations, they would inevitably reach the Pacific somewhat later than if they went direct to the U.S. Navy. Thus it could be represented that the allocation to Britain of a proportionate share of factory output would actually retard their use against the enemy and thus tend to frustrate the common purpose of the two nations. Yet Britain had willingly committed herself to play a part, and she would have to endeavour to replace such supplies as were denied her by the United States from her own factories, thus adding to the economic burden, which had already almost crushed her. It was an exceedingly difficult problem.

A matter had been discussed at Quebec which may be regarded as a red herring in relation to the immediate purpose of the Washington talks, but which yet in a subtle way may have affected them and certainly caused embarrassment to Keynes in his intimate relations with American leaders – Mr Morgenthau's plan for the de-industrialization of Germany. Mr Morgenthau was pleased with the progress which had been made at Quebec, and he showed some tendency in Washington to wish to interest Keynes in the furtherance of his scheme. Keynes, of course, had no brief for discussing such matters.

At the outset of these negotiations a situation arose which a lesser man might have deemed embarrassing. By a directive of the President and the Prime Minister, the Chancellor of the Exchequer was to lead the British side of the Committee, and Keynes was named as his deputy for the purpose. Meanwhile, there had come from Quebec, mainly bent on scientific investigations of more than top secrecy, Lord Cherwell, a man of great genius, a pioneer of the quantum theory in its earliest days, who was now the Paymaster-General in Britain and Personal Assistant to Mr Churchill. He gave advice on scientific aspects of the war effort and also on its economic aspects. He had advised the Prime Minister from the beginning on a balanced use of shipping and manpower resources, and his opinions often had a decisive influence on the conduct of events. He was thus well informed on the issues about to be discussed. Among his many gifts was an unrivalled courage of his convictions. Come the four corners of the world in arms, let all the experts in all the departments agree upon the answer to a question, if his own reason and judgement gave him a different answer, he abided in it utterly unmoved. As cool as a cucumber, and with gentle sarcasm, he would explain to the Prime Minister that all the departments were wrong. And they often were! It was clever of Mr Churchill to have such a man always at hand.[1]

He was self-effacing in official matters, but at this juncture in Washington, coming hot from Quebec, he regarded him-

---

1. It was no doubt this same courage of his convictions which led him to undertake the following experiment in World War I. When auto-rotation was little understood, and when an aeroplane seen to be spinning was regarded as doomed, Lord Cherwell, then on scientific work at the Royal Aircraft Establishment ('Factory'), worked out theoretically the proper actions for the pilot to take, asked leave to learn flying so as to test his theory, and within three weeks put a B.E.2 aeroplane into a spin at 14,000 feet and brought it safely out – repeating the action first right and then left. (My authority for this is Mr M. O'Gorman, who was O.C. Royal Aircraft Establishment at the time of the experiment.)

self and was regarded by the Americans as speaking for the Prime Minister. He began to take up the threads of the negotiations. Keynes was bound to write to the Chancellor of the Exchequer. Was the Chancellor conducting these negotiations, as authorized, through himself, or was the Prime Minister doing it through Lord Cherwell? It was characteristic of Keynes's complete lack of egoism that, having made the Chancellor cognizant of the situation, he advised him not to take the matter up. His personal relations with Lord Cherwell were good, and Lord Cherwell's relations with Mr Morgenthau and Mr Harry Hopkins seemed to be excellent. It would, therefore, be to the general advantage if he stayed, so as to get the first stage of the proceedings properly launched. Lord Cherwell had to return to the Prime Minister in England shortly afterwards, and from then onwards Keynes was in charge of the proceedings.

Mr Brand was his deputy and Mr Frank Lee, an able man of great energy and magnificent grasp of detail, was his assistant from the Treasury. Mr Ben Smith, then Minister Resident in Washington, had been appointed as the other Minister on the Committee. The main burden of the preparation of programmes of requirements fell upon Sir Robert Sinclair, and, to Keynes's delight, he brought as his assistant Keynes's old friend and pupil, and present colleague in the editorship of the *Economic Journal*, Mr Austin Robinson. A notable part on the supplies side was also played by Sir Henry Self, who had been for some time resident in Washington.

The first task was the preparation of 'a book of the words'. This was introduced by a magnificent account of Britain's ardours and endurances during five years of war. It was a faithful record, but the cumulative effect of the narrative was such as to astonish even the British, who had endured the privations described. It seemed hardly possible that we had suffered so much, yet it was all true. Was it the act of self-immolation on 3 September 1939 that had enabled us to go through it without self-pity? There was, however, a limit to this power. The document explained that it would hardly be possible to sustain morale throughout the Japanese war, to which the authorities at Quebec had in their wisdom given a duration of eighteen months after the defeat of Germany, without some easements. The main part of the paper consisted in an analysis of our resources and a statement of our requirements.

There ensued protracted negotiations, in which the various Missions in Washington played their part on numerous specialist committees. The members in chief of the American Committee were Mr Morgenthau, Mr Stettinius and the head of the Foreign Economic Administration, Mr Leo Crowley. The last named was in charge of Lend-Lease arrangements. In these complicated discussions there were three main issues of policy. One was the question of the proportion by which the American sustenance of the British effort should be reduced. This was mainly the concern of the F E A; Professor J. W. Angell had with forethought provided a formula which was agreeable to British ideas.[2] The second question was the effect of the total programme on the British reserve position, which was mainly the concern of the U.S. Treasury.[3] Keynes had to revive all his arguments of 1941 and bring them up to date, to the effect that Britain would be a broken reed in cooperation during the war and afterwards if deprived of the necessary minimum reserve. Finally, there was the complication caused by the mode of thought of the U.S. Navy Department. In detail there were many dozens of controversial questions, which often had to come to the highest level for final decision. The shipping experts, for instance, carried on a dog-fight all

2. There may have been a little prearrangement.
3. Keynes and White, with all their efforts, were unable to reach agreement on the existing volume of British resources, there being a difference, connected with Portuguese liabilities, of $300 million, which was irreconcilable and ran through all the discussions to the end!

through these months. One bright idea of Keynes's own was that the Americans should include prefabricated houses in their Lend-Lease supplies; this proposal to help the victims of a bombardment, from which they had not suffered themselves, appealed to their imagination.

Keynes entered with all the force of his nature into every dispute. Mr Lauchlin Currie recalls how he waited until the end of a dinner-party to communicate an adverse American decision. It was as though Keynes had received a physical blow. He put his hands to his chest, saying that he would break off the negotiations. He could not go on talking now and must be left alone for a few minutes to recover from the shock. Yet, despite reverses in detail, the British had the sense that they had received a fair deal. Those at home were satisfied that the work had been well done. One point that was particularly valued was the relaxation of the principles of the 'Export White Paper', so that Britain might begin to make efforts during the eighteen months ahead to reduce the vast gap in her balance of payments. Provision was also made for the requirements of Dominions, and Keynes received their expressions of gratitude for his good work when the Conference was over.

On one point there was disappointment. It was hoped until the end that the decisions would be embodied in a protocol to be initialled and have the status of a treaty, so that the British should know what they could rely on, and not continue to have month by month anxieties. On the very last day this hope was dashed. Once again American initials seemed to be in short supply.

During these negotiations there occurred an event which gave joy to British hearts – the re-election of President Roosevelt. Lord Halifax had Maynard and Lydia to the Embassy to listen in to the results, and Mr Isaiah Berlin was there to keep them amused with his ceaseless flow of scintillating conversation. Keynes, his mind not tired after a day's immersion in official statistics, demanded paper upon which to make calculations with the figures that came over the air. He had devised a patent method for determining the final result of the election long before anyone else could grasp the drift of the returns.

2

He had many threads to pick up on his return to England at the end of a year, so much of which had been spent in the United States.

This was the time at which he began the negotiations for the new Covent Garden scheme. The Royal Opera House at Covent Garden had been turned over to banal wartime uses, and there was some doubt whether its old function would ever be revived. A scheme was hatched out, with the cooperation of Messrs Boosey & Hawkes and the Arts Council, for establishing a new trust. It was hoped not merely to revive Covent Garden as an opera house, but to have a new kind of direction, which would make it available for a wider range of production, including ballet, and enable it to give more scope to native talent. In these negotiations, which were successfully conducted, Keynes played a prominent part. He became Chairman of the new trust and presided at the first production, which took place in February 1946.

Honours at this time began to crowd upon him. In April he was nominated for Honorary LL.D. at Edinburgh; in January of 1946 he received an Honorary Doctorate from the Sorbonne, and, crowning glory, in the same month he was awarded an Honorary D.Sc. by his own University. The Borough of Cambridge had already (1943) done him the signal honour of making him High Steward.

These recognitions gave a pleasant background to the daily toil; yet he could hardly relish them to the full, so pressing and fateful was the business in hand. The Stage II settlement had provided a brief respite, but the really formidable problem was that of Stage III. What would happen when Lend-Lease was terminated? How approach the Americans for indispensable aid when we had ceased to be brother soldiers in arms? The load of external indebtedness was growing to gigantic dimensions, and the gap in our current account was getting steadily worse. It would not do to wait until the war was over to reach settlement with the Americans. We should have to endeavour to get them to consider our problems at once. VE-Day came and went, lacking somehow that great surge of joy which had marked 11 November 1918. The authorities at Quebec had decreed a period of eighteen months for the hostilities with Japan after the war with Germany should be over. But they were not infallible. Might victory conceivably come sooner? In any case, the negotiations with the Americans were bound to be very protracted, and it was necessary to begin preparations at once. In March Keynes wrote and circulated a masterly document. All became busy at assembling materials to support our case. April was darkened by the calamity of Roosevelt's death.

This summer the country had the delight of a General Election. Keynes contributed a modest sum to the fighting fund of the Liberal Party. It was at this time that he had the opportunity of making another of his exquisite after-dinner speeches, recalling times past, on his retirement from Editorship of the *Economic Journal*.[4] I had decided to stand as Liberal candidate for Huddersfield, and he drove me in his car after the dinner to catch the night train from Euston. He expressed grave anxiety lest there should be returned a large number of the kind of Conservatives who were opposed to the principles of Article VII. 'What would you think of a Labour victory?' I asked him. He found no consolation in that prospect either, but he characteristically added, 'It might make all the difference if one or two "funnies" like you got in.' My little adventure seemed to give him genuine pleasure, and the warmth of his good wishes made a difference to the days of campaigning which followed.

When the voting was over, but before the result was an-

4. cf. pp. 227–8 above.

nounced, Mr Churchill proceeded to Potsdam. Later he was succeeded by Mr Attlee. Americans were there, and it seemed expedient to broach to some of them on their return through London Britain's problem in the post-war period. It was learnt that Mr W. Clayton and Mr E. G. Collado would be in London for a meeting of UNRRA. They completed their complicated business at Potsdam in the early hours of Friday 3 August, and reached London later that morning. Keynes made contact with them without delay and took up the question of post-war assistance.

Mr Clayton made the point, which had long been recognized in Whitehall, that assistance could not be obtained save in conjunction with a further undertaking by Britain to pursue a neighbourly economic policy. Here was an explosive question. Keynes judged that there should be a conference of the most responsible officials. The UNRRA meetings were to begin on Tuesday. Then the conference of officials must be on Monday, which was Bank Holiday. Keynes assembled twenty-one persons. There was much moaning and groaning. Sir Stafford Cripps was in the chair. Mr Clayton explained that, as a prerequisite of assistance, there must be some area of understanding about policy.

There were three main heads. 'Sterling balances' (viz. the vast accumulation of wartime debts by Britain to Allies and neutrals) must somehow be segregated, so that American assistance could be used to meet the genuine current needs of Britain, and not to pay off old debts. There was every prospect that the United States would wipe out all claims under Lend-Lease, and it was not fair that she should now be asked to make retrospective payments, directly or indirectly, to other United Nations for their previous contributions to the good cause.

Secondly, there must be an arrangement for making sterling convertible in due course. It was the American opinion that sterling convertibility would be one of the principal foundation stones of world reconstruction. It was a wise opinion.

Thirdly, there was the old question of commercial policy and 'non-discrimination'. The State Department would undoubtedly remain adamant. It is fair to say that this was not merely a selfish interest, but a genuine conviction that health could not be restored if the nations tied themselves up in bilateral deals, and that bilateralism tended to make economics the servant of power politics. A major war objective in the American mind had always been to eradicate the Schacht system; it would not do for Britain to rise like a phoenix out of its ashes and apply it on an even more far-reaching scale.

Keynes struck the Americans as on the whole sound on the convertibility issue. It was quite clear to him that Britain, with her great dependence on invisible income, and her vulnerability on the side of international capital movements, would not flourish, whatever controls she might introduce, unless sterling was a currency that gave satisfaction. It could not do that if it was not convertible. He always preached that the sterling area, which he greatly valued, could only be saved if sterling itself was sound. Without convertibility the sterling area would lead us ever more deeply into the morass. While Keynes appreciated that the problem of our external indebtedness was one that needed most delicate handling, he was of the opinion that it must not be allowed to stand in the way of convertibility, and that, in the last resort, it would be better to handle our creditors drastically, as, for instance, by freezing the balances, than forgo convertibility. It was not clear that all shared this opinion. In the American judgement the whole meeting seemed very wobbly on commercial policy. Keynes himself was still in doubt where Britain's interest lay.

On this same August Bank Holiday, while these experts were cudgelling their brains over the intricacies of finance, President Truman was announcing in Washington that a bomb had been dropped on Hiroshima. Keynes had not been wrong in thinking that there was need for haste; it was lucky that he had sought to galvanize the official world into activity in those earlier months. The immeasurable blessing of peace was now clearly within sight, and with it the prospect of financial ruin for Britain. All materials necessary for the negotiation had to be mobilized now with the utmost haste. VJ-Day was not long in coming.

On Sunday 19 August Mr E. G. Collado was having tea at a Cambridge teashop. He had come to Cambridge with some friends to do sightseeing. They were resting after an exhausting day. Their attention was attracted by news coming over the air ... What was this? It was incredible. What could have happened? The U.S. radio had carried the announcement that Lend-Lease had been completely stopped, and from now onwards Britain would have to pay for all supplies, including those in the pipe-line. Collado dashed for the next train to Liverpool Street and thence by tube to the American Embassy. On the platform of Bond Street station he ran into Harry Hawkins, who was looking extremely gloomy. Yes, he had seen the cable. The worst was true. Collado made for the Embassy; he was later joined by Mr Clayton, who had hastened up from the house of a friend, where he had been staying for the weekend. It was a sad occasion. Did Keynes know? They discovered that he had been informed earlier in the day. They suffered, these American friends of ours, perhaps more than the British, since it was their people who had done it. The British were inured to hard knocks.

What had happened? Mr Truman, who was still somewhat new to his high office of President, held a Cabinet, and relied on the advice of Mr Crowley concerning what should be done; Mr Crowley was the relevant authority as Director of the Foreign Economic Administration; he correctly reported that the law required immediate cessation. It is usually supposed that, had Mr Roosevelt still been President, or had Mr Truman already enjoyed a longer period of office, he would not have regarded Mr Crowley's reply as final and decisive on such a momentous subject, and would have found some way within the law of easing the transition – although doubtless this would have been exceedingly difficult. The State Department and the Treasury had both prepared long memoranda on what should be done in the circumstances; but events had moved too quickly and the documents remained in their pigeon-holes. Mr Vinson, also new to his job, having but recently succeeded Mr Morgenthau as Secretary of the Treasury, did his best to get some postponement. By a piece of bad luck this event occurred in the one week when Mr Dean Acheson was not a member of the State Department. His previous post there had terminated, and he had not begun his duties in his new one. He was away in Canada. Mr Clayton was in Europe. Thus those with the greatest knowledge of the broader issues were dispersed and our cause went largely by default.

On Monday morning, Mr Clayton took up the trans-atlantic telephone and vented the vials of his wrath. It was good to see the whole six-foot-six of him reinforcing the vehemence of his rebukes. He was able to do some good. It was agreed that the question of payment for goods in the pipeline should remain over for negotiation. Mr Clayton and Mr Collado had the appalling task of conveying their intelligence to the British Ministers. They were received by Mr Bevin and Mr Dalton, who looked very downcast; but no words of recrimination were uttered.

Keynes had to move with speed now. There was no time to be lost. He would go straight over and seize victory from the jaws of defeat. His brief was wanted at once. Peace had evidently not brought slothful ease for the officials con-cerned. Keynes's spirits mounted. The British case was overwhelming. He had found the Americans reasonable and on the whole amenable on the previous visits. There was no reason to suppose that their friendliness had disappeared. He would surely succeed.

His plan was to ask for £1,500 million as a free gift, or, failing that, as an interest-free loan. This was surely within reason. Mr Brand came to London with reports on the American situation, and he and Keynes faced the British Ministers at 11 o'clock one evening. Mr Brand gave warning that the task of obtaining assistance would be exceedingly difficult. But Keynes, with his winged words, persuaded them that he was capable of achieving the plan. They were impressed, although some doubted. Mr Bevin, ever shrewd, is reported to have said: 'When I listen to Lord Keynes talking, I seem to hear those coins jingling in my pocket; but I am not so sure that they are really there.'

Keynes has been criticized for painting too rosy a picture. He suffered from it himself, since, when his full hopes were not realized, there was some disillusionment and misunderstanding at home. He had persuaded them so successfully that the thing could be done that, when it was not done, they tended to think that it must be owing to his faulty negotiation. Thus there was reluctance to allow him to make the necessary concessions, and mutual vexation was the consequence. It is clear he should have stressed more carefully those three necessary conditions for assistance which had been stated at the August Bank Holiday meeting. Indeed, it was expedient, even at the cost of delay, to give those three conditions close interdepartmental scrutiny and establish a carefully worded British brief, on the basis of which the negotiations could proceed. Concessions going outside such a brief would no doubt have had to be made, but these could have been granted in good order, Whitehall having cognizance of each step. Keynes preferred to keep the matter more fluid. His brain seethed with all sorts of possibilities. He knew quite well that 'strings' would in fact be attached to the assistance, including a British commitment on open commercial policy; indeed he wrote a memorandum warning the Treasury to have no illusions on this matter. But he hoped to be able to divide the proceedings into two stages. In the first, British needs and difficulties would be explored, and it might be possible to reach some provisional idea as to how far the

Americans would go to help. The second stage would consist of formal negotiations in regard to the 'strings'. Things did not so work out. It may be that Keynes had not at this point fully appreciated the time factor; the agreement would have to be passed by Parliament by the end of December, since American adherence to Bretton Woods was conditional on other nations also having adhered by that date. Meanwhile he felt that he would be impeded in feeling his way cleverly towards the best solution by any cut-and-dried instructions. He was rightly confident that he knew better than any living man all the considerations that were involved; he assumed too hastily that the British authorities would trust him implicitly and accept what he obtained as the best available. In fact he was a little over-confident, and this led to grievous trouble.

His buoyant optimism was soon dispelled when he set foot on the other side and made contact with his friends. The atmosphere had in fact changed. There was still much kindly concern for Britain. But the war was now over; the Americans had suffered heavy loss of life; there was anxiety for the future. The dangers of inflation in the United States were vividly present to their minds. There might be serious labour troubles. Huge tasks lay before them. There was the feeling that the various nations, whose freedom and integrity had been saved from a deadly threat, must now fend for themselves and settle down with discipline to the task of repairing their own homes. Where there was acute distress and danger of starvation the Americans would give bountifully. The UNRRA programmes were being worked out. But to enter deeply into the financial problems of Allies, to sustain their balances of trade, to support welfare programmes, this seemed to be asking them to go rather far. They had their own problems. Britain had shown herself a mighty Power, with great economic reserves, during this long war. Surely she would not quail before the minor problem of rebuilding her homes and her trade, with no bombs or flying-bombs to distract her energies. The high

American officials, after four years of educational campaigning by Keynes and other British representatives, knew
better; but their power to assist depended upon the man in
the street and upon Congress. To those the British case
seemed, on the face of it, unconvincing. Thus it was felt by
the U.S. Cabinet in September 1945 that the project of
giving Britain even moderate assistance would be a very
difficult one to carry through. And so indeed it proved.
During the first half of 1946 the American leaders had to
devote a tremendous amount of hard work to campaigning
for the British Loan; it would be difficult to find in
history a parallel case of men in the topmost walk of life
undertaking such tireless exertions merely to help a neighbour.

It is important to remember that the atmosphere was
totally different from that which prevailed when General
Marshall propounded his European Recovery Programme
in 1947. In 1945 there were already, it is true, some rumblings
from Russia. But the American people did not regard
Russia at that time as a potential threat to the Western
democracies. Nor was the strength of the Communist
element within the western Continental countries appreciated. It cannot be gainsaid that the Marshall Plan, generous
and statesmanlike as it was, could be justified in the first
instance as necessary to the defence of the United States.
The European bridgehead must be preserved. Keynes had
not the advantage of the support which this fear of Russia
later gave to American programmes of assistance. If he was
to appeal to American interests, it would have to be on the
ground of much wider considerations. They wished for
world prosperity in order that their trade might expand;
they wished that the peace-loving nations should be strong,
as bulwarks against unknown threats in the future. Britain
could only contribute to the fulfilment of these aims if she
was saved from bankruptcy now. These were real considerations, yet hard to argue at a time when it was felt that the
United States would need to devote all her resources to her

own reconstruction, and that inflation was round the corner.

The opening meetings of the negotiations took place in the State Department on 11 September at 4 p.m. Mr Byrnes, the Secretary of State, was still away, and Mr Clayton took the chair. The Americans were also represented by Messrs Vinson, Henry Wallace, Crowley, Marriner Eccles and McCabe. On the British side were Lord Halifax, Lord Keynes, Mr Brand, Sir Henry Self and Mr Hall-Patch. Besides these, there was a vast concourse of assistants and secretaries. This was merely a preliminary meeting. It was decided that serious business should be opened by Keynes's statement of the British case on 13 September, in the Federal Reserve Building.

3

Keynes was mounting the marble steps in front of the Federal Reserve Building, a structure of beauty and dignity, albeit on a modest scale, perhaps the most successful of the splendid piles that flank Constitution Avenue. Deeply cut in the marble over the doorway were the two simple words, 'Federal Reserve'. Twenty billion dollars of shining gold! No one could deny that the Americans had earned this store of wealth by their hard work and enterprise. Well, he had come to ask for six of those billions, a substantial proportion. Britain too had been labouring and adventuring during the last years, but without remuneration.

Americans were also mounting the steps. 'Ah, there is Keynes; we shall have an interesting morning.' One or two may have had slightly different thoughts. 'Oh, look, there is that tiresome man again; we shall have to listen to him telling us in his precious voice and superior manner what we ought to do; but the war is over, and he will have to moderate his tone, if he wants the money.'

He was walking through the glistening corridors; the rarest marbles had been brought from the ends of the earth under the loving supervision of Mr Adolph Miller; every detail was perfect. And so into the great Board Room on the first floor. The fittings were luxurious but restrained. It was a worthy meeting-place for the Federal Reserve Board, which had to guide the monetary policy of this opulent nation, now the world's leader, and to harmonize the administrative and political outlook with that of the pure banker. From ceiling to floor heavy Venetian blinds screened the three large windows overlooking Constitution Avenue. Round the walls were charts showing forth the current economic position of the country, in frames designed by the architect as part of the structure. Only a few years ago this chamber had been the scene of another historic occasion, when Mr Churchill first met the American Chiefs of Staff after Pearl Harbour and had found 'an Olympian fortitude ... the mask of an inflexible purpose'.

And now he, Keynes, had to carry the heavy responsibility of speaking for Britain on this matter, which was also in its own way one of life and death. For the condition of Britain was indeed parlous, with her staggering load of foreign debt and her present inability to pay her way from day to day. Her exports would have to be quadrupled – that could not be done overnight. Those stupid Members of Parliament, who thought that we did not need assistance! If his negotiation was not successful, rations would have to be drastically cut; the factories would stand idle for lack of materials; there would certainly be inflation. Would there also be labour troubles and even civil strife? The servicemen who came home, and the civilians who had been so patient under bombardment, would demand something for themselves and their families with wrathful insistence. They could not be expected to understand the complicated economic system in which they were enmeshed. There might be violence of a kind unknown in the fair island for many generations. Its consequences could not be foreseen; many precious features of our civilization might be lost. There would have to be a long period of grinding poverty and mendicancy. One might think of the troubles of Germany in the early years after the First World War and the disruption in her social fabric which was their consequence. The British were tougher than the Germans, but they had already had more to endure. Was this to be a turning point of history? Would the Britain of Shakespeare and Newton lapse into being a secondary power, a slum of squalid living and brutish ways? He thought of the amiable life of the Sussex countryside and the labourers whom he loved, he thought of the millions of Londoners in their tubes and buses whose perils he had shared, he thought of the universities, still in the vanguard of science and humanity, with their precious modes of life, philosophy, civilized discussion; he thought of talks with Lytton by the fireside, he thought of the cultivated gentlepeople all over England, living modestly, loving books and music, disseminating sweetness and light. Were all these to be ground down by harsh distress and social strife? The next few weeks mattered much.

The room was beginning to fill up. There was Lord Halifax, looking so handsome and splendid. He understood these secret things. He would be a pillar of strength. There were American faces, which had become so familiar in recent years – Eddy Bernstein, with his atmosphere of bustle, Pete Collado, with his determined features, Harry Hawkins, Jim Angell, Frank Coe. These were men of ability and earnest purpose. They were of kindly disposition. The Americans were a kindly people, as kind as any. Perhaps things would not go too badly. He spoke to some of them without having the faintest idea what he said.

Lord Halifax was to sit at the middle of the long table with his back to the window; he would sit on Lord Halifax's right. Someone was pulling out the heavy yellow leather chair for him to take his place . . . He was there as a beggar, to beg for Britain, herself a beggar. For even if he failed to get a gift or an interest-free loan, the terms of assistance must contain a charitable element, if it was to serve its pur-

pose. This was an unwonted role. He must be very careful
and tactful, and deny himself wisecracks. It was a horrid
situation. But there was one redeeming feature. It was an
essential part of the British case that Britain was still poten-
tially a great Power and that support to her would assist
world stability and peace. There could thus be an element
of pride in the request for help. How should this be conveyed? Britain was indeed still a great Power. It was not
so long ago since Mr Churchill had spoken of her finest
hour. But that must not be his own theme on this occasion,
for in the interval thousands of brave Americans had died
heroes' deaths in all quarters of the globe. This was no
time for boasting. He could show that per head of population the British had made a larger exertion than the Americans, but such comparisons were odious.

There was one way and one way only in which he could
remind this audience, in these circumstances, of the greatness of Britain. If he could explain the whole extraordinary
case in plain, unvarnished terms, without embroidery, if
he could plead with dignity and composure, if he could
assemble his materials with supreme skill, summoning up
those powers of speech which he knew he possessed, if he
could revive here and now what was best in the sober British
mode of oratory, using all his memories and experience,
he might make his audience feel that they were in the
presence of a great tradition. He must somehow distil the
greatness of Britain into the form of words which he chose.
That was the only way. He must himself appear to be the
embodiment of those ancient virtues, for whose continued
sustenance he had come to plead.

His chair seemed sufficiently comfortable. Lord Halifax
was explaining that Lord Keynes had come from Britain
fully armed with all relevant information, prepared to
answer every question, instructed to conceal nothing either
of good or ill in the situation . . . He was there as a beggar,
just that. Where was the security of Harvey Road now? His
parents were living through a peaceful old age there; that

position at least could be secured. What would Henry Sidgwick or old Alfred Marshall have thought of this terrible impasse to which Britain had now come, despite her recent victory? Was the responsibility which he was carrying a greater burden than he could bear? Was he feeling ill? Lydia was somewhere near. She would minister to his needs.

Keynes was speaking now. The rustle of papers died down. His discourse lasted for three days. It was the pure gold of perfect English prose, describing a situation of vast complexity with the lucidity and good arrangement that only a master mind could have achieved. It was so easy and light and sparkling, that there was never a dull moment. Those most sympathetic and those least sympathetic agreed in thinking that this was the finest exposition to which they had ever listened or were ever likely to listen.

The characteristic of the statement which the Americans who heard it most wished to stress was its integrity. They had the feeling that he was doing his utmost to present the facts exactly as they were. Numerous questions were put during the course of the three days. If a figure was challenged, he would state exactly how it was arrived at; if there was an element of conjecture, he would admit it; perhaps the figure was too high, or again, it might be too low; it was their best estimate on the facts they had, which were admittedly incomplete. There was no attempt to exaggerate. How different from the Keynes of 46 Gordon Square, ridiculing the absurd behaviour of the Bank of England! It is comforting to think that one who had given so much enjoyment by his pleasant exaggerations in private life, could get the highest marks from a critical and discriminating audience for his absence of exaggeration. The metal was tested under the fire of this supreme ordeal and found good. The combination of waywardness in private talk with supreme accuracy on the great occasion was not altogether an accident. For to be absolutely truthful in strange circumstances requires imagination. The dullard is the victim of his own prejudices, and while he supposes himself to be stating the sober truth, often deceives himself. It takes imagination to re-question one's own beliefs and suppose that they may be wrong, imagination to see things as others see them. Keynes had the active mind, which was always ready to think again about a belief complacently held; thus he saw the true force of the American questions, and they saw that he was always ready to reassess his own proposition in the light of a valid objection. This was integrity in the highest sense, very rarely achieved by men. The Americans appreciated it, and it thus served Britain. A loan would have been forthcoming in any case; it is arguable that no other Englishman could have secured one on such favourable terms.

The Americans were also impressed by his willingness, for which he had authority, to place all the cards upon the table. The vast volume of British liabilities was fully set out; her assets were also tabled, including items which the Americans might never have discovered for themselves.

Then there was the extreme clarity of the exposition. Everything was presented with a sharp, memorable outline, often with some jest or metaphor to keep the memory alive. Britain's problems, and the policies connected with them, were so vividly stated, that the Americans could feel them as their own problems, and slipped into the frame of mind of saying, 'What on earth shall we do about that?' Mr Marriner Eccles testifies that the British case was so clearly engraved upon his mind, that when, some months later, he had to give evidence to the Committee of the Senate on the British Loan, he could enter into all sorts of details of the British case, without any reference to notes, just as if he was testifying about his own private affairs.

After this great opening to the proceedings, the meeting dissolved itself into separate commissions, one on financial problems, one on commercial policy, one on Lend-Lease matters, and one on surplus property disposal. There were also meetings of a small group of four consisting of Lord Halifax, Keynes, Mr Clayton and Mr Vinson. The whole negotiation lasted three months. It had already become evident that the Americans were not willing to tarry any longer in the phase of discussing British needs without reference to the 'strings'; Keynes's programme of two stages could not be carried out in the form he had intended; the negotiations which followed were much hindered by his not having caused precise instructions on these topics to be formulated before he left England.

Keynes had to recognize in time, not without a hard fight and renewal of hope week after week, that a gift or an interest-free loan was out of the question. For a period the proposal for assistance which should be part gift and part loan was carefully considered. The authorities at home were not easily persuaded, till the bitter end, that the decision to accept the loan at interest was inevitable. Keynes's initial optimism had planted dangerous illusions in their minds. In the final settlement the whole assistance took the form of a loan, but it could be argued that the terms were such as to amount in effect to about half being a gift. There was to be a period of six years without interest, which would then be charged at two per cent. There was a valuable waiver clause. No interest would be payable or carried forward in any year in which British exports, visible and invisible, did not suffice to buy imports from abroad of the pre-war volume. Furthermore, in the early years of repayment interest would be larger than the redemption of capital, and the waiver correspondingly more valuable. If Britain really succeeded in achieving the exports postulated, the additional exports required to finance the interest payments would be comparatively trivial (less than two per cent of her total exports); if she did not succeed, the waiver would come into operation. Furthermore, the vast British potential obligations under Lend-Lease were to be remitted in entirety.

When Keynes set out for Washington he had it definitely in mind that in certain circumstances it would be better to break off negotiations. The moment came when he considered very carefully whether this should be done, and he drafted a cable setting out the pros and cons. His verdict was against breaking off. Two points were borne in upon him, which made him feel that there would not be a substantial reason for breaking. One was that the Americans entirely agreed with the British that it was excessively undesirable to create a commitment that the British were unlikely to be able to honour. The other was that the insistence by the American negotiators on interest was mainly for window-dressing purposes and that they would go to great lengths to make the burden of the interest negligible for a long time to come. It would hardly be sensible to break with negotiators who were honestly in this frame of mind, on the ground that they insisted on charging interest!

The so-called 'strings' to the Loan consisted in nothing more than the reaffirmation and application of the policy to which Britain had pledged herself by the signature of Article VII of the Mutual Aid Agreement. All the Bretton Woods negotiations were based on the understanding that Britain would adhere to this policy, and the Americans had already conducted a nationwide campaign, with a most lavish expenditure of time and energy, to convert the American people to the advantages of Anglo-American cooperation on these lines. The British negotiators, however, at this time were not in the main thinking deeply about fundamental principles; their minds were concentrated upon the question of what it was sensible to try to do here and now and in the immediate future.

Meanwhile at home there appeared to be some confusion on these issues. The fact of the matter was that many members of the new administration knew little about the implications of Article VII and that even the survivors from Coalition days had been too much immersed in the war effort to follow the developments of Anglo-American post-war planning in detail. The issues at stake were complex; the Americans had clear ideas about the evils of the dis-

crimination, restrictionism and bilateralism that they wished
to eradicate; the average British parliamentarian, conscious
of the danger of too speedy a relaxation of wartime controls
and somewhat hazy, no doubt, about the implications of
'socialism' for foreign trading relations, had still much to
learn about what was at stake.

Keynes in his own person was favourable to sterling convertibility; in this he was in agreement with the Americans.
But when they declared that sterling should be made convertible at an early specified date, to use the words of an
American witness, Keynes 'hit the ceiling'. He poured forth
his eloquence on the appalling difficulties that would beset
Britain for a number of years, and on the dangers of premature convertibility. No twist or turn of argument was
neglected. But the Americans were obdurate. They took
the view, in my judgement quite correctly, that the establishment of sterling convertibility on a firm basis was the
first indispensable step towards a satisfactory reconstruction of the international economy. They were fearful lest
there should be a transition period, in which existing
bilateral arrangements and an unnatural pattern of trade
should be crystallized. For them, therefore, early convertibility was a key point. Eventually it was agreed to
make sterling convertible within a year of the coming into
effect of the Loan. After much struggle, however, Keynes
secured a clause providing for agreed postponement of
convertibility after consultation.[5] In justice to Keynes it
must be observed that Britain never asked leave to postpone
the date, in accordance with this provision, before making
her unsuccessful experiment in convertibility in 1947.

The most important question discussed in Washington
on this occasion was that of the 'sterling balances'. These
were the debts which Britain had incurred to foreigners in
the course of waging the war; they stood at £3,355 million
on 30 June 1945. To get a full account of the external cost
of the war to Britain, the proceeds of the sales of overseas

5. Cmd 6708, Clause 7.

investments during the war should be added, viz. £1,118 million, and part of the sterling balances outstanding in 1939 (£476 million) deducted.[6] Thus Britain had paid, or promised to pay, to Allies and neutrals, no less a sum than £4 billion or more for having helped her to win the war. Even the large figure of £1½ billion, originally asked by Keynes of the Americans, was small by comparison with this. The Americans had made their contribution in assisting Britain by Lend-Lease, the Canadians by successive gifts; but the other Allies pleaded poverty. Britain was expected, in addition to the mighty efforts and endurances which she had herself sustained, and in addition to sizable payments under Reverse Lend-Lease, to pay these vast sums to others for their having had the honour of making some contribution, direct or indirect, to the defeat of Hitler.

In the early drafts of White's Stabilization Fund, there had been clauses relating to this problem, but Britain had taken the line that it was her affair, which she must find means of settling for herself. Now that she was asking for special aid from the United States, it could be regarded as partly their affair also. It seemed unjust to the Americans that the British should have to pay out these huge sums, and it was certainly not their intention to give her the wherewithal to do so on a large scale. Consequently they argued, with some justice, that Britain must bind herself in the agreement to freeze these liabilities by a certain date, so as to make it quite certain that she would not be using American dollars to liquidate them. Once again Keynes 'hit the ceiling', and protested vehemently against any reference to matters which were primarily the concern of the Commonwealth and Empire. But the question was too serious to be left just like that. Keynes had a strong point when he argued that to embody in the Loan Agree-

6. Only part, and perhaps a small part; for a considerable proportion of these were withdrawn by their foreign holders for safety in the early months of the war.

ment a clause for freezing these balances on a certain date would be to tie Britain's hands in subsequent negotiations with her creditors in a disastrous way. The liabilities had many diverse origins, and the equitable considerations involved were various. It was for Britain to do her best to settle these different claims by negotiation in a variety of ways.

At the same time Keynes recognized and agreed to the substance of the American plea, which was that the money which they proposed to provide should not be frittered away, directly or indirectly, in meeting old debts. It was intended to help Britain to cope with her balance of trade problem in the transition period, during which she would redeploy her factories for peacetime production, with such repairs and reconstruction as were urgently needed. Accordingly, a statement of Britain's intention was drafted in rather general terms and embodied in the Agreement.

### 10. *Accumulated Sterling Balances*

(i) The Government of the United Kingdom intends to make agreements with the countries concerned, varying according to the circumstances of each case, for an early settlement covering the sterling balances accumulated by sterling area and other countries prior to such settlement (together with any future receipts arising out of military expenditure by the Government of the United Kingdom to the extent to which they are treated on the same basis by agreement with the countries concerned). The settlements with the sterling area countries will be on the basis of dividing these accumulated balances into three categories:

(*a*) balances to be released at once and convertible into any currency for current transactions;

(*b*) balances to be similarly released by instalments over a period of years beginning in 1951; and

(*c*) balances to be adjusted as a contribution to the settlement of war and post-war indebtedness and in recognition of the benefits which the countries concerned might be expected to gain from such a settlement.

The Government of the United Kingdom will make every endeavour to secure the early completion of these arrangements.

(ii) In consideration of the fact that an important purpose of the present line of credit is to promote the development of multilateral trade and facilitate its early resumption on a non-discriminatory basis, the Government of the United Kingdom agrees that any sterling balances released or otherwise available for current payments will, not later than one year after the effective date of this agreement, unless in special cases a later date is agreed upon after consultation, be freely available for current transactions in any currency areas without discrimination.

Thus some scaling down of the total liability was envisaged. In the course of the discussions Keynes gave figures, merely by way of example and without committing the British Government, for the amounts involved under the various subsections of this clause. These figures imprinted themselves on the memory of the Americans who were present. It is of interest to observe that he gave the figure of £200 million as the maximum amount of ready cash that Britain should provide in all towards paying off these balances prior to 1951. The all-important point was that Britain assured the Americans that she would have dealt with the matter in her own way and have it completely under control before the date on which sterling should become convertible, so that the success of the convertibility experiment could in no wise be jeopardized by the existence of uncovered liabilities. It was recognized by both sides that a complete cleaning up of this situation was necessary, if the convertibility experiment was to be a success, and that after one year no balances should remain which were not absolutely beyond the power of the creditors to realize save as and when the British agreed.

Mr Liesching and Professor Robbins were the principal British negotiators on the Commercial Policy Commission. This matter had been fairly fully discussed in Washington in 1943, and Mr Harry Hawkins had attended a series of

meetings in London early in 1945. The main lines were
already clear, but a number of special problems had to be
solved. Keynes listened to many of these discussions. He
was deeply impressed by the reasonableness of the Americans and by the success which these successive negotiations
achieved in finding means for mitigating the severities of
an open trading system in all cases reasonably requiring
special treatment. He had not given his mind very fully
to these problems in the preceding years. As he now sat
and listened, his thoughts underwent a change. After all,
he had always been an internationalist himself, and had only
despaired of a revival of greater freedom of trade because
he judged that other nations would be uncooperative. But
now the Americans were being extraordinarily cooperative.
Large new vistas opened up. We need no longer be content
with a nationalist experiment in Keynesian economics, implying some measure of autarky, but could take the better
path of an experiment in Keynesian economics on a world
scale and not forgo the full benefits which flow from international trade. His mind reverted to Adam Smith and to the
great truths which he preached. Of course they were truths;
but for him they had been submerged in recent years by
what seemed to be the more urgent problem of mass unemployment and trade depression. So long as the present-
day followers of Adam Smith refused to recognize these new
problems, he would not preach their gospel. Yet he would be
far happier preaching that gospel; and these conversations
during the Loan negotiations convinced him that he could
now do so without sacrificing any of his cherished principles
relating to employment and trade depression. The Americans seemed to be as fully convinced as he that a nation
should not be compelled by her open trading commitments
to take action likely to lead to domestic slump.

Marvellous to relate, it appeared that his battle had
already been won over a greater part of the field than he
had suspected. By various streams and rivulets his doctrines
had percolated. If one could judge the world climate of

opinion in Washington, it seemed that the old deflationist orthodoxy had been routed once and for all. One need no longer fear that one would be expected to deflate in order to implement undertakings of commercial policy. It was generally recognized that methods other than deflation would have to be sought when there was disequilibrium on foreign trade account.

If such was the case, of course it was better to re-establish an open international trading system. He was at the utmost pains to convey his new view of the matter as soon as he returned to England. Now was the time when the programme stated at my dinner table in Oxford in 1930 could at long last be implemented: having proposed measures to restrict imports on that occasion, he had added: 'When this phase is past, we can reverse the process.' But, alas, it was not now to prove so easy to do that. In his own mind he had formerly come to favour some degree of autarky as the *sine qua non* for domestic experiments in full employment policy. But the autarkists and trade controllers were now in the saddle. Even among his close followers there were those who, so far from rejoicing at his judgement of what the change of American attitude now rendered possible and expedient, were disappointed and shocked, as well as sceptical. It was going to prove harder to de-indoctrinate them than it had been to indoctrinate them with the baleful creed of economic nationalism.

Besides broad principles, there was a great mass of detail to be handled. There was the question of goods in the pipeline and the disposal of surplus stores, military and civilian. The pipeline was a large item; in the case of certain commodities, such as wheat, which was assigned to the British out of stocks, the pipeline might not be more than five or six weeks; in other cases it might be more than a year, extending from the placing of the order at a factory to delivery in Britain. The military stores belonged to a large number of categories. These computations were exceedingly complex. Mr Frank Lee, with his wonderful tenacity and grasp of detail, laboured for many weeks with Mr E. G. Collado and Professor Angell, and achieved solutions helpful to Britain. Keynes kept track of all the complicated discussions. On the whole, the British thought that they had a very fair deal.

Finally, there was the burning question of the total amount of the loan. Keynes had originally asked for $6 billion as a gift; but later, when it appeared that a gift was out of the question, the British settled down to pressing for a somewhat lower figure. Estimates had to be made of the prospective balance of payments, relief from concessions on pipeline items, the state of the reserve, etc., etc. In the end, Mr Clayton did not feel that Congress could be persuaded to grant more than $4 billion. Mr Vinson was rather more apprehensive of Congressional opposition. He thought that $3½ billion was the largest sum for which a watertight case could be made. These two figures were put to the President, who, adopting a time-honoured expedient, decided on the figure of $3¾ billion, which was embodied in the Agreement.[7]

During all this time acute difficulties were experienced with the Government at home. They still hankered after a gift or an interest-free loan, and were troubled about many points of principle and detail, particularly in regard to the 'strings'. They were unable to shake off Keynes's initial optimism; they did not credit the reports of the basic American attitude; they were reluctant to face the rigours of convertibility and an open commercial policy.

Certain difficulties may have been caused also by Keynes's extreme flexibility of mind. He was always ready to consider new expedients hitherto unthought of, whether they were put up by the Americans or devised by himself. He rightly felt that he had such a comprehensive and detailed knowledge of the situation that he could readily assess the bearing, for good or ill, of some wholly new proposal. To ordinary men what is novel is thereby suspicious. Even his colleagues

7. To this must be added $650 million on account of pipeline goods.

in Washington, still more the Government at home, were taken aback when he suddenly accepted a proposal, which had not previously been discussed, and then wanted to push on to the next item of business. His own versatility made him cocksure; new ideas streamed from him, and he was ready to decide one way or the other with a speed that baffled Americans and British alike. What was his vexation when, having devised a new gadget, about which he was abundantly clear that it would be greatly to our interest, long cables came back from London expressing doubt and refusing authority. He had the feeling that we were repeatedly letting slip advantageous opportunities because of the lack of understanding of those across the water. His idea was that any plan should be accepted that was reasonable in itself, whether or not it conformed to preconceived ideas.

At the end of each day's work, he took his papers back to the hotel. The next morning, lying in bed, he drafted the cables that should be sent home upon the points that had come up on the preceding day. He arrived at his morning meeting with his British colleagues with these cables already typed. He had explained the points at issue and formulated proposals. When the British studied these drafts together, he was always ready to accept amendments and showed no pride of authorship. The problem arose as to what kind of cables to send. If one sent a long cable, explaining all the points of detail, one exposed a large flank and knew that one would receive in reply another long cable, perhaps misunderstanding many of the points, so that the discussion across the water would become ever more tangled. But if one sent shorter cables, that was unsatisfactory also; those at home sought fuller information. It appears that on the whole his cables were too brilliant, mingling lengthy arguments of remorseless logic with sparkling coruscations, and they tended to confuse those who received them.

In the course of the proceedings Professor Robbins went

home for a fortnight to Britain to give an oral account of what was going on. This visit was helpful. Professor Robbins stated the whole position with the utmost fullness and believed that what he had said was understood. Yet it was to prove difficult to convey a thorough comprehension to those in London. Identical words spoken there and in Washington seemed to mean different things. For a week or two relations were smoother, but soon the bothers recurred.

There is no doubt that in this period Keynes approached the point of exhaustion. He had to use all his resources of ingenuity and dialectic to win assent for what he conceived to be his instructions, even beyond his own real conviction. Then, when he reported home, he found much misunderstanding. He seemed to have lost the confidence of those in London. He was fighting a lone battle. There was overwhelming evidence that it would be exceedingly difficult to get any vote of money through Congress. It was absolutely vital to get this money. Yet the British at home persisted in drawing red herrings across the path, making proposals which had no chance whatever of success and failing to appreciate the implications of the great policy of cooperation to which, under Article VII, we were committed. Not only had he to get the loan, but he had to force those in London to take it on the only conditions possible, and there were long periods when it seemed that he would not succeed. Yet he knew that the British must have the money and had no alternative plan. There was also a time factor; it was needful to bring the fruits of these negotiations to Parliament sufficiently soon for the Agreement to be passed and the Bretton Woods decisions ratified before the end of December.[8]

Hard pressed at last and faced with final decision, the British Government had resort to a new expedient. It occurred to them to think that they had better send someone to check over for them what had been happening in

8. Congress had made American participation in the international institutions conditional upon other members joining them by this date.

Washington. Accordingly they instructed Sir Edward Bridges to proceed to the U.S. Bridges had become Permanent Secretary to the Treasury[9] on the retirement of Sir Richard Hopkins earlier in the year. They could not have chosen a better man. Sir Edward Bridges, as Secretary to the War Cabinet, had stood very high on the list of those responsible for British victory. His work exceeded the normal powers of human endurance. He took no rest and had knowledge of every aspect of our great war organization. At two o'clock in the morning he was still ready to read a great file of papers, and, after half an hour of study, he could dictate a Minute upon them, which was as fresh and lucid as though he were beginning the day's work.

Among the Americans this move created the greatest offence. They knew the consummate ability with which Keynes had stated the British case. They had come to have the highest regard for him and for Lord Halifax. If at moments they were nervous when Keynes let his imagination take wing, there was always Lord Halifax at his side, with his feet firmly planted on the earth, whose very lack of knowledge of financial detail gave his support the weight of common sense. The Americans could not conceive that the British could be better represented than they had been by Keynes and Lord Halifax, and they regarded the action of the British Government in sending another emissary as a slight upon them. Accordingly, they got together and made a resolve that whatever facts or figures or arguments Bridges produced, they would make no concessions to him. It was a touching tribute by the Americans to these two men who had won their admiration and affection. Bridges reported home that there was no chance of further concessions, and the British Government gave its assent to the terms which had been negotiated.

Subsequent events have made it unnecessary to reply to the criticism that we did not need any assistance from the United States at this time. That the Loan was inadequate

9. This is the senior position in the British Civil Service.

may be granted, but this is not a criticism of those who negotiated it. American generosity was stretched to what at that point was its limit. Doubters may read the protracted hearings of the Congressional committees on the subject.[10]

The verdict of history is likely to be that the best was done that could have been done with the knowledge then available and in the atmosphere then prevailing. Controversy may continue on the subordinate question of whether Keynes was too optimistic in judging on the data at his disposal that the Loan might well see us through. The view, however, that the Loan was clearly quite inadequate cannot be sustained. That some supplementation would in any case have been necessary may well be true, but exaggerated ideas have recently been common. It is interesting to observe that Britain's total adverse balance of payments on current account in 1946, 1947 and 1948 together amounted to £1,130 million, while the total of the American and Canadian Loans was £1,250 million. In the last half of 1948 Britain had almost achieved an over-all balance on current account. The first impression given by these figures, of course, requires correction. It was clearly understood by the Americans that part of the Loan might have to be used to finance the sterling area deficit, if any, additional to that of Britain herself. Furthermore, although the difference between the over-all deficit and the hard-currency deficit was discussed in the Washington talks, the full magnitude of the problem of 'unrequited' British exports to soft-currency areas may not have been envisaged. It would have been rather difficult, however, to have asked the Americans to give more than was needed to finance the over-all deficit.

In my own opinion the Loan would have gone much further in bringing Britain to solvency if certain grievous mistakes had not been made. These are for the judgement of the future economic historian, but it is desirable to refer

10. Hearings before the Committee on Banking and Currency, U.S. Senate, on S. J. Res. 138, 5–20 March 1946. Ditto, U.S. House of Representatives, on H. J. Res. 311 and S. J. Res. 138, 14 May–7 June 1946.

to them in order to give material for a fair verdict on the achievement of our negotiators.

1. In the years immediately following, the British Government countenanced and planned domestic capital outlay on a far greater scale than was consistent with the kind of effective export drive that was necessary if the Loan was to see us through. It was impossible to free our industries to meet hard-currency orders when they were loaded with such heavy orders for capital reconstruction at home and in other parts of the sterling area. It is fair to add that in so far as the influence of American opinion was wafted across the Atlantic it was favourable to capital reconstruction here. It should have been firmly and continuously stated in public, both in the United States and Britain, that the Loan was not on a scale adequate to finance large industrial reconstruction, but was designed rather to finance urgent requirements for the import of consumable goods during the period in which British industry was transformed, with minimum expense, from the production of warlike goods to those required in our export markets.

2. Britain, in loyalty to her commitments to the other United Nations, continued to maintain large expenditures overseas. These should have been cut more quickly and more drastically.

3. The most crucial question was that of the 'sterling balances'. Keynes may have tended in Washington to underrate the difficulty of negotiating satisfactory settlements. In the immediately following period the British authorities should have strongly held it in mind that, if they were unable to reach perfectly watertight agreements with all our creditors before the date of sterling convertibility, they would freeze all the balances so as to make it totally impossible for them to be drawn down when convertibility was established. If, owing to unavoidable delays, it appeared that the freezing operation could not be carried out in time, Britain should have asked the United States to agree to postpone the date of convertibility in accordance with

the Agreement,[11] with a view to this freezing being carried out as quickly as possible. The British authorities may have acted with the best intentions for the common good and for the implementation of the Agreement, but their policy was, in my judgement, foolish and wrongful. I would add that in my own opinion it was unwise of the British authorities not to allow the delegates in Washington to include in the Loan Agreement a specific provision for the freezing of sterling balances on the day of convertibility. American instinct was surely right on this issue and the British wrong.

4. As soon as the Loan was through Congress the British should have entered at once into the closest cooperation with the Americans to secure the earliest possible coming into effect of the Bretton Woods arrangement and to combine with the Americans in putting pressure on other countries to make their currencies also convertible at the earliest possible date. The British policy of bilateral monetary agreements, even as liberalized by transferable accounts, does not appear to me to have been a helpful step towards inaugurating the full régime of the International Monetary Fund.

As one who has, during the last twenty-eight years, studied the thoughts of Keynes very closely, I record it as my opinion that he would have pushed very hard in all four directions had he lived. In regard to the second and third points, he made no secret of his opinions before he died. In regard to the first, he had certainly shown anxiety about over-lavish expenditure at home, while conscious of the need for manufacturing industry to have the best equipment. He did not have time to focus his mind upon all the problems consequent upon the Loan settlement.

When the long-drawn-out tussle was over and a final compromise was agreed upon, Keynes, who had fought toughly and sometimes fiercely, thought it fitting to pay tribute to the American team. He summoned up his powers of gracious compliment. The press noted his reference to

11. See p. 717 above.

Mr Clayton and Mr Vinson as 'great gentlemen'. He had a way of underlining the real virtues of his opponents with discrimination, so that they remembered his words as something more than conventional tributes. He also organized a dinner-party for the whole of the British staff employed in the negotiations, including secretaries and typists; he congratulated them upon their work, making them feel that they had played quite as important a part as he in achieving a satisfactory result.

### 4

It appeared that he would arrive in England in time to intervene in the debate in the House of Lords and he busied himself on the boat preparing a speech. When he landed on 17 December the Commons debate was already over. It had been pushed on quickly, partly because it was desirable to have access to the Loan as early as possible, and partly because, if Britain was to become an initial member of the International Monetary Fund and the International Bank, adhesion before 1 January 1946 was necessary. If the Commons debate on Bretton Woods had been disappointing, how much more so was that on the Loan Agreement. The undercurrent of anti-American feeling had become stronger, and the ignorance in regard to Britain's predicament and the Bretton Woods plans was, if anything, more profound. The story was current that he was asked by a reporter if the rumour was true that he had made Britain the forty-ninth state of the United States of America. 'No such luck,' Keynes replied.

He went to the Lords that afternoon to listen and discuss procedure. He was appalled by the misunderstandings that were rife. The speech which he had prepared on the boat clearly would not do; it presupposed some modicum of knowledge. He would have to begin again from the beginning and compose a new speech. But there was little time. As he drove to the House of Lords the next day he had to

sort out on his knee the various notes which were hot from
the efficient Mrs Stephens's typewriter. To his mother, who
watched him, it seemed impossible that an ordered speech
could emerge in a few minutes' time from this maze of
jottings.

In the event it was a graceful and persuasive speech, and
was deemed a truly great performance. He handled an
embarrassing situation beautifully; it was embarrassing because all knew that, although not a Minister of the Crown,
he had been personally responsible for the terms of the
Agreement. To magnify their virtues was to praise himself.
He tried to convey to the House the difference of outlook
and mood on the other side of the Atlantic. He showed very
effectively in a few sentences how utterly inadequate, and
indeed ludicrous, was the alternative policy proposed. Of
his own work he spoke in terms of faint praise, and not all
their Lordships were generous enough to understand that
he was not thereby damning his own handiwork, but dis-
playing some degree of modesty. It was a very elegant performance and certainly showed no decay of powers; it was
brief and only dealt in a cursory way with the main topics;
nevertheless, it made a profound impression and moved
opinion. The Americans who received copies were delighted
to find him speaking in terms so different from those of
Washington and using some of their arguments. Is it possible that, had our Constitution provided him with the
opportunity to propound the case in all the strength of its
detail for three days, as he had done in America, the British
would have begun to understand something of the true
nature of the situation and have acted more wisely in the
years that followed?

It is satisfactory that this great man had an opportunity
to make a lasting impression upon the minds of the Second
Chamber. Testimony to the consummate brilliance of the
speech has come from members of all parties. The biographer must be allowed a rueful comment. The speech was
indeed an excellent one, compounded of penetrating

analysis, tact and sagacity. But Keynes had been talking in this style about matters of grave importance to the well-being of the country for some twenty-seven years. Why had his words not been listened to with equal respect during all this long period? He was not an unknown figure living in a garret. After 1919 he had world-wide fame. He wrote and talked and lectured to academic groups and public groups, tirelessly and unremittingly. The country passed through many grave crises and its affairs remained in an unsatisfactory condition; he had views, too, about the European situation and about the disastrous effects likely to flow from the world slump and about how to overcome that slump. Yet all this wisdom was spilled upon the ground, and the nation struggled along without his guidance until the second war. The speech in December 1945 was excellent, but no more excellent than his utterances for twenty-seven long years. Were the mighty ones in the land merely indifferent to wisdom, or were they incapable of detecting it, except when it was adorned with a coronet?

He wrote to Lord Halifax giving him a gloomy account of the state of opinion in Parliament. There had been much misapprehension about the nature of the proposed Agreement. There were also in both the principal parties strong prejudices against the kind of settlement proposed. A section of the Socialists detected too definite a smell of *laissez-faire*. A section of the Conservatives were worried about Imperial Preference. As usual, he was able to find some consolation.

*J. M. Keynes to Lord Halifax*, 1 January 1946

*

Nevertheless it soon became obvious that both the above sections were minorities in their own parties and cut no ice whatever with the general public. The general public was upset solely because they were being told by those who ought to know, that, after all their past *and present* sufferings, they were being given a raw deal by their old comrades in U.S. As usual, there was not the smallest necessity for the party leaders to run away.

My strong belief is (though you may all be justified, as usual, in saying I am too optimistic) that the line I took in my speech met with an immediate response from genuine public opinion – more than was immediately obvious – and a lot of people quickly became rather ashamed of the way they had been talking. This was certainly so in the House of Lords. There cannot have been for many years such a crowded and excited sitting. Mingling in the division Lobby and as the House broke up, it seemed to me clear that practically everyone was voting Aye out of conviction, and not merely to avoid a constitutional crisis, and that, if there had been a free vote with no one abstaining, the majority would have been large.

Cranborne, by the way, made a most masterly speech by way of getting out of a silly situation. A pure Cecilian utterance, which A.J.B.(whose shade one could feel hovering near) could not have done so well . . . The combination of his diffidence with some inherent quality of dignity and authority, which few today can reach, produces a remarkable effect. Old Lord Salisbury, as beautiful and pure a picture as ever, was there to hear him. However, I am prejudiced. I have never in my life been able to resist a Cecil.

One final conclusion. My impression is that the *fait accompli* is now being accepted, at any rate in official circles and in the Bank of England, as something which must be loyally and sincerely carried out. I think you can reassure the Americans on this, if the public reception of the programme here leads them to doubt it. Political trouble there will certainly be, for the Cabinet is a poor, weak thing. But I am hopeful that the technicians will now turn their technique in the agreed direction.

For me, I think the time has come for me to slip out of the Treasury, if not suddenly, at least steadily. When I return to London from the country, I shall have to reach a clear notion what happens next. Being of a resigning temperament, I shall not last long in this *galère* in any case; so I had better go when I go genial and friendly.

The following memorandum written by Keynes in March on his return from his next visit to the United States is of some interest.

There had been considerable canvassing against the Loan in certain British quarters, both with members of the American delegation when they were in London and by British visitors to the United States. This was having quite a serious effect. It was, however, largely overcome by the firmness with which Mr Winston Churchill at every opportunity, public and private, took the opposite line. He told all his friends that he was in favour of the Loan, that we needed it and that the argument against lending to a Socialist Government was a wrong and invalid argument, with which he would have nothing to do. I am sure that this had a great effect in many quarters.

Keynes was deeply depressed at the state of opinion in Britain; it seemed to augur so ill for effectiveness in grappling with the situation. I had been watching his work and shared his distress. I ventured to take up my pen and write a little pamphlet,[12] protesting with some vehemence against Britain's apathy and potential backsliding in regard to Article VII. I told him of what I was doing, and he warned me that I should find the public 'invincibly ignorant', but supposed it was none the less one's duty to try to enlighten it. In an attempt to gain attention, I allowed myself to become somewhat cross and had qualms that my tone was too testy. I sent him a proof.

*J. M. Keynes to R. F. Harrod*, 28 January 1946

I like this very much indeed. There is nothing in form or substance which I want to criticize. It would, in my judgement, do us no harm in America if it were to be published at once. On the contrary, I think it would do good.

His main comment reflects his newly found enthusiasm for the Commercial Policy side of the international plans.

Any criticisms I have relate, not to what you have said, but to what you have not said. Chiefly, I think there is a certain want of balance in the attention you give to Bretton Woods compared with the International Trade Organization. I imagine the reason for this is that you wrote most of it before you had the text of I.T.O. in front of you. But the result is that the proposals of I.T.O., which you recognize as rounding off your argument, do

12. *A Page of British Folly*, publ. Macmillan & Co. 1946.

not get enough attention in detail to make much impact on the reader. Thus the paper reads too much like a defence of Bretton Woods and not sufficiently as an advocacy of the rounded whole policy, which is what you are really after . . .

Somewhat earlier he had proposed to me that he should write an article for the *Economic Journal* on the prospective balance of payments of the United States. We agreed that he would have to defer publication until the British Loan was through Congress. He took immense pains with the article, correcting and recorrecting many times, and checking his figures on his next visit to the United States. The final version reached me by post, two days after his death, in an envelope addressed in his own handwriting.

This article has a special interest, quite apart from being his last published work. He took the optimistic view that the creditor position of the United States was not likely to be as oppressive as most people feared. It has since seemed that his prognostication was, for once, at fault, but caution is necessary. One must remember his telescopic tendency in prediction, a counterpart to his own quickness of decision; so often what he prophesied did not come to pass so quickly as he foretold, but after a time-lag. He made an inadequate allowance for the slow development of events. He may yet be in the right about the U.S. balance. Only when ten years have passed will it be possible to give judgement on this article. He did not profess to be diagnosing the immediate future, but the likely long-run trend.

Another point of interest was his reaffirmation of faith in the eternal verities.

I find myself moved, not for the first time, to remind contemporary economists that the classical teaching embodied some permanent truths of great significance, which we are liable to overlook because we associate them with other doctrines, which we cannot now accept without much qualification.

Referring to the American proposals he wrote:

It shows how much modernist stuff, gone wrong and turned

sour and silly, is circulating in our system, also incongruously mixed, it seems, with age-old poisons, that we should have given so doubtful a welcome to this magnificent objective approach which a few years ago we should have regarded as offering incredible promise of a better scheme of things.

He was in Cambridge in February, and Professor Robertson,[13] who had taken over his old Monday Evening Club, invited him to come and address it. He was among old friends now and the choice spirits among the present generation of undergraduates, and there is no doubt that he spoke from the heart.

He made a forthright plea for the multilateral system. It was a lengthy academic discourse. He was assuming that the Americans would adhere to their offer of a sound international system and not retreat into isolationism. He emphasized that the sterling area could only be saved by Bretton Woods. Organized discrimination by Britain was not only not a plausible programme, but it was also a wicked programme. Other countries also would have the power to discriminate. Britain could only gain advantage where she dominated the market, and that was in a small part of the field only. The programme meant economic war with a large part of the world just when Britain was at her weakest and unable to use financial inducements.

To suggest that we had agreed to a restoration of nineteenth-century *laissez-faire* implied a grossly ignorant misunderstanding. The documents were stuffed with provisions for elasticity, requiring international cooperation. Furthermore, there was value in the old classical doctrines; there are in fact deep currents and there is an invisible hand, although it operates more slowly than the classical economists thought. Strains of adjustment were only intolerable if not eased. The long-run mechanisms of the classical system must be allowed to work; but it would only be allowed to work in the long run if short-run aids were supplied.

13. Now Professor of Political Economy in Cambridge in succession to Professor Pigou.

Economic liberalism was consonant with British traditions. A totalitarian unit would have to be large, and the British Empire was entirely unsuitable.[14]

He was making slow progress in this formidable task of re-educating Britain on trade policy; his work in promoting the arts was making more visible headway. 20 February was the opening night of Covent Garden under the new auspices. The *Sleeping Beauty* (Diaghilev's *Sleeping Princess*) had been chosen. Margot Fonteyn would dance the Princess, while Robert Helpmann was doubling the parts of Carabosse and the Prince. It was the Diaghilev conception with certain minor changes. Oliver Messel had designed some admirable *décor* and Keynes's old friend, Constant Lambert, was to conduct. The King and Queen, Queen Mary, the Princesses Elizabeth and Margaret were coming; and a great concourse of people of fashion, of ballet lovers and of the artistic world would be there. How lovely it would be to see Covent Garden in all its beauty on this great occasion. Were we beginning to be able to turn our backs on the grim squalors of war?

Keynes, as Chairman, accompanied by Lydia, was to receive the royal guests. Unhappily he had a slight attack and had to retire to his box, leaving Lydia to hold the fort. He revived in time to enjoy the evening.

The performance was beginning now. He heard Tchaikovsky's splendid trumpets which he knew so well, and the march proceeded. He was still feeling tired, and he closed his eyes ... He thought of Diaghilev's production. There had been a princess, so light and quick, so charming and piquant, so gay and unexpected. His whole being had been filled with joy and exhilaration. But somehow, as he watched her in his memory, the plot became confused. It seemed to be not the princess but Prince Florimund who was under a spell. On the face of the princess was an expression of

14. This brief account of Lord Keynes's address is derived from very full notes taken at the meeting by Mr H. G. Johnson of Jesus College.

gravity and loving anxiety; she was a gay princess, but also an attendant spirit, a nurse, who applied ice-packs and administered medicines. By the spell she must be eternally vigilant; if her attention failed even for a second, the prince would die and his people would be plunged in ruin.

He drew his attention back to what was proceeding. It was not *that* princess; it was Margot Fonteyn; she was dancing divinely – but it could not be quite the same. He no longer had the feeling of joy and exhilaration. Yet he had a deeply satisfying feeling, not present at that other performance, which gave him solid comfort. What was that? Oh yes, it came from the fact that it was through his own clever contriving and careful management that Margot Fonteyn was now dancing before the King and Queen of England. But was it really he himself that was the cause of all this? Surely the true cause was that other performance twenty-five years ago; because that performance had taken place then, this one was taking place now. That other performance had cast its spell upon him and determined his future course of action. It was a pleasant thing to be able to look back upon one's life and find in it symmetry and purpose fulfilled.

# [15]

## The Last Phase

### I

I WAS driving with him along the Thames Embankment on 12 February on a mission, which those of us who involved him in it may remember with regret. Tired from his exertions in America and heavily burdened with duties of the utmost importance, he was induced to devote all the energies of an afternoon to a dispute between the Royal Economic Society and the Royal Statistical Society. The latter body planned to establish a diploma and a certificate in statistics, which the former body viewed with suspicion. Keynes was heart and soul with the economists. The issues involved were less momentous than those of the American Loan negotiations, but in their own way they were exceedingly complex. Should a learned society issue diplomas? Should any institution which provided no instruction presume to examine? What would be the relation of such an award to those given by universities? And how would it be related to the Ministry of Education? At the root of the dispute was the economists' fear that this diploma would carry weight with governmental or business appointing bodies, which were more and more on the lookout for experts in economic statistics, and that it would gain positions for persons who, while efficient in statistical calculations, were devoid of the background of economic understanding necessary for such advisers. Excellent and well-qualified economists, on the other hand, quite sufficiently adept at figures, might be excluded from advantageous positions by lack of the diploma. The questions of principle were complex and the facts were complex. Keynes absorbed them all at a short session in the afternoon, and, having proceeded to the rooms of the Statistical Society, deployed the case in a speech of

739

easy mastery. It was a fine performance. Were we really justified in taxing his energies at that time for this purpose?

During the drive from Royal Society to Royal Society, he remarked to me that he had an *embarras de richesse* in the coming weeks. He could either attend the first meeting of the nationalized Bank of England or go to Savannah for the first meeting of the International Monetary Fund and the International Bank. 'I expect that you will think the latter the more important,' I remarked. 'I am not at all sure about that,' he replied; 'important matters of principle and procedure, which will guide all future action, may be formulated at the Bank of England meeting, while I think that the Savannah meeting will be just a pleasant party.'

It may be that the word 'pleasant' enlarged itself in his mind during the following days. He would enjoy seeing his American friends again. The beauties of Georgia, with its magnificent trees and Spanish moss, called to him; the very word Savannah had an appeal. Perhaps he would prolong his stay and have a little holiday.

All turned out quite differently. There was a clash of wills and bitter frustration. Mr Vinson, still Secretary of the Treasury, was to take the chair. We must dwell for a moment upon him. It is to be emphasized that this distinguished American was a friend of Britain. Although his figure for the Loan had been the smaller one, he was anxious that we should be assisted; he was keenly alive to possible difficulties in Congress and thought it better to have a moderate figure that was beyond challenge than a larger one which might court defeat. In the great battle in Congress over the Loan, which took place in the spring of 1946, he worked sedulously for the British cause; both before the Committee of the Senate and that of the House of Representatives – in the latter case for four long days – he submitted himself to gruelling cross-examination on our behalf; Mr Clayton, Mr Eccles and others did likewise; the two stout volumes of evidence [1] are a moving account of the

1. See p. 727 above.

heavy labour undertaken by these eminent Americans for our country; they should have been given wide publicity in Britain.

Vinson was the friend also of the International Monetary Fund and International Bank. Here again he had anxieties related to Congress. It was true that the Fund and Bank had now been passed into American law, but occasions might arise on which renewed Congressional support would be necessary. Moreover, proceedings in these institutions might in a subtle way affect the prospects of the British Loan, for they would all be regarded as part and parcel of America's new policy of economic internationalism, and undesirable developments in one field might damage goodwill in another.

A lawyer by profession, he was not an expert on the money question. His Secretaryship of the Treasury was likely to be a transitional phase in his career. To his mind it may have seemed that, these institutions having been set up, the task was now a relatively simple one, namely, to operate them in a businesslike way in accordance with the principles that had been agreed upon. Keynes saw the matter in an entirely different light. Formal agreement to the institutions was only a precarious beginning, and the main work had still to be done. That was to win the confidence of the nations for the institutions. If the Bretton Woods project was to come to life, nations, one and all, would have to make drastic alterations in their external economic policies. A most fundamental change of heart would be needed. Keynes knew well how gigantic the obstacles were. This winning of confidence would be a most subtle and difficult process, and much would depend on correct behaviour by the institutions in regard to what might superficially seem to be small points. It would by no means be sufficient for the Fund and the Bank to function in accordance with their Charters. That could happen and yet the institutions could be side-tracked and become of little importance. The nations might easily render them of no avail by formal compliance and practical neglect. What was needed, if internationalism was to replace the economic nationalism still rampant and growing and supported by what seemed dire necessity, was that the Fund and the Bank should come to occupy the centre of the picture and make the nations feel that it was important to cooperate with them fully in all their detailed plans. Thus their future was a matter still of great anxiety in Keynes's mind; he saw pitfalls and dangers on every side, which Vinson, with his smaller knowledge of such matters, could not be expected to appreciate in detail.

Personal relations were important in the drama which followed. Keynes had become fond of Vinson. He always referred to him in amiable terms. When, after the Loan negotiations, he had called him a 'great gentleman', he had meant what he said. If he had some misgivings, that was due to Vinson's lack of sufficient experience and not to any feeling of personal hostility or suspicion of his character. American admirers of Keynes, it is true, who had watched Vinson in the previous negotiations, had some feeling that Vinson did not appreciate Keynes's stature and dealt with him too roughly. Not that any marked deference by Vinson would have been in place. In the context Keynes was a professional negotiator, like any other, and it was not to be expected, and he did not expect, that he should be exempt from the rough and tumble which was proper to such proceedings. But there are fine shades. Without abating a jot of one's rights in speaking as negotiator to negotiator, and as equal to equal, there may be some subtle difference in the mode of speech, if one believes oneself to be addressing a great figure of the age.

> Ah, did you once see Shelley plain,
> And did he stop and speak to you?

Vinson's main interests had been in other fields and there was no reason why he should have had a proper appreciation of the great economist. But, however we may feel about his bearing to Keynes, it is certain that the latter was entirely unruffled by it. His kindly feelings to Vinson were undisturbed. It was not his wont to be offended by rough handling. Was he not an old College Wall who had revelled in the game? He did not mind having his limbs prised apart.

The same was not true of Vinson. He was the one American of those important in our negotiations who did not come to relish Keynes's banter and sharp sayings. He took them much amiss. At Bretton Woods Keynes had rebuked him on the ground that politics came too much into the American point of view. He felt this to be unfair. Then there was Keynes's concluding speech about lawyers in the United States; Vinson was a lawyer. During the Loan negotiations there were passages. At one of the meetings of the Big Four, Vinson, not yet fully realizing the magnitude of Britain's need, made a proposal which Keynes deemed to be altogether inadequate. 'Won't you first put that up to the Government of Guatemala?' he replied. Lord Halifax was there to come swiftly into the breach with consoling words of a more deferential kind. There was another brush, which did not end so happily. Keynes did not normally take an active part in the work of the Committee on Commercial Policy during the Loan negotiations, but he came to the meetings fairly regularly, largely as a learner. Speaking out of turn and without full knowledge of the previous discussions, he made what he felt to be an appropriate comment on certain American proposals for dealing with international cartels. 'This plan seems principally designed to make a paradise for the lawyers.' Vinson burst out with harsh and angry vehemence. Keynes had no right to make remarks of that kind; they were insulting and intolerable. There was, in fact, a scene.

Thus, there was a paradox in their mutual relations. The hard-bitten man of affairs with his long experience of the dust and heat of battle in the Law Courts, in Congress and in public service was extremely sensitive below the skin, while the fastidious intellectual, the don, the intimate of the most refined and cultivated circle of our age, could take hard knocks and blows in practical affairs without any sense of injury. So it may not have occurred to him that his formidable opponent required gentler handling. It would have been so easy to accord him special treatment to fit the case.

It is not yet time for the historian to presume to give a final verdict about the various strands of thought in the mind of Vinson when he was preparing for the Savannah meeting. Yet it is necessary to our purpose to make some assessment, and a surmise may be justified. Like Keynes, he probably anticipated a fairly straightforward affair; in place of the idea of a 'pleasant party', he may have had that of a businesslike and streamlined conference. There were certain points at issue which it was essential from the American point of view, and above all in order to keep Congress in the right frame of mind, to settle in a certain way. The British Loan was not yet secure, and Congress would continue to need careful and tactful handling. Thus, his intentions were thoroughly upright and praiseworthy.

It does not derogate in the least from this if we add that there may have been a touch of personal pride. This was to be *his* Conference. There is a tide in the affairs of men. His position in the Treasury was not likely to be a long-lasting one. Whatever he may have thought himself, there were others who, thinking for him judged that he might rise to higher things. Might he become Chief Justice? Might he even perhaps become President of the United States? His supporters would wish him to show his mettle by having to his credit the most efficiently conducted International Congress on record. Keynes himself had words of praise when all was over. Some of them were no doubt the product of conventional necessity; but when he said of Vinson's handling of the press. 'I have never taken part in a congress where this, sometimes difficult, task has been so well performed,' he was obviously making a genuine point.

Thus, Vinson aimed at an efficient conference. He had it in mind that he would have on his hands this tiresome person, Keynes, who was always dangerous and liable to make trouble. He must be handled absolutely firmly. There must be no nonsense this time. This personal preconception may have closed his ears, when the time came, to arguments which, if not thus pre-conditioned, he would have accepted as reasonable. Instructions based on these ideas were given to the American team.

Before the proceedings opened, a fact became known which caused great disappointment among the British, although with careful forethought it might have been foreseen. Harry White had not achieved that perfectly good understanding with Mr Vinson that he had had with Mr Morgenthau. There was his difficult side, and his aggressive and obstreperous tendencies were not likely to endear him to a chief of Mr Vinson's temperament. This lack of complete harmony may have contributed to the bad atmosphere of the Conference.

The cause of the disappointment was, however, different. It was learnt that Harry White would not be the Managing Director of the International Monetary Fund. Keynes had always tended to take it for granted that he would be, and had come to repose confidence in his outlook and his vigour; he felt that under White the Fund would be in safe hands. The reason for this decision was plain. It seemed necessary that the International Bank should have an American President. The total paid-up capital was small, and it was already clearly understood that it would have to supplement its resources by borrowing in the open market; in practice this meant borrowing in Wall Street. Therefore it was essential that Wall Street should have complete confidence in the management of the Bank. The Fund had its independent resources and would not depend directly on the goodwill of American investors. Therefore, if one or other of these institutions was to have an American head, it must clearly be the Bank. It would obviously be exorbitant for both heads to be American. Thus Harry White was ruled out by inexorable logic from the Managing Directorship of the Fund.

Another point which Keynes had tended to take for granted was that the Fund and the Bank would be located in New York. The British at Bretton Woods had reserved their position about the location of the Fund being in the United States at all. But this reservation must be deemed to have been waived by the passage of the Bretton Woods Act through Parliament in December.

. . . In New York they would be in the daily contacts which can be provided by a great centre of international finance; they would be sufficiently removed from the politics of Congress and the nationalistic whispering gallery of the Embassies and Legations of Washington; and they would probably be sufficiently near to the seat of UNO to be able to cooperate closely on the economic and statistical side of their work with the Economic and Social Council.

Passing through New York on our way to the Conference we discussed these ideas at the Federal Reserve Bank of New York, and found them in complete sympathy. No rumour had reached them of any site other than New York. No rumour reached us until a day or two before we left Washington for Savannah, when Mr Vinson told me that the American Delegation had decided that both institutions should be placed in Washington and that this was a final decision the merits of which they were not prepared to discuss. The U.S. Administration, he said, was entitled to decide for themselves what location within the U.S. was to be preferred.

At Savannah we soon found that a majority of the other Delegations (China, Poland and perhaps some South Americans were on the other side) shared our view that this was an unfortunate, indeed a very bad, decision. It also appeared that it was primarily a personal decision of Mr Vinson supported only by the Federal Reserve Board (which would find itself strengthened against the New York Federal Reserve Bank by the Washington location), and not supported on its merits by the rest of the American Delegation. Unfortunately Mr Vinson, before warning us or seeking our views, had thought fit to take his proposition direct to the President and to obtain his authority to make this an absolute instruction to the American Delegation from which they were not to be free to depart in any circumstances. This made it impossible for Mr Clayton, for example, to listen to our arguments, however much he recognized their force.[2]

Mr Vinson opened the proceedings in a dignified speech, which touched on man's progress in monetary matters, culminating in the present development. Keynes thought something in a lighter vein would be appropriate to the occasion. His mind reverted to Covent Garden, where he had been only a week ago. A christening with good fairies and propitious gifts! That would do. But the grim figure of Robert Helpmann came insistently before his mind. Yes, he ought to say something about Carabosse also; without her the speech would be too sentimental; besides he could use her for pointing a very necessary moral.

Mr Secretary Vinson, Governors, Alternates, Advisers – and Observers, –

Like several others here present, I have been intimately concerned with what will, I think, always be known as the Bretton Woods plan. The gestation has been long; the lusty twins are seriously overdue; they will have put on, I hope, as a result, a weight and strength which will do credit to their mixed and collective parentage. At any rate it is a privilege I would not have readily foregone to be present at the hour of birth, in some capacity whether as Governor or governess, along with the midwives, nurses, doctors and parsons ready to christen (and I shall always hold to the view that the christening has been badly done and that the names of the twins should have been reversed).

Hidden behind veils or beards of Spanish moss, I do not doubt that the usual fairies will be putting in an appearance at the christening, carrying appropriate gifts. What gifts and blessings are likely to be most serviceable to the twins, whom (rightly or wrongly) we have decided to call Master Fund and Miss Bank?

The first fairy should bring, I suggest, a Joseph's coat, a many coloured raiment to be worn by these children as a perpetual reminder that they belong to the whole world and that their sole

2. Memorandum by Lord Keynes on Savannah, 27 March 1946.

allegiance is to the general good, without fear or favour to any particular interest. Pious words exceedingly difficult to fulfil. There is scarcely any enduring successful experience yet of an international body which has fulfilled the hopes of its progenitors. Either an institution has become diverted to be the instrument of a limited group, or it has been a puppet of sawdust through which the breath of life does not blow. Every incident and adjunct of our new-born institutions must be best calculated to emphasize and maintain their truly international character and purpose.

The second fairy, being up-to-date, will bring perhaps a box of mixed vitamins, A, B, C, D, and all the rest of the alphabet. The children may faithfully wear their many-coloured raiment, yet themselves show pale, delicate faces. Energy and a fearless spirit, which does not shelve and avoid difficult issues, but welcomes them and is determined to solve them, is what we must demand from our nurslings.

The third fairy, perhaps much older and not nearly so up-to-date, may, like the Pope with his cardinals, close the lips of our children with her hand and then open them again, invoking a spirit of wisdom, patience and grave discretion, so that, as they grow up, they will be the respected and safe recipients of confidences, of troubles and of perplexities, a reliable and prudent support to those who need them in all times of difficulty. If these institutions are to win the full confidence of the suspicious world, it must not only be, but appear, that their approach to every problem is absolutely objective and oecumenical, without prejudice or favour.

I am asking and hoping, you will see, a great deal.

I hope that Mr Kelchner has not made any mistake and that there is no malicious fairy, no Carabosse, whom he has overlooked and forgotten to ask to the party. For if so the curses which that bad fairy will pronounce will, I feel sure, run as follows: 'You two brats shall grow up politicians; your every thought and act shall have an *arrière-pensée*; everything you determine shall not be for its own sake or on its own merits but because of something else.'

If this should happen, then the best that could befall – and that is how it might turn out – would be for the children to fall into an eternal slumber, never to waken or be heard of again in the courts and markets of mankind.

Well, ladies and gentlemen, fairies or no fairies, this looks like being a very pleasant party and a happy christening, and let the omens be good.

Vinson assumed that Carabosse had been intended for himself and was extremely angry. Once again he took Keynes to task.

Keynes fought a hard rearguard action upon the question of the location, drawing heavily on his reserves of strength. While all will be inclined to attach importance to his intuition in such a matter, there may have been good points upon the other side. Did Keynes, with his close contacts and friends in New York, sufficiently appreciate the intense distrust which the main mass of Americans, throughout their vast country, entertains for that vast city? They would deem that, if these institutions were established there, they would be under the thumb of wicked bankers and international capitalists. The opinion of the Federal Reserve Bank of New York was of little value in this context. Even some of the British had doubts. At a certain point, Monsieur Gutt, seeing that Keynes was wearing himself out, advised him to desist.

The next question was of graver moment, and the verdict of history will surely be on the side of Keynes. The conduct of the institutions was to be in the hands of Boards of Executive Directors. The American plan was to have twelve Directors for each institution, all with Alternates, also on whole-time duty and high pay. This was at complete variance with Keynes's view. It was not simply that this involved gross over-staffing; it would paralyse the efficient working of the institutions. His conception was that, while there should be an efficient technical staff conducting research and responsible for day-to-day routine activities, policy decisions should be taken by a Board consisting of part-time Directors. The essence of his view was that the institutions should in effect be run by high officials in the Treasuries of the participating countries. Only so could the objectives and decisions of the Fund and Bank be integrated with those of the Treasuries of the principal nations. The main work of these Directors would lie at home; the British one might be the head of the Finance Division of the Treasury. They would bring to the counsels of the international institutions intimate knowledge of the current problems confronting their own governments and of the real, and sometimes secret, motives and objectives of their current policies. Only so could the decisions of the Fund be based upon realities. And when they went home, having bathed themselves anew in the spirit of internationalism, they would be impelled to do their best in all the details of the daily work there to deflect the policies of their own countries, wherever possible, towards the direction desired by the Fund. It would not be at all easy to wean Treasuries away from a nationalist outlook; it was always their duty to think primarily of their own people; yet in the long run national interest must be deemed to lie with the international interest. But it was difficult to have that always in the forefront of one's view. These visits would keep the international objectives alive in the minds of these officials. They would be drawing part of their salaries from the international bodies, and, as a matter of ordinary conscience, would not lend themselves to policies designed to frustrate the intentions of those bodies.

Thus both interests, the internationalist and the nationalist interests, would be served by the close intermingling of purpose and policy, which would result from the same people being responsible for national policy and for the policy of the Fund and the Bank. On the other hand, if full-time Directors were appointed, they would tend to operate in glorious isolation. They would, no doubt, have plenty of time to study the defalcations of the various nations, to chivvy them and to upbraid them. But they would not know what each nation was really doing, where the shoe pinched, what was the secret motive; they would soon be operating *in vacuo* and pass into the limbo of other international institutions. Meanwhile, the national governments would harden their hearts and follow courses of immediate expediency, while the enthusiasms of Bretton Woods passed into scarcely remembered history.

There is some analogy between this problem and the time-honoured question of whether the Cabinet should consist mainly of the heads of great departments or of Ministers without departmental duties. During the war there were always hot-heads to be found who argued that the War Cabinet should consist of half a dozen men with nothing else to do than to brood upon the general problems of the war. The wiser took a different view. Such a Cabinet would soon lose touch with what was really happening. While it might be useful to have one or two Ministers without portfolio, it was essential that the majority should be able to contribute the knowledge gained over a wide front by the manifold activities of their own departments, and to speak with the authority of men who were playing their assigned roles in winning the war.

Can anyone doubt that Keynes was in the right? And can it be doubted that the institutions have suffered in their early years from the adoption of the opposite policy?

The Americans, on their side, pleaded that if these institutions were to play significant roles, they would be very busy and require the constant attention of full-time Directors. Keynes found it hard to see wherein all this busy-ness would lie; on the contrary, he judged that these Directors would draw large salaries for very light tasks. The Americans seemed to envisage that they would have to give great attention every time a nation used its drawing rights. But this implied slipping back to the old ideas of the schoolmistress. When international order was restored, important matters requiring Fund decision, such as a change in the par of a currency, would only come up occasionally. They could be foreseen in advance. The technical staff would devote its time to amassing all relevant information, making forecasts and warning the Directors of likely difficulties. Of course, if the American view of continuous high-level super-vision were adopted, then, no doubt, the Directors could be kept busy – vainly and foolishly busy. Had it not been on the explicit undertaking by the Americans to drop their initial idea of the schoolmistress that the British had agreed to the non-Unitas version of the Fund? Now the Americans were slipping back into their old bad ways of thought. It is not surprising that Keynes was maddened.

Closely associated with this issue was the question of salaries. If the men were to be on full-time, they must be properly paid. The Americans pleaded that it was neces-sary to secure persons of the highest calibre and that they could only be attracted by high salaries. There could only be one salary scale, and if this scale seemed fabulous to some of the poorer nations, that was unfortunate. One must not jeopardize the institutions by cheeseparing economies. Keynes opposed these views with the utmost vigour. He claimed that these scales would bring discredit on the in-ternational bodies from the outset. Here were these persons voting themselves into cushy jobs at large salaries free of income tax.

He fought hard and bitterly, but it was in vain. The American view was predetermined, and this fact was the bitterest of all. It seemed clear to him that, if the voting by nations had been truly free, as befitted an international organization, he would have obtained a majority for his principal points; but at that juncture almost all the nations were prospective applicants for benefit of some kind from the United States. Rebellion was out of the question. The Americans were 'railroading' their decisions through the Conference.

Thus, before his eyes, the warning of his critics seemed to be coming true. It was not only the close followers of Lord Beaverbrook, but a large number of level-headed Englishmen, perhaps a majority, who had continually be-sought him to beware. 'What the Americans are trying to do', they argued, 'is to make you sign away Imperial Pre-

ference, and indeed in large measure to sign away the
British Empire itself, on the expectation of the prize of
American cooperation. But, when all has been signed away,
there will be no further question of cooperation. It will then
be just doing what the Americans say. You will see . . .' Now
he was seeing.

He had always argued back vigorously against this contention. Through all these years of close negotiation, on
Lend-Lease as well as on post-war plans, he had found the
Americans magnificently cooperative. They were always
ready to see the opposite point of view, and, if it was strongly
held, to agree to a compromise. The younger generation of
Americans were fine forward-looking men; isolationism
was a thing of the past; he knew what he was talking about;
he had had the experience. So he had argued. Now, at
Savannah, it seemed that all his fine protestations on behalf
of American goodwill and cooperativeness were belied. They
no longer discussed; they decided matters in advance. His
castles were falling around him.

He argued the points at issue to the full limit of his
strength. Only on the question of salaries did he carry his
opposition to a vote; the British voted alone.

Could he have carried his opposition further? Could he
have threatened violent measures – resignation, repudiation,
public exposure of the American tactics? After all, he
wielded great power. Far and wide he was acknowledged as
the father of these institutions. It was to him and not to
Vinson, or to any American, that the world looked for the
devising of a workable alternative to pure nationalism and
autarky, and for the finding of a compromise by which
American cooperation could be ensured without American
domination. He had his 'silent constituents in all countries'.
On a single word from him, Britain, and most of the
Dominions, would immediately lose all interest, and in
many other nations those small flames of economic internationalism, which were still weakly and in need of coaxing,
would be quenched at once. The Americans would be left

with their immediate henchmen, to make the best of their so-called international plans.

He had no such thoughts. No drastic action of this sort could for a moment be contemplated. *The British Loan was not yet through Congress.*

It may be held that he over-estimated the probable ill effect of the decisions that were taken. He succeeded in gaining a small compromise on the management, whereby the Directors and their Alternates need not both be on full-time duty. It was conceivable that matters might be so arranged that he could get the substance of what he wanted. The question of 'railroading' was a graver one, if it was symptomatic of what was to come. Nevertheless, while the present must needs bulk larger in one's mind, the past remained true, and one should not let a single instance of the wrong spirit weigh down all the many instances of the right spirit, which he had previously experienced. When Keynes had returned to England, he began to take a more favourable view of the matter. The wrong decision about management could be circumvented, while a showdown on the 'railroading' issue could be reserved for a more propitious occasion.

But there at Savannah all seemed black. The place became hateful to him. Gone were all thoughts of prolonging his stay. On 18 March he caught the night train for Washington.

His sleeper was in the front of the train, and next morning, being hungry, he set out for the breakfast car, which was at the extreme end. Such an expedition on a long train of sleeping-cars always had a whiff of pleasant association – one thought of Italy or the Mediterranean and the days of one's youth. This journey was to be uncomfortably long, past sleeping-cars and Pullman cars, from coach to coach over the moving platforms, time and again. The train swayed heavily. He felt very tired and exhausted. He was buffeted about. It was becoming a torment. Would he ever reach the end?

Step by step, he struggled on. It was indeed a torture. This was surely the punishment of the damned, walking for ever onwards through moving passages in the entrails of the earth. Could he endure it? ... Ah, here at last was the breakfast car. He afterwards remarked that this walk along the train was the greatest agony that he had ever endured in his life.

He settled down to breakfast, and his strength revived. He was feeling much better now. He would have to do the return journey very gently. Back to his walk along the swaying coaches. Yes, it was a torment. He was buffeted to and fro. It was the punishment of the damned, walking through moving passages in the entrails of the earth, walking for ever. He did not have to walk for long.

They carried him to the nearest club car and stretched him on a couch. He lay there for some two hours. It was the worst attack he had ever had. It was uncertain what the outcome would be. Lydia was by his side. Mr Brand was at hand, ready to do anything that might be needed. And there, too, was Harry White, keeping patient vigil by his dear friend, full of sad anxiety. In the end Keynes recovered.

Some of those who were at Savannah detected in his passionate excitement about the issues at stake a symptom of physical sickness. It seemed contrary to his usual level judgement to be so much exercised about matters that might be deemed of secondary importance. The world would not fall to pieces if the International Monetary Fund was wrongly constituted. According to this view of the matter, his health had already been fatally undermined by the protracted labours and vexations of the Loan negotiations. There in Washington he had had to fight on two fronts. He had exerted himself to the full to wring every ounce of concession out of the Americans, adamant in adherence to the British view and perhaps sometimes pushing it beyond his better judgement. And then from Whitehall there had come a constant flow of telegrams full of misunderstanding, which refused to give him leave to make concessions that he knew were necessary. He seemed to have lost the firm basis of confidence at home. He was lonely and harassed. A mighty issue was at stake, the survival of Britain. In the end his efforts were crowned with some measure of success and it was recognized that he could not have done more; but this could not make good the havoc which those long-drawn-out months had wrought in his health. This lack of physical fitness may indeed be the true explanation of his emotional excitement at Savannah.

We must also bravely face an alternative possibility. We have to remind ourselves of the character of the man. All that lifelong outflow of energy in such incredible volume, and all that abounding zeal on behalf of cherished causes, interests and friends, cannot be regarded as extraneous phenomena, unrelated to his inner constitution. His logic, his fluency, his gaiety, these were admirable gifts; but it was not they that propelled him on his voyage, with its ceaseless labours, to discover amid the confusions of the twentieth century the means for a happier way of life. He had within him a flame of goodness exceeding that granted to most mortals. A soul thus endowed is indomitable, even to death, in the face of its supreme enemy. It cannot be placated by maxims of expediency. For Keynes the supreme enemy was the use of power for unworthy or irrelevant or trivial motives, to frustrate an opportunity for improving the lot of man. He regarded the Bretton Woods institutions, on which he had lavished so much work during four years, as such an opportunity; we cannot yet judge whether the decisions of Savannah have frustrated it. He regarded Anglo-American cooperation, with mutual give and take, as the only means of saving the world. Savannah seemed to show that this was an unattainable ideal. There he had seen power used, for irrelevant motives, to frustrate a good purpose, and he had been denied by the possibility of the defeat of the British Loan in Congress the weapons to which a combatant was entitled. 'I went to Savannah expecting to meet the world, and all I met was a tyrant.'

We cannot but be reminded of that other occasion in his life, when he had been confronted with the supreme enemy face to face – at Paris, in 1919. According to his judgement, Lloyd George was using his power, for unworthy political motives, to frustrate the opportunity of rebuilding a prosperous and peaceful Europe. Then, too, he had been powerless, and the consequence was a physical collapse. 'I distinctly looked over the edge last week, and, not liking the prospect at all, took to my bed instantly.' [3]

2

He was resilient, as always. In Washington he was discussing with Mr Frank Lee how to overcome the difficulties that flowed from the Savannah decisions. There, and in New York, he was obtaining up-to-date statistics for his *Economic Journal* article. On the boat he was able to rest; he had some pleasant talk with Professor Jacob Viner, who was travelling with him. Back in London, he gave an account of matters to Dr Plesch, to whom it was plain that he had had a very serious attack. However, he picked up the threads of work during the middle of each week in London and had a heavy week beginning on 8 April. He had meetings in the Treasury and at the Bank. He attended a meeting of the Provincial Insurance Co. and of the National Gallery Trustees; he dined with the Other Club, went to an Arts Council Exhibition, went to the French Ballet and the theatre. Monsieur Gutt, who was to be Managing Director of the Fund, paid him a visit on his way through London. The advice he gave him was always to have in his pocket a letter of resignation. He put the final touches to his *Economic Journal* article.

He composed a lengthy memorandum on proceedings at

3. cf. p. 295.

Savannah, which was sharply critical. But when it came to its preparation for circulation as a Cabinet paper, he began to relent. His paper must not be lacking in a sense of proportion, and then he recalled the fact that, if the Americans had their faults, so too had the British. The British had not really worked out the implications for action of their adherence to the Article VII policy – not that they had any coherent ideas about an alternative policy. It would be a mistake to discourage them too much. The trouble was that he was still fighting a battle on two fronts. Was there no other sane person in the world besides himself? In London the virtues of the Americans became much more apparent. They had the will, as well as the means, to create a better international economic order. They had an intelligible policy, which they were pursuing with resolution. It is true that many sections of the American public might still be laggard, but their democracy was so functioning that able men of high calibre were in charge of external policy and seemed capable in the last resort of translating their wishes into law. Their fault was ignorance about how the wicked world really wagged. They had the dangerous illusion that self-seeking nations and individuals, with all their diverse and subtle modes of self-advancement, could be converted by management in Washington into disciplined schoolboys, complying with a timetable devised there. Believers in *laissez-faire* at home, they naïvely thought that the British, the French and all the rest would submit themselves overnight to a benevolent American paternalism. It would not be so.

But the British, albeit more realistic, had no settled policy at all. They seemed to be altogether lacking in the broader vision that he had found on the other side. They had signed Article VII and authorized elaborate negotiations extending over years, which implied acceptance of that doctrine, and would have protested against any implication to the contrary. Yet it was doubtful if they were converted at heart. They did not seem to realize that, if the policy was to be made a success and the vast obstacles facing them were to be overcome, they would have to address their minds most actively to the problem and refashion their present policy from top to bottom. Instead, they seemed to regard this essay in reconstruction as no more than a list of specified commitments – with plenty of escape clauses – which would have to be fitted into the jigsaw of the policy of day-to-day opportunism that they were pursuing. Nor was it possible to read into their policy an astute and wary empiricism, which would rebuild the country by snatching every little advantage on her journey through the morass of difficulties. We had not returned to the canny policy of the Tudors. On the contrary, we still seemed to think of ourselves as the rich uncle, who could meet all requests with lavish generosity. We still had something of the pre-1939, or even the pre-1914, mentality. If we were failing to live up to the requirements of Article VII, that was not because we knew a better way of turning the situation to our advantage, but because, it seemed, we lacked the mental grasp to appreciate what had to be done. He looked in vain for capable leaders. Understanding of the broad lines of the policy upon which we had embarked seemed to be confined to a few academic economists – Robbins, Robertson, etc. – and these had already left the service. He knew from Dr Plesch that he was in no fit state to run the country. Yet, how otherwise was it to be run? He could not free his mind from grave anxiety.

Yet his spirit was filled with joy and a sense of peacefulness when he went down to Tilton. He spent weekends there, and finally he spent the whole week before Easter, having his mother to stay. He could not abandon work completely. Each morning brought a pouch from the Treasury, which demanded his attention for at least a couple of hours. It was a week of beautiful English spring weather. He strolled in the woodlands or about the farm, discussing plans for the betterment of the land and improved conditions for the workers. One morning, clad in his favourite country garments, complete with a jacket of Cambridge light-blue, bought in America, and a shady straw hat, he took his mother to see the supply of meat provided for an Easter feast in all the cottages on the estate. A calf had been killed, and on a long table in a barn joints of veal were laid out, which were being allocated to the families according to the number of members.

He discussed the political situation with Clive Bell. At the moment he was furious with the Government, on account of the decision which they had taken to nationalize the road-hauliers. His soul revolted against this act of regimentation, and he attached no importance to the plea that coordination was necessary. But he added characteristically: 'You must not count on my opposition as a settled policy; in a few months' time, on some other issue, I may be equally zealous in their defence.'

He sat about in the garden reading. His book-buying proceeded; he was concentrating on Elizabethan authors at this time and liked to read what he had bought. His greatest joy was to drive to the top of Firle Beacon on the Sussex Downs. In the old days it had been within the reach of an easy walk, and he always took his friends, who were staying, up with him while he discoursed volubly without loss of breath on the ascent. Thence one could wander far over the Downs. Now, alas, he had to drive up in his car.

It was his third ascent this week that he made on the Saturday before Easter Day. It was a lovely afternoon. The luxuriant country lay spread out before him, with its fine trees, clad in the green of spring. He saw the cattle browsing at the foot of the hills. It was a scene of ineffable beauty and peace, an ample reward for all his labours of this last winter. The drone of an aircraft could be heard overhead. There was no longer any need to ask whether it was an enemy bomber. Britain was at peace now. He would soon be able to free himself of the heavy load of duties, and to devote himself to this countryside and to his books and friends. He was already planning to resume work at Cambridge. The prospect was fair. He was feeling much better. It was a pity that our affairs were in such feeble hands. Would they succeed in dealing with those sterling balances before the period of convertibility began? If they did not, the national prospect would by no means be fair. He would have to do a great deal of prodding himself. The trouble was that occasional prods were not enough; ceaseless vigilance was necessary. He was not sure that he would not have to get a firm grip himself upon this whole complex problem of the sterling balances. That would be a formidable undertaking. Dr Plesch would not approve, but he was feeling much better. It was wretched to think that the country, after its successful emergence from its greatest ordeal, should be plunged into squalor and misery by its ineptitude in coping with this much smaller ordeal. From the days of Ricardo the Bank of England had always been a thorn in our flesh.

Then there were those Americans, with their schoolmistress ideas. But he was feeling more hopeful about them. They would learn much with a little more experience of international finance, just as they had recently learned to fight at sea and on land. There was a nice balance between the possibilities of a good and of an evil outcome. He might have to exert himself – that was the trouble. It was unreasonable not to have confidence that the forces of good would prevail.

His mind reverted to the cattle at the bottom of the hill, and his plans for the farm. He could see his own home, and, a little to the left, Charleston, where his friends had kept the torch alight through these sad years. Thither they had come long ago during World War I. Away to the left was Leonard Woolf, living at Rodmell – rather lonely now. He must see more of him. His life had been very full since that day when Leonard and Lytton had come to vet him for 'the Society'. He had not forgotten the things which they valued. He could see a unity of pattern in what he had achieved. He had been striving to make that civilization, of which 'the Society' was the pure essence, still possible. The pleasant ways of life of the English countryside could go on; in the harsh setting of the towns employment could at least be assured now, and little by little things of beauty, the drama and music, and possibly even – perhaps through his Arts Council – visual arts would percolate in and enrich the lives of those who dwelt there; and, above all, the Lyttons and Leonards, the young men at the universities, must have a setting in which they could think their thoughts, which were the leaven of the whole society.

Turning a little, he had a wide view of the sea. This precious stone! Recovery would surely come. He had faith in the English people. Their native energies and patience would not fail to bring back prosperity. This great scene, reviving the impressions that had come to him as he had surveyed it through so many years, brought him fresh vigour. He felt better than he had for many months. Should they walk down? It was a long time since he had done so. For him to ask such a question was to answer it in the affirmative. He felt well. His mother could drive home in the car.

Step by step, he carried his large frame down the steep path. He was talking to Lydia about a poem by Thomas Parnell, the first edition of which had just reached him.

Early next morning his mother heard a sound of coughing in his room. She went to seek Lydia, who was with him in a flash. An attack, such as he had often endured before, had just come on, but this time there could be no recovery. In a few minutes all was over. His features assumed an expression of beautiful peacefulness.

*

At the Memorial Service in Westminster Abbey John Neville Keynes, aged ninety-three, walked up the aisle with a firm tread, leading his wife, Florence. Amid the forest of grey ribs which sustain the great fan vaults of King's College Chapel, the matchless choir sang, and Sheppard (the

Provost) recited a passage from *The Pilgrim's Progress* in tones of simple gravity: '... I do not repent me of all the trouble I have been at to arrive at where I am. My sword I give to him that shall succeed me in my pilgrimage, and my courage and skill to him that can get it ...' Across the waters many Americans, as well as English, mounted the hill to the Cathedral of Washington to do honour to a man whom they had come to love so much.

In the streets and clubs of central London, whenever one friend met another the same words were on their lips ... 'We have had a great loss.' This was no empty formula, for in their eyes was an expression of anxiety. The country was still in grave trouble. She was far indeed from solvency, and difficulties seemed to be mounting. We were facing complete disaster. He would have found a way. He had the power of thinking things through and sorting out the tangled issues; he would have made a plan and have used his great powers of persuasion to get it accepted and implemented. Was there anyone to take his place? Foreigners visiting England had the same idea: 'Your country has had a great loss.'

It was surely a very astonishing phenomenon this, for which it would be hard to find any parallel. For here was a man whom all knowledgeable people had come to regard as a principal support of the realm, a man truly irreplaceable. Yet, he was an ordinary private citizen, holding no official position, having no organized support, scarcely knowing to what political party he belonged, living simply and unassumingly, just plain Mr Keynes – no, we had to call him Lord Keynes now, but that hardly seemed to make any difference. The authority that he exerted was solely due to his intrinsic qualities.

Indeed, his career gives the lie to adages that have been current from the dawn of history about the unhappy fate of the over-clever man, who will not cloak his cleverness nor toady to the powers that be. No one in our age was cleverer than Keynes, nor made less attempt to conceal it.

He would not abate one jot of his convictions to curry favour, and had the audacity to change them in the light of experience, sometimes in a sense opposite to the wind of fashion.

Some credit must be given to the British democracy. Happy is the land where a wise man can wield power, simply because he is wise, although he has no support from any political group or from any financial or trade-union interest. Credit must be given to the British Treasury in particular. It does honour to the great intellectual traditions and high disinterestedness of its officials that in World War I they welcomed an outsider and quickly promoted him to a position of great responsibility. If, in World War II, it was more difficult to fit in a senior man of doubtful health, in the end he attained a high, albeit unofficial, position, which would probably have enabled him, had he survived, to save the country from the blunders that were made in the years that followed.

Among the qualities which served him well were his known integrity and personal disinterestedness. If his plans were not accepted, he showed a lack of resentment, rather rare among men of genius, who are apt to become querulous and thereby difficult. If one plan was unacceptable, he went patiently to work to devise a new one. Throughout his career he made no effort at self-advancement. It was understood that whatever success he might have in promoting schemes to save the country, he would seek no personal advantage. He would continue to live his simple life with Lydia, happy in moderate circumstances, buying his books, seeing his friends, attending to his farm and to the affairs of King's. He had sampled all that the world of the great had to offer, and he preferred the mode of life that he had long since chosen for himself. If he continued to labour, that was solely for the good of his country, or of mankind. His services were at the disposal of those who wished for them, and he expected neither thanks nor requital.

His financial independence, achieved solely by his own

exertions, was an advantage. A man, however high-minded, may have to moderate his crusading zeal, if bread-winning requires it. Our planners of Utopia should think of Keynes before deciding that the best plan is to have all members of the community dependent upon a salary.

When on his death it was revealed that he had left nearly half a million pounds, some vulgar people were surprised. They had not conceived it possible, to judge from his way of life, that he had been so affluent. In fact, he was prodigal of his means in securing for himself all that would enrich his experience. Books and pictures he bought, and did not stint his support of good causes. He had been generous to friends in need when his means were still slender, and continued to be so when wealthy. At the same time, he was careful in the details of expenditure and husbanded his resources, as befitted a practical economist, so that he was able, subject to the life interest of his wife, to leave a noble endowment for his beloved King's College. This institution will have been doubly enriched through him, by his administration as Bursar and by his legacy.

He was passionately convinced of the value of collegiate life, and it was a deep satisfaction to him to be able to ensure that King's should not lack the means to provide the charmed way of existence which had meant so much to him in his youth. He could think that, long after he had passed from the scene, another would look forward to each new Michaelmas term and 'give way to unrestrained Fresher excitement', able to rejoice that 'never has a term opened with so fair a prospect'. There, on the bank of the slowly flowing river, new generations would continue to discuss books, philosophy, the nature of the good life and the characters of their friends. There they would learn to be critical and to entertain those crisp and bold ideas that each new age needed. He had never ceased to believe that the well-being of society depended on the strong, clear thinking of the few. There, too, in those happy surroundings, a love of the beautiful and of the gracious arts of life would be fostered. Such things become ever more important with the progress of democracy. After so many generations of toil and drudgery, the people, through the slow process of education and through the rising standard of living made possible by science, were coming within sight of the Promised Land. Only the artists and people of refined vision could keep that land fair and pleasant for them. It was a sacred trust. If art failed and intellect declined, the people would find that, after all their struggles, the promised inheritance had become a desert.

In making a final appraisement of Keynes's influence, some may seek to attribute it to a gift or special power that lies outside the range of normal human qualities; they may seek for some mysterious aptitude, some nameless gift, bestowed on him from the unseen world. He was a rationalist himself and would prefer a rational explanation.

In the first place, his remarkable constellation of qualities can but rarely have been matched. There was his logical faculty, which gave him a mastery in the realm of pure scientific abstraction. 'The most substantial joys I get are from the perception of logical arguments.' [4] This found vent in his work on Probability, and consummation in his *General Theory*. He combined this with a passionate interest in and ready absorption of a great variety of detail; thus he was an empirical scientist as well as a logician. He had a special flair, not always granted to statisticians, for understanding the realities of the marketplace and tracing out how ordinary men were likely to behave in given complex situations. Thus his qualifications for excellence in applied economics were no less than those which qualified him to be a pure theorist. Then he had in very high degree the power of exposition and persuasion. Pure scientists do not tend to excel in the forensic art. Had Keynes adopted Trevelyan's programme and been called to the Bar, there is little doubt that he would have become one of our greatest advocates. He had the gift for assembling arguments in their proper sequence, with

4. See p. 24.

logic and persuasive power in happy harmony. And then he had a gift which was different again, a supreme mastery of English prose. Some may think that it is as a prose writer that he will be longest remembered. The science of economics will develop, and in due course the landmarks of its progress will come to be of interest only to antiquaries; but some of his passages will surely live as literature for so long as the English language is understood. His literary gift was one facet of something larger, his artistic nature. Here again we have an unusual combination, the scientist and the artist. His own inner artistic urge found vent in his writing, and in his delight in the companionship of artistic people. His patronage of the arts and his work in organizing means for diffusing a wider knowledge of them sprang partly from the artist in him, but also from two other traits: his social impulse – to make the lot of people happier – and his appetite for administrative tasks. Another paradox! A scientist and an artist, surely he would spend his life in the clouds and eschew the dull details of routine administration. On the contrary, he loved such details; he was a capable administrator and was always seeking to bring more fields within his province. His speed of work was great; his scientific impulse and his artistic impulse could be satisfied in intense moments of concentration, and thus many hours of the day were left free for administrative tasks. There were hours, too, for the pleasures of friendship, and for trivial pursuits, playing cards or weeding his garden. Thus he had a very rare combination of gifts; his endowment in any one of them would by itself have made him a notable person.

This catalogue might give a wrong impression to one who did not know him, for such a many-sided efficiency might suggest someone inhuman, rounded off at every point, the perfect man, too excellent to be bearable. This was not so, for he had a very intense individuality. A little knowledge of him soon persuaded one that he was utterly unlike anyone else that existed or had ever existed. For his

friends the sound 'Maynard' instantly conjured up an extraordinarily intense flavour, almost comparable to a sensible
quality in its definiteness and precision – or should one
compare it to a symphony long familiar? It was not the
economist or the writer or the financier that the word
evoked. One knew all about that, of course. It was a peculiar
pattern of behaviour, physical and mental – the quick
twinkle, the arching eyebrows, the whole face expressing
his acute sense of the droll, the fun giving way to a period
of lucid exposition in his soft mellow voice, which culminated in its turn in another burst of the ridiculous; his kindly
expression, his beautiful steady eyes seeking agreement and
testing your appreciation; the rapidity of the movement of
ideas, yet always without strain; his enjoyment of the feast
of reason, his comfortable companionship. No doubt all
human beings have their own unique individuality for the
seeing eye. In Keynes, perhaps because all his qualities
were raised to a high point, the individuality was more insistent. Yet it often expressed itself in the enunciation of
what was purely and exquisitely reasonable, and reason is
supposed to be a universal quality, the same for all. We
may remind ourselves that the greatest masters, whose
words or works have had a universal appeal in many lands
and ages, were also most intensely individual, their signa-
tures being plainly visible on all their products. So it was
with Keynes.

A further quality has yet to be mentioned, which animated his great gifts – his abounding and unfailing enthusiasm. Or, perhaps, we ought to give it the name of that
virtue for which austere moralists reserve the brightest
crown, the virtue without which all other virtues are said
to be vain and sterile – the virtue of love. I do not refer
only to his feelings for those who were near and dear to
him. If some new subject was brought to his attention, he
had an implicit faith that, by a little study and by looking
below the surface, one would find an exciting and fascinating pattern. He was ever and again proved right. What he

learnt somehow became a precious and cherished possession. He had that affection for the many things he had
studied, small things as well as great, that the lifelong
specialist so often has for his own peculiar province. He
had the true inquirer's joy in discovery. And in the process
he almost always found something to amuse him. In the
sphere of human affairs he did not believe that one could
get an intimate knowledge unless one looked through the
spectacles of comedy as well as those of pure science. Americans may remember his jokes about the abstruse clauses
of financial documents. These were not the patter of a
compère or the preliminary jokes of a public speaker, designed to prepare his audience for a dry discourse. They
were an essential part of the way in which he thought that
any system or plan involving human beings should be
looked at, if a deep understanding of it was to be achieved.

Many scientists have a love of their subjects, while being
a little arid in their personal dealings. Keynes had a fund
of affection that was always ready to flow forth towards
his pupils, his colleagues or those with whom he was negotiating across a table. This was entirely different from the
outflow of the man who extends hearty greetings by way
of routine or for diplomatic purposes. If he gave an expression of friendliness, you could be sure that it reflected a
genuine feeling. To many who only had the opportunity
of a casual meeting or an interchange of small talk, he
appeared cold and aloof and sometimes even a little arro-
gant. But, as soon as the communication was a serious one,
and he began to learn from the interplay of the business in
hand something of the character of his interlocutor, then
the impulse of affection welled up. He got to love Melchior
in the negotiations with Germany, and he got to love many
Americans with whom he had to deal during World War
II. As an economist he sought to bring about the well-being
of mankind in the abstract; as a man he craved for the
well-being of those with whom he had contact. Thus his
work was infused with a spirit of warm feeling towards all

whom he taught or strove to persuade. It was this quality of love which may entitle us to raise him above the status of wise man and rank him as a prophet in our modern age. He put his hand on your shoulder and opened the book of life before you; with his delicate finger he traced its story; his delight in it was infectious, and his vision became your vision.

It was some two years after his death that I found myself lying outstretched one beautiful summer day on a slope of the Sussex Downs. High above me, seated on a fine white horse, was the handsome one-armed shepherd, now turned cowherd, Beckett Standen. He was talking with rural fluency about the herd, explaining how the farm had become self-supporting in feeding-stuffs, and describing Keynes's plans for its improvement and extension. He evidently knew something about high politics also. 'His Lordship would never have approved the way they frittered away that American Loan.' There was a pause in the flow, and his face grew a shade more serious; he was seeking the right words. 'But, apart from all that,' he said, 'you know that he was a *good* man; he'd sit on the edge of a stack and talk to me for a long time about things – very homely.'

# Appendix

## NOTE ON 'TREATISE ON PROBABILITY'

IT is impossible in a small space to give an adequate idea
of the scope of this book. I shall only touch on one or two
salient points.

It may be well to begin with two statements of indebtedness. One comes from Keynes's Memoir Club paper.[1] 'It
was an important object of Moore's book to distinguish between goodness as an attribute of states of mind and right-
ness as an attribute of actions. He also had a section on
the justification of general rules of conduct. The large part
played by considerations of probability in his theory of
right conduct, was indeed an important contributory cause
to my spending all the leisure of many years on the study of
that subject: I was writing under the joint influence of
Moore's *Principia Ethica* and Russell's *Principia Mathematica.*' In the preface to his *Treatise* he wrote: 'It may be
perceived that I have been much influenced by W. E. Johnson, G. E. Moore and Bertrand Russell, that is to say, by
Cambridge, which, with great debts to the writers of Continental Europe, yet continues in direct succession the English tradition of Locke and Berkeley and Hume, of Mill and
Sidgwick, who, in spite of their divergences of doctrine, are
united in a preference for what is matter of fact, and have
conceived their subject as a branch rather of science than of
the creative imagination, prose writers, hoping to be understood.'[2]

It was pleasant to pay a tribute to Johnson, the friend of
his childhood. The debt, which was a real one, relates mainly
to a series of detailed and subordinate, although interest-

1. op. cit. p. 95.
2. The last few words of this contain a thrust, no doubt, at the
Oxford school of idealists.

ing and novel propositions, rather than to matters of basic doctrine.

A further occasion of diffidence and apology in introducing this part of my *Treatise* arises out of the extent of my debt to Mr W. E. Johnson. I worked out the first scheme in complete independence of his work and ignorant of the fact that he had thought, more profoundly than I had, along the same lines; I have also given the exposition its final shape with my own hands. But there was an intermediate stage, at which I submitted what I had done for his criticism, and received the benefit not only of criticism but of his own constructive exercises. The result is that in its final form it is difficult to indicate the exact extent of my indebtedness to him. When the following pages were first in proof, there seemed little likelihood of the appearance of any work on Probability from his own pen, and I do not now proceed to publication with so good a conscience, when he is announcing the approaching completion of a work on Logic which will include 'Problematic Inference'.[3]

We have seen that Johnson was a philosopher averse from publication. But in his mature years (at the close of World War I) he had a very brilliant pupil, Miss Naomi Bentwich,[4] who succeeded in writing, or inducing him to write, the three notable volumes on Logic which appeared under his name.[5] Hence the embarrassment expressed in the foregoing quotation.

Moore's influence was at the opposite extreme, in that it was very general in character. It was natural for Keynes to express indebtedness in his preface, considering the very high regard, approaching veneration, which he felt for Moore. The Memoir Club statement concerning the 'important contributory cause' is not very convincing, since it is a platitude that right conduct must often depend on a balance of probabilities; it must be admitted, however, that

3. *A Treatise on Probability*, p. 116.
4. Now Mrs Jonas Birnberg.
5. These did not include his views on Probability, which appeared posthumously in *Mind*, 1932.

Moore's ethic makes the problems of uncertainty and probability more prominent than does an ethic which allows an intuitable duty, for by the latter a course of action can be known for certain to be a duty even if some of its consequences are uncertain; this is impossible on Moore's view.[6] Keynes also based some arguments (*Treatise*, p. 240) on the theories of Moore's paper on 'Objects of Perception', which had created so much excitement among the friends,[7] but here again the relevance is not very striking.

But there was one point on which Moore's influence was of quite paramount importance. Basic to all the arguments of the *Treatise* is Keynes's view that probability should be regarded as an indefinable concept. There can be no doubt that his confidence that it was legitimate to treat a concept of this kind as indefinable was due to the respectability with which Moore had endowed such treatment of a fundamental concept.

Many authors on Probability had not been at pains to define their basic concept (or to state that it was indefinable). But there was one school which had given a definition, namely, the Frequency Theorists. For them, to state that if an event *a* occurred, there was, say, a half chance of *b* occurring, meant to say that if *a* occurred a great many times, *b* would occur half that number of times. The kind of situation which arises on the tossing of a coin was generalized by them to cover the whole field of probability. Thus this school explains what we *mean* when we say probable by reference to frequency of occurrence. Keynes was strong in his attack on this theory. This was one source of Whitehead's misgivings, and a more refined version of the frequency theory was supplied by him to Keynes during the period between the two submissions of the thesis.[8] Keynes treated this version with respect, but still in a hostile sense.

6. I refer to the doctrine of *Principia Ethica*, not to that of the Home University Library volume on *Ethics* (see p. 90 above).
7. cf. p. 130.
8. cf. p. 154 and *A Treatise on Probability*, p. 101.

The question remains an open one. In my own person I cannot resist some uneasiness in regard to the indefinability of probability, and hanker after some form of the Frequency theory.

Ramsey reverted to a sophisticated form of it.[9] Unlike Keynes he held that the probability of a proposition may be defined by reference to the strength of belief in it. To say that a proposition had probability of value $\frac{a}{b}$ simply meant that the strength of belief in it had that value. He held that the strength of a belief could be given a precise numerical measure, by reference to the believer's action in the conditions of a controlled experiment. Consequently, unlike Keynes, he held that probabilities were capable of precise measurement. The Frequency theory was brought in as follows: 'Belief of degree $\frac{m}{n}$ is the kind of belief most appropriate to a number of hypothetical occasions otherwise identical, in a proportion $\frac{m}{n}$ of which the proposition in question is true.'

Ramsey turned the highly penetrating ray of his intellect upon the quintessentials of any problem. The essay from which I have quoted is extraordinarily elegant both intellectually and stylistically. The intellectual process is at white heat; but the style is delightfully cool, like that of some old naturalist taking one for a ramble in the country and making desultory observations. Ramsey concentrated his attention on one or two aspects; it is not so clear that he had Keynes's comprehensive breadth of vision and acute realism in the observation of what actually goes on in the mind in the varied processes of empirical thinking. Ramsey was a Planck in his methods of empirical logic.[10] Does that subject require a Planck or a Keynes?

9. *The Foundations of Mathematics*, by F. P. Ramsey, essay on 'Truth and Probability' (1926), Sections 1 to 4.
10. cf. p. 159 above.

The influence of Russell on the *Treatise* is pervasive. In the first place, it is seen in Keynes's adoption of a proposition rather than an event as that which carries the attribute of probability. This is of central importance. Throughout his elaborate mathematical development, in which the ordinary theorems used in mathematical probability are deduced from ultimate logical principles, he always includes a term which stands for the evidence on which a 'probable' proposition is based. This was a novelty and acclaimed by all connoisseurs of the matter as a most valuable innovation. His basic symbol is $a/h$, where $a$ stands for a proposition (or propositions) held to be probable and $h$ for the propositions constituting the evidence for $a$. Where $a$ may be deduced with certainty from $h$, the value of $a/h$ is $1$; where $h$ renders $a$ impossible, its value is $0$. Keynes insists that this expression may have values lying between certainty and impossibility that are incapable of precise numerical expression. Here he is at variance with the Frequency theorists. It is not simply a question of the value of this symbol being unknown to the thinker; it is held to be often in principle incapable of having any numerically measurable value.

The further influence of Russell is seen in the task that Keynes set himself, of deriving a body of familiar mathematical propositions from a small number of logical axioms.[11] *A Treatise on Probability* is offered as providing a theoretical basis for the mathematics of probability analogous to that provided for the general corpus of mathematics by the *Principia Mathematica* of Russell and Whitehead.

11. He was rebuked by his old friend, C. P. Sanger (review in *New Statesman*, 17 September 1921), for referring more than once to the *Principia Mathematica* as being by Russell, and a statement of historical importance was elicited from Russell himself. 'I take this opportunity to protest against Mr Keynes's practice of alluding to *Principia Mathematica* as though I were the sole author. Dr Whitehead had an equal share in the work, and there is hardly a page in the three volumes which can be attributed to either of us singly' (*Mathematical Gazette*, vol. xi, July 1922).

This part of his work was naturally much less massive than the *Principia Mathematica*, because the body of theorems to be derived from his fundamental logical propositions was much smaller. A higher status could not be claimed for this part of Keynes's *Treatise* than that of being an appendix to the monumental work of Whitehead and Russell.

Finally, it is necessary to refer to a doctrine which may, from one point of view, be regarded as the core of the whole book. We have to ask ourselves how, in the first instance, we come to perceive that *a* has any relation of probability to *h* at all. Once we begin with certain propositions expressing probability relations, then we may proceed with the mathematical apparatus provided for us to develop further arguments. But how begin at all? Why is anything evidence for anything else? Why, because in a particular case *x* has been found to be conjoined with *y*, is that evidence that it ever will be so again? Hume had an answer to this problem which Keynes treated with the utmost respect. His answer was that the conjunctions found in experience are no evidence for identical conjunctions outside experience. He was completely sceptical as regards the logical validity of empirical reasoning; the mind had a natural tendency to argue from the conjunction of two particulars to the conjunction of similar particulars in other cases. But there was no reason behind this; it was merely a psychological tendency.

Keynes set out to rescue us from this obliterating scepticism, and his main arguments are to be found in Chapter 22. In order to get us going, so to speak, on the path of empirical reasoning, he thinks that it will be sufficient if we are entitled to assume the hypothesis of Limited Independent Variety, which means that the experienced properties of things arise out of a *finite* number of generator properties. This limitation gives us a finite, albeit in the first instance low, probability in favour of a connection between two properties. Furthermore he holds that our general experience is evidence for the validity of the hypothesis in question. The hypothesis may be regarded as an attenuated form of the principle, exploited by many logicians, of the Uniformity of Nature. Keynes does not find this latter postulate fruitful, and considers that it may be boiled down to the statement that the location in space or time of a conjunction is irrelevant to its evidential character. None the less, there is an analogy between Keynes's argument from our general experience to the hypothesis of Limited Independent Variety and the argument used by logicians, such as Mill, from our general experience to the hypothesis of the Uniformity of Nature.

Ramsey had some doubts, which made Keynes uneasy, whether the hypothesis of a finite number of generators was sufficient to provide initial probability relations, from which to build up our general knowledge of the empirical world. He suggested that a more rigid and difficult hypothesis was required, namely, that there is a specific number of generators.[12] This is certainly a fundamental point. It bears upon the validity of the whole of science and all our ordinary opinions and assumptions upon everyday matters. Might those whose thoughts are directed to the far-reaching problems of humanity, and who cannot be bothered with all the nonsense of wars and economic crises, wish that Keynes had remained a logician? Might he have grappled successfully with the problems which were left unsolved in the *Treatise*? Might we have had a *General Theory of Induction, Analogy and Probability*?

Russell took the line in his review [13] that the hypothesis of Limited Independent Variety would not be required, if Keynes abandoned his hostility to the Frequency theory and to the precise numerical evaluation of probabilities. 'If he were mistaken on the first two points, it might be possible to simplify his theory of induction. His difficulty arises from the fact that the *a priori* probability of a generalization has to be *finite*, i.e. greater than some numerically measurable

12. I rely for this point on my own memory, which is confirmed by Mr Richard Braithwaite.

13. op. cit.

probability other than zero. If all probabilities were numerically measurable, this condition would always be fulfilled.' But surely Russell's condition is insufficient; for why need there be any probability relation at all between *a* and *h*? Keynes took Hume's scepticism seriously. His task was to find a good reason why we could ever initially say that *a* was evidentially favourable to *b*. Without some such basis as the hypothesis of Limited Independent Variety, there would be no probabilities whatever, numerically measurable or otherwise.

Ramsey, whose opinions I quote, not only because of his great eminence, but also because they alone made Keynes uneasy, moved towards the position of Pragmatism. Rejecting Keynes's attempt to find rational grounds for the validity of induction, he offered, in the essay which I have quoted, pragmatic grounds. Induction has proved a success in the practical conduct of our lives, and that is all there is to be said in its favour. I do not believe that Pragmatism will survive. Furthermore, a rational basis for induction is surely needed if we are to develop the theory of induction and distinguish good induction from bad induction.

Nicod also criticized the sufficiency of Keynes's Hypothesis on somewhat different lines. At one point Keynes postponed entering into an epistolary controversy with him, on the ground that his mind was too much occupied with other matters. I do not know if he ever studied Nicod's published criticism.[14] Unlike Ramsey, Nicod offered no alternative solution, leaving the matter indeterminate. More recently Professor Jeffreys has leant upon the prior probability of simplicity, as giving a starting-point for the inductive process. But there are very grave objections to this solution.[15]

The question is still an open one, and Keynes's work, which

14. *Foundations of Geometry and Induction*, by Nicod. 'The Logical Problem of Induction', pp. 266–81.

15. A fuller account of my views on this topic is to be found in *Philosophy*, January 1951.

is likely in any case to be for long unmatched in its scope and erudition, will remain of living importance as a starting-point for discussion, until a more satisfying logical solution of the central problem of human knowledge is found.

# Index

# Index

Exchange restrictions, Keynes
on, 523
Expectations, Keynes on
importance of, 535, 547
'Export White Paper' (1941), 597,
608, 699

Falk, O. T., xvii, 257–8, 271, 297,
336, 337, 338, 351, 354, 357, 379
Family allowances, Keynes
recommends, 583
Family wages, 427–8
Farming, Keynes' pursuit of, 454,
458, 568, 613
Farrer, Gaspard, 422
Fay, C. R., xvii, 59, 64, 70, 146,
168, 601
Federal Reserve Board, 403–4,
746
Federal Reserve Building, 709–12
Federal Reserve System, 195, 423,
463, 468, 486, 499, 516, 674, 676,
678; Bank of New York, 486,
746, 749
Feis, Herbert, xviii, 611
Fight the Famine Council, 337
Finance, Keynes' private, 150–51,
174, 179, 335–6, 345–54, 357–8,
764–5
Finance and Industry, Committee
of Inquiry into (Macmillan
Committee), 467, 469, 487
*Financial News*, 578 n.
Firle Beacon, 760–62
Fisher, H. A. L., 436
Fisher, Irving, 368, 399, 404
Fitzroy Square, No. 21, Keynes
has rooms at, 177
Fitzroy Square, No. 29, 203
Flecker, J. E., 133
Foch, Marshal, 272, 321
Foley, Aloysius, 528
Foley, Edward, 637
Folger Library, 658
Fonteyn, Margot, 737, 738

Food, conference on, 655
Forbes-Robertson, Jean, 561
Forbes-Robertson, Johnston, 108
Ford, Revd L. G. B. J., 41
Foreign Exchange. *See*
Exchange, foreign
Foreign Investment. *See*
Investment
Foreign Investments of Britain,
590–91
Foreign loans, Keynes devises
control over use of, 238
Foreign policy, Keynes on, 564
*Formal Logic*, by J. N. Keynes,
7–8
Forster, E. M., 72, 87 n., 98, 109,
127, 218
Fowler Commission, 193
Foxwell, Professor H. S., letter to
J. N. Keynes, 10–11
France, Keynes proposes
integrating finance with, 585
Frankfurter, Justice F., xviii,
339–40, 529, 597, 658
*Frankfurter Zeitung*, 235, 578
Free Trade: Keynes on, 112, 113,
397, 417; Keynes' change of
view, 500–8, 526, 554, 574,
671–2; further change, 554,
673 n., 720–22, 734–7
French Ballet, 757
French franc, the, Keynes on,
373, 439–40, 464
Frequency Theory of Probability,
773–4
Freud, Sigmund, 218
Fry, Sir Geoffrey, 257, 271, 351
Fry, Roger, 96, 211, 218, 264
Fuel rationing, Keynes on, 631
Funk's New Order, 595–6, 602–3
Furness, R. A., 66, 130, 138, 192

Galton anniversary, 565
Gaming-tables, 146, 274, 371
Gardner, W., xviii

# Index

## MORE ABOUT PENGUINS
## AND PELICANS

*Penguinews*, which appears every month, contains details of all the new books issued by Penguins as they are published. From time to time it is supplemented by *Penguins in Print*, which is a complete list of all available books published by Penguins. (There are well over three thousand of these.)

A specimen copy of *Penguinews* will be sent to you free on request, and you can become a subscriber for the price of the postage. For a year's issues (including the complete lists) please send 30p if you live in the United Kingdom, or 60p if you live elsewhere. Just write to Dept E P, Penguin Books Ltd, Harmondsworth, Middlesex, enclosing a cheque or postal order, and your name will be added to the mailing list.

Note: *Penguinews* and *Penguins in Print* are not available in the U.S.A. or Canada

# KEYNES AND AFTER

*Michael Stewart*

Second Edition

In 1936 John Maynard Keynes published *The General Theory of Employment, Interest and Money*, widely acknowledged to be one of the most important books ever written.

Why was it so important? What did it say? How did it change things? Was Keynes's analysis applicable only to the mass unemployment of the 1930s, or is it also relevant to contemporary economic problems? Can Western governments really maintain full employment? Does full employment mean continuously rising prices and perpetual difficulties over the balance of payments? How does economic growth fit into the picture?

These are the issues discussed by Michael Stewart in this new and completely revised edition of his highly successful Pelican book.

'A first-rate popular study of Keynes's work and ideas' – *Banker*

'A delightful and fascinating volume . . . excellently written' – *New Statesman*

'This excellent introduction . . . the author has achieved a greater degree of readability in dealing with inherently difficult problems than one would have thought possible' – *Financial Times*

'Witty . . . and instructive' – *Spectator*

# THE PELICAN BIOGRAPHIES

*Other Volumes in this Series*

ISAMBARD KINGDOM BRUNEL* *L. T. C. Rolt*

'As Brunel's biographer, Mr Rolt is almost too accomplished. He has every admirable quality. He is an excellent writer in love with his subject' – A. J. P. Taylor in the *New Statesman*.

RUDYARD KIPLING* *Charles Carrington*

'. . . A very good biography – we are not left, as we so often are when we have closed an official life, with the thought "here is a quarry where other men in the future may dig more profitably". Mr Carrington has dug with effect. The quarry is closed' – Graham Greene in the *London Magazine*.

TOLSTOY *Henri Troyat*

'Nothing less than this magnificent, massive, 700-page biography could even begin to do justice to one of the most complex, baffling and grand men that ever lived . . . a masterly book' – *Sunday Telegraph*.

*also available*

Lawrence of Arabia* *Richard Aldington*
Scott Fitzgerald *Andrew Turnbull*
Baudelaire* *Enid Starkie*
Joseph Conrad* *Jocelyn Baines*
Charles Dickens* *Una Pope-Hennessy*
Flaubert* *Enid Starkie*
Henry VIII* *J. J. Scarisbrick*
John Keats* *Robert Gittings*
Picasso* *Roland Penrose*
Prometheus: The Life of Balzac* *André Maurois*
Queen Elizabeth I* *J. E. Neale*
Richard Wagner *Robert W. Gutman*
W. B. Yeats *Joseph Hone*

*NOT FOR SALE IN THE U.S.A.

REMAINDER NOT FOR SALE IN THE U.S.A. OR CANADA